Acclaim for JOHN READER's

AFRICA

"A huge undertaking . . . an account of Africa that embraces . . . land forms and life forms, earth science, environmental history and the span of human evolutionary and social development." —*Los Angeles Times Book Review*

"Eye-opening. . . . This immensely rewarding synthesis is amplified by the author's deeply lyrical, quietly stunning photographs that evoke Africa's beauty and ancient roots." —*Publishers Weekly*

"Astonishingly absorbing . . . elegantly written."
  —*The Cleveland Plain Dealer*

"[C]ombines the best of academic research with a sense of Africa which is vivid and understandable."
  —*The Economist*

"Masterly . . . [Reader] displays a virtuosity that cannot fail to impress." —*National Review*

"Comprehensive, lucid and well-written . . . what is truly astounding is the manner in which Reader breaks down the artificial barriers between academic disciplines as he pulls together ideas and information from seemingly every area of human inquiry." —*Houston Chronicle*

"Formidably researched, always readable. . . . An almost stunning blend of disciplines from geology to anthropology to agronomy." —*Kirkus Reviews*

JOHN READER

AFRICA

John Reader is a writer and photojournalist.
Born in London in 1937, he lived and traveled
in Africa for many years. He currently holds an
Honorary Research Fellowship in the Department of Anthropology at University College
London. His previous books include *Missing
Links: The Hunt for Earliest Man* (1981), *Kiliman-
jaro* (1982), and *Man on Earth* (1988). He lives
in London.

AFRICA

A BIOGRAPHY OF THE CONTINENT

JOHN READER

VINTAGE BOOKS
A DIVISION OF RANDOM HOUSE, INC.
NEW YORK

FIRST VINTAGE BOOKS EDITION, SEPTEMBER 1999

Copyright © 1997 by John Reader

All rights reserved under International and Pan-American Copyright Conventions.
Published in the United States by Vintage Books, a division of Random House, Inc.,
New York. Originally published in hardcover in Great Britain by
Hamish Hamilton Ltd, London, in 1997, and subsequently in the United States
by Alfred A. Knopf, Inc., New York, in 1998.

Vintage and colophon are registered trademarks of Random House, Inc.

All photographs were taken by the author.

The Library of Congress has cataloged the Knopf edition as follows:
Reader, John.
Africa : a biography of the continent / John Reader. — 1st American ed.
p.   cm.
"Originally published in Great Britain by Hamish Hamilton Ltd, London,
in 1997"—P.
Includes bibliographical references and index.
ISBN 0-679-40979-3 (hc)
1. Africa—History. I. Title.
DT20.R43 1998
960—dc21   97-36892
CIP

Vintage ISBN: 0-679-73869-X

Author photograph by Jerry Bauer
Book design by Cassandra Pappas

www.vintagebooks.com

Printed in the United States of America
20 19 18 17 16 15 14 13

Contents

Table Mountain, and the Oranjezicht area of Cape Town in 1957, before the Group Areas Act banished "non-whites" from the immediate environs of the city

Preface

I am a white Anglo-Saxon male—the son of a London taxi-driver. On a damp Monday afternoon in July 1955 I boarded an 8,000-ton freighter in the Royal Albert docks and set sail for Africa. We were out of sight of land by the time I went on deck the next morning, the sky still overcast and the ship pitching and rolling with the heave of the Atlantic Ocean as we entered the Bay of Biscay. That day was my eighteenth birthday and it marked the first time I had left England. Indeed, it was the first time I had travelled more than a hundred miles or so in any direction, and the first time I had been so completely separated from family and familiar surroundings.

I lived in Cape Town for eight years, and was often in the company of a family on the fringes of the Afrikaner establishment. From time to time I was obliged to hear their defiant rejections of world opinion concerning apartheid. Only the Afrikaners knew how to treat Africa's *nieblankes* (non-whites), they would say. One, a wine-grower, boasted that he would never hesitate to use his sjambok (a rhino-hide whip) on farm workers old enough to be his father, or mine.

Later, I was based in Nairobi for ten years where, as the colonial period drew to a close and black Africa assumed the responsibilities of independence, the experiences of life in white-ruled South Africa were tempered by experiences of a broader kind. As a photojournalist covering all sub-Saharan Africa I travelled widely. I was under fire with Nigerian troops advancing to quell the Biafran secession; I saw Tom Mboya and Kwame Nkrumah buried; I shook hands with Idi Amin the day after Milton Obote was deposed. I met Julius

Nyerere, Jomo Kenyatta, Helen Suzman, Alan Paton, Steve Biko, Gatsha Buthelezei, and Ian Smith. I went to church with General Mobutu and his family; I attended Haile Selassie's eightieth-birthday celebrations; I saw refugees starving; I travelled down the Nile, up the Congo, through the Okavango delta and across the Kalahari. I watched Mary Leakey uncover the fossil footprints of human antecedents who lived more than 3.6 million years ago.

Africa has been a formative element of my life and career. This means that however much I may have tried to adopt an objective point of view, this book inevitably bears the mark of subjective influences. Not the least of these is a conviction that, throughout recorded history, Africa has been woefully misunderstood and misused by the rest of the world. Humanity simply does not recognize its debts and obligations to Africa. In western imagery, Africa is the "dark continent." A synonym perhaps, but also the potent symbol of a persistent inclination to set Africa and its inhabitants apart from the rest of humanity. The double meaning of the phrase is clear. The "dark continent" does not refer only to the depths of Africa's equatorial forest, to the density of its tropical shadows, to the blackness of African skin, or even to a widespread lack of knowledge concerning the continent. Above all, the phrase tacitly labels Africa as the place where a very particular form of darkness is found—the darkness of humanity. In this context, Africa is where people do terrible things, not because the aptitude for such behaviour is a characteristic of all humanity, but because Africa is believed to be inherently more barbaric and less civilized than the rest of the world.

That people have behaved barbarically in Africa is undeniable but, as events in other parts of the world have demonstrated time and again, this is not an exclusively African tendency. Indeed, civilization—as an expression of cultured behaviour—is a very transitory feature of the human story. Civilization is not a predetermined consequence of human progress, as the Victorians believed, with white Anglo-Saxons leading the way, the rest of the world following in their wake, and the Africans straggling several centuries behind. On the contrary, civilization is more like a protective skin of enlightened self-interest that all societies develop as they learn to regulate their interactions with the environment, and with other people, to the long-term benefit of all parties.

Once established for a few generations, civilization might seem durable enough to last for ever. But the skin of enlightened self-interest is very delicate, easily eroded, and the human capacity for unspeakable barbarity lies just beneath its surface. Africa's horrors are chilling examples of what people are capable of doing to one another when short-term exploitation has taken over from long-term regulation, when the notion of accountability has been swept aside and the promise of the future is hidden by the trials of surviving in the present.

Africa's tragedies diminish everyone, for humanity evolved in Africa, and we hold everything in common—not least our destiny, now that the limits of global exploitation are understood.

AS A "BIOGRAPHY" of the continent, this book presents Africa as a dynamic and exceptionally fecund entity, where the evolution of humanity is merely one of many developmental trajectories that are uniquely evident there. The narrative follows the development of the continent from its earliest manifestation to the present; it identifies the physical processes which have determined the course of the developmental progressions and, where relevant, defines the ecological context in which they occurred. Human evolution is an important case in point, because critical stages of human evolution were adaptive responses to the ecological imperatives of the African environment.

Quite apart from its inherent logic, pursuing processes (rather than the historical sequence of events, for instance) frees the narrative from the tyranny of time and place. The book does not deal with Africa region by region, period by period. Instead, it covers in detail the instances in which the process under discussion is most clearly demonstrated, leaving as implicit the fact that similar courses of development undoubtedly occurred elsewhere and perhaps at other times.

Though it is true that subjective passion was the motivating force of the book and personal experience often its narrative vehicle, it was the help and work of others that fuelled the endeavour. I could have made little or no progress without the scores of individuals and organizations I called upon personally, and the hundreds of published papers and books to which the academic libraries gave me access. Passages from Francisco Álvares's *The Prester John of the Indies* (1540), translated by C.F. Beckingham and G.W.B. Huntingford (1961), and from Gomes Eannes de Azurara's *The Chronicle of the Discovery and Conquest of Guinea* (1441–8), translated and edited by C.R. Beazley and E. Prestage (1896, 1899), are quoted with the kind permission of the Hakluyt Society.

Published material determined the direction of my own research, but it was generous and helpful people in Europe, the United States and—most of all—in Africa itself who enabled me to gather the material that transformed an idea into a book. Some of these individuals are mentioned by name in the text; others are identified by superscript numbers referring to the chapter notes at the end of the book, and the bibliography provides an alphabetical list of all source material. These acknowledgements fulfil a formal purpose, but they give no hint of the gratitude with which I remember the numerous instances of informal help and hospitality I have enjoyed. It is customary for authors to list the names of those to whom they are indebted, but in this instance the list would be very long indeed, so instead I want to offer a collective thank you to everyone, trusting that brevity might actually intensify the sentiments of gratitude and goodwill that I wish to convey.

J.R.

AFRICA

Prologue

THE ANCESTORS OF ALL HUMANITY evolved in Africa. The earliest evidence of their existence has been found in East Africa, at locations scattered north and south of the Equator; the evidence consists of fossil bones, stone tools and, most poignant of all, a trail of footprints preserved in the petrified surface of a mud pan. Three individuals—two adults and one juvenile—walked across the pan more than 3 million years ago, moving without evident haste away from the volcano which was puffing clouds of fine ash over the landscape behind them. Their footsteps took them towards the woods and grasslands which are now known as the Serengeti plains.

The human ancestors made their living from and among the animals with whom they shared the landscape. They were diminutive figures—neither large nor numerous—who existed nowhere else on Earth for over 4 million years. The modern human species, *Homo sapiens,* with large brain and a talent for innovation, evolved from the ancestral stock towards the end of that period.

About 100,000 years ago, groups of modern humans left Africa for the first time and progressively colonized the rest of the world. Innovative talent carried them into every exploitable niche. They moved across the Sinai peninsula and were living in the eastern Mediterranean region by 90,000 years ago. They had reached Asia and Australia by 40,000 years ago, and Europe by 30,000 years ago. They had crossed the Bering Straits by 15,000 years ago and had reached the southernmost tip of South America by 12,000 years ago. The last remaining large habitable land mass, New Zealand, was colonized 700 years ago.

By the early 1970s people had been to the moon. Such achievements, and all by virtue of talents which had evolved in Africa.

AFRICA IS ONLY the second largest continent, but it contains 22 per cent of the Earth's land surface. The Sahara desert alone is as large as the continental United States. In fact, the United States, China, India, and New Zealand could all fit within the African coastline, together with Europe from the Atlantic to Moscow and much of South America.[1] But Africa is much less densely populated, with less than one-quarter of the population of the other regions. Indeed, there are more people living in India (with one-tenth the land area) than in all of Africa (see map 1, page 686).

Distances within the continent are vast—7,000 kilometres from the Cape of Good Hope in the south to Cairo in the north, and approximately the same distance again from Dakar in the west to the tip of the Horn of Africa in the east. The Nile is the world's longest river—6,695 kilometres from source to estuary; both the Congo and the Niger rivers are more than 4,000 kilometres long and the Congo alone drains a basin covering 3.7 million square kilometres, which is larger than all of India (3.2 million square kilometres); on the world scale, only the Amazon basin is larger—7.05 million square kilometres.

Size is one thing, but the position a continent occupies on the globe is also vitally important in terms of the ecological potential it offers a human population. Antarctica, for instance, measures 16 million square kilometres and offers nothing. Africa, on the other hand, straddles the Equator and offers a great deal. It is the oldest and most stable land mass on Earth, and the evolutionary cradle of countless plant and animal species—including humans. And yet, although humanity evolved in Africa and is self-evidently an expression of the continent's exceptional fecundity, the species appears to have been unable to exploit its full potential within the boundaries of the continent—in terms of either numbers or achievements.

If modern civilization and technological culture are judged to be the epitome of human achievement, then it is unlikely that the material way of life to which most of humanity currently aspires would have developed if those small bands of modern humans had not left Africa 100,000 years ago. All the accepted markers of civilization occurred first in non-African locales—metallurgy, agriculture, written language, the founding of cities.

This is not to make a qualitative judgement. Who knows, but for the influence of the out-of-Africa population, a superior alternative to modern civilization and its technological culture might have evolved in Africa. Indeed, the civilized art of living peaceably in small societies without forming states that was evident in Africa prior to the arrival of external influences is a distinctively African contribution to human history.[2] And in any event, civilization, culture and technology are very recent—if not ephemeral—expressions of the human condition. Biology is far more relevant. But here too there are differences that must be explained, particularly in terms of human-population growth potential.

The imperial rulers of China conducted a census in AD 2 and found that at least 57.6 million people lived in China at the time. Written records similarly indicate that the population of the Roman Empire in AD 14 was 54 million.[3] The population of India during the same period cannot have been less than that of the Roman Empire, and probably at least the same number of people inhabited the Americas and Australasia.

Thus, the modern humans who emigrated from Africa around 100,000 years ago, though possibly numbering no more than one hundred when they left (see Chapter 10 below), had multiplied into a global population of more than 200 million people by the beginning of the modern era.

Such an impressive growth of numbers is quite within the range of human reproductive capacity (see Chapter 14) and it begs the question: if this was the extent to which the out-of-Africa human population had expanded, how fared the population which had remained within the continent?

It has been estimated that about 1 million people inhabited Africa when the emigrants left the continent 100,000 years ago (see Chapter 10). By AD 200 numbers are said to have risen to 20 million—of whom more than half lived in North Africa and the Nile valley (and thus would have been part of the Roman Empire population in AD 14), leaving a sub-Saharan population of under 10 million.[4] By AD 1500 the population of the continent is estimated to have been 47 million and in a state of "stable biological equilibrium," with population size fulfilling the potential of the environments that people occupied.[5] Meanwhile, the out-of-Africa population had risen to just over 300 million.

A massive disparity is evident. While the out-of-Africa population grew from just hundreds to 200 million in 100,000 years, and rose to just over 300 million by AD 1500, the African population increased from 1 million to no more than 20 million in 100,000 years, and rose to only 47 million by AD 1500. And the disparity persists to the present day (see map 1, page 686), though both groups were descended from the same evolutionary stock. Both groups inherited the talents and physiological attributes that evolution had bestowed during the preceding 4 million years in Africa.

Why did the migrant population grow so much faster? Or, to approach the disparity from another direction, what prevented the African population from achieving similar levels of growth? Since the ancestral genetic stock was identical, the divergent history of the two groups implies that Africa itself was in some way responsible. In this case a biography of the continent, tracing the processes of development—geological, biological, ecological and anthropological—from the beginning to the present day could throw some light on the issue, illuminating the history of human interaction with Africa in times past and perhaps offering some explanation for the state of the continent at the end of the twentieth century.

THE FOUNDING FACTORS

The Barberton Mountain Land in South Africa, where 3.4-billion-year-old strata contain the earliest-known clear evidence of the Earth's geological history

CHAPTER I

Building a Continent

THE PROCESSES WHICH CREATED the configuration of the continents and the prevailing terrestrial landscape are exceptionally well demonstrated in Africa, where the particularities of ancient geology have endowed the continent with immense deposits of mineral wealth.

Where Africa meets the ocean at its southernmost point, the sea has a tumbling, disorganized aspect, altogether lacking the orderly progression of swells that would seem proper where a large expanse of the south Atlantic first strikes land. There is nothing but ocean—and icebergs—between Cape Agulhas and the Queen Maud Land coast of Antarctica, which lies 35 degrees of latitude further south.

But the continental shelf of Africa actually extends 400 kilometres beyond the coast. The inshore waters are shallow—hence the turbulence whipped up by onshore currents and prevailing winds. The shelf has risen as tectonic forces have driven the Antarctic Plate southward, away from the African Plate. It is as though the toe of Africa has curled up, like an old boot. And immediately inland the high humps of the Cape Fold Belt mountains might be the creases that form across the toe of a curling boot. The Cape Fold Belt mountains were formed 300 million years ago. Together with the Atlas mountains on the northern extremity of Africa they constitute the last major mountain-building events which the continent experienced. Africa is the Earth's oldest and most enduring land mass. Ninety-seven per cent of the continent has been in place and stable for more than 300 million years, most of it for more than 550 million years and some for as much as 3,600 million years (see map 3, page 688). It is a story of accretion that records a large and significant fraction of the history of the Earth. Incontestable forces assembled a continent as millions of years flitted by. This is a timescale on which the average human lifespan is close to irrelevant. Consider: 5 million years spans all of human evolution; 670 million years encompasses the evolutionary history of all animal life; 3,600 million years goes back to the beginnings of life itself.

Africa has seen it all, and preserves the evidence. The mountain-building episodes and deep geological dislocations which distinguish the landscape of other continents are less evident in Africa. Rock formed more than 1,000 million years ago still lies in the horizontal plane—undistorted; many ancient sediments are hardly touched by metamorphic processes. No other part of the world reveals so much of the Earth's structure and history so clearly, from the beginning to the present.

Several large stable masses of rock, known as cratons, were already set within the modern continental outline of Africa 3,600 million years ago. Stability is of course a relative term. At that time the Earth was still undergoing the geological activity that accompanied its cooling from an incandescent primal mass. The surface heaved, erupted, coalesced and gradually hardened. The cratons remained inviolate, floating like corks amid the turbulence, never destroyed by it, but becoming the nuclei around which the cooling rocks solidified. By 1,100 million years ago this process of consolidation had created three massive cratons which together occupied more than half the area of the modern continent.

The West African craton stretched from the coastlines of Sierra Leone, Liberia, Ivory Coast and Ghana north to Mauritania. The Congo craton filled most of Central Africa, and the Kaapvaal craton formed the greater part of what is now southern Africa.[1] Consolidation continued, and the continent was effectively a single stable mass by about 550 million years ago, while the rest of the terrestrial globe was still in a state of flux.

Apart from the tectonic twitches which created the Atlas and the Cape Fold Belt mountains at the northern and southern extremities of the continent (affecting only 3 per cent of its area), the basic geological structure of Africa has been stable ever since: uplifted, eroded, sunk under sediments many kilometres thick, covered with massive lava flows, but fundamentally stable through it all and preserving the evidence of the African genesis to this day.

Some of the rarest evidence is preserved in the Kaapvaal craton, in southern Africa. In particular, the Barberton Mountain Land at the eastern edge of the craton is acknowledged to be the repository of "the earliest clearly decipherable geological events on the Earth's surface" and hence is a unique source of evidence as to the nature and evolutionary development of the primitive atmosphere, hydrosphere, lithosphere, and biosphere of the Earth.[2]

By 3,000 million years ago, the Kaapvaal craton was over 600,000 square kilometres in extent—almost as large as the state of Texas today and a good deal larger than any other then-emergent cratonic masses that geologists have identified around the world. It was big enough to qualify as a microcontinent in its own right.[3]

Geologists speak of a dramatic change in the Earth's manner of construction having occurred around this time. A revolution, a change in building style, the onset of plate tectonics[4]—it was all these. The change was revolutionary, though hardly abrupt and not simultaneous in all parts of the world. It began with the consolidation of the Kaapvaal craton 3,000 million years ago, progressed through Africa and Australia and ended in what is now North America some 400 million years later.

Essentially, a threshold in the Earth's cooling history had been crossed. Previously, the heat rising through the mantle had kept the surface of the globe in a state of flux. Now, as the Earth cooled, oceanic and cratonic crust became separate entities—distinguished principally by their weight. Volcanic eruptions continued to burst through fractures in the cratons, setting in their mass great bodies of material from the mantle. Erosion moved huge quantities of cratonic material down to the oceanic basins to be recycled on the mantle's convection currents, but the cratons were no longer part of that cycle.

The basins were settling, the cratons consolidating and the Earth was a decidedly inhospitable place: barren, fissured, pockmarked with meteorite craters and belching volcanoes; and searingly hot. Noxious gases and huge amounts of water vapour (released from hydrate compounds in the rocks), hung in clouds above the surface. The clouds condensed and rain fell, acid rain, laced with hydrogen sulphides and chlorides. Not so much rain, perhaps, as a weak solution of hydrochloric acid drenching the bare rock surfaces. Erosion was as much a chemical as an abrasive process, and rapid. No plants or soils impeded its action. The acid rain dissolved the rock on which it fell; salts were formed and swept away in solution; minerals were released from their parent rocks and sank to the beds of watercourses, concentrating there in the interstices of an evolving landscape.

An arc of mountains stood along the northern and eastern rim of the Kaapvaal craton at that time, and a lake the size of Ireland lay at its centre. Rivers flowed from the mountains to the lake, rapidly at their headwaters, then sluggishly, cutting channels like tangled braids across the flat bare alluvial lake shore. Flowing water sifts and deposits the material it carries according to weight and density as well as size. Heavy minerals collected in stream beds along with large pebbles. Lighter sands and gravels were deposited in the lake shallows; muds and silts accumulated in deeper water; chemical precipitates fell to the lake bottom far offshore.

At times the lake basin was open to the sea and subject to ocean currents and tides; at other times it dried out completely. Volcanoes and geological uplift compensated for the material eroded from the mountains, the lake basin sank beneath the weight of accumulating sediments. Ultimately, the sediments were nearly 6,000 metres thick—over 1,000 metres deeper than Mount McKinley is high. It seems a lot, but if the deposits had accumulated at an average rate of only one millimetre every ten years, the entire process would have taken just 60 million years.

THE SEDIMENTS THAT ULTIMATELY became the Barberton Mountain Land were deposited in a deep-water basin on the eastern extremity of the Kaapvaal craton, and over the next billion years a series of similarly large basins developed on the craton, successively, one after the other. It was as though cycles of volcanic activity, uplift and erosion, sedimentation, consolidation and quiescence had "migrated" across the craton from the south-east to the north-west, progressively inundating more and more of the surface. As the basins settled, each in turn was subjected to a massive bout of volcanic activity.[5]

Rocks which solidified from one of the earliest cycles of eruption (3,000 million years ago), tinged green by the chlorites they contained and known therefore as greenstones, were the original repository of economically important metals—gold in particular. Diamonds are another product of the ancient rocks. And neither gold nor diamonds could be formed in any other geological environment. The simple fact of the matter is that the geochemical processes by which these elements are created only occur in the conditions which prevail in the mantle under the cratons.

Diamonds form at temperatures of 1,000–1,150 degrees centigrade at pressures exerted by about 150 kilometres of overlying rock.[6] Gold requires the extraordinary hydrothermal capacities of superheated water under immense pressure,[7] in which state the commonplace liquid dissolves substances normally considered insoluble, transports them—without mixing—through bodies of other viscous matter and deposits them as concentrated veins of ore in the fissures of solidifying rocks. Greenstone belts and diamond pipes have been located around the world, but their presence is particularly evident in association with the cratons of Africa. The simple fact is that oldest rocks bequeath the greatest wealth, and Africa is especially well endowed.

Two thousand eight hundred million years ago the Kaapvaal gold was entrapped in the greenstone strata of mountains ranged in an arc around the northern shores of a lake which extended at least 600 kilometres west of present-day Johannesburg and averaged 250 kilometres across. This was the Witwatersrand basin. Its waters covered an area twice the size of Lake Superior, the world's largest freshwater lake today. Over the next 500 million years, the basin filled with sediments eroded from the northern mountains including, of course, the gold from the greenstone strata. The sediments ultimately accumulated to a depth of seven kilometres.[8] Heat and pressure transformed them to metamorphic rocks, and the centre of the basin gradually sank beneath their weight. As the centre subsided, the edges rose, to form a saucer, around the rim of which erosion has exposed the rock strata from which has come more than half the world's total gold production.

The Witwatersrand gold might be considered wealth enough, but geology had contrived to deposit even greater riches within the boundaries of what would become the Republic of South Africa. Just over the northern rim of the Witwatersrand basin a huge single mass of rock lies beneath the present land surface. It is a geological feature unmatched anywhere on Earth, and the repository of unparalleled mineral wealth: the Bushveld Igneous Complex.

Two thousand million years ago volcanic spasms squeezed magma up through the crust and forced it along planes of weakness in the sedimentary layers of the basin. The magma settled and solidified, creating an island of solid rock 400 kilometres long and up to 10 kilometres thick, all of one piece, set deep in the sedimentary strata of a basin on the Kaapvaal craton.

The Bushveld Igneous Complex has a surface area of 66,000 square kilometres. It is the size of Sri Lanka (surface area 65,610 square kilometres), but this is no well-formed teardrop: the Bushveld Igneous Complex is more of a ragged four-leaf clover, oriented so that the stalk (if it had one) would point to where Pretoria is situated today. And while Sri Lanka is a mixed bag of geological components assembled over a relatively recent period of time, the Bushveld Igneous Complex is a single homogeneous unit—the same rocks throughout its mass, derived from an identical root source around two billion years ago. It is this homogeneity and great age which gives the Bushveld Igneous Complex its distinctive and most valuable characteristics.

This extraordinary subterranean island is one of just nineteen such features known from around the world, of which nine are in Africa, five in North America, three in Scotland and one each in Greenland and Antarctica.[9] With its surface area of 66,000 square kilometres, the Bushveld Igneous Complex is twice as large as all the rest put together and eight times larger than the next largest, the Dufek Intrusion in Antarctica.

In geological terms, the Bushveld Igneous Complex is a layered igneous intrusion: igneous because it is composed of magma that erupted from the mantle in molten form; intrusion because the magma was forced between pre-existing subterranean rock formations (if it had erupted at the surface it would have been an extrusion); and layered because as the magma cooled, physical and chemical differentiation occurred. Out of the molten homogeneous mass came a variety of minerals which settled into distinct layers. As a result, the Bushveld Igneous Complex resembles a giant layer cake, with layering as sharp and perfectly ordered as the strata of a sedimentary rock formation. In fact, the term "pseudostratification" is often applied.

Igneous rocks are an important source of many valuable minerals, and the layering of the Bushveld Igneous Complex gives serendipitous access to huge quantities of some of the most valuable. It is truly one of the world's great treasure houses. Annual production of platinoid metals and gold, chrome, copper, nickel, tin, iron ore, fluorspar, and vanadium contributed over US$5 billion to the South African economy in 1995—less than 5 per cent of the country's gross national product, but more than the combined GNP of Malawi and Tanzania, whose total population is greater than that of South Africa.[10] Furthermore, the reserves of the BIC exceed 3 billion tonnes[11]—enough to support 1,000 years of mining at current production rates.[12]

In terms of the amount of labour (mainly black labour) which has toiled to extract the wealth locked in the treasure house of the Bushveld Igneous Complex, and the contribution which that wealth (mainly white wealth) has made to the support of a political system, the mark this inert subterranean mass has made on the social landscape of South Africa is as broad and deep as its impact on the physical landscape.

Social and physical landscapes are often linked, dynamically, though the shape of a landscape may appear to be no more than the setting in which people and society act out the dramas of their existence.

THE HUGE FORCES POWERING the emplacement of the Bushveld Igneous Complex subjected the surrounding landscape to tremendous strain. As the volume of the magma intrusion increased, the overlying beds of quartzite were thrust upward into a dome-like form; and then, when the weight of the intrusion passed a critical point, the underlying beds began to subside, and the dome collapsed. Equilibrium at the centre was re-established; now the strain was exerted at the periphery. Along the southern edge of the intrusion in particular the beds bent downwards under the pressure, then snapped like slabs of brittle toffee. With the release of strain the fractured edges sprang upward, creating steep jagged cliffs on the southern face, and an incline to the north that struck the horizontal landscape at a moderate angle and continued beneath the surface on a line that takes the mind's eye directly to the mass of the Bushveld Igneous Complex.

The uplifted jagged edges of the quartzite beds which fractured 2,000 million years ago are now the rounded humps and ridges of the Magaliesberg mountain range, stretching more than 300 kilometres from east to west around the southern edge of the Bushveld Igneous Complex. The city centre of Pretoria is set in a valley, and the suburbs extend well beyond. Commuter traffic rushes over and along the ridges of the Magaliesberg, through cuttings and around hairpin bends where among the roadside rubble there are slabs of rock on whose surfaces the ripples of an ancient sandy lake shore are preserved.

Where there was a lake two billion years ago, the emplacement of the Bushveld Igneous Complex has created a mountain range, with ecological consequences that have had a significant influence on the distribution of plants and animals in the region. The northern slopes of the Magaliesberg receive more direct sunshine and less rainfall than the steeper southern side; they are hotter and drier; the vegetation is sparse and more drought-resistant. The southern sides of the ridges are distinctly cooler and better watered; their vegetation is more lush.

This ecological differentiation has social implications too—people prefer to live on the cooler southern side of the Magaliesberg. The higher the better—if it is affordable. The state president, foreign diplomats and wealthy citizens occupy expansive shady residences scattered along the ridge, while to the north at least 350,000 of South Africa's less economically advantaged citizens are packed into a sprawl of hot and dusty townships and squatter camps.

The ridges of the Magaliesberg impose a predominantly east–west orientation on travel in the region. A fine fast road runs due west of Pretoria towards Hartebeespoort, where a sizeable block of the Magaliesberg has been dislodged by geological faulting, creating a ravine which gives access to the north side of the range. Early white settlers knew the place as a gap (*poort*) in the mountains where hartebeest congregated. Since the ravine was dammed, Hartebeespoort has been important primarily as a water-catchment reservoir for the cities of the Witwatersrand (the name, meaning "ridge of white waters," has long been a misnomer).

The Hartebeespoort dam fills the landscape south of the Magaliesberg with a considerable expanse of cool water. There are sailboats and fishermen, flourishing woodland at the waterside, holiday homes and ribbons of lawn kept green under a haze of sprinklers. The water backs up to the rim of the dam in the ravine, and the dam wall marks the ecological boundary created by the

Magaliesberg: water to the south; and to the north a landscape almost as flat as a lake surface, but hot and vast and dry. They call it the Springbok Flats—the springbok is adapted to the dry conditions; hartebeest could not survive there. Farmers irrigate the sandy soils, and beneath lies the Bushveld Igneous Complex.

Hidden, but not completely. Near Rustenburg, tall pencil-thin chimneys and shaft-head gear point to the underground treasure house. They tap into the Merensky Reef—a vast and distinct unit of the Bushveld Igneous Complex with half of it still untouched by mining activity. The reef is as thick on average as a six-storey building is high, and holds within that space the world's greatest reserves of platinum-group metals, with platinum itself comprising 59 per cent of the platinum-group output, palladium 25 per cent, and the rare metals ruthenium, rhodium, iridium and osmium making up the rest in decreasing order. As well as the platinum metals, gold is also present. So too are nickel, copper and cobalt. And as if these riches were not enough, the Merensky Reef lies on top of an equally extensive layer of chrome ore.

The chrome lies in dense seams which curve with the elliptical base of the Bushveld Igneous Complex and break surface almost exactly where the lower slopes of the Magaliesberg merge into the horizontal surface of the Springbok Flats. The seams run underground at an angle of about fifteen degrees along a front that extends for over 300 kilometres. Just one of several mining companies exploiting the seam has a total of 137 kilometres "on strike." Day and night, a continuous stream of ore flows along conveyor belts from the mine into a noisy maze of sheds and steel girder towers to reappear as a grey sand-like concentrate, pouring from hoppers into a line of forty-tonne trucks. Surplus production is stockpiled at the perimeter fence, like dunes. Catching the light, the grains of metal on the surface sparkle like flecks of silver scattered over heaps of grey clay. They sparkle so vibrantly that they appear to be moving.

It is the addition of chromium to the iron-smelting process that produces stainless steel, the demand for which increased rapidly during the 1960s and 1970s, when the apartheid regime ruled South Africa. Of the world's chrome-ore production, South Africa accounted for 40.5 per cent—5.086 million tonnes—in 1995, virtually all of which came from the Bushveld Igneous Complex (South African chrome reserves beyond the BIC are negligible).[13]

MINERAL WEALTH WAS the foundation of economies throughout Africa. At independence, the development plans of many African states were dependent upon the output of their mines, foremost among them: Gabon, Ghana, Mali, Sierra Leone, Zaire, Zambia, and Zimbabwe. Latterly, the discovery of diamond pipes in the Kalahari gave Botswana the fastest-growing economy in the world during the twenty years to 1994.[14]

Minerals financed South Africa's repressive political system—chrome, platinum, diamonds and, above all, gold. More than half of all the gold mined during all of history has come from the Kaapvaal craton alone—over 40,000 metric tonnes. The first of the gold strikes which was to influence the course of history in southern Africa was made in the Barberton Mountain Land on the eastern edge of the craton in 1883. A gold rush ensued, which ultimately ebbed west to exploit the more extensive reefs of the Witwatersrand that were discovered three years later. Gold is still mined in the Barberton Mountain Land, but the region is more relevant to a biography of Africa as the repository of evidence concerning the beginnings of life on Earth: the remains of the earliest-known living organisms are preserved in its most ancient rocks.

The Barberton Mountain Land is built of layers of sediment that were eroded from a pre-existing landscape and deposited in a marine basin, where they eventually accumulated to a thickness of more than five kilometres. In their original state, around 3.6 billion years ago, they probably covered nearly 20,000 square kilometres—an area the size of Wales, or of Massachusetts.[15] Then, around three billion years ago,[16] a series of massive plutons—huge plugs of hard-wearing granite—rose on all sides of the structure and squeezed the basin like hands tightening around a pile of pancakes. Eventually the basin was squashed into about one-third of the area it had originally occupied, and massive high mountains were created as the rock layers were folded and forced upward. Since then erosion has stripped them down. In some places the ancient oceanic deposits have gone completely.

In other places the older deposits remain; the oldest of all are found in a 3.6-billion-year-old geological formation known as the Fig Tree Group, whose most distinctive component is a heavy dense black chert. Chert is a kind of flint, formed from the silica-rich ooze that collected on the floor of the ancient basin. In the Fig Tree Group the chert occurs in very regular bands, indicating that it was formed in a very stable environment, with little or no current to disturb or break up the ingredients of the ooze. Some of the earliest-known forms of life evolved in the waters above; as they died, the remains of these microscopic organisms sank to the bottom and were fossilized as the ooze was transformed to chert. They are preserved there still—the earliest-known evidence of life on Earth, 3.6 billion years old, in Africa.

The tree fern (*Cyathea* sp.) found in the Mount Kenya forest today evolved more than 150 million years ago

CHAPTER 2

Transitions

SOME OF THE EARLIEST-KNOWN forms of life have been found in Africa, and its ancient rocks are the repository of evidence from all stages in the evolution of life forms. Africa was the "keystone" from which tectonic forces drove the other continents on their global wanderings. Dinosaurs and the earliest-known mammals were present on the continent 200 million years ago.

The fossils preserved in the 3.6-billion-year-old cherts of the Fig Tree formation are the relics of single-cell bacteria. They comprise the earliest-known evidence of life on Earth, marking the transition from a sterile to an ultimately fertile world. The exact process by which life came into being remains a mystery (most probably it was the product of chemical evolution),[1] but it is certain that for millions of years life was fuelled solely by the chemicals that the organisms absorbed through their cell walls.

Other feeding arrangements came into use around 3.3 billion years ago with the evolution of organisms able to manufacture food internally—the photosynthesizers, such as blue-green algae. Photosynthesizers use the energy of the sun to convert water and carbon dioxide into the simple sugars they require. And in the process they give off oxygen.

Until the arrival of the photosynthesizers the Earth's atmosphere had been devoid of oxygen (indeed, none of the earliest life forms could survive in oxygenated conditions), but over the next billion years the photosynthesizers became the dominant life forms, and produced so much oxygen that vast amounts of ferrous iron in the oceans oxidized, and sank to create the geological formations that have subsequently become the source of the iron ore upon which the industrial world is founded. By about 1.8 billion years ago the main phase of iron deposition was finished (and Africa preserves a large measure of the resource, much of it still unexploited). The free oxygen produced by the photosynthesizers now accumulated high in the atmosphere, eventually creating the ozone layer, which filters out the fraction of the sun's rays that is harmful to life.

With the transition from an oxygen-free to an oxygen-rich atmosphere another broad niche was opened, and the diversity of life increased accordingly. Organisms which could tolerate the presence of oxygen evolved, and then others which could not live without it. Between one and a half and one billion years ago a new level of cellular organization arose, and with it sexual reproduction. Until then reproduction had been a matter of self-replication, the DNA of one parent dividing to produce two identical offspring. Now the DNA of two individual organisms combined to produce one or more offspring. The splitting and recombination of the genetic code that this entailed greatly enhanced the chances of mutations arising between generations. The evolutionary process quickened, generating more major transitions.

Sometime around one billion years ago, after 2.6 billion years of existence solely in the form of single-cell organisms, life advanced to the multicellular level of organization. The advantages were considerable, and the transition from wholly single-cell to predominantly multicellular form marks a crucial shift in the story of life on Earth; it is the point at which the ground plan of the living earth becomes discernible. Life forms proliferated. Palaeontologists speak of an "evolutionary explosion" having occurred around 600 million years ago, which brought into being nearly all the major divisions of the animal kingdom subsequently known and virtually all existing invertebrates. And this evolutionary explosion of life forms also engendered a revolutionary transition in lifestyles: animals with the propensity to eat other living organisms evolved.

Until about 500 million years ago life had been entirely self-sustaining. There were autotrophs deriving energy directly from chemicals present in the water, and photosynthesizers using light and carbon dioxide. There was *Dicksonia,* for instance, the size of a bathmat but only two cells thick, rather like a very thin quilted mattress lying about on the sea bottom; perfectly harmless, producing its own carbohydrates, bothering no one—and then suddenly other things began eating away at its edges. Predatory carnivores.

The arrival of predators set evolutionary events moving towards the world we occupy today. The sensory system evolved in response to the need to both find prey and avoid becoming the prey of other organisms. The evolution of a musculatory system facilitated the chase and escape, and the skeleton held it all together.

Scientists[2] are hunting for the fossil evidence of the animals which had carried the pattern of life through that all-important transition from passive to predatory feeding in cherts from the period that are uniquely available in the South African geological formations. And the search for the fossils that mark the transition between important chapters in the story of life on Earth follows what might almost be called a tradition of African palaeontology—the search for missing links. Many have been found. In the Karoo basin, for instance, an unparalleled sequence of deposits covering the period from 260 million to 190 million years ago has yielded fossils which tell the story of the transition from reptile to mammal more clearly and in greater detail than anywhere else on Earth. And the leaves of *Glossopteris,* fossilized in the sediments of ponds over which the trees had leaned 250 million years ago, indicated a link between Africa, South America and Antarctica and engendered a theory of continental drift long before plate tectonics were shown to be the mechanism by which the continents had moved apart.

> If we look at a terrestrial globe or map of the world, we shall perceive that the projection of the western coast of Africa nearly corresponds with the opening between North and South America, opposite to the Gulf of Mexico; that the projection in South America, about Cape St. Roque and St. Salvador, nearly corresponds with the opening in the Gulf of Guinea; so that, if we could conceive the two continents being brought into contact, the opening to which I have referred would be nearly filled up, so as to form one compact continent . . . A consideration of these circumstances renders it not altogether improbable that these continents were originally conjoined, and that at some former physical revolution or catastrophe, they may have been rent asunder by some tremendous power, when the waters of the oceans rushed in between them, and left them separated as we now behold them.

No, not Alfred Wegener, the man most frequently cited as author of the continental-drift hypothesis, but Thomas Dick, a clergyman from Broughty Ferry in Scotland, who published the idea in 1838, in his book entitled *Celestial Scenery; or the Wonders of the Planetry System Displayed: Illustrating the Perfections of the Diety and a Plurality of Worlds.*[3] Thomas Dick deserves credit for the first published reference to the concept of continental drift, but Alfred Wegener[4] certainly was the man who first attempted to clothe the bare hypothesis in a suit of respectable fact.

Wegener proposed that the land masses of the Earth initially had been joined together in a single supercontinent, for which he coined the name

Pangaea, meaning "all lands" (see map 2, page 687). Subsequently the super-continent had split, he reasoned, with Laurasia drifting away to the north, and Gondwanaland to the south. Later still, Laurasia split, Gondwanaland frag-mented, and the continents drifted to the positions they have occupied in recent geological time.

Wegener devoted the greater part of his professional life to the under-taking, and was castigated throughout. His first outline of the hypothesis, pub-lished in 1912, was sceptically received. A fuller treatment, bolstered with evidence of geology, palaeontology, polar wanderings and gravitational anom-alies, gathered during more than a decade of research, was published in 1927. The work was rejected by his colleagues. Even his father-in-law, a fellow cli-matologist, considered that the primordial continent postulated by Wegener was nothing more than a figment of the imagination.[5] What was the problem?

No one denied that, yes indeed, there were geological formations in Scot-land identical to others in Labrador, and some in Africa which matched others in South America; the fact that fossils of identical plants and animals were found in deposits of identical age, all around the southern hemisphere, did indeed suggest that the southern continents may once all have been joined together—but if so, how had they become separated? Wegener's hypothesis lacked this one crucial factor: an explanation of the mechanism which had driven the continents apart. In terms of what was then known of the Earth's formation, the only conceivable explanation was that the continents had some-how ploughed through the rigid ocean crust, and this was rejected as simply preposterous.

But Wegener's theory was not entirely without its supporters. In 1929 the South African geologist Alex Du Toit reported that some coastal regions of Africa and South America were geologically more similar to each other than to their own hinterlands.[6] Du Toit concluded that Africa and South America had travelled 3,200 to 4,800 kilometres apart in the last 250 million years—by means as yet unknown. He wrote a book about it, *Wandering Continents,* first published in 1937, a very readable volume which established broad popular acceptance of the continental-drift hypothesis even while earth scientists splut-tered about causal mechanisms.

The scientists dismissed Wegener's hypothesis for over fifty years. And the divide between popular acceptance and scientific rejection became so en-trenched that the man who did most to bridge the gap, Princeton geologist Harold H. Hess, was so uncomfortable with the implications of his findings that he attached a whimsical self-deprecating label to the first of his seminal observations on the subject: "An Essay in Geopoetry."[7]

Hess had realized that the mid-ocean ridges discovered in 1959 marked a pattern of fissures emitting molten basalt from deep within the Earth. He concluded that as the basalt spread outwards from both sides of the ridge it pushed the older material ahead of it, thereby widening the oceans and moving entire continents. The discovery of sea-floor spreading was the key to the modern understanding of plate tectonics. The Earth's rigid outer layer, the lithosphere, in which the cratons are embedded, is a mosaic of slab-like plates floating on a hot, plastic layer of the Earth's mantle called the asthenosphere. The continents are the terrestrial portions of the plates. Sea-floor spreading drives them across the face of the globe at rates averaging a few centimetres per year.

Alfred Wegener did not live to see his hypothesis confirmed by the facts of plate tectonics (he died in November 1930 while attempting to cross the Greenland ice cap). Harold Hess saw his first tentative observations on sea-floor spreading become the firm basis of fact upon which a succeeding generation of scientists has constructed its own tentative theories concerning the movement of continents. A "supercontinent cycle" has been envisaged[8] in which the continents drift apart and then reassemble as Wegener's Pangaea every 500 million years or so. In this scenario the continents are now at their most widely dispersed and about to begin drifting back together again. Geopoetry indeed.

The supercontinent cycle is the ultimate determinant of Earth history. The inexorable process has established geological formations, built mountain belts, and shaped landscapes. In turn, mountains and landscape have induced climatic variation and thereby influenced the direction and nature of biological evolution—including, of course, human evolution. Africa is a primary source of evidence for the supercontinent-cycle hypothesis. Indeed, Africa is described as "the keystone of continental drift hypothesis" in general.[9] And "keystone" is the operative word. Africa has been the core from which the other continents have broken away and then returned. In the current cycle, Africa has been more or less stationary for at least 200 million years; stationary, but not unaffected by the heat that accumulated beneath its solid cratonic mass. Some heat has escaped in recent geological times through the fractures which mark the length of the Great Rift Valley; the remainder has lifted the continent upward.

Measured by the height of the shelf break (the true edge of a continent, where the shelf drops abruptly to the oceanic depths) relative to sea level, Africa overall stands about 400 metres higher than the other continents. Locally, the uplift within Africa has been far greater. All of southern Africa stood at 1,800 to 2,500 metres above sea level while Gondwanaland was still intact, and as thermal uplift maintained the elevation of the continent, erosion swept away an average of 2,000 metres of rock from its surface in the 60 million years following the break-up of the supercontinent.[10]

At the other end of the continent, massive uprising lifted North Africa (with the Arabian peninsula still connected) from the floor of the Tethys Sea (the ancient waterway separating Laurasia from Gondwanaland in the first stages of the supercontinent break-up) around 40 million years ago and created a wall of mountains along what is now the Red Sea Hills region.[11] The prevailing climate was wet and warm; the densely vegetated mountains trapped substantial amounts of rainfall; vigorous west-flowing streams and rivers developed, eventually carrying the waters which had fallen on the Red Sea Hills nearly 4,500 kilometres across Africa to enter the Atlantic near what is now the Niger delta.

The trans-African drainage system (TADS) was of Amazonian proportions: twice the size of the Congo drainage basin, three times the size of the Nile. Its major channels were hundreds of metres deep; its broadest valleys were up to thirty kilometres across. This immense waterway has been hidden for millions of years beneath a shifting landscape of forest, savanna and wind-blown sand. Its existence was implied by huge channels in the bedrock which oil-prospecting surveys discovered beneath the sands of the Libyan desert in the late 1960s, and the vast reservoirs of fossil water known to lie under the Sahara were another clue, but confirmation was not forthcoming until the 1980s, when radar imagery from NASA's Landsat programme revealed the network of ancient watercourses buried under the sands of the eastern Sahara. Ground surveys subsequently provided detail of their age, size and extent.

The trans-African drainage system flowed for at least 20 million years until about 15 million years ago, when it was disrupted by an episode of geological uplift. Large segments remained active, but how long the drainages might have remained integrated all the way to the Atlantic is beyond speculation. Around 5 million years ago the first of the rivers to flow on a north–south axis through eastern Egypt—the Eonile—cut a 2,500-metre-deep canyon running 700 kilometres from Cairo to Aswan, and possibly as far south as the second cataract of the present-day Nile. This topographical feature was longer and deeper than the present-day Grand Canyon on the Colorado River.[12]

The Eonile severed the still-operational parts of the trans-African drainages from the Red Sea Hills catchment. The waterways dried up, and ultimately filled with wind-blown sands, leaving radar shadows as clues to the previous existence of a transcontinental drainage system as great as any the world has known, and the fossil remains of an ancient landscape and its inhabitants—including some of the largest animals the world has ever known.

•   •   •

DINOSAURS ARE KNOWN from all over Africa, and include some note-worthy specimens. A complete skeleton of *Brachiosaurus* excavated in Tanzania (now standing in the Natural Science Museum of the former East Berlin) repre-sents one of the largest land animals that ever lived. Estimates put its weight at 80 tonnes (as much as twenty mature elephants), and with its eye level 12.6 metres above ground it was tall enough to look over a four-storey building.[13] The oldest-known dinosaur eggs were found in South Africa, two of them with embryos preserved within.

Yet though they ruled the Earth for 140 million years, the dinosaurs ulti-mately became extinct, leaving their dominant position to be filled by the mammals. The passing of the dinosaurs and the rise of the mammals marks another important transition in the story of life on Earth; it is fitting, therefore, that the earliest-known evidence of the mammals should have been found in close proximity to a dinosaur skeleton—almost cheek-by-jowl in Africa.

James Kitching and his assistant Lucas found the *Massospondylus* skeleton in a small hill above Borman's Drift, close by the Lesotho border. "In" is the key word. The fossil was an integral part of the rock on a forty-five-degree slope. Only a fraction of the skeleton was exposed. The rock was a dark red mud-stone, a consolidated mass of thick muds and silts which had accumulated to a considerable depth on the bottom of a lake basin nearly 200 million years before. *Massospondylus,* measuring four metres from head to tail, carnivorous, and capable of walking on its hind legs, almost certainly had waded into the lake to drink or feed and become stuck in the mud, where it died and sank beneath the surface.

Mud is an excellent medium for the fossilization process—often preserving whole skeletons intact. Unfortunately, however, its homogeneous plasticity means that when consolidated and hardened to a rock it becomes extremely brittle; it has no "grain" (having settled in a mass rather than in distinct layers), and therefore is likely to break at random into cubes rather than along dis-cernible planes.

The skeleton was extracted in a number of large blocks, each bound securely in swathes of cotton and plaster of Paris. The work took ten days. Occasionally Kitching and Lucas would take a break and spend an hour or two exploring other sites where the fossil-bearing mudstone was exposed. Across the drift, James Kitching strolled along the foot of the escarpment and very soon made one of the most outstanding discoveries of his career. "There was only part of the skull showing, with a part of the tooth row," he has recalled, "but I knew what it was right away—the primitive mammal, *Megazostrodon*. It was also in the red mudstone, so I didn't rush to get it out. I just brushed it clean and gave the whole block a soaking of dilute glyptal cement to consolidate the rock around the fossil."

Repeated soakings of glyptal impregnated and consolidated the brittle rock and eventually enabled Kitching to extract the entire block in which *Megazostrodon* was preserved. It was encased in plaster of Paris and Kitching returned in triumph to Johannesburg, bearing rare treasures: a complete skeleton of *Massospondylus,* and a unique specimen of *Megazostrodon.*

Many months later, after as much of the matrix as was feasible had been removed from around the fossils, and the specimens had been studied and described for publication,[14] the two specimens were put on display in the museum of the Bernard Price Institute for Palaeontological Research at the University of the Witwatersrand in Johannesburg. Their proximity in the museum hall reflects not only the contemporaneity of their lives nearly 200 million years ago, but also draws attention to the shift in life pathways that they represent. The two African specimens stand on opposite sides of the museum hall, and on either side of a portentous transition in the story of life on Earth.

Filling a single large case, *Massospondylus* is displayed just as it had been preserved in the rock. The twisted neck, distorted limbs and open mouth prompt a twinge of sympathy for a large powerful creature in its death throes, thrashing helplessly in the quagmire. Across the hall *Megazostrodon* also has a case to itself, spotlit, with a magnifying glass hanging conveniently to hand for the use of visitors wishing to acquaint themselves with the pertinent points of the specimen. The most pertinent is size. The skull of *Megazostrodon* is little more than 2½ centimetres long. The jaw measures about one centimetre and each tooth is a millimetre wide. Even with the benefit of meticulous laboratory preparation and a display expressly designed to highlight its significant features, the shape and orientation of the skull are difficult to discern. The teeth that caught James Kitching's eye that November morning are no bigger than pinheads. The block he impregnated with glyptal and extracted from the rock was the size of a grapefruit.

What sort of treasure is this? Well, *Megazostrodon* from Africa is the earliest-known mammal. The tiny shrew-like creature is the first identifiable link in the evolutionary progression of which humanity presumes to be an ultimate expression.

Throughout the dinosaurs' 140-million-year reign the mammals were never larger than a hedgehog. While the dinosaurs diversified in such spectacular style—armoured, crested, spiked, clawed; mostly large, some immense—

the mammals changed hardly at all. Perhaps it really was the period of repression that it seems, with the rise of the dinosaurs leaving little room for anything else. In this scenario the mammals were confined to the parts of the world that the dinosaurs could not reach: the interstices of their daylight world—undergrowth, rocky crags, holes in the ground—and the nocturnal world, when the cold-blooded dinosaurs were inactive.

The world of a small nocturnal mammal is and always was immensely demanding. Merely climbing in and out of a dinosaur's footprint would have called for a high order of coordination and agility. And because their metabolic rate is relatively higher, small mammals require proportionately more food than large animals (a shrew must eat at least the equivalent of its own body weight each day while an elephant can manage on between 5 and 10 per cent). *Megazostrodon* had the teeth of an insectivore, and it is certain that catching enough food would have called for a high degree of sensory perception, especially in the dark. Eyes were relatively large, hearing acute, the nose more sensitive, while whiskers heightened the sense of touch and spatial orientation.

In short, while the dinosaurs followed an evolutionary course that developed their physical hardware, the early evolution of the mammals concentrated on the software: brain and behaviour. As the reign of the dinosaurs drew to a close, the mammals were well equipped to take over. They emerged from the long shadow of the dinosaurs as small, but very agile, and very alert animals. Carnivores.

The palaeontological record shows that all innovations in the evolution of the vertebrates have started out as small creatures, and carnivorous. Herbivores have always evolved from the innovations but they never have been the originators of a new evolutionary progression. They have been the specialists, which evolved physical equipment specifically designed to exploit particular sorts of vegetation. The specialists flourished while the resources they exploited remained abundant, but when environmental circumstances changed, they were unable to adapt and became extinct.

Carnivores, on the other hand, have tended to retain a more general set of attributes: teeth that could cut as well as chew, physical agility and acute senses. They were able to adapt, even to innovate, but once an evolutionary niche was established its occupants tended not to change. After all, meat remains meat through even the most dramatic of environmental upheavals. A grassland, on the other hand, might be converted to forest—with serious consequences for the herbivores which are grazing specialists. The leopard, for instance, has not changed in 3 million years, while thirty species of antelope have come and gone.

The Aberdare range in Kenya straddles the equator, and its montane rainforest vegetation is correspondingly exuberant

CHAPTER 3

Missing Links

A LANDSCAPE OF tropical rainforest and meandering rivers that existed 40 million years ago in what is today the Sahara region of western Egypt was the cradle of the primates from whom the human line evolved. Tropical rainforests preserve the greatest plant diversity on Earth, but they never have been permanent fixtures—their extent and location varies with climatic change.

The modern world is home to about 4,500 species of mammal. Technically they are distinguished from all other living creatures by their high body temperature, their capacity to nourish their young with milk, their four limbs, a diaphragm used in breathing, a lower jaw made up of a single pair of bones, three bones connecting eardrum and inner ear, and almost always seven vertebrae in the neck. An unremarkable set of attributes, one might say, with which to mark off a group of animals that has climbed, run, burrowed, and swum into all the viable habitats that the Earth has to offer. In terms of behavioural innovation the mammals are the most conspicuously diverse and successful animals on Earth. Clearly, it is what they have done with their evolutionary endowment, rather than the physical equipment itself, which accounts for their success.

Reproductive strategies divide the mammals into three subclasses, among which the placental mammals are further divided into sixteen orders. These include the Primates, comprising 193 species—all but one of which are covered in hair. The exception is of course *Homo sapiens,* the naked ape.[1]

Humanity acquired the label *Homo sapiens* in 1735, courtesy of the Swedish naturalist, Carl von Linné (1707–78). In a work which applied his newly devised binomial system of biological classification to the animal kingdom,[2] von Linné listed all known animals by genus and species according to their perceived relationships and gave a brief description of each. In the scholarly fashion of the time, the work was published in Latin, the author became Carolus Linnaeus and the genus *Homo* was described with the single Latin phrase: "HOMO nosce te ipsum," meaning "MAN know thyself."

Though Linnaeus' Latin phrase was intended as description rather than instruction, his work marked a critical point in the development of humanity's efforts to know and understand itself. The binomial system of classification became the essential tool of zoological inquiry and thus the framework within which science has constructed a viable understanding of humanity and its place in nature.

In Linnaeus' day the Christian world believed that humanity was a divine creation, ensconced at the right hand of God, blessedly separated from the brutish world of nature. Darwin's robust theory of evolution eventually changed all that. The idea that evolutionary principles could explain the development and diversity of life aroused elegant contradiction and a good deal of vehement protestation for decades after Darwin published *On the Origin of Species* in 1859, particularly since it implied that humanity was closer to the gorilla than to God. But the accumulating evidence became increasingly hard to deny. And the confirmation of humanity's status as a part of nature became indisputable when genetic studies showed that in terms of the DNA which dictates their form, chimpanzees and humans are 99 per cent identical.

This remarkable convergence invites the observation that 1 per cent can make a lot of difference, but for those interested in unravelling the evolutionary history of humanity it also means that chimpanzees and humans diverged from a common ancestor only in the relatively recent past. Techniques enabling scientists to apply a temporal measure to the genetic differences between species show that chimpanzees and humans diverged from their common ancestor between 5 and 7 million years ago. The common ancestor marks the transition from ape to human; its fossil remains would represent the ultimate missing link; if any exist they will be found in sedimentary deposits laid down between 5 and 7 million years ago.

The trouble is, of course, that the closer you get to the common ancestor of ape and human the more difficult it will be to distinguish between the ape and human lines. They will be more and more similar as the point of divergence is approached. But no matter. The missing link is the icon of palaeoanthropological investigation, hunted with fervour bordering on the zealous. The first requirement has been to locate sedimentary rocks laid down where and when the ancestral primate had lived. Then it is simply a matter of finding the fossils.

TWO HUNDRED MILLION YEARS AGO, while the ancestral mammals skittered through the environments of a world ruled by the dinosaurs, Africa was still part of the vast single land mass that Alfred Wegener had postulated: Pangaea (see page 22). And although the tectonic forces responsible for the global pattern of land and ocean were already splitting Pangaea apart and driving the continents towards their present positions, land bridges persisted for many millions of years. Africa (with the Arabian peninsula attached) was joined to the Eurasian and North American land masses until about 120 million years ago, and parted company with South America some 20 million years later. Thus, although the earliest fossil evidence of an evolutionary transition may have come from Africa, examples have also been found elsewhere.

The primates are a case in point. Though the evolution of the chimpanzee and hominids definitely occurred in Africa, the earliest-known primates have been found in Europe and North America, in deposits from 65 million to 40 million years old. This could mean that the primates originated in the northern hemisphere and migrated into Africa, or that the fossil evidence of their earlier presence in Africa has yet to be found. Very few mammals of any kind have been found in Africa dating from between 65 million and 40 million years ago[3] (fossil deposits of that age are few and far between in Africa), whereas mammals including primates are widespread in Eurasia and North America throughout the period.[4]

A single tooth from 65-million-year-old fossil beds in the eastern Montana region of the United States is the earliest-known fossil to have been described as an ancestor of the primates. Dubbed *Purgatorius ceratops* because it was found on Purgatory Hill and lived at the same time as the three-horned dinosaur, *Triceratops,* the tooth is distinctively primate in form, though it has been pointed out that this could be a result of adaptation to a similar diet rather than evidence of close relationship.[5]

The most abundant and widespread early primates are *Plesiadapis* and related families from younger deposits. The name *Plesiadapis* is an unhappy misnomer applied by a founder of palaeontology, Georges Cuvier, in the 1870s to fossils from France now known to be more than 56 million years old. Cuvier believed he was dealing with an early relation of cattle. *Plesiadapis* means "half towards Apis [the sacred bull]."[6] More fossils and subsequent study have corrected Cuvier's interpretation but, by the rules of taxonomic nomenclature, the name must stand.

There are doubts concerning the ancestral status of *Plesiadapis,* but none concerning its younger relatives, the adapids, the omomyids and the tarsiids. In the words of Elwyn Simons, a world authority on primate evolution, these three families are the "first primates of modern aspect."[7] They are abundant and widespread in the fossil record of Eurasia and North America from about 40 million to 35 million years ago. Most were the size of squirrels, none was larger than a cat. Opposable thumbs and big toes indicate a capacity to grasp branches and climb trees: they probably were arboreal. Big round eye sockets suggest large eyes and hence a nocturnal way of life; frontal alignment of the eyes indicates binocular vision. Fingers and toes were equipped with nails rather than claws, and the teeth show an evolutionary trend away from the generalized pattern of their insect-eating predecessors towards leaf- and fruit-eating specialization.[8]

The affinities of the early primates from North America and Eurasia are indisputable. There is no doubt that they were the ancestors of the primate family, which includes the living lemurs, lorises, aye-ayes, and bush babies (known collectively as the lower primates), who still employ today the distinctive adaptations that are found in the fossil remains of their ancestors who lived 40 million years ago.

The higher primates (that is, the living monkeys, the apes and humans, collectively known as the anthropoids), on the other hand, have evolved quite different attributes and none of their distinctive characteristics are found among the 40-million-year-old primates of Eurasia and North America. The two groups probably share a common ancestor (which may or may not have lived on Purgatory Hill), but the higher primates cannot have evolved from their lower cousins. They must have diverged from the ancestral primate line *before* the lower primates first appeared. Where did this occur? In Africa, most probably. Some crucial links are missing, but the next firm piece of evidence in the record of primate evolution is *Aegyptopithecus,* a fossil ape found in the Fayum region of Egypt and dating from about 35 million years ago, when Africa was effectively an island cut off from Eurasia and North America by ancient seaways.

No primates older than *Aegyptopithecus* have yet been found in Africa, but since none of the older specimens from Eurasia and North America qualifies as an ancestor, the distinctive characteristics of the anthropoids are most likely to have arisen in Africa between 45 million and 35 million years ago. Inconclusive evidence of earlier forms dating from about 55 million years ago has been found in Morocco, but *Aegyptopithecus* remains the earliest undisputed link in the evolutionary progression of which humanity has proved to be such an influential expression.

The Fayum is about 100 kilometres south-west of Cairo, where fertile fields gradually give way to desert surrounding a large brackish body of water called Lake Qârûn (the name is derived from an ancient Egyptian word for lake: pa-yom). Forty million years ago, what is desert today was a well-watered landscape in which forest was interspersed with open glades. Many fossilized tree trunks have been found in the deposits laid down by the ancient rivers; some are nearly thirty metres long—the overall impression is of dense tropical forest lining the banks of meandering rivers.

The fossil remains found by palaeontologists show that fishes, turtles, dugongs, crocodiles, and their narrow-snouted cousins, false gharials, lived in the rivers. In the open areas there were carnivores the size of weasels, small and large cousins of the modern elephant and a four-horned herbivore as big as a modern rhinoceros. The forest was inhabited by bats, perhaps by tiny rodents, and by several species of primate. The fossilized bones of the primates are found in the sands of the former river beds. Of the scores of primate jaws recovered, only one, judging by the eruption and wear of the teeth, belonged to an individual that had lived to an old age. Most apparently originated with a young animal's misjudged leap through the trees beside the river, or carelessness while drinking.[9]

THE TROPICAL RAINFOREST HAS an aura of still, silent, unfathomable power. Massive trees. Huge living things crowned with a tracery of green; flickers of sunlight; a tangle of undergrowth; soft damp decaying leaf mould underfoot. Once among the trees, perceptions of distance are frustrated, a sense of direction is hard to maintain, location is difficult to establish. People are quickly disoriented. Lost—and not only in the physical sense: the close, absolute self-sufficiency of the forest also confuses the human sense of purpose and self-esteem. The forest is alive and growing and all-encompassing. It appears to extend for ever, and seems capable of living for ever. Primeval. Eternally recycling its beneficence.

No living system on the terrestrial Earth is as diverse as a tropical rainforest. Many of the trees look alike and have similarly-shaped laurel-like leaves with "drip-tips," but in fact almost every tree found in the forest is likely to be a different species.[10] Surveys have shown that large trees alone can number more than 200 different species in a five-hectare block, and the number continues to rise with the area surveyed: 300 in fifteen hectares, nearly 400 in twenty-five hectares. If smaller trees, vines, shrubs, herbs, fungi, mosses, etc., were included the numbers would be many times greater. By comparison, there are only 1,500 different native plant species[11] in the 24.48 million hectares land area of the United Kingdom.

But the tropical rainforest, though a wonderful example of the living world's capacity to generate diversity, is extremely selfish. It absorbs CO_2 and is self-sustaining, but gives very little away. It even makes its own weather: water vapour rising from the forest forms massive banks of cloud, and the rain they eventually release falls right back on the forest itself. "New" rain brought in from the oceans accounts for only about a third or a quarter of the rain which falls on a tropical rainforest.[12]

By far the greater part of the biomass of a tropical rainforest consists of standing timber, its benefits locked away for hundreds of years in a form totally indigestible to all but specialized invertebrates. Indeed, the tropical rainforest is so efficient at keeping available resources at work within the living community of plants that the soils in which they stand are virtually devoid of nutrients. Plants take their nutrients directly from the air and the rain, and from other living and dead vegetation. The compost accumulating on the forest floor is an important source of nutrients (reprocessed by a teeming host of micro-organisms), but dense networks of shallow feeder roots rapidly channel them back into the living vegetation. Virtually nothing is wasted or stored in the ground, and the process has been shown to be so thorough that even the ground water in a tropical rainforest is purer than commercial distilled water. In other words, rainforest vegetation can remove salts and "impurities" from water more efficiently than a modern distillation plant.[13]

The result of such total self-sufficiency is that the entire system is rooted in sand, and is much less stable than might be supposed. The tropical rainforest might be called a "climax vegetation" in so far as its impressive volume and diversity has arisen wherever and whenever conditions were congenial; and it is certainly true that it marks the upper limit of a progression in which the number and diversity of plant species in a given area increases with distance from the pole to the Equator. The tropical rainforest is undoubtedly the most diverse ecosystem on Earth, but this does not mean it is the most stable.

The popular impression of the tropical rainforest as a permanent fixture of the natural world derives largely from the fact that scientific knowledge of the living forest covers a very short time-span. The trees live for hundreds of years, and the stability of a system can only be judged on the basis of observations covering many generations. Meanwhile, the tropical rainforests have waxed and waned with remarkable rapidity throughout geological history, subject always to fluctuations in climate and the movement of the continents. The rainforests of Africa are a case in point which is particularly pertinent to their role in the evolution of the primates, especially concerning the primates that were the ancestors of the human line and lived in the forests of Africa roughly 45 million to 30 million years ago, when the continent was an island, completely isolated from the other continents.

AFRICA HAS HAD MORE of its land surface covered with tropical forest, for a longer period, than any other part of the globe. But the forests have not been static. They have migrated across the continent as the continent drifted about the face of the Earth. Africa, with the Arabian peninsula attached, has moved 14 degrees north during the past 65 million years. The Equator lay across what is now the Sahara to begin with, and then moved south as Africa drifted northwards. The belt of forests of which the Fayum deposits and *Aegyptopithecus* are relics, moved down the continent with the Equator to the location they occupy today. The internal tectonic forces of the Earth are thus the primary determinant of where the tropical rainforests are located; but how much ground they will cover, and for how long, is powerfully influenced by extraterrestrial factors, principally the sun.

The sun is the ultimate source of the energy that fuels the food chains of the living world, and the amount of radiant energy available to plants at any given point on the globe, at any given time, varies according to the Earth's daily spin around its own axis and its position on the annual orbit around the sun. The seasonal rounds of vegetation change are obvious enough, so too are the variations in the type and density of plant cover that are determined by their distance from the Equator. These variations are the direct result of a cause-and-effect relationship: the amount of available energy directly determines the quantity of living tissue that is produced at any given time and place. But there is another source of variation which is barely detectable on the timescale of seasons, or even in terms of a human lifespan: long-term climatic change.

Formerly captive chimpanzees have been successfully rehabilitated to the wild on islands on the upper Gambia River, in West Africa

CHAPTER 4

Origins and Climate

CLIMATIC CHANGE UNDOUBTEDLY HAS a major effect on the distribution and population size of all living species, but evidence from Africa indicates that competition for resources has had more influence than climate on the origin and evolution of species.

The global climate has varied widely throughout geological time, its regimes affecting not only the seasonal growth of plants, but also the evolutionary history of all living forms. Seasonal changes are determined by the Earth's orientation: which hemisphere—north or south—receives the greater proportion of incoming solar energy on which section of the Earth's year-long journey around the sun. Long-term climatic changes are determined by less obvious astronomical cycles that affect the total amount of solar energy striking the Earth overall, not simply its distribution during the year.

Three factors are involved: (1) the Earth's orbit is not a circle, but an ellipse whose degree of eccentricity is modified by the gravitational influence of the other planets, and varies according to their relative positions; (2) the Earth wobbles slightly as it rotates, so that the angle its axis makes with the plane of its orbit varies through time; and (3) the point on the Earth's surface closest to the sun at the equinox moves westward with each annual orbit (this is due to gravitational attraction between the Earth's equatorial bulge and the sun and moon). These three factors—eccentricity, tilt, and the precession of the equinoxes—create peaks in the amounts of solar energy striking the Earth that occur at intervals of 100,000 years, 41,000 years and 23,000 years respectively.[1] Furthermore, astronomers believe that the pattern of orbital variations has not changed appreciably over the last several million years.[2]

In 1948 it was observed that the ratio of the oxygen 18 isotope to the oxygen 16 isotope in a sample of calcium carbonate varies according to the temperature at which the chemical had crystallized.[3] Chalk is calcium carbonate formed from the shells of plankton, the marine organisms which have inhabited the surface waters of the oceans since the beginnings of life itself. Billions upon billions of these tiny shells sank to the bottom of ancient seas, creating ocean-floor deposits that are, in effect, a thermometer from which can be read the temperature of the oceans when the plankton was alive.[4]

More than two decades passed before the difficulties of retrieving and reading the thermometer were overcome, but in 1976 results from the analysis of cores recovered from depths of over 3,000 metres in the southern Indian Ocean were published,[5] showing conclusively that the temperature of the ocean surface waters had varied considerably during the past 450,000 years, with peaks occurring at periods of 23,000, 42,000, and approximately 100,000 years—almost precisely as the orbital hypothesis had predicted.

Deep-sea-core analysis has proved that changes in the Earth's orbital geometry are the fundamental cause of variation in the Earth's climate; it has revealed a direct correlation with the succession of ice ages for example, and revealed that global glaciation was a much more frequent occurrence than previously believed. On the basis of evidence from the Alps, the geological textbooks to that time had contended that just four glaciations had occurred in the past 800,000 years, for instance; now the deep-sea cores revealed eight major glaciations in the same period, and many more less-intense episodes before then, going back to 65 million years ago.[6]

Once the correlation between the Earth's orbital geometry and climatic variation was firmly established and dated on the broad scale, researchers began extracting greater detail from the geological thermometer. In 1994 "a consistent set of high resolution age models for the past six million years" was published,[7] "... fully orbitally tuned, providing a secure, absolute time scale ... for all those aspects of climatic and oceanographic variability that transfer the astronomical record of varying solar insolation into quasi-cyclic sedimentological variability."

In other words, a geological thermometer recording changes in ocean-surface water temperatures over the past 6 million years was now available, precisely dated and correlated to orbitally induced variations in the amounts of solar radiation striking the Earth. Scientists interested in the effects of climate change on the terrestrial world during the past 6 million years now had a "calendar of climatic events" to which they could refer when looking for answers to fundamental questions. If the geological record showed that a species had become extinct at a known date, it was now possible to check if the extinction coincided with a changing climate. Conversely, if the climatic conditions prevailing at a particular time were known, assessments of likely vegetation spread could be made, and more questions asked, such as how extensive were the tropical forests and savannas of Africa during that crucial evolutionary period, 5 to 10 million years ago, when the ape and human lines diverged from their common ancestor.

WHEN AFRICA (with the Arabian peninsula attached) bumped into Eurasia about 30 million years ago, the continent's long isolation came to an end. Africa remained joined to Eurasia for about 7 million years, then the continents parted again and Africa spent another 6 million years in isolation before rejoining Eurasia about 17 million years ago.

While the land bridges were in place numerous mammalian species moved in and out of Africa. Primitive elephants dispersed into Asia from their evolutionary cradle in Africa; early apes, previously known to have inhabited only the forests of the Fayum, moved into what are now the Siwalik Hills of northern Pakistan. From the other direction, ancestral horses and antelopes migrated into Africa for the first time, along with hares and modern forms of rodents and carnivores.[8] By about 15 million years ago the African fauna had begun to assume the kind of balance between large and small mammals, herbivores and carnivores, that characterizes the modern African savanna.[9]

The evidence of these movements lies in the fossil record, where the sudden appearance of families and genera clearly indicates a foreign origin (and distinguishes them from endemic species). In instances where the first appearance of an immigrant mammalian line can be dated, palaeontologists often have been able to trace its subsequent evolutionary divergence into different genera and species through a known period of time, as well as its dispersal across the geographical landscape. This information in turn has been applied to the all-important question: what triggers the evolution of a new mammalian species? Is it changes in climate affecting habitat which prompt populations to fragment and evolve into different species? Or could it be competition for resources which causes some members of a growing population to evolve different ways of making a living?

Africa is a good source of information on these issues. Long periods of isolation and a virtually stationary position on the globe, plus the size of the continent and the fact that extensive stretches of its terrain had lain within the tropical climate zone at all times mean that Africa has been a laboratory of mammalian evolution.

Oxygen isotope analysis of the deep-sea cores has provided a timetable for climatic events in Africa. When global temperatures fell abruptly between 7 and 5 million years ago, the Antarctic ice cap was established and a powerful current of cold upwelling water flowed along the west coast of Africa for the first time: the Benguela Current. The world's rainfall is primarily a product of evaporation from warm seas; rates of evaporation decline when ocean temperatures fall, and so the icy Benguela Current brought intensely arid conditions to the already dry south-west African coast. At times the Benguela Current travelled much further north, imposing periods of aridity on the equatorial forests of the Congo basin and adjacent regions. Temperatures rose for a time, then fell again around 3 million years ago, subjecting Africa to another bout of arid conditions.

There is no doubt that extended periods of aridity had a pronounced effect on the African vegetation. Forests and woodlands, dependent on abundant moisture, gave way to more drought-resistant forms of vegetation. The landscape became more open. Vast regions of dense equatorial forest were transformed into a mosaic of small isolated forests dotted across savanna woodland and grasslands. Animals were affected too; new species may have evolved in forest refuges and on savannas, but was their arrival determined principally by the influence of changes in climate and vegetation, or was competition for resources a more significant factor?

When viewed on the broad scale the deep-sea-core data did indeed show climatic fluctuations, with very distinct peaks which appeared to correlate with the advent of new species. However, further research has shown that the peaks merely represent the end of long gradual trends; evidence from Arctic deep-sea cores, for example, suggests that the North Atlantic ice sheets began forming between 5.7 million and 4.5 million years ago and were fully established by about 2.5 million years ago.[10] So the formation of the Arctic ice cap took at least 2 million years—hardly a sudden event.

And when temperature differences were measured more closely along the length of the deep-sea cores, it was found that the climate had fluctuated greatly in the short term too. For instance, although the broad scale showed global climate cooling steadily from 3.5 million to 2 million years ago, the fine detail showed that a total of twenty-six climatic cycles had occurred during that time, some with temperature variations matching those recorded at the extremes of the broad-scale trend.[11]

Furthermore, the effect of these climatic cycles would have been conditioned by other factors, such as tectonic uplift, which raised central Africa from near sea-level to about 2,000 metres above sea level[12] between 5 and 2 million years ago. This uplift alone would have had a tremendous effect on local climate and vegetation. So too would the uplift of the Himalayas, which is believed to have established the monsoon weather system around the same time. And then there were uncertainties about when a global warming trend would begin to affect the terrestrial environment: would it precede fluctuations recorded in ocean temperatures, or would it lag behind?

Finally, each cycle lasted for tens of thousands of years; however great the extremes, their effect on climate and vegetation would have been gradual, not sudden. Animals would have moved with the trends; there would have been time for competition to bring about the evolution of new species where resources became scarce.

And what of the primates? Climate change has long been a popular explanation for major events in hominid evolution. The human ancestor is said to have stood up and begun walking when forests shrank and grasslands expanded as the consequence of a changing climate, but more rigorous inquiry suggests that competition has always been the overriding factor—whatever the climatic circumstances.

A statistical analysis of the extent to which the available fossil evidence correlates with climatic change in the case of the primates concluded that

> where climatic change is an important factor, it operates through competition. Climatic change will alter the nature, abundance and distribution of environments and resources within those environments. This will lead to changes in competitive relationships between and within species, and it is these altered competitive relationships that are likely to lead to evolutionary consequences. The consequences might be extinction of populations as the most direct effect, or speciation as a less direct one arising either out of reduced intra-community competition or the opening up of new ecological opportunities. Competition, therefore, is always likely to be the immediate cause of evolutionary change, played out within a framework determined by, among other factors, the climate.[13]

Clearly competitive relationships can change independent of climate, or alternatively, the impact of climate change will vary markedly with geographical factors. In other words, it is probable that species appear and disappear as a result of local competitive conditions rather than broad global patterns of climatic change.

PART 2

HUMANITY EMERGING

Fossil skull and fragments from deposits more than 1 million years old at the Swartkrans site, near Pretoria in South Africa

CHAPTER 5

The Real World

THOUGH THE FOSSIL RECORD of human evolution in Africa is unique and extensive, it is also tantalizingly incomplete. Crucial stages are still a matter of speculation.

Both within the realm of science and beyond, the "African fossil record" is often referred to as though it was a distinct entity of continent-wide dimensions that could be traced back through millions of years, from each and every starting point. This is an exaggeration. Although the African fossil record is rich indeed, containing unique information on the evolutionary history of life on Earth, the evidence is fragmentary, and widely scattered across the geographical space of the continent, and revealed at only a limited number of moments in its geological history.

Fossil sites provide no more than a glimpse of what was going on at one location, at one particular period of time. The sites may be thousands of kilometres apart; their ages may differ by hundreds of thousands—or even millions—of years. With evidence of such uncertain provenance it is difficult to reconstruct the full history of an evolutionary line with absolute confidence. This is especially true of human evolutionary history. The fossil evidence from the Fayum (see page 33) is rich enough to give a fairly full picture of the state at which primate evolution stood between 40 million and 30 million years ago, but the fossil record is blank for many millions of years thereafter, supplying only occasional glimpses of what was going on.

Aegyptopithecus, from the Fayum of 35 million years ago, is the earliest-known candidate for ancestry of the ape and human lines. It was a small arboreal primate, about the size of a domestic cat, with a supple, sinuous back and long limbs; though certainly a quadruped, all four feet were capable of both grasping branches and conveying food to the mouth. The brain was larger as a proportion of body weight than that of any other mammal then alive. Males were significantly larger than females, and had much larger canine teeth, suggesting that *Aegyptopithecus* lived in family groups led by a large dominant male, much like gorillas and chimpanzees today.

At least 18 million years pass before the fossil record provides another glimpse of primate evolutionary history, and this evidence came from a site located over 3,500 kilometres south of the Fayum, on Rusinga island close to the Kenyan shore of Lake Victoria. The fossil is *Proconsul,* dating from about 17 million years ago.

Proconsul was about the size of a baboon; quadruped, arboreal, fruit-eating. It is represented by an unusually comprehensive set of fossils—amounting to virtually a complete skeleton—which has enabled anatomists to identify an intriguing combination of characteristics. With a backbone akin to that of a gibbon, shoulder and elbow joints like those of a chimpanzee, and the wrists of a monkey, *Proconsul* is quite unlike any of the living apes, but could be the ancestor of them all—and of humans too.

A small suite of fossils carries the evolutionary theme evident in *Proconsul* at 17 million years ago on to *Kenyapithecus* at 15 million years ago, and then the fossil record of primates fades again, to an almost complete blank, before revealing a first clear glimpse of *Australopithecus,* around 4 million years ago.

A fossilized trail of hominid footprints found in 1978 at Laetoli, Tanzania, dates from 3.7 million years ago. The type specimen of *Australopithecus afarensis* was found at the same site a few years earlier, so by association it is assumed that *Australopithecus* made the footprints. A striding bipedal gait is unique to humans; it is the foremost distinguishing characteristic of the lineage, and so the Laetoli fossil footprint trail is the earliest-known incontrovertible evidence of humanity's existence.

Laetoli marks the beginning of the most recent phase of human evolution, during which technology and culture developed. The fossil record for this period is relatively full. Sites in East, Central, North and southern Africa have provided an abundance of fossils: *Australopithecus, Homo habilis, Homo erectus, Homo sapiens.* Problems of interpretation abound, but they are stimulated by the availability of evidence, rather than frustrated by its absence. The same cannot be said of the 10 million years which elapsed before those early representatives of the human line walked across the Laetoli landscape.

Ten million years. This is the hidden epoch of human evolution, during which humanity acquired its foremost characteristic—the upright stance and striding bipedal gait. Fossil evidence of this crucial development is non-existent. It is as though a magician had drawn a veil over the process, ushered a shuffling arboreal primate behind one end of the veil, and called forth the bipedal ancestor of humanity from the other. The transformation certainly has magical qualities, even though it took 10 million years. Only more fossil evidence can counter speculation as to when, where, and how it happened.

Altogether, thirty years of exploration to 1994 produced fewer than twenty relevant fossils from the time period: four incomplete jaws with teeth, two fragments of lower-limb bone, and two of upper-limb bone, two sets of skull fragments, and seven isolated teeth.[1] These specimens are important in so far as they confirm the presence of a putative human ancestor where they were found, at a known time in the past, but they reveal nothing of the development of the bipedal gait, and very little else concerning human evolution during the crucial 10 million years. The primary problem is that this most important period is very poorly represented by geological deposits in which the fossils might be found.

Of Africa's 30,343,551 square kilometres of land surface, the total extent of all known fossil deposits covering the period between 14 million and 4 million years ago could be enclosed in a square less than 200 kilometres across—little more than 0.1 per cent of the continent.[2] These deposits are most extensively exposed in Kenya, with smaller sites known in Ethiopia, Libya, and Namibia. In each region, the deposits cover isolated intervals of varying duration; only one region preserves a more or less continuous succession of deposits through the entire 14 million to 4 million period: the Tugen Hills, in Kenya. The Tugen Hills are therefore a unique repository of information for that period of time (and for more recent times too: the youngest deposits in the succession were laid down about 250,000 years ago).

Though the Tugen Hills give only a narrow view of evolutionary events on a continent-wide scale, their physical proximity to Laetoli, and to sites at Hadar in Ethiopia, Lake Turkana in Kenya, and Olduvai Gorge in Tanzania, where fossil evidence of evolutionary developments in the past 4 million years has been found, makes them especially relevant to the broad picture of human evolution.

THE TUGEN HILLS ARE a product of the tectonic uplift and fracture which created the Great Rift Valley. They stand to the west of Lake Baringo in Kenya, about eighty kilometres north of the Equator. While the lake basin is unremittingly hot and dry, the hills are frequently smothered in cloud. Rainfall is high around its summits; the montane forest is dense; the glades are fertile. Agriculture traditionally has been productive enough to supply people on the lowlands as well as sustain the Tugen Hills population.

The fossil beds are found in a succession of distinct sedimentary units, separated from one another by layers of volcanic lava. The lavas can be dated, which gives a minimum age for the sediments beneath (and an overall chronological structure of the succession), while within the sedimentary units there are layers of volcanic ash—tuffs in geological parlance—which give more precise dates for fossils found close to them. In general, the beds consist of sediments that accumulated around lakes and along rivers, places where animals congregated and carnivores might lie in ambush. The oldest beds date back to more than 16 million years ago, the youngest were laid down within the past 250,000 years. During that time, sediments and intervening lavas accumulated to a total thickness that approaches 3,000 metres, but not all of it occurs in any one continuous sequence—the geological history of the hills is much too complicated for that.

Throughout the long period of deposition, varying local patterns of sedimentation, of volcanic eruption and geological faulting militated against the formation of a neat and orderly sedimentary sequence, and these relatively minor complications were compounded by the uplift and faulting associated with the creation of the Rift Valley. Massive disruptions left a huge fault block standing apart from the western wall of the Valley; the block tipped to the west, the accumulated sequence of lavas and sediments was exposed along the eastern side, and subsequently subjected to erosion and further episodes of sedimentation, volcanic eruption and geological faulting. The result was the Tugen Hills.

The potential of the Tugen Hills as a source of fossils that might contribute to the elucidation of human evolutionary history was first noted in the 1960s. The Hills were among several regions that were explored as the tide of interest aroused by the discovery of hominid fossils at Olduvai Gorge by the Leakeys in 1959 swept across East Africa. Louis and Mary Leakey's son Richard excavated a complete fossil elephant skeleton from a 1.5-million-year-old Tugen Hills site in 1967 (his first independent excavation), and described an entirely new monkey from a nearby site in 1969 (his first scientific paper).[3] Also in 1969, however, Richard Leakey's team began finding fossils in sedimentary deposits that he had identified to the east of Lake Turkana. The finds included not only elephants and monkeys, but also hominids from between 1 and 2 million years ago. Richard Leakey subsequently transferred his energies and enthusiasm to East Turkana—with impressive results, but nothing from the missing 10 million years.

Work in the Tugen Hills languished until the 1980s, when it was revived under the aegis of the Baringo Paleontological Research Project, directed by David Pilbeam of Harvard University. In 1985 it transferred to Yale University, under the direction of Andrew Hill.

MORNING CLOUD OFTEN MAKES the walk to school a damp and cold experience for the children of Kipsaramon, on the high ridges of the Tugen Hills. But the cloud lifts, and then children in the schoolyard can, should they choose, gaze clear across the Baringo basin to the eastern wall of the Rift Valley, fifty kilometres away.

Kipsaramon is perched more than 2,000 metres above sea level, on the rim of a cliff-face as steep as the side of a high-rise building. At sites in the foothills, over 1,000 metres below, palaeontologists retrieve fossils from sediments that were laid down from 7 to 1½ million years ago; up here, they excavate sites that are over 15 million years old. In the Tugen Hills the oldest sites lie close to the highest ridge, a geological paradox which demonstrates the degree to which this massive fault block has tilted over: the lava flows which formed the base of the succession are now the spine of the hills, with sedimentary deposits to either side.

Just east of the school boundary, at the edge of a steep muddy track winding past gardens of finger millet, corn and cabbages, lies the most diverse and densely packed accumulation of fossil bone in Africa. Lava flows above and below have been dated at 15.4 and 15.6 million years respectively, giving the bone-bed a probable date of around 15.5 million years.[4] The bed is about 20 cm thick and covers an area of at least 2,500 square metres, and is so densely packed that fossils have been found one within another: a rodent tooth between the cusps of a monkey tooth that lay in the hollow of an elephant tooth.

No one knows how the bone-bed was created—does it represent a sudden event or a gradual accumulation? And the fossils themselves merely compound confusion, representing a diversity of animals not normally found close together, either in life or in death. Elephants and turtles, crocodiles and rhinoceroses, antelopes and hippopotamuses, rats and monkeys, springhares and flying squirrels—all jumbled and glued together in a sparse matrix of sandy clay. Such a diversity of animal species confounds even the most basic analysis of environmental conditions. Springhares, for instance, inhabit thinly wooded grasslands, while flying squirrels live in dense tropical forest. What brought them together at Kipsaramon, 15.5 million years ago?

The Kipsaramon deposits are the oldest in the Tugen Hills from which substantial fossil evidence has been excavated. The bone-bed is unique, but an extremely puzzling source of information. Moving on through the sequence, as it is exposed on hillsides and in gulleys throughout the length and breadth of the Hills, progressively younger deposits have proved to be equally unique, less puzzling, and more directly informative.

The Ngorora Formation covers the period from 13 million to 9 million years ago. At Kabasero in the northern hills, 450 metres of Ngorora sediments are exposed, representing at least 4 million years of continuous sedimentation from a time period otherwise totally unknown in Africa. Tuffs dated at ascending horizons within the Formation document sedimentation up to 10.5 million years at intervals of between 100,000 and 200,000 years, thus adding an unparalleled degree of precision to results correlating the ages of sites and significant fossils.

At the 12.59-million-year horizon, the Ngorora Formation holds a unique record of vegetation. Fossilized *in situ* by the clouds of thick volcanic ash which had smothered the living plants, the site preserves a sample of the local vegetation from just a brief instant in time. The deposit extends for more than one kilometre and its wonders include entire branches with leaves still attached and so well-preserved that their shape and vein-patterns can be ascribed to species with the naked eye, while even more definitive fine structure is revealed by scanning electron microscope. At least fifty-five distinct tree species have been identified, their composition suggesting that a true lowland rainforest existed at that time, not one simply confined to river margins.[5]

The Ngorora Formation is rich in animal fossils too; documenting through its depth and time-span the transition from the archaic African fauna to one which more closely resembles the modern population (see page 39). As the archaic species dominating the lower levels disappear, they are replaced by modern kinds of elephant, antelope, hippopotamus, and pig among others. Immigrants from Eurasia arrive. The earliest ancestral horses known in sub-Saharan Africa have been found in Ngorora sediments dating from around 10 million years ago, along with pigs and various carnivores which also are known from deposits of similar age in Eurasia.

The transformation of Africa's animal population from ancient to modern began around 11 million years ago and was complete by 4 million years ago. This of course covers most of the hidden epoch of human evolution—that

10 million years during which the arboreal quadruped was transformed into the bipedal ancestor of humanity.

Seven of the eighteen hominoid specimens known from the period in question were found in the Tugen Hills: five teeth, one fragment of lower jaw, and one piece of upper arm bone. Though these scraps of fossil offer no direct evidence about the evolutionary development of the human line during that time, they confirm the presence of a candidate for human ancestry in the Tugen Hills throughout. The fossils came from four different levels in the succession, dated at 15, 11, 6, and 5 million years ago.[6] Furthermore, the jaw fragment at 5 million years is the earliest-known specimen representing the ancestor that left footprints at Laetoli, *Australopithecus afarensis*,[7] and a skull fragment from more recent deposits dated at 2.4 million years represents the earliest-known specimen of our own genus, *Homo*.[8]

All these fossils are isolated and fragmentary, but they establish continuity. Candidates for human ancestry were present in the region throughout the period during which the animal population changed from a predominantly archaic to a modern form. And while the fauna underwent major transformation, the human ancestor began walking on two legs, which raises interesting questions. Were faunal change and hominid acquisition of a bipedal gait related in some way? Could both have been the consequence of a single cause? Were environmental circumstances a determining factor? Information on the composition of ancient plant communities would help to answer these questions.

WHEN MICROBIOLOGISTS BEGAN unravelling the details of photosynthesis, it was found that the chemical formula of the energy production process follows different pathways in different plants. The differences are related to the availability of carbon dioxide at the leaf surface. Plants living where the supply is more or less constant apply the carbon dioxide absorbed through the stomata (leaf pores) directly to the energy production cycle. Plants in more stressful conditions (in a hot, dry climate, for instance, where the stomata must remain closed for long periods to prevent water loss) take in more carbon dioxide with each gasp (so to speak), which they then "fix" and transport to internal cells before it is used in energy production. Molecules with three atoms of carbon characterize the direct process, while the indirect process uses molecules with four atoms of carbon. Hence they are known as the C3 and C4 photosynthetic pathways.[9]

Virtually all trees, most shrubs, herbs, forbs, cool-season and montane grasses use the C3 pathway, while C4 plants consist almost exclusively of grasses favouring warm growing seasons; C4 plants are especially well adapted to conditions of intense sunlight, high temperatures and drought. In broad terms, C3 vegetation is largely forest and cool wooded grassland; C4 vegetation is tropical savanna, temperate grassland and semi-desert scrubland.

After death, the C3 or C4 signature of living plants is preserved as differences in the carbon isotopic composition of carbonates in the soils which supported them. Where soils are preserved in fossil beds, carbon isotope analysis thus offers a means of ascertaining which sort of vegetation had grown there. In the late 1980s the technique was applied to fossil soil deposits in the Siwalik Hills of northern Pakistan, and the results showed that a dramatic shift from C3 trees and shrubs to C4 savanna had occurred between about 7.4 million and 7 million years ago. Researchers suggested that this very striking ecological transformation must have been associated with the development of the monsoon climate system.[10] And their work alerted interested parties to the possibility that something of a similar nature might have occurred in Africa around the same time—which was, of course, precisely when Africa's animal population was transformed from ancient to modern and possibly when the human ancestor began walking on two legs.

The Baringo research team began a programme of carbon isotope analysis of fossil-soil carbonates from the Tugen Hills in the 1990s. Samples from 95 sites over an area of more than 800 square kilometres which spanned the entire succession—from 15.5 million years ago to the present—revealed a remarkably heterogeneous mix of C3 and C4 plants throughout, with neither type predominant at any time.[11] The dramatic change seen in the Siwaliks was not evident in the Tugen Hills. There was no abrupt replacement of forest by savanna 7 million years ago. The mosaic of grassland, woodland, and patches of forest which exists today has characterized the region for at least 15.5 million years. The authors concluded "that interpretations of the origin of hominids in East Africa during the Late Miocene [15 million to 5 million years ago] should be considered within the context of a heterogeneous mosaic of environments rather than an abrupt replacement of rainforests by grassland and woodland biomes." In short: "If hominids evolved in East Africa . . . they did so in an ecologically diverse setting."

The implications of these results were significant, not least for hypotheses suggesting that major climatic and environmental shifts had been the cause of faunal change and speciation.[12] The results also discredited a favoured explanation of why the human ancestor had evolved a bipedal gait.

Textbooks and television screens frequently show pictures of the ape that stood up: a dark hairy hominid standing in the shade of the forest edge, gazing out across the bare sun-burned savanna. In one of its most elegant presentations this has been dubbed "The East Side Story."[13]

"The East Side Story" proposes that the massive upheavals which created the Rift Valley also created a "biological barrier" between east and west. The sinking of the valley produced an upthrust of mountains to the west, disturbing atmospheric circulation and leaving regions west of the valley more humid and forested, while the eastern regions were transformed into hot and dry savanna.

In this scenario, the common ancestors of apes and humans were separated by the changed conditions, and each of the two populations developed a lifestyle that was suited to the particular environment they occupied. The western descendants of the common ancestors were said to have pursued their adaptation to life in a humid, arboreal milieu: these were the Panidae (ancestor of the chimpanzees), while their cousins in the east developed a completely new repertoire that was better adapted to life in an open savanna environment: these were the Hominidae (the human ancestor).[14]

A nice story, but conclusively repudiated by evidence from the Tugen Hills, where carbon isotope analysis shows no sign whatsoever of the savannas at 8 million years required by "The East Side Story." Uplift associated with the formation of the Rift Valley may have established broader and denser forests to the west, but it did not create challenging savanna environments to the east. In any case, the human ancestor did not have to adapt to the savanna environment. If a changing environment is proposed as the cause of evolutionary change, surely one has to consider that the ancestors had an easier option: they could have retreated to the west with the forest. The Rift Valley did not form overnight—there was plenty of time. And since these are reckoned to be arboreal creatures that spent their lives climbing trees they certainly could have climbed up the Rift Valley escarpment.

Indeed, the crucial speciation event might have occurred in the forests to the west. It could be that the bipedal gait evolved in the forest—not on the savanna. In any event, competition would have been the most likely incentive, not climate, not environment. And in this scenario it would have been competition for resources which ultimately forced them out of the forest. Some came down into the Rift Valley. They trickled in, small groups who are represented by the scattering of fossils that have been found from 5 million years ago. Finding the mixed environment congenial, they tended to congregate along watercourses and around the Rift Valley lakes where they could exploit a variety of resources: forest, woodland, grassland, and lakes; fish, fruit, roots, seeds, and animals. Competitive pressure led to population splits and the evolution of two or three different species as the ancestral hominids spread eastward across the

Rift, then north- and southward along its length. Their population density increased throughout, peaking in numbers between 2 million and 1 million years ago, which is the period from which the greatest number of fossils have been found.

This is all speculation, of course. Until more fossils are found, the only certainty is that the human ancestor emerged from behind the veil of the hidden epoch sometime around 4 million years ago—walking upright on two legs.

CHAPTER 6

Footsteps

THE UPRIGHT BIPEDAL GAIT OF humans is a unique and highly inefficient mode of locomotion, but the anatomy of modern apes, with 60 per cent of their body weight carried on the hindlegs, indicates that the common ancestor of apes and humans was pre-adapted to bipedalism. Environmental circumstances in Africa provide an explanation of why and how the fully upright stance and bipedal gait evolved in humans.

Laetoli lies roughly 500 kilometres to the south of the Tugen Hills. Late-twentieth-century walking enthusiasts could cover the distance comfortably in twenty-five days, and the journey certainly would not have deterred their ancestors, 4 million years before. Indeed, the safari must always have been enticing: south along the western wall of the Rift Valley; perhaps taking a slow route through the high forest, where there is fruit and honey in season, or moving more speedily through wooded grasslands bordering the foothills below. At intervals, perennial streams gush dependably from the Rift wall. There would have been (and are still) predators to be avoided, of course, but also their prey to be scavenged. The route rises up and over the Mau escarpment, where there is an option of following the forested course of the Uaso Nyiro River to Lake Natron, or turning towards the Loita Hills and the cool grasslands above the lake basin. Volcanoes dominated the landscape to the east of Olduvai; southward, herds of antelope and zebra congregated on the plain.

Andrew Hill made the journey by road in September 1976. At Laetoli,

Footprints made by hominids crossing a mudpan 3.6 million years ago at
Laetoli in Tanzania were fossilized beneath showers of volcanic ash

Mary Leakey and her co-workers were bringing the season of investigations to a close. The work that year had been inspired by the discovery of hominid fossils (among them a mandible subsequently described as the type specimen of *Australopithecus afarensis*)[1] during an exploratory visit made during the Christmas holiday of 1974.

A host of fossils had been found, including animals ranging in size from shrew to elephant, tortoises, a clutch of beautifully preserved eggs matching those of the modern guinea fowl, and tiny leaves identical to those on acacias in the woodlands today. The Laetoli fossil beds had been dated to between 3.59 million and 3.77 million years old—just the period during which the bipedal ancestors of humanity were consolidating their presence in the Rift Valley—but hominid finds were scarce at Laetoli: a few fragments of jaw and some isolated teeth were found in 1975, and some pieces of a juvenile skeleton in 1976. After a promising start, it seemed the potential of the Laetoli deposits was not to be fulfilled.

That was the state of affairs when Andrew Hill went for a stroll one evening with David Western, a wildlife ecologist also visiting the Laetoli sites. Their walk took them across a dry river bed in which an expanse of fine-grained volcanic tuff was exposed. Elephants had recently passed that way too, and had left a number of their cannonball-sized droppings scattered about the river bed. In equatorial Africa, a sun-dried ball of elephant dung appeals to the same instincts that snowballs awaken in northern latitudes. People fling them at one another and, unsurprisingly, wildlife ecologists tend to be more adept than most. Dr. Hill fell as he turned to avoid a particularly well-aimed missile from Dr. Western. While on his knees, pleading for a brief cessation of hostilities, he noticed a curious spattering of tiny indentations in the surface of the grey tuff. These were later identified as raindrop prints but, having attracted Hill's attention, they led him to examine the surface more closely. Amid the puzzling indentations he recognized an unmistakable series of animal tracks.[2]

People had crossed that indented tuff surface hundreds of times during the course of the previous two seasons, but always on the way to somewhere else, with a clear picture in mind of the fossils they were looking for. By chance, an airborne ball of elephant dung introduced a fresh point of view, instantly focusing the investigators' attention on the totally different fossil information that lay at their feet—fully visible, but hidden until then by the blinkers of preconceived notion. Dr. Hill's lucky fall redirected the thrust of the Laetoli investigations. Fossil bones were relegated to a level of secondary interest and during the final weeks of the 1976 season the identification of fossil footprints became the primary endeavour.

Hundreds of prints were found, representing more than twenty different animals, ranging in size from cat and hare to elephant, rhinoceros, and giraffe. Guinea-fowl prints were numerous, so too were the prints of small antelopes, hyenas, pigs, baboons, and hipparion, the ancestral three-toed horse. During the 1977 and 1978 seasons, seven distinct sites were located and mapped. Where desirable, overlying soils were removed. Mammal and bird prints occurred everywhere, wonderfully preserved in the fine-grained volcanic ash. Most wonderful of all was the trail, nearly fifty metres long, left by three hominids walking northward from the woodlands down to the plains.

The trail records a unique moment in time and its preservation is little short of miraculous. About 3.6 million years ago, a series of light ash eruptions from a nearby volcano coincided with a series of rain showers, probably at the onset of the rainy season. The ash filled depressions in the landscape, and the rain transformed them into mud pans. Animals crossed the pans while they were still wet, and their tracks were preserved as the ash dried hard as cement. The next shower of ash laid a protective covering over the tracks. A succession of ash and rain showers created at least six distinct surfaces on which prints are preserved; in total they are fifteen centimetres thick.

Sadiman and Lemgarut, the volcanoes whose ash created the Laetoli fossil beds, are no longer active, but the Laetoli landscape is otherwise not very different today from that which its inhabitants knew over 3 million years ago. The highland foothills are covered in dense acacia thornbush, and the upper slopes are swathed in grass that turns from green to golden as the dry season advances. Westward, the plain extends to a distant horizon, the broad undulating expanse broken here and there by huge steep-sided outcrops of granite and gneiss that rise from the grassland-like islands (indeed, in geological terminology they are known as *inselbergs*—island mountains): Naibardad, Naabi, and Moru, where there is always water. In shallow valleys, strands of woodland mark the watercourses along which the seasonal rains drain away to Olduvai Gorge, about forty kilometres from Laetoli. Elephants come down from the highlands; giraffes cross the plain, their legs blurred in the shimmering heat haze; lions lie concealed in the dun-coloured grass, herds of zebra and antelope mingle nervously, flocks of guinea fowl scatter noisily. Laetoli preserves a sense of the Earth in a pristine state, when humanity had but recently learnt to walk.

THE HUMAN CAPACITY TO WALK on two legs is unique. Kangaroos and a few other mammals are also habitually bipedal, of course, but their hopping is quite different from the human walking and running. Apes and monkeys also get up on their hind legs from time to time, and can walk bipedally, but their gait lacks the mechanical efficiency of human bipedalism. Nonetheless, the apes do seem pre-adapted to bipedalism. Even when moving about on all fours they carry an unusually large proportion of their body weight on their hind legs—about 60 per cent (making it relatively easy for them to stand up), whereas typical mammals such as dogs and horses carry most of their body weight on the fore legs, and only about 40 per cent on their hind legs. The apes' pre-adaptation doubtless was a characteristic of the common ancestor of the ape and human lines, and of course would have been the inherited pre-adaptation from which bipedalism evolved in the human ancestor.

Questions of how, why, and when the human ancestor acquired the bipedal gait are the hardy perennials of debate in the study of human evolution. Darwin effectively set out the parameters of discussion in *The Descent of Man* (1871):

> Man alone has become a biped; and we can, I think, partly see how he has come to assume his correct attitude, which forms one of his most conspicuous characters. Man could not have attained his present dominant position in the world without the use of his hands, which are so admirably adapted to act in obedience to his will ... But the hands and arms could hardly have become perfect enough to have manufactured weapons, or to have hurled stones and spears with a true aim, as long as they were habitually used for locomotion and for supporting the whole weight of the body, or, as before remarked, so long as they were especially fitted for climbing trees ... From these causes alone it would have been an advantage to man to become a biped, but for many actions it is indispensable that the arms and whole upper part of the body should be free; and he must for this end stand firmly on his feet.[3]

In Darwin's view, bipedalism was the defining characteristic of the human line, and he believed it had evolved before humanity acquired its other most distinctive feature: the large brain. Not all agreed with Darwin on this point; some felt certain that the enlargement of the brain must have come first. The issue was fundamental, but impossible to resolve by debate alone. Evidence was needed, such as fossils which would indicate precisely which came first, bipedalism or the large brain. In some quarters the debate had degenerated to rowdy argument by 1912, when some surprisingly conclusive evidence was found in a roadside gravel pit near the village of Piltdown, in southern England. When introduced to science at a meeting of the Geological Society in London, Piltdown Man brazenly confirmed the view that enlargement of the brain had preceded bipedalism in human evolution; and the specimen seriously hindered further investigation of the issue until 1953, when it was shown to be a fake.[4]

By then, ancient stone tools were acknowledged as the forerunner of modern technology, and two world wars had demonstrated that humans possess a horrifying capacity to slaughter their own kind. Some influential scholars inclined to the view that slaughter was an innate human tendency that had been inherited from distant ancestors; weapons probably had been the tools with which the course of human evolution had been defined, they reasoned, and the killer-ape theory of human ancestry emerged. Its foremost proponent was Raymond Dart (1893–1988), an Australian-born anatomist working in South Africa who had changed the course of human palaeontology in 1925 when he described a newly discovered fossil skull, *Australopithecus africanus,* as a link between apes and humans previously missing from the fossil record.[5]

Dart's 1925 paper was the first definitive affirmation of Darwin's suggestion that the human ancestor had evolved in Africa, and this historical significance lent weight to his 1953 assertion that the earliest stages of human evolution had been bathed in blood.[6] The australopithecines, he wrote,

> seized living quarries by violence, battered them to death, tore apart their broken bodies, dismembered them limb from limb, slaking their ravenous thirst with the hot blood of victims and greedily devouring livid writhing flesh.[7]
>
> The loathsome cruelty of mankind to man forms one of his inescapable, characteristic and differentiative features; and is explicable only in terms of his carnivorous, and cannibalistic origin . . . The blood-bespattered, slaughter-gutted archives of history from the earliest Egyptian and Sumerian records to the most recent atrocities of the Second World War . . . [proclaim] this mark of Cain that separates man dietically from his anthropoidal relatives and allies him rather with the deadliest of the Carnivora.[8]

Dart and his work inspired the Hollywood dramatist Robert Ardrey to write *African Genesis* (1961), a best-seller which introduced the notion of humanity's African origin to a large popular readership (and advised those consulting the index entry for "tools" to "*see* weapons"). The killer-ape theory of human origins reached cinema screens too, in the opening sequence of the film *2001: A Space Odyssey,* where a group of apes discovers that using bones and rocks to kill less able relatives has the immediate effect of reducing competition for available resources.

Dart's theory and its popular interpretations were founded on the assumption that bipedalism and brain enlargement had evolved together, in a cycle of cause and effect that was powered by the production of tools: the upright stance freed the hands to make tools, tool production required intelligence, intelligence led to bigger brains and bigger brains produced still better tools.

The killer-ape theory of human ancestry was distasteful to many who believed that cooperation, not competition, was most likely to ensure the survival of humanity and the planet; but its reasoning was logical and impossible to refute by argument alone. Logic sufficed until the 1970s, when the evidence from Laetoli and Ethiopia showed conclusively that the earliest-known hominids, although undeniably bipedal 3.7 million years ago, had very small brains. Furthermore, the small-brained bipedal ancestors did not use stone tools at that point in their evolutionary history. No evidence of stone tools was found in the Laetoli beds. The earliest-known tools have come from sites in Ethiopia and east of Lake Turkana in Kenya dated around 2.4 million years. This does not mean that the earliest hominids made no use whatsoever of sticks and stones and bones in their daily life, nor does it suggest that they did not fight among themselves, but it does demonstrate that for at least 1.3 million years these bipedal, small-brained ancestors of humanity existed without the benefit of stone tools.

So, after more than a century of speculation, evidence replaced theory and the links between bipedalism, tool production, and brain-size were broken. Far from evolving together in a cycle of mutual cause and effect, the three developments had arisen separately, over extended periods of time: bipedalism preceded stone-tool production by at least 1.2 million years, and hominids were making stone tools for at least 700,000 years before there was any substantial increase in brain size. But of course, breaking the cycle that had linked these three major evolutionary developments invalidated the all-embracing explanation and raised three separate questions in its place: Why a large brain? Why stone tools? Why walk around on two legs?

THE HUMAN BIPEDAL GAIT IS unique, possibly because it is such an inefficient mode of locomotion. In terms of the energy required to move proportionately equal units of body mass over given distances, humans are not much more efficient than penguins. Mice, squirrels, ponies and gazelles are significantly more efficient—dogs even more so.[9] Among the apes, gorillas use relatively more energy than humans when moving about on the ground in quadruped mode, but chimpanzees use 25 per cent less.[10] Furthermore, chimps are also faster and more agile.

Considered from the ancestral quadruped's point of view, the advantages of walking around on two legs rather than four would have had to outweigh the disadvantages of undergoing the necessary physiological adaptation. And it is not as though the common ancestor had possessed a physique that was equally well suited to either the quadrupedal or the bipedal gait. Far from it. Descendants that opted for the bipedal route to humanity had to adapt, while those on the ape line remained comfortably on all fours. And the transformation from quadruped to biped called for a number of profound and interconnected physiological adaptations.

The basic adaptations were skeletal, concerned with taking the weight on the hind limbs and balancing on alternate legs as each stride is taken. The head shifted so that it is balanced on the top of the backbone, and no longer held in position by powerful neck muscles (as in the apes); the backbone developed curves in the neck and lower back, giving it an undulating appearance and the function of a spring; the pelvis became broader, the arms shortened, the legs lengthened and the thigh angled inward from the hip to keep the knee under the weight of the body (rather than to the side of it, as in the apes); the foot lost its capacity to grasp and became a stiff propulsive lever. All of these skeletal adaptations were accompanied by equally demanding muscular adaptations.

Physiological considerations preclude any probability that the transition from a habitually four-legged to two-legged mode of locomotion could have been a gradual process, marked by intermediate stages. No candidate for hominid ancestry could have made regular and effective use of *both* quadrupedal and bipedal locomotion. One or the other had to predominate at an early stage. Thus the transition to bipedality as a habitual mode of locomotion must have been relatively rapid.[11]

A rapid transition to bipedal locomotion in turn implies that the selection pressure which provoked the adaptation must have been intense. It has been proposed that competition and the threat of extinction were responsible, with the development of the home base and female sexuality as contributive factors.[12] On a less theoretical level, the observations of ecologists working at the Serengeti Research Institute in Tanzania indicate that the opportunity of exploiting a hitherto "unfilled niche" in the ecosystem was a more likely incentive for bipedal locomotion.[13]

The Laetoli discoveries had shown that the conditions prevailing in the savanna ecosystems of nearly 4 million years ago were essentially the same as those studied by ecologists at the Serengeti Research Institute in the 1960s and '70s: the same vegetation pattern; the same structure of animal populations, with carnivores preying on a variety of herbivores. Savanna ecosystems are distinguished by the immense herds of migratory animals they support and the annual migration of wildebeest and zebra from the Serengeti to the Mara and back is one of the natural wonders of the world. Millions of animals are involved. On their yearly round they are preyed upon by carnivores and scavengers—lions, cheetahs, leopards, wild dogs, and hyenas—which feed very well when the herds enter their territories, but suffer lean times when they have gone.

The migrating herds move between ten and twenty kilometres a day. No hunting or scavenging carnivores can follow them constantly because their young grow slowly and cannot keep up with the adults in the group. Consequently, breeding carnivores are sedentary and territorial. Yet if they could travel with the herds they would have year-round access not only to the animals they could kill but also to the products of natural mortality.

Almost 70 per cent of carcasses found by researchers in the Serengeti were the result of natural deaths, not predation. Every day there was at least one such carcass within five kilometres of any point on the migration route. Vultures locate the carcasses, but they cannot easily break through the skin of intact carcasses and so this unexploited food source represents the vacant niche that a bipedal hominid able to follow the migrating herds would fill. Enterprising researchers who followed the migrations on foot in the 1970s found plenty of meat and suffered no serious conflict with wild predators and scavengers.[14]

The palaeontological record indicates that the situation was little different at that crucial point in human evolutionary history when the ancestral hominids acquired the habitual bipedal gait. So, from an ecological point of view, it is probable that although competition and the threat of extinction may well have driven the hominid ancestors away from their original home, it was access to a new, rich and reliable food supply that led to the evolution of bipedalism. Pre-adapted to bipedalism, in that 60 per cent of their body weight was already carried on the hind legs, exploitation of the new niche favoured individuals in which the upright stance and the striding gait appeared.

The ancestral hominid was on the road to humanity, but there was nothing predetermined about the evolutionary route which had been taken. It was nothing more than a response to prevailing ecological circumstance: some individuals took advantage of a hitherto unexploited resource, and natural selection favoured the evolution of habitual bipedalism. No predetermining social innovations such as the home base and heightened female sexuality were required, nor was the subsequent development of other human attributes inferred. The primary implication of the migration hypothesis is simply this: the earliest representatives of the human line were nomads.

Mares and yearlings of a zebra family in the Ngorongoro crater, Tanzania

CHAPTER 7

The Cutting Edge

THE ANCESTORS OF MODERN HUMANS were bipedal nomads and scavengers who discovered that sharp stone flakes were more efficient than teeth at detaching meat from a carcass. Tools were teeth in the hand.

In the course of three field seasons in the early 1970s, an international expedition under the joint leadership of Don Johanson from the Cleveland Museum, Ohio, and Yves Coppens of the Musée de l'Homme in Paris, discovered a veritable treasure trove of hominid fossils in the Afar depression, Ethiopia.[1] Star of the collection was a skeleton, 40 per cent complete, accession number A.L. 288–1, but more widely known as "Lucy" (the Beatles' song "Lucy in the Sky with Diamonds" was popular in camp that year).

The fossils have been assigned to the taxon *Australopithecus afarensis,*[2] the earliest-known candidate for human ancestry. The deposits in which they were found date from 3.2 million years ago, and the Lucy skeleton is complete enough to give a good estimate of the hominids' overall physique at that time. She stood no more than 122 centimetres in height—barely tall enough to see over the average garden fence; and weighed about 30 kilograms—less than the average eight-year-old child in modern developed countries. The configuration of the pelvis and lower limbs leaves no doubt that Lucy and her kind walked upright, but since her arms were long, relative to body size, and her fingers and toes were curved, it is also clear that *afarensis* had retained the ancestral primates' ability to climb trees.[3] Trees would have been their first line of retreat from threatening predators during daylight hours; and they certainly would have sought out the safety of trees, or rocky ledges, for sleeping at night.

Like modern apes and monkeys, the ancestral hominids occupied a diurnal niche in the rhythm of life on the African landscape. This was crucially important to their survival. While the carnivores hunted from dusk to dawn, the hominids slept in some safe retreat. During the day they would have encountered some carnivore activity from time to time, but competition for food need not have arisen, for the simple reason that while meat was essential to the carnivores it was of only secondary importance to the omnivorous hominids.

Meat is commonly assumed to be a "high quality" protein food that hominids would have eaten by choice in large quantities whenever it was available. In fact, although meat provides a direct intake of certain essential amino acids (the building blocks of proteins) otherwise assembled only from a combination of vegetable foods, a little meat goes a long way and too much can be dangerous. There is an absolute limit to the amount of meat that humans can eat on a regular basis and remain healthy. Liver function is seriously strained, for instance, when meat protein constitutes more than 50 per cent of daily total calorific intake for a prolonged period;[4] this is especially true when the meat consumed is low in fat, and a diet consisting solely of lean meat would kill humans in a matter of weeks.[5]

Fat is essential to good health (when relieving extreme hunger, Eskimos eat fat in preference to meat, it has been noted)[6] but African plains game are notoriously lean, with an average carcass fat content of less than 4 per cent—and most of that is contained in the brain and marrow. It is probable, therefore, that hominids sought animal carcasses as much if not more for their marrow- and brain-fat as for their flesh. And since marrow bones and braincases are the items most often left unconsumed when predators and scavengers have had their fill,[7] the hominids had access to a largely unexploited source of these essential dietary supplements. So although the frequency with which carcasses became available among large herds on migration could have activated the ancestral hominids' pre-adaptation towards a bipedal mode of locomotion and a nomadic way of life, the attraction would have been more in the line of wholesome snacks than main-course dinners. Plant foods would have constituted by far the greater part of the hominid diet. In fact, some plant foods contain a higher proportion by weight of protein than fresh meat. Baobab seeds, for instance, are 34.1 per cent protein by weight, while fresh meat is only 21 per cent. Likewise, the mongongo nut on which the !Kung (! denotes that the K is said with a "click") bushmen subsist for long periods is 28.8 per cent protein.

Indeed, the average protein content of over 150 species of roots, tubers, beans, nuts, and fruits known to have been utilized by hunter-gatherers in modern times is significant. The biological value and digestibility of vegetable proteins are inferior to those of animal protein, it is true, but a varied plant-food diet adequately compensates for any amino acid shortage or imbalance.[8]

Whether acquired from meat or plants, protein is unlikely to have been a problem for the hominids; likewise, carbohydrates, vitamins and essential minerals were available from roots and fruits; fats could be obtained from insects and reptiles and small animals, as well as from scavenged carcasses. The food supply was good, so long as the ancestral hominids kept moving—not simply to keep up with the migrating herds, but also to take account of the seasonal round of plant-food availability. From rainy to dry season, varying patterns of plant growth provide different sources of food, widely distributed across the landscape.

The ecotones between forest and savanna grassland would have been favoured regions, providing access to two different vegetation regimes, but even dry and apparently barren grasslands are surprisingly rich in food resources, particularly below ground. A semi-arid shrubland on which only between about 100 and 600 grams of vegetation per square metre is produced above ground each year produces between 250 and 1,000 grams per square metre each year underground. Furthermore, below-ground plants are relatively unaffected by grazing, fire, and drought and thus provided a measure of security, stability and independence for hominids that could have been an important influence on the evolution of the group,[9] provided they kept moving.

Indeed, there would have been little or no incentive to remain in one place for any length of time. Successful exploitation of the available food resources depended very much upon the hominids' ability to travel. Furthermore, anything resembling a home base, to which hominids returned daily, would attract the unwelcome attention of predators; even safe sleeping sites could be ambushed or held under siege. So in terms of food supply and security the logic of a nomadic lifestyle for the ancestral hominids is compelling; and the fossil evidence is no less convincing—for although the total number of hominid fossils so far discovered is small, their distribution in Africa is widespread.

It has been estimated that even if the population density of the early hominids was no greater than that of modern wild dogs, the ten fossil skulls found at East Turkana in Kenya, for instance, represent no more than one in every 100,000 of the individuals who lived there during the million years spanned by the deposits.[10] The East Turkana deposits are exceptionally rich, but hominid fossils have also been found at sites spread across the full extent of sub-Saharan Africa east of the Congo basin, from the Afar depression in the north, down the length of the Rift Valley through East Africa, across the savanna woodlands of Central Africa, more than 500 kilometres to the arid southern borders of the Kalahari. And those are only the places in which fossils were preserved and subsequently have been found. Who knows where else the hominids might have gone—into the forests, the mountains, the seashores? There are many parts of Africa where their remains simply would not have been preserved; or else have not yet been discovered. Lacking the hard evidence of fossils, we can be confident only that the ancestral hominids were widely dispersed, and constantly on the move. They were diminutive figures in the African landscape, an integral part of the ecosystem, whose special talents were a generalized ability to take advantage of diverse opportunities, and a unique form of locomotion—the bipedal gait. Nomads.

And the unchanging persistence of the distinctive hominid characteristics through time is as impressive as their physical dispersal across the landscape of Africa. The passage of time, from the 5-million-year-old australopithecine (the oldest known) found in the Tugen Hills,[11] to *Australopithecus ramidus*[12] at 4.4 million years ago, to Lucy at 3.2 million years ago, and on to *A. africanus* in South Africa at 2 million years ago, represents a span of 150,000 generations (assuming each generation to have been twenty years) without any physical change that would indicate significant shifts in the way of life. Changes in tooth size and enamel thickness have been identified (and interpreted as indicating variations in diet), but the overall lightweight form of the "gracile" australopithecines remained virtually unchanged throughout all that vast expanse of time and space. Clearly, the generalized (as opposed to specialized) form and lifestyle of these small bipedal primates functioned successfully whatever climatic and ecological variations they may have encountered during the passage of more than 3 million years.

The fossil record indicates that for the greater part of that 3 million years the gracile australopithecines were the only hominids in existence. Then, at about 2.5 million years ago, another, much more heavily built hominid appears in the fossil record. Its appearance is sudden, marked by a splendid specimen discovered on the western shore of Lake Turkana in 1985,[13] but clearly, this earliest-known specimen marks only the first occasion on which a member of the living population had died under the very rare circumstances that lead to organic remains being incorporated in the fossil record. The speciation event from which this quite distinct hominid had evolved must have occurred long before; and the cause was probably competition for resources within the ecological niche exploited by the hominids. One group hived off, found other ways of making a living, and natural selection favoured the evolution of appropriate characteristics.

The most immediately obvious characteristic of the newcomer is its heavily built physique, particularly in respect of the skull. Average height matched that of its gracile cousins, but its weight appears to have been up to 50 per cent greater. The skull is of heavy and solid appearance, with a broad flat face, solid cheekbones and brow ridges, a low braincase and a prominent crest of bone running from the forehead to the back of the skull. The crest was the attachment point for the powerful muscles which operated the massive lower jaw; the teeth were correspondingly large, with a chewing surface some four or five times greater than is found in modern humans or gracile australopithecines. In acknowledgement of their heavy build the newcomer and its kin were dubbed the "robust" australopithecines.

The structure of the robust australopithecine skull was entirely determined by the muscular forces required to operate the massive jaw and its array of heavy-duty chewing equipment: large teeth and heavy jaws require powerful muscles pulling on strong bone attachments. What were the robust australopithecines eating that required such powerful chewing equipment? The intuitive answer would suggest that it must have been very hard—nuts and seeds, even bone (to extract marrow) perhaps—any foodstuff that required a tremendous biting force. But this misses the true relevance of the large teeth.

In fact, a large chewing surface lessens rather than maximizes the force applied at any particular point. With a chewing surface four times larger than in modern humans, a robust australopithecine would have to apply four times the bite force to create the same pressure that a human could achieve. It follows, therefore, that the robust chewing equipment was never intended to maximize bite force, but had evolved to serve a quite different purpose: prolonged bouts of chewing. Now the pertinent question ceases to be, "What were they eating that was so hard?" and becomes "What were they eating that needed to be processed in such large quantities?" The answer is foodstuffs that contained a large proportion of indigestible material.[14]

Researchers who examined the chewing surface of teeth through an electron microscope found that different diets leave quite distinct patterns of scratches. When the patterns on robust australopithecine teeth were compared with those on the teeth of an orang-utan (a fruit eater), rhinoceros (grazer), giraffe (browser), cheetah (carnivore), and hyena (scavenger and bone eater), the greatest similarity was found with that of the orang-utan, indicating that the robust australopithecines had eaten fruit in large quantities without much preparation.

The fruits of most indigenous African plants are small, largely lacking in fleshy pulp, and are either encased in a hard shell or pod or consist of small seeds with individual hard protective cases. The robust australopithecines must have chewed up masses of this indigestible material. The chewing apparatus they employed represents a specialization that set the robust australopithecines apart from the more generalized ancestral hominids, and directed them towards a separate evolutionary path. The specialization served them well, for a time. The fossil record shows that by 1.6 million years ago they were present at sites ranging down the length of the Rift Valley and beyond—from Ethiopia to South Africa.

But specialization is a one-way affair that permits no turning back, and it can be a mixed blessing: while maximizing the exploitation of one set of opportunities it can close off access to others—with dire consequences. The fossil record of vertebrate evolution contains numerous examples of creatures which diverged from the generalized form and evolved into specialized forms that subsequently became extinct. The robust australopithecines suffered exactly that fate. They reached an evolutionary dead-end about one million years ago, when they disappear from the fossil record. Nothing like them is known from more recent deposits: they left no descendants.

Meanwhile, the gracile form had developed specializations of its own, but these were specializations which extended the advantages of the generalized form, rather than restricting them: tools, and intelligence.

A FRESHLY KNAPPED STONE FLAKE IS as sharp as a well-honed steel blade. The first deliberate production of a cutting edge marks the dawn of technology, and thus the beginning of a trend which ultimately produced the modern industrial state. It began in Africa, a very long time ago. The earliest-known tools come from sites in Ethiopia and East Africa from around 2.4 million years ago (at the latest), and they are a common feature of archaeological sites throughout Africa from about 2 million years ago. At Olduvai Gorge and Olorgasailie stone tools are so plentiful it is difficult to avoid stepping on them; the Harts River dam in South Africa has drowned sites that contained literally thousands of tools. Throughout the continent, any exposed stretch of ancient land surface is likely to contain stone tools from the age it represents. Farmers plough them up without regard.

Stone tools and robust australopithecines appear in the fossil record almost simultaneously, so it may be tempting to assume that robust australopithecines made stone tools. However, with the exception of the single instance of a robust australopithecine specimen found near deposits that contained tools at Chesowanja in Kenya,[15] stone tools have only ever been found in association with gracile hominids.

It seems remarkable that the bipedal ancestral hominids should have existed without the benefit of stone tools for more than a million years and then started making them precisely as the first robust australopithecines appear in the fossil record, but that period around 2.4 million years was a time when extinctions and first appearances were relatively numerous in the palaeontological record.

Something was going on—possibly a climatic blip that imposed competitive conditions leading to speciation among some species, and inflicted extinction on others. The number of hyena species, for instance, suffered a marked decline around this time,[16] which may have increased hominid scavenging opportunities and inspired the use of tools to break open marrow bones and slice up flesh. In any event, the arrival of the robust australopithecines and the advent of stone tools probably were both responses to some ecological perturbation, but completely independent of one another.

Because meat is consumed in large quantities today, we tend to think that hunting and the acquisition of meat would have been the primary incentive for making stone tools, but the appearance of stone tools does not necessarily reflect an abrupt or dramatic shift in food *acquisition* behaviour at all. What it does seem to show is a shift in food *processing* techniques. Stone tools certainly were used to process animal carcasses, but there can be no doubt that they were also important in making tools such as digging sticks and for processing vegetable foods, such as nuts and tubers.[17]

Essentially, stone tools enabled hominids to do with their hands what other animals did with their teeth—this is their fundamental contribution to the evolutionary history of humanity. The gracile hominids *externalized* the processing of food. While carnivores ripped open carcasses and tore flesh from the bones with their teeth, and as the robust hominids munched laboriously through mounds of nutritionally low-grade plant foods, the graciles took a stone, cut meat from carcasses, cracked open marrow-bones, and pounded plant foods to a pre-masticated pulp.

Assessments of the relevance of stone tools in the daily lives of ancestral hominids must take account of the fact that stone tools are the most durable items in the archaeological record. While organic material rots and fossils erode away to dust, the tools survive unscathed. Their ubiquity may overemphasize their relevance. They tumble out of river banks and accumulate in depressions—just waiting, it might seem, to stir the imagination of someone passing by. You can pick up a stone tool quite freely (it will not shatter, as a delicate fossil might), you weigh it in the hand, and imagine you are repeating the actions of an ancestor who stood on the self-same spot, two million years before. You see tools lying among scattered fossil bones on ancient lake shores, there are cut marks on the bones, and you are inclined to envisage an extended family feasting on meat provided by brave hunters—but the true interpretation is more prosaic.

Hunting is a recent and very sophisticated innovation. Two and a half million years ago the ancestral hominids were using very unsophisticated choppers—cobbles with the end knocked off to make a sharp edge—and flakes. These were tools for processing scavenged carcasses, not for hunting. And the hominid tool kit remained essentially unchanged for almost a million years—until around 1.5 million years ago—by which time the robusts had become extinct and there was more than one species of hominid on the scene.

CHAPTER 8

In the Mind's Eye

THE DEMANDS OF stone-tool manufacture were significant among the aspects of early hominid life which stimulated the development of cognitive abilities and the evolution of anatomically modern humans—*Homo sapiens sapiens*—in Africa.

Lake Turkana lies in the hot and inhospitable landscape of northern Kenya. The lake measures more than 250 kilometres from north to south, and is about 50 kilometres across at its widest point. In places it is 240 metres deep. Three volcanic cones stand as islands at intervals along its length. Rivers flow into the lake (primarily the Omo River which drains the highlands of Ethiopia), but none flows from it. Evaporation from the lake is excessive, and the salts left behind have turned its waters into a solution that wild animals drink with impunity but which humans find decidedly unpleasant—not least on account of its laxative properties. On most days, a fierce easterly wind is drawn across the lake by thermals rising from the baking landscape, and the surface waters are whipped to a choppy froth of erratic waves. Crocodiles frequent the shallows, preying largely on fish but always alert for the unwary zebra or antelope. The surrounding landscape rarely receives more than 100 mm of rain in a year. Fresh water is available only at a few widely separated natural springs; so the human population is limited to small groups of nomadic pastoralists, even though there is grazing and browse enough to support large numbers of wild animals.

Nonetheless, people have inhabited this region of northern Kenya for mil-

The classic "handaxe," a stone tool commonly found in deposits more than one million years old at Olduvai Gorge in Tanzania

lions of years, and the record of their existence has been preserved as fossils in the sediments that form the greater part of the landscape around the lake. In 1968, researchers working with Richard Leakey, the then director of the Kenya National Museum, began the challenging task of recovering and unravelling that record of human origins. A permanent camp was established on a grassy plain bordering the lake shore where a sandspit curves out into the lake, and pelicans glide in to roost as the wind drops each evening. The place is called Koobi Fora. From there, scientists representing a variety of disciplines fanned out across the landscape: geologists, palaeontologists, anthropologists, archaeologists, biologists, all working towards a long-term aim of assembling a multifaceted picture of the human condition through time. Early on, the archaeologist Glynn Isaac (1937–85) was witness to a dramatic example of how little the problems confronting humanity have changed at the subsistence level in Africa. While out surveying prospective archaeological sites, Isaac and his companions encountered a young Shangilla boy tending a herd of goats. In their presence, the herdboy found the carcass of an antelope that had been killed by lions during the night and freshly abandoned. The boy had no knife. "Spontaneously," Isaac reports, "he tapped off a very small flake from a lava cobble and proceeded to slit the skin covering a cannon bone, which he then peeled and cracked open to obtain marrow."[1]

The Shangilla herdboy demonstrated that the technology used to exploit the basic food resources of the Turkana basin had not changed in 2 million years; meanwhile, geological investigations have shown that the basin itself had undergone profound changes during that time.[2]

The present Lake Turkana is only a few hundred thousand years old—the latest of several short-lived lakes which have formed in the basin over the last 3.5 million years. A large perennial river and its tributaries dominated the system for the greater part of that period. The inflow was primarily from the north, draining the Ethiopian highlands as the Omo does today. At times the ancestral Omo flowed through the basin and east to the Indian Ocean (a connection which is confirmed by the presence in the Turkana deposits of fossilized ocean fish remains, such as the teeth of a stingray). At other times its waters remained in the basin in the form of rivers flowing down the length of the basin like tangled braids of hair, meandering through gallery forests and woodland; creating floodplains and ephemeral lakes.

The pattern of the waterways was dictated by tectonic and volcanic activity associated with the formation of the Rift Valley, and the bends of the main river "flip-flopped" back and forth across the floor of the basin as the underlying geological surface tilted, first one way and then the other. Volcanic activity peaked around 1.7 million years ago, and lava flows accumulating along the eastern boundary of the basin severed the ancestral Omo from its Indian Ocean outlet.

The ancestral hominids were living in the Turkana basin through all these perturbations; the events cover the period during which hominids began using stone tools and archaeologists have attempted to identify the circumstances that made stone tools important to them.[3] Tracing the evidence of fossils and technology across the landscape and through time, they found that the earliest examples, from around 2.5 to 2.4 million years ago, coincided with a conspicuous change to drier conditions and the onset of a marked dry season/wet season annual cycle. Further, the sites at which tools have been found were the more sheltered and well-watered parts of the ancient landscape, where tree cover was evident. The advantage here was not drinks in the shade for hominids—it was rather that closed habitats along bush- and tree-lined watercourses offer the best opportunities for scavenging from the carcasses of animals that carnivores had ambushed on the way to drink.[4]

Dozens of sites from the period 2.4 million years to 1.6 million years ago have been located among the Turkana deposits. The tools at the oldest sites were made from cobbles that the hominids could have collected from nearby riverbeds; the most distant sources were only up to four kilometres away. Throughout, the tools demonstrate a very basic level of manufacturing skill: modified cobbles and stones, and flakes struck directly from a stone, just as the Shangilla herdboy had done. This technology (first described from Olduvai Gorge by Mary Leakey as the Oldowan Industry) has been found at every site in Africa with archaeological material from the period 2.5 million to 1.5 million years ago, from northern Ethiopia to South Africa, unchanged for a million years. Such continuity implies that there was no incentive for change or innovation throughout all that time. So change, when it did arise, must have been inspired by a perceived need for something different—a different tool for a different task. Perhaps even a different toolmaker.

The earliest toolmakers—those gracile hominids who externalized the processing of food while the robusts evolved specialized chewing apparatus to deal with large quantities of coarse vegetative material—are known as *Homo habilis* ("handy man"). The first fossil remains of *Homo habilis,* consisting of a lower jaw, a partial braincase, a collarbone, and sundry other parts of the skeleton, were found scattered among fossil animal bones (mainly of the non-marrow variety) and a number of Oldowan tools at Olduvai Gorge in May 1960.[5]

Tools and fossils found together implied that the hominid specimen at the site had made the tools, hence the term *habilis.* Furthermore, its brain was appreciably larger than any other early hominid, gracile or robust. Together, brain size and the capacity to make tools were the accepted definition of humanity in its true and earliest expression—hence *Homo habilis.*

While bipedalism marks the divergence which led hominids away from the ancestral hominoid stock, brain size and toolmaking denote the ancestors of modern humans. *Homo habilis* had crossed the Rubicon. Reconstructions of the *habilis* braincase gave an average cranial capacity of 640 cubic centimetres, 55 per cent larger than that of the gracile *Australopithecus afarensis* with 413 cubic centimetres, 24 per cent larger than the robust australopithecines with 516 cubic centimetres.[6]

Homo habilis at Olduvai Gorge dates from 1.7 million years ago; the species is known from Lake Turkana too, most notably in the form of the famous KNM-ER 1470 skull (cranial capacity about 750 cc) which is about 1.88 million years old. At both Olduvai and Lake Turkana, robust hominids were present at the same time as *Homo habilis;* indeed, they appear to have shared resources across the great expanse of East and southern Africa for several hundred thousand years. Different ways of life probably minimized the chances of competition and conflict.

Around 1.6 million years ago, however, *Homo habilis* and the robusts were joined by a third hominid, *Homo erectus. Homo habilis* disappears from the fossil record shortly thereafter—presumably having become extinct. The robusts continued to occupy their specialized vegetarian niche for another half a million years, before they too became extinct about 1 million years ago. *Homo erectus* was then the sole surviving hominid, and destined to become the most widespread and longest-surviving of the known candidates for human ancestry.

Homo erectus is most splendidly represented by the skeleton of a boy, less than twelve years old, whose body became entombed in mud west of the present Lake Turkana about 1.6 million years ago.[7] The skeleton is the most complete specimen of an ancestral hominid ever unearthed and fully substantiates the prevailing view that *Homo erectus* had been sturdy and well-built. The Turkana boy was over 1.6 m tall and if the *erectus* growth pattern matched that of modern humans, would have become a 1.8 m adult had he lived. He had the long-legged build which is characteristic of humans in the tropics; the arms too matched those of humans today. Brain size was approaching 900 cc.

Homo erectus had of course evolved from the same ancestral stock as the robust and gracile hominids who also inhabited the region at that time, but *erectus* was set on a unique evolutionary path which extended yet again the distinctive characteristics of the hominid line. The capacity to cover distance was enhanced by increased body size; the potential for technological innovation was heightened by the greater cognitive abilities of a larger brain. *Homo erectus,* therefore, was both bigger and brainier than the other hominids, and it is tempting to conclude that competition must have led to the demise of the latter. Perhaps. The facts are only that while the robusts and the graciles dwindled to extinction, *Homo erectus* thrived.

Homo erectus is known from sites in South Africa, Tanzania, Kenya, Ethiopia, Morocco and Algeria. At an early but unrecorded date, some representatives of the species took the human line out of Africa for the first time. Their fossil remains have been found in Europe, Java and China; the oldest dates from 1.8 million years ago (Java);[8] the youngest (200,000 years old) comes from China. *Homo erectus* is a prime candidate for the immediate ancestry of the Neandertals, *Homo neanderthalensis,* who populated Europe from about 120,000 years ago; if this is true, then the *Homo erectus* line persisted out of Africa until about 30,000 years ago, when the Neandertals became extinct.

Homo erectus individuals were significantly bigger than their antecedents and contemporary cousins. Increased size was potentially beneficial, but successful exploitation of that potential depended heavily upon keeping benefits ahead of costs. There was a fine balance to be maintained. A larger body brought greater mobility and therefore access to more dispersed resources, but it also required larger quantities of food. The enlarged brain could tip the balance favourably by endowing a capacity to think and work out solutions to problems, but there was a cost here too: an enlarged brain meant that offspring would take longer to mature, and parents would be obliged to invest more time and energy keeping children alive until they were able to fend for themselves. Furthermore, the brain is expensive to run.[9] Though on average the brain constitutes only 2 per cent of body weight in modern humans, it consumes 16 per cent of the body's energy budget and, as an evolutionary innovation, must therefore have paid its way.

ONE AND A HALF MILLION YEARS AGO the brain of *Homo erectus* measured about 1,000 cc, which is on the edge of the modern human range for adults (1,000 to 2,000 cc), and roughly three-quarters of the modern average (1,330 cc). Brain size is not an absolute measure of intelligence, but it is reasonable to assume that *Homo erectus* shared a measure of the dependence upon intelligence that distinguishes humanity today. Only humans depend for their survival upon elaborate systems of culture and social interaction; only the human brain could organize and sustain such complex systems. No other animal possesses the human capacity for reasoned action—even the chimpanzees, with whom humans share 99 per cent genetic identity, are far, far less able to assess problems and formulate solutions.

Homo erectus marks the point at which the further existence of the human ancestor—an animal with very generalized physical characteristics—was entrusted to a single highly specialized organ: the brain. Humanity was set to become a specialist, and the species' survival would be increasingly dependent upon the brain's capacity to find ways of satisfying the body's needs. The earliest-known manifestation of this development dates from around 1.4 million years ago, with the arrival in the archaeological record of an entirely new style of tool manufacture, occasionally in direct association with the fossil remains of *Homo erectus*. The tools are known as "bifaces" (the peardrop-shaped hand axe is the most frequently illustrated example), and they introduce the key factors of preconception and planned manufacture to human technology.

Homo habilis had been fully capable of making tools from cobbles, and that talent served its need for more than a million years. The technology remained virtually unchanged throughout and while such conservatism may demonstrate the complete adequacy of the tool to the task, it could also demonstrate the lack of a capacity to envisage any improvement. *Homo habilis* made tools according to an arbitrary "least effort" principle: take a cobble, knock off some flakes, use whatever is produced. *Homo erectus,* by contrast, made bifacial cutting tools according to a predetermined pattern.

The toolmakers selected suitable pieces of stone, knocked flakes from both sides and consistently produced tools that were longer than they were broad, pointed at one end and rounded at the other; they had a sharp edge all around, were perfectly symmetrical, and curved from end to end and from edge to edge on both sides. There was nothing arbitrary about this manufacturing process. The long axis, the cutting edge, the point and the symmetry of the carefully controlled curves were imposed on the stone, they did not arrive by chance. Each blow struck on the stone opened up too many possibilities for that. The process could be controlled only by constantly comparing the work in hand with an image of the finished product that is fixed "in the mind's eye."

This capacity to visualize things that do not yet exist has been seen as the fundamental hallmark of culture.[10] Imagination. Combined with memories of the past and experience in the present, imagination enables people to plan for the future—tomorrow or years hence.

In *Homo erectus* the capacity to envisage and manufacture a desirable tool (and their tool kit was not limited to hand axes) was accompanied by a tendency to seek out and use specific varieties of stone. The source of raw materials used by *Homo habilis* was never much more than four kilometres away, but investigations at Olduvai Gorge have shown that by about 900,000 years ago, *Homo erectus* was making tools from stone found more than eight kilometres away, and by 600,000 years ago the Olduvai basin was criss-crossed with a veritable network of supply routes. Different rocks have different properties, and it seems they were being collected and used selectively.

Trachyte (a coarse-grained lava) was brought in from the Olmoti foothills, fifteen kilometres away; green phonolite (a fine-grained lava) was carried twenty kilometres from its source on Engelosen. These are distances measured as the crow flies; on foot, across the undulating landscape, they would have been greater, and certainly difficult to cover in less than a day when carrying heavy loads of stone. So *Homo erectus* must have been planning activities several days ahead, and the rewards must have been worthwhile. The raw material may not have been carried over the entire distance by members of a single group; indeed, the distribution pattern could indicate that some form of barter was taking place among groups camped closest to the sources of the various raw materials—a kind of "trade" in raw materials,[11] operating in Africa more than half a million years before it first appears in the archaeological records of Europe.

From their point of origin in East Africa, *Homo erectus* populations dispersed throughout Africa, into Europe and across Asia to India, China and Java. The most distant populations probably left Africa before *Homo erectus* began making bifaces, for the characteristic hand axes are not found in Java and China (and the 1.8-million-year date for the evidence of *Homo erectus* in Java would appear to confirm this probability).

Homo erectus was the longest surviving and most widely dispersed of the ancestral toolmakers. The species disappears from the fossil record around 200,000 years ago, and the hand axes which characterized the biface technology it had introduced cease to dominate the archaeological record at roughly the same time.[12] Small flake tools, scrapers, and—in particular—blades take over. Though present alongside the bifaces of *Homo erectus* for some time previously, by about 130,000 years ago the new tools dominate the archaeological assemblages and have assumed a form which represents a major advance in manufacturing technology. Most characteristic are long narrow blades which had been struck from a carefully prepared block (the Levallois technique), but all the new tools indicate a heightened degree of technological insight and the adaptation of existing techniques to fresh perceptions of need. "Hand axe–style" bifaces are still made, but they are smaller, heart-shaped or triangular with carefully flaked butts, suggesting that perhaps they had been used as adzes. There were fine slivers of stone, which could have been used for piercing skins; scrapers; and single-edged blades which seem designed for cutting and sawing. In a word, the new tool kit suggests refinement. It is as though the mind's eye had looked beyond the primary imperatives of life and seen a multitude of secondary needs. Animals were no longer simply food, but also a source of skins that could be fashioned into bags and coverings; trees supplied bark from which string could be twisted, and gum for fixing stone blades to wooden shafts.

And does the fossil record reveal a new species of hominid to whom these developments in the archaeological record can be assigned, in the same way that *Homo habilis* is said to have introduced the Oldowan tool kit 2.5 million years ago and *Homo erectus* is credited with the advent of biface technology around 1 million years later? Indeed it does. At about 400,000 years ago a variation on the *Homo erectus* form appears in the fossil record, very similar overall, but with differences in the configuration of the skull and face that are related to a significant increase in brain size. The brain averages 1,250 cc—close enough to the modern human average for the newcomer to be called "archaic *Homo sapiens*." And as *Homo erectus* disappears from the fossil record around 200,000 years ago, the trend towards humanity marked so distinctively by archaic *Homo sapiens* continues in the form of a third hominid, which makes its appearance about 130,000 years ago.

The skeleton of the newcomer is tall and slender, the chin juts forward, the face is short and tucked in under the skull, there is a high forehead but no brow ridges, and the brain measures between 1,200 and 1,700 cc—well within the modern human range. Indeed, the association is unmistakable. This is the first evidence of ourselves, anatomically modern humans, *Homo sapiens sapiens*— wise, wise man. And it is this species which carries the chain of primate evolution in Africa forward from the innovative talents that enabled *Homo erectus* to transform an image in the mind's eye into present and future reality.

Lesser flamingos on Lake Nakuru, Kenya

CHAPTER 9

Cool Systems

THERMOREGULATION AND ACCESS TO water were crucial determinants of human survival in the African cradle-land—and important preconditions for the evolution of the species' highly developed brain and social behaviour.

The human form is solid and substantial enough to have cast long shadows across the face of the earth, but people—like the surface of the planet itself—are more than 70 per cent liquid. Water is the largest structural component of the human body; plumbing constitutes a major proportion of the human frame: in total, the blood vessels, lymph and urinary tracts of a single human adult are long enough to encircle the globe—twice.[1] The water content of a healthy 65 kg human is nearly 50 litres—enough to fill 150 Coca-Cola cans. So much water, but no more than is essential for the transport of nutrients and the elimination of wastes.

The average person, in average temperate conditions, must take in and excrete about 2.5 litres of liquid each day (amounting to the replacement of about 5 per cent of total water content), and no matter how much the intake may vary the body's total water content remains remarkably consistent, deviating less than 1 per cent from the norm. Skin and lungs account for a proportion of water loss, but total water content is maintained at a consistent level primarily by the kidneys—the urine becomes more dilute when liquid intake is high, and more concentrated when it is low. But there are limits. A minimum daily urine output of about half a litre is essential, since anything less will not be enough to flush all potentially toxic waste products from the body.[2]

Indeed, maintaining the water content of the body at optimum levels is so critical that relatively small departures from the norm can be extremely dangerous. An absolute loss approaching 5 per cent of total water content will impair many functions, including the brain's ability to process information; death will almost certainly result from a loss of anything more than 5 per cent.[3] For the average person, in average temperate conditions, 5 per cent of total water content amounts to one day's average liquid intake: 2.5 litres, the equivalent of 7.5 cans of Coke. People can live for weeks without food, but without water they die within days.

In tropical conditions water requirements are correspondingly greater, for humans must sweat to keep cool. Here of course it is the maintenance of body temperature that is critical—every bit as critical, in fact, as the maintenance of water content. The human body maintains a core temperature of 37 degrees centigrade, and while most body tissues are relatively tolerant of slight variations from the norm, the central nervous system is particularly sensitive to rises in temperature. Normal functioning of the brain becomes progressively impaired by elevations above 37°C, and even a temperature of 40.5°C can be fatal.[4]

Just being alive burns energy and therefore generates heat. A person at rest, reading this book for instance, is equivalent to a motor or an electric-light bulb running at around 75 watts. When ambient temperatures are below core levels, the heat produced by the human motor is readily lost to the surrounding air, but additional cooling mechanisms are required when temperatures are high. We flush and sweat. Evaporation takes heat from the blood pumped up to and through capillaries at the skin surface, the cool blood flows back to the core, and a stable temperature of 37°C is maintained.

The efficiency of the human cooling system (not to mention its necessity) was convincingly demonstrated over 200 years ago by Dr. Charles Blagden, the then secretary of the Royal Society. Accompanied by a few friends and a piece of meat, Blagden spent forty-five minutes in a room that had been heated to a temperature of 126°C. Blagden and his friends emerged sweaty but otherwise unaffected. The meat was cooked.[5] The records do not disclose how much liquid the gentlemen imbibed before their body water content was restored to normal levels, but the quantities must have been considerable. Modern field studies have recorded sweating rates of up to 4 litres an hour among people spending short periods of time at extreme temperatures. A fit young man walking at 5 km per hour in temperatures of around 40°C lost 1.5 litres of sweat per hour, and various studies have shown that a water loss of

8 litres per day is average for young men maintaining moderate levels of activity in hot deserts.[6]

In a hot dry climate the evaporation of one litre of sweat can in theory dissipate 2,500 kJ of heat[7] (which is enough energy to run the average family refrigerator for three and a half hours), so the effectiveness of sweating as a cooling mechanism is not in doubt. But the cost is equally apparent. Every drop has to be replaced. Failure to replace the water loss within the 24-hour cycle produces serious dehydration and incapacitation; death is inevitable if a second day of high heat load is experienced.

On the open savannas of East Africa, where conditions approximate those in which the human ancestor lived 200,000 years ago, a study by physiologist Pete Wheeler reported air temperatures at ground level regularly exceeding 35°C for seven out of the twelve daylight hours. They reached 30°C shortly after nine in the morning, and soared to a peak of 45°C by one in the afternoon. The hottest period of the day was from 11 a.m. to 4 p.m.—five hours when the air temperature consistently remained above 40°C. Even at dusk, six in the evening, air temperatures exceeded 30°C.[8]

Keeping cool in such a temperature regime calls for prodigious quantities of sweat. A person weighing 65 kg would sweat (and must replace) at least 7 litres per day while active in such conditions.[9] The human ancestors, 200,000 years ago, may have weighed less and probably were better adapted to savanna conditions, in terms of both physique and behaviour. They probably required less water. Even so, they had to drink every day and this fact alone would have placed strict limits on the distance they could travel away from known sources of water. Thus, regular access to water must have been a primary determinant of early human evolution and behaviour; more fundamental than access to food.

Humans of course are not the only mammals to have confronted the problems of heat stress on the East African savannas during their evolutionary history. Grazing animals spend their days exposed to the full impact of the tropical sun. In some species of antelope, the core temperature rises to 45°C and above during the hottest hours of the day. They survive only because they have evolved elaborate ways of keeping their brains cool while their bodies become very hot indeed.

The long muzzle is the key to the savanna mammals' survival strategy. In the length of the muzzle, heat is lost by the evaporation of water from the moist linings of the nasal chambers. This evaporation removes heat from blood flowing beneath the nasal membranes, and the cooled blood then collects near the base of the cranium, in an expanded section of the jugular vein, called a sinus. The pool of relatively cool blood in the sinus conducts some heat directly from the brain; more important, it also acts as a heat-exchanger which cools the brain's own blood supply. The brain is supplied by the carotid arteries, which pass through the sinus, where they branch into a net of fine blood vessels, called the carotid rete. As arterial blood passes through the carotid rete, excess heat is transferred to the cooler venous blood in the sinus, and the brain receives blood at the critical temperature.

With a "radiator" in the nose and a "heat-exchanger" in the cranium most mammals are able to keep their brains cool even when their body tissue is very hot. Humans (and most primates), however, possess neither radiator nor heat-exchanger. As the face broadened and the jaw shrank during the course of primate evolution (as a consequence of dietary changes), the muzzle shortened to the point at which it no longer functioned as a radiator. Humans do not even bother to pant when they are hot. Furthermore, primates (including humans) lack a carotid rete. These factors speak of ancestry in a forested environment, shady and cool, where our closest cousins are still found. Chimpanzees, for example, are very poorly equipped to contend with overheating. Even when shaded from direct sunshine, environmental temperatures of just 40°C cause chimpanzees considerable distress. They sweat and breathe heavily as their temperature rises, but to little effect. Only the cool of evening brings relief.

If the immediate ancestors of the hominids were anything like modern chimpanzees they would have been under considerable evolutionary pressure to stay cool when they ventured from the forests on to the open plains of tropical Africa. The plains offer a broad spectrum of opportunity—tubers, nuts, seeds, and scavenged meat—but these foods usually are scattered or clumped across the landscape, not uniformly distributed; successful foragers must roam widely throughout the day, and must be able to remain active even while the sun is at its zenith. This was the ecological niche that the early hominids exploited (see page 62).

Obviously they did not move in overnight; the adaptations which kept bodies hydrated and brains cool in extremely hot and dry conditions evolved over time, and our own physiology is the living testament of their ultimate success. Humans are supremely well-adapted to energetic activity during the day in hot and dry environments. We have the most effective body cooling system of any living mammal.[10]

The fossil evidence conclusively shows that the ancestors of the hominid lineage existed only in Africa; therefore, our body-cooling system must have been an adaptive response to the environmental stresses of tropical Africa. And so modern physiological fact is indisputably linked to ancient fossil evidence. The significance of this conjunction has been explored by Pete Wheeler in research undertaken for a doctoral thesis.

Wheeler investigated the physiological aspects of hominid evolution from a functional point of view, assessing the basic capabilities and essential requirements of the ancestral hominid, and endeavouring to define the selective pressures and adaptations that had moulded ancestral characteristics into the modern human form. His research led to a string of publications which ultimately invite the conclusion that thermoregulation is at the root of all things human.

He began with assessments of the basic—even rather obvious—physiological attributes of the human form. For instance, since the upright bipedal gait bestows little advantage in terms of locomotive efficiency (see page 61), could it be that the upright stance is functionally advantageous in terms of heat load and cooling demands? Clearly, an animal walking upright exposes less of its body surface to the direct rays of the sun than an animal moving about on all fours, but how much difference does it make?

Wheeler made models of hominids which could be positioned in bipedal and quadrupedal mode and measured the area of their body surfaces that was exposed to direct solar radiation as the sun rose and fell through the course of the day in tropical Africa. The results showed that while the quadruped had around 20 per cent of its body surface exposed to the sun throughout the day, the biped started off with 20 per cent surface exposure but this declined rapidly as the sun rose. By noon, when the sun was directly overhead and solar radiation at its most intense, only 7 per cent of the biped's body surface was exposed to the sun. This meant that simply by standing upright, the bipedal hominids avoided 60 per cent of the direct solar radiation to which they would have been exposed as quadrupeds.

Furthermore, since wind speeds rise and air temperatures fall with distance above the ground, the upright stance exposed a greater proportion of the body to conditions under which relatively more heat was removed from the skin by convection. Wheeler measured the cooling effects of elevation above ground and found that a biped standing on an open grassy plain lost heat 33 per cent faster than a quadruped in the same location. And this benefit was further enhanced by the fact that the air at ground level was relatively humid, owing to water given off by transpiring vegetation. Consequently, although the quadruped may have sweated as much as the biped, the sweat would not evaporate as quickly and its cooling effect therefore was diminished.

Then there is the naked skin of humans to be considered. Fur serves savanna quadrupeds as a shield, reflecting and re-radiating heat before it reaches the skin. If the quadrupeds had lost their fur, melanin would have protected them from harmful UV-B radiation, but this would have decreased the reflectiveness of the skin, causing even greater energy gain. Together, these factors have precluded the evolution of large naked cooling surfaces in savanna quadrupeds,[11] but a biped could dispense with most of the shield, retaining hair only on the head and shoulders while benefiting from evaporative cooling over the rest of the body. The advantages, in terms of thermoregulation, are considerable.

Humans have as many hairs per square centimetre as the chimpanzee, but the hairs are shorter and finer. This functional nakedness, coupled with well-developed sweat glands, enables us to lose heat at the prodigious rate of 700 watts per square metre of skin, a rate not even approached by any other living mammal. Other savanna species do have sweat glands, but their fur inhibits the free flow of air over wet skin and sweat evaporates from the fur instead, taking most of its latent heat of vaporization from the surrounding air, rather than from the skin. In people, almost all the energy needed to evaporate the sweat comes from the body itself, making the whole process more efficient.[12]

Wheeler evaluated all these factors and published results which convincingly demonstrate that the upright stance and naked skin would have enabled a bipedal hominid to remain active in temperatures that would have driven a quadruped cousin to the verge of heatstroke. The naked biped could have roamed across the tropical savanna through the hottest hours of the day, foraging. But lunch was never free; and the price of this unique ability to forage for food under open tropical skies was an adequate supply of water—not something that is always widely available on the African savannas. Dehydration is a serious matter, with risk of incapacitation at even low levels (see page 85 above), so there must always have been a point beyond which the debilitating effects of water loss outweighed the benefits of food gained in further foraging.

The data assembled by Wheeler show that if an ancestral hominid (Lucy for example, who was 1.2 m tall and weighed 30 kg; see page 65) could have tolerated dehydration amounting to 4 per cent of total body mass (which is close to the limit of safety for modern humans), she could have travelled only 11.5 km between water sources as she foraged for food in the course of a day. Hominids became larger through time. Larger hominids need more water, but the advantage of a smaller surface-to-volume ratio means they dehydrate more slowly than smaller individuals and thus are able to travel relatively further. In fact, as Wheeler has shown,[13] a doubling of body mass from close to that of Lucy to that of anatomically modern humans (70 kg) more than doubled the foraging range to 25 km between water sources and increased the potential food-resource area by a factor of 4.73.

· · ·

THOUGH THE UPRIGHT STANCE AND naked skin enabled hominids to forage on the open savannas of tropical Africa at higher temperatures and over greater distances than virtually any other mammal, in terms of basic physiology they were simply the functional elements of a whole-body cooling system that protected the brain from heat stress. The system maintained an exceptional degree of body-temperature stability. It evolved while the hominid brain was still relatively small, and thus coincidentally established the precise conditions which favoured the evolution of *the* most definitive human characteristic: the large cognitive brain. This is not to say that temperature-control strategies *caused* the evolution of a large brain, merely that they removed certain physiological constraints and thus rendered enlargement of it possible.

The physiological constraints in question, present in every other mammal that evolved to live on the open African savanna, are the radiator and the heat-exchanger; that is, the long muzzle and the carotid rete. These devices enable savanna animals to cool blood selectively (see pages 85–86), keeping the brain cool while the body heats up. But selective cooling has physiological limits. The strategy depends upon the amount of blood that the carotid rete can cool to the critical temperature before it flows into the brain. Larger brains need a larger blood supply and therefore a larger carotid rete. However, since the rete functions by pumping blood through an ever-finer network of blood vessels, its maximum size is determined by the pressure and volume that can be accommodated. Wheeler's calculations show that if the blood supplying the modern human brain was cooled through a carotid rete, the jugular sinus in which it was situated would fill the entire diameter of the neck.[14] Clearly, the whole-body cooling system supported by the upright stance and naked skin was a more feasible strategy.

But while the thermoregulatory strategies which evolved in early hominids removed the physiological constraints on brain enlargement, the ensuing evolution of a large brain itself imposed physical demands of considerable magnitude.

Brain is "expensive tissue."[15] The modern human brain is six times larger than that of a typical mammal of comparable size, and although on average it represents only 2 per cent of body weight in modern humans, it consumes over 16 per cent of the body's energy budget. By comparison, skeletal muscle, where energy is more obviously expended, consumes less than 15 per cent of the body's budget, even though it constitutes 41.5 per cent of average body weight.[16]

Furthermore, the brain uses energy nine times faster than is average for the human body as a whole, and since it has no means of storing energy for future use, must be continuously supplied with high levels of fuel and oxygen. The evolution of an exceptionally efficient cooling system facilitated the evolution of the large hominid brain, but fuelling the brain soon became no less demanding than keeping it cool. In physiological terms, food intake could be expected to increase and keep pace as the large brain evolved, so that by now the stomach and digestive tract would be correspondingly large—relative to body size. But in fact, the human gut is almost exactly half the size that would be predicted to match the enlarged brain, a physiological deficiency which evolution has balanced with a suite of behavioural characteristics.

Hominids learned to seek out nutritious foods that need be consumed in only small quantities. Not for us the large bellies through which other primates process large quantities of leaves and grass, with only the occasional taste of something more nutritious. Our small gut runs exclusively on high-quality food, principally the rich reproductive nuclei of other organisms—seeds, nuts, tubers, and eggs—topped off with significant quantities of protein in the form of meat.

Paradoxically, satisfying the dietary demands of a large brain has called for a good deal of cognitive effort on the part of the brain itself. The success of this interactive relation is self-evident; it lies behind all human behaviour and achievement: technology, language, and culture. The fundamental characteristics of humanity evolved to keep the brain running, it seems, and the large brain evolved as adaptations to hot and dry environments lifted the constraints which limited the potential for increased brain size in every other terrestrial mammal.

". . . it is probably no coincidence," Wheeler concludes, "that today the mammal with the most highly developed brain and social behaviour is the species which possesses the most elaborate cooling system."[17]

CHAPTER 10

Out of Africa

GENETIC, PALAEONTOLOGICAL, AND LINGUISTIC EVIDENCE
indicates that anatomically modern humans existed only in Africa until
about 100,000 years ago, when some migrated from the continent and
progressively populated the entire globe.

The first fossil evidence of anatomically modern humans, *Homo sapiens sapiens,*
ever found is one of the most famous discoveries in palaeoanthropology: Cro-
Magnon Man, found in 1868. Cro-Magnon Man had occupied a rock-shelter
in the Dordogne region of southern France around 30,000 years ago, but of
course his ancestors had evolved in Africa, with highly developed brains and
elaborate cooling systems. The oldest known fossil evidence of their existence
has come from caves in the mountains of Zululand; from cliff-shelters on the
Indian Ocean shoreline of South Africa; and from the savanna environments of
the Rift Valley basins in Ethiopia, Kenya, and Tanzania.

Beyond Africa, the fossil remains of anatomically modern humans have
also been found in the Middle East, China, Borneo, Java, and Australia, as well
as in Europe.

The African fossils are up to 100,000 years old, while their non-African
counterparts are all significantly younger. This implies that anatomically modern humans from Africa were ancestral to all non-African populations and their
modern descendants. The German anthropologist Günter Bräuer investigated
this question, and published his "Afro-European sapiens hypothesis" in 1984.[1]

Bräuer reviewed the fossil evidence in detail, looking not only at specimens

Pelicans soar on thermals rising above Lake Nakuru, Kenya

of anatomically modern humans but also at *Homo erectus* and archaic *Homo sapiens* (see page 81). The African fossils he examined came from sites in Libya, Morocco, Algeria, Sudan, Ethiopia, Kenya, Tanzania, Zambia and South Africa. The specimens were numerous and dated from between 500,000 and 30,000 years ago. Some possessed features of an archaic nature, others were entirely modern.

Noting a trend of evolutionary development, Bräuer concluded that anatomically modern humans had evolved in East Africa from the pre-existing hominid stock not less than 150,000 years ago. Thereafter they spread rapidly throughout the length and breadth of the continent. From among those who exploited the resources of the Nile valley and reached the Delta, small numbers migrated along the shores of the Mediterranean into the Middle East, and thence into Europe, Asia, Australasia, and the Far East.

The fossil evidence shows that modern humans were present in the Middle East by around 100,000 years ago; populations that turned north from that point were well established in Europe by 40,000 years ago. Those that turned east had reached Australia by 35,000 years ago at the latest, and were in China before 30,000 years ago. From Asia, groups of modern humans crossed the Bering Straits into North America between 30,000 and 15,000 years ago, when sea levels were low, and had dispersed down to the tip of South America by 12,000 years ago.[2]

Bräuer had constructed his model of how modern humans had populated the world from the evidence of the past: fossils. Meanwhile, scientists in the United States were reconstructing the past history of human populations from evidence of the present: genes. A group of geneticists at the University of California at Berkeley analysed the mitochondrial DNA of different groups of people around the world, and found that more mutations had occurred among Africans than among or between any other groups.

The mitochondria are discrete parts of the cell which play a vital role in the energy production systems of living organisms. In effect, mitochondria are the "powerhouses" of the cell, and such a fundamental function has endowed them with a very stable structure. Furthermore, the mitochondrial DNA (abbreviation: mtDNA) molecules are identical in every cell of an individual; mitochondria themselves reproduce by cloning, that is, asexually, by division, but are inherited only from the female parent because the mitochondria in sperm cells disintegrate at fertilization.[3] Clonal reproduction and female inheritance leave mtDNA unaffected by the recombination of genes that occurs in the reproduction of nuclear DNA. Mutations pass intact from generation to generation. Each mtDNA molecule carries in its sequence the history of its lineage, which makes it a wonderful tool for determining the evolutionary distance between closely related species and populations.

The Berkeley geneticists counted up and compared mtDNA mutations in 147 women from different populations around the world.[4] The greatest degree of variation was found among indigenous people in Africa, and significantly less among non-Africans. In fact, the mtDNA of an individual born in England and another born in New Guinea was more alike than the mtDNA of two individuals from Nigeria.

These findings showed that a greater time-depth of mutation was preserved among people in Africa, while everyone else shared a predominance of mutations which had accumulated in the relatively recent past. Setting these measures of difference against calculations of the rate at which mutations occur,[5] the geneticists concluded that the entire population of the modern world was descended from a relatively small group of people that left Africa about 100,000 years ago. Extrapolating still further from the present into the past, they claimed that the distinctive form of modern humans had evolved between 140,000 and 290,000 years ago, in Africa.[6]

Furthermore, the geneticists concluded that every human being alive today carries the mtDNA of just one African woman who lived more than 10,000 generations ago. This does not mean that she was the only woman alive at that time (Eve accompanied by Adam, as Creationists might like to believe), simply that her mtDNA steadily became dominant as some maternal lineages disappeared with each succeeding generation (not every mother produces a daughter to whom the mtDNA is passed on). After about 10,000 generations all but one of the founding maternal lineages would have become extinct, so that all living progeny carried the mtDNA of a single founding female line.[7] The geneticists referred to this ancestor as "our common mother," but she quickly became more popularly known as "the African Eve."[8]

The genetic research convincingly supported the "Afro-European sapiens hypothesis" which Bräuer had formulated on the basis of the fossil evidence. The results were disputed by statisticians, who identified inaccuracies in the computing procedures by which the single African origin of human populations had been derived. However, while these objections drew attention to inadequacies of statistical method they did not invalidate the evidence. The greater genetic diversity of African lineages remained unchallenged.[9] Indeed, the significance of these findings was reinforced in 1991 by the results of another worldwide study conducted by a team of geneticists from Stanford and Yale universities headed by Luigi Cavalli-Sforza.

Cavalli-Sforza and his team analysed an entirely different set of DNA data, but also concluded that the "result is exactly what one would expect if the

African separation was the first and oldest in the human family tree."[10] Furthermore, they found that the distribution of genes among human populations correlates surprisingly well with that of languages. A genetic tree showing the evolutionary origins of forty-two populations from around the world closely matches their linguistic affiliations: the most recent language differences, such as have arisen among the Pacific islanders, for instance, replicate the extent of their genetic differences. And in both the genetic and the linguistic evidence, the largest and therefore oldest differences occur between the African group and the rest of the world population.

So the evidence from fossils, genes, and language all points to an African origin of modern humans in the relatively recent past. A group (or groups) of these migrant nomads left Africa, and their descendants populated the rest of the world. Just how numerous these migrants were was shown by the results of calculations based on the presence or absence of distinguishing characteristics on the DNA strand: the actual number of people who initially left Africa was probably very small indeed, possibly as few as fifty, with six individuals breeding at any one time over a period of 70 years, or no more than 500 over 200 years. Either way, this is "an astonishingly small number to be the ancestors of all non-African humans." Humans of course remained numerous in Africa, but out of the continent, they "may have once been very rare, very close to extinction. . . ."[11]

SEVERAL STRANDS OF EVIDENCE—fossil, genetic, and linguistic—point persuasively to the conclusion that every person alive today is descended from a population of anatomically modern humans that existed only in Africa until about 100,000 years ago. They were nomads, and they soon spread around the globe. Within the span of 4,000 generations modern humans reoccupied the regions where *Homo erectus* and archaic *Homo sapiens* had become extinct; they replaced pre-existing populations, and colonized lands that people had never occupied before. Humans dominate the Earth and have been to the moon. We see visions of the future in the mind's eye, and turn them to reality with the aptitudes and talents which evolution bestowed—in Africa.

PART 3

THE AFRICAN OPTIONS

Wild fig tree, granite kopje and Thomson's gazelles on the eastern Serengeti plains, Tanzania

CHAPTER 11

On Home Ground

AFRICAN ENVIRONMENTS DEMONSTRATE the universal relationship that exists between soils, rainfall, and vegetation in a natural environment, and the extent to which biological adaptations enable animals to take advantage of what is available.

The genetic evidence reveals that modern humans first migrated from Africa about 100,000 years ago. The fossil evidence shows that, by then, the hominid line had been evolving in Africa for 5 million years and modern humans were present throughout the continent. It is as though Africa was filled to the brim with this nomadic oddity, and some had spilled over, across the isthmus of Suez, and thence into the rest of the world. With time, as generations of migrants ventured progressively further from Africa, they moved away from their origins in more than just the physical sense. It was a matter of belief too. Africa became a foreign place; unseen, but occupying a fertile corner of the non-African collective imagination, where myth and misunderstanding flourished.

When European descendants of the migrants first landed on African shores in the fifteenth century, there was no sense of returning home. Nor were they welcomed. Africa could hardly have been more inhospitable to the rapacious, white-skinned, and thick-blooded northerners. The continent held them off for centuries more; not until they had filched the means of curbing malaria—quinine—from South America could they settle close to the heart of Africa with a reasonable expectation of remaining alive and in good health. Even then, the facts of their African origin remained unsuspected.

In 1969 Neil Armstrong took that short step which put a man on the moon, and finally, sixteen years later, geneticists revealed that mankind's giant leap actually had been launched—not from Cape Canaveral—but from tropical Africa, many thousands of years ago. Ten thousand generations had come and gone, and until the migrants' search brought their descendants full circle, back to Africa, the inhabitants of the continent had experienced no identifiable need for anything that lay beyond its boundaries. Africa was self-contained, self-sufficient. People lived in a web of ecological relationships; generation succeeding generation, like knots in a string. Populations were dispersed, varied in nature and disposition, some even antagonistic to one another, but they shared an unbroken history of interaction with their environment; and they all had remained closer to the circumstances under which humanity had evolved than had the descendants of the migrants who had left Africa 100,000 years before.

While the migrants had colonized the globe, pushing always at fresh horizons and challenging new frontiers, the imperatives of life in Africa had remained within the confines of ecological boundaries that had been identified long before. There was nothing new in Africa. The human dynamic was continuous, and unbroken.

Humanity did not lack space in Africa, but in terms of the ecological potential a land mass offers a human population, its position on the globe is more important than sheer size. Africa, unlike any other continent, is divided into two almost equal parts by the Equator. Since most of the continent lies within the tropics, it does not experience the wide fluctuations in temperature which typify the climates of Europe and North America. Temperatures generally range from warm to hot. Even so, climate and vegetation are far from uniform. Differences in altitude, prevailing winds and distances from the ocean have created practically every conceivable type of climatic condition and environment—some perhaps even larger than in popular conception, others smaller. Africa's deserts, for example, occupy 40 per cent of the continent. Rainforests—the jungle of popular myth—account for no more than 8 per cent of the land mass (see map 6, page 691). The most extensive areas of vegetation are savanna, open plains, and wooded grasslands, which stretch between the deserts and the forests across a series of undulating plateaux that geological uplift has raised to an average of about 900 metres above sea level throughout the continent. This elevation renders the savannas much cooler than they would otherwise have been at those latitudes.

Where conditions are congenial, vegetation flourishes. Relatively high and stable temperatures encourage growth when the soil is fertile and the rainfall is good. But there is a downside: the annual round of warm temperatures, with no seasonal change, means there is no relief from the activities of harmful bacteria or disease-bearing insects, such as hard winter frosts bring to temperate climes. Furthermore, the total decomposition of vegetable matter is rapidly accomplished in consistently warm temperatures, leaving no time for the accumulation of humus, with the result that extensive layers of deep fertile topsoil are rare in Africa.

Fertile topsoils represent local concentrations of nutrients, but the overall availability of nutrients (from which that concentration is drawn) is initially determined by the nature of the geological parent material. Ancient granites and cratonic rocks, and the sediments derived from them, are poor in nutrients. More recent igneous and volcanic materials tend to be richer. Africa is the world's most ancient and stable land mass, as we have seen earlier, with a greater proportion of exposed granitic shield and cratonic surface than any area of comparable size on Earth. Nutrient-impoverished cratons and granites, basement sediments and sands cover about 90 per cent of the African land surface;[1] areas of nutrient-rich volcanic and associated sediments are correspondingly limited, concentrated in particular along the length of the Great Rift Valley in East and Central Africa.

But although Africa's soils are inherently poor (see map 5, page 690), its vegetation has of course evolved to make maximum use of the nutrients that are available, and distinct patterns emerge, creating communities of vegetation and animal life that are in turn conditioned by the availability of rainfall. In general there is always a direct correlation between rainfall and the amount of standing vegetation in Africa: more rain, more vegetation. Variations in local topography and soil nutrient levels give rise to exceptions, but most regions that receive less than 400 mm of rain each year are covered with open bush and savanna; regions on which between 400 mm and 1,400 mm falls are covered with grass- and woodland of varying densities; and regions that receive more than 1,400 mm support forest or a patchwork of forest and savanna.[2]

The increase in vegetation biomass which generally accompanies the trend from arid to humid regions in Africa is accomplished more by the increased size of the plants themselves than by an increase in their numbers. With increased rainfall the predominant vegetation changes from annual to perennial grasses, then to low bush and woodland trees and on to the complex species composition and architecture of the rainforest. And as the standing biomass increases the generation time of the plants lengthens—trees live much longer than grass and so the nutrients in a rainforest are recycled more slowly than the nutrients in a savanna grassland. In fact, it has been shown that a typical African savanna recycles 30 per cent of its biomass each year, while the rainforest can manage no more than 8 per cent.[3] These percentages relate directly to the amount of mammalian biomass that the various environments can support. Only the proportion of biomass that is recycled each year (leaves and fruit) is available for mammals to eat, so the forest, with most of its nutrients tied up in woody material and long cycles of growth and death, supports relatively few animals. The savanna on the other hand, with nutrients recycling more rapidly through its expanses of waving grass, supports dense populations.

So there is a finely balanced relationship between rainfall and the primary production of an environment that determines not only the quantity of vegetation, but also its predominant form. The forests are well watered and shady, offering refuge from the critical problems of aridity and excessive solar radiation which afflict mammals in tropical Africa, but they can support only those animals that are able to climb trees and can subsist on a diet of leaves and fruit. The savanna offers more food, but only to animals that can withstand excessively hot and dry conditions.

But, of course, vegetation has never been a passive victim in its relationship with animals. Plants and animals evolved together. The manner in which grass grows, for instance, is a specific evolutionary response to the actions of the animals that eat it.[4] Indeed, it has been shown that the primary production of a tropical savanna grassland is actually stimulated by grazing.[5] Grass plants subjected to moderate levels of grazing produced twice as much edible material as plants (of the same species) which were left untouched.

And some grasses demonstrate an extraordinary ability to maintain their optimum production levels under conditions which a cattle farmer in temperate climes might have described as severe overcropping. The grass *Kyllina nervosa,* for instance, clipped daily, is capable of producing 11.6 grams of fresh growth per square metre—day after day. No other plant is known to sustain shoot growth when subjected to such intense clipping, much less produce optimum growth at that intensity.[6] Undoubtedly, this ability to maintain optimum growth while being cropped daily was an adaptation that evolved during a long period of intense herbivore activity. Some savanna plants have taken this adaptation to the extreme, and have become obligate grazophils whose occurrence is totally dependent upon regular cropping—in the absence of grazers they disappear from the sward.

The grass *Andropogon greenwayi,* for instance, commonly comprises more than 50 per cent of the savanna where grazers are active; when researchers built enclosures to keep grazers off the grass they found that the proportion of

A. greenwayi in the protected area declined rapidly. As the grasses grew, uncropped, *A. greenwayi* was overwhelmed by other species until eventually it disappeared entirely: 56 per cent of the biomass outside the enclosure, zero per cent inside.[7]

These instances describe the adaptive responses of plants which grow (and are grazed) under optimum conditions, where soil nutrients and rainfall are adequate. In less congenial circumstances other adaptive strategies have evolved. Toxic plants are a case in point. The edible parts of forest trees growing on impoverished white sand in Cameroon, for example, contain higher concentrations of distasteful tannins and hydrocyanins than those of forest trees growing on the rich soils of western Uganda. And these differences in edibility are matched by equally marked differences in the densities and feeding ecology of the animals which inhabit the two forests.[8]

BASICALLY, PLANTS ARE made up of two things: the metabolic material (consisting of proteins and soluble carbohydrates) required to fuel their life processes, and the structural material (cellulose and lignin, etc.) that holds it together. From the hungry herbivore's point of view, metabolic material is nutritious, structural material much less so, and the ratio of these two constituents therefore describes the food quality of a plant. The ratio varies as a consequence of environmental conditions: a plant's production of metabolic material is strongly influenced by the availability of soil nutrients, while production of structural material relies more on water and carbon dioxide and is much less dependent on nutrients in the soil. So here is a trend which modifies the significance of the increase in plant production that occurs in response to increased rainfall. While the total volume of plant production is determined by the availability of water, the food quality of plants is determined by the availability of nutrients in the soil. There are plants which grow large on poor soils, given an adequate supply of water, but their food quality is low.

This of course means that animals subsisting on low-quality foods must consume large quantities of inedible structural material in order to get the amounts of metabolic material their life processes demand. And they have evolved accordingly. Elephants and buffalo are prime examples; their capacious digestive systems and correspondingly large bodies are directly related to the poor quality of the food they eat. No mammal of smaller dimensions could survive on the poor-quality food that sustains elephants and buffalo (they could not consume and process enough raw material at the rate required to satisfy their metabolic demands). The corollary of this is that elephants and buffalo are the animals best suited to utilize environments in which low-food-quality vegetation predominates. And sure enough, the areas in which elephant and buffalo constitute more than 75 per cent of the total biomass are exactly those in which soils are poor but rainfall is high; conversely, where elephant and buffalo constitute less than 50 per cent of the biomass, soils are rich in nutrients and rainfall is low.[9]

So decreasing body size correlates with levels of rainfall and soil nutrients, and on the savanna grasslands of Africa these correlations mesh with trends in biomass turnover and generation length to create a web of ecological interactions in which the opportunities and potentials for diversity in the living system are more dynamically expressed than anywhere else on Earth. More plant species, more animal species, more diversity and total biomass per unit area, and materials moving through the system at an unparalleled rate. This is the environment in which humanity evolved.

Humanity is a key word here, for it hints at self-awareness and social behaviour that is concerned with more than the biological imperatives of existence. There is a cultural connotation. When anatomically modern man strode across the savanna 150,000 years ago, upright, with naked skin and a large cognitive brain, human evolution had added culture to the species' repertoire of survival strategies. The advantages of the wholly biological adaptations which had evolved during the previous 5 million years were to be increasingly enhanced by the suite of behavioural and social characteristics that we describe as culture. Biology remained the final arbiter, but the cognitive brain endowed humanity with a unique capacity to learn by experience, and to act according to a premeditated assessment of likely cause and effect, rather than instinctively, on impulse. Nurture took its place alongside nature.

CHAPTER 12

Word of Mouth

THE ADAPTATIONS WHICH facilitated the evolution and survival of humans in Africa also pre-adapted the species for speech and language. The evolution of speech had important social implications for all of humanity. The most ancient characteristics of language worldwide are rooted in surviving African languages.

As an undergraduate studying zoology at Oxford, Richard Wrangham was introduced to the ecological principles of animal behaviour by Niko Tinbergen who, with Konrad Lorenz and Karl von Frisch, shared a Nobel Prize in 1973 for pioneering work on the subject. After graduating, Wrangham worked as a research assistant on Jane Goodall's chimpanzee research project at Gombe National Park, in Tanzania. For Goodall, Wrangham studied sibling relationships among pairs of males and this work established a basis for the Ph.D. that he did under Robert Hinde, doyen of animal behaviour studies at Cambridge.

Wrangham's Ph.D. dissertation was on the ecology and behaviour of the Gombe chimpanzees.[1] He was especially interested in the relationship between food and social organization, and his results showed that social groupings and individual behaviour were highly dependent upon the availability of food. Though well-ordered stability is popularly assumed to characterize chimpanzee society, with lots of amusing antics and playful interaction among individuals, Wrangham's findings invite the conclusion that such behaviour is typical only when all members of the group are well fed and at leisure. At other times, chimpanzees behave less altruistically. The size and range of groups are

Lioness stalking prey in the Ngorongoro crater, Tanzania

not designed to ensure the mutual benefit of all, it seems, but vary according to the amount and distribution of food locally available. When food is scarce the behaviour of individuals is directed to maximizing feeding efficiency[2]—in other words, selfishness prevails.

With his doctoral dissertation completed and several papers published on the ecology and social behaviour of the primate species most closely related to humans, Wrangham was invited to join a team from Harvard University that was studying the ecology and behaviour of the Mbuti pygmies of the Ituri rainforest, in eastern Zaire.

Wrangham brought a zoologist's eye to the Harvard study; he observed the food gathering and social behaviour of the Mbuti bands in the same way as he had observed groups of chimpanzees in the Gombe forest. A comparative study was not the intention (it is not that pygmies are more like apes than other people, simply that they happen to live in the same environment as chimpanzees), but he could hardly fail to note significant behavioural similarities and differences between the two groups. The similarities were generally attributable to the imperatives of finding food and sustaining a viable population in the rainforest environment. The differences were of another order, however, and derived not simply from the physical characteristics of the human form, as might be expected, but from the single most distinctive characteristic of humanity: language.

The ability to communicate through the spoken word conditioned many aspects of Mbuti behaviour. Most significantly, it denied individuals the freedom to pursue selfish interests that is so evident among chimpanzees, and created a network of mutual obligation that none could avoid, except to their personal cost.

The significance of language struck Wrangham most forcefully on an occasion when a group of hunters had killed an elephant. This was a rare event. Word spread rapidly, and people from camps near and far soon gathered around the carcass. Excitement was intense, and appeared dangerously volatile as the animal was skinned and dismembered. In terms of activity and noise, the scene matched anything of a comparable nature that Wrangham had observed among chimpanzees. The hunters worked feverishly on the carcass, while tight knots of onlookers surged around them, pushing and shoving, gesticulating, and shouting. Others moved erratically between individuals in the group, grabbing an arm, shaking a shoulder, demanding attention, shouting. The noise was cacophonous, but amid the din patterns of negotiation became discernible. The hunters and those with immediate rights to a share of the carcass were told to honour the obligations of kinship and give meat to their relatives. Old debts and favours were settled in exchange for meat; new pledges were contracted. The talking went on for hours, doubtless reinforcing a long-standing web of reciprocal obligations that was fundamental to the social order of the region. Wrangham says:

> Chimpanzees in a comparable situation would have gone berserk. They would have screamed and squabbled and physical strength ultimately would have determined the distribution of the meat, and there probably would have been some violence between competing individuals. There may have been some bad feeling among the Mbuti too, but aggressive tendencies were constrained by the intervention of other individuals. They could talk about their differences, and bring in the issues of what happened in the past and what might happen in the future. In short—they could negotiate. Talking reduced the fighting.[3]

THE ORIGINS OF LANGUAGE lie in the suite of adaptations that enabled the hominid ancestors to exploit the resources of the African savannas. Teeth and jaws evolved to deal with a varied diet of vegetable and animal foods (see page 68); the naked skin and upright stance allowed hominids to forage widely throughout the hottest hours of the day (see page 88); the whole-body cooling system facilitated the evolution of a large cognitive brain in which reason could override instinct (see page 89). These adaptations were beneficial in their own right. Each evolved as a consequence of pre-existing circumstances; none was in any sense "designed" to facilitate future evolutionary developments, but together—fortuitously—they created the physiological circumstance from which speech and language evolved.

The supralaryngeal airway, or vocal tract, and the cerebral cortex of the brain are the two key features.

The vocal tract of humans differs from that of any other mammal. The larynx is longer, and lower in the neck; the palate is higher; the tongue is rounder; the mouth cavity is more cube-like, and open to the back of the throat. Because humans cannot isolate the airway from the mouth, they are the only mammals that cannot drink and breathe at the same time, and because food can fall from the mouth into the larynx, cutting off air to the lungs, they are also the only animals that are likely to choke while eating. But these dangers are more than offset by the improved articulation that is made possible by these modifications.

The physiological arrangements which deny humans the ability to seal off the airway to the lungs while eating, allow them to seal off the airway to the nasal passages while speaking instead, and the effect is distinctly advantageous.

The vocalizations of all other animals include a large nasal element; humans can produce purely non-nasal sounds, which are much clearer and more readily understood. Nasalized speech is inherently more liable to errors of interpretation: between 30 and 50 per cent of nasal vowels are likely to be misinterpreted, for example, as against 5 per cent for non-nasal vowels under similar conditions.[4]

Furthermore, the round human tongue, moving in the more cube-like space defined by the palate and the back of the throat, with the nasal airway sealed off, can make sounds that are uniquely suited for speech. The consonants K, G, B, P, D, and T, for instance, and vowel sounds such as I as in "meet," U as in "boo" and A as in "mama" can only be produced by the tongue in the mouth; they are the most common sounds, and the first children acquire.

And the system is fast. Humans transmit phonetic segments (the speech sounds, represented in writing by the letters of the alphabet) up to ten times faster than is attainable by any other signals in the auditory domain.[5] Such speed ensures that complex ideas can be transmitted within the constraints of short-term memory. For instance: a short sentence, such as this one, contains about fifty speech sounds. These phonetic segments can be uttered in two seconds. If the segments were transmitted separately at the non-speech rate, a listener might well forget the beginning of the sentence before hearing its end.[6]

The capacity to transmit information rapidly via speech is of course intimately related to the capacity of the brain to receive and process the information with matching rapidity. The two components of the system evolved in tandem, interactively. For the purposes of language, evolution "recruited" neural circuits of the motor cortex that performed other functions in non-human primate brains, and appropriated large segments of the expanding neocortex (the most recently evolved portion of the cerebral cortex), making the capacity for language the most important specialization of the human brain—and humanity.

The process appears to have begun around 1.5 million years ago with *Homo erectus,* whose fossils show some indication that the modified voice box may already have been present, and it was confirmed with the large brain of anatomically modern humans. Ultimately, the capacity for language became so deeply engrained that "people know how to talk in more or less the sense that spiders know how to spin webs."[7]

Language is as old as humanity, and just as geneticists have confirmed the fossil evidence of an African origin, so linguists have shown that the most ancient surviving languages are rooted in Africa. On the basis of shared words and linguistic structure, the world's several thousand languages have been grouped into twenty or so linguistic families; of these, four bear only the most distant relationship with all the rest. All four are African (see map 7, page 692)—Khoisan (spoken by the !Kung San bushmen); Niger-Congo (the Bantu languages); Nilo-Saharan (Maasai and other pastoralist languages) and Afro-Asiatic (Ethiopian and North African)—and all four families are represented by languages heard today in East Africa, close to the sites where the oldest fossils have been found.

The original "mother tongue" that was heard on the savanna 100,000 years ago has long since been swamped or swept aside by the rapid change and modification to which spoken language is particularly susceptible. Nonetheless, some linguists believe it is possible to identify elements of the mother tongue lingering in the modern languages of the world. These are root-words which occur in similar form throughout several linguistic families. The first word of all is believed to have been *tik,* meaning finger, which occurs as *toe* in English; *digitus* in Latin; *tik,* meaning index finger in Kuskokwim, an Eskimo language; and *dik,* meaning one among the Nilo-Saharan speakers of Fur.[8]

Though these claims are controversial, it is generally agreed that the roots of the mother tongue must have been set in Africa, perhaps among the ancestors of the Khoisan, of whose languages it has been said: "From the phonetic point of view these are the world's most complex languages. To speak one of them fluently is to exploit human phonetic ability to the full."[9]

The Khoisan, like the Mbuti, are hunters and gatherers, once widely distributed throughout Africa but in modern times confined to the marginally productive parts of the continent. One hundred thousand years ago everyone was a hunter-gatherer, and it is commonly supposed that language evolved among them because effective communication enhanced their food-gathering and survival prospects. Richard Wrangham's account of the Mbuti pygmies and their elephant suggests that other factors were responsible.

Though the Mbuti made a lot of noise around the corpse of the elephant, the hunters probably had tracked and killed the animal in complete silence. The information they needed for the act would have been gained primarily from previous experience. Indeed, precise verbal instruction would have been counter-productive, since it could not have predicted the exact course of events and thus would have inhibited the spontaneous reaction and cooperation of individuals on the hunt. There would have been some prior discussion of possible contingencies, but verbal exchanges during the hunt would have kept to an absolute minimum.

The hunt—particularly the hunt of dangerous beasts—is the stuff of folklore. The children of hunter-gatherers grow up with fireside tales of hunting prowess and adventure; they are inspired, but a novice on his first elephant hunt might soon realize that the tales are more about the hunters than the hunt. First and foremost, the tales encourage him to admire the brave and clever hunters, and inspire him to emulate their actions; he listens, but learns most about hunting by watching, playing, and doing. The same could be said of virtually all food-gathering activities. Language is not essential. Certainly, it enables gatherers to exchange information about the location of specific food plants, and enables hunters to discuss the whereabouts of prey, but it is difficult to see why language should have evolved specifically for these purposes among humans when other primates, and the social carnivores such as lions, manage perfectly well without it.

Robin Dunbar, Professor of Psychology at Liverpool University, investigated the conundrum of language and concluded that it is primarily a response to social imperatives, and only secondarily related to hunting and food-gathering.[10]

From research on the social behaviour of primates, Dunbar had noted a strong correlation between the size of the neocortex among primates, and the size and social complexity of the group in which they lived—the larger the neocortex, the larger the social group. Lemurs, for instance, with a small neocortex, live in groups of less than five; marmosets, with twice the ratio of neocortex to the rest of the brain, live in groups of around fifteen; chimpanzees, with four times the ratio, commonly live in groups of about fifty-five.

In evolutionary terms, the correlation between larger neocortex and group size suggests that the benefit of living in larger groups had been the selective advantage which favoured the evolution of the primates' large brain. And the trend begs a pertinent question: what size group does it predict for humans, given our very large neocortex? The figure works out at 148, and a trawl through the relevant literature provided Dunbar with evidence demonstrating that this is indeed the group size at which human societies appear to function most effectively.

Anthropological censuses show that the clans of hunter-gatherers and subsistence farmers consisted of 153 individuals on average; archaeological evidence showed that neolithic villages in the Middle East typically housed between 120 and 150 people. Historically, the basic fighting unit of the Roman army was exactly 130 men. In the modern era, the Hutterites, a group of North American religious fundamentalists who live and farm communally, regard 150 as the maximum size for their communities (beyond which they must split and establish a new colony),[11] and business managers know that companies with up to 150 employees function well on a person-to-person basis but need a formal management hierarchy when they grow larger.[12]

Optimum group size doubtless is related to the benefits it bestows upon individuals and, through them, to the continuing viability of the species. But these are not factors that individuals are consciously aware of. So what holds them together in groups of just the right number?

Among primates in general, and the Old World monkeys and apes in particular, individuals live in a web of interactive relationships that are formed and constantly reinforced by social grooming—those episodes of intense mutual attention that serve the practical purpose of removing parasites and keeping the pelt in prime condition, but also elicit expressions of pleasure and conciliation from the recipient. The chimpanzees whose frenetic behaviour around the elephant carcass Richard Wrangham had envisaged would have spent many hours grooming one another after the event, re-cementing fractured bonds.

The problem with social grooming as a means of maintaining social cohesion is that it is so time-consuming. The total amount of time devoted to grooming is of course proportional to the number of individuals in the group. Each chimpanzee can only groom one individual at a time, and in groups of around fifty-five individuals (the average size) any one chimpanzee may devote a full 20 per cent of the daylight hours to grooming. At this rate, social primates in human-size groups of 150 would find themselves devoting from 35 to 45 per cent of their time to grooming.

No animal that had to find food daily could afford to spend almost half the day on social interaction, least of all the human ancestor, who foraged far and wide throughout the daylight hours. Fifty-five individuals is probably the limit for primates who spend 20 per cent of their time grooming, and Dunbar concludes: "Any [further] increase in group size can only come through a shift in gear in the mechanism used for social bonding."[13]

Dunbar suggests that language was the gear change that took human evolution through the grooming constraint on group size; and the large brain with expanding neocortex was fortuitously available to accommodate the development.[14]

Language has obvious advantages as a social grooming mechanism: people can talk while they are travelling or are engaged in other activities; they can address several individuals at the same time—and they can resolve disputes at the elephant carcass. But if language really did evolve to service increased numbers of social relationships, its efficiency relative to grooming should mirror the size of human groups relative to the largest found among primates. Dunbar investigated.

If human groups typically number about 148 individuals, and chimpanzees about 55, then speech should be 148/55 times more efficient than grooming as a bonding mechanism. Grooming is a one-to-one relationship, so language should operate at a ratio of 1:2.7 and human conversation groups should consist of 3.7 individuals (one speaker and 2.7 listeners). Dunbar's observations confirmed these deductions. The conversation groups he monitored consistently averaged 3.4 individuals, with a striking tendency for groups larger than four to fragment into two or more smaller conversation groups. Sound levels also appeared to impose an upper limit on group size: when more than five joined a conversation, individuals were obliged to stand in a circle whose diameter exceeded the distance at which everyone could be heard clearly. Thus, not just language but the characteristics of speech itself seem closely tied to the size of the group required to maintain cohesion.

Dunbar monitored topics of conversation too, and found that social relationships and personal experiences accounted for about 70 per cent of conversation time—about half of which was about people not present. Call it gossip, but this fascination with human relationships and the capacity to exchange information about people who are not present are vitally important, says Dunbar, in that they allow humans to coordinate social relationships effectively among dispersed groups.

Rock painting made by hunting and gathering bands at a rock shelter near Kondoa, in Tanzania

CHAPTER 13

Ancestral Economies

HUNTING AND GATHERING WAS the founding economy on which human society is based; but hunters and gatherers were not "the original affluent society" as is popularly supposed; their numbers and distribution were determined by the "law of the minimum."

Honey is an extremely rich source of energy, and people have been collecting it for so long that some birds have evolved strategies to ensure that they too benefit from the human predilection. A bird could never invade a bees' nest, but the African honeyguide, for example, knows there is a rich meal of grubs in the combs discarded by honey gatherers. So, when people appear in the vicinity of a hitherto unharvested bees' nest, the honeyguide attracts their attention with characteristic flight and calls, then guides them to the honey. The gatherers invariably reward their benefactor by setting aside a pile of grubs.

The honeyguide's behaviour is innate, evolved over many generations, but each generation of honey gatherers learns of it afresh. The lessons begin at an early age, not least in the beguiling metaphors of the folk tale, where the desirable and undesirable elements of social behaviour are imposed on impressionable minds. In rural Africa the honeyguide is a potent symbol of the benefits that accrue from mutual cooperation—help yourself by helping someone else. Likewise, the honey bee itself occupies a symbolic position in the popular consciousness of the industrial world. It is an icon of industriousness. "As busy as a bee," we say, alluding with approval to the ethic of ceaseless toil and bustling productive activity that powered the industrial revolution—work, for the greater good of all.

But though folk tales and symbols drawn from the natural world can have a powerful influence on people, they need only be as true as contemporary depths of observation permit. The layman is easily convinced that bees certainly do bustle, for example, but entomologists have shown that the life of the honey bee is not all ceaseless toil. Bees spend a lot of time doing nothing but wander about the hive. Hard work is intermittent and adds up to no more than three and a half hours for any single bee between sunrise and sunset.[1] Bees are busiest in the popular consciousness of the industrial world, it seems, making virtues of hard work and selfless endeavour.

Hunters and gatherers have occupied a similarly iconic position in the popular consciousness of the industrial world, and perceptions of their status have changed as society has changed.

The Hobbesian view of life without the trappings of civilization as "nasty, brutish and short,"[2] for instance, was moderated for a time by Rousseau's noble savage, who peers from the surge of social enlightenment that swept through France in the late eighteenth century; and again by the "coconut tree" theory of human social origins, which developed from early-twentieth-century studies of people on tropical islands, whose needs were bountifully provided by nature as they lounged beneath the palms. But the bleaker view was subsequently re-established: "Only intense application makes survival possible," wrote M.J. Herskovits in an influential anthropological text.

> Thus food, to a South African Bushman or a native of Tierra del Fuego, who lives always in a state of potential hunger, is always of maximum value . . . there is little surplus of energy or resources available for . . . activities [other] than the food quest.[3]

In the 1960s, views of the hunting and gathering way of life changed again, radically. So much so that by 1968, the very same bushmen that Herskovits had put on the edge of starvation, were described by Marshall Sahlins as members of "the original affluent society," for whom "the food quest is intermittent, leisure is abundant, and there is more sleep in the daytime per capita than in any other conditions of society."[4] A stream of quantitative data, flowing from new studies on hunters and gatherers, was the principal force behind this change of view, but the studies themselves were directly related to a reassessment of social values then sweeping through western society as a whole.

The Second World War had left humanity with a lot of explaining to do: where had humanity gone wrong? And now that fascism had been crushed,

Soviet communism loomed threateningly in the East. Was history about to repeat itself? The United Nations Educational, Scientific, and Cultural Organization (Unesco) was committed to the end of racial prejudice; its constitution specifically stated that the war had been a consequence of the "doctrine of the inequality of men and races," and in 1952 Unesco published its "Statement on Race," affirming that humanity was a single species, a family of man—equal in all things and its members all equally entitled to a share of the world's resources.

Being a scientific organization, Unesco needed scientific facts to fulfil its mission. The "Statement on Race" was drafted by a group of anthropologists, psychologists, and sociologists from around the world, with input inferred from evolutionary biologists Julian Huxley and Theodosius Dobzhansky.[5]

Affirming the principle of a non-racial "united family of man" obliged the scientists to ignore widely read anthropological texts which explicitly defined the separate identity of the so-called races.[6] In the event, however, avoiding the newly perceived imperfections of the past implicitly identified the research priorities of the future: science should define man as a single species of inherently egalitarian nature, inheritor of the world's resources and capable of living in peace with itself. Attention focused on Africa,[7] where the earliest-known fossil evidence of human origins had been unearthed,[8] and where groups of bushmen still lived as hunters and gatherers in a supposedly pristine natural environment.

THE FORAGERS WHO LEFT stone tools and fossils on archaeological sites across the length and breadth of Africa, on mountains, coasts, and savannas, were almost certainly the ancestors of the modern hunter-gatherer populations,[9] but the connection is not one of seamless untrammelled continuity. By the 1950s, 2,000 years of remorseless advance by herders and farmers had reduced the foragers' territory to a fraction of its former extent, and the near-genocidal behaviour of European settlers had reduced their numbers to a matter of thousands: pygmies in the rainforests of the Congo basin; a few hundred Hadza along a remote portion of the Rift Valley in Tanzania; and a few thousand Khoisan in the Kalahari desert.

The archaeological evidence shows that foragers have been exploiting the resources of the Kalahari region for more than 20,000 years;[10] so the living Khoisan were not necessarily the descendants of refugees from the invasions and persecutions of farmers and settlers, their ancestors could have been there all along. Even so, they were no longer foragers living in a world occupied only by foragers, they were hunters and gatherers surrounded by agricultural, pastoral, urban, and industrial communities.[11] And the influence of their contacts with these groups would inevitably affect the validity of any contribution they could make to an understanding of human social evolution.

Researchers heading for the field insisted that the Khoisan were not "living fossils," whose behaviour replicated that of humanity's earliest ancestors; they were primarily an invaluable source of ecological and social data against which hypotheses about society and economy could be tested, whether or not the evolutionary record itself was enhanced.[12] But such caveats were lost in the warm and welcoming popular appreciation that greeted the results they brought back from the Kalahari.

The first wave of research began with a study on the ecology of the !Kung bushmen by John Marshall (from Harvard University),[13] a film, *The Hunters,* which was to become a standard ingredient of many anthropology courses, and a number of papers on the social organization of the !Kung by Lorna Marshall, but it achieved widest impact with a popular book, *The Harmless People,* written by E.M. Thomas, who had accompanied the Marshalls on the Kalahari expeditions. The book described definitively harmless people, living peacefully together in perfect communion with their environment. It was a wonderful salve for searing memories of mutual atrocity recently committed. The message was plain: this is how we were, this is how we must become again.

Laurens van der Post wrote of a "search for some pure remnant of the unique and almost vanished First People of my native land"[14] in *The Lost World of the Kalahari* (published in 1958), another widely influential book which reinforced the image of primal innocence stemming from the Marshalls' work, and in the early 1960s Richard Lee collected the first quantitative data which would demonstrate the economic validity of the peaceful idyll in which the Khoisan reportedly lived out their lives.[15]

Lee's first spell of field research (1963–64) was conducted during one of the most severe droughts ever recorded in southern Africa. In Botswana (then still the Bechuanaland Protectorate) crops had failed for the third successive year; 250,000 cattle had died, and 180,000 people (30 per cent of the national population) were being kept alive by a United Nations famine relief programme. And yet the thirty or so members of a group of !Kung San whose daily diet Lee monitored for four weeks during this period each consumed an average of 2,140 calories and 93.1 g of protein per day, an intake which amounts to 8.3 per cent more calories and 55 per cent more protein than the recommended daily allowance (RDA) for people of their stature. Moreover, the wild food resource was abundant enough to feed neighbouring families of agriculturists who began foraging with the !Kung when the famine-relief programme failed to reach them.[16]

Plant food comprised up to 80 per cent of the !Kung diet, derived from a total of 85 species although 23 species supplied 90 per cent of their vegetable diet. Furthermore, one single item—the mongongo nut—supplied half of all the vegetable food the !Kung ate during Lee's study. Weight for weight, the mongongo contains five times the calories and ten times the protein of an equivalent quantity of cooked rice or maize. The !Kung each ate about 200 g of mongongo nuts daily, Lee reported, equal to a meal of 1.13 kg of rice and nearly 400 g of lean beef. Furthermore, they shared food among the group, according to status, obligation, and need. All were catered for.[17]

And if the arid Kalahari desert begins to seem a Garden of Eden, the undemanding workload of its inhabitants surely confirms the image: Lee's study revealed that adults each devoted an average of fewer than 19 hours a week to the task of finding food, and even the most energetic individual (a man who went hunting on 16 out of 28 days) spent only 32 hours a week at the task. Harmless people, sustained in leisured innocence by a rain of mongongo nuts as thick as the coconuts of a previous era; like the bees, less trapped in ceaseless toil than cursory observation had suggested—the original affluent society.

Lee recorded a division of labour in the food-production economy of the San. Women gathered and men hunted, and analysis of daily activities leaves little doubt as to which sex made the greatest contribution to the overall nourishment of the group. When men went hunting they came back empty-handed four times out of five, while women always returned from a foraging trip with something to eat. Overall, women supplied 2.5 times more food than the men.[18] Given this striking evidence of the !Kung's dependence upon female gatherers, the title given to a 1966 symposium on hunters and gatherers, "Man the Hunter," reflects the hunters' iconic status in the popular consciousness, rather more than it introduces the insights of new evidence.

The "Man the Hunter" symposium was organized by Lee and his Harvard colleague, Irven DeVore. It brought seventy-five scholars to Chicago from around the world for "the first intensive survey of a single crucial stage of human development—man's once universal hunting way of life."[19]

In the book of the symposium, also entitled *Man the Hunter*, the organizers noted that the contributors (90 per cent male) seemed to share a feeling that the human condition was likely to be more clearly delineated among hunters than among other kinds of societies.[20] In other words, hunting defined humanity, and some contributors said so, explicitly. "Hunting is the master behavior pattern of the human species. It is the organizing activity which integrated the morphological, genetic, and intellectual aspects of the individual human organisms and of the population who compose a single species," declared one.[21] ". . . [O]ur intellect, interests, emotions, and basic social life—all are evolutionary products of the success of the hunting adaptation," said another,[22] ". . . for those who would understand the origin and nature of human behavior there is no choice but to try to understand 'Man the Hunter.' "

So the icon was embellished with new evidence, and in a roundabout way confirmed the validity of a prevailing social paradigm: the post-war nuclear family as an ancient feature of humanity—mother at home with the children, making occasional forays to the supermarket, while father was away on more difficult enterprises. But the role of women in western society was changing, and the assumption that male hunting had been the driving force of human social evolution no longer passed unchallenged. From the 1970s on, both the importance of males and the primacy of hunting were questioned in a swathe of new analytical research which asked, among other things, whether woman the gatherer might not have been more important than man the hunter.

Feminism shifted the emphasis of a number of prevailing social paradigms in western society during the 1980s and '90s. The ascent of women in anthropology, for instance, produced a corresponding rise of interest in the role of the female in human evolution. The implicit assumption that females and offspring are the beneficiaries of the system, dependent upon males for their well-being and survival, was less frequently encountered; the obvious fact that females and offspring are the measure and ultimate determinant of a species' survival was more generally acknowledged.

Data on !Kung population size and structure which formed an important component of Lee's study was collected by Nancy Howell, whose demographic analysis revealed highly pertinent factors that were directly related to the status of women in !Kung society.

Three censuses, conducted over a period of ten years (1964 to 1973), showed that from 8.7 to 10.7 per cent of the population was over sixty years old. This is an exceptionally high proportion by Third World standards, which certainly appears to contradict the Hobbesian view of life in the natural world as "nasty, brutish, and short." However, the high proportion of old people among the !Kung was matched by a low proportion of young people that was equally exceptional—only 29 per cent were below fifteen years of age, whereas the proportion approaches 50 per cent in the developing world as a whole (the figure for Botswana in 1985 was 49.7 per cent).

The population structure of developing countries typically resembles a pyramid, with the number in each age group declining gradually with advancing years. But the !Kung population pyramid was more like that of developed countries, such as the United States, bulging in the middle with people in the age group fifteen to fifty-nine. Distortion of this order meant that for every 100 young and old dependants among the !Kung there were 152 economically active adults to provide for them, an exceptionally low dependency ratio, almost exactly matching that of the United States (with 154 active adults for every 100 dependants) and far below that of Guinea (with only 96 active adults for every 100 dependants).[23]

In the short term, a low dependency ratio would benefit every member of the !Kung: active adults are not burdened with the need to support a high proportion of dependants; young people are not pressed into supplying food at an early age; and old people can enjoy a life of leisure and tender care. The long-term effects of a low dependency ratio are less attractive. As economically active adults grow older, there are proportionally fewer young people to take their place. The dependency ratio reverses, leaving a small number of active adults burdened with the obligation to support a large number of dependants.

The economic effects of a skewed population structure and low dependency ratio suggest an alternative to the Utopian images of affluence and leisure which have been drawn from Lee's researches among the !Kung. Perhaps the !Kung were not such a perfect iconic example of a hunting and gathering community living in harmony with a natural environment after all. The large number of old people, and the bulge moving up the population pyramid, could indicate that the population had been larger in the past; that a decline in the birth rate had occurred over the past few generations, and that the apparent affluence of the current generation was simply the consequence of there being fewer people exploiting resources that were capable of supporting many more. Whatever the case, the measure of the !Kung's viability as a population lay not in the number of old people, nor in the apparent affluence of its providers, but in the number of infants that were born and raised.

Here again, the statistics were remarkable: the fertility rate of the !Kung recorded by Nancy Howell was exceptionally low. Whereas women in Africa generally had an average of six live births during their reproductive lifespan,[24] !Kung women had only three on average. Furthermore, 40 per cent of their offspring died before reaching maturity and Howell calculated that the !Kung's high mortality and low fertility gave them a population growth rate of below 0.5 per cent per year[25]—less than one-fifth of the rate for Africa as a whole, not even half that of the United States (1.04 per cent per year, 1970–75) and matching only that of Switzerland (0.44 per cent per year 1970–75).[26]

The !Kung do not practise contraception or abortion. On the contrary, Howell reports,[27] they say they would like to have more, complaining that their god is stingy with children. The dearth of children among the !Kung directly contradicts the image of a well-nourished and flourishing community. Lee's investigations appeared to show that the !Kung were more than adequately fed, and did not have an excessive workload. A population should increase under such favoured circumstances, and the first signs of this would be relatively large numbers of children. Why did !Kung women have so few?

The key factor stood out starkly from Howell's demographic data. On average, thirty-seven months elapsed between successive live births among !Kung women, and a significant number of births were nearly four years apart. Such long birth intervals are a feature of modern industrial societies, not usually found in traditional communities that do not practise birth control. Confronted with yet another statistic which aligned the !Kung more closely with the industrial world than with other evidence from the world they occupied, Lee took a positive view and concluded that the !Kung's long birth interval was a biological adaptation of the hunting and gathering way of life which performed a positive role in that it ensured the well-being of individuals and furthered the long-term survival of the group.

!Kung women provide about two-thirds of all the food their group consumes, and routinely carry up to 15 kg of nuts, berries, fruits, leafy greens, and roots over distances that amount to at least 1,200 km in the course of a year.[28] Since !Kung children were breast-fed on demand and stayed with their mothers at all times up to the age of four, they added considerably to the foraging load and an individual woman was better able to care for each of her children if the births were far apart, Lee reasoned. Furthermore, long intervals between births dampened the population growth rate, thus helping to keep the size of the population in long-term balance with the available food supply, he said.[29]

But if the !Kung women wanted more children, and were sexually active within twelve months of giving birth, without employing any deliberate means of contraception, as Howell reported, why did they not become pregnant sooner? Lee suggested that breast-feeding was probably responsible. Citing evidence showing that ovulation was suppressed by hormones which the pituitary gland produced in response to the stimulation of strong and persistent suckling, he concluded that the demands of a child that was carried could contribute significantly to the birth-control effect, "rather like carrying your contraceptive on your hip."[30]

On the other hand, strong and persistent suckling could just as well reflect an inadequate production of milk,[31] which in turn would suggest that !Kung mothers were inadequately nourished, and that the !Kung lived in conditions of greater stress than first impressions had suggested. Images of Utopia and the original affluent society began to fade.

IN A RIGOROUS NEW ROUND of investigation, the validity of regarding the !Kung as representative of the pristine hunting and gathering way of life followed by all humanity until 10,000 years ago (a founding premise of Lee's study)[32] was questioned by socio-economic reports contending that the twentieth-century !Kung were simply an underclass, relegated to a foraging way of life by the pressures of the ranching and farming economies that encircled them. Interaction with these economies had changed the very foundation of their culture, irrevocably, long before, claimed Edwin Wilmsen, a leading advocate of the revisionist view, who wrote:

> Their appearance as foragers is a function of their relegation to an underclass in the playing out of historical processes that began before the current millennium and culminated in the early decades of this century. The isolation in which they are said to have been found is a creation of our view of them, not of their history as they lived it.[33]

Reassessments of nutrition levels concluded that "Lee's studies of !Kung diet and caloric intake have generated a misleading belief . . . that !Kung are well fed and under little or no nutritional stress." On the contrary, there were months every year during which their lives were predictably arduous and stressful;[34] and there were years when the mongongo harvest failed. Eighty individuals, weighed at intervals over the course of twelve months, lost up to six per cent of their body weight during the dry season.[35] Tales of hardship were reported, the !Kung begged—"look at us; thinness has taken us."[36] A re-evaluation of the !Kung women's foraging and subsistence routine identified a degree of physiological stress matching that which disrupts the reproductive functions of female college athletes.[37]

Even the much-vaunted food-sharing practices of the !Kung were found to be rather less egalitarian than previous accounts had indicated.

The frequent availability of meat in large quantities was a founding component of the "affluent society" scenario that was drawn from Lee's study of the !Kung. Lee reported:

> Throughout the year, the proportion of meat in their diet rarely falls below 20 percent, and during peak periods when the hunting is good may reach 90 percent, with a per capita consumption of over 2 kg per day! . . . overall, the hunt provides around 40 percent of the calories of the !Kung.[38]

From the point of view of western males, for whom the hunt is a ritualistic pastime and a slab of steak the epitome of a feast, these figures indicated that the !Kung males were having a good time and providing for their women and children exceptionally well. After all, the average American consumed only about 14 per cent of total energy in the form of protein, and even athletes in the days before carbohydrate loading became popular seldom exceeded 17 or 18 per cent.[39]

Meat is indeed the measure of affluence that graces a rich man's table. It is nutritionally important, in that it provides essential proteins that the human body cannot produce internally, and which can be converted into calories when carbohydrates are in short supply. But you can have too much of a good thing. There is a limit to the total amount of protein (animal and plant protein combined) that can be safely consumed on a regular basis. More than about 300 g, or 50 per cent of total calories, a day can be dangerous,[40] especially in times of stress, when other foods and water are in short supply. For pregnant women, the limit is much lower—about 20 per cent of total calories, above which the development of the foetus may be impaired and its survival threatened.

Thus, an instance[41] in which twelve !Kung each consumed 2 kg of meat (equal to about 420 g of pure protein) daily for seventeen days at the end of the dry season almost certainly describes a serious scarcity of other foods, not a welcome abundance of the most desirable.

Indeed, the Arctic explorer Vilhjalmur Stefansson has given a graphic account of how a diet consisting solely of meat has the effect of increasing hunger, not relieving it:

> . . . you eat bigger and bigger meals for the first few days until at the end of a week you are eating in pounds three or four times as much as you were at the beginning of the week. By that time you are showing both signs of starvation and of protein poisoning. You eat numerous meals; you feel hungry at the end of each . . . Diarrhoea will start in from a week to 10 days . . . Death will result after several weeks.[42]

Stefansson was describing a diet of lean meat; an added proportion of fat alleviates the problem. In a medically supervised experiment, Stefansson himself lived healthily for an entire year (1928–29) on just meat and fat; his daily protein intake provided about 25 per cent of the calories he needed; fat supplied the rest.[43]

Lean meat alone is poison; animal fat is the proper measure of affluence. Not only is it a critical source of vitamins and fatty acids that are essential to good health, fat is also a highly concentrated source of energy, supplying more than twice the calories per gram than either carbohydrate or protein. Fat makes food taste good, and leaves people feeling replete after eating. Fat is also, of course, the medium in which surplus energy is stored; females in particular need reserves of fat to meet the demands of pregnancy and lactation; indeed, a threshold of "critical fatness" has been postulated,[44] below which women cease to ovulate and so cannot become pregnant.

But fat is not abundant on the savannas and semi-deserts of Africa—neither in people nor in the animals they hunt. Antelope are notoriously lean, and what fat they do have is far from evenly distributed throughout the carcass, so that although the meat may be equally shared among a group of !Kung, not everyone is guaranteed an equal quantity of essential fats.

Furthermore, some of the nutritionally most valuable portions of an animal are not shared among the group at all. The tongue, brain, kidneys, and liver, plus the marrow fat, for instance, are eaten by the hunters at the site of the kill, or given to individuals who have rights to these more valuable parts because they made the lethal strike, or owned the weapon.[45] And then, over and above these limitations to equal sharing, there are taboos which withhold valuable nutrients from specific members of the group at precisely the times of life when they would have bestowed the greatest benefit. Children are denied meat and animal fat during critical periods of growth, for instance; and women may not eat meat or animal fat at puberty or when they are pregnant or breast-feeding an infant.[46]

When the German chemist, Justus von Liebig (1803–73), made his pioneering studies on the growth of agricultural crops he noted that plants grew poorly in fields that were short of phosphorus, no matter how well they were supplied with all their other requirements. From this observation he formulated his *law of the minimum,* stating that when several factors are involved in the development of an organism and one is available in only small quantities, that single factor will determine the organism's success or failure. In other words, the reproductive capacity and growth rate of a population is ultimately determined by the availability of the essential commodity that is least plentiful.

Among the !Kung in modern times, that essential commodity was fat.

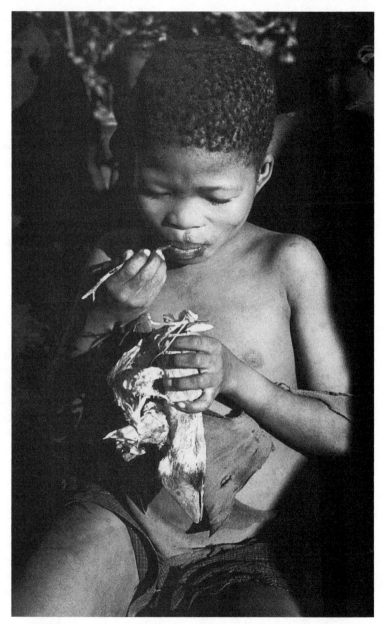

!Kung boy extracting marrow from an antelope cannon bone. Bone marrow is rich in essential fats that are not plentiful in the desert environment

CHAPTER 14

The Human Potential

NUTRITIONAL LIMITATIONS KEPT the human population of Africa at minimal levels for extended periods, but the population expanded rapidly when conditions permitted. Cycles of "boom and bust" were a commonplace factor of human existence.

Herbivores on the tropical savanna do not stop eating when the growth of vegetation exceeds their immediate needs, on the contrary, they eat no less voraciously and the surplus they consume is converted into reserves of fat which will be utilized during the harsh times that inevitably follow the good times. The animals' condition changes swiftly. At the end of the dry season savanna herbivores may be almost totally devoid of fat; when the rains are good and the vegetation recovers their reserves are rapidly replenished. Indeed, healthy animals that have fed exceptionally well even accumulate a layer of fat under the skin across the back (though the meat tissue itself remains lean).

The fat is deposited in a fixed sequence, and utilized in reverse order.[1] The back fat is the first to go; next the deposits that accumulated around the kidneys and at other points within the body cavity are mobilized. When the body fat has gone, marrow fat stored in the hollow core of the limb bones is utilized—again in a fixed sequence, moving progressively downwards from upper limbs to the extremities. A severely stressed animal will have fat remaining only in the marrow of the cannon-bones and the mandible, and in the brain.

The green vegetation of the tropical African savanna supports more than twenty species of large mammal, ranging from the elephant, rhinoceros, and giraffe to zebra and the numerous species of antelopes. They range across the landscape largely according to food preferences. Among the antelopes, for instance, the lechwe lives exclusively in and on the fringes of flooded plains; the dik-dik inhabits only dense-to-medium bush; the waterbuck and topi are found almost everywhere. Zebra and wildebeest in East Africa are migratory, following the cycle of rainfall that brings fresh grass to different parts of their range at different times of year. The impala are residential, moving only from a grazing to a browsing strategy—eating leaves instead of grass as the dry season advances across their home ground.

The standing biomass of large mammals in the National Parks where attempts have been made to preserve or recreate the African savanna averages nearly 9,000 kg per square kilometre;[2] the number of individual animals occupying an area at any one time will vary according to season and the type of standing vegetation, but the total numbers are huge. Even in modern times, when the areas available to wild animals are severely restricted by human activities, the number of migratory wildebeest and zebra in the 25,000 km^2 Serengeti ecosystem has averaged around one million animals. Since these animals live only about ten years at the most, at least 100,000 of them will die each year. Add the mortality of the other savanna herbivore populations, whose total biomass probably exceeds that of the migrating herds and whose turnover is more rapid in many cases, and the amount of dead meat lying about the savanna each year becomes substantial.

Popular imagery gives the large carnivores a dominant role on the African savanna but, in fact, they account for no more than one-third of all deaths among migratory herds in the Serengeti ecosystem. The remainder die from natural causes. Many of these carcasses are found by scavenging vultures, whose survival depends entirely on an ability to locate dead animals over great distances. Lions and hyenas follow vultures to the carcass, but not as frequently as might be expected. A study in the Serengeti found they did not appear at 84 per cent of the carcasses that vultures had located.[3] People, able to understand the behaviour of vultures and better adapted to the stress of remaining active through the heat of the day, could be expected to find them more frequently. Thus, scavenging supplied the animal-protein supplement that good nutrition demanded, and there was fat in the cannon-bones even when everything else had gone. Furthermore, meat could be dried and the marrow would keep for weeks in an unbroken bone; marrow bones could be stored in trees or rock crevices, "as we store meat in a fridge," said Louis Leakey.[4]

.   .   .

WITH THE EVOLUTION of the brain and language, the human adaptive strategy became one of endeavouring to make the environment and the food supply more predictable by learning how to control it. A progression of technological advances enabled people to manipulate natural processes and exploit sources of energy inaccessible to any other species; they learned how to survive and reproduce in environments where natural selection would otherwise have made human existence impossible. People could never circumvent the species' dependence upon a high-quality diet and a regular supply of water, but appropriate information broadened the field of opportunity. And specific information could be deliberately sought and acquired. Language, and the social arrangements it facilitated, meant that investigation could be collectively organized and directed towards specific ends.

People have always lived in groups consisting of families, and extended families. Men, women, and children related by kinship gathered together and stayed together in recognition of mutual need and the inescapable awareness that solitary existence was likely to prove short-lived. The marvel of language linked individuals in a web of interactions, concerns, and obligations; and the basic imperatives of food, shelter, and reproduction were fulfilled through increasingly complex patterns of behaviour for which the term "humanity" is an apt description.

Humanity and language created the novelty of a living organism that was capable of considering itself quite different from the rest of the natural world. But, although conscious thought, self-awareness, and a capacity for planned activity endowed people with a degree of self-determination in their individual lives, the continued survival of the species was always dependent upon the ecological determinants of the environments they occupied. In this respect humans were as much the product of natural selection as any other living organism.

Evolutionary biologists have grouped the ways of life which natural selection has favoured during the course of evolution into two broad categories: r- and K-strategies.[5]

As a general rule, organisms which have adopted r-strategies occupy unpredictable environments, reproduce early in life, have many offspring (of which only a few survive), tend to be small in body size and have short lives. They are opportunists, existing in minimal numbers for much of the time, but able to increase rapidly and move on to colonize other regions when conditions permit—annual grasses and the desert locust are typical examples.

K-strategists, on the other hand, generally occupy more predictable environments, where they maintain populations of near constant size which approach the carrying capacity of the region. They place greater emphasis on the survival of a small number of offspring, they mature slowly, are larger, and live longer. In essence, K-strategists place a high priority on preparation for the business of exploiting their present environment to the maximum[6]—they seek equilibrium and stability, not the increase and dispersal that distinguishes the opportunistic r-strategists.

Humans are said to be the quintessential K-strategists,[7] but they buck the trend at two crucial points: they evolved in a highly unpredictable environment and, though appearing to prefer a sedentary existence, their evolutionary history is one of constant migration and colonization. Progress was slow to begin with, almost as though the strategy was not so much migration and the colonization of one suitable environment after another, but unwavering expansion within the all-encompassing global environment the species would eventually occupy.

One hundred thousand years ago, when anatomically modern humans began moving across the isthmus of Suez, out of Africa and into the wider world, the number of people on Earth is estimated to have totalled less than one million.[8] The majority still lived in Africa, in clans of about 150 individuals (see page 112), made up of related but independent family groups, each probably averaging about 28 persons.[9] They could never forage more than one day's walk from water;[10] their population density, calculated from estimates of available food resources, was probably about one person in every five square kilometres.[11]

These rough-and-ready figures (intended to give an illustration of scale rather than precise measurement) indicate that each clan of 150 individuals would have required a home range of about 750 square kilometres, with water sources never more than about twelve hours' walking distance apart. Assuming the population of Africa to have numbered about 900,000 in total, the number of clans would have been 6,000 and humans would have inhabited a total of 4.5 million square kilometres. Since their evolutionary adaptations had fitted them for the savannas, wooded grasslands and woodlands that covered more than 15 million km^2 of Africa,[12] humans must have been very sparsely distributed. More than thirty clans could have inhabited a region the size of the Serengeti ecosystem, for instance. Clans and extended families could have been strung like beads along river banks, around lake shores and coastal estuaries. All indications suggest they could have multiplied and spread rapidly.

The human potential for population growth is considerable. Estimates to 1985 showed that women in Africa, for instance, each contributed an average of 6.43 children to the next generation, giving the continent an overall population growth rate of 3.01 per cent per year. Kenya had the highest annual growth rate, with 4.12 per cent, and could expect to see its population double in under fifteen years.[13]

Since the human population had been evolving in Africa for nearly 5 million years before amounting to the total of 1 million individuals it reached 100,000 years ago, it is clear that the overall population growth rate throughout that period was exceedingly low, far below the species' potential. As modern humans evolved from their hominid predecessors the original gene pool probably consisted of thousands of individuals, but even if it is assumed that the human population had begun with just two people, the biblical Adam and Eve (thus giving the maximum possible rate of increase), the annual population growth rate for the first few million years was still only 0.000015 per cent.[14]

The basic logistics of births and deaths are incapable of explaining this exceptionally low growth rate. Even if it is assumed that females did not begin bearing children until the age of eighteen; that over forty months elapsed between births; that infant mortality was high; and adults did not live beyond the age of thirty-two—even then the annual growth rate would be 0.52 per cent. At this rate a population could double in 130 years and a single clan of 150 would become a population of nearly 5 million people in less than 2,000 years.[15] Clearly, other factors were involved as well; cultural practices perhaps, such as birth control, abortion, infanticide, or even the ritual aggression of warfare. Or could it be that humans do not qualify as the quintessential K-strategists?

Perhaps the adaptive strategy of the species has not been to maintain populations of near constant size at or close to the carrying capacity of the region. In which case, humanity's evolutionary history would not be stamped with the hallmark of equilibrium and stability. Indeed, the evidence of human population growth patterns, modern as well as prehistoric, indicates that humans are supreme opportunists, who survive in numbers some way below the carrying capacity of the environment for much of the time, but whose growth rate potential enables them to multiply rapidly when circumstances permit.

These spurts of rapid population growth provoked migration and the colonization of hitherto unexploited regions. When the limits of expansion and carrying capacity had been reached the tide turned: there were more deaths, fewer births, and population size was drastically reduced.

The archaeological record bears witness to surges and lapses in population growth which would typify the early history of humanity in a regime of r-strategy adaptation. The density of sites increases abruptly with advances in stone-tool technology;[16] and there are distinct peaks in the "archaeological visibility" of human activity at about 215,000, 115,000, and 30,000 years ago, with troughs occurring thereafter.[17] The last of these surges began around 60,000 years ago, when the number of sites on the continent as a whole began to show a definite increase, and by 35,000 years ago there were virtually no regions or ecological niches that humanity had not occupied, except the depths of the rainforests.[18]

This colonization of the entire continent was accompanied by a technological development which, perhaps more than any other, opened new worlds of opportunity: the control of fire.

Fire had been an ever-present phenomenon throughout the evolutionary history of humanity: the fires started by lightning, the fire that erupted from volcanoes, the spontaneous fire that burst from heaps of critically damp though dead vegetation—wild fire, as Louis Leakey described it. Like many of us, with our gaze transfixed by the flickering flame, Leakey believed that all humanity shares a deep-seated fascination with fire. More than that, he believed fire had released humanity from fear, nurtured the spark of creativity and ignited the spiritual soul. In lectures, he described how people had captured wild fire and fed it "as we might feed a wild animal." They used it—this wild thing they had caught—but they could not make it.

Leakey was convinced that the ability to make fire sprang directly from the creative impulse to make ornaments; he described how the action of twirling a hard pointed spike between the palms will not only drill holes in shell and bone but will also heat a piece of soft wood beneath to the point of combustion—"a puff of smoke, and they had released the spirit of fire from the wood." Ostrich-eggshell beads, pierced bone, and other items with holes drilled through them all begin to appear in the archaeological record at precisely the same time as fire, he said.[19] From those beginnings, Leakey envisaged the spirit of fire burning steadfastly at the core of the human psyche, kindling a sense of fellowship, illuminating creative achievement, and, in historical times, lighting the candles of religious belief. On a less ethereal level, it is certainly true that the control of fire alleviated the dangers of the night.

As with food and drink, sleep is a physiological requirement that people cannot do without. In tropical Africa the nights are always close to twelve hours long and vary little in the course of the year; darkness falls abruptly. While most diurnal mammals take naps during the day and remain alert at night, the large primates devote the night-time hours exclusively to sleeping (as well as taking naps during the day). Chimpanzees sleep for about ten hours in total; gorillas for twelve. Humans are the least somnolent, able to manage on a daily average of about eight hours.

Chimpanzees and gorillas sleep in the trees, building a fresh nest each evening. The leopard is the only predator they need to be concerned about, and although leopards can climb trees, their numbers were not high enough to present an intolerable risk of predation. The ancestral humans doubtless slept in the trees too, especially when they colonized the savanna environments and thus entered the territories of predatory lions and hyenas as well as leopards. Cliffs and rock shelters—though few in Africa—were another option, but the need of a sleeping refuge always imposed severe constraints on the movement and distribution of early humans. Security at night was no less limiting than the demands of food and water.

But all animals have an instinctive fear of fire. Their experience of "wild fire," as Louis Leakey described it, was always potentially traumatizing—especially at close quarters. With the ability to make fires at night, wherever they chose, people gained greater security and extended the range of their activities through both space and time: they could forage further during the day and remain active even during the night; with burning torches they could explore caves, and establish bases that would be occupied for generations.

Burned bone excavated from the cave site at Swartkrans in South Africa indicates that hominids were making deliberate use of fire not less than 1 million years ago,[20] and evidence clustered around the edges of hominid expansion out of Africa from around 400,000 years ago[21] suggests that the use of fire may have been the technology that enabled *Homo erectus* and the Neandertals to penetrate the cold northern zones. But hearths, indicating the places where fires burned regularly and people gathered, are rare in the African archaeological record until after about 60,000 years ago, when they become more widespread and common. And Louis Leakey was right—with a proliferation of hearths showing that fire had been tamed, an accompanying expansion of social and cultural activity is apparent too.

A drilled bone from Libyan cave deposits more than 45,000 years old is the world's oldest-known musical instrument; it is a whistle, played for pleasure perhaps, or else to imitate the calls that would lure birds and animals into traps.[22] At the Diepkloof rock shelter in South Africa, thirteen fragments of a decorated ostrich eggshell were recovered from the remains of a hearth in which a fire last burned 42,000 years ago.[23] In Namibia, a stone slab found on a cave floor dated to 26,000 years ago bears the image of an animal with feline and bovine features. The image was drawn in charcoal, poignantly demonstrating the link between fire and the first sparks of human artistic expression.

THE SURGE OF population growth, territorial expansion, technological refinement and cultural awakening revealed in the heightened "archaeological visibility" that peaked around 30,000 years ago, occurred during a period when tropical climates changed rapidly from extremely arid to very humid. Beginning around 38,000 years ago, the cyclical perturbations of the Earth's orbit (see pages 37–38) brought three or four thousand years of steadily increasing warmth, the longest uninterrupted amelioration known to have occurred during humanity's evolutionary history.[24]

The ice sheets of the Mindel glaciation retreated, flooding the oceans with fresh water; sea levels rose worldwide; in Africa, the forests advanced, the savannas were well watered, the lakes and rivers were full. Initially, human population density was low, but the species' reproductive capacity ensured that humans exploited the opportunities presented by improved conditions. Biologically and culturally, humanity was poised—as never before—for a massive population explosion and territorial expansion. At the minimum probable rates of population increase calculated by demographers (see page 131), a single clan of 150 persons could have multiplied into a population of several million in the time available. No wonder they became so highly visible in the archaeological record.

Conditions remained broadly "favourable" long enough for the expanding human population to establish itself in virtually all the regions and ecological niches that Africa had to offer. Then the climate changed again, for the worse, lurching through a series of troughs that by 18,000 years ago had taken Africa from conditions of benign humidity to a state of extreme aridity (see chart, page 694). Astronomical perturbations had brought the last of the great ice ages to higher latitudes. In Africa, the human presence shrank to the point of almost total archaeological invisibility.

CHAPTER 15

Climate and Culture

PRONOUNCED CLIMATIC CHANGE prompted cultural responses. Evidence of hunting first occurs in Africa from 18,000 years ago, when the last ice age brought dry conditions to the continent, and the world's earliest-known evidence of organized human-on-human violence dates from 14,000 years ago in Africa, when deteriorating conditions provoked competition for resources among populations whose numbers had expanded during the intervening period of benign conditions.

Though climate was not the primary causative factor in the *evolution* of new species (see page 41), there is little doubt that it has played a significant role in the *history* of the human species, particularly in the early stages, when all humanity depended upon the gathering of plant foods and the occasional hunting of wild animals. Over thousands of years, changes in climate prompted a discernible pattern of cultural response. When the record of global climatic change preserved in the deep-sea cores is set alongside the archaeological record of modern humans since they first emerged in Africa, for example, a broad correlation becomes apparent, with distinct cultural developments occurring in both the good times and the bad times.

The good times were occasions for rapid population growth, migration, the manufacture of specialized tools, a deepening of social consciousness as signified by an increasing number of sites centred around the hearth, and the development of complex economic strategies, large-scale social networks, personal

Wildebeest and rain in the Amboseli reserve, Kenya

adornment and an expanded use of symbols in art and daily life. The bad times inspired major technological developments.

Africa's potential for providing abundant and varied food resources, combined with the continent's size and environmental diversity, ensured that the human potential for population growth described in the previous chapter was unhindered in the good times. Birth rates rose, death rates declined and the overall rate of increase was rapid; in these circumstances, a preponderance of children and old people quickly arose, and each active food-producing member of a group supported several non-productive dependants.

So long as water was always available and the food supply remained consistently adequate, the population could have enjoyed what has been described as a state of environmental equilibrium[1] for several generations. As the population expanded, groups migrated into unoccupied territory; throughout the continent, the partial isolation, self-sufficiency, and low density of the human population minimized the potential for competition between groups. Furthermore, since the available technology was fully appropriate to the level of exploitation that people employed there was no incentive for change, and the customary way of doing things was likely to have acquired the aura of tradition. There was time for ritual to develop, subtly reinforcing the validity of traditional ways.

While populations are stable, "cultural changes generally proceed slowly and with no major disruption of the traditional way of life."[2] Social exchange, song, dance, folklore, painting and carving all can flourish in the space that affluence and stability create, but this is not indulgence without function. On the contrary, these apparently non-productive activities all serve, explicitly or implicitly, to support the status quo by extolling the exploits of its past and present exponents. Established society is inherently conservative; abrupt changes in cultural practice are neither sought nor welcome.

But a long-term deterioration of the prevailing climatic conditions inevitably brought major disruption to early human populations in Africa. When the rains failed, season after season, water sources dried up, plant and animal resources became scarce; birth rates declined and death rates rose. Young children and the elderly were the first to die. Before long the population consisted entirely of the people who were best able to support themselves and resume population growth when the period of scarcity was past.

In these circumstances, necessity became the mother of invention. Cannibalism was an option which appears to have been exploited on occasion. Fossil human bones recovered from excavations at the Klasies River mouth in South Africa, for instance, show unmistakable signs of having been defleshed by someone using a sharp stone tool. The inner surface of a skull fragment shows breakage suggesting that the bone was broken while still fresh[3] to get at the brain. Cannibalism is believed to have been common among early humans at the Klasies site,[4] but the practice can only ever have been a short-term measure, simply because humans do not reproduce or mature fast enough to provide a sustainable food resource. Cannibalism can never have been more than a ritual or last-resort means of acquiring sorely needed fat and protein. Wild animals were a more sustainable source of supply.

The techniques of hunting and killing animals for food, as opposed to simply scavenging from natural deaths and predator kills, doubtless were critically refined during times of scarcity. Wild-animal populations were also severely reduced during extended periods of drought, of course; the survivors were scrawny, but the brains and the marrow fat of even the leanest animals were still a dependable source of essential nutrients (see page 127). Indeed, the glorification of hunters probably derives precisely from their capacity to provide the quantities of protein and fats required by Liebig's law of the minimum (see page 125) during bad times, when other sources of food were becoming scarce, rather than from their contributions during the good times, when luxuries of all kinds were abundant.

It has been proposed that the advent of hunting contributed to the extinction of numerous large mammalian species in Africa. At least twenty-six species disappeared from the fossil record between about 100,000 and 50,000 years ago, a controversial paper reports,[5] while only nineteen large mammalian genera disappeared during the preceding 1.5 million years. The deep-sea cores show that global climatic conditions had improved steadily for several thousand years up to about 125,000 years ago,[6] so human population densities in Africa can be expected to have peaked at the culmination of those good times (along with the populations of most other mammals). Thereafter, conditions deteriorated sharply; death rates rose and birth rates fell among all mammals, population densities were drastically reduced but, as has been noted above, the surviving populations were comprised entirely of those best able to support themselves and resume population growth when the period of scarcity was past.

Humans become less "visible" in the archaeological record[7] around this time, suggesting a significant drop in numbers and overall occupation of the landscape but, where they do occur in the record, there is evidence of important technological refinement and innovation. The amounts of faunal remains found at sites from the period, and the variety of animals represented among the bones, for instance, show that meat was a regular and significant fraction of the diet. Though the evidence had been equivocal hitherto, there is no doubt that animals were being deliberately killed as well as scavenged during this time of climatic and environmental stress. Tools were fashioned into weapons that enabled people to kill at a distance. Previously, ambush and trapping probably constituted the greater part of the hunting repertoire, each requiring a death blow at close quarters, and killing tools of a bludgeoning variety.[8] The new tools (doubtless a refinement of the small sharp blades used to skin and dismember carcasses) were made to be fixed at the end of a stick: the spear and, later, the arrow.

In southern Africa, the production of small, finely knapped blades capable of being hafted on to the business end of a throwing spear has been directly attributed to the variable and deteriorating environmental conditions which prevailed in the region around 70,000 years ago.[9] Staying alive while food resources dwindled placed increasing emphasis on the importance of acquiring meat, and thus the refinements of the microlithic industry found at Howieson's Poort in South Africa, for instance, are likely to have contributed to the extinction of animals whose populations had already been drastically reduced by the deteriorating conditions.

In central Africa, nearly 5,000 km north of Howieson's Poort, evidence recovered during the late 1980s from three sites at Katanda on the Upper Semliki River in the Western Rift Valley of Congo indicates that the period of cooler, drier climatic conditions during which the spear was invented and a slew of mammalian extinctions occurred was also the time at which people first fashioned barbed harpoons from bone and adopted the practice of spearing catfish that spawned in lake shallows during the rainy season each year.[10]

The Katanda sites are at least 75,000 and possibly as much as 90,000 years old,[11] an age which demands revision of some entrenched Eurocentric views on human cultural development. Hitherto it had been widely believed that although modern humans had evolved in Africa and first migrated from the continent around 100,000 years ago, the manufacture of specialized tools and the development of sophisticated cultural practices such as complex economic strategies, large-scale social networks, personal adornment, and an expanded use of symbols in art and daily life arose in Europe, central Asia, Siberia, and the Near East between 40,000 and 30,000 years ago.[12] The Katanda evidence contradicts this view, pushing back the invention of specialized tools at least 35,000 years and making Africa the origin not only of anatomically modern humans but also of modern human behaviour.

A total of over 8,000 pieces of worked stone and 7,369 mammal and fish remains were recovered from excavations at the 35.2 m^2 site, together with a series of ten worked-bone artefacts. The stone tool assemblage is primitive, lacking entirely the points, blades or microliths found at more advanced and younger sites, but the bone artefacts—though of equal antiquity—are very sophisticated indeed. One is part of a flat dagger-like implement, the remainder are harpoons, whole and fragmented, up to 19 mm in overall maximum length. Each artefact was made from the rib fragment or long-bone splinter of a large mammal; the sides and edges were shaped and smoothed with a grindstone, the barbs are precisely parallel and probably were fashioned with a sharp quartz flake. Shallow grooves were cut around the circumference of the butt ends, and it is possible that the artefacts served as harpoons, though probably with the barbed points permanently fixed to the shaft.[13]

The quantities of animal and fish bones found in association with barbed points suggest that the Katanda site was not only a sophisticated tool factory, evident in Africa at least 35,000 years earlier than is known from anywhere else in the world, but was also the site of the world's first factory canteen—with a preponderance of catfish on the menu. Two species of catfish constitute the greater part of the faunal assemblage. Only large mature fish are represented, which strongly suggests that they were speared during the annual spawning season, when catfish are easy to catch in the shallow reed-beds where they spawn. But the season is brief—just a few days—so that regular exploitation of the resource would have called for some pre-planning, and certainly the knowledge of how to smoke or otherwise preserve the surplus of the catch that could not be consumed on the spot.

The Katanda evidence dating from between 75,000 and 90,000 years ago documents human activity during a period when environmental conditions had been becoming drier for some time as the globe cooled and the ice sheets of the last major glaciation began to form at the poles.[14]

When conditions had been at their most benign some thousands of years previously (around 125,000 years ago), mean global temperatures were probably the same as today, or even higher. The climate in tropical Africa was generally warm and humid, rainfall and ground water was generally adequate, vegetation flourished and mammalian populations were well nourished and doubtless expanded accordingly.

The deterioration of climatic conditions began around 115,000 years ago, and reached its lowest point about 70,000 years ago. Conditions improved thereafter, sharply at first, then steadily for 30,000 years; human populations expanded during this period, reaching a peak of archaeological "visibility" (see pages 131–32) and presumed maximum density around 30,000 years ago. Then came another slump, with global temperatures plunging lower than ever before. Human populations crashed to near invisibility again, and the survivors acquired new skills.

. . .

OVERALL, THE CAPACITY TO adapt to different and changing circumstances is the fundamental characteristic of humanity. Aided and abetted by the brain, it has enabled people to identify and solve problems, to recognize and exploit opportunities, and to diverge and find new ways of doing things. The climatic crunch with which the long period of generally benign conditions was brought to an end sometime after 30,000 years ago was a founding test of humanity's capacity for adaptation; indeed, it was in its aftermath that the modern patterns of human economy, society, and culture were established—with agriculture, and the concomitants of ownership and territorial competition sharpening the human capacity for death-dealing conflict.

The period referred to here is the trough in which global temperatures languished during the last major ice age: the Würm Glaciation. Exactly how much temperatures fell at this time is a matter of debate—estimates range up to 8 and even 11°C below the average of recent historical times[15]—but the overall effects have been comprehensively documented.[16]

Minimum global temperatures and therefore maximum ice cover occurred around 18,000 years ago. The ice covered much of North America and Europe; glaciers flowed from the mountains of Asia, Australia, New Zealand, South America—and Africa. The continental ice sheets were about 1.5 kilometres thick on average, though the largest were up to five kilometres thick, and their immense weight depressed the underlying Earth's surface by a kilometre or more. Worldwide, one-third of the Earth's entire land surface was covered with ice at the glacial maximum (compared with less than one-eighth today), and fully half the surface area of the oceans. The volume of water locked up in all this ice amounted to more than 63 million km^3 (nearly two and a half times the modern total of about 26 million km^3),[17] and with so much water out of circulation, sea levels fell dramatically—up to 130 m overall.

Local effects of the glaciation of course varied with proximity to the poles, and the time lags inherent in atmospheric and oceanic circulations meant that the effects appeared later in some places than others, but no part of the world escaped its influence.

Throughout Africa, declining temperatures and decreased rainfall profoundly affected every type of environment, from desert to tropical rainforest. In addition to increased aridity, changes in atmospheric circulation brought a regime of high winds to the Sahara region, raising huge sandstorms in the central desert, and blowing great plumes of desert dust far out over the Atlantic—Sahara sand has been identified in cores taken from the middle of the ocean.[18] The Sahara itself advanced 500 km along its entire southern front, from Senegal in the west to the edge of the Ethiopian highlands in the east. Lake Chad disappeared, and the advancing dunes dammed back the Senegal, the upper Niger and Logone–Chari rivers, and even the Nile north of Khartoum. Indeed, the aridity was such that what is now the well-watered upper Nile basin became an area of inland drainage[19]—nothing flowed from it. Lake Victoria dried out almost completely, and the shorelines of Lake Tanganyika (the world's deepest lake) and Lake Malawi fell at least 400 m below present levels.[20]

The coastal shorelines of Africa fell up to 130 metres below present-day level, and the southern tip of the continent was over 100 km south of its present position at the glacial maximum.[21] With increased glaciation extending from Antarctica, the temperature of the always chilly Benguela Current, which carries water from the southern ocean northwards along the Atlantic coast of Africa, fell significantly. As a result, ocean-surface temperatures all the way up to the mouth of the Congo River fell too, evaporation from the cooler waters was reduced by up to 70 per cent, and the normally moist onshore winds brought much drier air and therefore less rain to West Africa. The south-west "monsoon" which currently brings rain to equatorial and West Africa from the Atlantic was suppressed.[22] Further south, rainfall was reduced to half the modern average,[23] and the already very dry Namib and Kalahari regions suffered even greater desiccation.

In fact, at the glacial maximum the sands of the Kalahari extended as far north as the riverine plains of the Congo River, near Kinshasa.[24] By this time, the great equatorial and tropical lowland rainforests of Africa, which today are mourned as an over-exploited symbol of environmental stability, occupied in total perhaps one-tenth of their present range.[25] Relic montane forests survived in the highlands, and a strip of coastal forest still graced the East African coast, but the continent's mighty lowland rainforests were reduced to a string of isolated pockets in West and central Africa. The largest of these was in the Congo River basin, straddling the mouth of the river, and covering an area of little more than 200,000 km^2 (compared with about 1.78 million km^2 in modern times).[26]

But even here the forest was not untouched by the climatic extremes then gripping the continent. Analysis of pollen samples from Lac Tumba in Congo, which lies at the very heart of the region that is presumed to have remained forested during the glacial maximum, suggests that woodland savanna was dominant at that time, with only some swamps and a scattering of gallery forest nearby.[27]

The glacial maximum was a bad time for vegetation and animals alike. The law of the minimum prevailed. Species that had exploited their population-growth potential during the preceding good times, and had extended their range across the continent, were cut back, remorselessly, to basic breeding stocks surviving in isolated territorial refuges. People were no exception: the human population of Africa probably had reached saturation point immediately prior to the last glacial maximum; with its onset, retrenchment occurred throughout the continent.

The effect on human populations was most severe on the continental fringes, and less so in the equatorial and tropical regions, where the long-term abandonment of sites is not evident[28]—probably because this was the evolutionary cradle of humanity and although temperatures fell and the landscape became drier, conditions remained within the parameters to which humans were physiologically adapted. It can be imagined that groups migrated from the region as human populations grew during the good times, while the size of the core population had hardly changed at all. With the onset of bad times some migrant populations died out, but the core population was simply cut back to survivor stock.

On the western edge of the cradle region, the early reliance on lake fish noted from the Upper Semliki valley (see page 140) continued unabated. In the east, snails, tortoises, and hyraxes feature in the menu, and a first occurrence of stones with holes bored through them suggests the innovation of a weighted digging-stick and therefore the more intensive exploitation of gathered food resources.

In southern Africa, severe frosts became a feature of conditions in the mountains and high exposed plateaux,[29] and the exceptional cold, coinciding with diminishing rainfall, provoked an exodus from the inland regions. People disappeared entirely from the elevated plateau of southern and central Zimbabwe, for instance, where their presence previously had been widespread.[30] Similarly, a general depopulation or at least a pronounced reduction in the occupancy of sites has been noted from Namibia, Botswana, Zambia, and Malawi.[31] Coastal sites were used throughout the glacial maximum, however, and a sustained dependence upon shellfish is indicated.

Average temperatures in southern Africa during the glacial maximum were possibly as much as 9.5 degrees cooler than at present; even today, temperatures in the region frequently plunge to zero, and it is certain that people 18,000 years ago could not have inhabited the southern African sites without protection against the cold. After all, humans originated in the tropics, where they evolved the physiological adaptations that enabled them to cope successfully with heat stress (see Chapter 9). As a consequence, people were ill-prepared for the cold conditions which prevailed in the subtropical regions of Africa during the glacial maximum. Fire would have provided temporary comfort, but clothing was the behavioural adaptation which offered permanent relief. And the manufacture of clothing of course placed an additional premium on the hunting of animals, not just for protein, or for fats, but also for their skins.

Doubtless, the skills required to prepare skins for clothing and other uses were behavioural adaptations that evolved at a very early stage (it has been claimed that slings for carrying babies and gathered foods were the first-ever technological inventions),[32] but it is significant that the appearance of polished bone points (which could serve as needles) in the archaeological record of southern Africa[33] coincides with the advent and duration of the last glacial maximum.

AS THE CLIMATIC CYCLE TURNED and the extremes of 18,000 years ago gave way to a period of more benign conditions in Africa, the change from desiccated landscape to a well-watered mosaic of savanna, wooded grassland, and forest was very rapid indeed. With persistently good rains, bare desert dunes were clothed with dense mature vegetation in no more than a few hundred years.[34] Animal populations expanded and extended their territorial range accordingly and, as the Earth entered a period of global warming which continues to this day, people and their activities became widely visible in the archaeological record once again.

The human populations of Africa which had survived the bad times of the last glacial maximum were well adapted to take advantage of the good times that followed. Their archaeological visibility increased rapidly, and a steady proliferation of rock engraving, painting, and decorative items in the record points to cultural systems of heightened sophistication. As for the food-production systems underpinning this population growth and burgeoning cultural sophistication, two innovations are particularly relevant, in that each represents an important stage of technological development and both are clues to the future course of humanity.

The first is the digging-stick weight, which is simply a large stone with a hole bored through the middle. The stone fits on the stick and its weight lends added force as the point is thrust into the ground. Digging-stick weights appear in the African archaeological record during the last glacial maximum, and their invention suggests that food-gathering technology had been improved in response to the greater importance of subterranean foods—roots, tubers, and corms—during the period of climatic stress.[35] The second innovation is the projectile point, made for use on the spear or the bow and arrow.

No remnants of either spear shafts, bows or arrows have been recovered from African sites of the period—African conditions generally did not favour the preservation of wood and other organic materials. In fact, the earliest-known such relics come from sites in northern Germany dated from 13,000 to 10,000 years ago, where arrows with points attached were preserved,[36] and from a Danish peatbog, where an elmwood bow dating from around 10,000 years ago has been found.[37] But even though spear shafts, bows, and arrows are absent from the African record, the evidence of projectile-point technology in Africa pre-dates that from any other part of the world.

Robust triangular points with a stem designed for fixing to a spear shaft are known from sites in North Africa dating back to about 44,000 years ago.[38] Finely made arrowheads recovered from sites near Kinshasa in Congo imply that the bow and arrow was used in West Africa by 30,000 years ago, and a site in Angola records the gradual refinement of arrowhead manufacture between 15,000 and 11,000 years ago;[39] but in fact, many of the microlithic blades and points (see pages 80–81) being made throughout the continent before those times could also have been used as spear points and arrowheads. Though their form is often indeterminate, the appearance of so many bladelets in the archaeological record at the onset of the last glacial maximum strongly implies that the widespread adoption of the projectile points was an adaptive response to the stress of environmental deterioration; and there can be no doubt that the spear and the bow would have made hunting a more reliable source of protein and fat during bad times.

But whatever the precise date and place at which the projectile point was invented and the weighted digging-stick became commonplace, their significance at the last glacial maximum was as precursors of modern human history. The digging-stick represents the beginnings of agriculture and the trend towards a sedentary way of life. The projectile point represents a refinement of the human capacity for taking life.

Though not the only factors involved, these innovations mark a critical point in human history. Previously, human populations had been an integral part of the ecological web defining the structure of their immediate environment, and they lived or died according to its precepts; now they lived at a stage removed from the web, still attached but able to modify the environment according to their perceptions of what was necessary.

Agriculture supported life, and the projectile point denied it. Both factors were evident during the millennia which followed the last glacial maximum. In climatic terms, the good times continued uninterruptedly, and the human population increased exponentially. The attempts to manipulate food production which mark the beginnings of agriculture encouraged extended use of areas that previously would have been visited only temporarily. Successful attempts raised population size above the carrying capacity of the land. Where they failed or could not be sustained, the inevitable competition for whatever resources were available was settled with the projectile point, denying the losers not simply the means of life, but life itself.

DURING THE 1960s, an international team of archaeologists discovered a burial ground about three kilometres north of Wadi Halfa in the Sudan, and about the same distance from a prominent hill known as Jebel Sahaba.[40] The site was in a small inset valley, framed on three sides by sandstone ridges and open to the valley of the Nile on the west; it then lay about one kilometre east of the river, but was soon to be inundated by the waters backing up from the Aswan Dam.

Excavations uncovered the skeletons of fifty-nine men, women and children, who had been buried in shallow graves under thin slabs of sandstone sometime between 14,000 and 12,000 years ago. The burial positions and orientation were remarkably uniform. Virtually all the bodies lay on their left side, head to the east, hands to the face, and knees flexed so that the heels touched the buttocks. The total number, sex, and age structure of the group indicated that they had belonged to a fairly large population, and the mode of burial demonstrates a high degree of concern for the dead. Less caring, however, was the manner in which they died. Most had died violently.

A total of 116 flaked-stone artefacts were found in direct association with twenty-four of the burials, either embedded in the bone or enclosed within the body cavity, and a further 73 similar items were indirectly associated with other skeletons. The artefacts were not "grave goods" left with the deceased for use in the afterlife: they were projectile points which, incontrovertibly in most instances, had been directly responsible for the death of the individual.

Points were found wedged in the spine, and embedded in the skull, the pelvis, and the limb bones. The killings showed no respect for age or sex. Two adult males had a total of 27 pieces either in their bones or in direct association. An adult female and a child buried together both had pieces embedded in the upper chest area. Two children, estimated to have been seven and twelve years old, had points in precisely the same position at the base of the skull, and both showed signs of having been struck about other parts of the body.

Violence on this scale, at this period, is not known from anywhere else in the world. It was almost certainly the consequence of a collapse in the proto-agricultural system which people had developed in that section of the Nile valley during the last glacial maximum.[41] The mainstays of the system were catfish and wetland tubers (and possible wild grass grains), which were abundantly available at certain times of year—catfish in summer, wetland tubers in winter—when surpluses were harvested and stored for consumption during the months of the year when food was less readily available.

Harvesting and storage mark the beginning of organized food production: agriculture. But at that stage of its development in the Nile valley organized food production was a high-risk strategy. Output was likely to vary unpredictably, and any increase in population size resulting from a succession of good years would inevitably lead to competition in less favourable times. The burials at Jebel Sahaba probably record one such episode of violent competition, or warfare, for the limited resources of a less than luxuriant Nile valley that was surrounded by an utterly inhospitable desert.

Ostriches incubate their eggs for six weeks. The chicks leave the nest within minutes of hatching

CHAPTER 16

The Beginnings of Agriculture

DELIBERATE CONTROL OF plant productivity dates back to 70,000 years ago in southern Africa, and the world's earliest-known centrally organized food-production system was established along the Nile 15,000 years ago—long before the Pharaohs—then swept away by calamitous changes in the river's flow-pattern.

Agriculture is essentially a process of manipulating the distribution and growth of plants so that greater quantities of their edible parts are available for harvesting and consumption. The world's earliest-known evidence of natural resources having been manipulated in this way comes from archaeological excavations at the Klasies River cave site in South Africa, where conspicuous deposits of carbonized material have been identified as the inedible residues of geophytes (buried plant foods, such as tubers, roots and corms) that are a feature of the region's long-established vegetation.[1]

The carbonized deposits at Klasies River cover a significant period of time around 70,000 years ago, and are absent on levels dating from before and after that period; the argument for their representing the earliest-known evidence of people having managed a natural resource rests upon the fact that the geophytes are perennial plants growing in extremely poor soils. A large proportion of their nutritious biomass is concentrated underground, but the resource is renewed very slowly under natural conditions, and exploitation on the scale evident at Klasies River could only have been sustained by some form of management, such as controlled burning of the surface vegetation.

The soils of the region are poor, but its mature vegetation nonetheless covers the ground with a dense profusion of long-lived plant species; seed is set annually, but germinates only when and where there is room. Burning clears the ground and causes hard seed-cases to burst, thus promoting the germination of seed that might otherwise have lain dormant for decades, and plant cover regenerates.

The fynbos, whose name is derived from the Afrikaans for "fine bush," is the richest, most varied, and concentrated area of vegetation on Earth. Covering just over 91,000 km² of the coast and hinterland to the north and east of Cape Town, it supports over 8,600 plant species, nearly 5,800 of which are found nowhere else. By comparison, the land area of the British Isles is three and a half times larger but has only 1,500 plant species in all, fewer than twenty of which are endemic. In fact, the Fynbos Biome (or the Cape Floral Kingdom as it is also known) is so distinctive that it has been named as one of the world's six botanical kingdoms. Even though so small, the Fynbos Biome is botanically on a par with the Boreal Kingdom, which covers approximately 42 per cent of the Earth's land surface and includes almost the entire northern hemisphere—53 million km² in all.[2]

Geophytes are a characteristic feature of fynbos flora; natural fields of them are found along the Cape mountains and in acid soils at the coast. Indeed, the distribution of these resource-rich patches is said to explain the distribution of human-occupation sites, while the lack of essential trace minerals in the region's very pure (and high pH) ground waters explains the coastal location of many sites: shellfish is thought more likely to have been a source of these essential dietary supplements than a staple resource. Hunting and scavenging provided the protein required to balance a subsistence diet high in carbohydrate.[3]

The exploitation of geophytes on the coastal hinterland of South Africa around 70,000 years ago is an early example of people directly manipulating their environment in order to produce more food, but it does not mark the beginning of a progression that can be traced, stage by stage, from the fynbos of the Cape Floral Kingdom to the realm of modern industrial farming. The early development of agriculture was erratic (in Africa and around the world generally); innovation occurred at various places at different times and seems to have been prompted by necessity: established practices persisted so long as they satisfied immediate needs, and change arose only when they proved inadequate.

Furthermore, there was nothing preordained about the advent and development of agricultural innovation; when it failed, or demanded more effort than the benefits justified, or simply exhausted the available resource, people reverted to the old tried and trusted practices. The Klasies River evidence is a case in point: people inhabited the site continuously for a very long time but exploited the geophyte resource intensively for only a relatively brief period. Before and after that time they pursued long-established food-gathering strategies.

The Klasies River evidence stands alone as a very early example of intensified food production, but Africa probably is littered with other examples as yet undiscovered. It would be surprising indeed if people had not occasionally manipulated the environment to their advantage in similar fashion throughout the millennia, and given the amounts of effort involved it is perhaps even more surprising that any should have adopted the strategy as a permanent way of life. Clearly, some exceptional factors must have been involved. Stress is the most likely candidate, either the stress of environmental degradation, or the stress of a population growing beyond the carrying capacity of a restricted environment. Either of these factors would impel people to intensify food production. Both were increasingly evident among the human populations of the eastern Sahara and the Nile valley from around 18,000 years ago, when the first signs of a move towards agriculture as a permanent way of life are recorded.

Though the verdant green course of the Nile appears to be the very antithesis of the bleached Saharan sands through which it flows, these two contrasting features have together constituted a primary force in the development of agriculture and settled human society in Africa. The Sahara acted as a pump, drawing people from surrounding regions into its watered environments during the good times, and driving them out again as conditions deteriorated (though not necessarily returning them to their point of origin). The Nile, for its part, was a refuge for people retreating from the desert, and then a reservoir from which the desert region was repopulated as conditions improved.

The Nile is commonly believed to have been a conduit along which the principles of food-crop cultivation had flowed into Africa along with the wheat, barley, peas, and lentils initially domesticated some 9,000 years ago in the "fertile crescent" of the Near East. It is true that the ancient Egyptian civilizations founded on the Nile over 5,000 years ago were sustained by the exceptional productivity of these crops, but they were a comparatively recent introduction, arriving long after the cultivation of indigenous African plants had begun further south.

Contrary to expectations, the earliest evidence of a shift towards a critical dependence on food production as opposed to food gathering comes not from the floodplain of the Nile, but from sites in what is now the empty and waterless Sahara. The development was complex, involving the domestication of plants and livestock, technological innovation, the establishment of villages, and an increasing level of social interdependence. "It was undoubtedly an optimal adaptation to this specific semiarid environment."[4]

The Sahara desert had been widely inhabited until the last glacial maximum, when conditions of increasing aridity drove people (and practically all animals) out of its previously productive wooded grassland and savanna environments. People moved from the desert in all directions. Essentially nomadic—though exhibiting some tendency to settle at lakesides and other sources of food and water—the groups moving to north and south continued to follow their established hunting and gathering way of life. The groups that moved east into the Nile valley, however, adopted a distinctly sedentary lifestyle. Indeed, they had no choice. The narrow strips of green floodplain flanking the Nile were bounded by waterless desert, and movement along the riverside plains was constrained by the presence of competing groups.

The Nile along which people congregated 18,000 years ago was a quite different river from that which flows through Egypt today. It was much smaller, and flowed more slowly through a tangle of braided channels across a wide elevated floodplain rather than along a single massive stream. The river carried a heavy sediment load, and the silts deposited along its length steadily raised the level of the river and its floodplain.

In effect, the Nile valley at this time was an elongated oasis: a sharply defined area of inhabitable territory beyond the boundaries of which human survival was impossible. The "oasis" extended all the way from the Sudan to Cairo—a distance of over 800 kilometres—but it was nowhere more than a few kilometres wide. Its food resources were varied and nutritious, though quantities and availability were always subject to seasonal variation and the vagaries of the Nile's annual flood. During the critical two to four weeks when the flood was at its height each year, people and animals were driven out of the wadis and valley of the Nile and crowded into the narrow band of inhabitable land that lay between the flood waters and the arid desert beyond.

People hunted large mammals for meat and hides but environmental and territorial constraints meant that only small numbers of a limited range of species were available. Indeed, large mammals constitute a very small proportion of the faunal remains found at archaeological sites (only about 1 per cent in one instance) and only three species are represented: the hartebeest, the dorcas gazelle, and the aurochs—wild cattle. Coots, and migratory geese and ducks, were caught regularly, but fish was by far the most important source of protein—primarily catfish. Harpoons such as were found along with catfish remains at the Katanda site on the Upper Semliki valley in Congo (see pages

139–40) were not present at the early Nile valley sites, but the fish could easily have been speared or even caught by hand when they congregated to spawn in the shallows.

For carbohydrates, the Nile valley offered its inhabitants a considerable variety and seasonal abundance. Twenty-five different seeds, fruits, and soft vegetable tissues have been distinguished among the archaeological remains from sites at Wadi Kubbaniya, and of those identified to species the tubers of the wild nut-grass (a sedge, *Cyperus rotundus*) are the most prevalent. Nut-grass is abundant in the Nile valley today, growing in dense swards at the water's edge. Its rhizomes produce small tubers which are rich in carbohydrates and fibre. The mature tubers are woody and contain a heavy dose of alkaloid toxins, but the young plants are tender and relatively toxin-free (though roasting or grinding before consumption is still advisable).

Grindstones bearing traces of starchy vegetables suggest that nut-grass tubers began to constitute a major part of the staple diet at Wadi Kubbaniya from around 19,000 years ago.[5] Certainly, the plant is impressively productive, capable of supplying 3.3 kg of tubers per square metre where it grows in dense swards (by comparison, modern barley achieves a maximum grain-yield of 3.5 kg per square metre), and a family armed with digging sticks could have gathered enough to meet several days' carbohydrate requirements in a matter of hours.[6] Furthermore, nut-grass thrives on exploitation. The soil disturbance resulting from the harvesting of tubers stimulates the production of yet more tubers, so that heavy annual harvesting would itself guarantee an equally heavy harvest of freshly formed tubers in the following year.

Wadi Kubbaniya provides a unique and unusually full record of how people lived in the Nile valley 19,000 years ago—14,000 years before the pyramids were built. The seasons followed not the elevation of the sun but the rhythm of the annual flood, which started to rise in early July, reached its peak (around seven metres or more above low water) six to eight weeks later, and usually had fallen to its previous level by November. Catfish were harvested as they congregated to spawn on the rising flood, and again as they retreated with the falling waters. Both these events were of short duration, in which every able-bodied individual in the community participated. Undoubtedly, more fish were caught than could be eaten immediately, and the surplus probably was sun-dried or smoked over hearths, thus providing a supply of dried fish for lean periods ahead, though it would not have lasted more than four or five months before spoiling.

During the flood, people collected dryland produce, such as dates and acacia seeds, but as the flood waters began to recede, they began harvesting the major carbohydrate component of their diet: the roots of wetland plants, whose growth had been stimulated by several weeks of immersion. Wild nut-grass tubers were the first to be harvested, followed by club-rush tubers. These plants are so prolific that—like the catfish—they doubtless were gathered in excess of immediate needs and stored for use in time of need. Later, as the water receded further, the Kubbaniyans had access to the edible rhizomes and flower-buds of water lilies.

As the wetland plants matured during October and November, they pro-duced edible seeds: nutlets of club-rush, nut-grass, and papyrus; grain from the wild millets, and seeds of water lilies. Waterfowl that stopped over on their southward migration would have been the target of hunters at this time of year.

In January and February, the rhizomes of cat's-tail, bulrush, papyrus, and common reed formed their starchy storage rhizomes. Some, at least, of these plants would have grown in extensive stands, and their rhizomes thus were also a resource that could be gathered for storage as well as for immediate con-sumption. Likewise, the fruit of the doum-palm, which was available from Feb-ruary through to April, was eminently storable, as were the edible seeds of acacia, which were abundantly available from March onwards. And then it was July, and time for the flood to rise again.[7]

Wadi Kubbaniya provides an exceptionally full insight into how a group of people lived along the banks of the Nile 18,000 years ago, but these were not the only people settled in the Nile "oasis," then or later. Many more occupation sites of various ages have been discovered (and doubtless still more remain undiscovered), and though the numbers are not large, it is clear that the sites became progressively more numerous and larger with the passage of time.[8]

In the course of the 2,000 years immediately prior to the last glacial maxi-mum 18,000 years ago, the number of sites in the Nile valley increased four-fold; during the following 2,000 years (18,000 to 16,000 years ago) the number almost doubled again, and it increased by yet another one-third between 16,000 and 14,000 years ago. By 12,000 years ago, the number of occupation sites along the Nile valley was more than ten times the number known from before the last glacial maximum, 6,000 years earlier.

Throughout this period the majority of sites had covered an area of about 400 m² (the home base for a group of perhaps forty people), but the size of the largest rose from 800 m² 18,000 years ago to more than 10,000 m² 6,000 years later—large enough to constitute a village. These increases in the size and number of sites clearly denote an increase in overall population size, and since the area of the Nile "oasis" would have varied little throughout the period in question, the growing numbers of people could only have been fed by increased food production.

Adaptation to the pressure of demands for more food was characterized by a more sedentary way of life and the development of food-production and storage strategies. As at Wadi Kubbaniya, people exploited the valley's wild resources, but increasingly from semi-permanent settlements close to the flood-plain and with a distinct shift to the utilization of grain as well as a greater reliance on fish and waterfowl. The adoption of this broad adaptive strategy provided the large food supply needed by a growing population,[9] but achieving maximum production called for a good deal of planning and the management of labour. This development marks the beginning of an organized food-producing system: agriculture.

Dating from more than 15,000 years ago, the evidence from the Nile valley is arguably the earliest comprehensive instance of an organized food-producing system known anywhere on Earth. Given time, this pioneering system might have developed into the stupendous civilizations that ruled ancient Egypt for two and a half millennia from about 5,000 years ago. But it could never be. Disaster struck the Nile valley as its population reached a peak, and by 10,000 years ago occupation density had plunged to a level only slightly above that known for the time of the Wadi Kubbaniya site.

The cause of the calamity originated more than 2,000 kilometres to the south, in central Africa at the headwaters of the Nile, where the climatic amelioration which followed the last glacial maximum had brought a very marked increase in rainfall. The Nile is peculiarly dependent on conditions at its headwaters and highly sensitive to changes in them. Its route through the desert means that no water flows into it for 44 per cent of its total drainage area.[10] Overwhelmingly, the Nile is fed by rain falling in its southern catchment. The Ethiopian highland provides most of the annual discharge via the Blue Nile and the Sobat; the smaller but less seasonal White Nile drains the east and central African highlands and sustains the river during the season of low flow. Changes in the amount and seasonality of either source can have a profound effect on the volume and character of the river downstream.[11]

Around 13,000 years ago, heavy and persistent rains which had already flooded even the desiccated Kalahari basin with a number of large lakes[12] moved steadily northward. The central African lakes rose tens of metres to unprecedented levels; the previously dry Lake Victoria filled and discharged massive quantities of water into the upper Nile. The effects downstream were catastrophic.

From a sluggish river flowing through shallow braided channels, the Nile was transformed over a period of five hundred years (12,000 to 11,500 years ago) into what has been called the "wild" Nile.[13] Extremely high floods were only the beginning of the problem. The heavier rains falling on the upper catchment area produced more vegetation; as ground cover increased, erosion was reduced and the Nile carried less sediment. Less silt was deposited downstream and, most catastrophic of all, the lightened, faster-flowing "wild" Nile began to cut a single channel through the valley.

With the Nile now flowing through a single deep channel, the extent of the floodplain was severely reduced. The quantities of available plant foods declined, and even the catfish became less plentiful with the shrinking of their spawning beds. The levels to which the human population had soared could not be sustained, and the pressure on resources mounted inexorably. Competition for food intensified, doubtless provoking conflict of which the massacre at Jebel Sahaba (see pages 146–47) is probably an extreme example.

THE NORTHWARD SHIFT OF the rain belt which had flooded the catchment basin of the Nile eventually extended to the Nile valley itself, and across the adjacent Sahara. Conservative assessments conclude that regular annual rains began to fall on the region from about 11,000 years ago;[14] additional rain in the valley can hardly have been viewed as compensation for the devastating floods its inhabitants had suffered, but in the desert increased rainfall produced an environment to which some of the survivors could migrate. The scene that greeted them, however, was not one of lush vegetation and teeming wildlife.

The Sahara was only partially transformed. Semi-desert best describes its open landscape of wild grasses and thorn bush, sparsely relieved by the occasional acacia and tamarisk tree, and inhabited only by animals that could tolerate arid conditions. Surface water was concentrated in and around the highlands, or in the lakes and ponds that formed in localized depressions. People congregated around these bodies of water, and were occupying such sites throughout the Sahara by about 8,500 years ago.[15]

Not all the newcomers were migrants who had left the Nile valley in the aftermath of the catastrophic floods. The flush of growth which the rains cast across the desert at that time attracted people from all around the Sahara, but the oldest-known sites from the period are undoubtedly those situated within a few hundred kilometres of the Nile; and the evidence of Nile valley food-production strategies is found also at younger sites across the breadth of the Sahara, suggesting that if not the people of the Nile themselves, then at least their cultural adaptations had played a role in the repopulation of the former desert.

The domestication of cattle, goats, and sheep was a crucial factor in the reoccupation of the Sahara at this time, for the herding of livestock was fundamental to the food-production strategies that enabled people to live permanently in the Sahara. Domesticated animals not only converted otherwise inedible vegetation into meat that could be harvested more easily than by hunting, they also constituted a resource that could be utilized on a continuous basis. As long as the animals had access to sufficient grazing and water they could provide people with supplementary supplies of nourishment, such as milk.

Dogon women returning from the well at Tii village, in Mali

CHAPTER 17

Renewable Resources

DOMESTIC LIVESTOCK WERE PRESENT in the Sahara during a wet phase 9,000–7,000 years ago, when African cereals were also domesticated in the region. The first villages are evident from this period, indicating the beginnings of a sedentary farming lifestyle, for which the invention of pottery was a crucial development. In particular, pots enabled people to make substitutes for mother's milk, thus shortening the weaning period and birth intervals and fuelling a growth in population.

The date at which domestic stock became a feature of human activity in Africa is an issue long fraught with controversy. Domestic cattle are descended from the wild aurochs, *Bos primigenius*, and the earliest-known evidence of the domesticated condition comes from south-west Asia (particularly Anatolia) and south-east Europe, where cattle bones have been found at several sites dating back to between 9,000 and 8,000 years ago.[1] The identification is made primarily on the basis of size, since domesticated animals generally are smaller than their wild progenitors, probably as a result of inadequate feeding and because people have tended to select and breed small animals that are easy to handle and house.[2] Furthermore, succeeding generations tend to become smaller when the gene pool is restricted, and modern attempts to farm wild game animals, such as eland, have shown that very few generations need pass before an appreciable size reduction becomes evident.[3]

Though the aurochs originated in Eurasia, it is known to have migrated into North Africa around 1 million years ago and may have survived there until Roman times.[4] People were hunting the wild aurochs in the Nile valley over 19,000 years ago, and the complete skeleton of a domestic cow found at Adrar Bous in the central Sahara shows that people were herding cattle in that region by about 6,000 years ago. These two observations raise an important question: were the cattle in the Sahara the product of a domestication process that began in the Nile valley, or were they migrants from the Near East, already domesticated, and drawn into the Sahara during its wet period via the isthmus of Suez and the Mediterranean hinterland?

The implications of the question are significant, since the introduction of a new but fully developed system of exploiting the resources of the region would have effects quite different from those that would result if the system had developed *in situ,* in Africa; the effect would be invasive rather than adaptive.

Those advocating indigenous domestication claim that every site in the Sahara from around 8,000 years ago at which there is a moderately large faunal collection has yielded a few bones of either wild or domestic cattle.[5] They point in particular to the remains of six very large wild cattle at a hunting site in the Nile valley near Esna dating from 19,100 years ago, and smaller adult specimens found at occupation sites in the valley dating from 14,500 and 10,500 years ago. The reduced size of the latter could be a consequence of domestication, and the discovery of human burials with cattle skulls as head-stones certainly suggests that people had developed a close attachment to the animals by that time.[6]

Furthermore, linguistic analysis of the Nilo-Saharan family of languages currently spoken across the region reveals root words for "cow," "to drive," "thornbush cattle pen" and "to milk" that are estimated (on the basis of the observed rate of change in languages during historical times) to have been in place by about 10,000 years ago.[7]

But not everyone accepts these claims for indigenous domestication. The linguistic evidence requires archaeological confirmation, say the critics,[8] and the available archaeological evidence is disputed on the grounds that the bones in question could just as well be those of buffalo or wild cattle.[9] Even more seriously, the claims are weakened by the antiquity of other domesticated stock in the Sahara, such as goats and sheep, which were unquestionably domesticated elsewhere.

Domestic goats worldwide are all descended from the scimitar-horned goat of western Asia, *Capra aegagrus.* As this wild goat has never inhabited any part of Africa, all domestic goats throughout the continent are descended from immigrants. Likewise, all domestic sheep are descended from an Asian progenitor, *Ovis orientalis*, which was never present in Africa.[10] The earliest evidence of domestic goats in the region dates from around 7,000 years ago, in the eastern Sahara. Indeed, their remains have been found at eastern Saharan sites on the same levels as those of cattle significantly smaller than any from earlier periods.[11] An obvious question arises: if domestic goats could have reached the eastern Sahara by 7,000 years ago, why not domestic cattle as well?

Goats, of course, are better adapted than cattle to the semi-arid conditions prevailing in the Sahara at that time (cattle have a greater absolute food and water requirement), so it is possible that the idea of domestication was brought in from the Near East by goats and applied to the wild cattle of the Nile valley. This proposition certainly lends weight to claims for indigenous domestication of cattle but it is confounded by the evidence of mitochondrial DNA. Just as mtDNA has proved able to show that all modern humans originated in Africa (see page 94), it shows that the domestication of European and African cattle was a single event.

In 1994, geneticists investigating the degree of differentiation separating humped and non-humped cattle (zebu, *Bos indicus*, and taurine, *Bos taurus*, respectively) examined mtDNA sequences from a number of European, Indian, and African cattle.[12] Hitherto, the various humped and non-humped breeds had been thought to represent two distinct species descended from a single domestication of the wild aurochs, *Bos primigenius*, around 9,000 years ago.

Far from confirming this relatively straightforward scenario, however, the mtDNA evidence revealed two very distinct geographic lineages that cut right across the humped and non-humped divide: all the African and European breeds fell into one lineage, and all the Indian breeds into the other. The degree of separation was large, suggesting that two subspecies of the aurochs had existed at least 200,000 years ago which were independently domesticated many thousands of years later, one to become the progenitor of domestic cattle in India, and the other to become the progenitor of domestic cattle in Europe and Africa.

The mtDNA evidence does not totally invalidate the possibility that the progenitor of European and African domestic cattle could have diverged yet again, permitting further domestication events to have occurred in both the Near East and the Nile valley, but, along with the early arrival of goats in the eastern Sahara and doubts concerning the palaeontological evidence, it does lessen considerably the likelihood of an indigenous domestication of cattle in Africa. The greater probability is that domestic cattle were introduced from the Near East.

But whatever the site and date of their original domestication it is inescapably true that people and cattle moved into the Sahara region together.

It was a symbiotic relationship which enabled the two species to inhabit an area where one of them, and probably both of them, would have been unable to survive alone.[13]

Cattle must drink every day if they are to thrive, or every other day if they are simply to survive. Annual rainfall over the eastern Sahara is estimated to have been about 200 mm at the time, enough to support a semi-desert vegetation and fill shallow ephemeral lakes, but not enough to sustain permanent standing water. People drove the cattle to water, latterly they dug wells; by way of return the cattle served as a reliable on-the-hoof source of protein in a marginal environment. Wild food plants provided essential carbohydrates, with a growing emphasis on the collection and eventually the storage of wild grass seeds.

These developments marked the beginning of the mutually dependent relationship between cattle herding and agriculture that would eventually replace hunting and gathering as the basic subsistence strategy throughout most of Africa. They are illustrated most vividly at Nabta Playa, 100 kilometres west of the Nile, where a number of archaeological sites have been extensively excavated and documented during the decades since their discovery in the 1970s.[14]

The Nabta Playa[15] is a kidney-shaped basin almost 10 kilometres long and 7 kilometres wide. It is devoid of vegetation and totally dry today, but during the times that periodically brought annual rains to the Sahara it filled with water draining from the surrounding higher ground, and was rimmed with vegetation. Rains probably became a regular feature of the seasonal round about 11,000 years ago, but people do not appear to have moved into the region much before 9,500 years ago. Plant remains identified from archaeological sites indicate that the vegetation at that time was diverse and in some seasons relatively abundant. Sedges and grasses favouring wet habitats grew around the playa itself; there were palms, tamarisk, acacia, and *Zizyphus* (which bears an edible citrus-like fruit) trees on drier ground, and annual grasses grew luxuriantly after the summer rains.

People lived in encampments that appear to have been almost continuously occupied from soon after 9,500 to around 7,000 years ago. Archaeologists found numerous open hearths throughout the inhabited areas, and durable dwellings were evident from around 8,000 years ago. Two long rows of saucer-shaped house floors were aligned in the form of a "street" that ran from east to west across the excavated area; adjacent to each house there were bell-shaped storage pits, most of which appeared to have been granaries. Wells two metres deep supplied the community with water; some had sunken access ramps, and one had a trough at ground level from which animals could have been watered.

The dwellings at Nabta Playa, the wells and the storage pits, are laid out in the logical and organized manner that might characterize a small village or hamlet. The suggestion is of a permanent or semi-permanent settlement occupied by a relatively large and disciplined community.[16] At the earliest sites, wild animals—gazelles and hares in particular—constitute almost 100 per cent of the faunal remains, suggesting a heavy dependence on hunting as a source of protein. At later sites, more than half the remains consist of bones identified as those of goats and cattle.[17] The goats must have been domesticated, derived originally from wild progenitors in the Near East, and the cattle are significantly smaller than earlier specimens, suggesting that they too were domestic.

So there was a village at Nabta Playa. People occupied a collection of wattle-and-daub dwellings with stamped mud floors on the shores of an ephemeral lake. They herded goats and cattle over the surrounding semi-arid grasslands; tended and watered the animals and encouraged them to convert inedible vegetation into nourishing milk and meat. The relationship favoured both parties. Neither people nor livestock could have lived permanently in the region without the other, but the people certainly got the poorer side of the bargain. Tending livestock was hard work, and although the animals were a dependable source of protein and fats, they contributed little towards the carbohydrate intake that fuelled the endeavour. The people were obliged to gather this essential part of their diet from the vegetative resources of the region.

Analysis of several thousand edible-plant specimens recovered from the floors of the houses at Nabta Playa has revealed that the inhabitants exploited forty-four different kinds of plants, including tubers, fruits, and seeds—and sorghum in particular.[18] Sorghum grains are larger than those of other grass species and for this reason probably were a preferred resource. The specimens recovered from the house floors were no different from wild sorghums in terms of size and shape, but chemical analysis indicates that they may have been cultivated.[19] Furthermore, the presence of weeds known to flourish in cultivated or similarly disturbed moist areas[20] makes it more likely than not that people were cultivating sorghum at Nabta Playa.

Whether wild or cultivated, the grains discovered in the houses at Nabta Playa are the earliest-known evidence of people gathering sorghum and indicate that the process of domesticating indigenous African cereal crops was under way, 8,000 years ago. And of course the importance of grain is not simply that it provides a nutritious source of carbohydrate for immediate consumption; it also can be stored to feed people when fresh foods are unavailable, or to barter for goods and services. In this respect, sorghum is a supremely useful crop.

In a single growing season a grain of wild sorghum no larger than a raspberry seed can produce a mature plant more than two metres high. Sorghum is superbly adapted to the semi-arid conditions and summer-rainfall regime of the African tropics in which it originated and evolved. It tolerates a wide range of soils and positively thrives on intense heat and drought once its extensive root system is established. Each wild plant produces many grain-bearing inflorescences—the largest up to half a metre long—but the stalk is remarkably sturdy and tough. Harvesting wild sorghum is exhausting work, suggesting that harvesting difficulties may explain the apparently late domestication of African cereals.[21]

Technology, and the organization of labour, were probably of greater initial importance than the genetic predisposition of the wild stock. The "sickle gloss" identified on small blades from early North African sites indicates that harvesting wild grains was a long-established practice, and evidence of deliberate cultivation and consequent domestication occurs only where people were living at permanent or semi-permanent sites, in association with livestock, as at Nabta Playa, and possibly were already under pressure to increase food production.

In every instance, the domestication of a food crop has been an extended process, not a sudden event.[22] As long as people simply harvested wild seed there was likely to be little or no selection effect, since it is seldom possible to harvest even half the natural production and ample seed was always left to maintain the wild stand.

In the early stages of the domestication process, people probably harvested grain by stripping it from plants in the field, but with the development of effective tools they reaped entire inflorescences and carried them away to be threshed. Sooner or later, the potential benefits of sowing some of the grain just harvested were noted, and with this development the process of domestication accelerated. People began to select and cultivate seeds from the plants that best suited their needs.

Plants that retain rather than drop their ripe seed are not common among wild stock, for instance, but they would always have been the plants that people harvested most successfully and so would make a disproportionate genetic contribution to the next generation. Similarly, selection towards a single terminal seed-head (rather than sprays of seed-heads) and simultaneous maturation would have been automatic once people began sowing the seed they had saved from a successful harvest. And when cultivators adopted the practice of selecting seed for the next planting before the crop was harvested, selection was total. The next generation grew only from seed with traits the cultivator deemed most desirable. The rest was eaten and so eliminated from the gene pool.

·   ·   ·

EVIDENCE DOCUMENTING the domestication of livestock and food plants in Africa (or around the world, for that matter) defies attempts to establish a neat and tidy chronology of the process. It is impossible to state definitively when and where a particular development first occurred; let alone whether the same development arose spontaneously in another location, or arrived there by cultural transmission via a series of intervening groups, or was brought in by immigrants. Nonetheless, there are some general observations that can be made. The essential preconditions for domestication seem not to be the availability of suitable stock or plants, but prevailing ecological conditions and the status of the human population.

Reflecting on why animals had not been domesticated in Africa, it has been said that since Africans were blessed with an environment supporting the greatest stock of game in the world, they had no incentive to innovate beyond the needs of hunting.[23] Around half of the world's species of wild ungulates are found in Africa. With such an abundance and diversity of wild meat, why would people bother to keep domestic animals? Maintaining a herd of livestock is very troublesome: the animals must be protected from predators, of which there are many species in Africa; and they have to be provided with food and water—all of which means that domestic livestock has to be owned. And ownership was perhaps the greatest discouragement of all. Ownership entailed settlement and an entirely different social and economic basis from that of the nomadic hunter and gatherer of wild foods.[24]

As with animals so too with plants. An abundance of wild food plants delayed the need for people to resort to the labour-intensive endeavours of cultivated food production. The domestication of indigenous food plants therefore was a relatively late development in Africa.

The conclusion must be that innovation leading to the beginnings of agriculture occurred in Africa only where and when there was demand for an increase in food production—and the same probably applies to its development everywhere else in the world. The demand could arise from the effects of deteriorating environmental conditions, from restrictions on territorial expansion, from a sudden spurt of population growth—or from a combination of factors.

NABTA PLAYA WAS QUITE LITERALLY an oasis surrounded by semi-desert in which people developed the innovative strategies that enabled them to live permanently on the resources of a marginal environment. The herding and farming strategies they developed have subsequently become the ways of life that sustain millions in the savanna and marginal semi-desert regions of Africa. The strategies are always interdependent, however, requiring the willing cooperation of people with very different land-use strategies. Whether herders and farmers are one and the same group, or each a separate population, neither is viable without the other: herders need carbohydrates, farmers need protein.

At Nabta Playa the success of the interdependent herding and farming strategies was significantly enhanced by the arrival in the region of a major technological innovation, perhaps the most important to have occurred in prehistoric times: pottery.

Finely made pottery dating from 12,000 years ago has been found in Japan, and examples are widespread throughout Asia and the Near East from the period around 10,000 years ago that saw the beginnings of livestock and food-plant domestication.[25] The earliest-known pottery in Africa was found in the central Sahara, at a site in what is now north-eastern Niger dating from 9,500 years ago,[26] and pottery appears at Nabta Playa from about 8,100 years ago, at first in small quantities, but in larger amounts from 7,500 years ago.[27] The earliest pottery found in any part of the Nile valley is younger still.

As with the domestication of livestock, the advent of pottery in the Sahara could denote an independent invention, or it could be a stage in the spread of the technology from the Near East via the Mediterranean hinterland across the Sahara and southward through Africa. Whatever the case, the significance of its diffusion and universal adoption by people throughout the continent is undeniable: wherever it first occurs in the archaeological record, pottery signifies that people were producing food, rather than simply gathering it.

Pots and bits of pottery are a ubiquitous element of African archaeological studies covering the past 9,000 years. Sorted into time-frames and typological categories, pottery has become the hard evidence according to which scholars have defined societies and traced their influence back and forth across the continent. Wavy-line and stipple, epipalaeolithic and neolithic, eastern stream and western stream, burnished, glazed, Cherekecherete, Gatung'ang'a, Musengezi, Urewe, and Zhizo—the bewildering terminology can boggle the mind, and the supreme functional relevance of the invention of the pot is submerged under a welter of intense academic discussion.

Gender could have something to do with this. The vast majority of archaeologists are male. Perhaps it required a woman to point out that the invention of pottery generated population growth and favoured a sedentary way of life.

Expounding this hypothesis, Randi Haaland of the University of Bergen notes:[28]

Pottery and the use of boiled food would influence the fertility of women and cause population growth because the development of ceramic containers enabled food to be boiled which might be substituted for mother's milk. This would reduce the breast feeding period and the duration of post-partum amenorrhea. Shorter birth spacing together with relatively abundant . . . resources and the constraints imposed on mobility by the new pottery technology constituted factors which favoured increased sedentism.

Randi Haaland was referring in particular to the evidence from Nile valley sites in the Sudan, where her excavations have documented the establishment of settled communities, the growth of populations, and the spread of technological innovation—especially pottery—but the observations apply with equal validity to sites further north, in the marginal environments of the Sahara, where Nabta Playa is the chosen example.

With domesticated cattle and goats, cultivated sorghum and the cooking pot, people living at Nabta Playa around 7,500 years ago might have considered themselves the beneficiaries of a system that could run for ever. Rainfall in the region matched the exceptional levels attained just prior to the last glacial maximum (see page 140) and, having established a permanent residential base, the problems of population increase and food production were balanced by the growth of the labour force. There were lessons to be learned in the counterpoint of individual rights and communal obligations and the founding principles of urban society were established (or perhaps not). In the event, whatever stage of social development had been reached at Nabta Playa during the good times, any further progress was rendered impossible around 7,000 years ago by a return of the bad times.

After 5,000 years of continuously improving conditions, throughout which the Sahara had been well watered and far more widely covered with vegetation than today, the climate changed abruptly (see chart, page 694). Within about 500 years the Sahara became a more arid and harsher desert than has existed at any period during historic times. The people and animals that had been drawn into the Sahara were pushed out again. Those in the eastern desert found refuge in the Nile valley, where their herding and cultivation practices fused with the long-established exploitation of the aquatic Nile resources to produce the unique and robust agricultural economy upon which the Pharaonic dynasties were founded.

The highly productive Near Eastern domesticates, barley and emmer-wheat, were incorporated into the Nile valley agriculture; there were cattle, sheep, goats, pigs, and dogs; the donkey, an indigenous African species, was domesticated. And, of course, there were pots in abundance. Permanent villages were established; at Merimde, on the western side of the Nile delta, people lived in two-by-three-metre mud-brick dwellings set on either side of narrow lanes and interspersed with storage pits, granaries, and open shelters which appear to have been workshops.[29] The number of people living along the Nile grew prodigiously. Whereas the entire human population of the western desert of Egypt was probably no more than 8,000 during the time Nabta Playa was occupied,[30] each village along the Nile now housed up to 200 people, and settlements big enough to be called towns could have supported at least 500 and possibly as many as 5,000.[31]

From ancient strategies that had evolved to cope with the stresses of surviving in river valley and desert, agriculture in the Nile valley flourished magnificently.

CHAPTER 18

The Pastoral Scene

THE DOMESTICATION OF LIVESTOCK enhanced early food production economies, but lactose intolerance and the tsetse fly restricted the spread of pastoralism among the people and habitats of Africa.

The wild aurochs, *Bos primigenius,* early inhabitant of Asia, Europe, and North Africa and ancestor of all domestic cattle, was a formidable beast. Standing up to two metres high at the shoulder and heavily built, with long curved horns pointing forward like two medieval impaling spikes, a full-grown male aurochs was larger and more ferocious than the largest animal that ever charged a Spanish bullfighter—lethal might be the appropriate term.

How people took the step from hunting these definitively wild beasts to the husbanding of tame individuals is a matter of conjecture and not a little wonder. They would not have been easy to capture, nor would they have willingly accepted restraint.

The first animal to have been domesticated was the dog, in western Asia about 12,000 years ago, and the most recent appears to have been the goldfish (in China about 1,000 years ago).[1] The progenitor of the domestic dog was the wolf and it probably entered the domestic state as pups caught in the wild and reared in the homestead. The wolf has a social system of dominant and submissive individuals not dissimilar to that of people—every individual knows his or her place in both the wolf pack and the human community. Wolves reared among people from infancy found an agreeable niche in the human

Fulani herdsman and cattle on the fringe of the Sahara desert at Tchin-Tabaradene, in Niger

hierarchy, and the wild temperament of their forebears was selectively eliminated from populations bred exclusively in captivity.

Dogs helped people to hunt, so their domestication served a useful purpose, but sheep and goats are more likely to have been domesticated because they were a nuisance. The earliest evidence of their domestic state occurs in western Asia, at sites dating from around 9,000 years ago. By then people were growing cereals where wild sheep and goats had previously roamed at will. Carefully herding the animals into corrals would have been an effective means of protecting the ripening crops; captured lambs and kids were reared to maturity in the settlement, and tame flocks ultimately displaced their wild antecedents.[2]

But by virtue of its size, ferocity, and solitary disposition,[3] the aurochs was not susceptible to either the herding or the rearing-from-infancy methods of domestication. The initial subjugation of cattle was probably brought about by putting out supplies of salt and water at fixed points in the neighbourhood, which encouraged free-ranging animals to stay near human settlements and gradually habituated them to people.

Even in modern times, people in the Assam hills entice mithans (*Bos frontalis,* a wild bovid found in the highland forests of India) from the forest by exploiting their craving for salt. The animals can be approached and stroked, and will even take salt from the hand. They are not milked or eaten, but are kept solely for purposes of sacrifice and barter. It is quite possible that the aurochs was originally tamed for the same purpose. Many early prehistoric societies undoubtedly venerated cattle. At Çatal Hüyük in Turkey, for example, horn cores associated with human figurines and fertility symbols are positive evidence for the ritual significance of cattle. A shrine with the horn cores of *Bos primigenius* set in a bench of clay dates from *c.*7,900 years ago.[4]

Çatal Hüyük provides the earliest incontrovertible evidence of domesticated cattle, and shows that cattle were a revered component of human culture 8,000 years ago. The earliest incontrovertible evidence of people using domestic stock as a source of milk, however, comes many centuries later, in dairy scenes depicted on seals, reliefs, and wall-paintings from the ancient civilizations of Mesopotamia and the Nile dating from around 6,000 years ago. Since some of this evidence clearly indicates that the people depicted made cheese and butter,[5] it can be confidently concluded that the knowledge of milking and dairy production was already well advanced and widespread by then. But the knowledge would not have been easily acquired. It is very unlikely that even a tamed aurochs would have allowed itself to be milked. Only considerable effort and guile will persuade a cow of an unimproved or primitive breed to let down her milk.[6]

Though it is difficult to imagine what use a captive herd of large and intractable aurochs could have served during the early stages of domestication, the advantages of pursuing the process to the point of breeding a tame dairy herd are readily apparent. Cows' milk can not only hasten the weaning of infants from their mother's breast, it can also sustain adults when other foods are scarce. Furthermore, as butter or in the fermented form of yogurt and cheese, milk can be stored or bartered—or sold. There is nothing in milk that cannot be obtained from other plant and animal foods, but because its primary purpose is to nourish infants during a critical period of growth it contains large amounts of the materials needed to build healthy and fully developed bodies. These include carbohydrates, fats, proteins, vitamins, and minerals, of which calcium is the most important.

Calcium builds bones; it can be obtained by eating plenty of leafy vegetables such as beet greens, turnip tops, and spinach, but milk solids are the most concentrated dietary source (and clearly the one most suitable for infants). Furthermore, milk also contains a substance which specifically promotes the absorption of calcium by the intestines: lactose (a milk sugar and thus also an important source of energy). Newborn mammals have soft bones which must harden and grow rapidly, and their mother's milk is a superb natural formula for promoting the absorption of calcium and maximum rates of bone growth (along with all other needs) during the time when an infant cannot provide for itself. Of course, the perfect matching of mother's milk to infant's need is no more than is to be expected of a dependency with a long evolutionary history. More surprising, perhaps, is the fact that many people continue to drink milk and consume dairy products long after the needs of infancy are past, when they are independent and perfectly able to fend for themselves. This is a cultural development that derives from the inadequacies of the diet on which people subsisted when they moved from food gathering to food production and the cultivation of crops.

The cereals that provide such a wonderful source of carbohydrate are, however, woefully low in calcium and iron. Moreover, the husks contain substances (phytate phosphorus) which can interfere with the absorption of whatever calcium may be in the diet. Set these deficiencies against the fact that mothers need significant *extra* amounts of calcium to pass on to their offspring during gestation and while breast-feeding and it becomes abundantly clear that women in early agricultural communities are likely to have been under severe nutritional stress. And indeed, a comparative analysis of bone from pre-agriculturist and agriculturist burials in north-east Africa has revealed widespread malnutrition and, in particular, a high incidence of osteoporosis and anaemia (resulting from low calcium and iron intake) among young females of the latter population.[7]

Insufficient calcium in the diet leads to rickets in children; legs become grotesquely bowed and stunted; the chest collapses and the pelvis becomes twisted. Once advanced, the condition is virtually irreversible. Adults who suffered rickets as children would be less likely to reproduce than their healthy counterparts; ricketic women who became pregnant, for instance, would be at risk of dying with an unborn child stuck in their distorted birth canal.[8]

By affecting the reproductive segment of the population so pronouncedly, the low calcium (and iron) content of the agriculturist diet restrained any potential for population growth that the community's increased food production otherwise might have fuelled. Adequate supplies of milk from domesticated livestock corrected the deficiency. Sheep and goats were the first step, and finally encouraging the domesticated aurochs to provide milk on demand established the value and viability of keeping animals principally for the milk they could provide (an appreciation of their value as providers of traction power and dung for field and fire would come later).

This is not to say that people began milking because they were aware of a calcium deficiency in their diet; it is simply that the benefits of the improved diet would have produced a population growth spurt among the people partaking of it. Their increased numbers in turn increased the prevalence of the practice. But before this could happen and milch pastoralism could become a dominant way of life in the semi-arid regions of the Middle East and Africa a not inconsiderable adjustment to human physiology was required.

THE LACTOSE MOLECULE WHICH ENABLES the human body to absorb calcium is itself unable to pass through the walls of the small intestine in one piece. It is too large and complex, and must first be broken down into its two major parts—the sugars glucose and galactose. Deconstruction is undertaken by an enzyme, lactase, which is secreted by the mucous membrane that lines the inner surfaces of the small intestine.[9]

Lactase is an enzyme which serves no function other than to break down milk sugars (lactose). So, from a physiological point of view, lactase production is superfluous once an infant has passed the age by which the majority of its kind are weaned from their mothers' milk. Accordingly, as this stage is reached, the gene determining lactase production is switched off in all mammalian species except one. The exception, of course, is humans. Large numbers of people continue to produce lactase beyond infancy and remain able to digest lactose throughout their adult lives—but not all. Others experience extreme discomfort whenever they drink so much as a single glass of milk. The undigested lactose accumulates in the large intestine, where it ferments. Flatulence, distension, severe intestinal cramps, and diarrhoea follow in rapid order, as the gut fills with water and the lactose is flushed from the body in liquid stools.

The first hint that milk might not be universally "good for you" was noted by western nutritionists during the 1960s, in the aftermath of international foreign-aid programmes which had shipped millions of tons of dried milk around the world and found their generosity greeted with less than total appreciation. While individual Americans and Europeans were drinking litres of milk every day, in the firm belief that it would build sturdy bodies, maintain good health, settle the stomach, calm the nerves, and relieve insomnia—among other things (and among other things, increased consumption also helped to soak up surplus production)—the inhabitants of impoverished countries around the world were complaining that it made them ill. Such ingratitude. In West Africa, a Peace Corps volunteer reported villagers concluding that the powdered milk from the United States contained "evil spirits" and should be avoided. In Colombia, large shipments were used to whitewash houses, after first adding small quantities of clay to give the wash a more desirable off-white shade.[10]

At first the donors attributed reports of the milk causing intestinal discomfort and diarrhoea to poor hygiene, dirty water, and lack of experience with a new type of food. But while shipping mountains of powdered milk abroad, the United States government was also distributing surplus whole milk to needy Americans, and by the mid-1960s blacks in the ghettos were also complaining of discomfort and diarrhoea after drinking milk. In 1965, a team of research physicians at the Johns Hopkins School of Medicine began to investigate, and soon found that 70 per cent of American blacks cannot digest lactose, while 85 per cent of whites can.[11] This pioneer study clearly showed that the European capacity to digest lactose is not universal; furthermore, it suggested that lactose tolerance and intolerance could be a measure of difference between ethnic groups.

The latter possibility was confirmed the following year by a study conducted at Makerere University College in Uganda which examined the capacity to digest lactose in two distinct ethnic groups: the cattle-herding Tutsi, and the agriculturist BaGanda.[12] The study found that while 80 per cent of the Tutsi could digest lactose, 80 per cent of the BaGanda could not. The issue of lactose tolerance and intolerance in adults now became a subject of worldwide study. The initial assumption (based on North American and European experience, where most people consume milk products without ill effects) was that tolerance must be the norm, but results soon began to show that this ability to digest lactose in adulthood was distinctly abnormal, and lactose intolerance was the norm. In fact, a review of the subject published in 1981 concluded that "the vast majority of humankind [is] lactose intolerant."[13] Functional levels of adult tolerance to lactose have been recorded only among northern Europeans and white North Americans (approaching 90 per cent), and nomadic pastoralists in Africa (80 per cent tolerant).

Back on the other side of the lactose divide, non-pastoralist Africans showed around 90 per cent intolerance, with the level approaching 100 per cent among the Igbo and Yoruba people of Nigeria.[14] Most North American blacks are the descendants of slaves from West Africa. Their reduced levels of intolerance (down to 70 per cent) indicate that either some north European genes have transmitted a degree of lactose tolerance to the black population since slaves were first sold into America 400 years ago (sixteen to twenty generations), or else that tolerance has evolved among the blacks as a result of their absorption into a dairying culture.

The ability to digest lactose depends, of course, upon the secretion of the enzyme, lactase; and the continued secretion of lactase beyond infancy is determined by whether or not the gene responsible for its production is left switched on. The genetic connection was established to the satisfaction of most commentators in the early 1970s by researchers from the medical schools at Lagos and Stanford universities. From their detailed surveys of cattle herding (Fulani) and agriculturist (Yoruba and Igbo) communities in Nigeria the researchers published results[15] showing that both lactose tolerance and intolerance were inherited. But the gene for tolerance was dominant, they found. In other words, if one parent was intolerant and the other tolerant, only the tolerant gene would be copied when they reproduced and all their children would be able to digest lactose as adults.

The implication of a dominant gene for lactose tolerance is that once the mutation had arisen, the number of people in a group sharing its benefits would increase, generation by generation, until all were lactose tolerant. Populations would have grown and dispersed, especially in the early days of agriculture, when livestock were newly domesticated and the capacity to exploit the nutritional benefits of their milk would have been very advantageous indeed.

The evolution of lactose tolerance can only have begun with the domestication of livestock around 10,000 years ago. Whether these crucial developments arose solely in the Near East, or in the Sahara as well (see page 160), they combined to expand the food resource potential of semi-arid lands throughout both regions. Cows converted dry grass and corn stalks into nourishing milk. As numbers of both cattle and people increased, nomadic pastoralists moved into ecological zones that could not otherwise be occupied in such numbers. The Sahara turned wet again between 6,500 and 4,500 years ago (see chart, page 694),[16] drawing people to its heart once more, fuelling population growth and nurturing what the geographer Frederick J. Simoons[17] has called the Saharan Pastoral Period.[18]

A SERIES OF WALLED CIRCLES, 30 to 40 metres in diameter, excavated at the Dakhleh (Dakhla) Oasis in Egypt have been interpreted as stock pens, indicating that large-scale pastoralism was practised in that part of the eastern Sahara from even before 6,500 years ago,[19] and evidence from numerous other archaeological investigations shows that pastoralism was widespread through-out the Sahara, from the Nile valley to Niger and Mali by 4,500 years ago.[20]

Rock paintings in the Acacus and Tassili mountains of the central Sahara dating from the Pastoral Period not only confirm the presence and herding of cattle in the region at that time, but also provide evidence of milking. Cows with large udders are shown. There are pictures of pots, enclosures, and huts and scenes of individuals closely associated with cows. One painting in partic-ular shows a person crouched behind a cow with arms extended, milking the animal into a pot; behind the cow stands a calf, whose presence probably encouraged its mother to let down her milk.[21]

But of course, not only cattle-herders were living in the Sahara during the Pastoral Period. There were hunters too. Watercourses and lakes in the central and southern Sahara were inhabited by hippopotamus, crocodiles, and fish. Gazelle and antelope were also plentiful, and the harpoons and finely knapped arrowheads recovered from archaeological sites indicate that wild resources were exploited throughout the region. Grindstones are found in profusion, suggesting if not always the cultivation of crops then at least the collection of wild grains. Pottery is equally common. People indulged in personal adorn-ment, such as beadwork and ivory bracelets. The dead were buried on their sides, in the foetal position, with large flat rocks or grindstones placed directly over them. One grave that was opened contained a skeleton with a single stone bead around the neck and fragments of goatskin leather tied around the ankles and the wrists.[22]

All in all, the Sahara appears to have been a veritable Garden of Eden dur-ing the Pastoral Period, with abundant wild resources, cultivated cereals, and cows which enabled people to fill their pots with milk as well as honey. Such affluence is probably an exaggeration, but the beginning of a mixed and inte-grated agricultural economy in the region is clearly evident.

• • •

THE SAHARAN ENVIRONMENT OF LAKES, streams, and ample grasslands spawned an enormous variety of local adaptations.[23] People were engaged in the specialized utilization of coastal shellfish; the exploitation of animals and fish in the inland lakes; game-hunting; wild-grass-seed gathering and grain-processing; and the herding of domestic animals. For the first time in Africa, distinct groups were following different lifestyles. Until 10,000 years ago, all had been hunters and gatherers; now, in the Sahara, a cultural landscape of subsistence specialists mirrored the ecological landscape of the region. Hunters, gatherers, fisherfolk, pastoralists, and agriculturists occupied distinct niches—each group dependent to some extent upon the others, though each no doubt developed a strong sense of independent identity and territorial right.

In this best-of-all-worlds scenario—with plenty of food and large pots to cook it in—a burst of population growth was inevitable. Climatic and ecological reconstructions of the ancient landscape, combined with figures on modern stocking levels in Africa, show that during the Pastoral Period (6,500 to 4,500 years ago), just over 3 million km^2 of the Sahara region was suitable for herding and could have supported a standing population of nearly 21 million cattle,[24] which in turn could have supported a human population of millions.[25] These figures are hypothetical and almost certainly were never approached, let alone attained, but people certainly extended their presence throughout the region during this period of population growth. The southward expansion of pastoralists was severely limited, however, by the tsetse fly and the sleeping sickness (trypanosomiasis) it carries, which is fatal to cattle, small stock—and people.

The preferred habitat of the tsetse fly is a mosaic of trees, bush, and open grassland which in tropical Africa requires a minimum rainfall of between 500 and 700 mm.[26] As rainfall levels have risen and fallen with the fluctuating climate over millennia, so the tsetse belt has advanced and retreated along the southern boundary of the Sahara.

The onset of lower annual rainfall and increasing desiccation brought the Pastoral Period to a close around 4,500 years ago, and by 3,300 years ago conditions very similar to those of modern times had been established throughout the Saharan region. The tsetse belt had moved 200 to 300 km southward, leaving in its wake a belt of undulating grassland savanna, studded with scrub and acacia woodland: the Sahel.

Varying between 200 and 400 km in breadth, its northern limits deter-

mined by the sands of the Sahara and its southern extent restricted by highlands, rain-fed vegetation, tsetse fly, and swamp, the Sahel extends in a gentle
curve across the continent from the mouth of the Senegal River on the Atlantic
coast to the Sudan shores of the Red Sea, a corridor of virtually unbroken
grazing lands, 6,000 km long and nowhere less than 200 km wide, the largest
pastoral zone in Africa. From the Sudan, the Sahelian corridor winds around
the Ethiopian highlands into Somalia, and opens southward into the grasslands of East Africa.

The desiccation of the Sahara which brought the Pastoral Period to an end
might, at first appraisal, seem to have been a wholly deleterious development;
but as it coincided with the growth of livestock and human populations in the
Sahara, and pushed back the tsetse belt, the onset and advance of drier conditions opened up a vast new ecological niche for the people who enjoyed the
benefits of lactose tolerance.

Pastoralists first moved into the present Sahel 4,000 years ago, when they
established camps in what is now the Tilemsi valley of northern Mali and at
other points along the southern boundary of the Sahara.[27] Evidence of pastoralist presence dating from shortly after 4,000 years ago has been unearthed
at sites to the east of Lake Turkana in northern Kenya (which provides a geographical and chronological link with early food-producing sites along the
Sudanese Nile),[28] and sites in southern Kenya indicate that pastoralism was
practised throughout the region from about 2,600 years ago.[29] But the early
pastoralists did not move into an uninhabited wilderness. Hunter-gatherers
had been living in this cradle of humanity longer than anywhere else on Earth,
and the evidence suggests that they were not slow to take advantage of the
new opportunities that the pastoralists introduced to the region; domestic animal bones, for example, were common among the wild fauna unearthed at
their camp sites.

Of course, the presence of domestic animal bones at hunting sites could
simply indicate that the hunters had themselves adopted the pastoralist way of
life, and were herding cattle (rather than poaching them), but the presence of
three distinct groups in the region, distributed according to the environments
they exploited and identified by the kinds of blade tools and pottery they
used—two groups of pastoralists, and one of hunters and gatherers—indicates
otherwise.[30] Of the pastoralists, one group utilized the lowland savannas, and
the other was confined to grasslands at higher elevations along the edge of the
Rift Valley, while the hunter-gatherers exploited the ecotone between lowland
and highland, savanna and woodland.

With each group primarily exploiting a different ecological zone, direct
competition between them was minimized and the development of stable

coexistence and symbiotic relationships assured. The archaeological evidence forming the basis for this interpretation of human social and economic arrangements in East Africa from about 2,500 years ago is sound, but it lacks evidence of one very important element. No pastoral society could survive for any great length of time without access to agricultural produce,[31] and although analysis of nitrogen isotope ratios in human skeletons has revealed a substantial plant-food component in the diets of people occupying the region during the period in question,[32] archaeologists have been unable to find any evidence of which particular plant food they were gathering or cultivating.

But what the archaeological evidence lacks, other disciplines can sometimes provide. And indeed, a sequence of population movements reconstructed from linguistic evidence reveals a Southern Cushitic-speaking population with domestic stock and possibly a knowledge of agriculture moving into northern Kenya from Ethiopia between 5,000 and 4,000 years ago, and thereafter spreading into central Kenya and northern Tanzania. During the latter part of this migration, a population of Southern Nilote-speakers moved down from the Sahelian region of the Sudan into the western highlands and Rift Valley of Kenya. The Southern Nilotes also kept domestic stock and may have cultivated sorghum and finger millet.[33]

It is quite possible, of course, that although these pastoralist groups had possessed the knowledge of agriculture as they advanced south through East Africa they lacked either the opportunity or the means to apply it. A mix of hunter-gatherer and pastoralist artefacts at a site could be indicative of hunter-gatherers with access to pastoralist resources, but it could also be evidence of impoverished pastoralists compelled by necessity to exploit hunter-gatherer strategies while rebuilding their herds.[34]

But whatever the status and interrelationships of the people occupying East Africa around 2,500 years ago, the archaeological and linguistic evidence undeniably shows that three of Africa's four linguistic families (see page 110) were represented in the region by that time: the Nilo-Saharan family of languages by the Southern Nilotic–speaking pastoralists from the Sahel; Afro-Asiatic languages by the Southern Cushitic–speakers from Ethiopia; and Khoisan by the indigenous hunter-gatherers.

For a period of several hundred years, East Africa marked the limit of pastoral expansion into the sub-Saharan regions previously occupied only by indigenous hunter-gatherers. The relatively rapid diffusion of food-production techniques from the Sahara and the Sahel came to a halt on the Serengeti plain, and did not advance further south until representatives of Africa's fourth linguistic family, Niger–Congo, arrived in East Africa: farmers speaking Bantu languages, and equipped with tools made of iron.

First stages in making a *makoro* (dugout canoe) on an island in the Okavango delta, Botswana

CHAPTER 19

The Impact of Iron

IN LESS THAN 3,000 YEARS the Bantu-speaking peoples expanded from their cradle-land that straddles the borders of present-day Nigeria and Cameroon and colonized virtually all of sub-Saharan Africa. The development of iron-smelting technology played an important role in their dispersal.

The nineteenth-century adventurers who set out to explore Africa from Zanzibar or the coastal towns of Bagamoyo and Mombasa had many difficulties to ponder, not the least of which was communication. Language. A basic grounding in the language spoken at the coast, KiSwahili, could be acquired while outfitting the expeditions, and European influence was already pervasive enough for there to be local agents and escorts who spoke English, French, Portuguese, or German and could act as translators. But deep inland, where even coastal traders had not ventured and ease of communication would be vital, language was likely to be a problem.

In the event, communication was surprisingly easy. Then as now, KiSwahili speakers could understand many of the languages and dialects encountered in sub-equatorial Africa: from Zanzibar across the continent to the Atlantic; from the Equator to the Zambezi, and around the Kalahari to the southernmost shores of South Africa. The reason for this vast swathe of mutual comprehension is that the people concerned all speak one or other of the Bantu languages, the most widespread of the Niger–Congo linguistic family. KiSwahili uses many loan words from foreign languages, particularly Arabic. The name itself comes from the Arabic *sahil*, meaning shore or coast, and could be translated as "coast dialect," but at root KiSwahili is a Bantu language.

The term "Bantu" is an exclusively linguistic label which has no ethnic or cultural connotation whatsoever. It was coined by the nineteenth-century German philologist Wilhelm Bleek as a name for the group of African languages and dialects among which the word-stem *ntu,* meaning some *thing* or person, is universal. The prefix *ba,* again common to all these languages, denotes the plural and so *ba-ntu* literally means "people." To Bleek this seemed an eminently suitable name for a family of languages spoken by so many groups dispersed over such a wide area.[1]

It was Joseph Greenberg, the leading modern authority on the classification of the African languages, who grouped Bantu with the Mande languages of West Africa in the Niger–Congo linguistic family; and it was also Greenberg who first defined the three other linguistic families in Africa: Khoisan, Nilo-Saharan, and Afro-Asiatic (see map 7, page 692).[2] As the name implies, the Afro-Asiatic family links Africa to Asia, including: Arabic; the Cushitic languages of Ethiopia and Somalia; Berber in North Africa; and extending around the western Sahara, where it is represented by the Tuareg and Hausa languages. The Nilo-Saharan family covers the central Sahara, the Sahel, and the Nile headwaters; Khoisan languages are spoken by the hunting and gathering populations who still inhabit the Kalahari, the Congo basin, and parts of East Africa.

The linguistic affinities linking Africa to Asia once supported a widespread belief that everything of any value in Africa had been imported. This was the Hamitic hypothesis.[3] "The incoming Hamites were pastoral 'Europeans'— arriving wave after wave—better armed as well as quicker witted than the dark agricultural Negroes," wrote the ethnologist Charles G. Seligman in his influential book, *Races of Africa.*

Seligman's book was first published in 1930, and subsequent editions up to 1966 all included the above statement, unchanged. But Greenberg's work, also published in 1966, showed that the most characteristic and specialized pastoralist strategies in Africa had developed among the Nilo-Saharans, not the Afro-Asiatics. It may well have been the Afro-Asiatics who introduced cattle, sheep, and goats to Africa, but it was the Nilo-Saharans who most fully exploited their potential. "The stereotype of the pastoral conquering Hamite must be abandoned," Greenberg demanded.[4]

Linguists prying ever deeper into Greenberg's four-family classification of African languages have concluded that, although the overall picture is very simple, the detail is not. Equal or greater degrees of linguistic complexity are found elsewhere in the world, "but nowhere is there such a geographically extensive area of linguistic 'fragmentation' as in sub-Saharan Africa."[5] Estimates of the total number of languages within the Bantu group range up to more than 600, depending upon where the line is drawn between a language and a dialect (some authorities believe that a figure of no more than 300 distinct languages is probably closer to the truth).[6]

But even the most distinct of the Bantu languages are no more different from each other than are the Germanic languages of northern Europe, such as Swedish, Norwegian, and Danish. Such close affinity, spread across the land mass of sub-Saharan Africa, separated at its extremes by 6,000 km of mountain, savanna, rivers, desert, and equatorial forest, and shared today among nearly 400 million people, is remarkable indeed.

All languages change over time, and the extent to which related languages differ is a measure of how long the people speaking them have been separated—the greater the difference, the longer the separation. Clearly, the shared affinities of the Bantu languages can only be due to their relatively recent dispersion. So was there once a single population of Bantu-speaking people? If so, where did they live, and when did they begin to spread out across Africa?

The answers to these questions lie in a four-volume comparative analysis of the Bantu languages compiled by Malcolm Guthrie,[7] which identified several hundred word roots that were common to a selection of representative languages from across the entire Bantu-speaking region. These word roots described culturally neutral items whose labels were least susceptible to change or replacement, such as "house," "district," "friend," "mother's brother," "bees," "clay," and so forth.

The percentage of word roots occurring with identical form and meaning among the languages is a measure of their linguistic proximity, and analysis of Guthrie's data shows that the greatest similarity is found among the languages spoken today in the Benue valley of eastern Nigeria, and in the adjacent grass-fields of western Cameroon. This is where the word roots survive most extensively in the least modified form, so this region must be the cradle of the Bantu languages.

Reconstructions of the original Bantu language—proto-Bantu—include terms for both root crop and tree cultivation, indicating that the proto-Bantu speakers were cultivators living on the forest margins. Domesticated crops such as yams and palm oil were an integral part of the diet, supplemented by the produce of the hunt. Bantu-speakers began dispersing from their cradle-land around 5,000 years ago, probably as a consequence of natural drift, as populations grew and villagers moved to new sites once or twice a decade, selecting natural clearings, riverside and forest-edge environments suitable for their main crops while at the same time avoiding areas that were already occupied.

The expansion appears to have been decidedly slow in the equatorial forest regions, taking 600 years to cover 1,000 km in one instance and advancing at an overall rate of no more than 22 km each decade.[8] Once beyond the forest, however, the rate of expansion accelerated. The distinct patterns of style and manufacture recognizable in the pottery they left at sites along the way[9] reveal the extent of their expansion, and radiocarbon dating gives a measure of its speed. Thus it is known that Bantu farmers were well established in the lakes region of central Africa by 2,500 years ago and had reached the southern limit of their dispersal by about nine hundred years later—in the 4th century AD.

In little more than 3,000 years Bantu-speaking peoples had colonized virtually the entire land mass of sub-Saharan Africa. From the Sahel, where their expansion was restricted by the presence of Afro-Asiatic and Nilo-Saharan-speaking pastoralists, to the south-west Cape, where their tropical crops were not viable in a Mediterranean climatic regime, the suffusion of Bantu languages and associated ways of life was total. Indeed, even the Khoisan languages of surviving hunters and gatherers are sufficiently imbued with word roots denoting food production to suggest long association with pastoral and farming communities.[10]

The suffusion of Bantu languages and settled farming throughout sub-Saharan Africa was an event unmatched in world history. Bantu-speaking peoples changed the human landscape of sub-Saharan Africa dramatically, from a region thinly populated by groups of hunter-gatherers to one that was dominated by farmers living in villages. Their language spread the word of their innovations; improved food supplies fuelled the dispersal of their influence, but a third factor was responsible for their overwhelming impact: iron.

THE EARLIEST-KNOWN INSTANCE OF people working with iron has been recorded in the Near East, where it was worked cold, hammered directly from meteorites into objects more valued for their rarity and curiosity than for their utility. The first evidence of iron smelted from ore also comes from the Near East, in the form of a blade dating from about 4,500 years ago found in Anatolia (Turkey).[11] Though the metal was soft and the blade probably more of a ceremonial object than a cutting instrument, its advent was ominous. By about 3,500 years ago, iron was being smelted on a large scale in Anatolia by the Hittites,[12] who managed to keep the process a secret for many years and thus ruled the region with their superior weapons and military force.[13] Throughout history, iron has bestowed power. Indeed, modern urban life could not have arisen nor be sustained without the tools, the weapons, and the industrial technology which iron made possible.

As is to be expected of a continent built with a high proportion of rock laid down when oxygen was accumulating in the atmosphere and mineral oxides were precipitating from overlying oceans (see pages 19–20), iron ores are abundant in Africa, though in a variety of forms, qualities and concentrations. The red earth that leaves travellers with an indelible first visual impression of Africa is composed of iron oxides, crumbling from the lateritic crust that covers so much of the continent. Iron ore also occurs in the form of haematite, a deep-red nodular material that throughout Africa is ground to make red-ochre pigments; haematite is found in surface and subterranean deposits. Another iron ore, magnetite, occurs in river sands and gravels, and limonite or bog iron can be recovered from swamps and lakes. But though the ores are plentiful, the process of extracting usable metal from them is complex.

Pure iron melts at 1,540°C, a temperature which remained unattainable until the invention of blast furnaces in the nineteenth century. Before then, iron was smelted by heating the ore between layers of charcoal to around 1,200°C until most of the impurities (the slag) melted and drained away, leaving a solid spongy mass of iron called the "bloom" that could be broken up and further purified by reheating and hammering in the forge. Even this limited operation placed a considerable demand on local resources, labour, and skills. The ore had to be collected; timber had to be felled to make the charcoal that fuels the furnace. A new furnace had to be built for every smelt and equipped with a ring of eight or ten tuyères (ceramic pipes through which hand-bellows pumped air into the combustion chamber); the ore and charcoal had to be carefully loaded into the furnace, layer by layer, two parts charcoal to one part ore, and once lit the bellows had to be pumped continuously for around sixteen hours. Even then a successful result was not guaranteed.

The most convincing explanation for the beginnings of metallurgy relates to copper and links the discovery of the smelting process to the manufacture of pottery. Early kilns were capable of reaching temperatures in excess of 1,100°C, at which metallic copper (melting point 1,083°C) would have been produced if a copper oxide such as malachite had been applied as a glaze, for instance, and a properly reducing atmosphere had been attained within the kiln.[14]

Copper was the first metal known to have been smelted (though lead may also have been important) and the remains of custom-built furnaces are an increasingly prominent feature of the archaeological record in the Near East from about 6,000 years ago. In the early 1980s considerable excitement was generated by claims that evidence of copper-smelting dating from up to 4,000 years ago had been discovered at Agadez, in the Air mountains of central Niger.[15] These claims implied an early use (and possible independent discovery) of the smelting process in Africa, but they were dismissed in 1988 by a more detailed technical study of the so-called furnace residues, which could find no definitive evidence of copper-smelting and concluded that the irregularly shaped baked clay structures thought to be furnaces probably were created when trees partially buried by termite mounds had been set alight by grass fires.[16]

If people in Africa had succeeded in smelting copper 4,000 years ago it is conceivable that subsequently they would have developed iron-smelting technology as well. Without that previous experience of more easily worked metals, however, an independent African discovery of iron-smelting is improbable. There is no precedent for mastering the techniques of smelting iron without a preliminary apprenticeship in more easily worked metals—even the remarkable skills developed by Andean metallurgists did not lead them to the discovery of iron-working before the Spanish conquest.[17]

On present evidence, iron-working in Africa was almost certainly an imported skill, introduced from its origin in the Near East via North Africa and the Sahara, courtesy of Phoenician sailors and Berber traders. The Phoenicians originated in the Lebanon. They knew both bronze and iron, built ships, and from about 3,000 years ago steadily acquired the status of a wealthy seafaring nation with a string of trading stations along the North African coast. The trading stations grew into settlements and eventually became colonies, virtually independent of the Phoenician homeland. The largest and most famous of these was Carthage, in present-day Tunisia, founded around 2,800 years ago.

At Carthage the Phoenicians had settled among the Berbers, agriculturists with a successful cereal- and livestock-based economy. Phoenicians, mixed with Berbers, now became Carthaginians, and Carthage became a base for further maritime exploration through the Straits of Gibraltar and around the coast of north-west Africa. Trade prospered. Passages in classical literature have been interpreted as evidence of voyages to the mouth of the Senegal River and beyond.[18] Herodotus (c. 485–425 BC) mentions a claim that a fleet of ships from Carthage had circumnavigated the continent. But this is improbable. The square-rigged ships of the day were incapable of sailing close to the wind, and would have had great difficulty returning north once they had sailed the full distance south. Herodotus himself doubted the truth of the claim and no archaeological evidence has been found to support it.[19] To date, the coast of Morocco is the southernmost limit of firm archaeological evidence of a Phoenician presence along the African coast[20] and so, although it remains possible that iron-smelting technology was brought to sub-Saharan Africa from Carthage by sea, a trans-Saharan introduction is more probable, by way of the Berbers.

The Sahara was less a barrier than a living space for the Berbers. Their inherited experience of the region encompassed the climatic fluctuations which had alternately drawn people into the region during periods of good rainfall and driven them out again when it reverted to desert (see Chapter 16). Contact with the highlands of the central Sahara and across the desert survived the climatic perturbations through a string of settlements, where pastoralist Berbers exploited the resources of isolated natural wells and oases.[21] These connections, along which goods already passed sporadically from group to group across the desert, were the ready-made foundation of trade routes that flourished when the Phoenicians arrived in Carthage.

Herodotus writes of the Berbers' Saharan trade, and their routes across the desert are recorded in paintings of loaded mules and horse-drawn carts (the camel was not introduced to the Sahara until the second century AD) discovered at rock-shelter sites along the way.[22] One route passed via Ghat in the Fezzan region of the northern Sahara, through the Hoggar mountains and down to the Niger River near Gao; another took a westerly route, skirting south of the Atlas mountains, through Morocco and Mauritania and on to the Niger River again. Salt, ivory, animal skins, and slaves are reported to have been the major items traded northward, while manufactured goods, including pottery, glass, and metalwork probably went south in exchange.[23]

Iron doubtless would have been among the most valuable items carried south across the Sahara by the Berbers, and sooner or later an enterprising trader would have sought to increase profits by smelting and forging the metal at the point of sale, instead of carrying the heavy finished product across the desert. Iron ore was abundant in the regions where the trans-Saharan routes struck the great southward curve of the Niger River, and the earliest-known evidence of iron-smelting in sub-Saharan Africa has been discovered in that region, at Taruga on the Jos plateau in central Nigeria. The residues from thirteen furnaces were excavated at Taruga and the oldest was found to date back to 2,600 years ago.[24] Several were younger, and the archaeological map of West Africa shows many other iron-smelting sites dating from the same period. When the technology finally became established in Africa south of the Sahara, it spread rapidly.

Meanwhile, the dispersal of the Bantu-speakers from their cradle-land in the Benue valley and the grassfields of western Cameroon also proceeded apace. The two tides, one technological and the other linguistic, were flooding across West Africa. At indefinable points in time and space, they merged and flowed on through the forest and the Sahel, into central Africa, East Africa, and then south to the tip of the continent. In a remarkably short space of time, Iron Age agriculture imposed on Africa "an economic revolution of devastating intensity."[25]

Archaeological investigations have opened a few small windows on the inexorable progress and impact of the revolution. In Gabon, for instance, numerous sites mark "streams" of iron-using farmers moving south from the Cameroon cradle-land around 2,300 years ago, abruptly replacing an indigenous hunting and cultivation economy based on stone-tool technology as they advanced through a region where iron ore is abundant.[26] In south-west Uganda, pollens identified from peat cores reveal major forest clearance beginning around 2,100 years ago.[27] It might be supposed that the land was cleared for cultivation, but felling as a source of charcoal for iron-smelting is much more likely.

Iron-smelting consumed immense amounts of charcoal. An experiment conducted in Malawi using ancient techniques found that one tonne of charcoal was needed to smelt barely enough iron to make three hoes.[28] A single set of ancient slag heaps in the Sudan has been estimated to represent a volume of iron-smelting that would have consumed 1,600 cubic metres of timber annually for 300 years.[29] Sixteen hundred cubic metres of timber is equivalent to about 100 trees twenty metres high. More prosaically, a former iron-smelter in south-west Uganda estimated that, as a rough average, one to one and a half trees were needed to produce sufficient charcoal for one smelt.[30]

Given that hundreds of iron-smelting sites are known in Africa—some containing thousands of furnaces—the capacity of any forest to sustain such offtakes must be in doubt. It has been claimed that the development of centralized states in the Sahelian region of West Africa was, in fact, aborted by ecological deterioration resulting directly from deforestation by iron-smelters.[31] On the other hand, forest clearance created grasslands, restricted tsetse-fly infestation and so facilitated the spread of cattle herding, which Bantu speakers were not slow to adopt.

The advent of iron technology doubtless hastened the spread of the Bantu speakers through Africa but, on balance, its direct benefits were small when compared with its indirect effect on the environment and on society. Iron hoes enabled people to produce food more easily than had been the case with stone tools, but the manufacture of iron hoes demanded the destruction of forests and the organization of a specialized labour force which in turn had to be fed. More iron, more people, more food—this self-perpetuating cycle of supply and demand was in itself enough to revolutionize the economy of a continent.

Surprisingly perhaps, it appears to have been a revolution in which weapons played little or no part. None have been found at archaeological sites from the period. The ironsmiths apparently were more engaged in making the tools that enabled people to produce more food than with forging the weapons that directed human affairs in other parts of the world with the onset of the Iron Age.

PART 4

AFRICAN CIVILIZATIONS

Murchison Falls, "where the Nile passes through the eye of a needle," Uganda

CHAPTER 20

The Nile

WHILE CIVILIZATIONS ROSE and fell along the Nile, their influence on sub-Saharan Africa was one of exploitation only—African commodities were traded north, but nothing of the Nile's culture and technology moved south.

Along the section of the Nile that measures 1,100 km between Aswan and the Delta, silts deposited by the annual floods had created 18,250 km² of cultivable land by about 5,000 years ago.¹ This strip of fertile soil winding through one of the Earth's most barren regions was almost as large as the state of New Jersey (19,340 km²), Wales (20,760 km²) or the state of Rheinland-Pfalz in Germany (19,840 km²). Scholarly estimates indicate that the region was inhabited by about 1.8 million people, who were concentrated most densely along two discontinuous stretches of the river: one extending 215 km north from Aswan, and the other comprising the 200 km upstream from the apex of the Delta,² where present-day Cairo is situated. In these regions the people and food-production innovations of the Sahara (see Chapter 17) and the Near East combined to fuel the rise of a unique civilization.

By about 5,000 years ago, the Nile valley was effectively a state unified under the control of a single ruler, the pharaoh, and an elite bureaucracy who often were members of the ruling family. The pharaoh was regarded as a divine being—the living personification of the sun-god Ra, and counterpart of Osiris, god of the land of the dead. This link between the living and the dead explains the immense importance the ancient Egyptians attached to the burial of pharaohs and preparations for their afterlife. The magnificence of the pyramids and the royal tombs of the Nile valley is a measure of the wealth and the concentration of human and material resources that the ruling elite had at their disposal. But none of this would have been possible without the Nile flood, whose silts rejuvenated the fields annually (though there were some years when the flood failed to materialize) and fed the state's huge labour-force of enslaved foreign captives and peasants working off their obligations to the state.

The system was rigidly hierarchical, and during the course of more than one hundred generations, millions of people effectively devoted their lives to the idea of a transcendental existence—an afterlife—for the pharaoh, if not for everyone. In the process, the ancient Egyptians discovered the principles of astronomy and mathematics, developed building practices that even now are not fully understood, invented a written language and created numerous pictures and statues depicting their society, culture, and beliefs. They employed the wheel and the plough, and invented the *shaduf* (a simple cantilevered water-bucket) and the *saqia* (an ox-driven waterwheel) to raise water from the Nile and keep fields in continuous production. They built lateen-rigged feluccas for the Nile and vessels more than fifty metres long[3] that were transported overland and sailed the length of the Red Sea.

The Egyptians worked with copper, and located gold mines 200 km south of Aswan, in the desert lying between the Nile and the Red Sea. They hoarded gemstones and made exquisite jewellery, but the utilitarian application of their metallurgical skills extended only to the manufacture of bronze. The advent of iron-smelting was delayed in the Nile valley, despite the region's proximity to Anatolia, where the technology was first developed. The primary reason was probably twofold: first, there was insufficient timber to supply the enormous amounts of charcoal required by the smelting process; and second, there was no serious demand for iron—bronze farming implements were perfectly adequate for working the soft alluvial soils of the floodplain, and bronze weapons were superior to those of any potential adversary.

This is not to say that iron was unknown in ancient Egypt—indeed, it appears to have been highly valued, but as an item of ceremony, not utility. Of two ceremonial daggers found in Tutankhamun's tomb (dating from 1323 BC), for instance, one has a blade of gold, and the other is made of iron.[4] But the Egyptians learned just how useful iron can be when they were overwhelmed in 670 BC by Assyrian forces wielding weapons of iron.

For 3,000 years the Egyptians reaped the produce of resources the Nile had brought to the valley from the very heart of Africa: water, and many million tonnes of fertile soil. With such a vast stream of lavish and unstinting benevolence flowing into the Egyptian economy from one direction, it is reasonable to wonder if anything was sent back by way of return. In other words, did sub-Saharan Africa benefit in any way from the Nile civilization it had sustained?

The mere presence of a great perennial river flowing from the heart of Africa to the Mediterranean suggests that the Nile must have been "the corridor through which men, things and ideas passed from the one world to the other."[5] Since Egypt and the eastern Mediterranean had been founts of civilization, topographical logic virtually demands that their influence should have flowed up the Nile and become responsible for such evidence of civilization as had been discovered in sub-Saharan Africa—from the concepts of state organization and divine kingship found in West Africa to the construction of Great Zimbabwe in southern Africa.

The concept of the Nile as a corridor through which the civilizing influences were conveyed to sub-Saharan Africa is the basis of an essentially Eurocentric interpretation of African history, implying that Africans were incapable of developing their own versions of civilization. It has an appealing simplicity, but is contradicted by the evidence.

In fact, the relationship between the Egyptians and the inhabitants of sub-Saharan Africa never rose above that of the pillager and the pillaged, with sub-Saharan Africa providing whatever trade commodities (including human beings) were currently required for the Nile trade. Nubians living along the intervening stretch of the river, between Aswan and Khartoum, doubtless regarded the Nile valley as a corridor of exciting interaction with Egypt to the north; but for Africa as a whole the Nile was a cul-de-sac.[6]

The earliest-known record of ancient Egyptian contact with Nubia and its hinterlands is carved in stone, on a tablet making brief mention of an expedition which returned from the land of Punt in the reign of the pharaoh Sahure, about 2450 BC.[7] This was at the height of Egypt's most flamboyant period, when the pyramids were erected and vast amounts of the state's manpower and wealth were applied to the culture of the divine ruler. On this single occasion, Africa, identified as Punt, contributed 80,000 measures of myrrh, 23,020 staves of timber and 6,000 measures of electrum (a natural alloy of gold containing about 20 per cent silver). Another expedition returned to Egypt with "134 slaves, male and female, 114 oxen, and calves; 305 bulls; . . . ivory, ebony, [skins] of the southern panther; . . . every good thing of this country; the harvest of this place likewise."[8] And one particularly noteworthy expedition included among its donkey-loads of incense, grain, ivory, and ebony, "a dancing dwarf of the god from the land of the spirits." The dwarf is presumed to have been a pygmy, captured for the curiosity of his stature. On receiving advance notice of this particular prize, the pharaoh ordered:

> Come northward to the court immediately; thou shalt bring this dwarf with thee, which thou bringest living, prosperous and healthy from the land of the spirits, for the dances of the god, to rejoice and [gladden] the heart of the king of Upper and Lower Egypt, Nerekere, who lives forever. When he goes down with thee into the vessel, appoint excellent people, who shall be beside him on each side of the vessel; take care lest he fall into the water. When [he] sleeps at night appoint excellent people, who shall sleep beside him in his tent; inspect ten times a night. My majesty desires to see this dwarf more than the gifts of Sinai and of Punt . . . [9]

Analysis of the available evidence persuasively locates Punt between the Red Sea and the southern Kordofan province of the Sudan, straddling the confluence of the Blue and White Niles and occupying a large portion of the north and north-west flanks of the Ethiopian highlands. Access from Egypt was either up the course of the Nile or by ship along the Red Sea coast. Neither route was without its difficulties. An expedition force might comprise several thousand men, including scribes, servants, functionaries, and contingents of militia who "cleared the way before me . . . vanquishing any opposed to the King," the high official Henu reported of an expedition undertaken on behalf of Montuhotep III c.1975 BC.

Henu provided each of his 3,000-strong force with a daily supply of water and bread, and included donkey-loads of sandals in the baggage-train to ensure that worn-out footwear was immediately replaced; but shoes and sustenance were matters of minor logistical detail compared with the problems of transport that Henu had to contend with. His ship was built on the Nile and sailed to Koptos, on the most easterly bend of the river, where it was taken apart and carried piece by piece across 150 km of desert to the Red Sea coast. With the ship reassembled, Henu sailed south to Punt—and back again. "When I returned from the sea," he reports, "I had achieved what His Majesty had commanded—I brought for him every product that I found on the shores of God's Land."

The most celebrated expedition to Punt was that ordered by Queen Hatshepsut c.1472/1 BC. As recorded in a series of carved reliefs and accompanying hieroglyphic text, five ships were carried across the desert from Thebes to the Red Sea coast with all provisions and equipment required for the voyage to Punt. The chief of Punt, Parahu, and his wife, Atiya, came to receive the royal expedition in obeisance, with bowed head, it is reported. They and other chiefs of Punt were presented with bread, beer, wine, meat, and fruit while the Egyptians

> Load[ed] the ships heavily with the marvels of the land of Punt: with [all kinds of] good herbs of God's Land and heaps of nodules of myrrh, with trees of fresh myrrh, with ebony and pure ivory, with "green" gold of 'Amau, with *tishepes* and *khesyt* wood, with *ihmt*-myrrh, incense and eye-paint, with baboons, monkeys and hounds, with southern leopard-skins, and with servants and their children.

The records indicate that Queen Hatshepsut dispatched her expedition to Punt via the arduous overland and Red Sea route because the Nubians controlled the Nile route between Aswan and Khartoum and were demanding payment on "the marvels of the land of Punt" in transit to Egypt. In other words, she wanted to cut out the middlemen, and the scale of her avoidance tactics must be a measure of the trade's value—to both the Egyptians and the Nubians.

For more than 1,000 years the Egyptians had maintained a colonial presence in Nubia, at first as a means of exploiting the resources of the region itself—principally gold, ivory, timber, animal products, and slaves—and subsequently to facilitate the transit of these goods from points further south when Nubian sources of supply were exhausted. But increasingly, as the Egyptian lines of communication lengthened and their authority abroad was weakened by political difficulties at home, Nubians took over sections of the trade. Eventually they controlled the entire trade route from Aswan to Khartoum and the lands beyond.

With only modest resources of their own, Nubians had become rich and powerful from handling the resources of others. Predisposed towards the Egyptian model of centralized authority and power, the local Nubian rulers had created a powerful independent state by 1000 BC, known to the Egyptians as Kush. Once they had assumed total control of trading and cultural links, the kings of Kush subsequently became powerful enough to conquer even Egypt itself in 730 BC, where they ruled for more than sixty years—a period of Egyptian history known as the twenty-fifth or Ethiopian dynasty. Kush domination ended with the invasion of the Assyrian armies, wielding weapons of iron, before whom the kings of Kush withdrew to Nubia, re-establishing their administrative centre first at Napata, and later (around 600 BC) at the southern provincial town of Meröe.

The move from Napata was probably inspired by a continuing threat of invasion from Egypt, and Meröe certainly offered a number of advantages.

The tract of land, 250 km broad, lying between the points at which the Atbara and the Blue Nile join the main stream of the White Nile is known as the "island of Meröe." To the security of distance and an enclosing arc of broad rivers on three sides, the southerly position of Meröe also offered its inhabitants the benefits of a well-defined wet season each July and August. In distinct contrast with the arid climatic regime of the Nile valley further north in Nubia, where the narrow floodplain offered limited opportunity for even irrigated cultivation, the island of Meröe lay within the zone of tropical summer rainfall. Total rainfall was never more than 180 mm, but this was sufficient to support rain-fed crops of indigenous sorghum and millet; furthermore, rain enabled the farmers of Meröe to extend their cultivation away from the immediate vicinity of the river.

With extensive rain-fed agriculture, and grasslands to east and west supporting herds of cattle and other livestock, Meröe was founded on a robust mixed-farming economy. Add to this the fortuity of access to the Red Sea and to the resources of the African hinterland at a time when rising Greek and Roman prosperity had created a demand for exotic goods, and the wealth and power of Meröe at its height during the last few centuries BC is not at all surprising, particularly since the island of Meröe was also richly endowed with both iron ore and the hardwood timber needed for charcoal.

Numerous iron tools and implements have been recovered from sites at Meröe, including the hoes and mattocks used by farmers; axes, adzes and chisels used by carpenters; sundry shears, tweezers, and the tiny rods with which women applied an antimony eyeliner. But weapons were much more plentiful than tools.[10]

The weapons consisted of swords, spears, and arrowheads, and the awesome significance of military might in Meröe culture is demonstrated in two reliefs flanking the doorway of a temple. The reliefs, five metres high and carved in Egyptian style, show King Natakamani and Queen Amanitere, each brandishing a sword and holding by the hair a cohort of thirty vanquished foes. And as if to reinforce this image of absolute autocratic power, each monarch is accompanied by a lion—with the beast at the queen's feet pawing her captives like a cat teasing a mouse, while the king's lion busily devours a human captive.[11]

Among the monumental ruins of a civilization lying today on the island of Meröe, huge mounds of slag testify to the scale of iron production that powered its rise and ultimately brought about its downfall. Meröe collapsed in the second century AD. Changing trade patterns in the Red Sea region (see next chapter) may have hastened its decline, but environmental degradation had already made collapse inevitable. Trees to fuel iron-smelting furnaces had been felled faster than new ones could grow. Deforestation led to erosion and a loss of topsoil. A region which had supported thriving agricultural populations for a thousand years could be farmed no longer.

MERÖE WAS EFFECTIVELY AN EXPRESSION of Egyptian civilization rooted in what the pharaohs had called the land of Punt—indigenous black Africa. Although the kingdom ultimately developed some distinctive religious and cultural features of its own, the Egyptian influence remained paramount. Gods were worshipped in Egyptian-style temples, and pyramids (small and flat-topped) were built over the tombs of rulers. Statues and stone panels were carved in the images of gods and kings, and hieroglyphic inscriptions recorded their exploits (developing ultimately into a cursive script—Meröitic—that remains undeciphered). Meröe was the southernmost expansion of a civilization founded on the bounty that had flowed down the Nile from the heart of Africa.

It has been argued that when Meröe collapsed, members of the ruling elite migrated across the Nile and west through the Sahel into sub-Saharan Africa, taking with them Meröe's technological knowledge and concepts of state organization which then spread throughout the continent.[12]

This hypothesis of course reiterates a belief that the development of civilization in the rest of Africa must have been externally inspired. It lacks factual support, however. Not a single item of material evidence from Meröe has been found west of the Nile.[13] Even iron-smelting technology, so powerful a formative element of the Meröe civilization, is older in West and central Africa and therefore cannot have been introduced from Meröe. An authoritative review of the evidence concerning the "corridor through which men, things and ideas were said to have passed from the civilized world to Africa,"[14] concludes: " . . . any residual feeling that Egypt or Nubia must have been responsible for developments in sub-Saharan Africa will have to be abandoned and Bantu-speaking people accepted as innovators in their own right."[15]

Traditional lateen-rigged *ngalaus* sailing from Vanga, Tanzania, on the southeast monsoon

CHAPTER 21

The Periplus of the Erythraean Sea

A MARINERS' HANDBOOK FROM the first century AD indicates that although trading vessels from Roman Egypt sailed to sub-Saharan Africa, the region offered meagre profits and attracted little interest.

Two thousand years ago the patterns of civilization founded in Athens and Rome radiated across Europe to the Rhine and Britain in the north, and to the Atlantic coast of the Iberian peninsula in the west. Trade routes carried their influence across Asia to link up with patterns of civilization developing independently in China and India. The Mediterranean world was of course entirely under the sway of Rome—including North Africa and the resources of the Nile.

At that time Rome had a population of close to 1 million people (no other city was as large until 1800, when a census recorded 959,310 people living in London) and the complexities of everyday life in Rome would not have been unfamiliar to residents of the modern urban world. Politics, commerce, religion; architecture, science, art and sculpture; drama and philosophy—there was a lot going on. Such large urban communities require a large food supply and must have access to an extensive agricultural system, especially grain crops, which are highly productive, relatively easy to transport and store for future use.

In the decades immediately prior to the birth of Christ the citizens of Rome and its immediate environs consumed 320,000 tonnes of corn each year—nearly 1,000 tonnes each day—more than 60 per cent of which

(200,000 tonnes) came by sea from Rome's North African colonies, and a further 100,000 tonnes from the cornfields of Egypt alone.[1]

Rome's huge and unremitting demand for grain was serviced by a minimum of 800 sailings across the Mediterranean each year,[2] in ships with capacities of up to 1,000 tonnes and more. The grain freighters were stout ships, built to withstand the worst of Mediterranean conditions, with massively strong hulls whose planking was held together by thousands of close-set mortise-and-tenon joints, a method of construction known only to Greek and Roman shipwrights.[3] The rig was similarly designed for safety, with a large square sail on a relatively short mainmast.

With maritime expertise and trade so well developed, it is hardly surprising that Rome's sphere of activity should have extended to include the Nile and Red Sea trade routes following the Roman conquest of Egypt in 30 BC. Other seamen had of course sailed these waters for centuries before the Romans achieved domination of the region. Arab and Indian seamen regularly sailed back and forth between their two countries on the monsoon winds, which blow from the south-west from May to September, then conveniently swing through 180 degrees to blow from the north-east from November to April.

Eudoxus of Cyzicus is reputed to have sailed from Egypt to India and back on the monsoons in 116 BC, a pioneering voyage which initiated a regular flow of Greek trade with the subcontinent. But the arrival of the Romans increased the volume of trade throughout the region several times over.

One hundred and twenty vessels were reported to have sailed for India and Arabia from Myos Hormos (a Red Sea port) in a single season around 25 BC, as compared with fewer than twenty in earlier times. And the quantities of contemporary Roman coins and pottery found in India are tangible evidence of an upsurge in maritime trading enterprise at that time.[4]

Indeed, within fifty years of merchants and shipowners from Roman Egypt entering the Red Sea and Indian Ocean trade, its extent and volume had expanded to proportions that merited a handbook of advice concerning routes and ports, giving details of the people likely to be encountered, the goods they had to offer, and the wares they would accept in exchange. An anonymous Egyptian-born merchant compiled such a handbook sometime between AD 40 and 70 (the date is known from the work's reference to a living monarch who ruled during that period).

The handbook was entitled *Periplus maris Erythraei*—a circumnavigation of the Erythraean Sea. "Erythraean" literally means "red sea," but ancient writers used the term more broadly than is the case today. Their Erythraean Sea encompassed not only the modern Red Sea, but also the Gulf of Aden, the

Arabian Sea and the Indian Ocean, from the western shores of India to the east coast of Africa.[5]

The author of the *Periplus* was a businessman, not a man of letters. He used a businessman's Greek: "purely functional, flat, and styleless, replete with repetitions and studded with technical language and trade terms."[6] But this gives the *Periplus* a unique status. Unencumbered by gratuitous praise of gods and kings, but full of pertinent detail (probably derived from personal observation), the *Periplus* was an equivalent of the modern-day commercial directories that investors consult before embarking on business ventures in foreign parts. Then as now, money determined the degree of involvement, and the *Periplus* is a measure of what the world beyond the Red Sea was worth to the merchants and sea-captains of Roman Egypt.

Africa appears to have been poorly rated. In a work of approximately 7,000 words, the author of the *Periplus* devotes just four paragraphs, 450 words, to the vast regions that lay beyond the Horn of Africa. A number of landmarks are listed, a few harbours, and just one port of trade—Rhapta— which is believed to have been in the vicinity of present-day Dar es Salaam, though no evidence of the port has ever been found.

This lack of interest in Africa was probably due to the fact that a return voyage to the East African coast could not be equipped and completed within less than two years, while ships could sail to India and back in less than twelve months.

It was the dog-leg turn around the Horn of Africa and through the Gulf of Aden that stretched the time required for the voyage down the East African coast. Although the north-east monsoon enabled ships to reach Rhapta within 100 days of leaving Egypt, they were obliged to remain in the region for not less than eight months, leaving Rhapta on the last of the south-west monsoon in order to catch the north-east monsoon for the westward passage across the Gulf of Aden. It was imperative that their arrival at the Horn of Africa coincided with the change of the monsoon.

Meanwhile, merchants and investors financing voyages to Arabia and India could expect to see a return on their money in little more than a year. Their ships sailed down the Red Sea on the end of the north-east monsoon, crossed the Arabian Sea on the rising south-west monsoon and returned when it changed to north-east again. And in addition to the advantages of a speedier turnaround, India and Arabia had more valuable cargoes to offer than Africa.

Ships bound for India filled their holds primarily with utilitarian goods for trading in foreign ports—clothing and household items, tools and raw materials such as brass, iron, copper, and raw glass—but they returned laden with luxury goods. The shippers of Roman Egypt wasted no space in their holds on cheap and mundane goods. They were first and foremost dealers in luxuries: frankincense and myrrh from Arabia, and a wealth of highly valued goods from India—spices and drugs; diamonds, sapphires, turquoise, lapis lazuli and onyx; pearls and tortoiseshell, fine cottons; silks, and even furs trans-shipped from China. Ships returned from India with cargoes of enormous value, on which substantial profits were realized—even after the Roman government had taken a 25 per cent import duty.[7]

By contrast, the African trade route, around the Horn of Africa and southward along the coast, offered mainly bulky and less valuable items, such as ivory and slaves, some rhinoceros horn, tortoiseshell, and a little nautilus shell. Frankincense and myrrh were also on offer, as well as cinnamon. Actually, the cinnamon was harvested in India and delivered to East Africa by Arabian ships. Indeed, Arabian influence in the region was already paramount. The East African coast was by "ancient right" under Arabian domination and governed by merchants from present-day Yemen, whose Arabian captains and agents were, "through continual intercourse and intermarriage . . . familiar with the area and its language."[8]

By virtue of its peripheral status, both geographically and economically, the East African trade probably was of interest only to the small-scale merchants of Roman Egyptian trade, who could afford only modest supplies of trade goods and chartered cargo-space at bargain rates on lowly freighters. And even their trading ventures are a matter of speculation—as yet lacking archaeological confirmation. In India, quantities of coin and pottery from the period confirm the presence of Roman Egyptian traders, but none whatsoever have been found in East Africa.

Although the *Periplus* is claimed to be of much interest and "great value for African historiography,"[9] its author saw very little in farthest Africa that was of interest and value to Roman Egyptian maritime traders operating out of the Red Sea. He devoted just 6 per cent of the *Periplus* to the region that lay beyond the Horn of Africa. With good reason: it was a bare and desolate stretch of coast, sparsely inhabited, offering scant opportunities for profitable trade. Furthermore, all the items of merchandise that were available along the coast could also be obtained without leaving the Red Sea at all, principally at Adulis, the port through which Meröe exported its produce. And as the fortunes of Meröe declined (see pages 198–99), another centre of commerce and political power rose, in the highlands of northern Ethiopia—Aksum.

CHAPTER 22

Aksum

THE UNIQUE ENVIRONMENTAL CIRCUMSTANCES OF northern
Ethiopia combined with the trading opportunities of the Red Sea to
fuel the rise of sub-Saharan Africa's first indigenous state.

The *Periplus of the Erythraean Sea* describes Adulis as a "fair-sized village," lying about 3½ km inland from a harbour which early commentators unhesitatingly identified with modern-day Massawa. The description perfectly matches the layout of the bay and islands comprising the harbour. Furthermore, Massawa is the only good natural harbour along the entire west coast of the Red Sea. In 1810, however, the British explorer Henry Salt came upon substantial ancient ruins some 40 km south of Massawa, at a place local people called "Azoole." Salt concluded[1] that this must be Adulis and indeed, archaeologists subsequently excavating at the site have uncovered evidence of a settlement that began modestly and grew into a large urban centre between the fourth and sixth centuries AD. The ruins lay 4 km from the shore, within a rectangle approximately 500 m long and 400 m wide[2] (large enough to accommodate more than twenty-five average-sized football pitches) and included the remains of impressive stone structures—buildings of black volcanic stone, with columns of marble and walls up to five metres high.

Evidence of the town's mercantile activity that visitors still pick from the salt-encrusted soils enveloping the ruins includes fragments of Roman amphorae imported from the Mediterranean, coins, glass, and beads of carnelian, but there is no harbour or landing place at an appropriate distance from

Detail of a portion of the massive stele which lies fallen and fractured at Axum, northern Ethiopia

the Adulis town site which matches the description given in the *Periplus,* merely a gently shelving beach on a shallow bay.

This apparent discontinuity is related to the water requirements of a growing urban centre. Although Adulis probably was sited near the port of Massawa in the first century AD, and only a "fair-sized village" when the *Periplus* was compiled, the growth in trade and urban development ultimately imposed unsustainable demands on the available water supply, and the trading and residential centre was subsequently relocated to the site where Henry Salt encountered it—on the banks of an ephemeral watercourse whose seasonal floods were large and dependable enough to replenish wells and fill cisterns. A reliable water supply more than compensated for the longer journey to the port.[3]

Finding and maintaining an adequate supply of fresh water has always been the foremost difficulty confronting people who live on the shores of the Red Sea. Massawa and Adulis lie just fifteen degrees north of the Equator, on the edge of a shallow marine basin that is surrounded by desert and mountains. Massawa's average year-round air temperature never falls below 26°C, and can soar to 47°C in August. Even the sea temperature averages 33°C all year; cool sea breezes are rare. The prevailing winds blow from across the Red Sea during the summer months; hot, damp and salty, they draw moisture from the body but do not cool it. Sparse vegetation offers scant relief in an eye-searing landscape of harsh gravel ridges, shimmering under the bulk of the Ethiopian plateau, which here constitutes the western escarpment of the Rift Valley, rising steeply just sixty kilometres from the Red Sea shore.

An average of 163 mm of rain falls on Massawa each year, but actual amounts vary widely. Many years pass without a drop of rain, while some have seen 600 mm fall in a single month. The only certainty is that the rain usually falls between November and February. If it does not, the rest of the year will certainly be dry; and August will be the driest and hottest month of all.

But if the crows that are to be seen around Massawa, clustered in the scanty shade with wings drooping, bills open and throats fluttering in their attempts to alleviate the cruel heat of midday in August, if these birds took wing and headed west, up and over the edge of the Rift Valley escarpment and across the Ethiopian plateau for less than 100 km, they would find themselves in a well-watered paradise of green fields and villages, where rainfall averages over 1,200 mm per year, and the greater part of it falls in August, when temperatures average less than 20°C.

By quirks of topography and climate the northern Ethiopian plateau is coolest and wettest precisely when the Red Sea coast is hottest and driest. One consequence of the close proximity of such contrasting regimes is that sub-Saharan Africa's first indigenous literate civilization was founded at Aksum in the highlands of northern Ethiopia, where agricultural potential was good, not at Adulis on the shores of the Red Sea, where trade was so profitable.

FROM INDIGENOUS AFRICAN ROOTS dating back many thousands of years, and encompassing the full history of hunting and gathering, herding and agriculture, Aksum[4] developed a civilization and empire whose influence, at its zenith in the fourth and fifth centuries AD, extended throughout the regions lying south of the Roman Empire, from the fringes of the Sahara in the west, across the Red Sea to the inner Arabian desert of Rub'el Hali in the east.[5] The Aksumites developed Africa's only indigenous written script, Ge'ez, from which the written form of the languages spoken in modern Ethiopia has evolved; they traded with Egypt, the eastern Mediterranean and Arabia, and financed their operations with gold, silver, and copper coinage—the first and only coinage known in sub-Saharan Africa until the tenth century, when Arabian coins were used along the East African coast.

The early Aksumites built in stone. They erected massive carved monoliths over the graves of their leaders (one was 33 metres long and weighed over 700 tonnes, arguably the largest single piece of worked stone ever hewn), but this practice appears to have been abandoned with the Aksum king's conversion to Christianity in the third century AD. The Orthodox faith adopted by the Aksumites is followed throughout Ethiopia to this day, unchanged by either the religious disputes of classical and medieval times, or the political upheavals of the twentieth century.

The impetus for the development of a literate civilization based at Aksum was internal. External influences were important—perhaps even vital—but they arrived by choice rather than by conquest or colonization. It was the fact of being so close to the Red Sea while yet so isolated from it that enabled Aksum to develop as it did. Ecologically isolated yet geographically adjacent, the Aksumites could exploit the Red Sea trading complex while remaining culturally independent. Adulis was their point of contact.

Though Adulis rose to prominence with the growth of the Roman maritime technology and trade, its history pre-dates Roman presence in the Red Sea region by a considerable margin. Four thousand years ago the settlement was already part of a cultural complex which spanned the Red Sea from what is now Saudi Arabia and Yemen, across to the coast of Eritrea, and through the Bab-el-Mandeb straits to Aden. The hard evidence for this connection consists of ceramic artefacts recovered from sites around the region which share enough common features (many with distinctly African affinities) to be ascribed to the same basic cultural tradition.[6] The implication of this shared cultural tradition is that people were sailing widely around the Red Sea long before Adulis became a major port on the Romans' trading network.

Meanwhile, a sequence of kingdoms extending back to about 1300 BC rose and fell in the mountain regions of Southern Arabia (present-day Yemen), culminating in the kingdom of Saba, which achieved its greatest prominence in the eighth century BC. The Sabaean kingdom flourished on the benefits of technological developments which maximized agricultural production. The fertile hillsides of the region were extensively terraced and irrigated to increase the area of available cultivable land, but principally it was the ox-drawn plough that enabled the Sabaeans to raise food production to maximum levels.

It has been argued that the plough underwrote the rise of civilization and the formation of states.[7] By extending the areas of cultivable land and increasing the productivity of the available labour force, the plough enabled agricultural communities to produce a surplus. The surplus supported specialist craftsmen, who made no direct contribution to the food production system; differences in individual ways of life and standards of living developed from this separation of roles, leading eventually to the stratification of society and the creation of social hierarchies that distinguished between people on the basis of their material wealth: a few royals at the top, hordes of peasants at the bottom.

If the plough was the mechanical prerequisite of civilization, literacy—in one form or another—was its defining cultural characteristic. The apparent antiquity of words for "plough" and related agricultural terms in Ethiopian languages has encouraged linguists to suggest that the plough may have been used, possibly even invented, by Ethiopians some time before the Aksumites were in contact with the Sabaeans of southern Arabia.[8] Archaeologists, on the other hand, are more inclined to suggest that plough agriculture arrived on the Ethiopian plateau as a direct consequence of contact with the Sabaeans, sometime between the eighth and third centuries BC.[9]

On the matter of literacy, however, there is no argument. The earliest inscriptions—found at a number of sites on the northern plateau dating back to the seventh century BC—are unmistakably Sabaean in style and content. The script is boustrophedon (literally "as the ox turns in ploughing," meaning script that reads from left to right and right to left on alternate lines), and the text uses traditional Sabaean terms. But signs of originality were evident from the beginning, and the Ethiopian inscriptions gradually developed their own distinctive characteristics, while the Sabaean influence faded. The boustrophedon style was abandoned (though it persisted longer in Aksum than in southern Arabia),[10] and eventually the Aksumite script developed into Ge'ez, the predecessor of the modern Ethiopian script.

With plough and literacy, Aksum possessed the prerequisites of civilization and state-formation. Subsequently, trade, territorial expansion, the growth of urban centres, and the rise of a social elite with a taste for luxury goods were as evident at Aksum as they have been in every other instance where the process has been observed.

Since Eurocentric predispositions have fostered a belief that any evidence of civilization found on the continent must have been introduced, it is important to note that Aksum is a defining example of indigenous civilization and state-formation in Africa. Its roots are set deep in the indigenous landscape, sustaining a system that remains viable to this day. Ecologically isolated from surrounding polities, though geographically close enough to note their good points, Aksum was uniquely able to graft foreign innovations on to its root-stock without damaging the viability of the system. Advantageous innovations thrived; the disadvantageous withered and died.

No other region of Africa fostered the development of an indigenous literate civilization, and its history spans more than 2,000 years. Such distinctiveness begs a number of questions: Why Ethiopia? Why not other regions? Are Ethiopians inherently different from the inhabitants of other parts of Africa; genetically predisposed, perhaps, towards the pattern of behaviour from which civilizations evolve? Or is the region they occupy the determining factor? Does the landscape of Ethiopia offer opportunities that would enable any group of people—regardless of origin—to create an indigenous literate civilization, simply by exercising the universal human capacity to exploit the potential of whatever resources are available? These questions must be considered in the context of Ethiopia's geological formation and ecological disposition, which also are unique in Africa.

AFRICA IS AN ELEVATED CONTINENT that has experienced a good deal of erosion in the course of its long geological history. Though the greater part of its land surface still stands between 500 and 1,000 metres above sea level, only a small proportion rises any higher; indeed, of the continent's 29.7 million km^2 land surface, barely 400,000 km^2 (1.35 per cent) stands 2,000 metres or more above sea level and only 28,545 km^2 (0.10 per cent) is higher than 3,000 metres (see map 4, page 689). Ethiopia, by virtue of its location on the edge of the Rift Valley, possesses a hugely disproportionate amount of Africa's high ground. Though representing barely 4 per cent of the entire African land surface, Ethiopia has 50 per cent of the continent's land above 2,000 metres, and just under 80 per cent of the land above 3,000 metres.[11]

In tropical regions, altitudes of over 2,000 metres are particularly conducive to the evolution of ecosystems that humans are able to exploit. At that altitude the temperature range is more congenial and the diseases common in the lowlands—such as malaria, trypanosomiasis, and bilharzia—are absent. Also, the tsetse fly, which renders cattle-raising impossible in much of Africa's wooded grassland, is not found at altitude. Furthermore, altitude not only creates a congenial temperature and disease regime, the elevated land masses also force moisture-laden winds up to levels at which clouds form and rain falls. The hot and damp Red Sea winds which make life in Massawa so uncomfortable during the summer months, for instance, rise when they strike the Rift Valley escarpment, just sixty kilometres inland, and are the source of the rain which falls on the plateau beyond.

The Red Sea winds are, of course, part of the monsoon system that enabled trading ships to sail across the Indian Ocean and down the East African coast. When the monsoon reverses, the moisture-laden ocean winds strike the continent from a southerly direction, bringing rain to the highlands of Tanzania and Kenya between February and May. During some periods of the region's climatic history, the rains brought by the southerly monsoons have extended as far north as the Ethiopian plateau. Aksum then enjoyed the benefits of two rainy seasons.

In the case of the Ethiopian highlands, the benefits of climate were combined with the fortuities of isolation. Rugged escarpments deny easy access to the plateau from north, east, or west, while a broad expanse of deserts and parched grasslands makes an approach from the south equally uninviting. In effect, the Ethiopian plateau has been encircled by natural barriers for several million years, and while geological upheaval, wind, and eroding rains have created a landscape of spectacular gorges, precipitous escarpments and tabletop plateau that is unique in Africa, evolution has populated the region with animals and plants that are no less distinctive.

During the millions of years before people began making an impact on the natural world, the common African flora and fauna were widely distributed throughout the continent, occurring wherever their preferred ecological conditions were to be found. Ethiopia was no exception. All common African animals and plants have inhabited Ethiopia at one time or another: from acacias, cedars, and grasses, to elephants and lions, crocodiles, giraffe, leopards, and zebra. But while providing suitable habitats for representatives of Africa's flora and fauna in general, the physical isolation of the Ethiopian plateau has also fostered the survival of species no longer found elsewhere in Africa and the evolution of some which only occur on the plateau. Ethiopia is home to a number of endemic animals and plants. Of the 219 mammalian species identified in the region, 28 (12.8 per cent) are found only in Ethiopia, for instance. Similarly, 23 (3.5 per cent) of Ethiopia's 665 breeding bird species are found nowhere else on the continent, along with significant numbers of amphibian, insect, and plant species.[12]

Of the plants endemic to Ethiopia, some have proved to be extremely useful—coffee is just one of them. Indeed, such is the distinctive nature of the region's vegetation that in the late 1920s the Russian plant geneticist Nikolai Vavilov described Ethiopia as one of just eight centres in which the world's stock of cultivated plants had originated. Vavilov reasoned that major food crops must have originated in mountainous regions where the greatest genetic diversity among wild ancestors and cultivated relatives had been noted. He organized a worldwide programme of plant collection and research to investigate the proposition and the evidence from Ethiopia convinced him that a number of species of wheat, barley, sorghum, millets, lentils, legumes, oil plants, spices, and stimulants had originated in the region.[13]

The appealing simplicity of Vavilov's research and the concept of "Vavilov Centres," as they became known, dominated debate about the origins of cultivated plants for almost half a century.[14] Eventually, however, the issue of plant origins and domestication was shown to be far more complex than Vavilov had supposed.[15] The revisions clarified the issues, but they did not dismiss Ethiopia and its vegetation as a unique source of opportunity for human exploitation. The region remains worthy of being considered "one of the world's greatest and oldest centers of domestic seed plants."[16] The status of coffee as an endemic plant first domesticated in Ethiopia is unchallenged; the oil-producing noog (*Guizotia abyssinica*) is another endemic, and ensete (*Musa ensete*), the so-called "false banana," whose starch-rich rootstock has for centuries been the staple diet of people on the southern portion of the Ethiopian plateau, is undoubtedly of Ethiopian origin. Among cereals cultivated on the plateau, finger millet (*Eleusine coracana*) probably originated there, and distinct cultivars of wheat, barley and sorghum certainly were developed locally from stock introduced from elsewhere (probably from the Nile or via the Red Sea—the physical barriers limiting access to the plateau were not insurmountable), but the cereal which contributed most to the historical development of the region was of purely Ethiopian origin and there is no doubt that it was first cultivated on the plateau, in the region where the Aksum state and civilization was established—teff (*Eragrostis tef*).

Even in the late twentieth century, teff is sown on more hectares than any other crop in Ethiopia, and for centuries it has been an exclusively Ethiopian crop. There is no evidence that teff was ever grown in South Arabia, for example, which invites the conclusion that teff was being cultivated on the northern Ethiopian plateau before the eighth century BC, when Sabaean influence first reached the plateau.[17] Indeed, it is more likely that wheat and barley were introduced to Ethiopia from South Arabia around that time, along with the plough, perhaps, and the techniques of terracing and irrigation. But although these new crops may have offered new opportunities, and the improved farming techniques would have increased productivity overall, wheat and barley could never supplant teff as the preferred crop, simply because teff evolved in the region and was best adapted to its environmental constraints.

The fields of teff which dominate the landscape of northern Ethiopia in the aftermath of the rainy season look more like hay meadows, rippling characteristically in the wind, than a cereal crop just a few weeks from harvest. The plant is light and delicate, and the grain it produces is tiny. Each seed is smaller than a pinhead; 150 equal the size of a single grain of wheat; 2.5 million teff seeds weigh one kilogram. But size is no measure of quality. In its value as a human food, teff is superior to any other cereal grown in Ethiopia. Carbohydrate and protein content matches and in some instances surpasses that of maize, sorghum, wheat, and barley and, even more important, its amino acid composition is closer to human dietary requirements. It is particularly rich in the amino acids which cannot be synthesized in the body and must therefore be ingested ready-made. These essential amino acids are among the foremost limiting factors of the human diet, but a single daily portion of teff supplies enough of them to sustain life without any other source of protein, while two daily portions are enough to ensure good health.[18]

During the nineteenth and twentieth centuries, when drought and famine have periodically brought devastating calamity to Ethiopia, the particular value of teff has been not so much its nutritional value as its capacity to produce a harvest when other cereals fail. The yield is substantially lower (averaging 910 kg per hectare, compared with 1,740 kg per hectare for maize, 1,460 kg for sorghum, 1,130 kg for wheat, and 1,180 kg for barley),[19] but teff is uniquely adapted to the climatic conditions most frequently encountered in the region. Teff will develop and ripen grain from every flower which has been pollinated even when no further rain falls while the plant is maturing. Other cereals commonly grown in Ethiopia will ripen either none (maize) or only some of the grain (barley and sorghum).

The most dependable portion of the region's rainfall blows in from the Red Sea during August and September, so farmers planting teff that flowers on the strength of those rains can be sure of a harvest, even if the rest of the year is dry. This capacity to produce a crop even in an ostensibly "bad" year is the quality valued most highly by the subsistence farmer. The high-yielding cereals so admired by agronomists and commercial farmers offer little or no benefit to subsistence farmers. High-yielding cereals perform well only in years when conditions are good (and even then they pose problems of storage and disposal). For the subsistence farmer, an adequate yield in years when conditions are bad is far more important.[20]

Teff is an indigenous plant that evolved in the region, so it is adapted to produce seed under the worst of prevailing conditions. Rain during the growing season is enough to provide farmers with a secure subsistence base. This has been important in the modern era—and no less so historically.

With areas of cultivation extended by terracing of the hillsides, and the scope of available labour augmented by the plough (pulled by oxen bred from cattle brought on to the plateau by pastoralists from the west), a sound agricultural base was established on the northern plateau by the time that South Arabian influence becomes evident at archaeological sites in the region from around 500 BC. Monumental temples were built at Yeha, Haoulti, and Mantara, with altars dedicated to a pantheon of deities almost identical to those known from the Saba kingdom of the period. At Haoulti, an elaborately decorated "throne" carved from a single block of fine-grained local limestone has been recovered, and among the remarkable quantity of metal objects found at the sites generally there are axes, adzes, sickles, and swords of bronze, and rings, scissors, swords, and daggers of iron—all indicating that the local metalworking industry was well-established.[21]

The large buildings, the tombs, sculptures and altars, the elaborate stone carving, the metalwork, and the use of writing at these sites all indicate that a very complex society, most likely at the state level, was firmly established on the northern Ethiopian plateau by the third century BC at the latest. Social stratification of the hierarchical variety is implied, and since some inscriptions tell of kings ruling over groups of people distinctly identified as "red" and "black," it may be concluded that the population was also divided on racial grounds.[22]

The influences of southern Arabia were almost entirely subsumed into the developing Aksumite culture by the first century AD. Through the coastal town of Adulis, Aksum maintained links with the Red Sea trading network, and was poised to become a key factor in economic and religious developments in the region, but its base remained firmly rooted on the Ethiopian plateau.

Meanwhile, the climatic conditions which sustained Aksum's robust agricultural system changed significantly during the first century AD. The analysis of sediments washed into drainage channels and archaeological sites in the Aksum region strongly implies that a more moist and possibly cooler climate prevailed from the first to the fourth century,[23] with consequences which might have seemed wholly desirable in the beginning but were to prove disastrous in the end.

DURING THE FIRST CENTURY AD, the monsoon which brought rain to East Africa early in the year regularly extended north to the Ethiopian plateau, so that Aksum's rainy season commenced in April or May each year, instead of July (when rains from the Red Sea began), and could be expected to continue through to September. The extension of the rainy season from three to six or seven months effectively doubled the length of the growing season, and with a vastly augmented surface and underground water supply, farmers could confidently plant and expect to reap two harvests each year.

The agricultural consequence of a temporary (though centuries-long) climatological perturbation explains how the inherently marginal environment of Aksum was able to support the demographic base of a far-flung commercial empire, and leaves little doubt as to why the empire eventually withered and died.[24]

The original, "natural" plant cover of the Aksum region was open, mainly deciduous woodland on well-drained soils, with evergreen elements such as cedars, figs, and palms occurring in concentrations along streams and in the vicinity of natural springs, and a more scrubby vegetation on steep or rocky slopes. Grasses predominated on poorly drained areas of flat open ground. Human impact has been accumulative, beginning with the terracing, plough agriculture, and irrigation of the south Arabian cultural influence, and intensifying with the rise of Aksum which followed the climatic perturbations of the first century AD.

Terracing increased the land area under cultivation; while irrigation and the onset of cooler and wetter spring weather improved the productive potential of soils not otherwise cultivable. At this crucial period, the growing season of the Aksum region extended from three or five to seven or even nine months,[25] and even poor-quality soils could produce two crops each year. Aksum, with its population and spheres of influence, expanded accordingly. An array of urban centres developed across the northern plateau, each doubtless controlling local farming and economic activities, but each in turn subservient to the authority of Aksum.

The *Periplus of the Erythraean Sea,* compiled in the mid first century AD, describes Aksum as a *metropolis* (an indication of size and importance that occurs rarely in the document).[26] Though situated on a far western spur of the plateau, 150 km from the nearest eastern access to the Red Sea, and then still 60 km from Adulis (an eight-day journey, says the *Periplus*),[27] Aksum exported considerable quantities of diverse goods from the plateau and the Sudan via Adulis into a maritime exchange network which dealt in commodities from as far afield as India, China, the Black Sea, and Spain.[28] The *Periplus,* and Pliny writing in the first century, specify ivory, rhinoceros horn, hippopotamus hides, and slaves as goods from Aksum shipped out through Adulis. Other sources refer to gold dust, frankincense, civet-cat musk—and even live elephants. One classical author describes a herd of about 5,000 elephants "pastured on a broad field" in the vicinity of Yeha.

The goods Aksum exported were acquired locally or from the hinterland in exchange for cattle, salt, and iron.[29] The geological evidence[30] suggests that iron probably was smelted on the plateau, but salt had to be collected from evaporation pans at the coast, or dug from deposits in the Danakil desert, and carried up the escarpment. Hence this dietary supplement was an especially valued commodity on the plateau and beyond, and remained an important medium of exchange well into the modern era.

Aksum ultimately became the commercial and administrative centre of an empire that controlled the exploitation of resources in the African hinterland and whose influence extended across the Red Sea to southern Arabia. Its rulers maintained close ties with the eastern Roman Empire, and in the third century achieved international prominence by issuing their own coinage, in gold, silver, and bronze; Persian leaders of the day described Aksum as one of the world's four most important kingdoms (the other three were Persia, Rome, and Sileos—possibly meaning China).[31] Aksum adopted Christianity in the fourth century, not long after Rome.

But while Aksum's commercial and territorial influence expanded, the food-production capacity and population size of the controlling central authority remained finite. By about AD 500 the city of Aksum covered an area of 75 hectares and housed about 20,000 inhabitants. The city was more extensive and more densely populated than its modern counterpart—and has never been larger.[32] Meanwhile, its rulers had developed what has been aptly described as a "mania for the gigantic."[33]

"Conspicuous consumption" is commonplace behaviour of wealthy people occupying the upper echelons of social hierarchies, and it is evident at Aksum in the size and grandeur of their residences, and in the variety and quantity of imported luxury goods that have been recovered from among the ruins of the buildings. These included glassware and ceramics; articles made of precious metals; fabrics and clothing; wine and sugar cane; vegetable oils; aromatics and spices.[34] Most of the luxury goods were imported from the eastern Mediterranean.[35] But although large amounts of the empire's resources were in effect

consumed by the ruling elite during their lifetimes, a more enduringly conspicuous proportion was dedicated to them after death.

At an early stage in its development, Aksum adopted the practice of bury-
ing its rulers in stone-walled tombs and marking their graves with monumental stelae (or obelisks). Over 140 stelae have been located in the city. All but a
few have fallen; some lie like stranded whales beside dry dusty streets, others
clog narrow ravines; fragments of some that broke have been incorporated in
church walls.

Most of the stelae are irregular in shape but perfectly smooth, with
rounded edges and curved sides and shallow undulations along their length.
Like works of sculpture, these stelae might have been carved to enhance the
proportion and form of the natural stone. The six largest are very different;
more indicative of an intention to revise rather than respect the natural form.
Each is precisely hewn, rectangular in section, and the surfaces are elaborately
decorated with bas-relief representations of multi-storeyed buildings.

One of the larger examples still stands among a number of smaller, undec-
orated stones in a neatly tended park at present-day Axum (the spelling used
when referring to the modern city). It is a single block of granite 21 metres
high, carved with geometric precision to represent a ten-storey building, with
a false door at the base. The fallen pieces of an even larger stele (24 metres
overall), similarly decorated, were taken to Rome in 1937, during the Italian
occupation of Ethiopia, and re-erected near the site of the Circus Maximus.
The largest of all—33 metres long, 3 by 2 metres in section at the base, and
carved on all four sides to represent a thirteen-storey building—lies broken in
five huge pieces, with smaller fragments scattered about the point of impact.
Whether this massive decorated piece of stone ever stood upright is uncertain;
archaeological investigations in the 1990s indicate that the stele fell and broke
in the process of erection. Less than 10 per cent of its total length would have
been below ground, too small a proportion to hold the stone upright and prevent it toppling from the perpendicular before the ground around the base
could be adequately consolidated.

Whatever the case, while still in one piece the massive Aksum stele
weighed over 700 tonnes and was "probably the largest single block of stone
ever quarried, carved and set up in the ancient world."[36] Its production called
for technological expertise and labour resources comparable with those which
built the pyramids. The granite block was cut from a hillside more than 4 km
west of Aksum, where the marks of quarrying are still evident. Dressing the
stone with the unsophisticated metal or stone tools of the time, and cutting
bas-relief designs between 10 and 20 cm deep into its entire surface area

(roughly 330 square metres) would have kept a sizeable corps of masons busy for months, if not years.

Exactly how the stone was moved from the quarry to Aksum and erected is a matter of conjecture. Rollers would have been employed, and elephants may have augmented the available human tractive power, but transporting such a massive stone over a distance of 4 km and then raising it to a vertical position was an undertaking that would strain the ingenuity and technical resources of modern engineers.

No two of Aksum's six great stelae are identical, either in size or in the complexity of their decoration, but when arranged in order of increasing size the sequence corresponds exactly with the stylistic development of the decoration. Each stele is larger and more elaborately decorated than the one before. This "mania for the gigantic" appears to have ended with the greatest of the six stelae; possibly because its fall was interpreted as a bad omen, possibly because its manufacture demonstrated the sheer impossibility of hewing, transporting, and raising anything larger. The end of the series also appears to coincide with the period during which Aksum turned from the deification of kings to the worship of Christ, a coincidence which may have been purely fortuitous, but could have been significant.

In any event, developments at Aksum were moving in a direction which made further pursuit of the gigantic impossible by the fourth century AD— whatever the whim of the rulers. The city and state was destined to become a victim of its own success. Environmental degradation was the instrument of its collapse.

During the period of conspicuous consumption, the region's woodland and forest had been stripped to fuel the charcoal-burning furnaces of iron-smelters and local glass, brick, and pottery manufacturers; people needed wood and charcoal for cooking and heating, and timber was also used in house-building and for furniture. The landscape was denuded, and while clearance initially made additional land available for crops to feed a growing population, it also exposed the soils to overcropping and erosion. Ironically, the extended rains which had nourished the growth of Aksum now hastened its decay. Nutrients were leached from the land; soil was washed from the hillsides. Rain that had been a blessing was now a curse.

"The breakdown of Axumite civilization was the result of a chance concatenation of mutually reinforcing processes that led to environmental degradation and precipitous demographic decline."[37] People were hungry, and Aksum's problems of food production at home could only compound the deleterious effect of commercial and political difficulties abroad. During the late sixth and early seventh centuries, war in the eastern Mediterranean reduced the market for luxury goods in the increasingly impoverished Roman Empire; then Persia gained control of South Arabia (threatening trade routes to India), and in the early eighth century Arab forces destroyed Adulis.

Aksum was isolated from the Red Sea trade. Gold coinage ceased to be issued, confirming the end of Aksum's commercial and military involvement in affairs beyond the escarpments of the Ethiopian plateau. And the region's degraded agricultural base could no longer support the extravagances of the social hierarchy it had fostered. Centralized power collapsed. Within a few generations Aksum and its satellite urban communities were reduced to loose clusters of villages, with a few residences of the elite established in defensive locations on steep hillsides.

Beginning around AD 750, the region's difficulties were exacerbated by a decline in annual rainfall. After centuries during which an extended rainy season had been the norm, the rainfall pattern reverted to the single season that had prevailed before Aksum rose to wealth and power. Agricultural production was reduced still further. Even where soil fertility had been maintained, only one harvest per year could be expected. With this reversion to the Ethiopian plateau's ancient rainfall pattern, the surviving population relied heavily on the food crop that had evolved in the region: teff, the cereal that would ripen all grain which had been pollinated, without further rainfall. Teff, the only cereal capable of producing sufficient grain in a bad year.

By AD 800 Aksum had almost ceased to exist. The elite and sections of the common people abandoned the denuded landscape in favour of settlement on the virgin soils of central Ethiopia, where the foundations for the thirteenth-century emergence of the modern Ethiopian state were laid. Aksum became a peripheral backwater, important only as a symbol of royal and religious authority.[38]

"Backwater" though it may still be, the enduring importance of present-day Axum as a symbol (and seat) of religious authority should not be overlooked. The royal authority of Haile Selassie and his feudal-style state was swept away by the army-led coup of September 1974 and replaced by a communist-inspired regime which soon proved to be no less repressive than its predecessor. With the simplistic confidence of a new broom, the new rulers denigrated and outlawed many aspects of the old social order—including religion.

Some aspects of reform were welcomed—even merited (especially land reform)—but the denigration of religion was a step too far. As the ugly nature of the new regime was revealed, church attendances soared, respect for the authority of the priests rose, and religion provided a network of shared belief through which dissent and opposition could spread and consolidate. The network drew its strength from Axum where, during the period of physical isolation that followed the collapse of the Aksumite empire and its mania for the gigantic, myth and reality had created a unique and durable foundation of Christian belief.

Aksum converted to Christianity only in the fourth century AD, but traditional belief says that its connection with the Bible dates back to the ninth century BC, when the Queen of Sheba travelled from her Ethiopian palace to meet King Solomon in Jerusalem. Their meeting is described in 1 Kings 10:

> And she came to Jerusalem with a very great train, with camels that b[o]re spices and very much gold, and precious stones: and when she was come to Solomon, she communed with him of all that was in her heart . . .
>
> And she gave the king [one] hundred and twenty talents of gold, and of spices very great store, and precious stones: there came no such abundance of spices as these which the queen of Sheba gave to king Solomon.
>
> And king Solomon gave unto the queen of Sheba all her desire, whatsoever she asked, beside that which Solomon gave her of his royal bounty. So she turned and went to her own country, she and her servants.

According to Ethiopian tradition, Solomon's gifts to the Queen of Sheba included the son to whom she gave birth on her return to Ethiopia. The child was named David and in due course ascended to the throne as Menelik I, founder of the Solomonic dynasty of which Haile Selassie was the last incumbent. And in later times, the link between Ethiopia and the roots of Christian religion represented by Menelik was strengthened by legend telling that while still a young man called David, Menelik had brought the fabled Ark of the Covenant to Aksum.

The Ark of the Covenant was the most sacred object of Old Testament times—and the most precious. A wooden box covered and lined with gold, it was made for the two tablets of stone on which the Ten Commandments had been written by the finger of God. After its construction at the foot of Mount Sinai around 1250 BC the Ark accompanied the Israelites through the wilderness, helping them to victory in every encounter, including the conquest of Palestine. King David took the Ark to Jerusalem, and his son Solomon installed it in the temple he was building when the Queen of Sheba made her visit. Legend tells that when David, son of Solomon and the Queen of Sheba, was a young adult he spent a year at the court of his father. On his departure he stole the Ark of the Covenant from the temple and carried it back to Axum, where it has remained ever since.[39]

So the story goes . . . It is a good story, but supported only by the fact that no other explanation for the Ark's disappearance from the record has been forthcoming. Even the Bible is silent on the subject. In fact, claims of its long and continuing presence in Axum rely entirely on the capacity to believe that it is so, despite the awkward contradictions of historical fact. The legend of Solomon, Sheba, and Menelik has no historical basis. The Queen of Sheba is a mythical figure; Aksum did not exist as a political entity while Solomon was alive, and the city of Aksum itself was founded several centuries after Menelik was supposed to have brought the Ark to it from Jerusalem. But belief is a powerful force. Monks guarding the sanctuary in which the Ark is said to rest insist the story is not legend, but history. A replica of the Ark is enshrined in each of Ethiopia's more than 20,000 Christian churches. Known as *tabots,* these replicas play a central role in major religious events, particularly at the feast of Timkat, when the *tabot* is carried in procession from every church, and the faithful bow and pray as it passes.

A replica of the Ark is used in the Timkat procession even at Axum. No one is ever allowed to see the original Ark of the Covenant; belief in its existence and its power is sustained by legend and the word of the priests.

People flock to Axum in their thousands for the Timkat festival. Crowds surge past the stelae, the huge hewn stones which offer tangible evidence of the region's ancient history, but there are no gestures of respect—leave alone reverence—for the relics of an ancestral civilization. "If it wasn't for foreign visitors we'd know nothing about these stones," a high-school student remarks. Ancient Aksum is forgotten. The relics of the past are highly visible, but the crowd today strives for just a glimpse of the *tabot*—a replica relic—and is more concerned with the promises that faith and belief offer for the future than with the evidence of the past.

The house in Timbuktu occupied by Gordon Laing in 1826. Laing was the first non-Muslim to visit the city; he was murdered soon after departing

CHAPTER 23

Cities without Citadels[1]

WHILE AKSUM WAS DISTINGUISHED by the conspicuous consumption of a ruling elite and its subjects toiled under the rule of despotic kings, the large, complex societies of the inland Niger delta developed a more egalitarian and less coercive political system.

The last chapter took a determinedly Afrocentric view of the social and economic developments that marked the rise of Aksum. The narrative emphasized the African input and treated the influences of southern Arabia as contributions which were incorporated into the Aksumite culture when advantageous, and discarded when not. Aksum achieved its moment of splendour, but the account of its rise (and fall) implied that Aksum would have realized its potential with or without the southern Arabian influence, simply by exercising its indigenous African talents and dynamism. The ecological assets of the Ethiopian plateau would have been exploited and Aksum would have made its mark on the region. An exclusively African phenomenon, instead of what it actually became—basically African, with more than a touch of foreign influence.

Of course, it could also be argued that without foreign influence the Aksumite state could never have been formed. Indeed, for anyone puzzling over the phenomenon of a rich city state perched high in the mountains of Africa this is the most obvious interpretation. Simple logic suggests that a curiosity so unlike anything else known from sub-Saharan Africa, possessing distinctive features also found in the ancient cities of Arabia and the classical world, is more likely to be an outpost of foreign influence than an expression of local endeavour.

Such logic as this conclusion possesses is derived entirely from established western precepts concerning the city, state-formation, and the rise of civilizations.

Moving on from the attractions of discovery (and plunder) that had excited western interest in the ruins of ancient cities around the world during the nineteenth century, scholars offered descriptions of the social and economic processes that encouraged people to live together in towns and build cities. A consensus view described the movement into towns and cities—urbanization—as a consequence of sustained increases in food supply. There had been a diversification of occupations, it was said, with people becoming specialized in specific tasks. As society became more complex, control became more centralized—and more coercive. Evidence of hierarchical social systems, in which the many were ruled by the few under varying conditions of benign or despotic authority, was found to be widespread.

In broad terms, the pre-industrial city was described as a centre of power and production, distinguished by a number of defining characteristics common to all. "Laundry-lists of attributes" were compiled, specifying the physical and organizational features essential to the rise and functioning of a city. Among them, writing was regularly cited as an important criterion, and monumental architecture was universally presented as a primary feature distinguishing the city from other types of settlement.

Monumental architecture expressed civic pride and identity, it was said, reinforcing the elite's dominance of the masses. Monumental architecture—especially the citadel—was a "signpost to permanence," reflecting and reinforcing the control ideology of the state.[2] The pyramids of Egypt, the civic buildings of Greece and Rome, the ziggurats of Mesopotamia, the plazas and temples of central America . . . all were intended to be enduring signposts of permanence, but all pointed to a common theme of coercive centralized control as well. If monumental architecture is indeed the primary defining characteristic of a city state, then Aksum was the only example ever to have arisen in sub-Saharan Africa.

But if cities are founded by people from different social and occupational backgrounds congregating to live in close proximity to one another, is a hierarchical social system and coercive centralized control the only way of managing the group's increasingly complex economic and social interactions?

In the classic definition of the urbanization process, centralized—often despotic—control is deemed to have been the norm, with the many ruled by the few and the ideology of the city state reinforced by monumental architecture. This definition is confirmed at archaeological sites around the world, but does the prevalence of one interpretation obscure even the possibility of an alternative? Is there perhaps an alternative management strategy, more practical than ideological, that would direct the growth of complex societies along routes that rendered monumental "signposts to permanence" unnecessary?

The history of people exploiting the resources of the inland delta of the Niger River, in West Africa, suggests that there is an alternative route. One which not only reveals a unique, wholly indigenous, wholly African process of urbanization, but also discredits a long-standing interpretation of early West African history.

HITHERTO, IT HAD BEEN widely believed that the economic and cultural development of West Africa was largely a consequence of the trans-Saharan gold and slave trade initiated by North African Arabs in the eighth century AD.[3] No towns or complex social and economic networks were believed to have existed before the arrival of the Arabs. It was assumed that the history of trade and towns in West Africa dated back no further than the trans-Saharan trade and scholars concentrated their efforts on confirming the existence of towns, states, and sources of luxury goods mentioned in Arab documents.

West African history was "unshackled from the Arab stimulus paradigm" in the 1970s, when evidence of "cities without citadels"[4] was uncovered, wherein the transformation to a complex urban society began 1,000 years before the arrival of Arab traders from across the Sahara, and a large urban centre remained active for centuries after "the signposts to permanence" erected by the rulers of Aksum had become totems of failure.

At Jenne-jeno, a large archaeological site adjacent to the modern town of Djenne on the inland Niger delta in Mali, about 350 kilometres south-west of Timbuktu, excavations have revealed evidence of urbanization that spans 1,600 years without a break.[5] At its most densely populated (around AD 800) Jenne-jeno housed up to 27,000 people. There is no evidence of a hierarchical social system and centralized control, no monumental architecture, no citadel.

Remarkably similar settlement processes appear to have characterized the urbanization process at sites of similar age in China,[6] suggesting that this alternative to the hierarchical social system and coercive centralized control strategy of classical definition may have occurred worldwide, but only in Africa, at Jenne-jeno and its hinterland on the inland Niger delta, have the origins and dynamics of the process been unravelled and described in meticulous detail. And the results show that, as with so much of indigenous African history, it was the opportunities and constraints of the regional environment that determined the initial form and pace of developments, not trade and external influence.

THE NIGER RIVER RISES FROM the foothills of the Tingi mountains, on the border between Guinea and Sierra Leone. One of Sierra Leone's major rivers, the Sewa, rises from the same mountains, at a spot less than 10 km from the source of the Niger, but on the opposite side of the watershed. The Sewa flows southward, dropping rapidly from the mountains to the lowland, then meandering across a humid and densely vegetated coastal plain to the Atlantic Ocean, not more than 250 km from its source. The Niger, meanwhile, carries its share of the Tingi waters to the north and, supplemented by the inflow of its tributaries, takes a grand circuitous route to the ocean: north-east through the Sahel and along the fringes of the Sahara to Timbuktu, then curving east and south-east across Niger and through Nigeria to join the Atlantic on the Bight of Biafra. The Niger covers a distance of 4,200 km in all.

The Tingi mountains from which the Niger rises are part of the massive Precambrian formation which comprises the West African craton. These are some of the world's most ancient land surfaces (see page 10). As with cratons generally, the unique chemical and physical processes of their formation laced the craton with veins of economically important mineral ores.

Over millions of years, erosion stripped substantial quantities of rock from the craton, breaking down its chemical components in the process, dissolving out the soluble substances, and washing away the mineral residues. As a result, iron and aluminium ore are commonplace throughout the region; rich deposits of gold and diamonds are known and exploited, and sedimentary sands and clays have accumulated to the north of the craton in such quantities that their weight has caused the underlying basin floor to subside. This feature, known to geologists as the Taoudeni Syncline, is one of the largest of its kind in the world.[7]

The landscape through which the Niger River flows across the Taoudeni Syncline is notable for its sandstone outcrops and escarpments, elevated river banks and expanses of gentle undulation. The diversity of these landforms belies the underlying uniformity of the basin. In effect, the sediments filling the basin have settled like sugar in a bowl. Over its total expanse, the surface is remarkably level. Where the course of the Niger veers north-east around the Bandiagara plateau, the river drops just 10 metres over a distance of more than

200 kilometres—five centimetres in each kilometre: an incline of 1:20,000.[8] Over this broad and gently sloping section of its long journey to the sea, the Niger assumes the character of a delta, spreading itself in a tangle of meandering streams which shift their course from time to time but are always reunited near Timbuktu, where the Niger flows along a single course once again.

Like the Nile, the Niger brings to its arid reaches the water that rainfall denies, and is similarly powered by seasonal high rainfall in the highlands where the mainstream and its tributaries originate. In the case of the Niger, an average of 1,500 mm of rain falls in the catchment each year. With the onset of the rains, the river swells substantially but remains confined to the course it has cut through the bedrock as it tumbles from the highlands.

The character of the river changes dramatically, however, when the flood reaches the level expanse of the basin. The meandering streams soon fill to overflowing and the rising waters steadily inundate the adjacent low-lying dry land. In a year of average rainfall, the Niger flood transforms 30,000 km^2 of parched Sahel into an intricate lattice of channels, flats, ponds, marshes, and lakes, interspersed with tracts of dry land and islands on which groups of tightly packed houses are perched. This is the inland Niger delta—as big as Belgium, 25 per cent larger than the state of Vermont.

By virtue of its origin in a region of ancient rock and heavily weathered soils, the Niger brings very little silt to the inland delta. While the Nile, for example, carries about 770 g of sediment per cubic metre from its catchment in the younger, more easily eroded volcanic highlands of East Africa, the Niger carries an average of only 75 g per cubic metre. Annual sedimentation in the Nile delta is measured in centimetres; in the inland Niger delta it amounts to less than one-tenth of a millimetre per year (about one metre in 5,000 years).

The Nile is a turbid river; the Niger and its major upstream tributary, the Bani, run clear, pouring 70 billion cubic metres of water into the inland Niger delta each year, of which only about one-half flows out where the Niger becomes a single main stream again, near Timbuktu. The other half is lost to evaporation and to the voluminous infiltration which soaks the soil and augments the ground-water reservoir[9]—but whether lost or flowing on, the annual passage of the flooding waters creates a vast, diverse and immensely productive ecosystem.

The flood begins to rise in September, but because the area it covers is so vast, and the slope away from the main channels so slight, the waters rise and fall very slowly. Elevated and distant areas of the delta are flooded for only a month or two, but the lowest ground may be submerged for more than six months under three metres of water. Maximum depth and extent is attained in early November, and levels everywhere then begin to fall; by May the delta is so dry again that even the main distributaries of the delta are less than ten metres across, and barely knee-deep.

As the flood rises and spreads over the parched delta landscape, the water is enriched with nutrients released from the breakdown of decaying vegetation, organic matter, and the droppings of animals which grazed on the floodplain. The nutrients fuel an explosive growth of bacteria, algae, zooplankton, and vegetation. In areas flooded for six months or more, the growth of highly productive grasses known collectively as *bourgou* keeps pace with the rising waters, their photosynthesizing surfaces and seed-heads always at the surface of water often more than three metres deep. The *bourgou* vegetation produces up to 17 tonnes per hectare each year. In areas flooded less deeply for three to six months, the indigenous wild rice (*Oryza barthii* and *O. breviligulata,* both unrelated to any species of Asian rice) is dominant, with an annual biomass production of about 10 tonnes per hectare. By contrast, the annual biomass of the mixed Sahelian vegetation of acacias, palms, scrub, and savanna grasses growing on high ground watered predominantly by rain, rarely exceeds 5 tonnes per hectare.[10]

The prodigious productivity of the inland Niger delta offers human populations several ways of making a living. Farmers sow the domesticated West African rice, *Oryza glaberrima,* on soils moistened by the summer rains as the flood approaches; during the flood they harvest wild rice and the *bourgou* cereal *Echinochloa* spp. from canoes; as the flood recedes, millets and sorghums are grown as *décrue* crops on the newly saturated soils (*crue* is French for "flood"; *décrue* refers to the recession of the waters after the flood). For pastoralists the retreat of the flood coincides with the advance of the dry season in the Sahel regions they exploit to the north, exposing *bourgou* pasture and crop residues for their herds to graze upon when there is precious little fodder anywhere else. Farming and pastoralism are two of the predominant food-production strategies that are employed in the delta. Fishing is the third.[11]

In the dry season fish are confined either to the bed of the river, where the flow may be broken into pools, or they are trapped in small isolated lakes, ponds, and swamps on the floodplain. Either way, their numbers are very low indeed for five or more months of the year—amounting to hardly more than a basic breeding stock—but their status changes dramatically with the arrival of the flood.

The flood not only releases the delta fish from their dry-season retreats, it also stimulates the production of enormous quantities of food: algae, plankton, aquatic plants and insects, even other fish. As they disperse through the delta the fish grow very rapidly; they spawn, and the eggs of most species hatch within about two days, thus ensuring that the juvenile fish are born when food is plentiful and plant cover offers maximum protection from predators.

High water, when the abundance of food is greatest, is the main season of feeding, growing, and fattening for nearly all the delta fish species. Their growth is very rapid and stores of fat are laid down as reserves for the dry season ahead. As the flood subsides, the aquatic habitat shrinks. Fish concentrate in channels that run back to the rivers. Food supplies dwindle and a mass exodus begins. The large carnivorous fish are the first to move downstream, where they lurk at the exits of channels through which the very abundant young-of-the-year must pass. This is also the main fishing season for other hunters, such as birds (which also have young to feed) and people.

Huge quantities of fish are taken; according to an FAO report, 54,112 professional fishermen each landed 1.66 metric tons in an average year—a total catch of 90,000 tonnes. The report was compiled from catches recorded in market statistics only; it is probable that half as much again was caught and consumed by subsistence fishermen. Yet more fish are stranded in rapidly shrinking pools on the floodplain, and mortality is also very high in the dry-season refuges, where food and cover are limited.

The inland Niger delta fishery survives this massive offtake year after year because it exploits the juvenile young-of-the-year, more than 90 per cent of which is superfluous to the recruitment needs of the breeding population. The fish species sustaining the fishery are typical r-strategists (see page 129) capable of very rapid population increase, able to colonize new habitats and to cope with fluctuating environmental conditions, as opposed to the more stable K-strategist populations found in the deep-water African lakes.

Fishing, farming, and pastoralism: in each activity the inland Niger delta offers opportunities for successful and sustained food production. The tendency has been for people to specialize in one or other of the three, and since the activities are complementary—even symbiotic—networks of exchange have developed, with each specialist group supplying for barter essential items that the other two cannot easily obtain. But the relationships were not as easily established and sustained as might be supposed.

The general terms and statistical averages that have served in describing the ecology of the inland Niger delta up to this point may seem to support a popular belief that ecosystems always tend towards harmony and a state of "natural balance," in which they will persist unchanged for centuries, if not millennia. In this scenario the delta appears to be a fully self-sustaining ecosystem, functioning to the benefit of all parties, with the added wonder that people appear to have found ways of reaping its harvests without disturbing the "natural balance."

Sadly however, generalities and averages give an unrealistic view of the inland Niger delta. In this ecosystem (and many others) the general view is always qualified by a number of specific caveats, and the average almost never pertains. Take the example of rainfall. Some rain generally falls on the delta between June and September, but not always on every part of it and the dates of commencement and cessation vary widely from year to year. Annual total rainfall at Mopti (in the delta at the confluence of the Niger and Bani rivers) ranged from 360 mm up to 962 mm over a period of twenty-five years. In eleven of those years, rainfall was 25 per cent or more above the average; in seven it was 25 per cent or more below. In only seven of the twenty-five years did it fall within 25 per cent of the average.[12]

Annual rainfall does not tend to cluster around the average. There may be long periods of high rainfall followed by periods of very low rainfall. Such unpredictability may be manageable in rain-fed agricultural systems that are geared to produce a crop at even minimal rainfall levels (as with teff in the Aksum system—see page 213), but in the inland Niger delta, where fishing, farming, and herding activities are dependent upon rising water, not falling rain, the inability to predict conditions from year to year is a serious constraint.

The extent and duration of the flood is of course determined by rainfall in the catchment area, which varies just as widely as the rainfall over the delta itself but with a disproportionate effect on the height of the flood reaching the delta. Because roughly the same amounts of water are lost to evaporation and infiltration whatever the rainfall, a 15 per cent drop in rainfall over the catchment actually leads to a 33 per cent fall in the amount of water flowing into the delta.[13] Records show that over a period of 85 years (between 1877 and 1962) the Niger's contribution to the delta flood was within 10 per cent of the annual average only seventeen times, while the totals ranged from 37 per cent below average to 77 per cent above.[14]

Because of the complexity of mechanisms affecting the flood regime of the delta, many of the factors which affect the day-to-day life and decisions of its inhabitants are profoundly unpredictable, so much so that even group memories of cycles of drought and flood cannot identify useful precedents.[15] And yet they developed systems of food production and social interaction which sustained high population densities for 1,600 years.

Remarkably, it was the unpredictability of the delta regime itself which was responsible for the robust subsistence system that its inhabitants developed. In other words, the problems of making a living in the delta were so great that only sound adaptive strategies were effective. Sound adaptive strategies tend to endure, and in this instance have been the context for an indigenous transformation to a large, complex, but non-coercive urban settlement at Jenne-jeno—

a viable alternative to the hierarchical social system and coercive centralized control strategy that distinguished the transformation at Aksum and elsewhere.

In each of the delta's three basic subsistence strategies (farming, herding, and fishing), only deep, sharply focused knowledge of the effects and potential of prevailing environmental circumstances on the particular activity could ensure long-term adaptive success—in other words, specialization. But concentrating on a single highly specialized strategy in unpredictable conditions is also a recipe for frequent and disastrous failure. Diversification—spreading the risk of failure across a wider range of options—would be a better strategy but, since success with any food-production system called for a high degree of specialization, no single group could hold and exercise the necessary degree of specialized knowledge in more than one activity. There is a paradox here. The demand for diversification is incompatible with the requirements of specialization; yet each is fundamental to survival.

The paradox was resolved in the inland Niger delta by the development of special relationships between specialists. These relationships allowed each group to pursue its occupation exclusively, while sharing bonds of mutual obligation which included accommodating the occasionally inconvenient demands of each other's speciality.

Permanent settlement in the delta, resulting in the formation of *tells* (large mounds consisting of the accumulated remains of ancient settlements), was initiated by people who entered the region during the last 500 years BC. They made pottery similar to that found at earlier sites along the southern fringe of the Sahara, suggesting that the immigrants were part of a southward movement of herders, fishermen, and cultivators that began with the accelerating desiccation of the Sahara and Sahel regions around 2000 BC. They also made and used iron tools, a factor which enhanced their capacity to exploit the resources of the delta. Farmers probably began cultivating the wild West African rice (*O. glaberrima*) at an early stage. The plant almost certainly was domesticated in the region, and it is clear that rice cultivation was well established in the inland Niger delta by the first century AD as part of the farming, herding and fishing complex that remains dominant to this day.[16]

In the most productive basins of the delta, the cultivated West African rice (*O. glaberrima*) has successfully held off the diffusion of the higher-yielding Asian varieties, largely because of its greater genetic variability and capacity to produce a crop under a wide range of conditions. More than 41 distinct varieties of *O. glaberrima* are known, among which some will survive variations in water depth of from one to three metres, compared with a maximum of one metre for the Asian rice, *Oryza sativa*. The delta's rice-growing specialists, the Marka people, sow a mixture of varieties in the same field, each with different growing periods (from 90 to 210 days), varying tolerance to soil porosity and pH, and sensitivity to the timing of the flood. Their fields are long and narrow, cutting across several soil types along a progression of potential flood levels. The multiple sowings are made at intervals of several days or weeks. The procedure and timing of Marka rice cultivation are determined to some extent by intricate cosmological observations; this and other aspects of their activities are kept secret. Most tellingly, they are not freely shared outside the Marka community.

Secret knowledge, and subtleties of environmental response in the delta, are also prevalent among the Bambara millet and sorghum farmers, the Fulani and Tuareg herders, and the Bozo and Somono fishermen.[17]

Classic anthropological definitions of symbiosis among groups require that each should occupy a distinct niche, both in terms of occupation and territory;[18] without such separation hostility is predicted. This is yet another definition that is contradicted by evidence from the inland Niger delta. Once population densities had passed a critical point, the different groups occupying the delta were living cheek-by-jowl. The demands of their occupations, and the need to work and move with the flood, had engendered a profusion of land-use strategies—often relating to the same piece of territory at the same point in time. The potential for inter-ethnic conflict was extreme. In terms of classic definition, the inland Niger delta should have been a "morass of interethnic hostility."[19] But what distinguishes the delta throughout its 1,600 years of archaeologically recorded history is not the frequency of conflict, but the maintenance of peaceful and reciprocal relations.

This is not to say that conflict never occurred between the groups occupying the delta, only to remark that where it occurred the result was not the imposition of despotic coercive rule by the victors. Most groups have come into conflict in the past. Inter-ethnic clashes feature prominently in the myths, legends and stories of the delta, for instance, but the message is adaptive. The stories tell of conflict arising from differing priorities of land use, but emphasize the negative consequences of deviating from the established patterns of inter-ethnic behaviour, not the glories of victory. They are parables of instruction wherein victory is not the only virtue, some even tell of victors who assumed the identity of the vanquished.

The myths and legends of the delta are in fact "ecological abstractions" which incorporate the realities of existence—namely a highly unpredictable environment and the incompatible strategies of specialists exploiting it—into systems of belief. In effect, they transform the potential of conflict between groups into expectations of appropriate behaviour, which in turn defines ethnic identity in terms of obligations to others. People know how to behave because they know they are different and this mutual respect allows specialization to flourish and material symbols of group identity (hairstyles, scarification, dress, etc.) to develop. Together, myths and material symbols remind all involved of the expectations that bind the regional community. Herein lies the origin of *in situ* ethnic elaboration, and the device that maintains ethnic boundaries.

Ethnic identity has become a divisive and inflammatory feature of society in the modern world, but it has often been a unifying social phenomenon—as in the inland Niger delta of Africa. Indeed, the counteracting forces of ethnic identity in the delta—where the demands of specialization pushed groups apart while the requirements of a generalized economy pulled them together—created a dynamism that ensured growth and the establishment of urban settlements. And they were non-coercive settlements. Groups congregated by choice. This is an instance of transformation from a rural to an urban society that did not establish a hierarchical society and coercive centralized control, with the many ruled by a despotic few. The process in the delta and at Jenne-jeno in particular, was one of "complexification" rather than centralization.

JENNE-JENO IS a true *tell*, with the evidence of human occupation rising layer upon layer to a height of six metres above the sterile floodplain. An arc of permanent water fills a depression on the eastern side of the mound. Mango trees line the rise—someone's hopeful enterprise that has not been very fruitful (this is not a place for mangoes)—their exposed roots revealing both the degree of erosion down the slope and the trees' tenacious grip. Two trees stand on either side of a gully running several metres into the body of the mound.

The ancient occupation levels are so clearly revealed in the gully walls that it is hard to find a patch that does not contain some fragments of pottery; there is some bone, and some ash too, but pottery predominates: thin, thick, decorated or plain; rich russet-brown shading to black; polished, rough, coarse-grained or fine—it is the quantity and diversity that strikes the untutored eye. That and the tangible link with an earlier age that they represent. Stand in a gully or in the archaeologist's trench and the wall before you represents over 1,600 years of people living and dying, making a way for themselves, dreaming and arguing.

They took mud from the plain and built houses. When one fell, or threatened to fall, they built another. Depressions were created where the bricks were made, and a mound rose where the houses had stood. Sixteen hundred years are exposed in the wall of a gully, a slice of time the eye scans in a second. Bee-eaters burrow nesting tunnels in the deposit.

Dust raised by the strengthening wind softens the landscape to a monotone grey, with a shading of ochre here and there. The skyline of modern Jenne, two or three kilometres to the north, is a low, light-grey medley of angular mud-block buildings and the round heads of trees. The mosque is centrally placed; three spires, a tower in the south wall, crenellations and buttresses. In the near distance, beside the causeway that raises the main road to Jenne above the flood, three women are firing new pots. The kiln is a heap of rice-straw, burning at a slow smoulder and the internal heat evident only when the wind raises a sudden flush of orange to its surface.

The Jenne-jeno mound covers an area of about 33 hectares. The surface is covered with fragments of pottery; so densely covered, in fact, that you cannot avoid walking on them. Grindstones and iron slag are plentiful too. The visitor's eye is constantly distracted by some striking pattern, or novel configuration underfoot. The fragments generally are just a few centimetres across, but if a piece preserves a segment of the rim and you hold it at eye level, edge on, with the arc of the rim horizontal, the mind's eye can follow the profile of the curve, reconstructing the breadth and depth of the pot as it was when whole—straight from the kiln.

Specialized craft skills from the very earliest times are evident at Jenne-jeno. Pottery from the lowest levels is finely made and delicately patterned, generally of a quality suggesting that highly skilled potters were engaged in its manufacture. Abundant quantities of iron and slag likewise indicate that some members of the community had the knowledge and skill to smelt and smith the metal; others must also have had the time to obtain the ore, the closest sources of which were at least 50 km away. Later, the evidence for craft specialization increases and diversifies. Potters and smiths were joined by artisans working initially in solid coursed mud and subsequently in unfired brick. Many stone beads and hundreds of sandstone grinders of uniform size and shape were found (again indicating journeys beyond the immediate hinterland, since the delta is devoid of natural stone and the nearest source more than 50 km away). Fired-clay net weights indicate the presence of fishermen; similarly, loom weights and spindle whorls demonstrate that weavers were also at work in the community.

Copper and gold ornaments were found in the deposits, though it is impossible to tell if they were crafted at Jenne-jeno from imported materials, or were brought in ready-made. In any event, the large amounts of other foreign material clearly indicate that a well-organized trade system was operating from

Jenne-jeno well before AD 800, when the settlement was most densely occupied. Crowded cemeteries and an increasingly complex layout of house foundations indicate that occupation of the mound became very dense indeed at that time. Houses were built close together, with narrow alleys in between. The effect was like a warren of alleys winding between tightly packed compounds of round and square houses linked by walls.[20] There may have been an open market place in a central location. The whole residential sector was enclosed by a wall built of solid rows of cylindrical mud brick, 3.6 metres wide at the base.

The wall is something of a puzzle. It could have been the most prominent architectural feature at Jenne-jeno, but certainly it was not a monumental "signpost to permanence." No concomitant evidence of social ranking or authoritarian institutions such as a "temple elite" has been found. Nor is there any evidence of external threats to Jenne-jeno, so if the wall was built for defensive purposes, it probably was with the intention of protecting the settlement from high and destructive floods; or else the wall served to control access to the market place and trade.[21]

THE MOUND THAT ROSE from the Niger floodplain with the growth of Jenne-jeno did not stand alone. Indeed, it was surrounded by twenty-five smaller mounds, all within a distance of one kilometre, all occupied simultaneously. The total surface area of Jenne-jeno and its satellites was 69 hectares; the total population when most densely occupied approached 27,000.[22] This was large enough to qualify as an urban centre, but urban cluster is the term that best describes Jenne-jeno. There is no topographical explanation for the siting and separation of the mounds. The arrangement was purely a consequence of human choice. The surface of the floodplain was equally suitable throughout, people could have settled wherever they chose; indeed, there was nothing to prevent them congregating to make Jenne-jeno a single settlement.

Analysis of the type and concentration of artefact found on the mounds in the Jenne-jeno cluster has revealed that residence was related to trade or craft. Whether they were fishermen, metallurgists, farmers, potters, or weavers, each group occupied sites that were distinct from the others. Several crafts usually were represented on mounds larger than 1.5 hectares, while those smaller than 0.5 hectare rarely demonstrated convincing evidence of any specialized craft activity. On mounds of between 0.5 and 1.5 ha, however, there was evidence of exclusivity, with sites tending to be dominated by one or another specialized activity.[23]

The mounds of Jenne-jeno, separate but in close proximity and occupied simultaneously, functioned as a city, whose diverse population supplied diverse services and craft products to the hinterland.[24] Drawn as they were from the food-producing communities that inhabited the hinterland, and dependent still on the supplies of rice, fish, and cattle that sustained the entire delta, the specialist groups who congregated at Jenne-jeno each retained their ethnic identities—sustained by their shared beliefs. They settled within shouting distance of each other, but avoided assimilation into a single urban entity.

With none of the centralized authority that elsewhere controlled the social tensions generated by the emergence of urbanism, clustering allowed a diverse population to congregate for economies of scale, and to draw upon the services of other specialists without surrendering their independent identities, the whole thereby functioning as a city, and providing a variety of services and products to a wider hinterland. In effect, the "push" of specialization produced occupational castes and ethnic distinction, while the "pull" of economic integration produced a web of shared myth and belief that emphasized both individual ethnic identity *and* mutual interdependence.

THE PEOPLE WHO INHABITED the inland Niger delta left no monumental public architecture, extravagant burials, or incised tablets praising kings and recording feats or conquests, but the archaeological record speaks no less eloquently (and certainly more impartially). The history of Jenne-jeno appears to have been extraordinarily peaceful. While evidence of dwellings razed to the ground is commonplace at urban sites elsewhere, with level after level of burning, not a whiff of such disaster is evident at Jenne-jeno throughout its 1,600 years of occupation.

The abundance of subsistence food supplies in the delta trade, and the containment of trade largely within the boundaries of the delta ecosystem, contributed significantly to the peaceful longevity of its society and economy. Trade dealt overwhelmingly in the subsistence produce of the floodplain. Grain, fish, oil, meat, and other animal products were traded in volume; exotic and luxury items hardly at all. It was a remarkably robust system. Why then did it collapse? Between the twelfth and fourteenth centuries the population of Jenne-jeno fell to one-tenth of its size in the eighth century; similar levels of decline in population are evident at other mounds in the delta.

It could be that climatic change and an extended regime of severely reduced floods contributed to the decline, creating environmental circumstances which even skilled specialists could not counter. External influence and economic domination could have been responsible. By the fourteenth century, the inland Niger delta was part of a trade network with extensive links throughout West Africa and across the Sahara. Arab sources chronicle the rise and fall of empires and the sad history of wars and slaving that racked West Africa, but there is no evidence of such collapse at Jenne-jeno. The modern town of Jenne (sited on an adjacent mound and occupied by AD 500) converted to Islam in the thirteenth century, but the decline of Jenne-jeno dates from before that time.

Alternatively, the cause of the decline could have been more insidious, only indirectly attributable to human agency. The Black Death was advancing from Asia around the Mediterranean, along the North African coast and into Europe during the thirteenth century. The pestilence could have hitched a ride across the Sahara.[25] Disease has always been a major constraint on the expansion and congregation of communities in Africa.

Carved door in Enndé, a Dogon village in Mali

CHAPTER 24

Disease and Affliction

BECAUSE HUMANS EVOLVED in Africa, their parasites and diseases are uniquely prevalent there too. Disease spreads rapidly among people congregating in large numbers and has been a major constraint on the establishment of urban centres in Africa.

The imperial rulers of China conducted a census of the country's population in AD 2, and surviving documents show that at least 57.6 million people lived in China at the time. Similarly, written records show that the population of the Roman Empire when Augustus died in AD 14 was 54 million.[1] The population of India during the same period cannot have been less than that of the Roman Empire, and probably at least the same number of people inhabited the Americas and Australasia. Thus the bands of anatomically modern humans (*Homo sapiens sapiens*), who migrated from Africa around 100,000 years ago (see Chapter 10), though relatively few when they left, had colonized the globe and multiplied into a population of more than 200 million people by the beginning of the modern era.

Such an impressive growth of numbers is quite within the range of human reproductive capacity (see page 131), and it begs the question: if this was the extent to which the emigrant population had expanded out of Africa, how fared the parent population that remained within the continent?

The population density of hunter-gatherers in modern times suggests that about 1 million people inhabited Africa 100,000 years ago, when the emigrants left the continent and everyone lived by hunting and gathering. By AD 200 numbers are said to have risen to 20 million, of whom more than half lived in North Africa and the Nile valley (and thus would have been part of the Roman Empire population in AD 14), leaving a sub-Saharan population of under 10 million.[2] By AD 1500 the population of the continent is estimated to have been 47 million and in a state of "stable biological equilibrium," with population growth fulfilling the potential of the environments that people occupied.[3] Meanwhile, the out-of-Africa population of the world had risen to just over 300 million by AD 1500.

A massive disparity in population growth rates is evident. While the out-of-Africa population soared from just hundreds to 200 million in 100,000 years, and rose to just over 300 million in the next 1,500 years, the African population increased from 1 million to no more than 20 million 100,000 years later, and to only 47 million in AD 1500. And yet both groups were descendants of the same evolutionary stock. Both groups inherited the talents and physiological attributes that evolution had bestowed during the preceding 4 million years in Africa. So why did the migrant population grow so much faster? Answer: because they moved out of Africa.

By leaving the tropical environments of the cradle-land in which humanity had evolved, the migrants also left behind the many parasites and disease organisms that had evolved in parallel with the human species. Throughout their evolutionary history humans have been opportunists, whose numbers were kept low by environmental factors for much of the time, but whose potential for population growth ensured they would multiply rapidly whenever circumstances permitted. In short, humans are adapted to maximize numbers and colonize new territory. In Africa this adaptation was dampened by debility and disease. Out of Africa, beyond the reach of the insects and organisms which had reinfected generation after generation,[4] the multiplication of human numbers quickly assumed a hitherto unprecedented scale.

Of course, the initial absence or near-absence of organisms capable of living on or inside the human body was a passing phase. In time, as is all too evident, biologically and demographically significant diseases developed among the migrant populations too. But by then they had had more than a head start. Meanwhile, contemporary populations in the tropical African cradle-land remained constrained by debility and disease. That is why the African population grew so slowly, and it also explains why the rise of indigenous cities and civilizations in Africa had hardly begun when the migrants returned with foreign ideas of how it should be done.

·   ·   ·

THE TROPICAL ENVIRONMENTS OF Africa have seen the evolution of the greatest number and diversity of life forms on Earth. Although humans are a relatively recent expression of the continent's fecundity, the array of organisms that evolved to take advantage of their existence is no more than might be expected to result from five million years of co-evolution. Parasites and disease affecting humans are uniquely prevalent in Africa. The afflictions are numerous; the means of infection bewildering and various.

Though the "boom and bust" tendency of ancestral human populations in Africa does not exactly qualify them for description as quintessential r-strategists, the tsetse fly—carrier of the microscopic parasites, trypanosomes, which cause sleeping sickness in humans and domestic cattle—is undoubtedly the consummate K-strategist (see pages 129–30). Equilibrium and stability are the distinguishing characteristics of tsetse populations, and the success of their strategy is amply demonstrated by the small numbers of offspring each generation contributes to their near constant numbers.

Tsetse flies do not lay large numbers of eggs from which only very few mature flies will result. Indeed, the female tsetse lays no eggs at all. Instead, a single fertilized egg develops into a larva within her abdomen. Each female tsetse fly produces only four or five larvae in her lifetime, such is the certainty of her contribution to the next generation. She is impregnated only once, and stores the sperm for fertilization of an egg as and when conditions are amenable. At the appropriate moment, the larva is deposited in moist shady ground, pupates immediately, and over a period of five weeks matures into an adult fly.[5] The larvae are deposited at random—small solitary organisms in a large and diverse environment. Their arrival is not simultaneous, their numbers are never large—factors which mitigate against predation (and have frustrated eradication programmes in modern times).

The tsetse fly occurs only in tropical Africa, where it currently infests more than 10 million km^2 of the continent's potentially most productive land. Wherever its preferred temperature range prevails (see page 177), the tsetse attacks its victims from the shade of the forest fringe and savanna woodland. The arrival is silent, often noticed only when the insertion of the proboscis strikes a nerve. But of course it is not the tsetse itself which causes disease— the trypanosomes that transfer to the host's bloodstream while the fly takes its meal are the culprits.

Once inside the human body the trypanosomes breach the immune defences that normally eliminate malign intruders by constantly changing their coats. Trypanosomes are enveloped in a protective layer whose antigenic character they can change in order to frustrate the antibody response of their host. The host's immune response may destroy one wave of parasites, but the population recovers as trypanosomes with different antigenic qualities reproduce. Trypanosomes are capable of producing at least one hundred variable antigen types, and possibly even thousands.[6]

Though the trypanosomes can kill humans and cattle, the fly in which they hitch a ride to their host is unaffected. Likewise, trypanosomes do not cause sickness in the many species of antelope that they also parasitize. There are many situations in which host and parasite live in each other's presence indefinitely with no significant effect on the normal activity of either. Humans, for example, carry a massive population of bacteria in their lower intestines, with no noticeable ill effects. Such benign associations indicate a very long period of co-evolution, during which the parasite became totally dependent on its host, and the host developed immunological reactions (and in some instances even derives benefit from the association).

Trypanosomes, tsetse flies, and antelopes have all been present in Africa far longer than hominids. Their relationship doubtless was firmly established before even the ancestors of humanity moved from the forest (where the triad were not present) to the savanna (where they were). The fly was the principal beneficiary of the hominids' arrival and doubtless soon transferred trypanosomes from antelope to hominid. From the parasite's point of view, however, the introduction was counter-productive: when hosts died entire populations of parasites died with them. The hominids, for their part, kept away from tsetse-infested regions and so never acquired immunity. The strategy avoided the risk of trypanosomiasis, but also denied humans access to almost two-thirds of the potentially food-producing regions of sub-Saharan Africa.

While the trypanosomes restricted the growth and development of human populations in Africa by limiting the extent of land area available for them to occupy, the primary effect of other parasites has been to debilitate the people themselves, and thus lower their capacity to produce food. It has been claimed, for example, that where bilharzia is endemic the disease can cause an average loss of 40 per cent of an adult's capacity to work. A study of sugar-estate workers in Tanzania quantifies the point in more direct terms: workers infected with bilharzia earned at least 11 per cent less in bonuses than those who were not infected.[7]

Bilharzia, known medically as schistosomiasis, has a long record of association with humans. The parasite probably originated in Africa. Eggs of the schistosome fluke were found in the kidneys of two Egyptian mummies from the XXth dynasty (1200 BC),[8] and the parasite's complex—not to say devilishly elaborate—life cycle certainly suggests an extended process of co-evolution.

The fluke's life cycle involves water-snails as well as people, moving from one to the other through water, in two distinct free-swimming forms that seek out their snail and human hosts respectively. The egg that parasitizes the snail produces two or more generations of arrow-shaped schistosome larvae (called cercariae). Tiny, but readily visible with a magnifying glass, the larvae penetrate the skin of people who drink or frequent the infected waters, and pass into the bloodstream, where they develop into flukes up to 2 cm in length. The flukes lodge themselves in blood vessels around the intestines and bladder and begin producing numerous showers of eggs. Most of the sharply pointed eggs penetrate the bladder or intestinal walls and are discharged with the urine or faeces; those that find themselves in a watery environment seek out snail hosts and begin a new cycle. Eggs that fail to make their way from the body die and are washed back into the host's bloodstream, ultimately accumulating in the liver and spleen (and even the brain), causing enlargement and malfunction (those lodged in the brain often cause epilepsy).

Schistosome infestation is fatal to the snail. Among humans the disease peaks in childhood then persists in a debilitating but not necessarily lethal form for years thereafter. The disease occurs wherever standing water facilitates the propagation of the host snail. It is so commonplace that a brisk haemorrhage from the bladder was regarded as a sign of puberty in boys, analogous to menstruation in girls, a colonial medical officer reported from East Africa. He continued:

> The victims' bellies swell to accommodate a damaged, swollen liver; energy is replaced by apathy; the community becomes weighed down by its load of parasites and its industry languishes. Worse, a vicious circle sets in: less food is grown by these tired people; they come to suffer increasingly from malnutrition and lose hope . . . [9]

Hookworms, another parasite that evolved in Africa, are equally capable of debilitating a human population. A Unesco survey revealed an 80 per cent infestation rate among villagers and pygmies in the West African rainforest.[10] The worms themselves are about 1 cm long and inhabit the small intestine, where they attach themselves by means of their hooked teeth and live for several years sucking the blood of their host. One person may be host to thousands of worms; suffering bouts of abdominal pain, diarrhoea, and anaemia that could even lead to heart failure. Each female worm produces about 30,000 eggs per day. Deposited with the faeces, the eggs hatch, the larvae disperse and all that is required for their transfer to another human host is a misplaced foot. The larvae burrow through the skin and begin an incredible two-day journey to their final destination in the small intestine.

Adapted to inhibit immunological reaction, they travel with the bloodstream to the heart and then on to the lungs, where they break through the capillary walls and transfer from the bloodstream to the pneumonic system; from the lungs they crawl up the trachea (presumably secreting an anaesthetic that inhibits the cough reflex), across the larynx and into the pharynx, where they are swallowed and so reach the stomach. While acids and digestive enzymes break down most of the stomach's contents, the worms pass through unscathed, and finally lodge themselves in the small intestine.[11]

THE MICROSCOPIC, SINGLE-CELL ORGANISMS OF the genus *Plasmodium* that cause malaria in humans are probably among the oldest of human and prehuman parasites. They date from at least 60 million years ago and appear to have begun their careers in the guts of reptiles.[12] They were transferred to avian and mammalian species when susceptible predators ate an infected reptile, and ultimately evolved into a variety of forms, some of which entered the bloodstream, where they parasitized red cells. Blood-feeding insects are known from at least 55 million years ago, and the earliest clearly recognizable mosquitoes date from about 35 million years ago. At some indefinable date the *Plasmodium* parasite coopted the mosquito as a means of dispersing its numbers from host to host, and in due course all susceptible species were infected.

Among the 3,000 species of mosquito that are known, only a few of the *Anopheles* genus transfer the malaria parasite to humans and only via the female. She must have a meal of blood before she can lay eggs (the male is a vegetarian who dines on the nectar of flowers). Exhalations of carbon dioxide direct the bloodthirsty females to their victims, and moisture, warmth, and aroma enable them to choose a suitable point of attack. The proboscis which she thrusts into the skin actually consists of six slender probes; two are used to pierce the skin, two saw the wound open, and the third pair suck out the blood—but only after a minute quantity of anticoagulant saliva has been injected into the wound to prevent the blood clotting into an indigestible mass in her stomach.

In a single meal the female mosquito ingests about two and a half times her own weight in blood. If the feed contains malaria parasites, some will feed and grow and reproduce within the insect's body until they are ready for injection into a new human host with the anticoagulant saliva.

The arrangement does not cause the mosquitoes any distress. Their activities are not diminished by the parasites maturing within them, nor are their lives shortened. But then, if the *Plasmodium* is to reach a new human host, the mosquito carrying it must be vigorous enough to fly normally. A seriously sick mosquito simply could not fulfil its role in the malarial cycle. This benign association of mosquito and malarial parasite indicates that they have shared a process of co-evolution which extended over many millions of years. Humans became part of the cycle relatively recently, so they are correspondingly more severely affected by the malarial parasite.

In humans, the parasite's life cycle involves the periodic destruction of millions of red corpuscles, provoking waves of fever and debilitating weakness in the host as the parasites circulate freely in the bloodstream for a day or two before taking up residence again in new red corpuscles. Of the four different forms of *Plasmodium* that infect humans, one is far more virulent than the others. *Plasmodium falciparum* can kill, and almost always does in its most severe form, when the parasite invades the brain and causes cerebral malaria.

Falciparum malaria is the most common form of malaria in the tropics. In endemic zones nearly all children are infected by the time they are two years old.[13] Such widespread intensity can be partially explained by the fact that the parasite is carried from host to host by a female mosquito that feeds by preference on human rather than animal blood: *Anopheles gambiae*. This particular mosquito also prefers the kind of open, moist, and well-vegetated environments that people created as they began farming. Forest clearings increased the number of breeding places available to the mosquito. Indeed, *Anopheles gambiae* has been described as a "weed species" proliferating in the gashes that farmers made in the natural environment.[14]

With the advance of agriculture *Anopheles gambiae* supplanted mosquito species accustomed to feeding on creatures other than humans. Falciparum malaria attained unparalleled intensity but, while practically all newcomers to infested regions who are bitten are seriously affected, large numbers of permanent residents appear to escape its most deleterious effects—they have evolved a degree of resistance to the parasite.

In the human populations which have become resistant to malaria, the gene that determines the structure of red blood cells has mutated into a form which distorts the normally globular cells into a crescent or sickle shape. These cells rupture when the malaria parasite attempts to enter, thus denying the parasites a living site and reducing the debilitating effects of the malarial infection.

The advent of the sickle-cell gene is an evolutionary response to a changed environment, but its benefits are not without cost. The distorted sickle cells which deny parasites a living site also block capillaries and cause a variety of dangerous conditions, ranging from anaemia to heart failure. The dangers are particularly high among individuals who inherit the sickle-cell gene from both parents; most die in infancy from what is known as sickle-cell anaemia. Those who inherit the gene from just one parent, however, are resistant to malaria.

The selection process is severe, but acts to retain the sickle-cell gene: those who inherit the gene from both parents are liable to die from anaemia, and those without it may succumb to malaria. Both groups will be eliminated from the breeding population, while those who inherit a mixture of normal and sickle cells survive. The catch is, of course, that each breeding generation must contain a significant number of individuals who have survived malarial infection but do not have the sickle cell. This explains why the incidence of sickle cell does not exceed 20 per cent in susceptible populations.[15]

The sickle cell has been described as the first-known genetic response to an important event in human evolution.[16] That event, of course, was the development of agriculture, which brought people together in greater numbers than before and created settled communities. The nomadic foraging groups of early humans probably supported a range of parasites closely resembling that which infects the higher apes and they must have been exposed to the full range of disease present in the environment. But the small size and scattered distribution of foraging groups limited the capacity of any infection to become endemic, killing or seriously debilitating generation after generation. Modern estimates suggest that measles, for instance, requires a community of roughly half a million people with 7,000 susceptible individuals annually to sustain an endemic infection.[17] Among scattered foraging groups of no more than 150, a specific disease would disappear with the passing of the individuals it infected.

Agriculture, and permanent villages and towns, swept aside this natural limitation on the spread of disease. And the introduction of domesticated animals increased human exposure to disease even further. Most and probably all of the distinctive infectious diseases of civilization were transmitted to human populations from animal herds.[18] One source lists a total of 296 such diseases.[19] Measles, for example, is related to rinderpest; smallpox and cowpox are closely connected; and pigs harbour influenza.

The close confines of urban centres guaranteed both exposure to infection and sufficient numbers to sustain endemic disease. Towns and cities were decidedly unhealthy places (to cite a modern example: laboratory tests have shown that a typical Nigerian banknote harboured bacteria responsible for gastro-enteritis, boils, sties, and conjunctivitis).[20] Even in second-century Rome, average life expectancy was probably under twenty-five years.[21] Everyday life in pre-industrial towns and cities depended heavily on a large labour force, but the places were so unhealthy that until very recently, when improved sanitation and medical advances have dampened urban death rates, they could not maintain an adequate labour force without a substantial inflow of people from the surrounding countryside. Thus the establishment of urban centres not only relied upon rural populations to produce food above and beyond their own needs for consumption by the town-dwellers, the process also depended upon there being a surplus of children in rural areas, who would move into town and so sustain numbers. Thus rural communities were doubly blighted by the rise of urban centres, obliged to intensify food production on the one hand, denied the labour of their children on the other. Only the application of coercive force could have persuaded them to comply. It need not have been much, once Africa's unique prevalence of disease had begun to sap the energy of farming communities. Indeed, the power of the pharaohs probably rested on the fact that their subjects spent much of their lives paddling about in bilharzia-infested waters.

South of the Sahara, the same principle might have applied to the inland Niger delta and Jenne-jeno, except that developments there were among the first signs of intensified agricultural activity and urban settlement in sub-Saharan Africa. Disease had not yet tightened its grip. The seasonally changing character of the environment discouraged the establishment of large permanent settlements. As described in the previous chapter, people were kept apart by virtue of their occupations and their ethnic identities. Sedentary communities, though clustered, were dispersed. To an extent, the flood washed the place clean every year, and the dry season sterilized it.

Throughout the greater part of its evolutionary history, the human population of Africa has lived in relatively small groups, demonstrating that people are perfectly capable of living peacefully in small communities for millennia without establishing cities and states. Indeed, the most distinctively African contribution to human history has been precisely the civilized art of living fairly peaceably together *not* in states.[22] Since Africa was the cradle-land of humanity it would be comforting to believe that small peaceful communities were an ideal mode of existence. But of course, like everything else in human evolutionary history, small peaceful communities in Africa were an ecological expedience; ensuring survival in a hostile environment of impoverished soils, fickle climate, hordes of pests, and a more numerous variety of disease-bearing parasites than anywhere else on earth.

In Africa, people were constrained. Because they had evolved there as an expression of the continent's ecological diversity, in parallel with an infinite number of other organisms, any attempts to exploit the system to their exclusive benefit risked disaster and extinction. Their continued survival was a consequence of expedience, and of their ability to accommodate the ecological realities confronting them, including predators, parasites, and disease. The migrants who left the continent 100,000 years ago threw off the yoke. That is why they had multiplied from just hundreds to over 300 million by AD 1500 while the population of Africa had risen from 1 million to only 47 million.

CHAPTER 25

Successful Harvests

SUBSISTENCE FARMING IN Africa often demands more labour than can be fed with the food that farmers produce, but where conditions have been amenable, innovative agricultural practices have overcome this problem and established a highly successful community. Until comparatively recent times, elephants have been a major constraint on agricultural development in Africa.

The human population of Africa has never approached the size that the continent seems capable of supporting. Not in prehistory, when people lived exclusively from hunting and gathering, nor in AD 1500, when 99 per cent of the world's population was sustained by agriculture and the population of Africa stood at 47 million. In the view of agronomists at the International Institute of Tropical Agriculture,[1] Africa remains underpopulated even at the end of the second millennium, with a population approaching 900 million. Certainly the food-production potential of the continent has yet to be fully exploited. An FAO survey published in 1991 reported that only 22 per cent of land in Africa suitable for agriculture was actually in production (the comparable figure for south-east Asia is 92 per cent).[2]

Though Africa has extensive tracts of impoverished soils derived from ancient land surfaces, it also has the blessing of a varied native vegetation which evolved *in situ* and is therefore adapted to take best advantage of Africa's soils and highly variable climate. Foragers had long been familiar with the edible component of the continent's native vegetation; this experience became the

Elephant cows and calves in acacia thicket, Lake Manyara National Park, Tanzania

foundation of an indigenous African agriculture that was developed in Africa by Africans domesticating African plants.

The modern distribution of wild and domestic varieties indicates that Africa's indigenous crop plants were domesticated throughout a broad zone extending from the Atlantic to the Indian Ocean, primarily within the Sahel and savanna belt (see map 6, page 691).[3] The agricultural complex spread throughout Africa, and some elements even crossed the Indian Ocean. The drought-resistant sorghum and millet initially domesticated in Africa, for instance, subsequently became the staple food of millions in the drier region of India.

By virtue of its origins in the Sahel, Africa's indigenous agriculture was basically savanna agriculture, utilizing indigenous savanna plants, including cereals, pulses, roots and tubers, vegetables, oil crops, stimulants, medicines, and plants used for ritual purposes.

Sorghum is a savanna crop, domesticated in the Sahara region (see pages 163–64). So too is pearl millet, which is dominant along the Sahara fringe and among the most drought-resistant of all crops; African cotton is a savanna plant. African rice was domesticated from varieties that grow wild in savanna waterholes. Even yams, a staple food of people in the West African forest belt, were originally savanna plants, whose large tubers evolved to ensure survival through the dry season and periodic burning. The baobab and the tamarind are savanna trees; the oil palm was originally a tree of the forest margin which spread into the forest with the advance of shifting cultivation. The cowpea, the hyacinth bean, and the bambara groundnut are also plants from the forest margin. Indeed, the only true forest plants represented in the African agricultural complex are the kola nut (a stimulant), coffee, and malaguette (a spice and medicinal plant).

Unlike the pattern of agricultural development in the Near East, which can be traced to a specific area and the domestication of specific cereals and livestock, indigenous African agriculture developed over a wide area as a mosaic of crops, traditions, and techniques without a centre, nuclear area, or a single point of origin.[4] The distinction has important implications. Centralized coercive authority took control of affairs where agriculture was established in the Near East and beyond, and its rule was enshrined in the tenets of religious belief. In Africa, where unpredictable climates and widely varying environmental conditions called for a range of farming strategies, diversification was more appropriate than centralization: diversification of crops and the specialized knowledge required to grow them successfully; diversification of beliefs and ethnic identity, as the example of the inland Niger delta indicates (see pages 232–33).

The accommodations that Africa's indigenous agricultural system made to the problems of impoverished soils, an unpredictable climate and the effects of disease might appear to demonstrate that indigenous farmers in Africa had achieved a state of "biological equilibrium," wherein everyone was well fed and population levels remained stable, comfortably below the carrying capacity of the environment.

The Garden of Eden scenario is attractive: Africa as the paradise lost that the migrants turned their backs on 100,000 years ago. Africans learned how to live in balance with nature; they are the keepers of the fount, preserving the last vestiges of humanity's true and pure identity from the depredations of the migrants' descendants, who returned to plunder and despoil. The implication of the atavistic myth is that prior to the advent of foreign influences, Africans had achieved a higher order of association with the natural environment than humanity had forged elsewhere. That Africans are different. Left to itself, "Africa works."[5]

The genetic evidence convincingly demonstrates that Africans are no different from the rest of humanity. And the evidence of archaeology, human biology, and ethnology shows that African populations are subject to the same biological imperatives that have influenced the growth and development of human populations everywhere.

"Civilization is the daughter of numbers," wrote Fernand Braudel.[6] Applying the principle to Africa, the historian J. Ki-Zerbo has noted that:

> The very vastness of the African continent, with a diluted and therefore readily itinerant population living in a nature at once generous with its fruits and minerals, but cruel with its endemic and epidemic diseases, prevented it from reaching the threshold of demographic concentration which has almost always been one of the preconditions of major qualitative changes in the social, political and economic spheres.[7]

Watching a man with a hoe attack the hardened surface of land that has not seen rain for six months, the visitor begins counting the number of blows required to turn over a square metre of soil. Fourteen, twenty, twenty-eight— and even more where the job is made more difficult by perennial weeds and stout shrubs that must also be removed.

Three hectares of land (including fallow) is considered enough to feed a family and produce a surplus in any part of Africa where mixed agriculture is a viable option,[8] but the amount of labour required to keep that amount of land in production seriously restrains a family's ability to satisfy its needs. Pioneers clearing land for cultivation in the East African highlands invested up to 150 man-days of labour per hectare, according to anecdotal reports.[9] The annual round of planting and tending yam crops at typical locations in south-east Nigeria absorbed an average of 230 person/days per hectare.[10] Weeds are a curse. Cleared ground creates conditions for profuse growth, especially in the humid tropics. In recorded instances, African farmers devote up to 54 per cent of their total labour input to the tiresome business of weeding, a greater proportion than weeds demand of farmers in any other part of the world.[11]

A year-long study of energy expenditure among villagers cultivating clearings in the forest flanking the Gambia River in West Africa found that the effort required for some tasks exceeded the workers' physical capacity by more than 50 per cent. Their body weight rose following the harvest, when food and leisure time were plentiful, but fell steadily when land preparation began again and the workload increased. Food stocks diminished rapidly and were almost exhausted during the period leading up to the harvest, when the workload was most demanding. At any one time in the course of a year the villagers were either enjoying an excess of food or enduring a deficit, hardly ever in balance.[12]

Producing enough food to sustain the existing workforce is the first principle of subsistence agriculture. When production consistently fails to keep a community well-nourished, the seasonal round becomes a vicious circle: weakened by their inability to produce more food, farmers produce less and are trapped in a wearying struggle to prevent the circle becoming a downward spiral.

Nutritional deficiencies are particularly hard on childbearing women, whose pregnancies inevitably span at least one period when food is scarce and their workload high. The interval between births can be up to four years among women living under consistently stressful conditions (see page 122). In terms of a woman's reproductive effectiveness, extended birth intervals should not simply limit the number of children born, but also ensure that as many as possible survive. Even so, evidence from comparable situations in modern times shows that more than 30 per cent of infants probably died before reaching the age of five.[13] The result was that although women married and began bearing children soon after puberty, they raised far fewer to maturity during their reproductive lifespans than was theoretically possible.

Children were precious, and the drive to reproduce became a central feature of African culture and social order. Woodcarvers celebrated the fecundity of the round-bellied and full-breasted female form; fertile young women were valued members of the community that prospective husbands must pay for; polygynous marriages gathered several childbearing women together in a single economic unit; women prayed for children at priapic shrines in secret groves; society measured a man's standing by the number of children he had produced.

From the time that Europeans first set foot in Africa, travellers have commented upon what they saw as an excessive interest in sex among Africans. Though the comments could just as well indicate a no less acute interest in sex on the part of the commentators themselves, the emphasis on reproduction is more than adequately explained by the circumstances of the people concerned. With population growth rates adding no more than two or three per thousand to the human population each year, the separate but interdependent groups of farmers needed all the extra hands they could produce. This imperative of course fed back into the system: successful harvests produced surpluses that enabled farmers to buy more wives.

Assessments of subsistence farming in Africa that fail to take note of the constraints under which it operates have occasionally attributed the apparently undeveloped state of African agriculture to lethargy and an inability to innovate. The absence of the wheel and the plough from sub-Saharan Africa, for instance, is cited in a context suggesting inherent backwardness and ineptitude. A closer look shows that the wheel and the plough were never an option for the indigenous sub-Saharan farmer—not simply because many African soils are difficult to plough and domesticated draught animals would be susceptible to endemic disease; a more pressing reason was that feeding the animals would place unsustainable demands upon the food-production system.

In terms of the energy input and output budget of subsistence farmers in tropical Africa, human manual labour is far more efficient than an animal-drawn plough. Sorghum sown and tended manually produces fourteen times more energy than went into it, for instance, while the energy value of a crop produced with the help of oxen falls short of its cost.[14] The point is that for draught animals to have been a viable option, Africa's indigenous farmers needed ancillary crops equivalent to the highly nutritious and easily grown oats, turnips, and clover that revolutionized agriculture in Europe.[15]

In the absence of such benefits, Africa's farmers made extremely good use of the opportunities that were available to them. The specialized production systems and complex interrelationships of groups exploiting the resources of the inland Niger delta are an example (see pages 228–29). There are others. All the strategies for intensifying food production developed during the agricultural history of temperate zones were also developed in Africa, independently.

Archaeological evidence affirms that the building of terraces and irrigation canals in sub-Saharan Africa pre-dates external influence;[16] and there can be little doubt that crop rotation and the manuring of land has an equally ancient history.[17] Wherever appropriate conditions prevailed, Africa's farmers exploited the opportunity of intensifying food production. The opportunities were few, however, and always circumscribed by the prevalence of disease, but in at least one notable instance—on Ukara, an island in Lake Victoria—a community of sub-Saharan farmers built terraces and irrigation canals, rotated their crops, manured the land, stall-fed their cattle (and even grew forage to maximize manure production). According to oral histories, the overall population density of Ukara exceeded 200 people per square kilometre long before foreign agricultural advisers arrived on the scene. Homesteads in the main settlement were so close together that "fire could be passed without walking from one fireplace to another," it was said.

UKARA IS AN ISLAND lying off the south-eastern shore of Lake Victoria, part of what is now Tanzania. Roughly square in shape, it has a total land area of just under 80 km^2 and measures only 10 km across at its widest point. The total number of people living on the island has exceeded 16,000 at all times since the permanent farming systems of the island were first noted by German colonial authorities. Following World War I, Britain assumed control of the territory. German East Africa became Tanganyika. A census conducted on Ukara in 1925 recorded a population of 17,755;[18] in 1948 the figure was 16,501;[19] in 1957 the population stood at 16,052.[20]

Meanwhile, a constant stream of people had been leaving the island—between twenty and thirty families (approximately 140–210 individuals) every year, according to a district officer's report of 1934. Eighty-one families left in 1955, and another forty in the first six months of 1956. In 1975, a dubious piece of government policy forcibly removed 1,000 families from Ukara, but still the official census of 1988[21] recorded a total of 16,546 people living permanently on the island.

The population of Ukara remained constant despite significant emigration. Not only was the island able to sustain an exceptionally high rural population density, it also produced a surplus population that moved out and settled elsewhere. In effect, Ukara has been exporting people from the island at least since records began and probably for centuries before. "It was always like that," said Manyasi Burimbe, a sixty-three-year-old farmer whose Ukaran origins go back to the beginning of traditional accounts. "My people were always on Ukara," is his answer to the visitor who asks "How long?," though scholarly evaluation supposes that the island was initially a refuge for people escaping slave-raiders and warring neighbours, and became densely settled only in the seventeenth century.[22]

There is no spare land awaiting clearance and cultivation on Ukara; nor has there been for as long as records are available. The first survey was conducted by the German colonial authorities and published in 1913.[23] In 1934 a British district officer noted that the island was practically devoid of natural vegetation, "except [for] a weak growth of grass between the boulders on the hills";[24] and a 1968 survey based on aerial photography showed that 98.6 per cent of the total land area of the island was being used. Only 1.4 per cent was unproductive—consisting of rocky outcrops, sandy river-courses, settlements, and small areas rendered worthless by erosion. Of the land area 73.6 per cent was rain-fed, and devoted predominantly to millets (traditionally the staple crop, but overtaken by cassava in the 1980s); 6.7 per cent was irrigated land producing rice and vegetables; 18 per cent was grazing land; and 0.3 per cent meadows producing cattle fodder.

The irrigated terraces laid out along the island's rivers consist of deep soils, rich in organic matter, but soils on the greater part of the island's land surface are derived from the Precambrian core of the island: acid, deficient in nutrients, so coarse and sandy that a farmer's iron hoe-blade is worn to nothing in a year. Rainfall averaging 1,500 mm per year is sufficient to produce a crop on the rain-fed land even in dry years, but the inherently poor soils could support continuous cropping only with careful management.

Each household farms an average of about 2.5 hectares in total, which is divided into about ten plots held at various locations. Millet rotated with bambara nuts (*Voandazeia subterranea,* an indigenous African groundnut similar to peanuts) and other nitrogen-fixing legumes, and a proportion of plots were left fallow for one or more seasons. Between seasons farmers sowed green manures, selecting from a number of leguminous plants whose dense cover protected the ground from erosion and was dug in when showers had moistened the soil. These measures notwithstanding, however, the greatest contribution to the soil's resilience was the regular application of animal manure. Cattle and manure are the key to the success of the strategies developed on Ukara.

Each household ideally possessed at least three or four head of cattle, whose primary purpose in life was to supply manure for the fields. Milk and meat, though consumed appreciatively, were in effect the by-products of a manure production system. The cattle were (and still are) housed in stables consisting of circular stone-lined pits almost one metre deep and roofed with thatch. The animals were tethered to the central roof support-post and fed twice a day on a diet of grass, leaves, weeds, and crop residues. They almost never left the stable. Their manure accumulated, and in four to six months filled the pit to ground level. The cattle were then led to pasture for a day or two (muzzled to prevent them snacking on someone else's land along the way), and the manure removed from the pit and piled up to compost.

There were no carts or pack animals on Ukara. People transported the manure to the fields in baskets carried on their heads. A single basket-load of manure weighed 15 kg, and the members of a typical family between them carried eleven baskets of manure to the fields each day: a total daily load of 165 kg. In the course of a year their cattle provided about 20 tonnes of manure, enough to ensure that each field was manured every two to three years. And the amount of work involved ensured that the Wakara each spent an average of more than ten hours per day on agricultural tasks throughout the year.

On the return journey each basket was filled with fodder for the cattle. Water-meadows are a particularly important source. The Wakara are the only people in the African tropics known to practise water-meadow farming. Flooded terraces along sections of the island's principal rivers maintain a permanently moist strip of land that is sown with forage grasses. Close to the lake shore, pits have been dug down to the water-table, and these too are sown with grasses. The pits may be up to four metres deep, and some cover an area of 50 by 100 metres. Planting on the water-table guarantees moisture year-round, and growth is further boosted by flooding the pits with water channelled from the lake. The cultivated fodder consists primarily of elephant grass (*Pennisetum purpureum*), which grows to the height of a man in a matter of weeks and can be cut four times each year.

Trees are another important source of fodder for the cattle and it is remarkable that while firewood demands have stripped rural areas bare of trees throughout Africa, Ukara remains notably wooded. Indeed, a visitor will be struck by the contrast. Mature trees up to fifteen and twenty metres high line the trackways (there are no made roads on Ukara) and offer refuges of deep shade beside streams and in the folds of the uplands; saplings flank cultivated plots; each homestead is surrounded by trees—and all this living wood on a tiny, densely populated island where trees are a source of cattle fodder, building materials *and* firewood. What is the explanation?

The fact that every tree is privately owned ensures that the use of this indispensable resource is sustainable. Every tree is protected by vested interest. Indeed, the ownership of some trees is shared among as many as three individuals. Trees are rented for their leaf harvest. Building poles, timber, and firewood are bartered and sold. Every individual has an interest in trees, both as owner and utilizer, and it is in everyone's interest to ensure that the crucial renewable resource does indeed renew itself.

The same principle of private interest applies to the land. With the exception of springs, river and pond water, communal buildings, and the main trackways between villages, every square metre of the island is privately owned.

Even the rocky outcrops and the bushes around them belong to known individuals.

Traditional systems of land tenure among indigenous farmers throughout Africa granted only rights of use—rights that could be revoked, or were forfeited if the land was left uncultivated. Africa's indigenous farmers were more concerned about using land than owning it.[25] By contrast, all the land on Ukara belonged to individual families and could be sold or even left uncultivated with impunity. Ownership was vested in the oldest male in the family, who divided the property among his sons when they established families of their own. In some instances the repeated division of land ultimately reduced plots to the size of squash courts, but prudent marriages (often arranged while the partners were still infants) consolidated holdings too.

There were no chiefs or centralized authority on Ukara that dictated how people should manage the land. The system had evolved in response to the limitations of the environment and functioned to serve the needs of individual families. Community was a secondary matter, and the resource base was neither big enough nor rich enough to encourage the emergence of a ruling elite or even a centralized authority.

THOUGH A SHORTAGE OF land stimulated the development of intensive and sustainable agricultural strategies on Ukara, there were other factors contributing to its success. The absence of the tsetse fly and trypanosomiasis, for instance, enabled the islanders to keep cattle. Stabling obviated the danger of fevers that have made cattle-dips and vaccination obligatory elsewhere. The prevalence of human disease on Ukara in historical times is not quantified, but the rate of population growth certainly suggests that infant mortality was low.

Over and above such factors, the absence of wild animals was especially important. There were no dangerous carnivores on the island, nor any of the large herbivores for whom standing crops are an irresistible attraction. Elephants in particular have severely hindered the development of indigenous subsistence agriculture throughout Africa.

Elephants dominated the African landscape throughout the evolutionary history of humanity. Cohabitation verging on shared destiny has given the elephant a position of respect—even reverence—in people's minds. The Mende of West Africa, for instance, believed that their ancestors were elephants and that people became elephants when they died. Elsewhere, folklore tells of wild seed in neat packages of elephant dung initiating the domestication of cereals and the first tentative steps towards agriculture. Thereafter the relationship changed, principally because elephants and Africa's early farmers were competitors with identical preferences. Farmers were attracted to precisely those areas which elephants most wanted; conversely, there was little elephants liked more than a crop of grain or roots ready for harvest.

For centuries, much of Africa's potential farmland was a continuously changing patchwork of mutually exclusive human and elephant occupation zones, with the elephant limiting opportunities for agricultural expansion and thus restraining the growth of the human population. The situation was reversed only in modern times.

> Geographers on Afric Maps
> With savage Pictures fill their Gaps
> O'er uninhabitable Downs
> Place Elephants for want of Towns.

Jonathan Swift doubtless was taking a satirical swipe at early-eighteenth-century cartographers when he jotted down these lines but, if the author of *Gulliver's Travels* (published in 1726) had read William Bosman's *New and Accurate Description of the Coast of Guinea* (published in 1705), he would have known that the Gaps were real, and the uninhabited if not uninhabitable Downs were exactly where elephants were most likely to be found.

William Bosman had gained first-hand experience of the geography and society of the West African coastal regions over a period of fourteen years at the end of the seventeenth century. He had noted that "the wilder and less inhabited the Lands are, the larger Quantity of Elephants and wild Beasts are found"; there were fewer between Ante and Accra, he reported, "because this Place hath long been reasonably well-peopled," except for the country of Fetu, which had lain almost waste for the past five or six years "wherefore there is a much larger number of Elephants there at present than formerly."[26]

The distribution of elephants is thus an indicator of the relationship between African populations and their natural environment during historical times.[27] The changing pattern of town and village sites in Ghana, for instance, suggests that communities there never quite succeeded in establishing a long-term equilibrium with their environment. Instead, "a sort of chessboard effect" developed, with people occupying one set of squares and elephants the other. Each human settlement was surrounded by a zone of potential farmland, not more than one-sixth of which was in production at any one time, while the rest was lying fallow and steadily became covered in thick secondary bush.

Elephants feeding on lush secondary growth on fallow land inevitably were also attracted to the fresh young crops sprouting from adjacent cultivated fields, and communities barely large enough to provide the labour needed to feed themselves would be incapable of keeping elephants from all their scattered fields, all the time. The result was that wherever people settled and began growing crops the elephant became a major constraint on agricultural expansion and human population growth.

ELEPHANTS LIVE AN AVERAGE MAXIMUM of about sixty-five years. Puberty in females occurs at eleven to twelve years, the gestation period is twenty-two months and females are fertile up to the age of forty-nine years.[28] These and other relevant factors give elephants a theoretical maximum potential population growth rate of 7 per cent per annum.[29] The elephant population of the Addo National Park in South Africa (where the animals are fed and completely protected from poachers and other dangers) has grown from 100 in 1979 to 212 in 1995,[30] an annual rate of increase of just over 5 per cent. And even in Kenya's Amboseli basin, where they are entirely dependent on natural resources and have been subject to human harassment, elephant numbers rose from 400 to 800 between the 1970s and the 1990s, with immigration from surrounding areas contributing only about forty animals to that rise.

Darwin chose the elephant as an example that would demonstrate the basis and function of natural selection. In *The Origin of Species* he pointed out that although the elephant was the slowest breeder of all known animals, its minimum rate of natural increase would produce a standing population of 15 million individuals from a single breeding pair in just five hundred years.[31] Since elephants were nowhere near as numerous as they could be, Darwin reasoned that some natural process must be controlling their numbers.

Modern studies of the ecology and behaviour of African elephants have shown that access to water is the principal mechanism by which natural selection controls elephant numbers. Disease and predation take their toll, but the effects are slight compared with the massive die-offs that occur in times of drought. Elephants consume 150 kg of vegetation daily and must drink at least every second day. As vegetation is depleted in the immediate vicinity of waterholes and rivers, the distance between browse and water increases by the day. Driven more by thirst than hunger, all the animals grow weak from lack of food as they trek back and forth between food and water; the old, the ill, and the very young die. When the long rains failed to replenish water supplies in Kenya's Tsavo East National Park in 1971, the distances between water and browse reached a peak of 48 km. Of 13,500 elephants in the park before the drought, at least 3,000 died.[32]

The concentration of elephants in Tsavo East in 1971 was partially artificial, brought about by the expansion of farming activities in surrounding areas.

This in itself serves to demonstrate that a principle of "competitive exclusion"[33] applies to the relationship between farmers and elephants: when two species simultaneously exploit the same resource, competition becomes more acute as the population of either increases, until a point is reached at which one of them either moves away or becomes extinct.

Except where agriculture developed, people did not compete with elephants for resources. Early hunting and gathering groups certainly killed elephants for meat when they could, but did not impinge upon the needs of the elephant population; and the relationship between nomadic pastoralists and elephants was mutually facilitative, in that elephants converted bush country to grassland, while the nomads' cattle in turn stimulated the regrowth of bush preferred by elephants.

Farmers, by contrast, were in direct competition with elephants. Their preferred habitats were the same: medium to high rainfall regimes, soils capable of producing edible vegetation, and access to drinking water. Thus agriculture in Africa advanced at the expense of the elephant's population size and range.[34] Every hectare cultivated was a hectare lost to elephants. Conversely, since elephants found virtually all human food crops palatable, they inhibited expansion of the farmers' population size and range.

Early farmers had recourse to spears, arrows, poison, fire, and noise, and they could dig pit-traps, but their capacity to keep a herd of hungry elephants at bay was always compromised by an inadequacy of numbers. In short, elephants compounded the problems of labour shortages and unpredictable environmental circumstances already restraining the development of agriculture in Africa and, from earliest times, were therefore a formidable obstacle to human population growth and expansion on the continent.

In the Great Lakes region of central Africa, where land and climate suited both the agricultural ambitions of farmers and the natural preferences of elephants, oral histories recount how farmers succeeded in raising crops to maturity only when their fields were close together and the local community was large enough to supply the people needed to repel raiding elephants. Lone farmers stood little chance, and if conflict or disease reduced a community's manpower, elephants rapidly completed its collapse.

The "elephant problem" was a major concern of colonial authorities throughout Africa. In Uganda, firearms and free ammunition were issued to farmers, who were encouraged to kill marauding elephants. The policy ran from 1912 to 1921, when it was deemed to have failed—despite the death of several thousand elephants. Professional white hunters were hired, but even their increased rate of slaughter failed to moderate the elephant problem. In

1925 the government established an elephant-control department, which was soon renamed the Uganda Game Department although, for the next forty years, the killing of elephants remained its primary function.

It was not until the 1950s that the principle of competitive exclusion finally began to tip the balance in favour of people over elephants. In East Africa, where the process has been most thoroughly documented, elephants ranged across 87 per cent of the region in 1925. By 1950 their range had been reduced to 63 per cent and in 1975 it stood at 27 per cent. In 1925, people farmed islands in a sea of elephants. The islands expanded and coalesced until in 1975 elephants occupied fragmented and shrinking islands in a sea of people. By the turn of the century elephants will be extinct in all but the National Parks and the few forested and otherwise challenging areas where farming is impractical. The rise in human population densities mirrors the decline in elephants with such precision that the nadir of the elephant is predictable. Taking rainfall and environmental factors into account, calculations show that elephants in Zimbabwe face extinction when human population density reaches 18.9 people per km^2. In Kenya the figure is 82.5 per km^2.

The authors of the provocative study from which the details of the above paragraphs are taken claim that it was not ivory poaching which caused the calamitous decline of elephant population throughout Africa during the 1980s. It was the sheer force of human numbers, they say.[35] Ivory was merely a by-product of the struggle between farmers and elephants that had been going on in sub-Saharan Africa for more than 2,000 years.

CHAPTER 26

The Implications of Trade

CROPS, CATTLE, AND IRON formed the matrix around which African society and economy developed. A gerontocratic social order prevailed. Salt probably stimulated the first instances of long-distance trade between groups; camels facilitated the exploitation of Sahara deposits.

The generally hostile and unpredictable environment of sub-Saharan Africa inspired a highly conservative approach to the business of making a living. Sustaining existing levels of population was difficult enough, and the communities which endured were those that directed available energies primarily towards minimizing the risk of failure, not maximizing returns. For them, innovation and change were unacceptable risks. But conservativism need not imply stagnation.

The examples of Ukara and the inland Niger delta, though special cases, amply demonstrate a significant potential for innovation and social transformation. Elsewhere in sub-Saharan Africa, where circumstances were less propitious, that potential was expressed through social systems that persistently defied the trend towards coercive centralized control and the formation of states. And they functioned for 1,000 years. Indeed, remnants are still evident at the end of the twentieth century, despite a second thousand years of external interference—faded but still interpretable images of the political order that once dominated human society in all of sub-Saharan Africa.

Tuareg herdsmen wait to water their camels at Tchin-Tabaradene, on the southern Sahara, Niger

Constant movement was its primary characteristic. The seasonal round kept nomadic foragers and pastoralists on the move, while the demands of shifting agriculture committed even the ostensibly sedentary farmers to a cycle of periodic resettlement which, in turn, was assisted by the iron-makers, whose demands for charcoal were an incentive to clear new areas of forest. Many if not most of the numerous communities that marked the spread of the cropping, herding and iron-making complex throughout Africa formed initially around small groups who moved from established communities to the relatively unpopulated frontiers.[1] The movements could be local, or they could involve migration to frontiers a considerable distance from the original community.

Two factors shaped the social order of the new group: the traditions they brought with them, and the principle of precedence, of being first, that bestows legitimate authority in African societies.[2] Immigrant groups constantly sought to recreate the social order of the parent community they had moved away from, but variations inevitably arose in the course of their efforts to define a physical space and identity for themselves in relation to the land and to other groups who were already settled in the vicinity. In such cases the social order that developed was not solely a consequence of internal influences. It was significantly shaped and changed by external factors—by the social and cultural relations between the source area and the frontier, and by the size and organization of any societies already inhabiting the frontier region. Some hierarchical systems evolved, for instance, from the willing tendency of new immigrants to adopt positions of subservience to groups that had initially settled in an area.[3]

The emergence of a hierarchical system could in turn signal the emergence of lineages to whom the principle of precedence granted status above the rest of the community. And this development gave rise to the institution of chieftaincy. Chiefs had status, but little authority or power over the community in general, beyond the respect they may have earned in their everyday dealings. Indeed, as though to counter the frictions likely to arise if authority and power were vested in certain chiefs and lineages and thus flowed vertically, from the few at the top to the majority at the bottom, a system emerged whereby authority and power were spread horizontally throughout the group as a whole, touching every lineage and family. This was the age-grade system: a political structure uniquely suited to the social and economic conditions of sub-Saharan Africa.

The age-grade system divided all males into groups, each of which included all individuals within a particular range of ages (the range often covered five, seven, or fourteen years). Each group was allocated a standard set of social and political duties. As individuals advanced in years they changed duties until those surviving had progressed through the complete set. Thus the system sustained no permanent or hereditary rulers or office-holders.

A widely known example of the age-grade system is the moran age-set of the Maasai in East Africa, whose duty was to keep cattle and community safe. Overall control of the moran, however, lay with the elders—men who had been moran themselves in the recent past and now had the authority to impose their political judgement upon the actions of the moran.

The rites of passage through which individuals were conveyed from one age-set to the next were timed to occur simultaneously among groups over a wide area, each group giving the event its own distinctive character. Above Tii, a Dogon village on the Bandiagara escarpment in Mali, a cleft in the rock face opened on to a cave then narrowed again to an exit on the far side. "Our operating theatre," said Martin, a beneficiary of higher education. "You went in through the entrance as a boy and left through the exit on the other side as a man." It was a one-way, one-time experience—deeply symbolic. No boy passed through the cave before his moment of circumcision was decreed; no man ever made a reverse journey through it.

Individuals with qualities of leadership and astute judgement emerged in each age-set, but their talents were converted to power or authority only at the behest of the age-set, and exercised only with its prior approval, not by their individual right. Some individuals acted so effectively on behalf of the community as they progressed through the senior age-sets that they achieved the status of wise men, whose judgements were universally respected.

With its respect for the wisdom and judgements of the oldest members in a group, the age-group system established gerontocracy as the dominant form of political organization in sub-Saharan Africa. Since it was mutually recognizable among different groups, regardless of their origin or present status, the age-group system deposed the vertical authority of family lines, transcended the divisive nature of ethnic boundaries, and even provided a basis for compatible interaction between groups speaking different languages.

Gerontocracy was in fact a unifying characteristic of sub-Saharan Africa, holding in its thrall the numerous distinct groupings that had emerged among people living in generally hostile and fickle environments. Respect for the elders and their way of doing things was the essence of the principle. This was not an attitude that encouraged innovation or change. Indeed, Africa's gerontocratic form of social and political organization was (and remains) highly conservative, which, of course, explains why it and the cropping, herding, and iron economy on which it was so firmly ensconced remained unchanged and functionally efficient for so long.

The abiding strength of the gerontocratic system was that it functioned on a basis of compromise not coercion, and was disseminated by a process of consent, not conquest.

Aggressive and avaricious behaviour among the early farmers of sub-Saharan Africa was controlled by the authority of the elders, and even enmity the elders might have deemed justifiable was controlled by the limited availability of warriors and weapons. It was a matter of costs and benefits, and minimizing the risk of failure. Among communities already pressed by constraints of population size and environmental circumstance, none could afford to lose the people, time, and weapons that serious conflict demanded. People possessed clubs, bows and arrows, and spears, true, but these were articles of value used in acquiring food. They were neither so numerous nor so easily replaced that their availability as provisioning tools could be risked in conflict with the neighbours—no matter how aggravating their behaviour.

The historian Leonard Thompson has noted: "There are no traditions of devastating warfare among the mixed farming people in Southern Africa before the nineteenth century."[4] And in the last decade of the nineteenth century itself, when Africa was in the throes of colonial annexation, Frederick Lugard, then advancing British interests in East Africa, noted in his diary that "when Wakikuyu fight a man gets his skull cracked perhaps at most. If the British fight, and bring guns many many men die."[5] This unfamiliar aversion for death-dealing conflict does not imply that the indigenous people of sub-Saharan Africa were universally peaceful. Raiding was evident across the continent and throughout the first millennium, raiding for cattle, for goods, and possibly for women.[6]

A typical village of around AD 500 made no provision for defence, however, beyond providing enclosures for the protection of livestock. At the Broederstroom site in southern Africa,[7] houses of any one period were scattered in a random pattern about an area of perhaps 200 metres in diameter. As houses reached the end of their useful life, they were abandoned and new ones built on the fringe of the village, so that the occupied area moved progressively eastward. The circular houses were up to six metres in diameter, made of wattle and daub, with a stamped dung floor and occasionally a fireplace in the centre. Under the floor of some houses there were dung-lined pits which were used to store grain.[8] Rubbish tips, ash heaps and graves have been identified; slag heaps and the remains of furnaces denote the presence of iron-workers; but there is no evidence that market places or professional merchants were a feature of African village life in the sixth century AD.

So long as barter remained the principal means of exchange in sub-Saharan Africa, trade did not stimulate the emergence of professional merchants.[9] Individuals and groups exchanged produce and services directly among themselves, item for item: a week's labour for a share of the harvest; a goat for a hoe. The barter trade was mostly between local communities, mostly in essentials, but isolated exotic items found at a number of sites indicate that these local links were connected to networks that spanned the continent. Sites excavated in the Tsodilo Hills on the northern fringe of the Kalahari, for instance, contained glass beads from the Indian Ocean coast and shells from the Atlantic—unequivocal evidence of indigenous transcontinental travel.[10]

But it was the goods that travelled across Africa, not the traders. The nonessential items and foreign durables found at sites remote from their points of origin were traded from village to village, in relays, as part of what was certainly a vigorous trade in essential goods between local centres. There is an important distinction to be made between local and long-distance trade.[11] Local trade refers to transactions which took place within distances which could be covered in one day by foot or by donkey, while still allowing time to exchange goods and return home—about sixteen kilometres from the area of production. Beyond this radius it was necessary to make arrangements for overnight stops, to reallocate work in the household, and sometimes even to hire people to help with the load.

Additional effort meant that the returns had to be proportionally greater, so that long-distance trade was feasible only if it involved rare items of high value or substantial volumes of low-value goods. And even then the barter system's lack of a common negotiable currency meant that traders always faced the risk of having to exchange goods for items they did not want.

Local trade, on the other hand, was part and parcel of the social and food-production systems that evolved among communities. The farmers, herders, and fishermen of the inland Niger delta, each pursuing their specialized activity to the exclusion of all others, depended absolutely upon the exchange of produce between the groups (see pages 231–33). And even among apparently more homogeneous communities, in regions where the opportunities for food production were the same over a wide area, even here there were inequalities. Not all farmers were equally competent. For some, the strategy of planting enough to survive the poor years regularly produced a surplus during average years. Others failed to produce all they needed even in good years.

Local barter systems enabled communities to balance these inequalities. Surpluses were made available to those in deficit, either by an exchange of goods or services, or in charitable distributions, at harvest festivals or similarly ritualized ceremonies. It is unlikely that the perfect balance hypothesized here ever pertained for long—if at all. Avarice and greed are certain to have been as manifest among sub-Saharan Africa's indigenous farmers as they are in the modern world of industry and high finance. But imperfections and abuses were contained. The unpredictabilities of production and an inescapable need to barter for essentials, for instance, limited the likelihood of individuals or groups accumulating wealth in a form and quantity that would enable them to control the lives of others. Furthermore, the collective authority of the age-set dampened overreaching ambition.

Thus local trade had the capacity to reinforce both the integrity and interdependence of groups. Goods and services were paid for in local "currency" and circulated within the system. As long as there was no external drain on resources the political order of participating communities was impregnable. But no system was entirely self-contained; there were always some essential items that must be acquired from far afield. Glass beads and shells from distant shores were dispensable trinkets that hardly caused a ripple as they moved from centre to centre through the relay trade network. Other items were more disruptive: iron and copper, for instance, but most especially salt. In many instances salt travelled long distances between source and consumer, exciting the entrepreneurial interest of ambitious individuals along the way. Ultimately, the demand for salt broke the barriers of self-sufficiency.[12]

THROUGHOUT HISTORY AND around the world, salt has been the most sought-after food supplement known. Indeed, it has been described as humanity's earliest addiction—"the primordial narcotic."[13] Wherever salt was not readily available, the desire for it has been a strong incentive for the development of trade. Although direct evidence is lacking, it is generally assumed that the distribution of salt marked out the earliest and most frequently travelled long-distance routes in Africa. Certainly they were sufficiently well defined by the sixteenth century for Portuguese explorers to make a practice of following the salt routes into the interior.[14]

The constituents of salt, sodium and chloride, are critical to many physiological functions and must be replaced when lost in urine or sweat. A daily intake of about 12 gm will meet the requirements of an average person, even in tropical regions, where acclimatization substantially reduces the amount of salt lost in sweating. Most people get enough salt from their everyday diet—especially those who consume relatively high proportions of milk and meat, which are naturally saltier than vegetable foods. Consequently, Africa's nomadic herders had less need of supplementary salt than sedentary farming populations. On the other hand, their stock required relatively large quantities of salt, regularly. So, although the nomads needed less salt themselves, the needs of their stock obliged them to know where salt was available in large quantities.

In turn, the animals provided the means of transporting supplies of salt to people who had none. A source, a market, and a means of travelling between the two was the basis of long-distance trade.

Wherever people have developed a taste for salt, they consume more than their physiological requirement. A history of salt production and trade in the central Sudan sets a figure of 4.5 kg as the average amount of supplementary salt consumed per person per year in the region.[15] At this rate a community of 250 people required just over one tonne of salt each year. Amounts used to preserve food and for medicinal purposes probably doubled the requirement, and the needs of livestock would have doubled it again.[16] Thus, to cover all its needs, a community of 250 people required at least four tonnes of salt per year. One thousand people required sixteen tonnes; one million required 16,000 tonnes.

By the time the Bantu farmers had dispersed from their cradle-land (see pages 183–84) throughout sub-Saharan Africa, and the cropping, herding, and iron complex was established as the dominant way of life, the total number of people using salt cannot have been much less than 10 million. The annual salt requirement of 10 million people would be 160,000 tonnes. On the backs of donkeys, which are capable of carrying about 50 kg, this yearly requirement amounted to over 3 million loads. For the human porters who were employed where the tsetse fly and lack of pasture militated against the use of pack animals, the annual salt-budget represented 8 million loads. For camels, it was 800,000 loads.

The sources of salt in Africa are in no way distributed to the convenience of the human population. Indeed, by definition, saline regions are precisely the places that people in general and farmers in particular would avoid. Crops do not thrive in salty conditions. And since salt production and marketing did not readily combine with farming activities it attracted a cohort of specialists and generated a fraternity of traders.

The oceans contain a 3.5 per cent solution of various salts, of which 2.5 per cent is sodium chloride. On tidal flats, on lagoons and estuaries around the continent, wherever conditions were conducive, people built shallow dams or channelled sea water into ponds and produced salt by solar evaporation. In equatorial regions, where higher levels of humidity, cloud cover and rainfall made solar evaporation impractical, salt-makers were obliged to boil sea water. William Bosman reported that people on the coast of Guinea used "earthen pots, which they set ten or twelve next another; thus making two rows, being all cemented together with clay, as if they had been done by a bricklayer, and under the pots is something like a furnace of fire."[17] Salt production in these circumstances was a time-consuming and labour-intensive process, involving not only the salt-makers themselves, but also potters and woodcutters.

Away from the coast, people throughout the savanna regions made salt from a grass, *Zaleya pentandra,* which grows on saline soils and accumulates salt in its stalks. The grass was burned, the ash dissolved and the solution repeatedly filtered and boiled until only a residue of salt remained (vegetable salt is also derived from crop residues and dried dung).[18] Salt was extracted from saline soils by a similar process of dilution, filtration, and boiling.[19]

Wherever they occurred, saline springs were also exploited (by either evaporation or boiling), though their sodium chloride content was often very low—less than one-quarter of that of sea water in the case of springs in the Benue region of Nigeria.[20] Salt-makers at Kibero, on the Ugandan shore of Lake Albert in East Africa, increased the salt concentration of their spring in carefully tended *ebibuga,* meaning "salt-gardens."[21] Loose dry earth was spread over moist salt-impregnated surfaces each morning and scraped up again each evening. During the day the dry earth absorbed saline moisture from the ground, which in turn evaporated in the sun. Over a period of days the salinity of the earth increased to the point at which salt could be leached from it in quantity, after which the soil was dried and the process started afresh. In effect the salt-makers at Kibero "farmed" salt.

The Kibero salt works have been in production for under 1,000 years, according to the archaeological evidence. Eight hundred kilometres due south, brine springs rising from underlying volcanic formations around the confluence of the Malagarasi and Ruchugi rivers near Uvinza in western Tanzania have been exploited for over 1,500 years. The Uvinza brine is abundant and concentrated, and so pure that it needs no filtering; partially evaporated in shallow clay tanks, then boiled in large earthenware pots, it produced a fine white salt that made the region a centre of commerce. "A very good white salt, the best of any I have seen in Africa," remarked Verney Lovett Cameron, a traveller who passed through Uvinza in 1874 while searching for David Livingstone. "This salt is carried far and wide . . . There are some other places in these districts where salt is produced, but that of Uvinza is so superior that it always finds a ready sale."[22]

The production and distribution of salt stimulated economic activity throughout sub-Saharan Africa, but its effects were most profoundly evident on the fringes of the Sahara desert, along the broad swathe of Sahelian grassland that extends from the Atlantic Ocean to the Red Sea, and south into the forests of West Africa.

The Sahara desert is the greatest repository of salt on the continent. When the lakes and waterways which characterized the Sahara landscape during the wet period began to dry out with the onset of less humid conditions, the receding waters leached salts from the soil and the lake waters became increasingly saline. In effect, desiccation transformed lake basins into immense salt pans. The lake that filled the basin north of Bilma in Niger 10,000 years ago was at least 120 km long and 20 km wide, for instance; as it dried out, the lake bed became permeated with salt at concentrations of around 50 per cent to depths of more than six metres. The total quantity of salt deposited in the lake basin is estimated to be more than 1 million tonnes and possibly as much as 6 million tonnes.[23]

Similarly vast Saharan salt deposits are located at Taoudeni and Teghaza in northern Mali, and at Tichitt in Mauritania . . . high-quality salt in plenty. The pity for sub-Saharan Africa's indigenous farmers was that it was located so far away, in the heart of the Sahara, where neither food nor water was regularly available for man or beast, and working conditions were appalling.

PICTURES OF CARTS ENGRAVED OR painted on rocks in the southern Sahara indicate that the region's artists were familiar with the concept of wheeled transport in the last centuries BC, but anyone who has attempted to ride a bicycle through dry sand must doubt that trans-Saharan traders made much use of the idea. Even the beasts pulling the carts would have found the going difficult, and would have transported loads more efficiently on their backs than in carts towed behind. If carts did cross the Sahara (rather than just an artist's impression of them), logic demands that the traffic must have been very light. In fact, of the thousand or so known sites of rock-drawings in the Sahara and its approaches, only about fifty have representations of wheeled transport—and they all look more like racing chariots than traders' carts. Furthermore, the images become more and more abstract as the distance from the Mediterranean increases.[24] In the most realistic of the rock-paintings, the chariots were drawn by horses rather than oxen—which would have been the most effective draught animals.

The skeleton of a horse found at the ancient Egyptian settlement of Buhen dates from about 1675 BC, and from this time onwards the horse was associated with high status, and with the ceremonial chariot so frequently shown in the art of ancient Egypt, Greece, and Rome. The horse certainly would have been known in North Africa during the same period, but its advent in sub-Saharan Africa is uncertain. Linguistic evidence suggests the horse crossed the Sahara at least 2,500 years ago.[25] A few teeth found in association with pottery from about 2,000 years ago could indicate the contemporary presence of domesticated horses, or they could have come from a zebra. The earliest irrefutable evidence of horses in sub-Saharan Africa comes from Arabic texts, beginning with the writings of Al-Muhallabi from about AD 985. By then, however, the horse was a highly valued prestige animal, and camels were the vehicle of trans-Saharan trade.

Archaeological evidence indicates that relays of Berber nomads were trading goods across the Sahara from Phoenician times (see page 187), but the evidence is scanty, suggesting once again that the volume was slight. The arrival of the camel opened a new dimension of opportunity. Indeed, the camel might have been the best means of getting a cart across the desert—dismantled, with the pieces slung either side of the animal's hump.

The origins of the camel lie not in Africa, however, nor in Arabia as might be supposed, but in North America, where the fossil remains of a rabbit-sized creature recovered from 50-million-year-old deposits have been identified as the progenitor of the camel family. By about 2 million years ago, the descendants of these diminutive ancestors had spread via the Bering Straits throughout the semi-arid regions of Asia and the Middle East (another branch of the family spread southward, to become the llama and alpaca of South America). Of the two species of camel known today, the bactrian with its thick coat and two humps is ideally adapted to the temperate deserts of its central Asian habitat, which can be extremely cold in winter. The single-humped dromedary is equally well adapted to the extreme heat of deserts in lower latitudes.

The wild dromedary was domesticated in southern Arabia not less than 4,000 years ago. Being able to carry twice as much as an ox at double the speed across terrain impassable to any wheeled vehicle, it soon superseded the ox-drawn cart as the preferred means of long-distance transport throughout the Near and Middle East,[26] and certainly was well established in southern Arabia when the Sabaean rulers were extending their influence across the Red Sea in the eighth century BC (see page 209).

A 92-cm length of camel-hair cord dating from about 600 BC was recovered from excavations in the Fayum region of northern Egypt in the 1920s,[27] and dung pellets dating from 770 BC (at the latest) were found at Qasr Ibrim in the Nile valley region of southern Egypt during the 1980s.[28] The implication is tenuous, but the south-to-north chronological orientation of these two scraps of evidence supports a widely accepted contention that the camel moved from its cradle of domestication in southern Arabia directly across the Red Sea to Africa. It became established first in the Horn of Africa, then spread across the continent via the Sahel and the fringes of the Sahara—west to the Atlantic, north to the Nile valley.[29]

The camel's endurance is legendary. T.E. Lawrence (of Arabia) wrote of an animal that carried its rider a distance of 450 km in thirty-nine hours, practically without a stop; another travelled nearly 230 km between sunrise and sunset in one day, rested the second and then returned on the third. These were exceptional instances, but even an average working camel could keep up a steady walk of about 6 km per hour for sixteen hours a day for ten or twelve days (a total of 960 to 1,152 km), Lawrence noted, and could be confidently expected to cover nearly 2,500 km in a month of daily travel. In Lawrence's experience, if the camel was strong, it was the rider who gave in first.[30]

In terms of its physiology the camel is probably the most resilient creature on Earth.[31] It can drink over 100 litres of water in a single session, then go without water for up to nine days. This means it can forage up to four and a half days from the nearest water, giving it a food-gathering range of over 400 km (compared with the elephant's range of less than 50 km—see page 260). Camels cope so well without water because they tolerate heat without perspiring. Instead, their body temperature tracks the ambient temperature, rising from 36°C in the morning to as high as 41 or 42°C in the heat of the day. Furthermore, their kidneys are super-efficient filtration plants, and do not need large quantities of water to flush wastes from the system; when operating at the limits of hydration, a camel's urine is more sludge than liquid.

As with water, so with food. Camels are adapted to eat a lot when they can, and to survive on nothing when they cannot. A specialized enzyme system enables them to adjust rapidly to fluctuating conditions of want and plenty. Only the pig matches the rate at which a camel converts surplus consumption to fat; and when it comes to utilizing fat reserves the camel is on its own. Other ruminants must use amino acids (the constituents of proteins) to break down fat, and so lose muscle tissue when starving; the camel's enzyme system bypasses this requirement; they can live off their fat reserve until it is exhausted without losing muscle tissue and condition. Cattle and sheep and other true ruminants can get by with a third of their normal maintenance diet, but camels can get by with nothing.[32]

The only drawback to human exploitation of the camel's unique attributes has been its reluctance to reproduce. They breed slowly. Left to themselves, camel numbers would be low—but stable. Indeed, the camel is the quintessential K-strategist (see page 130), superbly adapted to maintaining a small stable population in a hostile environment. Females are not sexually mature until the age of five years; each pregnancy lasts thirteen months; therefore, since camels mate only in the spring, their birth interval is a minimum of two years. And even that is not guaranteed.

Female camels release a mature egg only *after* copulation has occurred, the process in some way triggered by an ovulation-inducing factor in the semem

But the males' inclination to copulate is awakened only briefly each year, and copulation is not an act for which either the male or female domesticated camel seems at all predisposed. The act is performed with the female in a seated position, legs folded under her. Though aroused by the proximity of a female in heat, male camels lack the instinct that should direct them to the appropriate orifice and have to be assisted—manually. Authoritative sources suggest that only this human intervention has saved the camel from extinction since the species was domesticated, though some say camels are just bone idle and if someone is willing to lend a tactful hand, you will not hear a camel say "no."[33]

In East Africa, and across the Sahelian belt from Somalia to Senegal, camels enabled nomadic pastoralists to exploit arid regions where cattle could not survive, adding another dimension of opportunity to the existing network of interactions that characterized the cropping, herding, and iron dynamic of society. Along the fringe of the Sahara in West Africa they were an impetus to trade that revolutionized the character of society itself.

Berber-speaking forebears of the present-day Tuareg are believed to have introduced camels to the Saharan trade routes, sometime between the second and fifth centuries AD.[34] The routes had been lightly used until then, limited by the forage and water requirements of pack animals between oases. Camels extended both the volume and the radius of trade.

The volume of the Saharan salt trade during the early centuries of its expansion is a matter of speculation, but by the nineteenth century as many as 70,000 camel-loads of salt (more than 6,000 tonnes) were exported annually from the Bilma region alone, according to eyewitness accounts of the German explorer Gustav Nachtigal.[35] The Bilma salt travelled due south, supplying primarily the salt-deficient Sahelian regions of Niger, Chad, and northern Nigeria, with significant amounts traded onward to the forested Bantu cradle-lands of Cameroon and south-eastern Nigeria, where pure salt was equally scarce. Rock salt from deposits in the western Sahara at Tichitt, Teghaza, and Taoudeni also travelled due south, to join trade routes supplying the Sahelian and forested regions extending from Senegal to Nigeria. The Niger River was a major artery of the trading networks through which salt from the western Sahara was distributed. Timbuktu, poised where the Niger curves eastward in its sweep around the ancient rock core of West Africa, was the clearing house.

Tens of thousands of camels congregated at Timbuktu to join the biannual salt caravans. Once en route these caravans themselves spanned over 50 km of the 800-km desert trail to Teghaza and Taoudeni, and they returned to Timbuktu with between 4,000 and 5,000 tonnes of salt each year.[36] This was pure rock salt, in the form of slabs weighing about 30 kg each, white and smooth as marble gravestones—and indeed, they might have been gravestones for the men that died in the hellish labour of extracting them from seams at subterranean levels.

The trade continued through the twentieth century. Caravans were still bringing salt to Timbuktu in the 1990s, though in much reduced quantities. Men were still extracting salt from the Taoudeni mines, labouring under the system of debt bondage which was surely the only way that anyone was ever induced to work at Taoudeni. In exchange for food and transport, destitute men mined salt for their creditors six days a week. Salt mined on the seventh day was theirs to keep. With it they bought extra food, sugar, and tobacco—but at greatly inflated prices. They were rarely able to pay off their entire debt, and when they were no longer able to work, the debt devolved on to their sons who were likewise snared in bondage if unable to pay it off in cash.[37]

Mohamed Ali runs a caravan of 150 camels between Taoudeni and Timbuktu. Each camel brings back four slabs of salt; each slab sells for just under US$10 (February 1994). In a house built of concrete blocks on the northern edge of the town, three nephews are visiting. The floor of the house is sand—deep Saharan sand, so fine that it holds the print of a hand pressed into it. The nephews snuggle together on mattresses with Mohamed Ali's two sons, like a basketful of puppies, supple, and just as innocent—heads in laps, arms and legs intertwined. Ibrahim, in blue robes and indigo turban; Alous in sparkling white; Aladu, in camouflage trousers and canvas fatigue boots, wears a bullet on a cord around his neck. A lot of touching, hand-slapping, and laughing accompanies the young men's animated conversation. Tuareg music plays on the radio Alous has brought from Cotonou. What are they singing about? "Oh, life, camels, women—the desert." A taller, darker-skinned man sits apart, on a low chair near the doorway. "That's Marushad, one of our slaves," Mohamed Ali's son explains, "he came to us with his family five years ago, when he was hard up."

TIMBUKTU WAS ALREADY a trading centre of notable size in the eighth century AD. Its origins probably lay in a cluster of farming, herding, and fishing communities such as distinguished the inland Niger delta at that time (see pages 228–32), but its subsequent growth and status is almost entirely attributable to the salt that the Tuareg camel caravans brought to its markets. From the backs of camels the salt was trans-shipped to canoes for distribution through the hundreds of kilometres of navigable waters on the Niger River system.

Throughout recorded history the Niger has carried a voluminous river trade. In modern times, sawn boards are imported from the forests of Guinea and the Ivory Coast and fashioned into large flat-bottomed vessels at riverside towns. Before the advent of saws and road transport, dugouts were made wherever the tree was felled and manhandled to the nearest river. West Africa has a long history of boat-building. A dugout canoe found by well-diggers five metres below the land surface at Dufuna, a village on the Komadugu Gana River in north-eastern Nigeria, dates from 6,400 years ago.[38] This is the oldest-known canoe in Africa; and is second only to a boat found in Holland as candidate for the oldest-known man-made boat in the world.

The Dufuna canoe is over eight metres long and half a metre wide; it could carry at least five and possibly even ten camel-loads of salt, and there can be little doubt that craftsmen on the Niger were capable of producing canoes of equal if not greater capacity even before the salt trade reached Timbuktu. European captains who explored West African lagoons and rivers in the early sixteenth century reported seeing dugouts over twenty-five metres long, with complements of one hundred men or more. On the upper reaches of the Niger River, where large trees were scarce, dugouts made from two trees were stitched together with cord.[39]

The middle section of the Niger, linking Timbuktu to Djenne (about 400 km upstream), and to Gao (about the same distance downstream), was the busiest inland waterway in West Africa. Hundreds of craft have been in use on this stretch of the river since historical times and probably earlier.[40] Some carried 20 to 30 tonnes of merchandise, including foodstuffs as well as items of long-distance trade. With its development, water transport transformed the middle Niger into one of the great centres of indigenous trade in Africa. It encouraged the growth of specialized occupations, such as the building and operation of canoes; it led to the development of specialized ports on the waterways; and it contributed to the political and economic homogeneity of the region.

The Niger River probably has been a major north–south transport route for millennia, and there seems little doubt that the development of the ancient urban centre at Jenne-jeno (adjacent to modern Djenne, see page 234) was intimately related to the commercial importance of the inland Niger delta as the river trade expanded.[41]

The delta was important to river trade not only for its navigability, but also because its rich fishing grounds and agricultural hinterland were a source of dried fish and rice, among other staples, which were exported to both the Sahara and savanna regions. Jenne-jeno's location at the south-western extreme of the navigable and agriculturally productive inland Niger delta was critical, indicating that the town developed as a point of exchange where Saharan commodities like salt and copper could be traded for dried fish and rice from the delta, and where savanna commodities, including iron in particular, could be obtained in exchange for goods of either Saharan or delta origin.

From its origin in the Sahara, salt was carried by camel to Timbuktu, by canoe to Jenne-jeno, by donkey to the edge of the tsetse belt, and by porters to its most distant points of distribution. At each stage its value was inflated by the mark-ups of middlemen and the rising cost of transportation. By the time a slab of Saharan salt reached Kong in what is now the Ivory Coast, or Gonja in modern Ghana, it had travelled the best part of 2,000 km and was as much an article of prestige as of utility. Arabs visiting Gao in the tenth century reported that to avoid waste, rock salt was always licked, never ground and sprinkled.[42] Even in recent centuries, salt was sold in Gonja for sixty times its price at the point of production.[43]

With imported salt achieving such inflated value, most people continued to rely on the local sources that had served them hitherto; it was an inferior but always affordable component of the local trade network. Some, however, acquired the means of purchasing the prestigious imported variety. How did they pay for it?

For every piece of expensive, high-quality salt that came into the region, something of equivalent value had to go out. Ivory was one item that found a market, providing farmers with a modicum of profitable return from the elephants that invaded their cultivated clearings. Another was the kola nut, an addictive stimulant whose intensely bitter taste relieved thirst and became a symbol of hospitality throughout the Sahel and Saharan regions of West Africa. The nut stimulated long-distance trade as well as hospitality, and by the thirteenth century was regularly transported across the Sahara to markets in North Africa. By the late twentieth century its influence had embraced the planet, as an ingredient of the world's most popular soft drink: Coca-Cola.

The kola nut is exclusively a product of the equatorial rainforest, a delicate and highly perishable crop which must be packed in damp leaves of a certain kind, and repacked every five days if it is to reach distant markets in acceptable condition.[44] The value of the kola nut at its most distant points of distribution trade eventually approached that of Saharan salt. The price increased as the crop was transported north. In markets closest to the sources of Saharan salt, kola nuts were sold at forty times their cost in Gonja.[45]

Long-distance trade required people to collect the goods and porters to carry them to distant markets. That these demands for labour were satisfied implies a growth in population and a major shift in the social and economic relationships of local trading networks. Increased food production resulting from improved farming methods fuelled population growth, and the shift in social and economic relationships probably was initiated by successful members of local cropping, herding, and iron systems who began investing their surpluses in the accumulation of wealth, and in conspicuous consumption, rather than in the social networks to which they were beholden.

A vertical stratification of society came into being, creating sharp discontinuities in the horizontal layer of gerontocratic authority that previously had restrained individual ambition. Some people became more equal than others, controlling rather than sharing resources. Once the trend had begun, resources inevitably fell under the control of fewer and fewer individuals, culminating in the centralization of authority and the exercise of coercive power by a ruling elite. Power was exercised most coercively by traders who sold the porters as well as the goods they had carried to distant markets.

Bronze casting dating from between twelfth and fifteenth centuries AD, Ife
Museum, Nigeria

CHAPTER 27

Outposts and Inroads

THE ANCIENT SETTLEMENT at Igbo-Ukwu in Nigeria was an outpost of West Africa's long-distance trade routes. The inroads of the
trans-Saharan gold trade stimulated the inception of centralized states
in the Sahel; environmental constraints predicated their demise.

The Igbo[1] people of south-eastern Nigeria developed neither towns nor states
until recent times. Despite food production and barter systems capable of sustaining high population densities, and notwithstanding the fact that positions
of prestige and status were important in Igbo society and could be inherited or
attained by the accumulation of wealth—despite factors which elsewhere have
led to the formation of ruling elites, kingdoms, and states, Igboland remained
resolutely egalitarian: a landscape of villages clustered in areas where production and economic concerns were best served, but without the nuclei of settlement and activity from which urban centres develop.

As was common throughout sub-Saharan Africa, political authority among
the Igbo was exercised through the age-grade system and reinforced by a pantheon of guardian deities and oracles. General meetings of all eligible adults
decided major issues, though the elder and important household heads tended
to have greatest authority.[2] The weight of an individual's opinion was measured by the multiple criteria of age, wealth, and ability; status without ability
was acknowledged, but not much respected.

Prestige could be achieved by those who had acquired wealth and converted it into less tangible symbols by buying "positions" in exclusive secret

societies. Social position was also reflected by other objective indicators, such as the loyalty of a significant number of people: wives, children, kinsmen, friends, in-laws, and the indebted. For the many who possessed neither wealth nor the loyalty of a following, prestige could be achieved by feats involving personal risk that were performed in the interests of the village. Young men, for instance, who confronted interlopers—human or otherwise—were admitted to select groups.

The subtleties and strengths of Igbo social order are expressed beautifully in Chinua Achebe's novel *Things Fall Apart* (1958). The system did indeed begin to fall apart under the influence of external pressures in the colonial era, as Achebe describes, but its capacity to define a distinct ethnic identity is still evident at the end of the twentieth century. Such an enduring sense of collective esteem suggests that its origins are set deep, yet the earliest-known evidence that can be attributed to the Igbo contradicts their reputation as an egalitarian group whose political system subverted the rise of centralized authority and powerful rulers. At the very least, the evidence recovered from a tenth-century burial site at Igbo-Ukwu[3] in the heart of the Igbo region is the exception which proves the rule.

The burial chamber contained remains from a single individual and a collection of grave-goods that even authors contributing to staid archaeological journals have inspired to describe as "sumptuous."[4] Elephant tusks, copper anklets, a copper breastplate, beaded armlets; a crown, a fan-holder, a leopard's skull fashioned in bronze, and a bronze sword-handle in the form of a man on horseback. In the close vicinity of the burial chamber a storehouse of sophisticated regalia was discovered, along with a pit in which a hoard of items associated with the burial had been disposed. The finest of the objects from Igbo-Ukwu are exquisitely ornamented bronze castings made by the lost-wax technique, demonstrating a level of technical skill and artistic expression for which there are no antecedents or immediate successors in the region. Igbo-Ukwu is unique. The bronzes have been ranked among "the most technically accomplished and daring castings ever undertaken."[5] As a collection Igbo-Ukwu stands alone, without parallel in any other part of the world.

Early reactions to the implications of the Igbo-Ukwu evidence doubted the accuracy of the dating[6]—it seemed much more likely that the artefacts should have come from the thirteenth to fifteenth centuries, when work of a similar nature and quality was being made elsewhere in Nigeria. Subsequently, however, the source of the metals used in the castings has been located, and dating of mining debris shows that the mines were active sometime between AD 895 and AD 1000,[7] precisely when the Igbo-Ukwu burial was said to have taken place.

Pending further evidence the Igbo-Ukwu burial must remain something of an anomaly. It could represent the existence of a group otherwise unknown; or it could mark the moment at which the centralization of wealth and authority was abandoned, and gradually replaced by the egalitarian political system for which the Igbo became renowned. The durability of the new system could in itself reflect a determined reaction against the system it replaced.

But whatever the status of Igbo-Ukwu as regards the antiquity of the Igbo political systems, one central fact is clear: Igbo-Ukwu marks an outpost of long-distance trade. The sword-handle cast in the form of horse and rider, though made locally, indicates familiarity with an aspect of foreign influence still rare in sub-Saharan Africa at the time. And 165,000 pierced beads made of glass and carnelian found among the hoard of items recovered from the pit beside the burial represent an influx of foreign wealth that would be remarkable at any period during the prehistory of sub-Saharan Africa.

The beads must have reached Igbo-Ukwu through the indigenous trade network, but where had they come from? From the eastern Mediterranean via the Sahara is the most reasonable probability, and two glass beads found at Jenne-jeno establish a conceptual link between human activity in the Niger's inland and estuarine deltas which is pleasing to note, though of course this does not mean there was ever a direct connection between the two sites. In fact, the two beads at Jenne-jeno and the 165,000 at Igbo-Ukwu span a gap in both time and space throughout which not a lot is known with certainty of events in Africa. These are the dark ages of African history when, as in Europe, the archaeological evidence is sparse and often equivocal, and the histories written centuries later can be assumed to reflect the contemporary beliefs and suppositions of the historians writing them, as much as they represent a true record of past events.

ACCOUNTS OF AFRICAN HISTORY during the first 1,500 years AD draw heavily upon the reports of Arab geographers and clerics, many of whom put pen to paper long after the events they described and few of whom wrote from personal experience. Furthermore, the writers' concept of plagiarism allowed "many degrees of permissiveness . . . " in that "it is not always possible to determine whether additional information in the text was derived from an independent source, or simply from the imaginative elaboration by one writer of material contained in the work of a predecessor."[8]

Nonetheless, Arab manuscripts are the primary basis for accounts of African history during the relevant period given in modern history books. The successive rise and fall of states and kingdoms is depicted: ancient Ghana (no connection in time or space with the modern nation) in the eleventh century was succeeded by Mali and then Kanem-Bornu in the fourteenth century, which in turn fell to Songhay in the fifteenth century.[9] Military strength is assumed to have been the decisive factor in the rise and fall of these states. One chronicler reported that "the king of Ghana, when he calls up his army, can put 200,000 men into the field, more than 40,000 of them archers."[10] How the men were assembled, fed and deployed is not revealed. The figures probably are a tenfold, or even a twentyfold exaggeration.[11]

The archaeological evidence shows that large complex social formations did indeed succeed one another in the Sahelian region of West Africa during this period, but does succession necessarily imply conquest? A review of the evidence relating to the fall of Ghana in particular concluded that it did not. "Putting it very bluntly," the authors reported,[12] "we have discovered no sources, whether external or internal, which unambiguously point to such a conquest. A handful of sources suggest some link between the rise of the Almoravids [a group alleged to have conquered Ghana before the rise of Mali] and the decline of Ghana, but with a puzzling vagueness—a vagueness which decreases as the number of centuries between the alleged event, and the reporting of it increases."

Ecology, not conquest, brought about the fall of Ghana. The herds were too big, there were too many people. The more successful they were, the more certainly their fate was sealed.[13]

But the Arab chroniclers of early African history paid little attention to the dynamics of food production and population size that ultimately determine the fate of every community. Arab chroniclers were as subject to the bias of human interest as are journalists today. It was splendour, dramatic events, and stirring conquest that made the news, not drab everyday life and demographic change occurring over the years and decades. Meanwhile, the vagaries of climate and the afflictions of disease exercised their remorseless control of human population trends.

The persistently arid conditions which for centuries had been a primary determinant of human population trends and movements in sub-Saharan Africa yielded to more amenable conditions around AD 300. Rainfall increased and became plentiful during the period up to about AD 1100, promoting the expansion of both local and long-distance trade networks.[14] Population densities increased too—of both humans and livestock—and a conjunction of internal and external influences transformed the political structure of some ethnic groups from the age-set system which dispersed authority through the community to a system favouring centralized control and the formation of states.

Long-distance trade was a primary influence in this transformation—most especially the export of commodities for which Africans had no use but which were in demand abroad, such as ivory, "surplus" human beings, and gold.

IT IS NO ACCIDENT that the development of the first indigenous African states coincides with the rising importance of gold as a medium of exchange in the economies of the Mediterranean and beyond. Furthermore, all five regions known to have been producing gold before the colonial period are also the regions in which the first notable indications of indigenous state formation occur in sub-Saharan Africa: Aksum on the northern Ethiopian plateau, ancient Ghana, Mali and Asante in West Africa, Zimbabwe in south-east Africa.

Gold embellished the cultures of ancient Egypt, Greece, and Rome, but it was never a feature of indigenous African culture, and apart from sources supplying the Nile and early Aksum trade, the greater part of Africa's extensive gold deposits were untouched until foreign demand stimulated exploitation. Herodotus (c.485–425 BC), for instance, alludes to salt-mining in the Sahara and records a trans-Saharan crossing, but makes no mention of gold. The Carthaginians were striking gold coins at various mints in Sicily, Sardinia, and Spain from about 350 BC and in Carthage itself from 260 BC, but there is no evidence of their having used gold from across the Sahara. No classical author mentions a trans-Saharan gold trade—not even those who were born in North Africa, or who were personally familiar with the region—and the poet Lucan, writing in about AD 60, explicitly stated that no gold was mined in Africa.

The conclusion must be that the trans-Saharan trade in gold did not exist before the end of the third century AD, when the introduction of the camel and improved climatic conditions made trans-Saharan journeys a practical and profitable proposition.[15] Gold coinage struck in Carthage intermittently between AD 296 and 311 is probably the first indication of a trans-Sahara gold trade. The amount of coinage was minimal to begin with, but the increasing volume of gold circulating in North Africa from the fourth century AD onward indicates a substantial trans-Saharan trade in the metal—no other source could have sufficed.

Legal texts from the Roman period show that landowners and traders were obliged to pay taxes in gold at the end of the fourth century AD, and gold currency appears to have been abundant by that time. Carthage minted the *solidus* (and fractions thereof), which was destined to become a widely accepted medium of finance and exchange, and although production ceased during the Vandal occupation of North Africa from 439 to 533, the Carthage mint produced a copious stream of gold coinage until 695, when the Arab invasion of

North Africa brought the production of *solidi* to an abrupt halt. Immediately thereafter the Arabs opened a new mint at Kairouan in Tunisia and began producing *dinars*. Clearly, the Arabs had commandeered the Carthage gold supply, and since Arab geographers cite the trans-Saharan trade as the source of Arab gold in North Africa, it may be concluded that this had also been the source of the Carthage gold.[16]

Arab demand intensified the production of gold in West Africa during succeeding centuries, and the trans-Saharan trade was further boosted when Europe began minting gold coins for the first time since the disintegration of the western Roman Empire: at Florence in 1252, in France from 1254, and in England from 1257. Between the eleventh and the seventeenth centuries West Africa was the leading supplier of gold to the international economy, and in the later Middle Ages accounted for almost two-thirds of world production.[17]

Ancient Ghana was the first source of West African gold to be exploited by the trans-Saharan trade. Ibn al-Faqih, an Iranian scholar compiling material for an encyclopedia of the Muslim world, wrote *c.*900:

> It is said that beyond the source of the Nile is darkness and beyond the darkness are waters which make the gold grow . . . to the town of Ghana is a three-months' journey through deserts. In the country of Ghana gold grows in the sand as carrots do, and is plucked at sunrise.[18]

The Arab chronicles report[19] that Ghana was ruled by a king who adorned himself, his pages, and his court with gold, held audiences in a pavilion surrounded by horses caparisoned in gold, and even possessed a single gold nugget so large that it served as a tether for his personal mount. The nuggets found in all the mines of his country were reserved for the king, only the gold dust being left for the people. The best gold found in his land came from a town eighteen days' travelling distance from the king's town, over a country that was inhabited throughout.[20]

According to the chronicles, the capital of Ghana consisted of two towns— the king's and the traders' towns—which were situated on a plain, 10 km apart, with continuous habitations in between. Archaeologists have located what is believed to be one of these towns at Koumbi Saleh, in Mauritania.[21] The region is arid Sahelian scrub today, occupied only by nomadic pastoralists in recent times, but excavations and aerial surveys have revealed the remains of a large town covering an area of about 250 hectares with stone buildings, some of them two storeys high, the ground floors of which appear to have been used as stores for merchandise. The houses were close together, the streets narrow; there was a mosque, and extensive cemeteries.

Koumbi Saleh was occupied from the sixth to the eighteenth century AD[22] and home to between 15,000 and 20,000 people when it was most densely inhabited. Artefacts recovered from the site included many fragments of Mediterranean pottery, stones inscribed with Koranic verses and a number of glass weights so small in size that they must have been used for weighing gold. The evidence clearly indicates that Koumbi Saleh had been occupied by a rich commercial Muslim community who were involved in the trans-Saharan trade.

If Koumbi Saleh was the traders' town, then the king's town has yet to be found. Indeed, there must be some doubt as to whether it ever existed in a form as durable as Koumbi Saleh. In fact, the traders' town was probably an extension of a long-established local settlement, stone-built in the North African fashion while the local people continued to construct their dwellings from the traditional mudbrick and thatch. It is quite likely that the king was simply the richest individual in the local community; a man who lived more grandly than anyone else, to whom a significant proportion of local people owed loyalty: wives, children, kinsmen, friends, in-laws, and the indebted. They brought him gold; he served them well. Such a man would inevitably become the individual with whom Arab traders had most contact, and his regal behaviour doubtless imposed an obligation of careful formality if not obeisance upon foreigners wishing to trade with him.

That a single astute and respected individual should be the representative of local interests in dealing with Arab traders simplified matters for both the buyers and the producers of gold. However, the pomp and gold trappings that so impressed the Arab merchants were also a measure of the very limited value that African communities had traditionally attached to gold. Though locally abundant, the metal served no practical, ritual, or even ornamental purpose in the affairs of people in sub-Saharan Africa until demand from the north reached the region, and even then it remained solely an item of trade. The king and his court were ancient Ghana's shop window.

Iron and copper were the metals most valued in sub-Saharan Africa: iron for its practical use; copper and copper alloys as a medium of exchange, power, and art.[23] Indeed, copper appears to have been foremost among the goods most readily exchanged for gold, and the demand was considerable. The abandoned loads of a twelfth-century caravan discovered deep in the Sahara in 1964 contained over 2,000 bars of copper and brass, weighing almost a tonne,[24] and a source from the early fourteenth century reports that copper was exchanged for two-thirds its weight in gold.[25]

In the early stages of the trans-Saharan gold trade the metal was simply collected in the form of nuggets and alluvial gold dust by rural communities, for whom it was at best a seasonal and part-time occupation, filling periods of the day and the year when the labour demands of food production were relatively slight. The rewards are also likely to have been relatively slight, and most likely were in the form of local essentials rather than expensive imported goods. Thus imported goods tended to accumulate as the property of gold dealers—rather than gold producers—and became a measure of their wealth. The sources of gold were widely dispersed across the landscape and exploited independently, perhaps even secretly, so that the opportunities for any one individual to gain control of a substantial level of production were limited. As demand increased, however, specialization entered the equation wherever the deposits were rich enough to merit concentrated effort.

Asante miners in the eighteenth century dug slanting pits with broad steps to depths approaching fifty metres. Ore dug from the bottom was loaded on trays and passed to the surface along a human chain. In the Bure goldfields, parallel vertical shafts about twelve metres deep were joined underground by horizontal tunnels from which the ore was extracted and hauled to the surface in calabashes or baskets. Ores were crushed, washed, screened, and packaged as gold dust, or else smelted and made up into bars or wires.[26]

Intensified gold production called for a substantial full-time workforce and a considerable degree of specialization and coordination within each production unit. Given that the metal had no value in African society, it can only have been instigated in response to foreign demand, at a time when local climatic and environmental conditions were favourable—in other words, when there was food and labour to spare in sub-Saharan Africa. Those favourable conditions prevailed from about AD 700 to AD 1100, and so coincided with the Arab conquest of North Africa, and the establishment of Islamic rule. Gold was a spur to Arab ambition in North Africa.

For over 700 years up to 1450 the Islamic world was virtually the only external influence on sub-Saharan Africa, but the African system was resilient enough to absorb the foreign influence without suffering destructive distortion. African traders bought goods they wanted, and sold commodities they did not need.

CHAPTER 28

Merrie Africa

THE IDEA THAT GENERATIONS of Africans enjoyed congenial lives in well-integrated, smoothly functioning societies prior to the era of European exploitation is widespread but wrong. Few communities had sufficient labour to satisfy their needs. Life was arduous and unpredictable. Slavery was commonplace.

Administrators endeavouring to establish the infrastructure of government during the early colonial period faced a severe shortage of labour. Every district and provincial administrative centre required cohorts of people to make roads and construct office and residential buildings, as well as a permanent staff of clerks, carriers, cleaners, and cooks. Willing volunteers were hard to find. And committed workers no less difficult to attract, for the minority whose status in the local community gave them the time to work found the levels of pay derisory, while the majority who could have used the money were totally committed to their obligations within the local subsistence and barter economy. Money had yet to impinge upon the aspirations and interests of most Africans, and they had little enthusiasm for toiling on foreign eccentricities which had no apparent relevance to their lives.

Confronting the realization that indigenous labour was either unforthcoming or at best unreliable, while foreign labour was impossibly expensive, administrators resorted to the only option they could see available to them: forced labour. Forced labour, either in the sense that individuals were physically coerced into service, or by the more devious strategy of imposing a hut

Girl at a Rendille encampment in the Kaisut desert, Kenya. The Rendille
people herd camels on the arid lands of northern Kenya

tax, whereby heads of households were obliged to earn money since the tax had to be paid in cash. And, of course, only one source of paid employment was locally available to them.

Forced labour in Africa during the early colonial period was different only in degree to the slavery that the western world had abolished on humanitarian grounds not so many decades before. The colonial mind resolved this paradox by declaring that while slavery was uncivilized, forced labour was the only practical means of bringing the benefits of civilization to primitive people.[1]

The colonial administrators were, in fact, confronting the problem that communities in Africa had confronted ever since cropping, herding, and iron had become the predominant way of life on the continent, some 2,000 years before. The labour requirements of subsistence agriculture were high; population growth rates were low. With the notable exception of Ukara (see pages 255–58), agricultural communities in sub-Saharan Africa were barely large enough to feed themselves, let alone supply labour for extraneous activities. Even at the beginning of the twentieth century, average population densities in tropical Africa were of much the same order as those of England in the decades after 1066, when William ordered a census of his newly conquered domain, the evidence of which suggests that England was inhabited by fewer than 2 million people.[2]

Average population densities in Africa were always very low indeed, so that individual well-being was very much dependent upon the number of people with whom households and communities were economically integrated. Even an abundance of good land and adequate water could not be exploited without sufficient labour; a surplus of sorghum was worthless without a local trade network in which to exchange it for other goods. The wider the net, and the smaller its mesh, the more security it conferred upon those within it.

The imperatives of participating in the benefits accruing to large communities affected people at every level of society. But in order to participate, people had to "belong." Some belonged *in* the community, by virtue of birth or kinship; others belonged *to* it, having been recent immigrants, the destitute, orphans, or persons acquired by purchase or capture. All members of the community benefited from the security of numbers, but the people who belonged *to* rather than *in* the group were, in effect, slaves.

A history of slavery in Africa claims that between 30 and 60 per cent of the entire population were slaves during historical times.[3] If this is correct, the number of people enslaved in Africa far exceeded the number taken from the continent by the slave trade. In fact, given the volume of the demand for slaves within the continent, the shipping of slaves across the Atlantic should perhaps be seen as an extension of the internal market.[4]

·   ·   ·

DEFINITIONS OF SLAVERY ARE dominated by the indelible images which the Atlantic trade has imprinted upon the popular consciousness. It was a despicable trade, but the enormity of its crimes should not be allowed to obscure the fact that slavery in various guises existed in Africa and elsewhere long before the Atlantic trade got under way, and has continued ever since it was abolished. The trade which transported millions from Africa to the plantations of the Caribbean and the Americas was a grotesque instance of opportunistic exploitation; it carried existing practices to extremes, but was widely condoned for 300 years because a sufficient number of people believed that slaves were a necessary component of society.

Aristotle, to whom generations of thinkers have turned for ethical guidance, believed slaves were indispensable. "The slave is . . . an instrument of instruments," he said. "If every instrument could accomplish its own work, obeying or anticipating the will of others . . . if . . . the shuttle would weave and the plectrum touch the lyre, chief workmen would not want servants, nor masters slaves."[5]

In western imagery slaves are commodities that may be bought and sold and disposed of at will. Slaves have no control over their destiny, no choice of occupation or employer, no rights to property or marriage, and no control over the fate of their children. They may be inherited, given away, or sold without regard to their wishes, and may be ill-treated, sometimes even killed, with impunity. Furthermore, their progeny inherit their status.

The converse of slavery is freedom. Free individuals cannot be bought or sold, inherited or mistreated by another person; they can choose their occupation, own and dispose of property at will, marry whomsoever they wish, and raise children as they see fit. Freedom means autonomy. But where is the totally autonomous individual in any society?

The children of free men in ancient Rome were free, not slaves, but fathers had the right of life and death over their children. A woman in Victorian times assigned control of her property (and most aspects of her life) to her husband upon marrying, but supposedly remained a free woman. The dynamic family firm, that ubiquitous feature of pre-industrial and industrial society worldwide, functioned on captive family labour; some extended family firms grew into industrial empires, with hordes of workers who received a wage but enjoyed only a limited degree of freedom in their lives. Wherever wages are low and the workload excessive, people complain of being made to work like slaves.

Money is a determining factor in perceptions of slavery, it seems, and western attitudes to adoption are an illuminating illustration of this point. Voluntary adoption grants total control over an unrelated person's life, but it is perfectly acceptable provided no money changes hands. If parents gave their children out for adoption in exchange for money, it would be considered a sale, and thus akin to selling a slave; if adoption for money became common practice the system would be described as a trade in children. Yet if prevailing checks and restrictions on adoption remained in place, the exchange of money would change nothing in the relationship of adopted children to their adoptive parents. The children would be as much loved or mistreated as before.

In short, western attitudes to adoption indicate that while individuals may gain control of others by means of employment or marriage, they cannot use their wealth simply to increase the size of their households. Other societies, at other times and in other places, applied less exacting standards. The social histories of sub-Saharan Africa, for instance, indicate that it was customary practice for people to augment their households by acquiring people "ready-made," as Marx put it.[6] And from a Marxist perspective, the practice could be justified in terms of both society and economy. Rates of natural population growth achieved by marrying and begetting were consistently low, and where food production was locally variable and unpredictable, the child of an impoverished household who was exchanged for a supply of grain enhanced the survival prospects of both the parents and the child: was this slavery, or charity?

Among the Sena people who live along the southern bank of the Zambezi River in Mozambique, the allocation of land and the ability to mobilize human resources traditionally has been the principal factor distinguishing one community from another. Communities rarely exceeded 200 households. Land in itself had no intrinsic value, but was significant only as a means of attracting and supporting a large following. Levels of agricultural production varied greatly. In this part of Africa famines were frequent and made terrible depredations, but occurred in some areas more than in others, and people from the affected lands would crowd into unaffected areas where food was to be found. They bought food with anything they possessed, including their own freedom, voluntarily making themselves the slaves of those who would give them sustenance. Desperate individuals would even destroy an item of value belonging to a wealthier neighbour, knowing that the punishment for this symbolic act would be enslavement.[7]

Slavery in Africa has been described as "simply one part of a continuum of relations, which at one end are part of the realm of kinship and at the other involve using people as chattels. Slavery is a combination of elements, which if differently combined—an ingredient added here or subtracted there—might become adoption, marriage, parentage, obligations to kinsmen, clientship, and so forth."[8] All these relationships confer upon one person some right of control over another.

Rights-in-persons are a feature of society everywhere.[9] Children have the right to expect support and protection from their parents, who have a reciprocal right to exercise varying degrees of control over the child's activities. Husbands and wives have reciprocal rights; to a lesser degree so too have cousins, and even neighbours. In the west the rights are exercised by implicit mutual understanding and the reciprocal entitlements are at best imprecisely defined. In Africa, however, rights-in-persons tend to be explicitly recognized and precisely defined in customary practice; furthermore they are the subject of complex transactions between the parties involved.

Transactions in rights-in-persons are an integral part of African systems of kinship and marriage, for instance. When a prospective husband pays bridewealth, he and his kin group acquire certain rights in his wife from her kin group, and clearly defined rights to the children. The precision and complexity of the transactions varies widely, but the common characteristic is that they measure people as a form of wealth.

Kinship, adoption, the acquisition of wives and children are all inextricably bound up with exchanges that involve precise equivalences in goods and money.[10] Furthermore, the rights-in-persons acquired by payment are transferable. Individuals or kin groups could sell or exchange the rights they own in a person to others who were totally unrelated to the individual—and the relationship established by the exchange was first and foremost economic. A lineage in need of money, or forced to pay compensation for a crime, or unable to feed all its members in time of famine, for instance,[11] might transfer all its rights in a person to another lineage in return for goods or money. The individual, usually a child, would now "belong" to the recipient lineage, and would be totally at its disposal, to do with howsoever it might choose.

Alternatively, the transfer of such rights could be temporary. This is usually called "pawning" in the anthropological literature and was extremely widespread in Africa. In exchange for a loan, a kin group would transfer to its creditor a pawn—often a girl—who could be redeemed later. If the debt was never repaid, the pawn remained permanently and totally transferred to the creditors. The pawn was not a hostage to ensure good behaviour but an object of equivalent value to the loan, and the whole transaction was a pecuniary one.

But rights-in-persons were also obtained by means other than as a part of the arrangements formalizing marriage or adoption, compensation, loan, or pawn—not all of them benign. The Igbo, for instance, acquired slaves principally by capture, kidnapping, purchase, and political intrigue. Prior to the

eighteenth century inter-village raids had been common among the Igbo—
not for conquest or domination but to capture men and women. It was customary to spare the children, but such niceties were swept aside during the
eighteenth and nineteenth centuries, when the demands of the Atlantic trade
transformed customary slavery into profitable business. Corps of mercenaries
were recruited from particular regions of Igboland expressly to loot and
capture slaves. The incidence of warfare and slave raids increased correspondingly.[12]

Once enslaved, the treatment a person might expect varied widely. First-
generation slaves almost universally belonged to, rather than in a community,
but the distinction was less rigid for second and third generations. Born in the
community, knowing no other language or culture, having no outside ties
or exotic knowledge, nor any hankering for a lost past—the offspring of
acquired slaves were not strangers except by origin,[13] and were more readily
accepted as belonging in the community. Some slaves with specialized skills
acquired economic power in their own right; slaves with the appropriate aptitudes held important positions of trust and authority, and some even owned
slaves of their own.[14]

Among the nomadic Tuareg, slaves did all the hard work but were integrated into Tuareg society at the level of the family. Slaves used kinship terms
to address members of the family. The owner assumed responsibility for
bridewealth payments. He treated the wives of his male slaves just as he treated
his real daughters-in-law. A man could marry a slave even though she was considered to be his "daughter," and the children of the marriage assumed their
father's status.[15]

Once acquired, the Tuareg rarely sold or otherwise disposed of their slaves
since the principal reason for acquiring them in the first place was to assimilate
them into the lineage and increase the size of the family unit. Other ethnic
groups acquired slaves for very different purposes. For instance, the forty-one
young women whose remains—clothed and adorned with jewellery—were
discovered at the bottom of a well in the city of Benin in Nigeria were almost
certainly the victims of ritual sacrifice as practised by a powerful centralized
authority.[16] The remains date from before AD 1200, but documentary evidence
shows that the practice of throwing sacrificial victims into pits continued in
Benin until as recently as 1897.

VIEWED IN THE CONTEXT OF the unpredictable climatic conditions, arduous environmental circumstances, and endemic disease that restrained population growth among agricultural populations in sub-Saharan Africa, the

readiness of Africans to trade rights-in-persons among themselves doubtless began as an adaptive response to low overall population densities. There simply were not enough people.

Thus, the roots of Africa's servile institutions lie in the need for wives and children, the wish to enlarge one's kin group, and the desire to have clients, dependants, servants, and retainers. Indeed, in circumstances where the opportunities for converting agricultural surpluses into material wealth were limited, control over people was an alternative option. This was the niche that came to be occupied by the "big men" of the community, the individuals who accepted large-scale social responsibility, and thereby acquired elevated social status. In the languages of some ethnic groups in the Congo basin, for instance, the modern word for king stems from older terms meaning "ancestor," "grandparent," and "he who groups people around him."[17]

The ease with which exotic aspects of African society and culture can be attributed to a basic economic function that ultimately benefits every participant is responsible for what has been described[18] as the "Merrie Africa" view of African history. In this nostalgic scenario the centuries preceding the slave trade and Europe's exploitation of the continent were Africa's Golden Age, during which generations of Africans enjoyed congenial lives in well-integrated, smoothly functioning societies. The means of livelihood came easily to hand, for foodstuffs grew wild and in abundance, and this good fortune enabled the inhabitants to concentrate on leisure pursuits which, if some sources are to be believed, consisted of interminable dancing and drumming.

Merrie Africa, of course, mimics the myth of pre-industrial England as a country of prancing Morris dancers and rosy-cheeked yokels supping cider under the caring eye of the landed gentry: Merrie Englande. Both myths are based on the supposition that human society is capable of developing economic systems that are mutually beneficial to all participants—and indeed, assessment of the unpredictable climatic conditions, arduous environmental circumstances, and endemic diseases confronting early agricultural communities in sub-Saharan Africa invites the conclusion that a large measure of cooperative effort and mutual respect must have contributed to their survival. Communities survived because their members knew they "belonged" together—in the fullest sense of the term. There was little choice. Individuals could not live alone; nor even families for any length of time.

The dynamics of the local barter network kept the system running, and a gerontocratic political system, tempered by the authority of the age-set, kept it under control. But inevitably, instances arose wherein external factors distorted the system irretrievably. A succession of good harvests, for example, or a large influx of impoverished individuals, and the attractions of long-distance trade, all tended to heighten inequalities within the community. As that happened, the strategies which had ensured the survival of the majority became the devices that enriched a minority.

By the eleventh century there already were traders on the Sahara-Sahel margin who owned more than 1,000 slaves; they were not the first to accumulate wealth in the form of slaves, and in later centuries there were traders who owned even larger numbers. These were the men who ate meat and traded in kola nuts, Saharan salt, and slaves; they dressed in imported cloth, adorned themselves with expensive trinkets and lived "la vie de château."[19]

Wide economic and social inequalities prevailed. The poor, whom the Merrie Africa scenario presumes never to have existed in pre-colonial Africa, were a conspicuous feature of African society when the Portuguese established Europe's first direct contacts with Africa in the early 1500s. Francisco Álvares, a Portuguese priest who visited Ethiopia in 1520, wrote of more than 3,000 destitute people seeking help at a shrine near Axum.[20] In West Africa, visitors noted[21] that while the rich were well dressed and lived in substantial houses whose interiors were furnished with fine-quality mats and three-legged stools covered with oxhide, the poor lived under open shelters, wore grass skirts when even goatskins were beyond their means, and subsisted on meagre, inferior diets. Whether by the compulsion of fate or force, many of the poorest gravitated inexorably towards enslavement.

Elizabeth Bagaya, a princess in the former Toro kingdom of western Uganda and briefly a minister under Idi Amin

CHAPTER 29

Bananas and Cattle

BANANAS AND PLANTAINS, introduced to Africa from south-east Asia more than 2,000 years ago, produce high yields with minimal labour. They revolutionized food production throughout the equatorial regions and rapidly became a staple food—most especially in Uganda, where cattle simultaneously became valued as symbols of prestige and wealth.

"Very delicious to eat . . . soft to bite, as if it were made of a mixture of flour and butter . . . the smell is like that of roses and very good but the taste is even better."[1]

Pieter de Marees, a Dutch traveller, was writing of bananas, which he ate for the first time during a visit to West Africa in 1601. The banana was virtually unknown in Europe at the beginning of the seventeenth century, but in Africa the fruit was already the staple diet of millions (though not the sweet variety that de Marees had enjoyed, but rather the more substantial plantain and cooking bananas). But bananas and plantains had not always been familiar to Africans. In fact, they were introduced from south-east Asia (their cradle of origin) about 2,000 years ago and are a classic example of the extent to which new crops can influence the population dynamics and economy of a region.

In modern times, Africa produces 35 per cent of the world crop, and where bananas and plantains are the staple diet Africans eat about 250 kg per person each year (in the United States average consumption is about one banana per week—roughly 11 kg per year).[2]

Bananas and plantains are an excellent energy food, second only to cassava in calorie yield, well ahead of other root crops and between two and three times more productive than cereals. They are also a good source of potassium and vitamin C, though very low in iron and calcium and practically devoid of protein and fat; a good supply of supplements is essential to the nutritional well-being of people for whom bananas are the dietary staple.

The value of the banana as a staple crop, however, does not depend solely upon its nutritional attributes. The small amount of labour it demands is equally important, and the ease with which subsistence farmers can produce a regular supply of bananas in large quantities more than adequately compensates for the dietary shortcomings of the crop. Bananas are a perennial crop; indeed, in the case of Uganda, where the banana is especially productive, eternal may be a more appropriate term. A banana garden maintained in good cultivation will produce good crops for thirty years or more, and instances are known of satisfactory yields still being obtained from gardens that were fifty and sixty years old. But the figure of thirty years probably reflects the observation that gardens appeared to last at least a working lifetime, though when well tended they would probably go on growing and fruiting indefinitely.[3]

Such ease of cultivation has enabled generations of African farmers and their families to subsist upon the banana. A young man wishing to establish a household for himself and a wife would clear up to about one hectare of vacant land and plant it with banana rootstocks, from which several stems would soon sprout. In ten to eighteen months each stem would be bearing fruit and he was then set up for life. Maintenance of the grove was left almost entirely to his wife (or wives), and primarily involved systematically returning dead vegetation to the soil. Stems which had fruited were chopped down and split lengthwise to make a continuous floor, a simple operation which smothered weeds and prevented run-off erosion as well as preserving fertility. The growth of the suckers in a mature grove could be manipulated so that there were stems at every stage of development all year round. Feeding the family then consisted of simply cutting a bunch of bananas that was ready for cooking. Unlike grains and tubers, bananas did not need to be pounded before they were cooked, and the energy thus saved could be more profitably applied to the preparation of relishes—leaf vegetables, cowpeas, dried fish or meat—that compensated for the protein and fat deficiencies of the banana.

The banana plant can survive a moderate drought, but does not fruit while the soil is dry. So, although it is grown throughout much of Africa, it can be relied upon as a year-round staple food only where rainfall is more or less continuous and temperatures always relatively high. Equatorial conditions, in other words, and most especially those prevailing in the broad crescent of land extending from the northern and western shores of Lake Victoria to the lakes under the western escarpment of the Rift Valley and the foothills of the Ruwenzori mountains. This is indeed a fertile crescent—Uganda. Here an ancient plateau has crumbled into deep, well-structured loams that are better supplied with plant nutrients than is usual in Africa. Annual rainfall varying from 1,000 to 1,500 mm according to locality is well distributed throughout the year—even the two short "dry seasons" are rarely completely rainless.

Ugandans were growing about sixty cultivars of banana by the time their activities became a subject of interest to agronomists and plant geneticists in the mid twentieth century. And to the surprise of everyone it was discovered that none of the sixty cultivars exists anywhere but in Africa.[4] In fact, the African cultivars constitute a larger pool of diversity among cultivated bananas than is known anywhere else in the world.

West of the region in which the banana attained such remarkable levels of diversity, the diversity and social influence of the plantain (another species of edible banana) is even more impressive. From the lakes and the Ruwenzori mountains to the Atlantic coast, throughout the equatorial rainforest, the plantain is a staple food found growing profusely in every village. The total number of plantain cultivars grown in the region is about 120, and most have not been found elsewhere.[5]

Plantains—even more than bananas—are perfectly adapted to equatorial rainforests. Unlike the yam (initially a savanna plant, see page 251), the plantain is not affected by the absence of a dry season. Indeed, it flourishes in drenching, year-round rainfall. Forest need be only partially cleared, as compared with total clearance for yams, and the plantain requires far less attention after planting. Furthermore, plantain yields exceed those of yams by a factor of ten, while the crop absorbs only a fraction of the labour demanded by yam cultivation. All in all, the plantain was the ideal crop for rainforest agriculture and it enabled farmers to colonize all its potential habitats throughout West Africa.

The cultivation of plantains and bananas was a major component of developments that made a tremendous impact upon the human demography of equatorial Africa during the thousand years up to AD 1500. With generally favourable climatic conditions, plus the benefits of iron tools and burgeoning trade networks, the plantain and the banana provided an impetus to agricultural productivity that raised population growth rates and increased the size of predisposed settlements beyond the constraints of numbers. Wherever the advantages of banana and plantain cultivation took hold, the numbers of people belonging in and to a community at last began to exceed the number labouring to feed it. Increased productivity raised birth rates of successful communities and attracted hungry inhabitants from the less successful; surplus production was sold along the local trade network and fed the porters who carried it.

Growing populations also fuelled an intensification of the activities for which time had been limited hitherto. People could hunt elephants, rather than simply chase them from their gardens; collecting ivory, gathering kola nuts, panning and mining gold could engage people full-time.

THE NUMBER OF DIFFERENT BANANA and plantain cultivars identified in Africa has been described[6] as by far the highest level of diversification due to somatic mutation alone[7] yet detected. Such an extraordinary degree of diversity could only have arisen from a long period of cultivation involving large numbers of plants and intensive human selection for desirable characteristics, which seems to imply that African bananas and plantains were first domesticated and brought into cultivation on the continent. Even among scholars, those advocating another origin for the plants are likely to be accused[8] of wilfully denying Africa the illustrious honour of having given the world one of its most valued crops.

But the evidence is incontrovertible, and not at all dismissive of African achievements: yes, the number and diversity of unique cultivars in Africa is greater than in any other part of the world. No, the edible bananas were not domesticated in Africa, and could not have been, simply because their wild progenitors are found only in south-east Asia.

All edible banana species are derived from two wild species—*Musa acuminata* and *Musa balbisiana*—whose range spans south-east Asia from India to New Guinea. *M. acuminata* is found in the more humid regions, while *M. balbisiana* occurs more frequently in drier zones. The wild species flower and are fertilized to produce fruit containing seeds like virtually all wild flowering plants—seeds, after all, are the primary purpose of the flowering and fruiting process. But the edible descendants of the wild bananas are parthenocarpic, i.e., their fruit develops from female flowers without the benefit of fertilization. Without fertilization there can be no seeds; energy is diverted to the bulk of the fruit itself, and it is of course this characteristic which made the fruit attractive as a source of food.

Plant geneticists disarmingly admit that the development of parthenocarpy and seedlessness in edible bananas is not fully understood, but the implication is clear enough: without seeds the edible bananas can only reproduce by vegetative means. In this process the root stock of the plant, a rhizome, sends up suckers which mature as the parent stem dies after fruiting. In theory the process could continue indefinitely, but in practice the bulk of the rhizome builds up with each generation of suckers until it is wholly above ground; the rhizome dries out and the plant dies. But suckers can be transplanted as they appear, and by adopting this practice human intervention has preserved and propagated the edible banana. Since the plants could not reproduce themselves, propagation could only have been initiated where the wild progenitors occurred, and thus the presence of edible bananas beyond their cradle of origin could only be due to human intervention.[9]

The introduction of edible bananas to Africa involved the transportation of live suckers from south-east Asia to equally congenial locations on the African coast. Madagascar was proposed as a likely way station, it being clear that the island had been settled many centuries ago by immigrants of Indonesian extraction who would have been familiar with banana cultivation. From Madagascar it was a relatively short hop to the African coast and the banana could have spread in stages via the Zambezi and the Rift Valley to its centre of dispersal in the Lake Victoria region. It is an appealing proposition. However, a comparative study of cultural lexicons indicates that Africans knew all about the cultivation of bananas some time before they learned of the existence of Madagascar, so the Malagasy could not have introduced the banana to Africa.[10]

In fact, the banana probably reached Africa via the Indian Ocean and Red Sea trading voyages of which the *Periplus of the Erythraean Sea* preserves a record from the first century AD (see Chapter 21 above). Bananas are not mentioned in the *Periplus,* but that does not prove their absence. Farmers on the Ethiopian plateau cultivated ensete, an endemic African plant remarkably similar to the banana in its form and habitat requirements (though only the corm is edible), and probably were capable of growing bananas with equal success. The earliest piece of written evidence for bananas in Africa is their reported presence at Adulis, Aksum's Red Sea port (see pages 205–8), in AD 525.[11] The text is accompanied by a drawing which makes identification certain, but this sliver of information merely confirms the presence of the banana in Africa at that time, while the profusion of African cultivars known today indicates a far longer history of cultivation on the continent.

Vegetative propagation effectively produces clones of the parent plant. The suckers are made of identical genetic material. There is no unzipping and recombination of the genetic code such as occurs when seeds are produced by the cross-fertilization of two individual plants. The chances of new varieties arising from vegetative propagation are thus severely limited, since the genetic mutations which cause variation must arise entirely within the sucker itself, rather than from the mixing of genetic material inherited from two parents, as is the case in sexual reproduction.

Extrapolating backwards from the numbers of cultivars presently known in Africa, and applying rates of mutation deduced from laboratory experiments, banana specialists have calculated[12] that between 1,500 and 2,000 years were required for the present diversity of edible bananas to have arisen in the equatorial centre of dispersal alone—which barely leaves time for the farmers themselves to have become established in the region and leaves unanswered the question of how bananas got from the coast to the equatorial lakes.

Bananas and plantains cannot survive either the cold nights of high altitudes or dry seasons of more than two months' duration, so the plains and highlands of East Africa would have been a formidable barrier to a steady diffusion of banana cultivation from the coast to the congenial equatorial regions. Suckers may have been transplanted from patch to patch over a period of time, moving steadily from favourable habitat to favourable habitat, bypassing unfavourable locales. Alternatively, they may have been transported from the coast to the Great Lakes region in one dash, although this implies a degree of organized high-speed long-distance trade that seems improbable.

But even if the arrival of edible bananas in Africa could be precisely dated and the manner of their transfer to the lakes region exactly defined, an intriguing puzzle remains: how is it that African farmers generated in not more than 2,000 years a profusion and diversity of cultivars which surpasses even that found in Asia, where edible bananas originated? In the absence of definitive evidence, speculation suggests that new environments may have provided more opportunities for exploiting the potential of the plants; an absence of specialized pests, for instance, would have reduced the incidence of crop failure. Alternatively, it may have been solely a matter of human initiative: Africans exploited the potential of the crop more expediently than their Asian counterparts.

David Schoenbrun, whose Ph.D. thesis[13] on the history of the Great Lakes region between c.500 BC and AD 1000, brought together linguistic, ecological, and archaeological strands of evidence, has published convincing reconstructions[14] of the historical context in which the advent and exploitation of the edible banana occurred. The region was occupied by food producers more than 3,000 years ago, he reports, and large-scale forest clearance began around 2,000 years ago, first in Rwanda and Burundi, then steadily extending across the region, creating a mosaic of fallow secondary forest, grassland, and cultivated fields. Iron-smelting contributed both to the clearance of the forests (with its demand for charcoal), and the development of agriculture (with the production of hoes). In fact, the "intense and shocking" environmental impact of early iron production inspired changes in farming, herding, and land-use practices which in turn powered the subsequently rapid development of communities in the region.[15]

Food-production systems exploiting the inherent potential of the region were highly developed by about AD 500, with different ethnic groups specializing in different modes of production (a pattern already noted in the case of the inland Niger delta). The different groups spoke different languages. Indeed, three of Africa's four major language families (see pages 109–10) were represented in the Great Lakes region—Nilo-Saharan, Afro-Asiatic, and Niger–Congo—and the fourth (Khoisan) was spoken within contact distance.

The Khoisan language family was represented by the Hadza, remnants of ancient hunting and gathering populations. Speakers of Nilo-Saharan languages depended mainly on growing cereals, but also raised some livestock, while those of the Afro-Asiatic group gave decidedly greater emphasis to cattle in particular but probably also grew some cereals.

The fourth group, speaking Niger–Congo languages, included agriculturists who grew root crops and cereals, kept some livestock, and fished. These were the Great Lakes Bantu, among whom the edible banana was destined to become a staple crop.

The linguistic evidence[16] indicates that familiarity with the varieties of banana suitable for cooking and making beer developed between AD 500 and 900 among the Great Lakes Bantu. The process probably began with only sporadic cultivation of the crop, but was confirmed by an elaboration of terms describing banana varieties, their cultivation and preparation which occurred between AD 800 and 1300. There are some sixty terms for banana varieties alone, and another thirty to forty terms which describe parts of the plant and the preparation of bananas for food and brewing. All these terms are unique to the languages of the Great Lakes Bantu, denoting a trend towards specialized production which culminated in the establishment of the banana gardens and plantations around which the history of the region pivoted from about AD 1300.

Uganda's banana gardens represented invested labour and the generation of surplus value stored in the form of perennially fruiting trees. They were "islands of fertility and wealth," which the family heads controlling them used to attract and support large followings. But banana production was not the only specialized activity which rose to distinctive heights of achievement in the Great Lakes region during this period. While some farmers experimented with bananas and established firmly rooted islands of wealth, others developed alternative strategies that used the intervening grasslands to create and accumulate movable wealth: cattle.

Two thousand years of increasingly sophisticated and refined cattle-rearing strategies are embedded in the languages of the region,[17] beginning with the development of words for selected breeding lines and culminating in numerous terms describing the horn shapes and hide colour patterns of individual animals. Six terms referring to horn shape, and "not fewer" than seventeen cattle colour terms were coined between AD 800 and 1450 in the region which today covers Rwanda, northern Burundi, north-west Tanzania, and south-west Uganda. So much linguistic innovation over such a large area implies "an astonishing explosion of interest in pastoralist pursuits."[18]

The grasslands from which this explosion of pastoral pursuits erupted are among the lushest in Africa. Better watered than the savannas which often are regarded as the "proper" home of pastoralism, yet fortuitously avoiding the scourge of the tsetse fly, the high productivity of the Great Lakes grasslands enabled people to maximize the potential of cattle, rather than simply employ them as a means of utilizing environments that were otherwise uninhabitable. Here more than anywhere else in Africa it has been possible to maintain highly specialized herding in coordination with cultivating communities and to select medium-sized cattle of a not especially drought-resistant breed.[19]

Nomadic pastoralists, such as the Fulani in West Africa and the Maasai in East Africa, developed the skills necessary to keep their stock and thereby themselves alive on minimal resources. Their achievements were considerable—after all, sustaining a milk supply means keeping cows sufficiently well-nourished to conceive and calve, which is no easy task under semi-desert conditions—but theirs was a survival strategy, designed to supply basic requirements under even the worst conditions (and usually dependent also upon some exchange-and-barter arrangements with settled farmers).

Pastoralists herding cattle on the Great Lakes grasslands were not totally dependent upon their stock for survival, and therefore could afford to develop a maximizing strategy. Even before the advent of the banana, agriculture and fishing could be relied upon to provide an adequate food supply. The grasslands were surplus to basic requirements, and the cattle raised on them were a non-essential resource, a luxury destined to become symbols of wealth and power among the people owning them. In these regions it was cattle-wealth, rather than, as elsewhere (see pages 278–79), the influences of long-distance trade, that shattered the egalitarian authority of the age-sets and created progressively more centralized and coercive political systems.

Cattle were already established as a major presence in the Great Lakes region by AD 1000,[20] and throughout historical times they have been accorded a degree of prestige seemingly out of proportion with their economic relevance as a source of food. Herding was regarded as a noble pursuit. The herders became rulers who emphasized their attachment to the pastoral life, and not only measured wealth in the size of the herds, but also valued the distinctive, even aesthetic, qualities of the animals themselves. In short, cattle became objects of adoration.

From the basic long-horned and humped zebu stock (*Bos indicus*), the herders bred for size—not only body size, but also the size and shape of the horns. In modern times, horn spreads of over two metres have been noted; lyre-shaped, bow-shaped; curving upward, curving downward; pointing forwards or backwards. Each configuration (and combination thereof) has its terminology, genealogy, and passionate admirers. In folk history and legend, cattle were elevated to almost reverential status; they were the wonderful companions of royal heroes and the godlike personalities of antiquity from whom the pastoralists claimed descent.

Several archaeological sites in Uganda attest to the early development of specialized pastoralism in the Great Lakes region. At Ntusi, 200 km west of Kampala, vast amounts of cattle bones litter the surface over a large area, together with equally numerous fragments of pottery and a substantial number of grindstones. There are the remains of a smelting industry on the fringe of the inhabited area, and rich iron-ore deposits nearby. Many hundreds if not several thousands of people lived at Ntusi from the eleventh to the fourteenth or fifteenth centuries AD.[21]

At Bigo, about 20 km south of Ntusi, massive ditchworks and ramparts enclose 300 hectares of land that backs on to a papyrus swamp (which both provided the Bigo inhabitants with water and inhibited approach from that direction). Some of the ditches were dug five metres into the bedrock; their overall length exceeds ten kilometres. Construction of the earthworks and occupation of the site is estimated to have been concentrated between the thirteenth and sixteenth centuries.

Bigo means "the defended place" and folk history tells that this was where the ancestors kept their herds. Clearly, the massive ditches and earthworks were intended for protection, and Bigo certainly appears to have been a centre or refuge to which rich cattle-owners could retreat with their herds in times of insecurity.[22] The scale of the works indicates that the cattle-owners were able to conscript a large labour force equipped with a good supply of the iron hoes needed for constructing and maintaining the ditches and ramparts.

IN ALL THEIR FORMS, specialized herding practices and the prestige attached to owning cattle were dependent upon substantial populations of cultivators and, therefore, pastoralism as an exclusive way of life could be pursued by only a minority who had access to the services and produce of a non-pastoralist majority.[23] Pastoralists required the services of craftsmen for iron tools and pots; they depended upon agricultural communities for supplies of essential carbohydrates, and needed to maintain good relations with populations round and about who would absorb people from the pastoral populations which the grasslands could not support, and provide relief during successive drought years or following heavy losses through cattle disease. By way of return the agriculturists could expect a reciprocal supply of animal products (blood, milk, meat, and hides) and services (not least a manuring service) from the pastoralists.

Given the extent to which pastoralists depended upon agriculturists, it follows that herding and the reverence of cattle cannot have been a predominant way of life that pre-dated all others in the region; it must have been a late development resulting from polarization within a mixed economy. Ntusi, where large numbers of cattle were brought into an essentially agricultural community, may illustrate the early stages of the process.[24] Bigo and other sites where earthworks are evident represent a later stage in the process, following which decentralization occurred; the large sites were abandoned and numerous smaller centres are evident in the archaeological record from the fifteenth and sixteenth centuries. It was during this period that banana cultivation began to exercise its influence on affairs.

The expansion of banana cultivation in the region led to "spectacular demographic increase."[25] By the eighteenth century the power of pastoral leaders was being eclipsed by the power of leaders controlling dense agricultural populations in the highlands of the Rift Valley escarpment to the west and along the shores of Lake Victoria to the east. A number of distinct polities emerged from this conjunction of pastoral and agricultural interests; some were elevated to the status of kingdoms under colonial rule (1890s to 1960s): Buganda, Bunyoro, Nkore, and Toro.

THE GREAT LAKES REGION WAS perhaps the largest, most richly endowed, most developed and most densely populated of indigenous agricultural systems in Africa. It was also one of the last to be "discovered" by Europeans. John Hanning Speke was the first white man to enter the region. In the company of James Grant he travelled around the west and northern shores of Lake Victoria in 1862 with the avowed purpose of establishing that Lake Victoria (which he had discovered in 1858 while making a solitary side trip from Richard Burton's expedition) was indeed the source of the Nile, as he claimed (and others, including Burton, denied).

Speke established that Lake Victoria was indeed the source of the Nile (by the simple expedient of following its course from the lake to the Mediterranean). During his stay in the lakes region he also recorded detailed observations on the people he encountered, on their social and political organization, and on their history. Combining prejudices formed as a British army officer in India with propaganda from informants representing the interests of ruling elites, Speke surmised that the ruling minority had some time previously invaded the region from Ethiopia. Speke thought it likely that they were a branch of the pastoralist people he had encountered while accompanying Richard Burton to Harar in 1854. His view on the matter is encapsulated in a chapter subheading: "Theory of Conquest of Inferior by Superior Races."[26]

> In these countries the government is in the hands of foreigners, who had invaded and taken possession of them, leaving the agricultural aborigines to till the ground, whilst the junior members of the usurping clans herded cattle [Speke wrote].[27]
>
> It may be presumed that there once existed a foreign but compact government in Abyssinia, which, becoming great and powerful, sent out armies on all sides of it, especially to the south, south-east, and west, slave-hunting and devastating wherever they went . . . [one branch of these armies] . . . were lost sight of in the interior of the continent, and, crossing the Nile close to its source, discovered the rich pasture-lands of Unyoro . . . where they lost their religion, forgot their language, extracted their lower incisors like the natives, changed their national name . . . and no longer remembered [their original names]—though even the present reigning kings retain a singular traditional account of their having once been half white and half black, with hair on the white side straight, and on the black side frizzy . . . Believing, as they do, that Africa formerly belonged to Europeans, from whom it was taken by negroes with whom they had allied themselves, [they] make themselves a small residue of the original European stock driven from the land— an idea which seems natural enough when we consider that [they] are, in numbers, quite insignificant compared with the natives.

This view of African history compounded a prevailing belief that whatever was commendable in black Africa must have been introduced from somewhere else by lighter-skinned and (it is implied) more intelligent people. This Hamitic myth has a long and enduring history;[28] indeed, the notion of a separate origin for the pastoralist elites, and their superiority over the cultivators of the lakes region, persists to this day. The idea was reinforced by the colonial regimes and since independence the elites themselves have seized every opportunity to perpetuate it.

Yet there is no firm historical evidence to support the idea, and linguistic analysis strongly contradicts it.[29] No traces of a Cushitic substratum related to Galla or any other Ethiopian tongue have been detected among the languages of the region; furthermore, the region possesses a remarkable degree of linguistic continuity.[30] From north to south, through the pastures, parklands, and forested foothills of the Rift Valley escarpment to the western shore of Lake Victoria, essentially a single language persists, transcending the distinctions that have been imposed during recent times. In Rwanda and Burundi, for instance, the pastoralist Tutsi speak the same Bantu language as the Hutu cultivators; both groups are descended from farmers who began cultivating the region 2,000 to 1,500 years ago.

CHAPTER 30

Cattle and Gold

CATTLE CONVERTED GRASS into items of wealth that could be owned, exchanged, and inherited. In the extensive grasslands of southern Africa a new order of values emerged, characterized by a degree of social stratification that is epitomized at Great Zimbabwe. The gold trade initiated by Arabs calling on the East African coast introduced a disruptive dynamic to the region.

During the first centuries of the modern era, cattle became an increasingly important component of human systems in Africa. They provided nomadic pastoralists with a means of exploiting the Sahel and other semi-arid regions, and contributed to the social and economic developments in the Great Lakes region of East Africa described in the last chapter. Farther south, the exploitation of cattle achieved even greater significance, inspiring a belief that cattle were the root cause of the strife that becomes increasingly evident in the archaeological record of the region from around that time.[1]

Prior to the advent of cattle-herding on the grasslands of southern Africa, societies had lacked any kind of surplus or economic wealth that was worth fighting for or defending. In those circumstances, disputes led to dispersal rather than conflict. But cattle converted expanses of otherwise worthless grass into items of wealth that could be owned, controlled, and inherited. A new order of values emerged, characterized by a greater stratification of society and an increasing incidence of conflict between groups.

The high stone walls of Great Zimbabwe were built by the indigenous
population between the thirteenth and sixteenth centuries AD

The underlying factors which distinguish cattle-exploitation practices in southern Africa from those employed around the Great Lakes or across the Sahel were environmental: conditions in the southern African grasslands more closely approximated those of southern Europe and the Near East where the wild progenitors of domestic cattle had evolved. Cattle thrive in temperate regions; cold suits them better than heat; wetness better than aridity. In the Sahel and the Rift Valley regions of East Africa, cattle confront conditions that are generally both very hot and very dry; they survive, but only within the physiological constraints of an animal that evolved in temperate regions. In hot conditions, for instance, cows drink not only to avoid dehydration but also to cool themselves by passing huge volumes of water through their bodies. As their water intake rises with temperature there is a parallel increase in urination. One study[2] recorded an instance in which urine output increased fivefold, rising from 25 to 125 litres per day. Selective breeding has produced cattle that are adapted to arid conditions and can go without water for two days or more, but water deprivation puts a significant strain on the animals—they eat less and lose condition rapidly.

The highlands of East Africa are better watered than the Sahel, and the grasslands of the Great Lakes region in particular are rated among the lushest pastures in Africa.[3] But these lush pastures straddle the Equator; so that even here cattle achieved maximum productivity only to the extent that an equatorial climate allowed.

By contrast, the high savanna grasslands extending from Zimbabwe in the north, and southwards across the Transvaal and the Orange Free State to the Natal coast of South Africa lie between fifteen and thirty-five degrees south of the Equator. The soils are derived from ancient granites—less fertile than the volcanic soils of the Great Lakes region but capable, nonetheless, of producing large quantities of forage that cattle find highly attractive.

The grasslands of southern Africa have been classified as "true climax grassland,"[4] i.e., they represent a mature and stable form of vegetation ideally adapted to the prevailing ecological circumstances. Wild animals, and hunters and gatherers had exploited these environments for millennia, and agropastoralists and farmers had been present in surrounding lowland regions since around AD 300, but settlements dating from the tenth century which have been excavated at Mapungubwe in the Limpopo valley represent an intensification of farming activity. Cattle were the enabling factor.

The Mapungubwe settlements were built around a sandstone hill that rises abruptly from the Limpopo valley. On the summit of the hill, excavators found richly adorned burials among the remnants of buildings, and evidence of further settlement extended in a broad swathe beneath the ten-metre cliffs on the south-western side of the hill. The deep, stratified deposits showed that the houses had been built and rebuilt over many decades. Radiocarbon dates indicated that the first buildings were constructed beneath the hill in the eleventh century, and the settlement had expanded to include the summit of Mapungubwe by the early twelfth century.[5]

Mapungubwe appears to have been the largest in a widespread local hierarchy of settlements which were established during the warm and moist conditions that characterized the climate of the region from AD 900 to 1300.[6] During the late twentieth century the area has been a "drought trough," incapable of supporting a resident population, but 900 years ago it was populated by thousands of farmers.[7] By AD 1175, if not sooner, Mapungubwe was the capital of a state with several district centres.[8] Settlement at the district centres was intensive. At Mapela, for instance, 85 km north-west of Mapungubwe, all the slopes of the 100-metre-high hill had been terraced with roughly piled stone walls to provide level building sites.[9]

Hierarchical distinctions were evident within settlements, as well as between them. Houses on the highest terrace at the core of the Mapela settlement, for instance, were built with thick floors and walls—upper-class residences, they might be called, quite distinct from the flimsy wattle and daub dwellings of their neighbours. At Mapungubwe, ninety-seven individuals had been buried at random throughout the settlements at the foot of the hill; their skeletons were found in what had been cattle enclosures, living areas, and ash heaps. Another twelve skeletons were all found close together on top of the hill, in a graveyard, and they had been buried with an assortment of grave goods and adornments.

The striking differences in housing at Mapela, and in modes of burial at Mapungubwe, point to the presence of socially distinct groups which enjoyed more congenial living conditions than the rest of the community and had a measure of wealth at their disposal.

Cattle thrived and people adapted their social and economic patterns to the advantages and constraints of the new system. Mapungubwe preserves a record of the beginnings of the cattle culture in southern Africa, whence it spread rapidly across the grasslands wherever the distribution of the tsetse fly permitted, from what is now Zimbabwe to the Cape of Good Hope.

AS IS THE CASE EVERYWHERE ELSE, the cattle of southern Africa converted an inedible resource—grass—into produce of value. But unlike the nomadic pastoralists of the Sahel, the pastoralists of southern Africa were more interested in meat than milk. This distinction between what are known respectively as carnivorous and milch pastoralism has significant implications, both in terms of herd management and the social organization of the people involved.

Since the sex ratios of cattle are virtually 1:1 at birth, nearly 50 per cent of a herd's reproductive capacity is not wanted by the milch pastoralist. A Maasai family of eight persons requires a minimum of forty animals to sustain milk production at the optimum level, but the herd need contain only one bull.[10] Herd ratios of fifty females to one male are not uncommon among milch pastoralists; 40 per cent of male calves "disappear" before they are a year old, according to one study, compared with only 5 per cent of females.[11] For the most part, male animals are a waste of grass for pastoralists whose priority is milk, especially in marginal regions where resources are barely able to support needs, let alone subsidize waste. Even the bull, whose presence is essential for only a few brief moments each year, consumes grass that cows could more usefully convert into milk.

The pastoralist herding cattle primarily for consumption as meat suffers none of these constraints. Every animal born can be raised to maturity; the numbers of animals slaughtered or sold each year can be matched to the number born. Furthermore, the beef herd is less demanding in terms of labour. Milch cattle must be tame, and are therefore incorporated into a structure of domestic relations: boys tend the calves; adults drive the cattle to pasture and water, and protect them from predators; women milk the cows morning and evening. Except for the need for protection from predators, a beef herd requires far less attention.

The distinctions between milch and carnivorous pastoralist are obviously related to environmental circumstance and invite the conclusion that carnivorous pastoralism maximizes production from *prime* habitats while milch pastoralism is a strategy that utilizes *marginal* habitats to best advantage. Thus, milch pastoralism guarantees a basic level of subsistence for existing populations, while carnivorous pastoralism can sustain expanding populations.

The expansion of the Mapungubwe population coincided with the extension of Arab trading voyages southward along the East African coast. By the tenth century the "Land of Zanj" (the present-day coastal region of Kenya and Tanzania), was exporting slaves, leopard skins, tortoiseshell, and ivory to Arabia and India, according to contemporary reports.[12] But Kilwa, 300 km south of Zanzibar, marked the southernmost limit of travel for Arab dhows sailing from the Persian Gulf and back on the seasonal monsoons. Beyond Kilwa trade was conducted by intermediaries who had access to the "Land of Sofala" and its fabled "meadows of gold."[13] Al-Idrisi, who compiled a book of travels in the early twelfth century based on the experiences of other informants, indicated that the Arabs had by then described a number of landing and trading points along the coast as "Sofala."[14] The name probably stems from the Arabic for "shoal" and thus warned of dangerous inshore waters, but it was eventually attached specifically to a landing point and trading post located on a bay near the present-day city of Beira, in Mozambique.

Sofala gave traders access to the produce of the Limpopo basin, which was the first region of the southern African interior to be integrated into the trade network of the Indian Ocean. Mapungubwe was strategically placed on the route along which goods and produce began travelling to and from the coast in the tenth century. Gold was the product most in demand at the coast.

Sofala's "meadows of gold" could as well have been a metaphor for the grasslands that supported such a wealth of cattle, but it was the metal that the traders wished to harvest. Even so, the association of cattle and gold in Zimbabwe is more than just metaphor or simple coincidence. Gold originates exclusively in ancient cratons such as that which comprises the solid core of southern Africa (see pages 10–11); grasslands favouring cattle production are the climax vegetation of soils derived from ancient cratonic rocks.

At the Mapungubwe sites, glass beads made in India and Egypt testify to the community's involvement in long-distance trade. The appearance of gold as a commodity of significance to the local community itself is demonstrated by a number of items recovered from the hilltop burials—including a unique gold rhinoceros. The rhino is crudely made of small gold plaques hammered to shape over a wooden maquette and pinned in place. The wood has long since decayed, but the image of the animal remains evocative—head lowered and tail raised, as if preparing to charge.

The Mapungubwe rhino dates from around AD 1200 and is the earliest-known evidence of an indigenous use of gold in southern Africa. Furthermore, its presence coincides with the first mention of gold in Arab records of East African trade.

The inhabitants of Mapungubwe probably found their gold initially in the form of nuggets, or recovered it as gold dust from the Limpopo and its tributaries. This alluvial gold had been washed down from the highlands. Ultimately people discovered that the metal was more readily available at sites along a ridge of hills and mountains that geologists have called the Belingwe Greenstone Belt, in what is now south-central Zimbabwe. The Belingwe greenstones are 2.7 billion years old, and laced with veins of gold. The name Belingwe is a transliteration of Mberengwa, meaning "a place bearing great weight, or carrying great expectation."[15]

•   •   •

THE MAPUNGUBWE COMMUNITIES OF the Limpopo basin fade from the archaeological record around AD 1250. The warm moist epoch that had sustained inhabitants of the Limpopo basin for 400 years was drawing to a close; conditions now favoured the expansion and consolidation of communities on the highland plateau to the north, close to the greenstone belt and the gold. This was crucial to the development of the Shona state. Cattle were central to the economic and social life of the Shona; unique stone buildings are a lasting testimony to their presence and widespread influence.

The Shona term *dzimba dzemabwe* means "houses of stone"; a related form, Zimbabwe, became the name of the nation at independence in 1980, but initially the term had been applied to the stone-walled enclosures that are a common feature of the Zimbabwe landscape. More than 300 have been found in all; the best known is also the oldest and the largest: Great Zimbabwe, situated among a complex of rocky hills and valleys on the southern edge of the plateau.

There was gold in the mountains and river valleys near Great Zimbabwe, and its location certainly offered the opportunity of participating in or controlling the flow of gold from richer deposits to the west, but it was not gold or trade which initially determined the location and establishment of Great Zimbabwe. Control of the gold trade was a corollary of success in the meat trade.

The distribution of *zimbabwe* settlements throughout the Shona region correlates to a striking degree with the ecological conditions that optimize cattle production. A survey has shown[16] that the majority of *zimbabwe* were located within daily herding distance of the contour line above which ambient temperatures limited distribution of the tsetse fly. The plateau was, in effect, a tsetse-free peninsula, whose boundaries moved back and forth with the tide of seasonal and long-term climatic variation. The location of the *zimbabwe* accommodated these variations while affording best access to the grassland resource. There were few in the west, or close to the densely wooded and infertile Kalahari sands, but a clear concentration on the north-east and south-east edges of the plateau. Great Zimbabwe is at the centre of the latter concentration, close to a large river system and in a position to benefit from convection rains carried by winds from the coast.

Thus the Shona appear to have practised a form of pastoralism on the Zimbabwe plateau that effectively harvested the resources of the grasslands in self-propelled packages of concentrated protein and fat that could be consumed at will (unlike milk, which must be collected twice daily and consumed almost immediately). No other farming activity could have exploited the resources of the Zimbabwe plateau so effectively. The Shona also grew cereals and vegetables, but it was carnivorous pastoralism that enabled their *zimbabwe* settlements to achieve such permanence and high population densities in what was essentially a savanna environment.

ARCHAEOLOGISTS CONDUCTING EXCAVATIONS at Great Zimbabwe in the 1960s and 1970s recovered about 140,000 pieces of animal bone from a midden on the lower slopes of the hill on which the so-called Hill Ruin is situated. Of these, 20,359 were examined closely and all but 263 were found to have come from cattle. (Domesticated sheep or goats were most common among the more recognizable non-cattle bones, along with domestic dogs and a limited range of wild animals.) Among the cattle bones to which an individual age at death could be assigned, almost 80 per cent of the animals had been slaughtered when they were between twenty-four and thirty months old,[17] the age at which beef cattle are at their prime.

Evidence of intensive meat consumption has been found at other *zimbabwe* sites, indicating a widespread and intensive beef-producing economy in which cattle were bred for meat and herds produced a regular surplus of animals for slaughter.[18] Most of the animals had just reached maturity and were slaughtered while still approaching full body weight, before hardly another blade of grass was wasted on their sustenance. The prevalence of young adults among the *zimbabwe* cattle remains is strikingly different from the pattern found among milch pastoralists, who slaughter cattle only on occasions of special significance, and then only mature or aged beasts.

It has been noted, however, that young cattle remains are found only in middens within close range of the *zimbabwe* structures themselves; elsewhere in the wider inhabited surroundings, cattle bones of any age are rare. This distinction not only confirms that the communities were socially segregated, but also points to the presence of a ruling elite—perhaps even a royal court[19]—which lived in the seclusion of the *zimbabwe* walls and fed regularly on prime beef.

At its greatest extent, Great Zimbabwe covered an expanse of seventy-eight hectares,[20] but the earliest occupation was confined to a whale-backed granite hill, crowned with massive boulders and with a steep, smooth rock face on its southern side, overlooking several broad valleys and lower granite hills nearby. A village was established on the hilltop in the late eleventh century. As the status of Mapungubwe faded from its zenith in the twelfth century, and Great Zimbabwe achieved greater importance during the thirteenth century, occupation of the hilltop settlement intensified. Drystone walling filled the gaps between the boulders, and terraces levelled the site into an intricate and teasing maze of living areas.

During the fourteenth century the Great Enclosure was constructed on a shoulder of level ground 600 metres from the hill settlement. The massive outer wall is 244 metres long, 5 metres thick and 10 metres high at its largest points, and forms an irregular ellipse with a maximum diameter of 89 metres, making it by far the largest single prehistoric structure in sub-Saharan Africa. Two high parallel walls restrict access from the north-west entrance to a narrow single-file running along one-third of the enclosure's total circumference. The passage opens on to a small enclosed space containing the enigmatic Conical Tower: 5.5 metres in diameter, 9 metres high, solid stone throughout, beautiful regular coursing and once decorated around the top with a *dentelle*-patterned frieze (now collapsed). Behind the tower, stone walls divide the internal space into a number of smaller enclosures; there are *daga* platforms and the ruins of huts.

The construction of Great Zimbabwe was facilitated by an ample supply of suitable stone within carrying distance of the site. Indeed, the largest and most striking hills in the vicinity are smooth rounded domes of granite, formed by the exfoliation of thin layers of rock under the marked daily changes of temperature caused by tropical sunshine (hot days) and clear skies (cold nights). Parallel-sided slabs of granite up to eighteen centimetres thick split off the domes (much as an onion peels), and slid down to collect as scree at the bottom, where they could be broken down to manageable size. The fracture planes of the granite ensured that the broken pieces all had a very regular cuboidal shape, with parallel surfaces, vertical sides and a standard thickness. Thus the blocks not only were an easily obtainable material, they also were ideal for building techniques based on more or less regular horizontal layers of stone.

The outer wall of the Great Enclosure is certainly the largest single structure of comparable age in sub-Saharan Africa, but in terms of age and architectural significance the most striking feature of Great Zimbabwe is simply the fact that it is in Africa. Drystone building is an ancient craft—there are large structures in the Orkneys that have been standing for more than 5,000 years. India, China, and Egypt all developed sophisticated techniques for building in stone long before the modern era; and the Incas of South America demonstrated the finesse that can be achieved in the handling of massive granite blocks.

Great Zimbabwe was built between AD 1275 and 1550,[21] when the great medieval cathedrals of Europe were also under construction. By the end of the nineteenth century, when the first definitive records of the site were made, much of the Great Zimbabwe structure was already falling down; energetic rebuilding and conservation programmes are responsible for its subsequent preservation.

In terms of what drystone construction can achieve, Great Zimbabwe is not well built: the stones were not selected and laid with consideration for their relative sizes; vertical joints often run continuously through three or more courses (the joints of each course should be offset); there are no tie-stones linking the face surfaces of the walls and the void in between is very loosely filled. Even the amount of labour required was not excessive. Presented with detailed plans of the site, a modern drystone building contractor estimated that a workforce of eighty-four men on a six-day week could build the entire complex in two years. And the cost, employing skilled manual craftsmen working to higher standards than were applied to the original buildings and using 50,000 tonnes of stone, would be £3,907,000.[22]

EXCAVATIONS AT GREAT ZIMBABWE have produced numerous artefacts which throw light on the nature of Shona society during the period of its ascent and supremacy. Quite apart from the everyday pottery and iron items that are to be expected of a large settlement, seven carvings of birds from the eastern enclosure of the hilltop settlement suggest an element of religious ideology. The birds are about 35 cm high and carved from a soft green-grey soapstone that is not found less than 24 kilometres from Great Zimbabwe. They are the only sculptures of any size or displaying any attempt at representation from Great Zimbabwe or any other site of similar age in southern Africa, although they are stiff, crude "diagrams"[23] rather than attempts to analyse, depict, or recreate a natural creature.

On the other hand, the Great Zimbabwe birds have been described as ceremonial items symbolizing the role of the ancestors as interceders between the spiritual and the physical world.[24] Shona symbolism reveres birds as messengers, and so the birds could have commemorated distinguished ancestors who lived before Great Zimbabwe was established.

Elsewhere on the site, evidence of more secular affairs has been uncovered. In July 1903 archaeologists found a cache of the most varied and numerous articles ever discovered in south-central Africa.[25] The cache was buried more than one metre deep in an area near the north-eastern rim of the Great Enclosure known as Renders Ruin. Imported items included a glazed Persian bowl with thirteenth- or fourteenth-century inscriptions, several Chinese celadon dishes, some sherds of Chinese stoneware, fragments of engraved and painted Near Eastern glass and several tens of thousands of glass beads. There was also a piece of coral, cowrie shells, an iron spoon, an iron lamp holder suspended from a copper chain, a copper box, two copper finger rings and a quantity of brass wire. Thirty thousand glass beads were found in another part of Renders Ruin that was excavated in 1941.

The extraordinary assortment of exotic items found in Renders Ruin is securely dated to the thirteenth or fourteenth centuries, and thus demonstrates that Great Zimbabwe was in direct contact with trading centres on the East African coast by that time. Spindle whorls indicate that travellers or traders had brought the craft of spinning to Great Zimbabwe, and an early-fourteenth-century Arab coin minted at Kilwa in what is now southern Tanzania certainly suggests that trading connections had been established.[26] Furthermore, a sudden increase in building activity at Great Zimbabwe during the fourteenth century coincides with a no less sudden expansion of Arab trading centres on the East African coast, particularly at Kilwa. The most likely explanation for such a coincidence of prosperity must be that there was a "close economic connection."[27]

But if exotic artefacts and circumstantial evidence confirm the importation of goods into Great Zimbabwe, what was being exported? Gold was the most likely commodity. The Renders Ruin hoard included twenty small pieces of perforated gold sheathing, some gold wire, and a handful of gold beads. No other gold has been found at Great Zimbabwe. But if the settlement elite were primarily concerned with trading gold, rather than making personal use of it, the metal is unlikely to be widely evident in the archaeological record. Indeed, a large quantity of utilitarian goods recovered along with the Renders Ruin hoard strongly suggests that the Great Zimbabwe traders were middlemen who bought gold from miners and sold it on to traders from the coast.

An early inventory of the Great Zimbabwe finds listed about 25 kg of iron wire and about 100 kg of assorted hoes, axes, and chisels, items which would have been of value to farmers and miners living farther afield. As such they suggest that Great Zimbabwe was the focal point for a substantial internal African trade. Furthermore, "cakes of copper" and other items bearing strong affinities with artefacts characteristic of Zambia, the Congo basin, and West Africa, invite the conclusion[28] that Great Zimbabwe was on the eastern edge of a widespread and complex internal trading network which substantially predated the external trade that was founded primarily on gold.

AT THE TIME OF its pre-eminence in the fifteenth century, at least 11,000 and possibly as many as 18,000 people are said to have lived at Great Zimbabwe.[29] The massive stone-built enclosures were in fact only the central feature of an extensive urban sprawl of huts and living space[30] that covered an area of about seven kilometres in circumference.[31] Great Zimbabwe was large enough to be called a town, or even a city, but this was urban living at its most basic and unhealthy. The huts were so close together that their eaves nearly touched.[32]

Such a dense concentration of human activity imposed tremendous demands on the natural resources of the surrounding regions. The land suffered from excessive cultivation and overgrazing; water supplies became inadequate or contaminated; and unrelenting demands for firewood cleared progressively more distant woodland. As the site grew larger, people were obliged to travel ever further to tend fields and gather firewood. Ultimately the system became unsustainable; the centre could not hold and political authority gravitated to the periphery.

Great Zimbabwe flourished for little more than one hundred years. When the stone enclosures and surrounding urban sprawl were abandoned in the late fifteenth century, the ecological damage that just three or four generations of human inhabitants had inflicted upon the landscape was such that certain tree species will not grow in the area to this day.[33]

With the collapse of Great Zimbabwe two other Shona states rose to prominence on the plateau: Torwa, centred on Khami, about 250 km west of Great Zimbabwe; and Mutapa, 400 km north. Both states were founded on cattle-herding economies; both expanded with the growth of the gold trade; both rose and fell in 250 years: Torwa c.1450 to c.1650, Mutapa c.1450 to 1700.

It was during the period of Torwa and Mutapa prominence that the full extent and richness of the Zimbabwe gold deposits became apparent. Shona miners worked at more than 1,200 reefs and alluvial sites on the plateau,[34] and it is estimated that by the time industrial gold production began in the 1890s they had produced at least 200 million grams for the internal and export trade.[35] These were the Sofala "meadows of gold" which had attracted the Arabs and which would eventually come to the attention of European adventurers. In 1497, while on his pioneering voyage along the coastline of South and East Africa, Vasco da Gama found Arab dhows at the Zambezi delta "laden with gold dust."[36]

PART 5

FOREIGN INFLUENCES

Horses are exercised on the beaches of Togo in West Africa, where they were exchanged for slaves, 500 years ago

CHAPTER 31

"I Speak of Africa and Golden Joys"[1]

CHINESE FLEETS VISITED East Africa in the early fifteenth century, and took a giraffe back to Beijing in 1415; Portuguese caravels began exploring the coast of West Africa during the same period. The Portuguese sought gold, but found Africans willing to supply slaves as well. Nearly 1,000 African men, women and children were shipped to Portugal between 1441 and 1446.

In an essay[2] exploring the contemporary knowledge of Africa and Africans which had informed the Elizabethan writers from whom Shakespeare might have taken the many references to Africa that are scattered through his work (including, of course, *Othello*), the literary scholar Eldred Jones noted that although inquiring readers had access to an impressive body of authentic information by the end of the sixteenth century, legendary ideas and fancies were still firmly entrenched in the popular imagination.

Before the middle of the sixteenth century, the Bible and the classical historians constituted the sole source of information on Africa. In the first century AD, the author of the *Periplus* offered a small contribution (see Chapter 21) and Pliny described Africa and its inhabitants in his *Summary of the Antiquities and Wonders of the World*. A popular edition of the work published in 1556 brought some extraordinary ideas to the attention of a wide audience:

> Of the Ethiopians there are divers forms and kinds of men. Some there are toward the east that have neither nose nor nostrils, but the face all full. Oth-

ers that have no upper lip, they are without tongues, and they speak by signs, and they have but a little hole to take their breath at, by the which they drink with an oaten straw. There are some called Syrbote that are eight foot high, they live with the chase of elephants. In a part of Affricke be people called Ptoemphane, for their king they have a dog, at whose fancy they are governed . . . Toward the west there is a people called Arimaspi, that hath but one eye in their foreheads, theye are in the desert and wild country. The people called Agriphagi live with the flesh of panthers and lions: and the people called Anthropomphagi which we call cannibals, live with human flesh. The Cinamolgi, their heads are almost like to the heads of dogs . . . Others called Gramantes, they make no marriages, but all women are common. Gamphasantes they go all naked. Blemmyis a people so called, they have no heads, but have their mouth and their eyes in their breats. And others there are that go [walk] more by training of their hands than with their feet.

With greater prescience than the author could have guessed, William Waterman's *The Fardle of Fashions* (1555) quoted philosophers who:

Affirmed the Ethiopiens to have been the first of all men. For they conjectured that the ground of that country lying nearest the heats of the sun must needs first of all other wax warm. And the earth at that time being but clammy and soft, through the attemperance of that moisture and heat, man there first to have been formed . . . when all places were as yet strange, and unknown . . .

"What a feast of wonders! Shakespeare never forgot them," exclaims Eldred Jones. By Shakespeare's time, however, a body of more sober (and less memorable?) information was available. European mariners and merchants not only had visited Africa but also had published accounts of their voyages that described personal encounters with the peoples of the coastal areas. They had met African kings, had made friends with ordinary people, had dined on oysters, and had brought back pepper, gold dust, and ivory.

Between 1509 and 1513 a Spanish-born resident of Morocco, Leo Africanus, made two journeys to West Africa. He wrote an account of his experiences which was published in Venice in 1550 (in Italian) and subsequently translated into many languages; an English edition entitled *A Geographical Historie of Africa* appeared in 1600. Here Leo describes the region, which was commonly believed to be populated with monsters:

Moreover, the land of Negroes is divided into many kingdoms: whereof albeit a great part be unknown unto us, and removed far out of our trade . . . I myself saw fifteen kingdoms of the Negroes howbeit there are many more, which although I saw not with mine own eyes yet are they by the Negroes sufficiently known and frequented. Their names therefore (beginning from the west, and so proceeding eastward and southward) are these following: Gualata, Ghinea, Melli, Tombuto, Gago, Guber, Agadez, Cano, Casena, Zegzeg, Zanfara, Guangara, Burno, Gaoga, Nube.

Leo's description of his visit to "the kingdom of Tombuto" (Timbuktu) gives the impression of a well-ordered, prosperous, and civilized society in which learning flourished as well as trade:

> Here are many shops of artificers, and merchants, and especially of such as weave linen and cotton cloth. And hither do the Barbarie merchants bring cloth of Europe ... Corn, cattle, milk, and butter this region yieldeth in great abundance, but salt is very scarce here; for it is brought hither by land from Tegaza, which is 500 miles distant. When I myself was here, I saw one camel's load of salt sold for 80 ducats. The rich king of Tombuto ... keeps a magnificent and well-furnished court ... Here are great store of doctors, judges, priests, and other learned men, that are bountifully maintained at the king's cost and charges. And hither are brought divers manuscripts or written books out of Barbarie, which are sold for more money than any other merchandise.

An account of a visit to the kingdom of Benin made by the English merchant captain, Thomas Windham, in 1553 was published two years later:

> When they came they were brought with a great company to the presence of the king, who ... sat in a great huge hall, long and wide, the walls made of earth without windows, the roof of thin boards, open in sundry places, like unto louvers to let in the air ...
>
> And now to speak somewhat of the communication that was between the king and our men, you shall first understand that he himself could speak the Portugal tongue, which he had learned of a child. Therefore after that he had commanded our men to stand up and demanded of them the cause of their coming into that country, they answered by Pinteadao [Windham's pilot, formerly a captain in the Portuguese navy] that they were merchants travelling into those parts for the commodities of his country for exchange of wares which they had brought from their countries, being such as should be no less commodious for him and his people.

In 1554 John Lok captained a voyage to West Africa and returned with "four hundred pound weight and odd of gold, of twenty-two carats and one grain in fineness; also thirty-six butts of grains [pepper] and about two hundred and fifty elephants' teeth of all quantities." He also brought back an elephant's skull, complete with tusks weighing about 2 cwt (100 kg), which inspired the publisher Richard Eden to embellish Lok's somewhat bleak report with detailed description of elephants: their appearance, habits, and their continual war with dragons who "desire they blood because it is very cold."

In his compilation of voyages (including those of Windham and Lok quoted above) Richard Eden mixed fact and fancy in a manner which might have been designed to supply his readers with a good measure of both information and entertainment. His 1555 publication in particular marks the beginning of a process by which new facts gradually replaced old beliefs about Africa and Africans. But progress has been slow—and the whiff of prejudice is detectable in some quarters even at the end of the twentieth century. As Eldred Jones comments: "Legends die hard in the popular mind, while facts tend to languish in books."

EUROPE'S INVOLVEMENT WITH Africa was preceded by the Arab incursions, of course, and—more unexpectedly perhaps—by the Chinese. Chinese porcelain is a ubiquitous feature of the material recovered from early trading locations in East Africa; Arab reports and Chinese trade figures indicate that large quantities of African products were reaching China by the tenth and eleventh centuries[3]—almost certainly via India, which Chinese Buddhists had been visiting from the fourth century AD. By the twelfth century, however, Chinese vessels capable of carrying up to 600 persons were sailing to the Indian ports; their captains doubtless knew of the Arab trading settlements on the east coast of Africa and the tremendous expansion of maritime activity which occurred during the early part of the Ming dynasty (1368–1644) made direct contact inevitable.

In the closing decades of the fourteenth century, local governments of the eastern coastal regions of China were ordered to build ocean-going vessels; 1,180 ships of various types and sizes had been constructed by 1405,[4] and between 1405 and 1433 seven fleets sailed to the "Western Ocean" under the command of Cheng Ho, a military leader who had been castrated at the age of ten and thereafter assigned to the emperor's service. The first fleet comprised 63 large ships and 255 smaller vessels carrying a total of 27,800 men, including 95 commanders, 543 military officers, 868 civil officers, 180 medical officers and assistants, sundry ambassadors, secretaries and servants and more than 26,000 soldiers.[5]

Cheng Ho's first voyage cleared the way to India, his second (1407) and third (1408–11) gave China an influential position in the maritime trade of the Indian Ocean; the fourth (1413–15) and the fifth (1416–19) extended Chinese direct trading contacts to Arabia and the Red Sea, while his sixth (1421–24) sailed beyond them to East Africa and established official relations between the Ming court and official figures at Mogadishu, Malindi, Mombasa, Zanzibar, Dar es Salaam and Kilwa. Internal dissent delayed the launching of a seventh voyage until 1431; this time a score of states were revisited including those along the coasts of Arabia and East Africa, but Chinese interest in far-flung dominions was waning. Cheng Ho, who was already in his sixties, died in Calicut, India, and the return of the fleet marked the end of the most extensive maritime activities in China's history.

Contemporary documents and charts indicate that although Chinese mariners did not venture beyond Kilwa during the period of maritime expansion, their knowledge of the East African coast extended to the southern tip of the continent, and they were even able to produce a tolerably accurate impression of Africa's west coast. The evidence implies that the Chinese, with their knowledge, superior ships and navigational instruments, were even capable of sailing around Africa at the beginning of the fifteenth century but desisted—at first because the Indian Ocean provided enough trade to satisfy their interests, and latterly because of the internal isolationism which "cast its shadow [over] the unfolding horizons, and [left] Africa . . . to be 'rediscovered' by the daring sea captains from Portugal," nearly a century later.[6]

Of all the documents and reports linking Africa with China none is more evocative than the image of the giraffe which arrived in Beijing in October 1415. Envoys from Malindi had joined Cheng Ho's fourth voyage at an Arabian or Indian port with a variety of gifts for the Chinese emperor, including "a magnificent specimen of a giraffe." A contemporary painting on silk[7] shows the giraffe with halter and lead-rope standing calmly beside its Chinese handler; and the painting's inscription congratulates the emperor on the arrival of such an auspicious beast.

The emperor is reported to have received the giraffe in person from the Malindi envoys, at the gates of the inner palace, amid scenes of acclamation. This occasion of intercontinental accord coincided almost exactly with Henry the Fifth's less than friendly encounter with the French at Agincourt, and with the capture of Ceuta, a trading centre on the North African coast, by Portuguese forces under the leadership of another royal Henry, Prince Henry, later to be known as Henry the Navigator.

On returning to Portugal from North Africa in the 1430s Henry established his household on Cape St. Vincent, near Sagres. Here, it is said, he always wore a hairshirt next to his skin and lived a virtuous and chaste life, without ever knowing a woman or drinking wine or indulging in any other vice.[8] At Cape St. Vincent he founded the world's first naval academy, instigating a programme of innovation and enterprise that within the span of little more than three generations opened the entire inhabitable globe to European mariners— from Portugal's first tentative voyages around the bulge of West Africa in the 1430s, to Columbus's discovery of America in 1492, and the Spanish circumnavigation of the globe in 1521.

Prince Henry's interest in maritime affairs is said to have been awakened in Ceuta, where he heard alluring tales of the gold that traders brought to North Africa from Timbuktu, on the other side of the Sahara. This information indeed may have inspired the idea that mariners should be directed to pioneer a sea route down the western coast of Africa which would outflank and thus divert the gold trade from the trans-Sahara caravans to the Portuguese caravels.

Such overtly pecuniary incentives for maritime exploration were later subsumed, however, under the more noble enterprise of looking for Prester John, the fabled Christian priest-king whose domains were believed to lie beyond the realm of the Islamic powers which then ruled from Morocco to the Black Sea, cutting off Christendom from direct contact with Asia and the isolated Coptic Christian kingdom of Abyssinia. From 1402 onwards, Abyssinian monks and envoys had travelled to Europe (and at least one reached Lisbon in 1452), but the location of Prester John's kingdom was still undefined. Henry wanted his ships to sail around Africa, join forces with Prester John and thus outflank and eventually overwhelm Islam.

Under Henry's direction, Portugal pioneered the major advances in shipbuilding and navigation that would enable mariners to fulfil his aims. The caravel, 20 to 35 m long and 6 to 9 m broad, with little freeboard and shallow draft, was fitted with three masts and Arab-style lateen sails, a combination which made the vessels highly manoeuvrable and ideally suited for reconnaissance along unknown coasts.[9]

Navigation remained a problem, however, for until the invention of an accurate chronometer (in 1760) no precise means of determining longitude (east–west) was known. Latitude (north–south) could be measured by finding the angle of the sun above the horizon at noon. With precisely formulated tables giving the sun's declination at stated latitudes for each day of the year, mariners could determine their position in relation to the Equator to within about 50 km—even with the comparatively crude sighting instruments then available. Longitude remained a guess, but whereas navigators previously had followed the coastline, they now could sail long distances across open ocean, well beyond the sight and dangers of the coast, and then steer along the appropriate line of latitude towards the desired landfall.[10]

The pioneering voyages to Africa instigated by Henry the Navigator (he did not sail with the voyages personally) from the 1430s onward were in fact preceded by more than a century of European seafaring along the coast of Morocco and to the Canary Islands and Madeira. In 1291 two brothers from Genoa, Vadino and Ugolino Vivaldi, sailed out through the straits of Gibraltar with the avowed intention of circling Africa. They were never seen again. In 1336, another Genoese mariner, Lanzarote Malocello, followed in the wake of the Vivaldis and, recording more success than his predecessors, ultimately made landfall on the island which still bears his name, Lanzarote, the most north-easterly island of the Canary archipelago.

Lanzarote and its immediately adjacent neighbour, Fuerteventura, are about 80 km from the African coast. The islands were inhabited when Malo-cello arrived, by a group of people known as the Guanche, whose ancestors are believed to have settled in the Canaries from the African mainland over a period of centuries, a seaborne immigration that began no earlier than 2000 BC and was concluded by the first centuries AD. The Guanches had brought with them cereals, beans, and peas; goats, dogs, and possibly sheep. They made pots, but knew nothing of cloth or metal tools (not least because there are no ore deposits on the Canaries).[11]

Lanzarote Malocello settled among the Guanche, but maintained contact with Europe, exporting hides and tallow derived from the Guanches' large herds of livestock and quantities of an indigenous lichen, orchil, a most valu-able item which, depending on the method of processing, yielded a variety of blue, violet, purple, and scarlet dyes and was much sought after by medieval weavers and dyers.[12]

In 1341 the King of Portugal, Afonso IV, declared the Canaries to be within Portugal's domain and dispatched a slave-raiding expedition to the archipel-ago. In the decades that followed, Europeans of many nationalities joined forces to raid the Canary Islands for captives.

Europe was desperately short of labour at the time, the Black Death (1347–51) and its aftermath having swept away more than one-third of its agri-cultural workforce, thus creating a ready market for slaves. Demand was espe-cially high in southern Europe; nowhere more so than in the sugar plantations. Europeans had learned about sugar cultivation and processing from the Mus-lims during the Crusades, and established their first plantations at Tyre, in what is now the Lebanon, in 1123. From there, sugar production spread steadily westward through the Mediterranean, never able to keep pace with the soaring demands of Europe's sweet tooth; always needing more battalions of slave labour.

Plantations in Syria, Cyprus, Sicily, and elsewhere in the Mediterranean were at first worked by captive Muslims and Slavic peoples ("slaves") acquired at Black Sea ports. By 1404, when Portugal granted Giovanni della Parma, of

Genoa, a royal licence to establish a sugar plantation in the Algarve[13] the Canary Islands were a primary source of slaves. The Guanche resisted, but slave-raiding, combined with warfare and disease, had reduced the population of Lanzarote to 300 by 1402,[14] and the indigenous Guanche population of the Canary archipelago had been all but annihilated by the early 1500s.[15]

Meanwhile, the Portuguese were attempting to establish settlements in the Madeira archipelago which, unlike the Canaries, had been totally uninhabited by people when the first prospective settlers landed on the islands in the 1420s. Until then the islands must have been a microcosm of biological evolution, such as that which inspired Charles Darwin in the Galapagos. The two main islands, Madeira and Porto Santo, were covered in forest and their indigenous flora and fauna probably included numerous species that were unique to the islands. Any chance of their being saved for the interest of science was, however, soon destroyed by the settlers' pursuit of what they believed to be their own best interests.

Bartholomeu Perestrello, recipient of settlement rights to Porto Santo (and future father-in-law of Christopher Columbus), released a family of rabbits, intending that they should become a source of meat.

> [The rabbits] in a very short time multiplied so much as to overspread the land, so that our men could sow nothing that was not destroyed by them [a contemporary chronicler reports].[16] And it is a marvel [he continues] how [the settlers] found in the year following their arrival, that although they killed a very great quantity of these rabbits, there yet remained no lack of them. Wherefore they abandoned that island and passed over to the other isle of Madeira . . . twelve leagues [sixty kilometres] distant from Porto Santo.

When the settlers first landed on the shores of Madeira they found it so densely wooded that "there was not a foot of ground that was not entirely covered with great trees." "Ilha de Madeira" is Portuguese for "island of timber" but, like Porto Santo before it, Madeira was not destined to retain its pristine character for long.

> It was therefore first of all necessary, when it was desired to people it, to set fire to the [forest], [the chronicles report][17] and for a long while this fire swept fiercely over the island. So great was the first conflagration, that . . . this Zuanconzales, who was then on the island, was forced, with all the men, women, and children, to flee its fury and to take refuge in the sea, where they remained, up to their necks in water, and without food or drink, for two days and two nights or thereabouts, to escape destruction. By this means they razed a great part of this forest, and cleared the ground for cultivation.[18]

The settlers introduced sugar cane from Europe, slaves from the Canary Islands and by 1455 Madeira was producing nearly 70 tonnes of sugar per year; a shipment landed at Bristol in 1456 was one of the first to supply the parlours of England. By 1472 Madeira's annual sugar production was approaching 200 tonnes, and in the first decades of the sixteenth century it exceeded 1,600 tonnes per year.[19] The so-called civilized world was becoming addicted to sugar, and awesome consequences would unfold.

Voyages serving the commercial enterprises of Madeira, the Canaries and later the Cape Verde Islands and the Azores, were the background of regular maritime activity against which Henry the Navigator's pioneering exploration of Africa was set. In 1433 the Canary Islands marked the southern limit of known human habitation in the Atlantic. No one had ventured beyond Cape Bojador, a barren coastal landmark some 200 kilometres due south of the Canaries. A contemporary account[20] explains why:

> Beyond this Cape there is no race of men nor place of inhabitants: nor is the land less sandy than the deserts of Libya, where there is no water, no tree, no green [sward]—and the sea so shallow that a whole league [5 km] from land it is only a fathom deep, while the currents are so terrible that no ship having once passed the Cape, will ever be able to return.

Such fears notwithstanding, in 1433 Henry sent out a vessel under the command of Gil Eanes, whom he instructed to sail past Cape Bojador. On approaching the fateful Cape, however, Eanes was "touched by the self-same terror" that had afflicted earlier voyagers. He abandoned his mission and sailed instead to the Canary Islands, where he took some captives and returned home to Portugal. Next year, 1434, Henry bade him try again:

> You cannot find [Henry told him] a peril so great that the hope of reward will not be greater ... Go forth, then, and heed none of their words, but make your voyage straightaway, inasmuch as with the grace of God you cannot but gain from this journey honour and profit.[21]

Eanes went forth, "doubled the Cape, despising all danger," and returned with tales of a desolate and uninhabited coast. In 1435 he went forth yet again and sailed 250 kilometres beyond Cape Bojador; here he went ashore and found "the footmarks of men and camels."

"As you have found traces of men and camels," Henry remarked on Eanes's return, it is evident that the inhabited region cannot be far off; or perchance they are people who cross with their merchandise to some seaport with a secure anchorage for ships to load in, for since they are people, they must of necessity depend upon what the sea brings them, and especially upon fish, however bestial they may be.[22]

The inhabitants of West Africa received the first intimations of Portuguese ambition the following year (1436), when a vessel under the command of Affonso Gonçalvez Baldaya sailed beyond Cape Bojador, beyond the point reached by Eanes the previous year, and found safe anchorage in an extensive inlet, nearly 400 km south of Cape Bojador. Baldaya named the inlet Rio d'Ouro ("River of Gold") on the assumption that, first, it was a river and, second, it flowed from the African goldfields.[23] Both assumptions were wrong.

Henry had supplied the expedition with two horses. Baldaya had them put ashore and ordered two youths to ride inland, looking for villages or people. The youths (neither of whom was more than seventeen years old) followed the course of the "river" for seven leagues (35 km), "where they found nineteen men all banded together without any other arms of offence or defence, but only assegais [short stabbing spears]." The youths attacked with swords and lances; the group retreated to the security of some rocks, where fighting continued until late afternoon, when the youths broke off and returned to the ship. One of them was wounded in the foot, but this "did not go unavenged," the chronicler reports,[24] "for they wounded one of the enemy likewise."

While leaving unquestioned the assumption that the nineteen Africans were an "enemy" of the Portuguese, the chronicler acknowledged a degree of common humanity when he wondered how they might have regarded the youths—" . . . what would be the fancy in the minds of those men at seeing such a novelty, to wit, two such daring youths, of colour and features so foreign to them; what could they think had brought them there . . . [?]"[25]

The reason for the Portuguese presence was made abundantly clear in 1441. A young captain, Antam Gonçalvez, led a party of nine armed men ashore and captured a man and a woman. Days later, Gonçalvez joined forces with Nuño Tristão, captain of a caravel newly arrived from Portugal, and led a night attack on two small African encampments.

And when our men had come nigh to them [the chronicler reports], they attacked them very lustily, shouting at the top of their voices . . . the fright of which so abashed the enemy, that it threw them all into disorder. And so, all in confusion, they began to fly without any order or carefulness.

Four Africans were killed and ten taken prisoner. No Portuguese injuries were reported. Antam Gonçalvez was knighted for his enterprise and valour.[26]

The captives were delivered to Henry, and one of more noble demeanour than the rest soon learned enough Portuguese to promise that if he were returned to Africa his people would give five or six slaves in return for his freedom. And a similar ransom would be given for each of two other captives, he said. Antam Gonçalvez sailed for Africa with the three captives. The noble (finely dressed) was set ashore at the boundary of the land where the ransom was to be made, and Gonçalvez sailed on to anchor in the Rio d'Ouro. Eight days later an African on a white camel arrived with a message to the effect that others would arrive to make the ransom the following day.

Antam Gonçalvez received ten slaves for his captives, plus an oxhide shield, ostrich eggs (subsequently served to Prince Henry "as fresh and as good as though they had been the eggs of any other domestic fowls") and "a little gold dust."[27]

News of the slaves and gold that Antam Gonçalvez brought back to Portugal awakened a surge of commercial interest in Henry the Navigator's explorations of the West African coast. Portuguese merchants who previously had been scornful of the notion now applied to Henry for a licence to send trading voyages to Africa. The first was granted in 1444 to one Lançarote, who probably had a better idea than most of the trade's value, since he was the receiver of customs at the Portuguese port of Lagos, where Henry's captains unloaded their cargoes.[28]

Lançarote took a fleet of six armed caravels to West Africa and returned with 230 slaves. This expedition marked the beginning of the West African slave trade as a part of European commerce. Gomes Eannes de Azurara, chronicler, royal librarian, and keeper of the archives of Portugal witnessed the unloading of the human cargo at Lagos on the eighth of August 1444:

> . . . very early in the morning, by reason of the heat, the seamen began to make ready their boats, and to take out those captives, and carry them on shore, as they were commanded . . . But what heart could be so hard as not to be pierced with piteous feeling to see that company? For some kept their heads low and their faces bathed in tears, looking upon one another; others stood groaning very dolorously, looking up to the height of heaven, fixing their eyes upon it, crying out loudly, as if asking help of the Father of Nature; others struck their faces with the palms of their hands, throwing themselves at full length upon the ground; others made their lamentations in the manner of a dirge, after the custom of their country. And though we could not understand the words of their language, the sound of it right well

accorded with the measure of their sadness. But to increase their sufferings still more, there now arrived those who had charge of the division of the captives, and who began to separate one from another . . . fathers from sons, husbands from wives, brothers from brothers.

And who could finish that partition without very great toil? For as often as they had placed them in one part the sons, seeing their fathers in another, rose with great energy and rushed over to them; the mothers clasped their other children in their arms, and threw themselves flat on the ground with them; receiving blows with little pity for their own flesh, if only they might not be torn from them.

And so troublously they finished the partition; for besides the toil they had with the captives, the field was quite full of people . . . who for that day gave rest to their hands (in which lay their power to get their living) for the sole purpose of beholding this novelty. And with what they saw, while some were weeping and others separating the captives, they caused such a tumult as greatly to confuse those who directed the partition.[29]

Azurara declares that a total of 927 captives were shipped to Portugal from West Africa between 1441 and 1446. With the exception of the few that were ransomed, no captive was taken without a fight, and many others died resisting capture. Among the Portuguese, three captains and over thirty seamen were killed on slave-raiding expeditions during the same period.[30]

CHAPTER 32

Portuguese Initiatives

THE PORTUGUESE OUTFLANKED the trans-Sahara gold trade when they reached the Gold Coast (modern Ghana) in 1472. The first European buildings in Africa were erected at El Mina (the mine) with materials imported from Europe; gold and slave-trading contacts were firmly established in West Africa while the Portuguese carried European influence around the southern tip of the continent: the Cape of Good Hope.

As West Africa became more widely known as a region where fortunes might be made, Henry the Navigator maintained a determined interest in the trade. His regulations stipulated that trading vessels which sailed beyond Cape Bojador without a licence were liable to have all their goods confiscated, and even traders sailing under licence were required to give Henry a "fifth" and a "tenth" of all commodities acquired in trade.[1]

In the matter of slave cargoes, the royal chronicler's account indicates that Henry distributed the greater part of his shares to others,[2] retaining only a few for his service—such as those deemed likely to be of use in the further exploration of the African coast. Royal standing orders instructed captains on turning from the farthest point they reached "to contrive to bring away a negro, by force or persuasion, so that he might be interrogated [through an interpreter], or in the course of time might learn to speak [Portuguese], so that he might give an account of his country."[3] Once trained, African interpreters sailed with subsequent voyages, serving not only as interpreters, but also as trading intermediaries and guides through unfamiliar waters. By the late 1440s, these

337

Eclipse of the sun over the Koitokol Hills, Samburu district, Kenya

grumetes (as they were known) were indispensable to Portuguese navigators and traders.[4]

As voyages of discovery advanced along the unknown coast of West Africa, trading voyages followed in their wake, and the guile of merchants replaced the rapacious behaviour of the pioneers. In 1448 Portuguese merchants built a trading post and fort from local materials on Arguim Island, a barren speck of land 6 km from what is now the Mauritanian coast in the bay that lies between Cabo Blanco and the mainland. Fish were a primary incentive for the location, for the Canary Current brings cold oxygenated waters to the continental shelf of the Mauritanian coast; plankton flourishes and feeds a rich fishery in which tuna—in particular—abound.

Voyaging captains replenished their provisions with fish caught and salted on the banks, and the rich resource even enticed Portuguese and Spanish fishermen to make the long voyage to Arguim. Furthermore, the fish sustained large populations of seals—colonies of maximum density that had never been attacked—and the early voyagers regularly carried large quantities of sealskins and oil back to Europe. In 1436, for instance, Affonso Gonçalvez loaded his ship with skins taken from a colony of some 5,000 seals among which his men made "a very great slaughter . . . because they were very easy to kill."[5]

From their base on Arguim, the Portuguese established business relations with Arab traders and nomadic groups known today as the Tuareg, who told them

> that when for the first time they saw sails, that is, ships, on the sea . . . they believed that they were great sea-birds with white wings, which were flying, and had come from some strange place: when the sails were lowered for the landing, some of them, watching from far off, thought the ships were fishes. Others again said that they were phantoms that went by night, at which they were greatly terrified. The reason for this belief was because these caravels within a short space of time appeared at many places, where attacks were delivered, especially at night, by their crews . . . Perceiving this, they said amongst themselves, "If these be human creatures, how can they travel so great a distance in one night, a distance which we could not go in three days?" Thus, as they did not understand the art of navigation, they all thought the ships were phantoms.[6]

Trade flourished and the merchants prospered. It has been estimated that returns were hardly ever less than 50 per cent and sometimes as high as 800 per cent. Highest returns were registered between 1450 and 1458, when ten to twelve ships were sent out each year and the traffic yielded from five to seven times the invested capital.[7]

The Portuguese shipped woollen cloths, cotton, silver, cloaks, and carpets to Africa and "above all, corn, for they [the Africans] are always short of food." In exchange they acquired civet-cats (prized for the musk used in perfume-making), hides, beeswax, gum arabic, fish, ostrich eggs, goats and, valued above all else, gold and slaves.[8]

In medieval Europe it was considered perfectly in order to enslave anyone who was not a Christian; and their suffering was justified by the spiritual salvation which Christianity offered. Prince Henry "reflected with great pleasure upon the salvation of those souls that before were lost,"[9] and the crusading inspiration of his desire to circumnavigate Africa and thus join forces against Islam with the mysterious Christian potentate, Prester John (see page 330), was explicitly recognized by Pope Nicholas V in the papal bull *Romanus Pontifex* issued on 8 January 1455.

Pope Nicholas commended Henry's achievements to date and granted the King of Portugal and his successors the jurisdiction to build churches, monasteries, and other pious foundations, not only in the lands already conquered, but also in those to be later acquired. The papal bull also recognized the commercial motive inherent in the Portuguese expansion, however, by granting Portugal the exclusive right to trade with the inhabitants of the newly discovered regions, subject only to the proviso that the sale of war materials to enemies of the Christian faith was forbidden.[10] To the chagrin of Spain and the subsequent frustration and exasperation of France and England, Portugal had gained a monopoly of trade in West Africa's valued commodities.

Early Portuguese voyagers had been obliged to conduct their own slave-raids on African communities, but the establishment of a trading post on Arguim Island encouraged Africans to do the job for them. In due course, horses became a primary medium of exchange. Alvise da Ca' da Mosto (also known simply as Cadamosto), a Venetian who sailed with Portuguese caravels to West Africa in the 1450s, reported that rulers in "the Land of the Blacks" would readily give ten or fifteen slaves for one horse, "according to their quality."[11]

Though the Portuguese caravels were capable of transporting only seven to ten horses at a time, the animals attracted trade away from the trans-Saharan route and towards the West African coast. Rulers and elites from among the Jolof people who occupied the savanna and agricultural regions south of the Senegal River, for instance, were eager to obtain horses as a means of attaining and maintaining a dominant role in the region.

With growing cavalry forces and the need for captives to barter for new mounts (a horse's lifespan in West Africa was short), as well as for saddles and other accoutrements, the Jolof elites took to slave-raiding as a means of both accumulating wealth and expanding their territory. In the 1450s Cadamosto had noted that the "negro chiefs . . . have very few horses," but by the end of the century the Jolof were said to have a force of 10,000 mounted horsemen—an exaggeration, no doubt, but nonetheless indicative of a formidable reputation.[12] Jolof ambitions fuelled the slave trade, and by the 1460s the Portuguese were shipping 1,000 slaves per year from Arguim.[13]

Henry the Navigator died in 1460, by which time Portuguese mariners had explored and produced charts of the West African coast from Cape Bojador to present-day Sierra Leone and Liberia. The previously uninhabited Cape Verde Islands, 600 km due west of Senegal, were settled during the 1460s and became an advance base for the African trade. West African captives were brought in for labour and settlers in the archipelago rapidly developed economic, social, and cultural links with the mainland; miscegenation between Portuguese men and captive African women produced a growing population of Luso-Africans whose African heritage was to be of inestimable value in dealing with related groups in West Africa.[14]

The Cape Verde settlers harvested and exported orchil, the dye-producing lichen that grew on the cloud-enshrouded peaks of the archipelago, and introduced sugar cane, doubtless hoping to match the achievements of plantations in Madeira, but the more arid climate of the Cape Verde islands precluded large-scale sugar production. The settlers had greater success with cotton, however, and by the early sixteenth century were supplying West African markets with woven cloth and exporting raw cotton by the tonne to Flanders.[15]

After Henry's death, the direction of Portugal's African trade and exploration passed to his nephew, King Afonso V. But Afonso was more interested in affairs closer to home and, although keen to retain the profits of Henry's ambition, he was unwilling to assume liability for the costs of further exploration. Hence he leased the royal privilege of African discovery and trade to one of his subjects—a wealthy merchant of Lisbon named Fernão Gomes. The five-year lease, drawn up in November 1469 (and extended an extra year in 1473), obliged Gomes to advance along the coast from Sierra Leone (then the farthest known point) a further 100 leagues (500 km) each year. In return for 500 leagues (2,500 km) of discovery Gomes was granted exclusive rights to trade in the lands which his agents might discover, subject only to royal customs dues and the stipulation that all ivory was to be sold to the crown at a fixed price.[16]

Gomes had made a good deal. His well-organized voyages advanced rapidly around the Gulf of Guinea. At an early stage his agents developed a profitable trade in an African species of pepper, malaguetta (*Aframomum melegueta*). These "grains of paradise," as they were known, found a ready market in Europe as an alternative to pepper imported from the East via the

Mediterranean. The seaboard of what is now Liberia became known as "the Grain Coast," the primary source of malaguetta pepper.[17] Further east, the Ivory Coast was identified as the source of yet another valuable commodity, and in January 1472 the vanguard of Gomes's exploratory voyages anchored off the estuary of the Pra River, near "a town called Samaa of some 500 inhabitants where the first gold in this country was obtained in barter."[18]

Gold mines were located nearby. The trading centre became known as El Mina, and the seaboard as the Gold Coast (now Ghana). Forty years after Henry the Navigator had established his naval academy at Cape St. Vincent with the intention of exploring and exploiting the African coast, the Portuguese had at last located the foremost source of gold in West Africa and outflanked the trans-Saharan trade.

The gold trade at El Mina rapidly assumed major proportions.[19] From 1487 to 1489 an estimated annual average of almost 8,000 ounces reached the royal treasury in Lisbon. By 1496 the figure had risen to about 22,500 ounces and mariners in the first years of the sixteenth century reported that between 24,000 and 30,000 ounces of gold was reaching Portugal from El Mina each year. These anecdotal reports may have been inflated, but none of the computations took account of shipments lost at sea, or of smuggling and unofficial trade, and the fact remains that within the space of a few years a small fishing village on the coast of West Africa had been transformed into a principal supplier of bullion to the world market, and was exporting more than half a tonne of gold annually. It has been suggested that the Portuguese probably captured about half of West Africa's gold exports while in control of the Gold Coast.[20]

The Portuguese at first had a problem paying for the gold. Horses could not survive the equatorial climate and there was a limit to the amounts of cloth and sundry goods that the Akan people who controlled the Gold Coast trade would accept. Weapons were eagerly requested, but banned by papal edict. Perversely, however, the Portuguese discovered there was an African commodity that the Akan would readily accept in exchange for their gold; furthermore, it was a commodity that was abundantly available to the Portuguese a relatively short distance (up to 800 km) along the coast: slaves.

The Akan were engaged with expansion of their own when the Portuguese arrived on the Gold Coast, expansion that required labour for forest clearance and agriculture in particular. They were already accustomed to acquiring slaves from the north in exchange for gold; now they acquired them from the south as well. During the 1470s the Portuguese established trading contacts at anchorages along the Bight of Benin and the Niger delta, where the Benin and Igbo people were very willing to sell them captives taken in military and territorial raids.

Thus the seaboard of what is now Benin and Nigeria acquired the sobriquet that still identifies it on some reputable atlases[21]—the Slave Coast—and the Portuguese became maritime middlemen in a network of indigenous exchange.[22] Between 1500 and 1535 (the only period for which such records exist) they shipped 10,000 to 12,000 slaves across the Bight of Benin from the Slave Coast to the Gold Coast, and sailed onward to Portugal with rich cargoes of gold, ivory, and pepper.

THE LONG EASTWARD CURVE that the Portuguese had followed around the bulge of West Africa might have encouraged some mariners to believe that they had reached the southernmost limit of the continent, eastward of which they would meet the Indian Ocean and could sail north to the land of Prester John, or east to India. But from the Niger delta the coastline turned abruptly south again and the southernmost limit of the continent was still a good way off.

During the 1470s Portuguese mariners discovered the islands of Fernando Po, Príncipe and São Tomé in the Gulf of Guinea; they crossed the Equator in 1474,[23] but sailed no farther than Cape Santa Caterina (two degrees south) in present-day Gabon on that adventure. For a time, attention was more closely focused on harvesting the wealth of the Grain, Ivory, Gold and Slave Coasts, and in furtherance of this aim it was decided that a permanent fort should be built at El Mina, on the Gold Coast.

Accordingly, a fleet of nine caravels and two urcas (the urca, or bark, was a large provision ship of up to 500 tonnes) set sail from Lisbon for West Africa on the 1st of January 1482. The urcas carried cargoes of dressed stone, lime, tiles and bricks, timber, tools and nails. Those sailing on the voyage included a full complement of crew plus 100 stonemasons and carpenters and 500 soldiers, whose orders were to build, provision, and garrison a fort to guard Portuguese interests at El Mina. The Pope, probably in response to a specific request, had granted a full indulgence for their sins to all Christians who might die on the expedition.[24]

Strenuous opposition from the indigenous population notwithstanding, the surrounding walls of the fortress, along with a large central tower and spacious warehouse, were finished and available for defensive purposes within twenty days, it is said, and on completion the fort was proclaimed "the first stone building in the region of the Ethiopias of Guinea since the creation of the world."[25]

Setting aside any moral and ethical difficulties that might be attached to the construction of a fort in foreign territory, the technical difficulties confronting the Portuguese deserve a moment's contemplation: the bay was full of shallows, ships were anchored some distance offshore, and all materials were laboriously transferred to boats and rowed ashore; average daytime temperatures hovered around 30°C and are unlikely to have fallen below 24°C at night; humidity was constantly high and malaria rife; drinking water was scarce, "many of the people sickened and some died."[26]

While the majority of the fleet and its crews were engaged with building the fort at El Mina, two vessels under the command of Diogo Cão were sent off to discover what lay beyond Cape Santa Caterina. Each carried in its hold a *padrão*, a stone cross just over two metres high. These crosses were to be erected at the expedition's important and farthest landfalls. Prior to that time the Portuguese had been content to erect wooden crosses, or to mark the progress of their discoveries with inscriptions carved on trees. King John II, who took the throne on the death of Afonso V in 1481, wanted to leave a more permanent record of Portuguese progress. Each *padrão* bore an inscription:

> In the year 6681 of the world, and in that of 1482 since the birth of our Lord Jesus Christ, the most serene, most excellent and potent prince, King John II of Portugal did order this land to be discovered and these [*padrãoes*] to be set up by Diogo Cão, an esquire of his household.[27]

It was 1483 before Cão sailed beyond Cape Santa Caterina and another six months before he encountered any landmark worthy of a *padrão*. Five degrees south of the Equator, he found the country densely wooded and thickly populated with both people and elephants; high red cliffs lined the coast; twelve leagues (60 km) beyond the red cliffs two thickets with exceptionally tall trees stood behind a rugged beach, and twenty-five leagues (125 km) south-south-west of the thickets a large river flowed into the ocean—of so great a volume that the surface water was still noticeably fresh at a distance of thirty leagues (150 kms) from the coast. Diogo Cão erected a *padrão* on the south-eastern shore of the estuary and accordingly named the river Rio do Padram. The fishing was good, but the region very liable to fever. Inland, Cão noted, lay the kingdom of Conguo, whose people called the river he had discovered "Nzadi," meaning "great river." Today it is called the Congo.[28]

South of the Congo estuary Cão noted the good fishing that a powerful cold current (the Benguela Current) brought to the waters off present-day Luanda, in Angola, and erected his second *padrão* on a promontory he named Cape Santa Maria—thirteen degrees and forty minutes south of the Equator—thereby extending Portugal's claims to more than 8,000 km of coast that had been charted in the thirty-eight years since Cape Bojador was first rounded in 1441.

Diogo Cão sailed home believing he had reached the southernmost tip of Africa (his evidence for this belief is not recorded) and must have been sorely disappointed to discover on returning to Cape Santa Maria in 1486 that the coast not only extended southward without apparent limit, but also became increasingly arid. He erected a third *padrão* at Cape Negro 100 km north of the border between modern Angola and Namibia, where "the surrounding country is all sand except at the point of this Cape where there is a black patch";[29] and a fourth at Cape Cross, on the southern fringe of the forbidding Skeleton Coast. Diogo Cão died at Cape Cross; the *padrão* he erected there was removed by German officials during the colonial period and sent back to Berlin, where it was displayed for many years in the museum of the University's oceanography institute.[30]

On the return of Cão's expedition in 1486, King John II immediately ordered that further exploration of the sea route to India must continue. Three vessels were prepared and command entrusted to Bartolomeu Dias. The expedition sailed from Lisbon in August 1487.[31]

The Portuguese took with them two male Africans kidnapped by Cão from the shores of modern Angola, and four females taken from the Slave Coast. The intention was that the six should be landed at intervals along the coast, dressed in European fashion and equipped with samples of gold, silver, and spices that might help to locate sources of these items along the coast. Women were the predominant choice for this local exploration because it was hoped they would be more respected in the event of conflict.

Information on the Dias voyage is lamentably sparse. Though the voyage has been described at length in popular books,[32] no contemporary sources have survived, and the only available knowledge is derived from a few odd references in the logbook of Vasco da Gama's voyage (made ten years later), and from names appearing on contemporary maps.[33] These meagre sources indicate that Dias followed the coastal route to beyond Cape Cross and raised his first *padrão* on the promontory of Lüderitz Bay in modern Namibia. The two male Africans and two females were set ashore at unspecified points on these first advances into unknown territory, and a ship with stores for the return voyage was left in Lüderitz Bay with a caretaker crew of nine (who are said to have been given seeds and instructions to start a vegetable garden ashore).

Proceeding south from Lüderitz, contrary winds blew Dias and his caravels out of sight of land, and a storm then carried them southward for several days. When the storm abated the caravels edged cautiously eastward for some days, expecting to regain sight of the north–south coastline. None appeared, so Dias ordered another change of course—due north—and a couple of days or so later caught the first glimpse of a coastline that filled the horizon from east to west.

Dias had rounded Cape Agulhas, the southernmost point of Africa, and made landfall in a bay that he named Bahia dos Vaqueiros (Bay of Cattle), on account of the large numbers of cattle and herdsmen seen on the surrounding grassland. But there was no fresh water available in the vicinity, so the caravels weighed anchor and sailed along the coast until a source was found in what is now known as Mossel Bay. Dias named the promontory sheltering the bay Cabo de São Bras (Cape of Saint Blaize), and since the Portuguese customarily named landmarks after the saint's day on which they were sighted, it can be stated with certainty that white men first set foot in South Africa on the 3rd of February 1488.

Herdsmen and their cattle gathered above the shore as the caravels anchored in the bay, but rapidly dispersed when a party landed to take on fresh water. Some herdsmen returned a little later, however, and began to bombard the Portuguese with stones from a hillside above the watering point. Royal regulations for the voyage had instructed Dias to cause no harm or "scandal" to the Africans he encountered, but Dias was so incensed by the stone-throwing that he shot a bolt from his crossbow at the assailants and killed one of them.[34]

Leaving Mossel Bay, the last of the African women (the other had died on board) was put ashore to join two local women seen gathering shellfish, and the two caravels continued along the coast, pursuing an easterly course that satisfied the captains but raised a state of alarm among the crews. Having reached the end of the continent they wanted to see an end to the voyage. Wearied by their struggles with the sea, and rotten with scurvy, they turned upon their commander "with one voice," declaring that provisions were hardly sufficient for the voyage back to the store-ship, while 2,000 kilometres of new coastline was more than enough of pioneering exploration. Rather turn back, they urged, and discover the cape they had missed, where the southern trend of the continent veered eastward.[35]

Compromise allowed Dias to proceed for two or three days more. He erected a *padrão* on a promontory now called Kwaaihoek (where its shattered fragments were found 450 years later),[36] thereby adding more than 2,000 kilometres of African coastline to the limit of Portuguese discoveries that Diogo Cão had marked out, and turned about.

In April 1488 the caravels anchored beside the attractive and well-watered cape they had missed on the outward voyage. Dias named it the Cabo de Boa Esperança—the Cape of Good Hope—in acknowledgement of the promise it offered mariners on both their outward- and homeward-bound voyages. A *padrão* was erected on the brow of a prominent cliff, then the caravels rounded the Cape and at last turned north for home.

Of the nine men that had been left with the store-ship in Lüderitz Bay, only three were alive when Dias and his caravels rejoined them, after an absence of nine months, in July 1488. Six had been killed by Africans when they ventured ashore; and the survivors were so weak that one is said to have died of excitement when the caravels returned.[37] The fate of the Africans who had been set ashore, dressed in European fashion, and bearing samples of gold, silver, and spices, is not known.

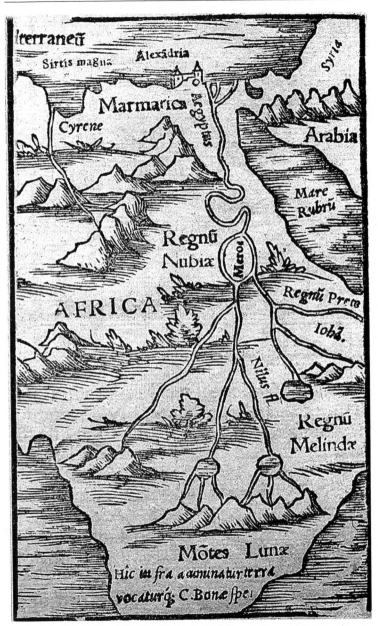

A map published by Sebastian Munster at Basle in 1544 shows (right-centre) the kingdom of Prester John as *Regnu Pretr, Ioha*

CHAPTER 33

In Search of Prester John

THOUGH EUROPEANS FIRST VISITED Ethiopia in 1407, Ethiopians had been visiting Europe since 1306 at the latest. These early visitors told of a great Christian King, Prester John, who ruled Ethiopia. Portuguese voyages around the continent were intended to make contact with Prester John and gain his support for the Christian crusade against Islam.

Squeezed by historical circumstance on to the far western corner of Europe, with suspicious neighbours at their backs and a seaboard facing the unexplored expanses of the Atlantic, the Portuguese were isolated from the Mediterranean and defined by the Atlantic. Thus it was no more than to be expected that they would have an affinity for the ocean and develop the maritime technology and expertise capable of taking men around the toe of Africa. And no less predictable that they would have a very poor idea of what to expect on the other side.

Merchants travelled freely through the straits of Gibraltar, supplying Portugal with exotic commodities and an abundance of tantalizing allusions to the wonders of the eastern world. Reliable information was more difficult to acquire. European contacts with Ethiopia—the land of Prester John—were established during the thirteenth century, but Portugal shared few of them. Information on north-east Africa accumulated in the archives of the Mediterranean states during the fourteenth and fifteenth centuries, but Portugal knew little of its substance.

In fact, contemporary accounts indicate that while Henry the Navigator and his successors had only a hazy impression of Prester John and his domain, the rest of Europe were fully aware that a vigorous and literate Christian state controlled the highlands that lay south of Egypt, between the Nile and the Red Sea.

The ancient Aksumite state had collapsed in the ninth century AD under the strain of its overextended ambitions (see pages 218–19), but the Coptic Christian faith adopted by King Ezana in the fourth century survived. Indeed, while the region's much-reduced population fell back upon the unique ecological circumstances and indigenous resources of the Ethiopian plateau for subsistence, the church became their fount of influence and authority. Kings acquired divine status—the Priest-King.

The earliest-known reference to Presbyter Iohannes (medieval Latin, meaning Prester, or Priest, John) appears in an 1145 manuscript of Otto, Bishop of Freisingen, referring to him as a powerful Christian priest-king ruling a vast empire vaguely supposed to be somewhere in middle Asia. A letter said to have been addressed to the Greek emperor Manuel by Prester John himself in 1165 claimed, among other things, that the wonders of his empire included the fountain of youth, a river whose bed consisted entirely of gemstones, ants that dug gold, pebbles that gave light or could make a man invisible, and a mirror that enabled Prester John to see what was happening anywhere in any one of his seventy-nine kingdoms.[1]

However much credence (or lack of it) was given to the more fantastic elements of the myth surrounding Prester John, his identity was conferred upon the kings of Ethiopia when medieval Europe learned of the Christian kingdom that lay beyond the realm of Islam.

In considering the relationship between Africa and Europe, received wisdom suggests that Africa was a dark and passive continent, supine with tropical lethargy, awaiting the enlightenment that European discovery and exploration ultimately would bring. The truth is otherwise. Far from being passive, Africa responded vigorously to European attempts to establish a presence on the continent; furthermore, Ethiopians were exploring the city streets of Europe long before Europeans visited Ethiopia or any other part of sub-Saharan Africa. The first European to visit Ethiopia was an Italian, Pietro Rombulo, who made the journey in 1407; Ethiopians had visited Italy in 1306—101 years earlier.[2]

The evidence is scarce and always brief, but documents preserved in various medieval archives indicate that Ethiopians were travelling abroad from an early date. Most evocatively, a summary[3] of a document written in the early years of the fourteenth century describes how a priest in Genoa had interviewed a group of thirty Ethiopians who were returning home from visits to

Avignon and Rome, but had been forced to wait at Genoa for a favourable wind. The year was 1306, but the records suggest that the thirty Ethiopians may have been only slightly less commonplace than modern travellers on an unscheduled stopover at a foreign airport.

> A certain priest [Giovanni da Carignano], the rector of St. Mark in Genoa, a truly excellent man, published a treatise . . . Among many things written in it about the state of this nation [the Ethiopians] he reports that Prester John is set over that people as Patriarch; and he says that under him are 127 arch-bishoprics, each of which has twenty bishops . . . It is said that their emperor is most Christian, to whom seventy-four kings and almost innumerable princes pay allegiance, except those kings who observe the laws of Mahomet but submit to the emperor in other things. It is known indeed that this emperor, in the time of Clement V [Pope, 1305 to 1314] and the year of our salvation 1306, sent thirty envoys to the king of the Spains and offered him aid against the infidels. They also presented themselves reverently before Pope Clement V at Avignon and, instructed by many apostolic letters, came to Rome to visit the churches of Peter and Paul. Having seen these they set forth joyfully to return to their own country. But as they tarried many days at Genoa awaiting fair weather for sailing, they were questioned and left (so it is said) many things in writing about their rites, customs and regions, which the same author has published.

The fact that the Ethiopians Giovanni da Carignano had met were travelling so widely in such numbers, presumably with interpreters or able to converse in a common language (probably Latin), at the command of a king seeking a western alliance—all suggests that their journey had been preceded by other fact-finding missions.

Ethiopians regularly visited Egypt and Cyprus, and made pilgrimages to the holy places of Palestine, where they met European travellers and established links between Ethiopia and the rest of the Christian world. These contacts gave Europeans exaggerated notions of the decisive role Ethiopians could play in a united Christian alliance against Islam in the eastern Mediterranean. It was commonly believed, for instance, that the Ethiopians controlled the flow of the Nile. A typical report stated that "if it pleases the Prester John, he could very well make the river flow in another direction."[4]

In the year 1400 King Henry IV of England sent a letter to the "king of Abyssinia, Prester John." Evidence of the letter preserved in the British royal archives indicates that Henry was seeking King David's (the then Prester John) participation in a crusade against Islam, but the bearer of the letter was instructed to convey this in person, for security reasons.[5] It is not known if Henry's letter reached Ethiopia, but in 1402 King David himself sent envoys to

Italy, presumably asking for technical aid (apart from any political purpose) and is known to have received a number of Florentine craftsmen at his court. The Ethiopian chronicles report that a young Italian named Pietro Rombulo arrived in Ethiopia in 1407 and remained there for thirty-seven years, when he was sent on a mission to India and China by David's successor, Yishaq. After returning to Ethiopia, he was back in Naples on another mission in 1450, now a grey-haired man in his sixties who told his story to a Dominican monk, Pietro Ranzano.[6]

Vatican records indicate that letters of safe conduct were given to at least three parties of Italians who travelled to Ethiopia between 1451 and 1453, and a traveller who visited Ethiopia in 1482 reported on his return that he had met ten Italians there who had been in the country for twenty-five years.[7] The French sent missions to Ethiopia too; during the 1420s the Duke of Berry dispatched a Neapolitan by the name of Pietro who not only reached Ethiopia successfully, but remained there for some years and actually married an Ethiopian.[8]

These fragments of evidence add up to a clear indication that continuous relations were firmly established between Ethiopia and Europe during the first half of the fifteenth century. Furthermore, Europe's relatively sound and extensive knowledge of the land of Prester John is shown on two contemporary maps: the Egyptus Novelo, drawn in Florence c. 1454; and the Mappomondo drawn in Venice in 1460.[9] Though the Egyptus Novelo shows only north-east Africa while the Mappomondo gives a representation of the entire world, both contain details of Ethiopian geography and the location of towns that could only have been acquired from first-hand knowledge.

Even more significantly, the Mappomondo shows Africa surrounded by ocean, confirming a medieval assumption that the circumnavigation of Africa was a practical proposition.[10] It was this assumption that had inspired the Vivaldi brothers who set sail from Genoa in 1291, never to return (see page 331); and which Henry the Navigator and his successors were determined to confirm. But, although the Portuguese doubtless shared European assumptions concerning the possibility of sailing around Africa, they lacked detailed information on Prester John and the lands he ruled. They had papal blessing for their enterprise (see page 340), but little or none of the intelligence to which the Pope might have had access. If the Portuguese knew of the many Europeans who had travelled to Ethiopia and beyond by the end of the fifteenth century, they were not privy to the maps and reports that had been brought back. Strong support for this contention is implied by the simple fact that in 1487 King John of Portugal dispatched what are popularly referred to as "two spies" to the unknown land of Prester John.

Pero de Covilhã and Afonso de Paiva, both of whom spoke Arabic, travelled as merchants through a network of contacts the king had established around the Mediterranean. Their instructions were to discover whatever they could of Prester John, East Africa, and the route to India and report back to the king.[11] The intelligence clearly would have been helpful to Portugal's seaborne expeditions.

The two agents travelled safely through Alexandria, Cairo and Suez to Aden, where they parted. Paiva crossed the Red Sea en route back to Portugal while Covilhã sailed to India, where he collected details of the spice trade before taking a ship to Sofala on the East African coast. Believing that Paiva had by then returned to Portugal, Covilhã too began to make his way home. In Cairo he was contacted by two Jewish agents of King John who told him that Paiva had failed to reach Portugal and was believed to be dead. Covilhã sent one of the agents back to Portugal with his report on India and East Africa, and returned to Aden with the other. From Aden he travelled alone to Ethiopia, where he confirmed that Paiva was indeed dead and had not been able to send a report back to Portugal before his demise.

Covilhã was taken to King Iskindir[12] (the then Prester John), and appears to have got along well with his Ethiopian hosts, so well in fact that he was given land and a wife with very great riches, raised sons and was still alive and well thirty years later, when another Portuguese traveller, the priest Francisco Álvares met him in Ethiopia and recorded his story.[13] But Covilhã never lost a passionate desire to return to Portugal, Álvares reports. He repeatedly begged King Iskindir and his successors for permission to leave, but his pleas were obstinately refused.

A lack of news from Covilhã and Paiva in part explains the lapse of more than ten years between Bartolomeu Dias's rounding of the Cape of Good Hope and the departure of an expedition instructed to pursue the route Dias had opened to the east (finance and the king's failing health also contributed to the delay). In hopeful expectation of valuable first-hand information from Covilhã and Paiva, four vessels were prepared for a major voyage of exploration around the coast of Africa. Two ships were built specifically for the enterprise, and contemporary accounts report that nothing was spared.

> They were built by excellent masters and workmen, with strong nails and wood; each ship had three sets of sails and anchors and three or four times as much other tackle and rigging as was usual. The cooperage of the casks, pipes, and barrels for wine, water, vinegar, and oil was strengthened with many hoops of iron. The provisions of bread, wine, meat, vegetables, medicines, and likewise of arms and ammunition, were also in excess of what was

needed for such a voyage. The best and most skilful pilots and mariners in Portugal were sent on this voyage, and they received, besides other favours, salaries higher than those of any seamen of other countries. The money spent on the few ships of this expedition was so great that I will not go into detail for fear of not being believed.[14]

The fleet set sail from Lisbon on 8 July 1497 under the command of Vasco da Gama, who carried letters for various potentates (including Prester John), detailed instructions and all available information on the eastern and western seas but lacking any word from Covilhã and Paiva.

An officer of the fleet was assigned the task of compiling a *Roteiro,* a log of the voyage. The identity of the author is not known, but a copy of the document made at the beginning of the sixteenth century has been preserved; in it are navigational details and a day-by-day account of the voyage that reads more like a personal diary than a ship's log. The *Roteiro* thus provides a unique eyewitness account of the expedition's encounters with Africa and Africans.[15]

With Dias having recorded the latitude of the Cape of Good Hope, da Gama was free to follow the prevailing winds from the Canaries in a broad curve to the south Atlantic before turning east towards the tip of Africa. The crews sighted land on the 4th of November and cast anchor four days later in a wide bay. The anchorage was named Saint Helena Bay after the saint's day on which it was located and the fleet remained there for eight days while the ships were careened and cleaned, sails were repaired and firewood supplies replenished. There were a number of Khoisan people camped nearby, and each group—African and European—was avidly interested in the activities of the other.

The inhabitants of this country are tawny-coloured [the diarist reports].[16] Their food is confined to the flesh of seals, whales and gazelles, and the roots of herbs. They are dressed in skins and wear sheaths over their virile members. They are armed with poles of olive wood to which a horn, browned in the fire, is attached. Their numerous dogs resemble those of Portugal, and bark like them . . . The climate is healthy and temperate, and produces good herbage.

On the second day the Portuguese seized a man they had found gathering honey. They took him on board ship, fed and dressed him well, then put him ashore again.

On the following day fourteen or fifteen natives came to where our ships lay. The captain-major landed and showed them a variety of merchandise, with a view to finding out whether such things were to be found in their country. This merchandise included cinnamon, cloves, seed-pearls, gold, and many other things, but it was evident that they had no knowledge whatever of such articles, and they were consequently given round bells and tin rings. This happened on Friday, and the like took place on Saturday.

On Sunday about forty or fifty natives made their appearance, and having dined, we landed, and in exchange for the *ceitils* [small copper coins] with which we came provided, we obtained shells, which they wore as ornaments in their ears . . . and fox-tails attached to a handle, with which they fanned their faces.

One of the Portuguese wanted to find out how the Khoisan lived. He followed them from the bay, but when some distance from the ships they indicated that he should follow no farther. By the time he got back to the beach (accompanied by some of the Khoisan), the rest of the shore party was on board again. He shouted for a boat; his shouts were mistaken for cries of help; a "rescue" party rushed ashore in such haste that the Khoisan feared attack. They responded by throwing their assegais and wounding four or five men. "All this happened," the diarist concludes,[17] "because we looked upon these people as men of little spirit, quite incapable of violence, and had therefore landed without first arming ourselves."

The fleet sailed from St. Helena Bay on Thursday, 16 November, rounded the Cape of Good Hope (200 km to the south) against contrary winds and on Saturday, 25 November, anchored in the bay of São Bras, the modern Mossel Bay, where they remained for thirteen days.[18]

On Friday . . . about ninety men resembling those we had met at St. Helena Bay made their appearance. Some of them walked along the beach, whilst others remained in the hills. All, or most of us, were at that time in the captain-major's vessel. As soon as we saw them we launched and armed the boats and started for the land. When close to the shore the captain-major threw them little round bells, which they picked up. They even ventured to approach us, and took some of these bells from the captain-major's hand. This surprised us greatly, for when Bartolomeu Dias was here the natives fled . . . Nay, on one occasion, when Dias was taking in water, close to the beach, they sought to prevent him, and when they pelted him with stones, from a hill, he killed one of them with the arrow of a crossbow [see page 346] . . .

The captain-major did not land at this spot, because there was much bush, but proceeded to an open part of the beach, when he made signs to the negroes to approach. This they did. The captain-major and the other captains then landed, being attended by armed men, some of whom carried crossbows. He then made the negroes understand, by signs, that they were to disperse, and to approach him only singly or in couples. To those who approached he gave small bells and red caps, in return for which they presented him with ivory bracelets, such as they wore on their arms, for it appears that elephants are plentiful in this country. We actually found some of their droppings near the watering place where they had gone to drink.

On Saturday about two hundred negroes came, both young and old. They brought with them about a dozen oxen and cows and four or five sheep. As soon as we saw them we went ashore. They forthwith began to play on four or five flutes, some producing high notes, the others low ones, thus making a pretty harmony for negroes who are not expected to be musicians; and they danced in the style of negroes. The captain-major then ordered the trumpets to be sounded, and we, in the boats, danced, and the captain-major did so likewise when he rejoined us. This festivity ended, we landed where we had landed before, and bought a black ox for three bracelets. This ox we dined off on Sunday. We found him very fat, and his meat as toothsome as the beef of Portugal ... The oxen of this country are as large as those of Alentejo [in Portugal], wonderfully fat and very tame. They are geldings and hornless. Upon the fattest among them the negroes place a pack-saddle made of reeds, as is done in Castile, and upon this saddle they place a kind of litter made of sticks, upon which they ride.

During their visit, the Portuguese erected a *padrão* and a cross on Cape St. Blaize; the *padrão* was of stone and the cross was made out of a mizzen mast, and very high. As the fleet was preparing to sail, ten or twelve Africans attacked the cross and the *padrão* and had demolished them both before the ships had cleared the bay.

ON SATURDAY THE 16TH OF DECEMBER 1497 da Gama and his fleet passed Kwaaihoek, where Bartolomeu Dias had erected a *padrão* nine years before, and by Christmas Day they were more than 500 kilometres beyond the mouth of the Keiskamma River, where Dias had turned back.[19] The coast they were tracking was green and wooded, with knolls of rock and prominent red sand-bluffs; da Gama called it Terro do Natal,[20] for the Day of the Nativity. Natal, one of South Africa's provincial regions, is named after this sighting. The crews made a good catch of fish behind the sheltering headland of Durban bay on the 28th of December and on 11 January the fleet anchored to take water from a river flowing into Delagoa Bay, possibly in the vicinity of present-day Maputo (identification of the exact site is disputed).[21]

This country seemed to us to be densely peopled [the author of the *Roteiro* declares].[22] There were many chiefs, and the number of women seems to be greater than that of the men, for among those who came to see us there were forty women to every twenty men. The houses are built of straw. The arms of the people include longbows and arrows and spears with iron blades. Copper seems to be plentiful, for the people wore [ornaments] of it on their legs and arms and in their twisted hair. Tin, likewise, is found in the country, for it is to be seen on the hilts of their daggers, the sheaths of which are made of ivory. Linen cloth is highly prized by the people, who were always willing to give large quantities of copper in exchange for shirts. They have large calabashes in which they carry sea water inland, where they pour it into pits to obtain salt [by evaporation].

The fleet stayed five days; some of the Portuguese were lodged in a nearby village where they were fed millet porridge and chicken. Da Gama named the country Terra da Boa Gente—Land of Good People. Sailing on (along the coast of modern Mozambique), they found the country low and marshy, and covered with tall trees yielding an abundance of fruits.

> These people are black and well made. They go naked, merely wearing a piece of cotton stuff around their loins . . . [They] took much delight in us. They brought us in their [canoes] what they had, whilst we went into their village to procure water.

Saturday the 2nd of March 1498, and da Gama's fleet dropped anchor in the harbour of Moçambique town. Many of the men had become ill, the *Roteiro*'s author reports,[23] "their feet and hands swelling, and their gums growing over their teeth, so that they could not eat." Scurvy. But here was a town and markets, offering the prospect of fresh provisions, while four Arab dhows anchored in the harbour added a promise of success to the voyage. At last, the Portuguese were in direct contact with traders from the east.

The ships in the harbour were of considerable size, owned and manned by Arabs and as well, if not better, equipped than the Portuguese, with compasses, charts, and extremely efficient navigating instruments. They were loaded, so the Portuguese were assured through a crew-member who spoke Arabic, with gold and silver, with pearls, seedpearls, and rubies, and with cloves, pepper, and ginger. The Portuguese were also informed that Prester John held many cities along the coast to the north, from which his residence could be reached on the back of camels. So much good news. The author of the *Roteiro* confessed:[24]

> This information, and many other things which we heard, rendered us so happy that we cried with joy, and prayed to God to grant us health, so that we might behold what we so much desired.

Relations between the Portuguese and the people they encountered as they sailed onward were not propitious, however. This was the Swahili coast, where local Africans followed Islam and merchants were wealthy enough to dress in rich linens and cottons with borders of silk embroidered in gold. The Portuguese were impoverished by comparison. A dignitary who visited the ships in Moçambique harbour dismissed with contempt the hats, corals, and sundry items he was offered as gifts and demanded better; "of which we had none," the diarist laments. In Mombasa, where the fleet anchored on the 7th of April, a sheikh sent a sheep and great quantities of oranges, lemons, and sugar cane to the ships. In return for these items and a guarantee of peace he was presented with a string of coral beads. This was a gross insult; akin to offering a lump of coal to the owner of a coal mine.[25]

Clearly, the Portuguese had little or nothing of value to offer the people they now found themselves beholden to for safe anchorage, water, and provisions. Furthermore, they feared anti-Christian enmity from Arab seamen and Muslim Africans alike. Portuguese fears provoked Arab suspicion, to which the Portuguese responded aggressively. The town of Moçambique was bombarded with cannon and plundered before they sailed on. While anchored off Mombasa, boiling oil dripped upon the skin of two Arab hostages produced confessions of Arab plans to capture the Portuguese as reprisal for the damage done at Moçambique.

Forewarned, the Portuguese repelled the attack. Two days later they sailed from Mombasa and exacted revenge of a kind by capturing a vessel in which

we found seventeen men, besides gold, silver, and an abundance of [grain] and other provisions . . . also a young woman who was the wife of an old Moor of distinction, who was [also] a passenger. When we came up with the boat they all threw themselves into the water, but we picked them up from our boats.[26]

Having learned from his captives that four vessels belonging to Christians from India were currently anchored in Malindi harbour, da Gama promptly began negotiating for the pilot and provisions he needed for the voyage to India and it was agreed that, in return for their release, the captives would persuade the Malindi authorities to provide not only a pilot, but also water, wood, and all other necessities for the voyage.

The old Moor was set ashore to arrange matters and, over several days of haggling, the hostages were released, the vessels were reprovisioned and a pilot was taken on board. The *Roteiro* reports that the fleet sailed from Malindi for the south Indian port of Calicut on Tuesday, 24 April. "On the following Sunday we once more saw the North Star, which we had not seen for a long time."[27]

The man who piloted da Gama's fleet to India has been identified as Ahmad Ibn-Madjid, not a Christian, but the most famous Arab pilot of his day, and one who knew the Indian Ocean better than any other. Thanks to his guidance, the Portuguese reached Calicut without further difficulty. Their arrival inaugurated an age of European maritime power in the region; not surprisingly, Ibn-Madjid has been blamed for his contribution to Europe's ascendency. Fellow-countrymen and co-religionists cursed his memory; and in his old age, Ibn-Madjid himself bitterly regretted what he had done.[28]

The pioneering Portuguese fleet spent several months in India and returned to East Africa in January 1499 (without a local pilot). The passage across the Arabian Sea took nearly three months, owing to calms and contrary winds. By the end of the crossing scurvy was rampant. Thirty men had already died of the disease, and another thirty died before the fleet sighted the African coast near Mogadishu. Only seven or eight able-bodied men survived to handle each vessel.[29]

Fortunately, the authorities at Malindi were welcoming when the vessels arrived on 7 January 1499. Meat and oranges, chickens and eggs, were sent aboard, and da Gama found the people so well disposed that he asked for an elephant tusk to be given as a present for the King of Portugal, and for permission to erect a *padrão*. Both requests were granted.[30] The *padrão* still stands. The fleet lay at Malindi for five days, recuperating, then sailed on beyond Mombasa, and anchored in the neighbourhood of modern Tanga for fifteen days. Deaths had now reduced the crews to the point that made effective handling of three ships impossible. The crew and contents of one were distributed among the other two, and the empty ship burnt.[31]

The two vessels rounded the Cape of Good Hope on 20 March. "Those who had come so far were in good health and quite robust," the author of the *Roteiro* reports, "although at time nearly dead from the cold winds which [they] experienced." The journal ends abruptly shortly after this entry, but other sources indicate that da Gama entered the Tagus at the end of August 1499.[32]

Vasco da Gama was given a hero's welcome; honours were showered upon him. He had opened the sea route to India and the East and proved that there was gold in south-east Africa. On the other hand, the voyage had been a dismal failure in diplomatic terms. Not one alliance or agreement had been negotiated with any of the states he had visited. There was an "understanding" with Malindi, it is true, but this fades to insignificance when compared with the opportunities that had been missed or squandered by his actions. Furthermore, da Gama had made enemies of Islam and East Africa.

Rendille women tie in the framework of a hut at an encampment in the Kaisut desert, Kenya

CHAPTER 34

Harnessed to Europe

THE PORTUGUESE HARNESSED Africa to Europe. The continent and its people were assessed in terms of their significance to Europe, but the stress of ecological imperatives on human society in Africa remains strikingly evident from documentary evidence, which joins archaeology as the principal sources on African history.

Following the pioneering voyage of Vasco da Gama, the Portuguese proceeded to consolidate their position on the East Africa coast by the blatant use of force and terror. They sailed their heavily armed vessels into the harbours of the important Swahili towns, demanded submission to the rule of Portugal and payment of large annual tributes. Towns that refused were attacked, their possessions seized and resistant Muslims killed.

Zanzibar was the first Swahili town to be taken in this manner (in 1503). Malindi formed an alliance with the Portuguese which hastened the fall of Mombasa in 1505; Barawa (on the Somali coast, south of Mogadishu), Kilwa, Moçambique and Sofala were all taken in the same year. The towns were incapable of repelling a determined attack from ships armed with cannon, and the long-standing rivalry that existed between them as trading centres militated against cooperative efforts of defence.

The Portuguese justified their actions as battles in the Christian war against Islam, though some of the methods they employed could be more accurately described as crimes against humanity. On his second voyage to India, for instance, Vasco da Gama encountered a ship laden with pilgrims going to

Mecca. There were 380 men on board, besides many women and children. The ship was primed with gunpowder and then blown up, with the pilgrims on board. Islam shuddered at the news of Portuguese atrocities,[1] and the tremor travelled far afield.

Though the Portuguese described their activities as Christian and right-eous, their motives were mercenary. In 1506, a Portuguese commander reported that Sofala was capable of supplying over 4,000 tonnes of gold per year. The king of Portugal was ecstatic at the news, writing of "infinite gold" from Sofala.[2] It was anticipated that gold from Sofala would buy goods and luxuries from India which would be sold in Europe—a lucrative prospect, with the added attraction of circumventing if not usurping Muslim trade via the Red Sea.

To defend Portuguese interests, a fort was built at Sofala (and in due course others were constructed at Moçambique, Kilwa, and Mombasa); but the East African gold trade never amounted to more than a fraction of its alleged poten-tial. Of the prospective 4,000 tonnes, a mere 2.6 kg was shipped from Sofala in the fifteen months from the founding of the station to the end of 1506, and exports appear to have been equally meagre throughout the succeeding peri-ods for which records are available—up to 1513.[3]

But whatever the vagaries of trade they experienced, the Portuguese unquestionably harnessed Africa to Europe. Their voyages overlapped the Arab presence; they erected crosses around the shores of the continent, like charms on a necklace, and claimed rights of possession and exploitation in the name of God and King. The coastline was known, and the dimensions of the interior thereby established. The continent was huge, its resources appeared infinite. In West Africa a significant portion of the trans-Saharan gold trade had been diverted to Portuguese outlets at the coast; in East Africa, Arab and Swahili dominance was challenged.

THE EARLY SIXTEENTH CENTURY, when Portugal's involvement with Africa was at its height, marks an important shift in the study of African his-tory. This is the period during which the written word begins to supersede archaeology as the most accessible evidence of human affairs on the continent. Evidence for the first 4 million years of human existence consists entirely of artefacts and scientific deduction; but from the sixteenth century onward, European exploration (and the printing press) produced substantial amounts of documentary evidence, from the eyewitness accounts of life in Africa recorded by visitors, and the histories of communities transcribed directly from the mouths of their living representatives.

The shift in emphasis, from archaeological to documentary evidence, produces a dramatic (and possibly unrealistic) change in the picture of human society in Africa that history presents. For the period during which the evidence of human activity is purely archaeological, interpretations tend to imply that the size and distribution and behaviour of communities was overwhelmingly conditioned by prevailing climatic and ecological circumstances: human population densities were low; people were highly mobile; settlements were small, scattered, and ephemeral; problems of food production and disease militated against the establishment of large sedentary communities. From the time that documentary evidence becomes available, however, humanity's joys and woes in Africa are largely attributed to the behaviour of people themselves.

Assessing the relative validity of the contrasting interpretations is fraught with difficulty; both are likely to be coloured by the quality of the original evidence, by the predispositions of the people who unearthed or recorded it, and by the partiality (or wishful thinking) of those currently interpreting it. A book such as this, for instance, can choose to imply that violent conflict between communities became a feature of human social behaviour in Africa only with the intensification of trading demands that Europeans imposed upon the continent from the late fifteenth century. And it is certainly true that, with the exception of the Jebel Sahaba massacre of 12,000 to 14,000 years ago (see pages 146–47), no direct archaeological evidence of humans killing humans has been found in Africa (and the Jebel Sahaba massacre could be attributed to unique circumstances in the Nile valley).

There are grounds for believing that episodes of serious conflict occurred in Africa only when people began to accumulate conspicuous surpluses in the form of cattle herds (see page 311). Before then, while human settlements were small, scattered and ephemeral, dispute led to dispersal rather than conflict. Once cattle-owning societies began exercising control over access to grazing and water, however, opportunities for dispersal were limited and the potential for conflict intensified. But even then, the evidence of conflict is equivocal. Spears found at Great Zimbabwe, for instance, could be ceremonial symbols of authority, not lethal weapons.[4] Similar ceremonial items were recovered from excavations in the Middle Senegal Valley, and the numerous spears found throughout the 1,000-year sequence are as likely to have been used for hunting animals as for killing people.[5] The same could be said of spears and arrowheads recovered from other sites.

But while the archaeological evidence of violent conflict between groups in Africa is either totally absent or at best equivocal, the documentary evidence is full of it: foreign visitors record instances of strife, and the oral histories glorify traditions of conquest. This could mean one of two things: either the documents record activities of which there is no sign in the archaeological record, or the documentary evidence records the moment when violent conflict became a repeated and significant feature of African affairs. If the latter is true, as is at least possible, it points to the conclusion that the arrival of Europeans incited Africans to a level of conflict not previously evident.

But a surfeit of violent conflict *after* the arrival of the Europeans does not imply that peace and harmony reigned throughout the continent during the preceding centuries. "Merrie Africa," like Merrie Englande, was always a myth. Dispersal, insufficient manpower, or the lack of anything worth fighting for, certainly would have repressed the human propensity for conflict, but hardship was widespread nonetheless. And hardship, though revealed in the archaeological record only by the implications of climate and potential food shortages, is unmistakable in the documentary record. Foreign visitors write of impoverishment and suffering, as well as of warring despots; oral histories tell of famines as well as conquests.

FATHER FRANCISCO ÁLVARES, priest, represents a more recognizably Christian aspect of Portugal's foreign enterprise than was evident in the exploits of da Gama and his colleagues. Like the mariners, Álvares sailed to Africa at royal command, but while the king's captains sought territory and profit, the priest had a less directly acquisitive interest in the material world. He collected information. For six years, from 1520 to 1526, Álvares travelled around Ethiopia as part of a thirteen-man diplomatic mission to Prester John. He recorded everything of relevance that he saw. His account of the journey appeared as a book, first published in Lisbon in 1540.

"I decided to write down everything that happened to me on the journey," he declared in the preface,

> things seen and things found, by sea and on land, and the kingdoms, lordships and provinces, cities, country houses and places where we went, and the nations and peoples, their clothes, manners and customs, whether Christians, Moors, Jews or heathens, the customs of each of them. Whatever I have been able to learn I shall vouch for as something I saw if I saw it, or if it was something I heard I shall tell it as something I heard. So I promise and swear in my soul I shall tell no lie, but what I write I shall vouch for as the truth.

Álvares wrote a great deal: 151 chapters filling 441 pages of the modern two-volume English translation.[6] The book is the first extensive documentary account of conditions of Africa. Álvares's observations on everything from gate fastenings to the rituals of the royal court are remarkable for their objectivity—and compare favourably with some modern accounts of foreign travel. Indeed, the only false note is struck by Álvares's repeated mention of "tigers" (known only in India), when he must have been referring to either leopards or hyenas.

"In all the country there is much bread, wheat and barley," Álvares reported in a summary presented as the final chapter of his book,[7]

> ... and where wheat and barley are somewhat lacking, there is much [tef] ... pulse, beans, kidney beans, chickpeas and all vegetables ...
>
> Birds, partridges of three kinds, like ours, other fowls which we call guinea fowl ... quails, pigeons, turtle-doves, sparrowhawks, falcons, kites, golden eagles, thrushes ...
>
> There is much basil in the thickets (and plenty of other sweet-smelling herbs ... not known to us). There are none of our trees ... except cypresses, plum trees, and willows by the rivers; there are no melons, cucumbers, or horse-radish ...
>
> There is flax there, but it gives no fibre, and no cloth is made with it; there is much cotton, and cloth made of it; there is much coloured cloth, and there is a very cold country where they wear burel [a coarse woollen cloth].
>
> There is a great quantity of honey in the whole country, and the hives are not in apiaries, but inside the houses, where the peasants live, up against the walls on the inside, through which they have a way to the outside ... there are also many bees in the woods and mountains, and the men put hives in the trees and fill them with bees, and they bring them up to the houses.

Álvares travelled through millet fields thick and tall as a man;[8] he visited regions where cereals were sown and harvested all year round;[9] he saw "very beautiful fields, all irrigated by channels of water descending from the highest peaks,"[10] and he passed "beautiful herds of cows," so numerous that "the multitude there is cannot be believed."[11] And yet not all Ethiopia was a land of milk and honey:

> In these parts and in all the dominions of the Prester John there is a very great plague of locusts which destroy the fresh crops [and trees] on a very big scale. Their multitude, which covers the earth and fills the air, is not to be believed; they darken the light of the sun. They are not general in all the kingdom each year, for if it were so, the country would be a desert in consequence of the destruction they cause: but one year they are in one part, and another year in another ... Sometimes they are in two or three of these provinces. Wherever they come the earth is left as though it had been set on fire ...[12]

We travelled five days through country entirely depopulated, and through millet stalks as thick as canes for propping vines; it cannot be told how they were all cut and bitten, as if bitten by asses, all done by the locusts. The wheat, barley and *tafo* [tef], as though they had never been sown there, the trees without any leaves, and the tender twigs all eaten, there was no trace of grass of any sort ... This country was entirely covered with locusts without wings [the hopper stage], and they said these were the seed of those which had been there and destroyed the country, and they said that as soon as they had wings they would at once go and seek their country ... the multitude of those without wings is not to be believed ... The people were going away from this country, and we found the roads full of men, women, and children, on foot, and some in their arms, with their little bundles on their heads, removing to a country where they might find provisions (it was a pitiful sight to see them).

[Another time] ... in a town named Aquate, there came travelling thither such a multitude of locusts as cannot be told ... Next [morning] they began to depart, and at midday there was not one there; and not a leaf remained upon a tree. At that moment others began to arrive, and they remained like the others ... and these did not leave any corn with a husk, nor a green blade. In this way they did for five days, one after the other ... After these had passed we learned the width of the passage of these locusts and saw the destruction they had caused. The breadth of this exceeded three leagues [15 km], in which there remained no [leaf or] bark on a tree, and the country did not look burned, but very snowy with the whiteness of the wood and dryness of the grass.[13]

Álvares was told that were it not for the threat of locusts and hailstorms, farmers would need to cultivate only half the area of land he had seen in production. But natural disasters were not the only threats to their survival that farmers had to contend with.

The stress of famines caused by hail, drought, and plagues of locusts was often exacerbated by plagues of a more insidious nature. Leprosy was commonplace.[14] Disease and epidemics were rife. People attributed these and the hazards of famine to the will of God, and prayed for relief. Álvares reported[15] seeing "more than 3,000 cripples, blind men, and lepers" gathered at a religious shrine near Axum,[16] but was not unaware of the relief that secular authorities denied the poor and disadvantaged of Ethiopia.

"There would be much fruit and much more cultivation in the country, if the great men did not ill-treat the people," he wrote, going on to note that:

In no part that [we] went about in were there butchers' shops, except at the Court, and nobody from the common people may kill a cow (even though it is his own) without leave from the lord of the country.[17]

When Francisco Álvares finally left Ethiopia in April 1526 he took with him a letter[18] from Prester John addressed to the king of Portugal. Opening with florid greetings and salutations, the letter expressed the hope that "we might tear out and cast forth the evil Moors, Jews, and heathens from [our] countries," and offered trading opportunities as an enticement. Prester John concluded his letter with a request:

> Lord brother, hear another word now: I want you to send me men, artificers, to make images, and printed books, and swords and arms for all sorts of fighting; and also masons and carpenters, and men who make medicines, and physicians, and surgeons to cure illnesses; also artificers to beat out gold and set it, and goldsmiths and silversmiths, and men who know how to extract gold and silver and also copper from the veins, and men who can make sheet lead and earthenware; and craftsmen of any trades which are necessary in kingdoms, also gunsmiths.

Álvares noted that although Prester John could muster a sizeable army and possessed plenty of spears, shields, bows and arrows, of modern weaponry he had only a few swords and helmets, two small cannon, some poor-quality mail and fourteen muskets bought from the Turks.[19] Prester John wanted technical and military aid.

Ethiopia, by the early 1500s, was a despotic and hierarchical Christian state whose rulers wished to import what they saw as the benefits of European civilization to their corner of Africa. From the rise of Aksum to modern times, its history spans 2,000 years; no other region in Africa has seen such continuity. The Ethiopian state owed its origin and continued existence to a unique agricultural heritage, its ascendency to foreign trade, and its domination of the regional population to a set of traditional Christian beliefs that had been formalized in Africa's only indigenous script (see page 208).

Food supply, trade, religion, and literacy—these are not determinants, but certainly among the essential characteristics of every state that vies for regional power and influence. Of the four, food supply was the only wholly African characteristic that had contributed to state-formation in Ethiopia. The other three were either wholly or partially of foreign origin. Since Ethiopia is the oldest state in Africa, does the fact that foreign influence contributed so much to its formation imply that states as they are known elsewhere could not have developed in Africa without foreign influence?

Communities in sub-Saharan Africa were always small and dispersed. Even in the Ethiopian empire at the time of Álvares's visit they were not large. "In all the country there is no town which exceeds 1,600 households, and of these there are few, and there are no walled towns or castles, but villages without number," Álvares reported.[20]

The archaeological evidence indicates that while communities throughout Africa maintained strong kinship and trading links over wide areas prior to their contact with external influences, the centralized and coercive regional control so typical of early state-formation elsewhere was not a feature of African social development. Unpredictable ecological circumstances and the need to maintain voluntary and cooperative barter and trade relationships militated against the emergence of groups powerful enough to rule others; while the age-set system ruled against the emergence of dominant lineages within groups (see pages 265–66).

By AD 800, however, when Arabic sources begin referring to sub-Saharan Africa and the trans-Saharan trade began to introduce external pressures of supply and demand to the system, the reciprocities of give and take sustaining the indigenous trade-network system were already under strain. By the early 1500s, when documentary evidence becomes an important source of information, Africa—wherever contact was made—was already demonstrating that its future lay along the route that Europe had taken: centralized states; monarchies; hierarchical social structures.

Mali, Kongo, Benin, Yoruba, Asante, Zimbabwe, Zulu, Buganda . . . across the continent, all the ethnic groups which have been described as states have origins (or moments of ascendancy) that cannot be disentangled from the influence of external trade and foreign contacts. Among them, an impressive variety of kinship and inheritance patterns, and social and cultural practices which may well pre-date the advent of foreign influence, has been described, but state-formation is a recent development in every case. Inevitably, its consequences have percolated through to every other group on the continent, including those with no predisposition towards state-formation whatsoever: nomads, hunters and gatherers, fishermen. At the end of the twentieth century there is no group in Africa which is not in some way affected by the continent's attachment to Europe. Could Africa have developed differently?

Were it not for the importunities of Europe, Africa might have enlarged upon its indigenous talents and found an independent route to the present—one that was inspired by resolutions from within rather than examples from without. The moment passed, however, during the fifteenth century and cannot be retrieved. Since then the history of Africa has been the story of an ancient continent and its inhabitants trying to accommodate the conceits of modern humans whose ancestors left the cradle-land 100,000 years ago (see Chapter 10), and who came back 500 years ago, behaving as though they owned the place.

CHAPTER 35

Nothing Else to Sell

EUROPEAN DESCRIPTIONS OF rich and densely populated kingdoms notwithstanding, the exigencies of human ecology kept Africa
thinly populated. Rural settlements were dispersed, urban centres small,
population growth rates low—but the foreign demand for slaves
became relentless.

Though printed books became an increasingly important source of information on Africa from the sixteenth century onward, and were numerous (and
voluminous) enough by 1600 to excite the imagination of Shakespeare and
awaken the mercantile interest of his contemporaries (see page 326), genuine
accounts of Africa and the lifestyles of its inhabitants were few and often inaccurate.

With the notable exception of Álvares's journey through Ethiopia
described in the last chapter and the journeys made by Leo Africanus in West
Africa (see pages 326–27), few accounts dealt with more than the coastal strip
and its immediate hinterland. Furthermore, the limitations of quantity were
compounded by dubious quality. Where direct information was lacking,
authors tended to fill out their accounts with passages (sometimes imagina-
tively embellished) taken from books by previous visitors to the continent.
Very few works can be regarded as sources of original material.[1]

Limitations notwithstanding, however, a precedent was established that
described African society in terms that Europeans would most readily understand. History books, both popular and academic, persistently told of states

Map and description of the Congo, published in London by John Morden, 1688

and kingdoms, of armies and conquests, of great wealth and exotic ritual when writing of Africa as it was when Europeans first made contact with the continent.[2]

Even today, books on early African history invite comparison with images of medieval Europe, with its feudalism, kings, and glory. But is the comparison valid, even for the coastal areas covered by early first-hand accounts? And what of the vastly more extensive interior regions, where no contact at all was made until much later, and social organization may have been different (and more typical of the continent as a whole) but was assumed to share the characteristics of places already described, areas rich with gold and slaves, ruled by kings.

In the absence of either adequate archaeological evidence or reliable historical documents, human ecology provides the surest means of reconstructing a broad picture of society throughout the interior of Africa when Vasco da Gama added a last *padrão* to the necklace of European influence that Portugal had strung around the continent: how did the imperatives of human biology and society respond to the opportunities and constraints of African ecology? The facts of human ecology make a briefer, less colourful and less detailed reconstruction than one patched together from other sources, but it is a sounder base upon which to set the history of Africa from that moment forward, as Europe began to pull the necklace tight.

Extrapolating backwards from population-size and growth-rate estimates for the period between 1900 and 1935, demographers have calculated[3] that the total population of sub-Saharan Africa in 1500 was in the order of 47 million. This figure had risen to 165 million by 1935, and the majority of people still lived in small village communities. Even in 1945 there were only forty-nine cities in the entire continent with populations of more than 100,000. Of these, twenty-five were in North Africa and eleven in South Africa. Between the Sahara and the Limpopo only thirteen had reached this size—four of them in Nigeria.[4]

If most Africans were living in small villages in 1945, when the population of sub-Saharan Africa was around 250 million, and cities established by colonial administrations and commerce had introduced the attractions of urban living to the continent, it is improbable that large and permanent urban centres were a common feature of the African landscape in 1500. Francisco Álvares noted that few communities in Ethiopia consisted of more than 1,600 households (see page 367) in 1520–26, even though Ethiopia was a large Christian state with regional centres of authority and a uniquely productive food supply, which had been exposed to the urbanizing influences of literacy, religion and foreign trade for more than 1,000 years.

Elsewhere in sub-Saharan Africa the opportunities for urbanization were even more limited. Inherently low population-growth rates, compounded by the problems of food production and the threat of disease, inhibited the formation of urban centres (see pages 246–47). The "boom and bust" characteristic of the species prevailed (see pages 131–32), with populations expanding rapidly when conditions were favourable, but shrinking back to fundamental numbers even more rapidly when conditions deteriorated. Food-production and social strategies had evolved to enhance prospects of survival when only minimal resources were available. Maximizing numbers was not on the agenda. Relatively large (but still not very large) urban-style communities identified at Jenne-jeno and Great Zimbabwe were exceptions; they arose where special conditions had pertained (and even here the influence of foreign trade cannot be ruled out).

Roland Oliver, a pioneer of the modern study of African history, believes that monarchies are an idea "which seems to have occurred naturally to the human mind the world over" and were an ancient feature of indigenous African society.[5] By the end of the colonial period (c.1960), he says, perhaps half the total population of Africa was living in monarchical states, most of them consisting of communities of 5,000 to 10,000 people, among whom one family had been elevated above all others by virtue of prior settlement or later conquest. The question is: were such social arrangements truly monarchical, and how were groups subject to such rule *before* Eurocentric concepts and ambitions began to influence the structures of African society?

In the BaGanda language, for instance, the only word which approximates a European understanding of the word *reign* is *mirembe,* which actually means a period of peace between succession struggles. Primogeniture is rare in Africa. In most systems several members of the "royal" family are eligible to become monarch when the throne becomes vacant. Sometimes the choice was peacefully arranged by an inner circle of councillors, but very often it was decided by warlike means.[6] All of which suggests that the reigns of kings were aberrant eruptions from the standard pattern of events in Africa, provoked by unusual circumstances (such as high levels of food production or external influences).

The semblances of monarchy that existed in Africa before foreign visitors began describing them as such were prominent arcs on a cycle of constant social renewal, not stages on a progression leading inexorably from village via monarchy to empires and the nation state. But wherever European adventurers encountered cooperative leaders they named them kings and lent them power, breaking the self-perpetuating cycle and creating a progression that all too often led only to disaster. The story of the Kongo people who lived south of the Congo River in West Africa is a case in point.

•   •   •

FOR AS LONG AS PEOPLE had farmed in West Africa, Malebo Pool on the lower Congo River had been a virtual Garden of Eden. Soils on the margins of the forest and savanna woodlands were fertile and the rainfall was sufficient to support banana plantations as well as produce regular cereal and root crops. The river and its tributaries encouraged the development of fishing. There were sources of copper, iron, and salt within trading distance and the Malebo Pool was itself a major trading crossroads for land and river trade.

Once established, the agricultural communities at Malebo Pool also began to export people. Descendants of the founding populations migrated southward, across the Congo River and into the uplands beyond. By the mid-1400s the BaKongo, as the migrants became known, were the dominant group in the region and comprised a loose confederation of villages linked by language, kinship, and trade. There was a concentration of economic activity at a place called Mbanza Kongo, to which the Portuguese directed their attention in the late fifteenth century.

Diogo Cão had visited Mbanza Kongo after erecting a *padrão* at the estuary of the Congo River in 1483 (see page 344), and the region had commended itself to the Portuguese for its trading and evangelical prospects. From 1490 onward, numbers of missionaries were dispatched, along with masons, carpenters, and other skilled artisans. Two German printers from Lisbon emigrated voluntarily with their press to São Tomé in 1492, presumably intending to work in or for the Kongo kingdom. Several Portuguese women were sent out to teach local ladies the arts of domestic economy as practised in Portugal.[7]

The Portuguese built a town of stone amid the mudbrick and thatch villages at Mbanza Kongo, which they called· São Salvador, and converted a receptive ruling elite to Christianity. Not all of the converts regarded Christianity as more than an adjunct to beliefs already held, but one at least was wholly devout, and was converted not only to the ideals of Christian belief but also to the ambitions of a European-style monarchy. Nzinga Mbemba was baptized as Afonso in 1491 and took the throne as King Afonso I of Kongo in 1506.

Afonso ruled as an ardent Christian until his death in 1543. He is described as a genuine, fervent, and intelligent convert to Christianity who did his utmost to implant the new religion by precept and example. Afonso adopted Portuguese dress and manners, welcomed missionaries, traders, and workers warmly, organized his court along the lines of the European monarchies, and even sent selected young Kongolese nobles to Portugal for their education— one of whom was in due course consecrated Bishop of Utica, in Portugal, in 1518.[8]

Christianity achieved a remarkable degree of acceptance in the Kongo kingdom during Afonso's reign and thereafter. Its success stemmed first from the ease with which Catholic rituals and sacred objects could be incorporated into customary ceremonies and shrines, and second from a Portuguese willingness to accept the indigenous character that Christianity gradually acquired in the Kongo.[9] It was a unique melding of cultures. The Kikongo catechism published in 1555 was the first printed transcription of a Bantu language.[10]

For a time, there in the early sixteenth century, it might have seemed that the Kongo was destined to become a fully westernized kingdom. Unfortunately, however, there were never quite enough missionaries, instructors, and artisans to turn that prospect into a reality. Afonso repeatedly pleaded for more to be sent out, but they came only in small numbers and many of those soon died from the tropical diseases that were rife in the Kongo. Furthermore, not all the Portuguese visitors travelled to Africa with a sense of Christian vocation; even some missionaries were inspired by more secular interests. And Afonso himself was not above using the Portuguese to further his earthly ambitions.

With the aid of Portuguese mercenaries and firearms Afonso was able to extend and consolidate his influence over the region, a process of expansion which, by way of return, provided the Portuguese with plenty of slaves for the sugar plantations they had established on the island of São Tomé, off the coast of modern Gabon.

The Portuguese introduced sugar to São Tomé in the 1490s, and had populated the island with settlers, including some 2,000 Jewish children taken from their parents in an era of infamy that culminated in the expulsion of Jews from Portugal in 1496.[11] During the early 1500s São Tomé became the largest single supplier of sugar to the European market; most of the slaves working on the plantations at this time came from regions beyond the boundaries of the Kongo kingdom, obtained by barter from ethnic groups to the north-east, or by raiding and trading to the south. By 1526, however, when up to 3,000 slaves were being shipped to São Tomé from the Kongo each year, King Afonso's own subjects and even some of his relatives were being enslaved.[12] Afonso addressed a letter of complaint to his "brother monarch," the king of Portugal:

> ... in our Kingdoms there is another great inconvenience which is of little service to God, and this is that many of our people, keenly desirous as they are of the wares and things of your Kingdoms, which are brought here by your people, and in order to satisfy their voracious appetite, seize many of our people, freed and exempt men; and very often it happens that they kidnap even noblemen and the sons of noblemen, and our relatives, and take them to be sold to the white men who are in our Kingdoms ...

And as soon as they are taken by the white men they are immediately ironed and branded with fire, and when they are carried to be embarked, if they are caught by our guards' men the whites allege that they have bought them but they cannot say from whom ... and so great, Sir, is the corruption and licentiousness that our country is being completely depopulated ... That is why we beg of Your Highness to help and assist us in this matter ... because it is our will that in these Kingdoms there should not be any trade of slaves nor outlet for them.[13]

The king of Portugal dismissed Afonso's complaint, and far from offering even the slightest support for his wish that the Portuguese trade in slaves from the Kongo should cease, replied to the effect that the Kongo had nothing else to sell.[14] If the king wished to continue receiving goods and services from Portugal, the Kongo would have to continue exporting slaves.

Women promenading in the cool of the evening, Dakar, Senegal

CHAPTER 36

The Atlantic Slave Trade

OVER NINE MILLION SLAVES WERE shipped across the Atlantic between 1451 and 1870. Another million or more did not survive the voyage, while untold numbers died on the journey from their point of capture to the coast. Europe's taste for sugar was the principal incentive of the trade.

Madame Honoria Bailor-Caulker, former Paramount Chief of the Shenge district of Sierra Leone, exemplifies the extent to which the value and strengths of the feminine role are entrenched in African society. Throughout Africa, women traditionally have been the providers of sustenance and education; in many parts they also have controlled a large fraction of the market economy, and inheritance through the female line has been a restraint on the accumulation of wealth and power by men. "A man belongs to his fatherland," wrote Chinua Achebe, "and yet we say Nueka, 'Mother is Supreme.'"[1]

Shenge is a small coastal village not 100 km south of Freetown, capital of Sierra Leone, as the crow flies, but isolated by the full day's rough circuitous journey that swamps and estuaries oblige motor transport to make. The Shenge villagers are not numerous; their homesteads are scattered among coconut palms and breadfruit trees; their houses are mud-walled and thatched with palm fronds and their activities are basic: they fish, maintain a stand or two of bananas, and grow some cassava or millet. Children attend a local primary school.

During her years as Paramount Chief, Madame Honoria regularly embellished her official duties with displays of traditional splendour. Swathed in voluminous silks, with turban and ornate jewellery, she was carried through the white-sand lanes of the village in a palanquin, borne at a trot by relays of her subjects, and accompanied by a large entourage, with dancers and drummers all joyfully performing, singing and clapping. At the Shenge District Court, Madame Honoria heard and gave judgement on cases of local grievance. At public meetings she promised that water and electricity services would soon be coming to Shenge, now that she had been elected district representative.

Madame Honoria was invited to the United States in 1977, to speak at an American Anthropological Association meeting on women in government and politics. Most of the speakers were academics who read papers which, by and large, threatened to put the audience to sleep, she says. Madame Honoria did not have a talk prepared. She had no paper to circulate; no slides, no charts or graphs to show—nothing but her formidable presence and a map of Africa on which she could point out the location of Sierra Leone and Shenge.

Taking the podium, Madame Honoria opened her talk by explaining that, as a Paramount Chief, she was accustomed to entering any forum to the accompaniment of singers, dancers, and drummers. "Where are they today?" she asked. The audience laughed and, having grabbed their attention with a joke, she asked them to join her in a song—a hymn. "The national hymn of the United States," she said, "Amazing Grace." The audience sang with good humour, if not with the volume and vitality that would have accompanied the Paramount Chief as she processed through Shenge. When the singing was over, and the audience had settled down, Madame Honoria let the silence extend to the point at which concentrated attention was turning into quizzical discomfort: whatever would she do next?

> The man who wrote that hymn, John Newton, was a slave trader before he became a man of the church [she told her audience]. He took a lot of his merchandise from Shenge and assembled them in a slave pen on Plantain Island—just offshore from Shenge; ships would then come and take them away to America. Plantain Island was the last piece of Africa on which the slaves had stood. Today it is the first thing the Shenge people see through the church doorway on Sundays, as they turn from their prayers and leave our small church.

Paramount Chief Madame Honoria Bailor-Caulker enjoys recounting this story.[2] The talk was very well received. Her introductory remarks linking the horrors of the slave trade to the history of the Shenge community evoked a lot of sympathy for her current efforts to improve amenities in the district, she says. But probe a little deeper in the family history of the Bailor-Caulkers and it becomes apparent that the sympathy that the conference had felt for the enslaved was, in fact, directed towards one of the enslavers.

> Yes, the Caulkers were slavers [Madame Honoria admits]. They ruled the shores of Yawri Bay between the Sierra Leone Peninsula [on which Freetown is located] and the Sherbro estuary, and their territory included Plantain and Banana Islands. These islands were busy slave-trading centres, regularly visited by ships from Europe; the Caulkers grew rich and powerful on the slave trade. We bought the slaves that others brought from up-country and sold them to the ships. Yes, we were slavers.

She speaks of her family history defiantly, while listeners might find shame more appropriate. But history cannot be eradicated, she says; furthermore, powerful chiefs frankly prefer their ancestry to be rooted among the strong that ruled rather than among the weak that were enslaved. Ordinary people too, when an argument becomes a shouting match, are not always able to restrain the taunt: "Just remember, my fathers sold your people!"[3] In Sierra Leone, such distinctions have been profoundly disruptive.

Freetown is so named because it was the port at which slaves were set ashore as free men by the English fleet which patrolled the shipping lanes off West Africa and seized slaving vessels after England and America abolished the slave trade in 1807 and 1808 respectively. Though diverse in origin, the freed slaves were bound together by experience and formed a community which regarded itself as morally superior to the indigenous population. With British inducement, Christianity, literacy and education advanced more rapidly among the freed slaves than among those who had never been enslaved, creating a social divide that would inevitably colour the political future of the country— slavers and the enslaved. Liberia experienced the same fate.

IN 1441 ANTAM GONÇALVEZ AND HIS CREW acquired the dubious distinction of being the first to enslave Africans on the west coast of Africa and take them away by sea (see pages 334–35). For 400 years thereafter slaves were considered to be legitimate items of commerce for Europeans trading with Africa. Philip Curtin, whose 1969 publication[4] remains a reference point for all other studies in the field, puts the total number of slaves landed in the Americas between 1451 and 1870 at 9,391,100. Paul Lovejoy estimates that 11,863,000 were shipped from Africa, of whom between 9,600,000 and 10,800,000 were landed in the Americas, the rest (between 10 and 20 per cent of the total captured) having died on the Atlantic crossing.[5] Further research has raised the figure,[6] and as historians investigate sources closer to the point of supply, and discover more about the ramifications of the trade, the higher their estimates are likely to become. "It may finally prove that up to 13 million slaves left Africa for the Atlantic," an authoritative commentary notes.[7]

During the early decades of the trade the Portuguese shipped significant numbers of slaves to Europe; contemporary censuses show that by the 1550s, for instance, African slaves comprised nearly 10 per cent of the Lisbon population and a large part of the country's agricultural workforce.[8] The majority at that time, however, were shipped to the Gold Coast, the Cape Verde Islands, and Madeira. On the islands, the slaves supplied labour for the sugar plantations established by Europeans, but on the Gold Coast they satisfied domestic African demand. In the early days the Portuguese were primarily interested in gold, and slaves purchased from the rulers of Benin were a convenient local merchandise with which to buy gold from traders on the coast of modern Ghana who wanted both porters to carry their goods inland and labourers to clear forest for agriculture (see pages 342–43).

By the early sixteenth century the Portuguese were buying slaves on the Slave Coast and selling them for gold on the Gold Coast at a rate of 500 to 600 slaves per year. When Benin restricted supply, the Portuguese turned to sources farther south; the Kingdom of Kongo came on stream, supplying slaves to the São Tomé plantations as well as other islands and the Gold Coast. Contemporary ships' logs and customs returns reveal that four to six vessels were continually transporting slaves from Kongo via São Tomé to the Gold Coast between 1510 and 1540. Some were caravels capable of carrying only from thirty to eighty slaves, others were vessels that could accommodate up to 120.[9]

The Kongo in their turn had become an unreliable source of slaves by the 1550s, and the Portuguese looked south again, to the hinterland of the modern Angola coast. They established a presence at Luanda. Meanwhile, the demand for slaves soared, and they began to flow from African slaving ports like blood from a stab wound.

The Atlantic slave trade, though awful to contemplate whatever its dimensions, had remained relatively small in volume during the first 150 years of its existence. Lovejoy's estimates show that an average of about 2,500 slaves were exported each year between 1450 and 1600; but this figure rose to 18,680 per year for the period 1601 to 1700, and reached a peak of 61,330 per year during the following century (1701 to 1800); even at the end of the nineteenth century (ninety years after abolition) it was still running at an average of 33,300 slaves per year.[10]

The surge in numbers can be attributed to the discovery of the Americas and the European taste for sugar. Columbus discovered the Caribbean islands and North America for Spain in 1492; Pedro Álvares Cabral discovered Brazil for Portugal in 1500. Both the Caribbean islands and the Brazilian coastlands were ideally suited for the production of sugar; both regions were inhabited by people whom Pêro Vaz da Caminha (a chronicler who sailed with Cabral) described as "people of good and pure simplicity [with] fine bodies and good faces."[11] But their natural attributes were no defence against the disease and labour demands of the Portuguese settlers, who began to establish sugar plantations in Brazil during the 1540s. Both there and in the Caribbean the Amerindians died, and were replaced by Africans. Vast numbers of Africans, as seafarers from other nations scrambled for a share of the highly lucrative trade that Portugal had instigated in the Atlantic. It was a triangle of trade, with a potential for multiplying returns on each of its three sections: manufactured goods from Europe were exchanged for slaves in Africa; slaves were exchanged for sugar in Brazil and the Caribbean; sugar was sold for cash in Europe.

The Portuguese had a head start and for a time their interests were protected by the papal bull of 1455 (see page 340) which granted Portugal an absolute monopoly of trade on the African coast. They attempted to conceal news of their discoveries from other seafaring nations with an official policy of secrecy. Sailors were warned to be silent; facts about the discoveries were carefully garbled; maps and navigation charts were removed from contemporary books, and the making of globes, maps, and charts became the privilege of a single family, whose loyalty to the Portuguese crown was unquestioned.[12] Direct action included standing orders which instructed Portuguese sea-captains to seize all foreign vessels encountered on the West African coast and cast their crews into the sea.[13]

But of course word did leak out, and vessels of other nations persistently defied the Portuguese monopoly. After 1492 the attention of an avaricious neighbour, Spain, was diverted from West Africa by the discovery of the Americas, but the French and the English, the Dutch and the Danish, would not be kept out. Often they not only traded in the territories that Portugal had claimed but took additional profit by seizing Portuguese vessels as well. Between 1500 and 1531, for example, French ships alone captured more than 300 Portuguese vessels in West African waters and along the coast of Brazil.[14]

During the sixteenth century the Portuguese expanded their empire to include territories spread around the globe from South America to the Spice Islands of the Far East. Best estimates suggest that up to 10,000 Portuguese were working abroad at any one time. Ten thousand, when the population of Portugal was only around 1 million, and large numbers were continuously leaving to replace those who died abroad. The empire imposed a drain on manpower and resources that Portugal could not sustain—and the empire collapsed. The wonder is not that it collapsed, a history concludes, "but that it flourished for exactly a century and lasted as long as it did."[15]

Portuguese domination of the West African trade was steadily eroded by interlopers during the sixteenth century and shattered entirely during the first half of the seventeenth century. For a while the Dutch reigned supreme. In 1617 Dutch traders negotiated an agreement with local rulers that allowed them to establish a trading post on the island of Bir, off present-day Dakar. They renamed the island Gorée (from the Dutch *goede reede,* meaning safe anchorage), and in 1639 built a fort and slave-handling facility which in modern times has become a symbol of the slave trade—a Mecca for American blacks. The Dutch also took El Mina in 1637; in 1641 they occupied Luanda briefly.

From the 1640s Dutch traders and shipping provided a source of cheap slaves for sugar plantations newly established in Barbados by the British and in Martinique and Guadeloupe by the French. Not surprisingly, these developments attracted the attention of British and French traders, who gradually supplanted the Dutch as the foremost shippers of slaves across the Atlantic. In due course, the output of the first sugar islands was overtaken by that of Jamaica, the major British slave colony, and especially by the French colony of Saint-Domingue (formerly known as Hispaniola), which imported nearly 1 million slaves during the eighteenth century and in 1791 was the scene of the only successful slave revolt in history. Today, Saint-Domingue is known as Haiti.

Philip Curtin's figures show that of the 9,391,100 slaves shipped across the Atlantic, fewer than 5 per cent were landed in what is now the United States of America. The largest proportion, 42 per cent, was sold to plantation owners on the sugar islands of the Caribbean. Thirty-eight per cent were shipped to Brazil (by the Portuguese).[16] Between 10 and 20 per cent died en route.

CHRISTOPHER COLUMBUS IS SOMETIMES credited with having carried the first African slaves across the Atlantic—a not unlikely proposition since slaves were numerous in both Spain and Portugal at the time of his first voyage, and one or two could easily have sailed as crew. The exact date at which African slaves began crossing the Atlantic as items of merchandise is not known, but it must have begun before 1502, for in that year the governor of Hispaniola, Nicolas de Ovando, requested that the importation of Negroes should be suspended, since they were inciting the indigenous Amerindians to rebellion. Trade resumed in 1505, however, when seventeen were sent out, with a promise of more. In 1510 King Ferdinand of Spain ordered that 250 Negroes should be shipped to Hispaniola, and in 1513 he imposed a charge of two ducats per head on slaves shipped there; the Spanish government thus began exploiting the trade as a source of revenue. Trade became brisk as colonists demanded labour and courtiers at home recognized a source of rich profit.[17]

During these first decades of the Atlantic trade slaves were shipped from Portugal and Spain, not direct from Africa. Indeed, ordinances granting Nicolas de Ovando permission to carry Negro slaves "born in the power of Christians" implicitly outlawed the direct importation of African slaves to Hispaniola. The restriction was lifted at the request of missionaries on the island who supported the colonists' pleadings for more labour to work on the sugar plantations. The missionaries wrote to the king, requesting:

> . . . that leave be given to them to bring over heathen negroes, of the kind of which we already have experience. Wherefore here it is agreed that Your Highness should command us to grant licences to send armed ships from this island to fetch them from the Cape Verde Islands, or Guinea, or that it may be done by some other persons to bring them here. Your Highness may believe that if this is permitted it will be very advantageous for the future of the settlers of these islands, and for the royal revenue; as also for the Indians your vassals, who will be cared for and eased in their work, and can better cultivate their souls' welfare, and will increase in numbers.

On the 18th of August 1518 the king of Spain granted Lorenzo de Gomenot, governor of Bresa, the right to ship 4,000 Negroes to Hispaniola, Cuba, Jamaica, and Porto Rico "direct from the isles of Guinea and other regions from which they are wont to bring the said negroes," requiring only that customs duties are paid and "that the said negroes male and female, have become Christians on reaching each island."[18] Lorenzo de Gomenot promptly sold his privilege to Genoese traders in Seville for 25,000 ducats. The Genoese fulfilled the contract through Portugese agents and are said to have made a profit of 300,000 ducats.[19] Slaves were assembled in the Cape Verde Islands by Portuguese traders for sale and shipment to the Caribbean in either Spanish or Portuguese vessels. The Portuguese also began shipping slaves to Brazil during the 1510s.[20]

The trade in slaves to the Spanish Caribbean may have reached 10,000 a year by 1540, though estimates are conjectural.[21] Many special licences were granted; traders were vying for contracts. In 1552 Fernando Ochoa was granted a seven-year monopoly of the trade, under which he contracted to deliver 23,000 slaves to the Spanish possessions and pay a duty of eight ducats on each. Ochoa was unable to fulfil the contract, and his failure can be seen as a measure of demand during a critical period, when English adventurers decided to seize a slice of the trade.

William Hawkins was one of a small group of pioneering English merchants trading to Brazil by the 1530s. Alone among English fleets, his vessels made stops at the Cape Verde Islands or the Senegal coast on several outward voyages[22] and the story of these enterprises inspired the buccaneering scheme that his son, John Hawkins (then aged thirty), proposed in 1562.

> And being amongst other particulars assured that Negroes were very good merchandise in Hispaniola, and that store of Negroes might easily be had upon the coast of Guinea, [John Hawkins] resolved with himself to make trial thereof, and communicated that device with his worshipful friends of London ... All which persons liked so well of his intention, that they became liberal contributors and adventurers in the action.[23]

Hawkins sailed from England in October 1562 with a fleet of three ships crewed by a total of "not above one hundred men for fear of sickness and other inconveniences, whereunto men in long voyages are commonly subject." Touching first at Tenerife, "where he received friendly entertainment," Hawkins sailed on

> to Sierra Leone, upon the coast of Guinea ... where he stayed some good time, and got into his possession, partly by the sword, and partly by other means, to the number of 300 Negroes at the least, besides other merchandises which that country yields. With this prey he sailed over the Ocean sea to the island of Hispaniola [where he] made vent of the whole number of his Negroes; for which he received ... by way of exchange such quantity of merchandise, that he did not only load his own three ships with hides, ginger, sugars, and some quantities of pearls, but he freighted also two other [vessels] with hides and the like commodities, which he sent to Spain.[24]

Hawkins left a very sparse account of his first adventures in the slave trade, hardly two pages in all with fewer than sixty words on the procurement of his merchandise on the Sierra Leone coast "partly by the sword, and partly by other means." Complaints made to England by the Portuguese government provide a little more detail on the Hawkins mode of operation. According to the Portuguese Hawkins acquired his cargoes more by piracy than by trade or capture. On the coast of Guinea-Bissau he seized a vessel carrying two hundred Negroes and other goods to the value of 15,000 ducats, they said. In Sierra Leone waters he captured three vessels with seventy Negroes each, one with many Negroes, and one with ivory, wax, and 500 Negroes. A Spanish document confirms Hawkins's piratical behaviour, listing no less than thirteen vessels he was alleged to have seized.[25]

Hawkins's first slaving voyage did nothing for Anglo-Iberian relations, but its profits engendered enthusiastic support for his second voyage, raising £4,990 for expedition costs over and above the capital value of the ships and the cost of the cargo. The fleet sailed on the 18th of October 1564: four ships, 150 crew, cargo and provisioning which included one and a half tonnes of beans and peas as food for the 500 slaves they expected to ship from Africa to the Caribbean, plus shirts and shoes with which the merchandise would be outfitted.[26] Hawkins and his ships arrived off the coast of Sierra Leone in the second week of December.

> ... We stayed certain days, going every day on shore to take the inhabitants, with burning and spoiling their towns ... we sojourned unto the one and twentieth of December, where having taken certain Negroes, and as much of their fruits, rice and meal, as we could well carry away (whereof there was such store that we might have laden one of our [ships] therewith) we departed.[27]

Sailing a short distance down the coast, two Portuguese caravels "loaden with Negroes" were captured on the 22nd of December, and on the 27th a combined force of Hawkins's men and the Portuguese attacked a town where they believed a great quantity of gold was to be taken, as well as 100 slaves. But this time, resistance was severe. While one contingent of men attacked the town, those who had remained with the boats

> were suddenly so set upon that some with great hurt recovered their boats; others not able to recover the same, took the water, and perished by means of the [ooze]. While this was doing, the Captain who with a dozen men, went through the town, returned, finding two hundred Negroes at the water's side, shooting at them in the boats, and cutting them in pieces which were drowned in the water, at whose coming, they ran all away: so he entered his boats, and before he could put off from the shore, they returned again, and shot very fiercely and hurt divers of them. Thus we returned back somewhat discomforted ... having gotten by our going ten Negroes, and lost seven of our best men [including one ship's captain], and we had twenty-seven of our men hurt.[28]

Hawkins sailed from Sierra Leone with a cargo of about 400 slaves[29] on the 29th of January 1565, sold the slaves in the Caribbean despite Spanish objections and returned to England, dropping anchor at Padstow in Cornwall on the 20th of September:

> God be thanked, in safety, with the loss of twenty persons in all the voyage, and with great profit to the venturers of the said voyage, as also to the whole

realm, in bringing home both gold, silver, pearls and other jewels great store. His name therefore be praised for evermore. Amen.[30]

The voyage was alleged to have made a 60 per cent profit for Hawkins and his sponsors.[31] Hawkins was knighted, becoming Sir John Hawkins in 1565, with African slaves prominently depicted on his coat of arms.[32]

Hawkins initiated England's involvement in the slave trade (and also helped Francis Drake to defeat the Spanish Armada in 1588). In his day, slave traders had exchanged their cargoes for treasure, but during the seventeenth century sugar became the principal medium of exchange. Europe had developed an insatiable taste for sugar and expansion of the plantations and slave-deaths were such that the islands constantly demanded more labour.

In 1654 Dutch traders were selling slaves to French settlers on Guadaloupe and Martinique at a rate of 2,000 lb (909 kg) of sugar per head.[33] Planters on Santo Domingo were paying 6,000 lb (2,727 kg) per head in 1684, and insisting that they needed from 2,500 to 3,000 new slaves each year, though this would absorb a full 60 per cent of their annual sugar production of 20 million lb (9,090 metric tonnes).[34] The number of vessels operating the slave route increased correspondingly, predominantly British and French. The trade passed from direct control by the Crown into the hands of private merchants granted royal charters to trade in specific regions. In 1672, 200 men of substance pledged £111,600 to the formation of the Royal Africa Company, attracted by the prospect of profit from slaves and sugar.[35]

JOHN NEWTON HAD AMBITIONS to join the Royal Africa Company, but as a seaman, not a shareholder. Born in London in 1725, sent away to sea as a cabin boy at the age of ten, he was press-ganged into the Royal Navy at seventeen and two years later deserted, hoping to be taken on by the Royal Africa Company. Before he could reach the company offices, however, he was arrested by a military patrol, sent back to his ship and flogged. In those days the Royal Navy would rid itself of troublesome sailors by exchanging them for merchantmen at opportune moments. Newton was rated troublesome; in Madeira he was transferred to a vessel sailing to Sierra Leone for slaves.[36]

He was no less troublesome on the slaver it seems, and escaped the threat of being transferred back to a warship only by agreeing to enter the service of a white slave-trader resident in Sierra Leone. The trader's name was Mr. Clow, and he lived on Plantain Island with an African woman who took a violent dislike to Newton and prevailed upon Mr. Clow to use him as a slave. For more than a year Newton worked with other slaves on Mr. Clow's lime plantation, unpaid, badly fed and inadequately clothed—but finding solace in mastering the first six books of Euclid, whose figures he drew with a stick in the wet sand of the seashore.

Mr. Clow finally released Newton to another trader operating further south. In due course he was returned to England, became a devout Christian, married the girl he had loved since his early years, and was appointed captain of a slave-trading ship. He was twenty-five, the year was 1750, the slave trade was at its height and not only respectable, but also a key aspect of English prosperity.

Newton made three voyages between 1750 and 1754; illness spared him from a fourth on which the captain who took his command died, along with most of the officers and many of the crew. Newton attributed his salvation to divine intervention, and thereafter his mounting dislike of "an employment that was perpetually conversant with chains, bolts and shackles" was transformed into a conviction that the slave trade was inhumane and morally wrong.[37] He became a minister of the Church, composed hymns, and his book, *An Authentic Narrative,* published in 1764, and a pamphlet entitled *Thoughts upon the African Slave Trade* (1788) offered powerful support to the abolition movement which the British government did not feel obliged to recognize until the late 1780s. Newton told a House of Commons committee in 1790:

> The people [of Sierra Leone] are gentle when they have no communication with the Europeans . . .
>
> The intercourse of the Europeans has assimilated them more to our manners: but I am afraid has rather had a bad than a good influence upon their morals; I mean they learn our customs, they wear our apparel, they get our furniture; but they are generally worse in their conduct in proportion to their acquaintance with us . . .[38]

On each of his three voyages Newton spent between six and eight months sailing back and forth along the Sierra Leone coast, buying slaves from traders who had settled in the region and who acted as intermediaries for African suppliers—including Mr. Clow and his wife on Plantain Island. Slaves were supplied singly, in twos or threes, rarely in batches of more than five at a time and Newton did not buy every slave he was offered. Women who were "long breasted and ill-made,"[39] men who were lame, old, or blind, children who were too small, were all rejected.

The trade was slow. During the first twelve weeks of trading on his first voyage Newton acquired barely a dozen slaves; four months later he was begging the odious Mr. Clow and his wife on Plantain Island for help in making up the desired number, explaining in his journal that: "Our slow purchase and the pressing season reduces me to court those whose behaviour I have reason to resent and despise."[40]

Newton sailed with 174 slaves, of whom twenty-eight (16 per cent) died on the notorious "middle passage" of the trading triangle. Of his thirty-man crew, seven died—23 per cent. The second voyage carried 207 slaves and Newton left the number of deaths unrecorded in his private journal, which suggests the figure may have been embarrassingly high. On his third and final voyage, however, Newton took only eighty-seven slaves across the Atlantic, none of whom died. His original intention had been to carry 220 slaves, Newton later told a government inquiry, adding: "Had I remained there till I had completed my purchase there is little doubt but I should have shared largely in the mortality so usual in vessels crowded with slaves."[41]

Crowded vessels compounded the fear, cruelty, and disease that sent more than a million slaves to their deaths on the "middle passage." They came to the ships weighed down with fetters and manacles, and fearing not only the pain of captivity but also the fate they believed awaited them. A Danish surgeon, sailing on a slave ship in 1787, reported:

> In their own country they have themselves heard such dreadful tales of how the slaves are treated . . . that one is appalled when one hears them. I was once asked by a slave, in complete earnest, if the shoes I was wearing had been made of Black Skin, since he had observed that they were the same colour as his skin.[42]

Stories of white men from the ships eating their black captives were legion in the slave homelands. Huge copper kettles stood boiling on the foredecks, they had been told; African meat was salted, and fed to the crew; red wine was African blood; cheese was made from African brains; the victims' bones were burned and became

> the ashlike, lethal gray powder that, when placed in iron tubes, transformed itself back into the flames from which it had come and spewed pain and destruction against any who tried, unprepared, to resist their demands.[43]

The number of slaves a ship could carry was of course determined by its size. How many human beings could be packed in the holds? Two slaves per gross ton is an often-quoted rating; ships averaging from 200 to 300 tons, specifically designed and constructed for ferrying Africans across the Atlantic, could carry between 500 and 600 slaves, a Liverpool shipper told a British government inquiry in 1789.[44]

The *Brookes* was a Liverpool ship of about 320 tons, for example, whose slave-deck layout was carefully worked out by her architects. The drawings survive, depicting a meticulous concern for mechanical efficiency that ranks with the Holocaust for its callous inhumanity. The bodies lie in tightly packed ranks, more like corpses than living beings, their positions showing more respect for the demands of geometry than for the needs of people being transported across an ocean. Not a metre of space is left vacant, from bow to stern. Where the ship's side bulged outward, an extra "shelf" of slaves was slotted in. The drawings gave the *Brookes* a capacity of 454 slaves, but in 1783 she sailed with 150 over and above that rating—600 in all.[45]

But this is not to say that shippers were unaware of the dangers of "tight-packing." The relationship between crowding and mortality was recognized, though slaves did not succumb to cramped conditions alone. In fact, "They were more sensitive to the adequacy with which captains provisioned their ships with food, and especially with water."[46]

Captains earned commission on the slaves they landed; so some packed their ships, gambling for maximum returns, in the knowledge that slave mortality was a loss to the company whose goods had paid for them in Africa, not to themselves. In attempts to restrict this tendency, the Royal Africa Company in 1713 issued instructions stipulating that each slave should be allowed "five foot in length, eleven inches in breadth, and twenty-three inches in height"[47]— most coffins are bigger.

In 1788 the British government passed legislation ruling that slaves should be transported at a ratio of five slaves per three tonnes up to 200 tonnes, and then one slave per additional tonne thereafter. Surgeons were to be carried, and the legislation provided for bonuses of £50 and £25 to be paid to captains and surgeons respectively on voyages which achieved mortality rates of under 3 per cent. Over a period of seven years (1791–97) about 50 per cent of British vessels qualified for the bonus.[48]

The slaves themselves might have preferred to die. On board they were chained together in pairs, but not always side by side, with the right hand and foot of one chained to the left hand and foot of the other, as would have been most "comfortable." No. John Newton describes how hands and feet were sometimes fettered right to right or left to left, so that the slaves were in effect chained one behind the other, and could not "move either hand or foot, but with great caution, and with perfect consent. Thus they must sit, walk, and lie, for many months (sometimes for nine or ten), without any mitigation or relief . . . "[49]

Newton prepared his ship for the "middle passage" by having the slave holds scraped and fumigated with a mixture of tar, tobacco, and sulphur, then washed out with vinegar.[50] But with slaves loaded, "the infamous stink"[51] soon pervaded the entire ship. The slave holds were not ventilated; toilet facilities typically consisted of "three or four large buckets, of a conical form, being near two feet in diameter at the bottom, and only one foot at the top, and in depth about twenty-eight inches; in which, when necessary, the negroes have recourse."[52]

With slaves cramped and chained together, dysentery rife and seasickness taking its toll, not every slave managed to reach a bucket in time. Some did not even try. Heat, perspiration, and the odours of unwashed bodies added to the stench; candles would not burn in the fetid air and even the ship's surgeon could bear to visit the slaves only briefly. A surgeon reported:

> The deck, that is the floor of their rooms, was so covered with blood and mucus which had proceeded from them in consequence of the [dysentery] that it resembled a slaughterhouse. It is not in the power of human imagination, to picture to itself a situation more dreadful or disgusting.

The slave pen on Plantain Island from which John Newton collected his merchandise occupies a small rocky bluff on the island's northern tip, separated from the main body of the island by a sandy causeway across which the sea floods at high tide. These days the bluff is used as a communal latrine, since facilities are otherwise lacking on the island and the community disapproves of people using the beach. Heaps of ordure at varying stages of desiccation await the unwary foot at every turn. The bluff reeks—the pen especially so—and the visitor's gasp for air is a pungent personal encounter with the depravity of the slave trade.

The pen is a square of stone walls, ten metres along each side and over two metres high, mortared and plastered: stout solid walls, with sharp fragments of eighteenth-century bottle-glass still firmly embedded along the top. Trees have taken root in the space where slaves once stood and sat and slept and lived out their last days in Africa; the trees shade the entire floor today, but there was never a roof to shelter the succession of slaves that occupied it more than 200 years ago—sun or rain.

Slaves entered and left the pen through a single opening in its south wall. A turn to the left on exiting and they faced east, where the sun rose and warmed the bulk of Africa; turn right, and a path hewn through the boulders led to the jetty, pointing west to where the sun sets and ships disappeared into the ocean.

CHAPTER 37

African Slave Traders

AFRICAN ENTREPRENEURS GREW PROSPEROUS on the slave trade; slaves were exchanged for European goods by barter—a fickle method of trade to which the cowrie shell brought a standard measure of value when it was introduced from the Maldives in the 1510s.

For students of Africa's economic history "the remarkable expansion of the slave trade in the eighteenth century provides a horrific illustration of the rapid response of producers in an underdeveloped economy to price incentives."[1] In other words, European slave-traders offered incentives their African counterparts were not inclined to refuse. But it was not simply slaves that were sold; no less significantly, the African traders also sold whatever those slaves might have contributed to the indigenous African economy. During the course of centuries, the slave trade effectively denied Africa the labour of 11 million extra pairs of hands. In return, the influence of imported goods brought wealth and power to traders, chiefs, and kings.

Given that slavery, in a variety of modes, was a widespread and entrenched feature of African society (see Chapter 28), and that long-distance trading opportunities had already stimulated the rise of wealthy individuals in communities across the continent, the student of economic history could not be surprised that the labour demands of sugar plantations in the Americas and the Caribbean were answered by willing suppliers in Africa. Nor could the student of human nature be surprised to find that the suppliers' motive was depressingly familiar: individual self-aggrandisement.

Cave on Zanzibar in which slaves from the mainland were held while awaiting shipment to Arabia or the Indian Ocean islands

The first slaves taken from Africa by Europeans had been captured by Portuguese seamen, in raids on coastal villages (see pages 334–35). The numbers were small, and the raids not without considerable danger to the raiders on occasions when the Africans were sufficiently prepared to resist attack and capture. If the Atlantic slave trade had depended upon European raiding expeditions as a means of acquiring merchandise it would never have become a viable enterprise. But, to their eternal shame, Africans in effect conducted slave-raids on behalf of the European interlopers; employing in the first instance not the force of arms, but the force of custom and political authority.

Chiefs and wealthy elites took people whom customary practice had enslaved within the indigenous economy, where the practice bestowed at least a measure of benefit on all parties, and sold them abroad for goods that brought little benefit to anyone other than the traders themselves—indeed, it could be argued that the inflow of foreign goods seriously disrupted the development of indigenous economies.

Like asset-strippers on Wall Street, African slave-traders plundered the accumulating human resources over which they had gained control with no thought for the wider implications and long-term consequences of their actions. They sold their brothers, their cousins, their neighbours, the only conceivable justification being that slaves were a commonplace feature of African society—chattels, valued less highly than the goods offered by European traders.

Slaves, millions in total, left Africa via the Sahara, the Red Sea, the Atlantic and the Indian oceans. The exchange of human beings for material wealth was the base common denominator of all instances, but the procedures involved were most thoroughly documented in the case of the Atlantic trade.

Horses were foremost among the items which Africans were keen to acquire in exchange for slaves in the earliest instances of the Atlantic trade. Horses for slaves had been a familiar component of the trans-Sahara trade for centuries, and readily became a feature of trade along the coast when Portuguese caravels arrived off Mauritania and Senegal in the mid fifteenth century. Contemporary chroniclers report that each horse landed at the trading post established on Arguim was worth between ten and fifteen slaves in the 1450s (see page 340); as the Portuguese ventured farther south and around the bulge of West Africa, however, the horse became a less attractive item of merchandise—difficult to transport and never able to thrive in humid equatorial conditions. In those regions textiles and hard goods became the common currency of trade.

Although the Portuguese shipped 1,000 slaves annually from Arguim during the 1460s, and established plantations on the Canaries, the Cape Verde

Islands and São Tomé with the labour of African slaves, the commercial objective driving their exploration of the West African coast was gold. Indeed, as was mentioned in a previous chapter (see pages 342–43), the Portuguese transported up to 12,000 slaves from the Slave Coast to the Gold Coast between 1500 and 1535. Thus, ironically perhaps, the first Europeans to participate in the purchase and sale of human beings on this particular stretch of coast were suppliers for a domestic West African slave trade. The Portuguese bought slaves first from the rulers of Benin; when that source dried up supplies were acquired from trading contacts established in the wake of the advancing edge of Portuguese exploration: in the Niger delta region, Igbo country, the estuary of the Cross River, the Cameroon coast, Kongo, and ultimately as far south as Angola.

The Portuguese sold slaves to Akan communities on the Gold Coast for gold, having purchased them with a variety of European goods, among which textiles and metalware appear to have constituted between one-half and two-thirds of all goods over the longest period of time.[2] By the early 1500s, when Portuguese commercial activity steadily became concentrated at three points in West Africa (the Gold Coast, Benin, and São Tomé) a seemingly "insatiable market" for copperware in particular had developed.[3] Warehouse records from El Mina, for instance, list consignments including 1,582 shaving bowls, 290 copper kettles, 25 copper water jugs, 722 barber's basins, 3,192 chamber pots, and 5,683 urinals.[4]

Copper and brass manillas (heavy open bracelets shaped like horseshoes, with bulbous ends) were shipped in by the tonne. El Mina received 287,813 manillas over a thirty-month period between 1504 and 1507, and an inventory from 1513 records a stock of 302,813 manillas weighing over ninety tons. Shipments to Benin and São Tomé appear to have been more modest—a mere 16,000 manillas shipped to São Tomé on one occasion, and 13,000 to Benin. Manillas entered the local economies as a form of currency, and were a highly profitable item of trade. Copper production in Europe was expanding rapidly at the time; unit costs were low, so that manillas bought for ten units of currency apiece from foundries in Europe sold for gold to the value of 120 units at El Mina.

The price differential between gold and copper on the Gold Coast was matched by a weight differential which had important implications for local labour markets. In the 1550s the Portuguese were paying forty manillas for an ounce of gold.[5] Since manillas during that period weighed around twenty ounces (567 g) apiece[6] it will be readily appreciated that what one man could carry from the mines to the coast in gold, would require twenty men to carry in copper on the return journey.

Portuguese shipments of slaves from Benin and points beyond supplemented the indigenous Gold Coast labour force (as well as providing labour for Akan agricultural expansion), but the rising cost of slaves complicated the equation. In the early 1500s the Portuguese were buying slaves from traders on the Grain Coast for two barber's basins apiece; a few years later the price was four or five basins. In Benin and the Niger delta the price of a slave rose during the same period from twelve to fifteen manillas to about fifty-seven by 1517; the Portuguese tried to set an official ceiling of forty manillas per slave, but soon had to raise it to fifty.[7]

With slaves costing as much in manillas as an ounce of gold, profit margins on shipping them to the Gold Coast from Benin and points beyond narrowed to vanishing point. Meanwhile, however, plantations on São Tomé and across the Atlantic in newly discovered Brazil offered more lucrative markets for the Portuguese slave trade, and the cost of obtaining slaves had fallen markedly with the introduction of a new currency: the cowrie shell.

CONTEMPORARY SHIPPING CONTRACTS INDICATE that the Portuguese introduced the cowrie shell to West African commerce just after 1515 at the latest; by 1522 "they had become as important as manillas in Portuguese trade with Benin."[8]

Cloth and copper, in whatever form, offered some utilitarian value in exchange for the slaves they purchased, but it would be difficult to find anything more useless than the cowrie shell. On occasions they have been crushed to provide lime for cement and mortar, it is true, but in the parts of Africa where cowries were exchanged for slaves they served only as decoration and a form of money.

In 1520 Portuguese traders bought slaves from the Forcados River, on the western edge of the Niger delta, at the standard price of 6,370 cowrie shells per adult;[9] in 1920, the flexibility of Britain's "indirect rule" colonial policy permitted wealthy Muslims in northern Nigeria to continue purchasing concubines according to their customary practice at a price of between 200,000 and 300,000 cowries each.[10]

During the intervening four centuries thousands of tons of cowries were shipped into West Africa, which at roughly 1 million shells to the tonne represents billions of cowries and millions of slaves. Inflation and problems of transportation eventually rendered the cowrie impractical as a commercial medium of exchange, a development which is aptly demonstrated by the plight of a British official who wished to sell a horse in northern Nigeria in the 1890s: "The trouble is that we cannot sell it, as its value in cowries would require fif-

teen porters to carry, to whom we should have to pay all the money they carried, and a great deal more besides."[11]

The money cowrie is a thing of beauty in its own right—pleasing to look
at and satisfying to handle—but the shell's attraction as a currency encompasses much more than its aesthetic qualities. The shells can be accurately
traded by weight, by volume, and by counting; their colour and lustre do not
fade as rapidly as in other species and although each shell weighs little more
than a gram (880 per kilogram) their durability compares favourably with that
of metal coins. "Survivability tests" have confirmed that money cowries are
very difficult to break and can be "poured, sacked, shoveled, hoarded in heaps,
kept buried in the soil, chuted like gravel" while remaining "clean, dainty,
stainless, polished, and milk-white." Unharmed by water, even bilge-water, a
ship could carry cowries as ballast in the holds and a washing at voyage end
would render them as clean as though stored in casks en route.[12]

Money cowries are much easier to lift off a flat surface than metal coins and
impossible to counterfeit—it is simply not worth the effort. The value per shell
was so very low, even thousands of kilometres from the point of origin, that
one unit of cowrie currency would be worth far less than any metal coin that
could be produced. Furthermore, unlike other commodity currencies, such as
gold, silver, iron, copper, cloth, tobacco, or alcohol, etc., cowries had no practical value *other than* as a currency.

Uniqueness, durability, ease of handling, portability, no other practical use,
and difficulty of counterfeiting were properties of the ideal commodity
money; properties that the cowries of the slave trade possessed in full measure.

THE COWRIE WAS ESTABLISHED as a monetary unit of the commercial
world well before Linnaeus began imposing his system of binomial nomenclature upon the natural world. About 200 species of cowrie have been recognized and given Latin names according to the Linnaean system, and the money
cowrie is identified by its economic function: *Cypraea moneta.* The generic
name, *Cypraea,* derives from the island of Cyprus, where Aphrodite was worshipped as the goddess of fertility. The cowrie's long slender orifice was
likened to the female vulva in some societies, and a cowrie worn around the
neck was said to promote conception and ease childbirth.[13] Hence some people used the cowrie as a fertility charm; in West Africa, however, *Cypraea moneta*
was first and foremost "the shell money of the slave trade."

The money cowrie occurs throughout the warm waters of the Indian
Ocean and the Pacific: from the Red Sea to Mozambique in the west, to northern Australia, Japan, Hawaii, and the Galapagos Islands in the east. There are

none in the Atlantic. In most locations *Cypraea moneta* is found together with another small cowrie, *Cypraea annulus*, with a yellow-orange ring around the crown of the shell (*annulus* is Latin for "ring") which has not the same exclusive attraction as a unit of currency. Sorting one from another is time-consuming, a simple fact which explains the predominance of the Maldive Islands as suppliers of the money cowrie.

Cypraea moneta is abundant throughout the Maldives (a string of small coral atolls whose central point lies about 800 km south-east of Sri Lanka), and on several atolls it occurs in relatively pure stands, with very few *annulus* specimens that need to be sorted out. Furthermore, a combination of water temperature and depth in the Maldive lagoons produces a mature cowrie that is significantly smaller than the average *C. moneta* specimen found anywhere else in its range. This combination of small size, abundance, and ease of collection gave the Maldives an unmatchable advantage over all other sources of supply.

A French seaman, François Pyrard de Laval, who survived a shipwreck on the Maldives in 1602 and remained on the islands for five years, published an account of the cowrie harvest:

> There is another kind of wealth at the Maldives [in addition to the products of the coconut palm], viz., certain little shells containing a little animal, large as the tip of the little finger, and quite white, polished and bright; they are fished twice a month, three days before and three days after the new moon, as well as at the full, and none would be got at any other season. The women gathered them on the sands and in the shallows of the sea, standing in the water up to their waists. They call them *Boly*, and export to all parts an infinite quantity, in such wise that in one year I have seen thirty or forty whole ships loaded with them without other cargo. All go to Bengal, for there only is there a demand for such a large quantity at high prices. The people of Bengal use them for ordinary money, although they have gold and silver and plenty of other metals; and what is more kings and great lords have houses built expressly to store these shells, and treat them as part of their treasure. All the merchants from other parts in India take a great quantity [from the Maldives] to carry to Bengal . . . When I came to Malé [the Maldive capital] for the first time, there was a vessel at anchor from Cochin, a town of the Portuguese, of 400 tons burthen; the captain and merchants were [half-castes], the other Christianised Indians, all habited in the Portuguese fashion, and they had come solely to load with these shells for the Bengal market. They gave 20 [kegs] of rice for a parcel of shells . . . [14]

The total dry-land area of the Maldive Islands is 298 km² (population in 1993: 240,000). The quantities of rice and other goods with which traders purchased the cowries enabled the islanders to settle on islands that were otherwise uninhabitable. The cowries just kept on growing. At the spring tides entire village communities would wade into the lagoons and pick cowries from the coral, marine plants, and ocean debris to which they were attached in their dozens. Fifty villagers could harvest over 50 kg in a day. The live cowries were buried in shallow pits for several weeks, then washed in sea water to remove dead organic matter and in fresh water to restore their pristine colour and lustre. The shells emerged from the second washing clean and bright, like "money fresh from the mint."[15]

A contract drawn up in 1515 allowed Portuguese merchants to ship 24 tonnes of cowries per year from the Maldives to West Africa,[16] and thereafter the Portuguese dominated the trade for most of the sixteenth century. The Dutch and British East India Companies began calling at the Maldives for cowries in the early years of the seventeenth century and, with the decline of the Portuguese authority in the Indian Ocean, became principal suppliers to the slave trade during the eighteenth century, when West Africa's cowrie imports averaged 110 tonnes per year.

The cowries were shipped to West Africa via Europe, since prevailing winds obliged captains to sail far out into the western Atlantic on the return voyage and calling at the West African coast on the way home was impracticable. Slave traders bought their cowries at markets centred on London and Amsterdam, where the prices paid indirectly established the value of the slaves that were to be shipped across the Atlantic.

The cowrie currency was in use over a wide area more than a century before slaves were being shipped across the Atlantic in large numbers, but the expansion of the slave trade during the eighteenth century was without question a major reason why cowrie imports also reached record levels during the same period.[17] Fifty-two per cent of the total Atlantic slave trade was transacted during the eighteenth century, when an average of some 61,000 slaves were exported from Africa each year.[18] During the same period, Africa imported more than 11,000 tons of cowries—more than ten billion shells.[19] In the 1710s a slave could be bought for 40–50,000 cowries; by the 1760s the price had risen to the equivalent of about 80,000 cowries, and in the 1770s traders were paying from 160,000 to 176,000 cowries per slave.[20] Since 176,000 cowries weigh approximately 200 kg, eight porter-loads could be earned from the sale of a single porter.

Although the price of a slave may have been stated in cowries, they usually constituted only a proportion of the actual payment, the remainder being made up of other goods to the value of so many cowries. Nonetheless, the Royal Africa Company found the shells themselves almost a sine qua non for trading on the Slave Coast, the proportion required for a single transaction ranging up to one-half of the purchase price, though generally limited to about one-third or lower for most of the eighteenth century.[21]

The predominant status of the cowrie in the slave trade was restricted primarily to the Slave Coast itself—the 1,000-kilometre stretch of coastline extending from the mouth of the Volta River to just east of the Niger delta and encompassing along its length the notorious slaving ports of Ouidah, Lagos, and Benin. Elsewhere, other commodities were predominant among the goods exchanged for slaves, and they became the measure of the trade.

On the Plantain Islands and elsewhere along the Sierra Leone coast, for instance, John Newton traded in terms of bars. The bars in question were originally bars of iron, which were bartered at an agreed number of bars per healthy adult male slave. By the 1750s, however, when Newton made his three slaving voyages, slaves were selling at a stated price of up to eighty bars apiece—though iron no longer constituted more than a fraction of the goods that made up the payment. Defined quantities of cloth, wrought metal, manufactured goods, guns, and other commodities were all assigned agreed values in terms of bars and together made up the amount required to purchase a slave. Purchases thus entailed a series of complex barters for which the African traders—though lacking the benefits of literacy—demonstrated a consummate talent.

The complexities of barter were compounded by the African traders' seemingly fickle demands. The variety of goods deemed acceptable were likely to change from voyage to voyage and from port to port. Describing trade on the Sierra Leone coast in the 1780s, one captain declared: "Custom has authorized what fancy began in assigning to almost every separate district in Africa a different choice of goods." Furthermore, " . . . what is quite the rage one year will the following one, most probable, be rejected with the greatest disdain," wrote another, while a third concluded (with the exaggeration born of exasperation): "You might starve in one place with bales of goods that would purchase kingdoms in another."[22]

On the Gold Coast, where a trade in gold and slaves began simultaneously in the early 1500s, with the Portuguese exchanging Benin slaves for Akan gold, a rough equivalence of one ounce (28.35 g) of gold for one adult male slave appears to have established a baseline for what subsequently became known as the "ounce trade." By the early 1700s, when the Gold Coast began exporting more slaves than gold, the ounce was divided into sixteen angels, or ackies; a male slave cost four ounces and gold did not feature in the transaction. Records show that in 1714 two male slaves were acquired for fourteen guns, sixty pounds of gunpowder, forty pounds of brass, one length of cloth and two firkins of tallow, valued in total at seven ounces and four ackies.[23]

In the 1770s slaves were sold on the Gold Coast at a rate of nine ounces and fifteen ackies for a prime male, and two ounces less for a prime female.[24] But although the price was ostensibly measured in ounces of gold, the trading reality was now reversed—while the Portuguese originally had traded slaves for gold, the merchants currently active on the Coast found themselves obliged to trade gold for slaves. The flow of gold from the hinterland had ceased, probably because the Asante who controlled the mines were retaining the metal for use in their own economy. Before 1740 an ounce of trade might still have purchased an ounce of gold. By 1770 European slave-traders had to include gold in practically every barter at the rate of two ounces of trade for one ounce of gold,[25] a development which rendered the cost of slaves much higher than before.[26]

An indication of the complex deals that African traders negotiated in exchange for slaves on the Gold Coast is preserved in the barter lists of Richard Miles, an agent of the Company of Merchants (which succeeded the defunct Royal Africa Company in 1750) who resided on the coast continuously from December 1772 until April 1780.[27] During those eight years Miles purchased 2,352 slaves on behalf of British traders and kept a meticulous account of virtually every transaction, recording more than 18,000 entries in all. Gold appears in 96.3 per cent of the barters Miles negotiated at the stations from which he operated along the coast, together with a bewildering range of other goods.

The barter lists show that Miles was an adept trader, as well as a meticulous accountant. He would sell anything for a profit. One of his barters included a cow, another a hat, but most were drawn from a list of seventy-five commodities, including thirty-six varieties of cottons and silks from India; woollens, cotton, and linen from Europe; unworked iron, lead, copper, brass, and pewter; guns and gunpowder; basins, chains, padlocks, knives, pans, and tankards; pipes, tobacco, brandy, and rum. On 16 January 1779 Miles recorded a typical assortment of goods required for the purchase of a prime male costing eight ounces: a roll of tobacco at two ounces, an ounce of gold at two ounces trade, a neganpaut or bejatepaut (an Indian cotton/silk mixed-weave cloth) at one ounce, two eight-ackey short pieces of textiles of any sort for one ounce, two ankers of rum at one ounce, a quarter barrel of gunpowder at eight ackies and a box of (tobacco) pipes at eight ackies.[28]

The barter lists are fascinating for the detail of European trading strategies they provide, but they contain detail concerning the African side of the trade too, detail which is rarely included in other records of slave purchases and never so comprehensively. Richard Miles recorded the name of every individual dealer from whom he bought slaves during his eight years on the Gold

Coast. The total of 2,352 slaves he purchased were the proceeds of 1,308 separate barters—an average of under two slaves per barter. The barters were made with no fewer than 295 different individuals, only eleven of whom sold slaves frequently enough to be considered regular suppliers. Roughly half of Miles's purchases were made from strangers or individuals from whom he bought fewer than five slaves overall.[29]

Historians have tended to regard the supply-side of the slave trade as the strict preserve of a wealthy and powerful African elite.[30] This may have been true of states such as Asante, Dahomey, and Benin, and it is also true that the governing elites of slaving ports enriched themselves by demanding from each ship a payment in goods to the value of 50 to 100 slaves merely for permission to trade,[31] but the detail contained in the barter lists of Richard Miles indicates that small-scale traders and individual entrepreneurs supplied significant numbers of slaves on the Gold Coast. Doubtless some traders who sold slaves to Miles were members of a wealthy elite, but the great majority were small or part-time traders—or even private individuals—who supplemented their regular income by buying or selling the odd slave or two.

It is as though anyone who was able to acquire slaves did so whenever the opportunity arose, and kept them on hand, for sale as required. And there is no reason to suppose that the same practice was not adopted throughout the greater part of the slave-trading region. Indeed, John Newton's account of cruising back and forth along the Sierra Leone coast for six months and more, acquiring slaves in twos and threes, confirms the contention—as do many other accounts of slaving voyages.[32]

The Africans who sold slaves to the European traders left virtually no records of their activities (unsurprisingly, since most could not read or write), but a rare exception supports the contention that the sale of small numbers of slaves by large numbers of part-time traders and private individuals constituted a significant proportion of the slave trade. Antera Duke, who sold small batches of slaves to ships calling at Old Calabar in eastern Nigeria, kept a diary in a ship's logbook he had been given by an officer from a slave-trading vessel. The diary recorded brief day-by-day details of his activities during the years 1785 to 1788. Sometime in the nineteenth century it was found by a missionary and taken to Scotland, where lengthy extracts of its idiosyncratic pidgin English subsequently were transcribed and "translated" into a more generally understood form of English. The original was destroyed in air raids during the Second World War, but the transcription survived. Its rediscovery and publication[33] in 1956 has been hailed as "an outstanding historiographical event."[34]

Antera Duke was a member of the Efik ethnic group which occupied the islands and hinterland of the Cross River estuary, close to the modern border between Nigeria and Cameroon. Today the Efik are a minority group among the inhabitants of the Cross River State whose affairs are administered from Calabar, the state capital. In the eighteenth century the Efik were a major supplier of slaves to the Atlantic trade, plundering the human resources of the region from a collection of small waterside towns known as Old Calabar. The name "Efik" derives from a verb root in their language—*fik*—meaning "oppress."

Antera Duke had been selling slaves for nearly two decades before opening his diary in 1785. His name appears among those of thirty African traders who sold slaves to a Liverpool ship, the *Dobson,* which brought a cargo of slaves from Old Calabar in 1769. The *Dobson* was at Old Calabar for one week short of six months, and the purchase of 566 slaves during that period is meticulously recorded in the ship's account book (preserved in an obscure collection of papers in England).

The *Dobson* accounts record 328 separate sales, averaging about eleven sales per trader and fewer than two slaves per sale—in fact most sales were of one to three slaves, and six was the largest number recorded for any single transaction. Since there were about thirty African traders, each averaged a total sale of nineteen slaves. A few sold only up to five slaves, but most were not sharply differentiated by the number sold. Antera Duke traded on only a few days during each of the six months that the *Dobson* was buying slaves: once in July; twice in August; three times in both September and October; four times in November; and once in December—a total of just fourteen days in all. He sold thirty-seven slaves: sixteen men, fifteen women, four boys, and two girls. The cost of slaves at Old Calabar was expressed in copper bars, the price ranging from 65 to 120 "coppers" per slave (paid in quantities of guns and gunpowder, metal goods, alcohol, and cloth). Antera Duke earned 4,400 coppers from his sales to the *Dobson.*[35]

By the time Antera Duke opened his diary in 1785 he had acquired wealth and status enough to build a house of materials imported from Liverpool and entertain ships' captains to supper.[36] He makes note of more than twenty sailings from Old Calabar between 1785 and 1788, on which a total of more than 7,000 slaves were carried. "Before night Captain Tatam went away with 396 slaves," Antera Duke wrote on the 27th of June 1785; "Captain Fairweather was going away with 440 slaves," he notes on the 20th of March 1786; and on the 16th of July 1787: "Captain Aspinal's ship goes away with 328 slaves." Antera Duke's contributions to these cargoes are rarely mentioned; he writes occasionally of agreements made with specific captains for the supply of slaves, and on some days notes that a relative or an agent had arrived with a captive or two from upriver, but throughout the diary, Efik political and ritual affairs are a more prevalent theme. Antera Duke writes of human sacrifices he has attended more frequently than he mentions slaves he has sold.

The Efik believed in a supreme God, in the power of the ancestors and other supernatural beings, in magic-medicine, reincarnation, sorcery, and witchcraft.[37] Torture and execution were the recourse of customary justice; human sacrifice placated wrathful gods and accompanied revered but departed members of society on their journey to the afterlife. Slaves were the sacrificial victims, and their dispatch is noted by Antera Duke with guileless candour. When one of the Efik elite died and was buried in July 1786, "nine men and women went with him," Antera Duke reports. The wake was held four months later:

> About 4 a.m. I got up; there was great rain, so I walked to the town palaver house and I found all the gentlemen here. So we got ready to cut heads off and at 5 o'clock in the morning we began to cut slaves' heads off, fifty heads off in that one day. I carried 29 cases of bottled brandy, and 15 calabashes of chop [food] for everybody, and there was play in every yard in town.

Two days later:

> ... I saw Jack Bakassey come and bring one woman slave to be beheaded in honour of my father, and I sent my Yellow Hogan Abasi [a family member] to market. All the gentlemen had dinner at Egbo Young's. We heard news about a new ship. Three more heads were cut off.[38]

In July 1787:

> ... we saw Robin Tom, King John and Otto Ditto Tom; King John sent them to come and make a play in honour of Duke and my father, and Egbo Young's mother; so they cut one woman's head off for Duke and seven Bar Room men were to be beheaded for my father. So they played all night.[39]

Antera Duke's diary documents an extraordinary double life: one day he might participate in the ritual sacrifice of slaves, and the next might find him just as confidently donning "whiteman trousers" to drink tea and discuss business with Liverpool ships' captains. No embarrassment is evident in the diary's innocent prose. Indeed, Antera Duke represented not a clash of cultures but the coalescing of two unrelated but horribly compatible cultural moralities. Slavery was an enduring feature of African society. Europeans exchanged slaves for trade goods. To both parties the trade seemed fair and proper, each profited but there was a hidden cost that Africa was left to pay.

A carved panel made by the Malinke people of West Africa

CHAPTER 38

Africa Transformed

THE SIGNIFICANCE OF THE SLAVE TRADE for Africa lay less in the number of people lost than in the changed social patterns and reproductive capabilities of those who remained behind. The importation of firearms had a profound effect on these developments.

By the time the Atlantic slave trade was running at its peak average of over 60,000 transactions per year during the eighteenth century, the trade and its ramifications had touched every region and every community in Africa. This statement cannot be proved beyond all reasonable doubt, but the export of slaves via the Sahara and the East African coast ensured that the influence of the trade pervaded the continent from three out of four cardinal directions, and given what is known of the trade routes that criss-crossed Africa before the advent of the slave trade, it is improbable that slavers and the proceeds of the slave trade did not also travel just as widely.

Seashells found at a northern Kalahari archaeological site indicate contact with the Atlantic or the Indian Ocean coast (or both) and a capacity for transcontinental travel by the ninth century AD[1] at the latest; at that rate, word of mouth, if not always actual involvement, would have spread a fearful awareness of the slave trade across the entire continent by the eighteenth century.

On a map of West Africa, the area in which cowries became the shell money of the slave trade during the eighteenth century extends 1,000 kilometres inland from the coast, then spreads like a broad ugly stain along the Sahelian latitudes: 1,500 kilometres west across Upper Volta and Mali to the borders of Senegal, and another 1,500 kilometres east across Nigeria and northern Cameroon and into Chad.[2] Trade goods, cloth, copper, iron, guns, and gunpowder spread even more widely. In this way the slave trade commercialized even those local indigenous economies which were not directly involved, creating a demand for imported goods which, ultimately, could be supplied only by the export of slaves. Commentators write of Africa developing "an unquenchable thirst for foreign imports" which tended "to gain an uncontrollable momentum."[3]

The mass of information that has been extracted from archival records of the slave trade—trading invoices, shipping manifests, customs declarations, and so forth—provides substantive detail on the volume and execution of the trade but gives no conclusive answer to one very important question: what effect did the slave trade have upon human society in Africa? Academics who venture to express a definitive opinion on this question tend to group in two camps: one believes that the slave trade transformed African societies from whatever they might have been into societies that relied on slavery more extensively than ever before; and the other contends that the impact of the slave trade, though horrific in its totality, was spread so thinly through the centuries and across vast areas that it could not have transformed African society. Historian Paul Lovejoy formulated the transformation thesis; economist David Eltis is prominent among those opposing it.

Lovejoy believes the interaction between enslavement, the slave trade, and the long-established practice of domestic slavery in Africa stimulated "the emergence of a system of slavery that was basic to the political economy of many parts of the continent."[4] Although the export trade in slaves was abolished in the nineteenth century, African enslavement actually increased during the late 1800s, Lovejoy claims, and the use of slaves in Africa became more common. Fellow historian Patrick Manning goes further, and sees the heritage of slavery manifest even in Africa today,

> in the distribution of population, in marriage patterns, in continuing class distinctions, and in total population size, which remains relatively low despite its recent rapid growth ... African labour systems [have] retained important continuities with slave labour [he says], including reliance on migration, on compulsion, on low pay, and on uneven sex ratios.[5]

Countering the transformation thesis, Eltis acknowledges the evidence for an increased use of slaves in Africa during the nineteenth century, but claims that if this does indeed mark a transformation in African society it must be attributed to causes within the continent, not to the external trade and its cessation.[6] Eltis pursues an economic argument,[7] constructing a model of economic development for the pre-colonial period which leads him and a co-author to conclude: "The majority of Africans . . . would have been about as well off, and would have been performing the same tasks in the same socioeconomic environment, if there had been no trading contact [with Europe]."[8] In short, Eltis contends that neither the Atlantic trade nor its suppression had much influence on African history.[9]

Both transformationists and non-transformationists call upon the same body of evidence to support their contentions, and as successive cohorts of researchers extract more and more material from the archives the amount of detail that the arguments must encompass expands proportionately. The opposing points of view are mutually exclusive; as yet, however, the available evidence does not support either more conclusively than the other. So judgement becomes a matter of what one chooses to believe. The protagonists of course believe absolutely in the validity of their argument and the strength of the supporting evidence, but for the lay observer the issue is not so simple. Both arguments are persuasive, but neither will be totally convincing until the other is shown to be invalid. Until then the issue is a matter of belief, and this narrative takes the view that the transformation thesis is the more believable.

The implications of the transformation thesis are profound. It may be possible to verify and even measure the effect that the slave trade had on indigenous African economies and population growth, as this and following chapters will attempt to show, but there is no way of establishing the extent to which the trade affected African social and cultural life. They too could have been completely transformed, and since virtually all the direct evidence of living African societies has been gathered since the advent of the slave trade (and often in the context of the trade) there must always be a possibility that only vestiges of that evidence relate to previous times.

Archaeology provides hard evidence of where and how people lived, but the anthropological evidence is softer. Linguists caution that oral histories are not reliable to more than two or three centuries in the past;[10] origin myths, such as those of the Asante in West Africa, the Kikuyu in East Africa and the Basuto in southern Africa, for example, put the beginnings of these groups in the seventeenth and eighteenth centuries, when the disruptions of the slave trade were already being felt across the continent.

Slavery was already an established fact of African life before the advent of the slave trade, it is true, and the influence of the trade was spread thinly over wide expanses of time and space—even at its peak. But enslavement for sale and the importation of foreign goods in large quantities were radical departures from everything that had gone before, and their influence permeated the social, political, and economic fabric of the continent.

Joseph Miller describes the "slaving frontier" as a demographic wave which surged inland from the coast, bearing on its crest the seaborne goods of the Europeans:

> It tossed people caught in its turbulence about in its wildly swirling currents of political and economic change. Like an ocean swell crashing on a beach, it dragged some of its victims out to sea in the undertow of slave exports that flowed from it, but it set most of the people over whom it washed down again in Africa, human flotsam and jetsam exposed to slavers combing the sands of the African mercantile realms left by the receding waters . . . By the middle third of the nineteenth century, the wave had tumbled populations all the way to the center of the continent. There it rose to towering heights of chaos as its force combined with a similar demographic surge flooding the area from the Indian Ocean . . . [11]

Though an average of over 60,000 slaves were shipped across the Atlantic each year during the 1700s, when the slave trade was running at its peak volume, they represented a very small proportion of the population from which they were taken. In the case of regions supplying the Angolan ports in particular, an average of perhaps no more than 6 people per 1,000 of population were taken each year. Adding to this an equal number who were seized but left to reside in other parts, a community of 100 people could thus expect to suffer the loss of one able-bodied man in the course of each agricultural cycle or two. "A community of ten or so settlements linked by economic and affinal ties would mourn the abduction of six to a dozen neighbours and kin every year," Miller concludes. "Every settlement would have been touched in this way, some more than once," and as the slaving frontier advanced, "It became virtually inevitable that a close relative or friend would vanish without trace during one's adulthood."[12]

Since deaths from disease and other natural causes probably accounted for 50 people per 1,000 of the region's population each year, the enslavement of another 6 per 1,000 may not seem an excessive threat to individual peace of mind. Indeed, in statistical terms, an individual villager in eighteenth-century west-central Africa was less likely to be enslaved than a modern American citizen is likely to be killed on the highway.[13] But road deaths are a risk, while enslavement was a threat. Road deaths are not arranged for the profit of the perpetrator, nor are modern Americans living at subsistence level and already subject to the vagaries of wildly unpredictable environments. For Africans, enslavement was a threat that compounded the uncertainties of existence—a fear at the back of the mind, dulled by familiarity perhaps, an ache that induced a lingering fatalism in society as it passed from generation to generation.

Kidnapping, capture, and enslavement threatened villagers in various parts of West Africa for up to 400 years: twenty generations lost some of their kinsmen to the slavers, or saw their neighbours routed. The influence of the trade came later to the more distant reaches of the continent; first the word and then the reality; fear intensified by the waiting.

The fear and the reality spread like the tide, reconfiguring the status and structure of every community they touched. The distinctive, insular, identity of the Dogon people, for instance, developed in the fastnesses of the Bandiagara escarpment in central Mali, where rocky terrain and cliff-face villages provided security against the mounted slaving expeditions which raided the surrounding lowland regions. Sahelian agricultural communities were especially at risk.

> For the slave-raiding of entire villages, mounted warriors typically surrounded a settlement, then burned it, and during the attack ran down on horseback those who sought to escape. Captives were then tied together in coffles [lines] and attached to the tails of the warriors' horses. For small-scale raiding into agricultural fields, warriors needed to strike quickly, to stuff smaller children into sacks and tie them on the horses' backs and, if exigencies permitted, to abduct the larger children and adults as well, and then flee quickly in order to escape the wrath of the raided community.[14]

The subsequent fate of captives such as these is recounted by Mungo Park, who travelled with a slave merchant from the western corner of present-day Niger via the Gambia River valley to the coast. The merchant had thirteen slaves, the last of a much larger contingent captured in raids by the Bambara army of Segou on the Niger River, south-west of the Bandiagara escarpment in which the Dogon had found refuge. The captives had been kept at Segou, in irons, for three years before they were sold to merchants from a variety of places. Some may have been sold to nomads from the Sahara, others had already been sent to the coast. The remainder contemplated their fate with trepidation, unwilling to believe that they would cross the salt water alive and be employed in cultivating the land. "They would not believe me," Park reports,

> and one of them putting his hand upon the ground, said with great simplicity, "have you really got such ground as this to set your feet upon?" . . . [they believed] that the whites purchased Negroes for the purpose of devouring them, or of selling them to others that they may be devoured hereafter, [which] naturally makes the slaves contemplate a journey towards the coast with great terror.

In due course the caravan left for the coast, Park noting that the slaves were secured by putting the right leg of one and the left of another in the same pair of fetters. By supporting the fetters with a string they can walk, though very slowly. Every four slaves are likewise fastened together by the necks, with a strong rope of twisted thongs, and in the night, an additional pair of fetters is put on their hands, and sometimes a light iron chain is passed around their necks.[15]

The autobiography[16] of a freed slave, Olaudah Equiano, gives a telling indication of the extent to which the fear of enslavement pervaded an African community:

Generally when the grown people in the neighbourhood were gone far in the fields to labour, the children assembled together in some of the neighbours' premises to play; and commonly some of us used to get up a tree to look out for any assailant, or kidnapper, that might come upon us; for they sometimes took these opportunities of our parents' absence to attack and carry off as many as they could seize . . . But alas! ere long it was my fate to be thus attacked, and to be carried off, when none of the grown people were nigh. One day, when all our people were gone out to their works as usual, and only I and my dear sister were left to mind the house, two men and a woman got over our walls, and in a moment seized us both, and, without giving us time to cry out, or make resistance, they stopped our mouths, and ran off with us.

Equiano and his sister were concealed in a forest hut overnight; on the journey next day:

I discovered some people at a distance, on which I began to cry out for their assistance: but my cries had no other effect than to make them tie me faster and stop my mouth, and then they put me into a large sack . . . The next day proved a day of greater sorrow than I have yet experienced; for my sister and I were then separated, while we lay clasped in each other's arms. It was in vain that we besought them not to part us; she was torn from me, and immediately carried away, while I was left in a state of distraction not to be described. I cried and grieved continually . . . [17]

Olaudah Equiano was aged eleven when he was enslaved, son of an Igbo farmer in south-eastern Nigeria. Domestic slavery had long been a feature of Igbo society (see page 295) and by the time of Olaudah's capture even commercial enslavement had been incorporated into the customary practices of the group. The phrase commonly used in modern times by people who feel they have been financially betrayed—"sold down the river"—originally meant exactly that: appellants who lost their case at the last court of appeal in the

Igbo judicial process risked being sold to slave-traders who would transport them down the river for shipment across the Atlantic.[18]

Such practices were widespread. Francis Moore, who bought slaves on the Gambia in the 1730s, noted that:

> Since this Slave-Trade has been us'd, all Punishments are chang'd into Slavery; there being an Advantage on such Condemnations, they strain for Crimes very hard, in order to get the Benefit of selling the Criminal. Not only murder, Theft and Adultery, are punish'd by selling the Criminal for a Slave, but every trifling Crime is punish'd in the same manner.[19]

"The Black Traders of Bonny and Calabar . . . come down [the river] about once a Fortnight with Slaves; Thursday or Friday is generally their Trading Day," William James reported from the Slave Coast in the 1760s,

> Twenty or Thirty Canoes, sometimes more and sometimes less, come down at a Time. In each Canoe may be Twenty or Thirty Slaves. The Arms of some of them are tied behind their Backs with Twigs, Canes, Grass Rope, or other Ligaments of the Country; and if they happen to be stronger than common, they are pinioned above the Knee also. In this Situation they are thrown into the Bottom of the Canoe, where they lie in great Pain, and often almost covered with Water. On their landing, they are taken to the Traders Houses, where they are oiled, fed, and made up for Sale.[20]

The widespread impact of the slave trade on African society can be judged by the fact that in 1850 over 200 different languages were identified among the 40,000 or so former slaves then living in Freetown district.[21] Though virtually all had been enslaved after the transatlantic slave trade had been abolished in 1807–8, their origins covered most of West and West-central Africa and included even a few outlying areas of East Africa.

Not only the languages of the former slaves was noted, but also the manner by which they came to be enslaved. One-third had been "taken in war," most of them in the raids which horsemen from nomadic groups in the Sahel launched against agricultural communities; another third had been kidnapped, either as children in the manner which Olaudah Equiano had described, or as adults travelling outside their homeland. The remaining third had not been enslaved by direct violence, but had been sold by relatives or superiors, sometimes to meet a debt—often not their own; sometimes after conviction as criminals[22]—though they themselves need not have been the criminals. Two men had been enslaved because their kinsmen had been convicted of witchcraft.[23]

•　　•　　•

HUMAN POPULATIONS IN AFRICA have always suffered from a lack of numbers. There were never enough people to contend with the problems of living in fickle environments. And yet, when presented with the opportunity of acquiring imported goods, Africans chose to sell people. Why sell people, rather than use them at home? The answer of course lies in the political systems which distributed the rights and obligations of *belonging* among members of a community.

With the development of agriculture and trade, chiefs and ruling elites emerged, upon whom the community at large was dependent for administration and security; imported goods embellished those positions of authority, and enabled ambitious individuals to offer patronage to less wealthy neighbours and thus enlarge their circle of dependants. In short, imports attracted followers. Sadly, however, they also attracted upstarts—men on the margins of established routes to wealth and power who now seized the opportunity to get ahead. The irony, and the tragedy, was that many new men could maintain their access to the goods that gave them power only by selling the very people whose allegiance as dependants they had set out to gain.[24]

It seems as though the slaves exported from Africa were seen as a "free good," like fish in a lake, there for the taking, at no cost to the enslavers beyond their incidental expenses.[25] Africa paid the actual cost, and it was massive—in terms of both actual losses and the trade's impact on African society. Patrick Manning has calculated, for example, that the shipping of 9 million slaves across the Atlantic between 1700 and 1850 actually incurred the capture of some 21 million Africans, of whom 7 million were taken into domestic slavery and another 12 million died within a year of capture.[26]

Manning developed a computer simulation model which used data on the size and composition of the export slave population as a means of estimating the size and composition of the population remaining in Africa.[27] The results show that, owing to the slave trade, Africa south of the Sahara and north of the Limpopo experienced virtually no population growth at all between about 1750 and 1850; furthermore, perhaps 10 per cent of the population—6 or 7 million people—were in slave status as a result of export demands during that period.[28] How large would the population of Africa have been if it had not suffered the losses of the slave trade?

The total number of slaves exported from tropical Africa between 1500 and the late 1800s is put at 18 million: 11 million from West Africa, 5 million from the savanna to the coast and via the Sahara or the Red Sea, 2 million from the East Coast. Assuming a growth rate for African populations of 5 per 1,000 (0.5 per cent) from 1700, the population of sub-Saharan Africa would have been close to 100 million in 1850, double the actual figure of about 50 million. Even when the constraints of domestic slavery, drought, and famine are taken into account, and the population growth rate assumed to have been only 3 per 1,000 (0.3 per cent), the 1850 population would have been 70 million—40 per cent more than the actual figure. In fact, the calculations show "that no growth rate of less than one per cent could have counterbalanced the loss of slaves in the late eighteenth century."[29]

But the cost of the slave trade was more than just the numbers of slaves exported and the loss of potential population growth; it also included the transformation of African economic, political, and social systems. Indeed, "the demographic significance of the transformation for Africa lay less in the aggregate population losses, than in profound changes in settlement patterns, epidemiological exposure, and the reproductive capabilities of the populations who remained behind."[30]

With reference to western-central Africa in particular, where the demand for slaves in Portugal's Brazilian plantations sustained high volumes of slaving until the late 1800s (and the trade is well documented), Joseph Miller describes the changes wrought by the slave trade as nothing less than a violent revolution.[31] The pre-existing political economies in which chiefs and elites commanded the respect and occasional material tribute of their subjects were transformed into systems controlled by warlords and powerful merchants who obliged indebted chiefs and elites to collect slaves as payment against forced loans. The violence of the revolution probably drove more western-central Africans into hiding than it exposed to seizure and shipment to the west. And the same probably holds true for most of the regions from which the slave trade drew its merchandise.

THE PAIN OF THE ECONOMIC, political and social transformations which the external slave trade inflicted upon Africa was mitigated to some extent by two crops which the Portuguese introduced to African agriculture from the Americas: maize and cassava (also known as manioc). Both crops were first introduced during the sixteenth century,[32] but dissemination appears to have been slow; neither was a significant contributor to the subsistence diet much before the eighteenth century.

Of the two new crops, cassava offered more advantages to Africa's agricultural communities. Capable of producing harvestable tubers at any altitude from sea level up to 1,800 metres, in soils grading from rainforest humus to savanna sands, with rainfall ranging from 300 mm to 9000 mm per year, cassava broadened food-production opportunities in every habitat that farmers had occupied. Furthermore, it was readily propagated from short lengths of stem simply stuck into the ground and its mature tubers could be left underground for up to two years or more. No other African crop could be stored for so long, and at a time of violent social transformation it was better to have crops in the ground than grain in the granary, where raiders could find it.

Maize also offered storage advantages, but its greatest attraction was high productivity, the absence of indigenous pests, and a husk which protected the cobs from birds. By virtue of these features maize could provide nine times more grain per unit of labour than either millet or sorghum,[33] but only where soils were sufficiently fertile and well-watered. Unlike cassava, maize cannot tolerate poor soils and drought.

The Portuguese who introduced maize to Africa did not rate the grain very highly as a food. Indeed, Duarte Lopez noted in 1591 that "maize was the vilest of grain and fit only for swine."[34] But the grain was not primarily intended for European tables; its introduction was more pragmatic than that. Traders needed a cheap staple food for the slaves they were shipping across the Atlantic in ever-increasing numbers, one that was easily transported and stored well. Maize fitted the bill admirably. John Barbot, writing of voyages to West Africa in the late 1600s, observed "that Indian corn rises from a crown to twenty shillings betwixt February and harvest, which I suppose is chiefly occasion'd by the great number of European slave ships yearly resorting to the coast . . . "[35] The amount of maize consumed by slaves when the trade was at its greatest volume is estimated to have been no less than 9,000 tonnes per year—a sizeable proportion of which was used to feed slaves en route from the hinterland and while awaiting shipment on the coast.[36]

If the prevalence of cassava and maize cultivation in Africa during modern times is any measure, the introduction of the crops amounted to an agricultural revolution. Maize enabled more intensive use to be made of fertile well-watered land, and cassava brought hitherto unproductive regions into use. Imported iron facilitated the dissemination and production of the new crops.

It might be supposed that the importation of iron would have put African iron-makers out of business. And indeed it did, but only in so far as the smelting of iron was concerned and this in itself was beneficial, for without the need to smelt ore the demand for charcoal fell dramatically. Whole forests were saved while the smiths concentrated on the production of agricultural implements. Trading records from the early eighteenth century indicate that the demand for iron was greatest in the planting season.[37]

The dietary contribution that maize and cassava made to African agriculture was almost all bulky carbohydrate, but when eaten with a relish of protein-rich leaves, beans, or fish the new crops improved nutrition, reduced infant mortality, and generally increased survival rates in regions otherwise too marginal for continuous habitation. In short, the increased production of maize and cassava during the eighteenth century probably stimulated the first pronounced spurt in overall population growth that the human population of Africa had ever experienced. Sadly, however, any benefit which this increase in the amount of available labour might have brought to the indigenous economy of Africa was lost in the demands and disruptions of the slave trade, which also experienced an unprecedented spurt of growth in the eighteenth century.

IN THE TORTUROUS LITANY of depredation which the slave trade visited upon Africa, the influence of one particular category of imports has yet to be mentioned: guns and gunpowder. Firearms in one form or another effectively rendered the transformation of African society irreversible: when the foreign slave trade was abolished, the guns which had hastened its expansion became the means by which powerful men maintained the positions they had bought from the trade. There was no turning back from the barrel of a gun.

The Portuguese had found Africans eager to purchase guns when they began trading for slaves from Benin in the late 1400s, but the Pope had ordered them to desist, lest the weapons should fall into the hands of hostile Muslims.[38] The Pope correctly acknowledged the terrible potential of firearms, but those early firearms were less effective than he supposed. The matchlock ignition had serious disadvantages, especially in night attacks, when its glowing wick was a giveaway to sentries and even its burning smell would carry for some distance. The matchlock could not be used in rain or high winds, and was always dangerous near gunpowder. Nonetheless, it was the only firearm available until about 1610–15, when the flintlock was invented in France.[39]

By then, the Pope's interdiction had been swept aside by events; firearms had become a common item of European trade with Africa, where the flintlock was adopted even more rapidly than by the armies of Europe. Though relatively wind- and waterproof, and without the matchlock's telltale open flame, the flintlock entered the arsenals of Europe's military establishments quite slowly, replacing the matchlock completely only after 1700. In Africa the "flintlock replaced the matchlock on the Gold and Slave Coasts in the 1690s,"[40] and remained the weapon of choice for centuries thereafter. Very few changes in the flintlock muzzle-loading musket were introduced for a century and a half after the 1690s; in fact, guns of the same type were still being exported to West Africa in the twentieth century.[41]

Firearms introduced a new order of psychological terror to the slave trade. Many of the guns sold to Africans were neither reliable nor accurate—an official check of trade guns stocked in Luanda in 1759, for example, found only 200 out of 4,000 which met military standards of reliability;[42] but fear was surely the gun's most significant contribution to the slavers' armoury. The surprise attack at dawn, sudden volleys of gunfire, the noise, the panic, the threat . . . Clearly, raids which resulted in fatalities would be counter-productive, so raiders employed "field of fire" tactics rather than aiming at individuals, and probably loaded their muskets with shot rather than with a single lethal ball, hoping to stop fleeing victims without necessarily causing fatality.[43]

The inaccuracy, tedious loading procedures, and cumbersome nature of early firearms have persuaded some commentators in modern times to conclude that they were used principally for ostentatious show or ornamentation, or for the protection of crops (the introduction of maize being related to firearms, it was said).[44] Analysis of customs records, shipping invoices, the records of gun manufacturers and reports from agents resident in West Africa make it abundantly clear, however, that guns were an important feature of the slaving operation. "The import of firearms into West Africa in any significant numbers began at much the same time as the large-scale export of slaves . . . and there is an obvious connection between the two," a paper on the subject reports.[45]

The astonishing speed with which guns became a dominant feature of the slave trade is demonstrated by the sheer numbers which appear in shipping manifests and the prices at which they were sold. In 1682, for instance, guns were valuable items of merchandise which were exchanged for slaves at a rate of two guns for one male slave. By 1718 they were so common that anything between twenty-four and thirty-two guns were being exchanged for one slave.

In 1704 the director of Dutch slaving operations on the Gold Coast promised his masters in Amsterdam that he could fill six ships full of slaves within four months, if supplied with sufficient quantities of fine guns and powder. A year later he reported on trading developments:

> Concerning the trade on [the Gold Coast], we notified your Honours already that it has completely changed into a Slave Coast, and that the natives nowadays no longer occupy themselves with the search for gold, but rather make war on each other to furnish slaves . . . [46]

In 1721 the British trader John Atkins put guns and gunpowder at the top of his list of goods which "are everywhere called for." Guns and gunpowder were included among the goods worth 4,000 coppers Antera Duke received for the slaves he sold to the *Dobson* in 1769–70 (see page 402); indeed, the *Dobson* shipped a total of 1,570 guns to Old Calabar on that voyage.[47]

Richard Miles, who was resident on the Gold Coast from 1772 to 1780,

buying slaves for British traders (see page 400), repeatedly advised his corre-
spondents in London that "guns were an absolute drug on the market."[48] Guns
and gunpowder featured in 78.5 per cent of Miles's barters, but the actual number of guns he sold was small, averaging below 0.7 guns per slave, probably
because the demands of the American War of Independence had left British
manufacturers with little capacity to supply guns to the African market during
that period; or it could have been that Africans had acquired the gunsmithing
skills required to maintain the weapons they already possessed, rather than buy
new stock. Either way, the slump in gun sales that Miles's barter lists reveal
does not mean that the use of guns had declined. The slump was not matched
by a decline in the demand for gunpowder, nor by a decline in the production
of slaves.[49]

In total, British traders alone are estimated to have shipped between
283,000 and 394,000 guns per year to West Africa between 1750 and 1807,
and another 50,000 to the Congo and Angola region. A yearly average of
nearly 400 tons of gunpowder and 91 tons of lead shot were shipped from
Britain to West Africa during the same period.[50]

The export of guns by other European nations and to parts of Africa other
than the West Coast has been less thoroughly researched, but best estimates
put the total number of guns sold to African merchants during the era of the
slave trade at no less than 20 million.[51]

The effect of the gun on African affairs was first felt in a relatively small
area of West Africa in the 1600s, but its influence reverberated through the
continent during the succeeding centuries no less profoundly than the outbreak of war in Europe affected world history during the twentieth century.
Consider the extent to which the Second World War, of just six years' duration,
has pervaded the consciousness of the developed world for two generations,
and imagine how four centuries of slave-trading might have seized the entire
social and cultural ethos of an undeveloped continent.

Asante swords of state are adorned with symbolic emblems cast in solid gold.
The *Ahwehwebaa* sword, made in 1799, bears the effigy of a defeated warrior

CHAPTER 39

The Aftermath

THE SLAVE TRADE COMMERCIALIZED African economies; after abolition indigenous slavery kept the economies turning—throughout the continent the incidence of slavery increased.

"The production, or, more accurately, the harvesting of slaves was one of the biggest commercial ventures launched in Africa during the pre-colonial era."[1] Since no other venture that could be described as "commercial" in the European sense of the term had ever been launched in Africa, the phrase "one of" is a qualification which its author probably introduced in order to temper the brutal fact that the slave trade shackled Africa to the commercial and political ambitions of Europe. Permanently. The slave trade created an economic system in Africa that diverted resources from indigenous applications towards the coast, where their exchange for European goods represented a net loss to the continent.

Africans brought gold, slaves, ivory, beeswax, gum arabic, dyes, timber, and foodstuffs to the coast and exchanged them for goods of which the continent previously had no need: textiles, metal goods, alcohol, and, most influential of all, guns and gunpowder.

There were aspects of this exchange trade which multiplied European benefits while serving only to heighten its negative effect on Africa. Distilled spirits, for instance, introduced new levels of inebriation to Africa. Rum, a by-product of the Caribbean sugar plantations for which Africa had supplied the labour, was a particularly profitable item of trade. Textiles constituted at least

50 per cent by value of African imports,[2] creating a huge market which helped to stimulate the industrialization of textile production in Europe while simultaneously inhibiting the expansion of indigenous production in Africa (local weaving persisted,[3] but the mass market it could have served was dominated by cheap imported goods). Similarly, the African market for metal goods contributed to the development of mass-production methods in Europe, whose low unit costs effectively eliminated commercial incentive for the development of such enterprises in Africa. Even the export of beeswax had a detrimental effect, since gatherers flushed out the bees with fire and responded to demands for more wax simply by seeking more nests to destroy, rather than by adopting intensive and less wasteful methods of production,[4] such as putting out reusable hives.

The influence of Europe during the era of the slave trade left a permanent mark on every community it touched; some flourished, others disintegrated. The kingdom of Kongo, for instance, never recovered from its rulers' attempts to establish a European-style monarchy in Africa (see page 374). A network of provincial administrations enabled the Kongo kings to gain control of extensive territory and diverse communities as the tide of trade flowed inland during the sixteenth and seventeenth centuries, but could not hold it together as profits were spread more thinly. Splits developed within the ruling elite, and outlying communities rebelled against the authority of centralized control.

At its prime the Kongo state had a standing army of some 5,000 men, including 500 mercenary musketeers, but ultimately even Portuguese military assistance could not halt the disintegration of the kingdom, and its fate was sealed when the greatest concentration of Portuguese slave-trading activities shifted to Angolan ports in the south during the early eighteenth century. Control of the region over which the Kongo kings had aspired to rule reverted to local group and village chiefs, with the difference that the unrelenting problems of food production in regions of extreme and highly unpredictable environmental conditions were now exacerbated by threats of enslavement, and by the demands of an economic system that was obliged to find some way of paying for the foreign goods its participants found so attractive.

The Oyo state of what is now western Nigeria collapsed during the era of the slave trade; also as a result of overextended ambition. Oyo was an inland Yoruba state which had become a major supplier of slaves to the Atlantic trade by the early seventeenth century, exporting its captives through a corridor of conquered territory which led to the Slave Coast ports of Ouidah, Porto Novo, and Lagos. The sprawling Oyo empire was administered by regional chiefs whose personal ambitions and military power grew no less rapidly than the profits of empire. Chiefs competing for supremacy tore the political system apart, subject communities broke away, and a revolt of Oyo's numerous Muslims overran the capital. "Internal structural tensions, imperial expansion, and militant Islam had together destroyed the state."[5]

The slave trade led to a fusion of political and commercial power in major trading states, either as a consequence of rulers taking control of trade or by traders acquiring political power.[6] The Efik community of Old Calabar to which Antera Duke belonged (see pages 401–2) is an instance of the latter development. When the European demand for slaves reached the Calabar River, the Efik adopted the role of wholesalers, exploiting the natural advantages of their estuarine location and excluding rivals from direct trade with the European traders. They occasionally launched raids, but mostly bought slaves from other suppliers and by the eighteenth century had established a network of contacts which extended over 300 kilometres inland.

The slave trade enriched the Efik community, but not every member, and with the passage of time a diminishing group of individuals acquired increasing concentrations of wealth and power. There were about a dozen important African dealers in Old Calabar in the mid eighteenth century, but only three by the end of the century and only one in the early nineteenth century. The survivor, Duke Ephraim, was the greatest trader, and the sole collector of customs duty.

Duke Ephraim was in effect ruler of the Efik, but not king. Political control was vested in an institution known as Egbo (or Ekpe in some texts), which brought together in a single organization all the leaders and potential leaders of the community. No man in Old Calabar, however rich and powerful, could afford not to be a member of Egbo (Antera Duke makes frequent reference to it in his diary; see page 402) and thereby submit to its control. Political authority was exercised solely through the society, subject to unanimous agreement. Like the age-set system of a previous era (see pages 265–66), Egbo set individual ambition firmly in the context of collective obligation. Recognizing that prospects of wealth inspired greed, Egbo restrained rivalry and prevented the development of factions and political feuds which might split the community. Feuds conflicted with the main interests of Egbo, which required peace and order so that its members could proceed with their business of trading and making money.

The sanctions imposed on those judged guilty of breaking Egbo were severe, ranging from trading boycotts to execution, either by straightforward decapitation or by a particularly horrible form of fatal mutilation in which the offender was left tied to a tree in the forest with his lower jaw cut off.[7]

Political and commercial power also fused in Dahomey during the era of the slave trade, but here authority was highly centralized and vested in a single individual—the king—and, unlike the Oyo and Kongo states, Dahomey never created an empire. Dahomey's forces, armed with muskets and including bands of fierce female warriors (dubbed the Amazons by Richard Burton[8] and others), raided its neighbours for slaves but remained a small kingdom, largely confined to the narrow strip of West African territory that is today known as Benin.

Royal succession in Dahomey was largely by primogeniture; only ten kings reigned between 1650 and 1889[9] and although pragmatic political considerations may have restrained the kings' territorial ambitions, their trading and religious authority was unfettered. Dahomey vies with Benin City as the most infamous of the slaving states, always keen to maximize trade. When King Agaja sent an unsolicited gift of forty slaves to George I in 1726, his accompanying letter (written for him by an English agent) offered "forty times forty" slaves and assured the English monarch that there was no prospect of "any want of slaves"; indeed, he would purchase quality goods "even to a thousand slaves for any single thing."[10]

Archibald Dalzell, who was on the Slave Coast in 1763, estimated that from 10,000 to 12,000 slaves were exported from Dahomey annually.[11] In 1770 the king demanded customs duty to the value of 14.5 slaves from every ship wishing to trade at Ouidah and his merchandise was valued at the rate of 25 guns, or 100 kg of gunpowder, or six anchors (a contemporary measure) of brandy, or assortments of cloth, or 80,000 cowrie shells per slave.[12]

It was alleged that the king of Dahomey customarily sold his own people into slavery,[13] but this can hardly have been a more unwelcome fate than that visited upon the hundreds who were sacrificed in the annual round of ritual and ceremony. Richard Burton, who visited the Dahomean court as British Consul in 1863, concluded that although its sacrificial customs had been greatly exaggerated, "the annual destruction is terribly great." Nocturnal executions which took place during Burton's visit (but not witnessed by him) accounted for an estimated total "butchery bill" of seventy-eight or eighty individuals, and he estimated that not less than 500 were ceremonially slaughtered in average years, and not less than 1,000 during years of grand ceremony.[14]

Still more were executed in the "normal" course of events. When the king was ill, for instance, the witchcraft responsible would be rooted out by the deaths of all suspect individuals, and should the king have some interesting piece of news he wished to pass on to his forebears he would whisper it to a messenger who was then immediately dispatched to the afterworld.[15]

Burton concluded: "It is evident that to abolish human sacrifice here is to abolish Dahomey." But he saw some hope:

During the last reign the victims, gagged and carrying rum and cowries for the people, were marched about, led with cords, and the visitors were compelled to witness the executions. In 1862–63 the wretches were put to death within hearing, if not within sight, of the white visitors. In 1863–64 the King so far regarded the explicit instructions which I had received that no life was publicly taken during the daytime. This is, let us hope, the small end of the wedge.[16]

Asante,[17] in what is now Ghana, was another West African state which rose to prominence during the era of the slave trade, and whose reputation was dragged low by accounts of human sacrifice. Visitors described Kumasi, the capital of the Asante region, as "a monstrous golden bowl filled with the blood of human sacrifice." Thomas Bowdich, who travelled to Kumasi in 1817 as a representative of the Africa Company, saw 100 men sacrificed during the annual yam festival, and their blood directed into the holes from which the harvest had just been gathered. Each year men were sacrificed in the royal mausoleums, in a manner which deliberately splattered their blood over the blackened stools and skeletons of past kings. It was said that when the king died up to 3,000 subjects accompanied him to his village. Such allegations can never be checked, but the rampant fear and alarm which ran through the Asante region following the death of the last Asantehene (king) in 1970 suggests they have left a mark on the popular consciousness that time has yet to erase. Executioners were among those holding traditional roles who presented themselves for duty when the death of the Asantehene became known. "The sheer presence of the *abrafoo* (executioners) often makes people scared," a correspondent complained to the *Kumasi Pioneer*. "You claim they have discarded their inhuman practices. This is not easy to believe."

But the grisly fascinations of human sacrifice were but a secondary aspect of European interest in Asante—gold was always the primary concern. It was gold from the Asante mines which the Portuguese had purchased with slaves from Benin in the early sixteenth century (see page 343) and which gave that part of the West African littoral its name: the Gold Coast.

Though Gold Coast trading connections began with the sale of gold for slaves, the flow reversed in the early eighteenth century, when traders found themselves obliged to include quantities of gold among the goods they exchanged for slaves (see page 400). The Asante rulers had recognized the value of gold as a medium of exchange, rather than a disposable commodity, and were accumulating the metal in their own treasuries.

This reversal of values can be dated back to the late sixteenth century, when Asante emerged as the dominant power among the Akan people of the Gold Coast. The newly introduced flintlock muskets contributed significantly to their success, but gold of course underwrote the purchase of weapons and the significance of gold to Asante is immortalized in the legend of the nation's origin. As the warrior king Osei Tutu sat pondering the problem of uniting (if not actually conquering) the groups from which the Asante felt entitled to claim obeisance, a stool made of gold tumbled from the sky and landed at his feet. "This is the *sunsum* of a new Asante nation," his soothsayer declared, "if it is ever captured or destroyed, then just as a man sickens and dies without his soul, so will the Asante lose their power and disintegrate into chaos."

Under the leadership of Osei Tutu the Asante advanced from strength to strength. When the last strand of indigenous opposition was overcome in 1701 they became the most powerful of the Akan states, controlling both the resources of the hinterland and the trading ports on the coast.

The amount of gold mined in Asante is legendary. Even at the end of the twentieth century Ashanti gold is Ghana's foremost foreign-exchange earner. In the early nineteenth century Europeans on the Gold Coast variously noted that in one group of Asante mines each miner was expected to produce two ounces daily; in another 10,000 slaves were said to be employed. Quite apart from mining production, taxes, tithes, tributes, and fines all swelled the flow of gold into the royal coffers. One province was reported to have paid an annual tribute of 18,000 ounces to the Golden Stool; another poorer province paid a mere 450 ounces. A poll tax of one-tenth of an ounce was collected from each married man in each village. In the courts, gold fines were imposed for petty offences and a person found innocent was expected to make a "thank offering" to the Golden Stool. Those found guilty and condemned to death could buy their acquittal for 500 ounces.

Asante is the only part of Africa whose inhabitants found both mineral and agricultural resources in abundant quantities. Kumasi, situated near the fringe of the rainforest, had access to both forest and savanna produce. Imported slaves (bought with gold initially) cleared the forest for agriculture, and transported its produce—especially kola nuts—to distant markets. Kumasi became the centre of a trading empire which at its maximum extent of more than 250,000 km^2 in 1820 was larger than the present-day United Kingdom (244,755 km^2) and only slightly smaller than the state of Wyoming (251,200 km^2).

Goods were transported from Kumasi to savanna regions in the north along four main roads (not trails), and another four roads provided for trade southwards to the coast. The roads also facilitated Asante control of its subjugated territories but, although Asante was always a military society with a harshly militaristic ideology, the kingdom's chief strength lay in its political institutions. Unlike the divisive system which brought about the collapse of Oyo, the Asante system did not set king and chiefs in structured opposition;

instead, they were integrated in a national council, the Asantemanhyiamu. The Asantehene was king in council. He was chosen from among the eligible matrilineal candidates by the Queen Mother and prominent chiefs—a system which averted the dangers of succession disputes that have destroyed other African states.

But whatever the value of its agricultural base and the strength of its political institutions, it was certainly the use of gold as a medium of exchange that was responsible for the long-term stability of Asante. Everything, even a few bananas, had their price in gold dust. The Asantehene bound ambitious followers to him with loans of gold. When converted into slave labour, gold enabled Asante to conquer the encircling forest. When converted into muskets, it defended the kingdom against its enemies. Gold accumulated by a chief belonged not to his descendants but to his chiefdom or the state; private success was therefore public virtue. Gold gave the Asante a means, notably lacking to most African societies, of channelling individual competitiveness into the service of the state.[18]

IN EUROPE AND AMERICA, popular pressure for the abolition of slavery gathered irrepressible momentum during the last decades of the eighteenth century. In Britain pressure was sustained by an impassioned campaign organized by the publicist Thomas Clarkson and the parliamentarian William Wilberforce. First-hand personal accounts of slavery published by former slaves such as Olaudah Equiano (see page 410), and slave-traders such as John Newton (see page 387), were valuable contributions to the campaign, as were the many details of the inhuman trade that spilled from evidence given to parliamentary select committees, but the public-relations skills of Clarkson and his colleagues spread their message more widely than might otherwise have been the case.

Two centuries before piles of direct mail began covering domestic doormats, the abolition campaign was the first to promulgate its cause by means of letters written to potentially receptive members of the community; and two images reinforced the message of the campaign—and have been enshrined ever since in the iconography of slavery.[19] The first was a small medallion which showed a black man on his knees and in chains, raising his hands and his eyes in prayer. "Am I not a Man and a Brother?" the caption asks. The design was approved by the anti-slavery committee in October 1787 and put into production by Josiah Wedgwood, founder of the famous ceramics company. The second was a poster which reproduced the drawings of the slave ship *Brookes* and showed how 450 slaves had been accommodated on that notorious vessel—jammed head to toe, elbow to elbow, in every available space with hardly room to turn (see pages 388–89). Though the placement of slaves as shown on the poster was inaccurate and could not have been used in practice,[20] this did not affect its impact, especially when it was revealed that the *Brookes* had in fact carried 609 slaves on one of her voyages.[21]

While campaigners campaigned and legislators debated, slaves themselves were the first to make a successful move towards the abolition of slavery. In 1791 slaves rebelled on the French island of Saint-Domingue, one of the oldest and most lucrative of the Caribbean sugar economies. It was a rebellion that could not be contained. The last European forces were evacuated in 1798, and the independent black government of Haiti was established in their wake. The tide was now flowing in favour of abolition.

Legislation abolishing the slave trade was enacted by Denmark in 1803, and by Britain in 1807; the United States abolished the trade in 1808, the Netherlands in 1814, France in 1818. A series of treaties signed by Britain and Portugal led to the cessation of legal trading by the Portuguese and newly independent Brazil in 1830, and pressure thereafter was directed towards the abolition of slavery per se, not simply the slave trade. In the slow-moving trend towards global compliance, India abolished the legal status of slavery in 1843; Egypt banned public slave markets in 1854; the thirteenth amendment to the Constitution of the United States abolished slavery in 1865; Portugal abolished slavery in 1878; Sierra Leone in 1896, Zanzibar in 1897. Forty-four countries ratified the League of Nations slavery convention in 1926, and in 1962 Saudi Arabia became the last country to abolish the legal status of slavery.[22]

Clearly, passing laws did not end the trade overnight, or even over decades; in fact, more than 3 million slaves were shipped across the Atlantic during the nineteenth century, fully 28 per cent of the total shipped between 1450 and 1900.[23] In a worthy attempt to curtail the illegal trade, a squadron of British naval ships patrolled West African waters continuously for nearly sixty years after the British abolished the slave trade in 1807, with orders to intercept ships suspected of carrying slaves. Many slipped through the net, but the navy nonetheless succeeded in capturing 1,635 ships and freeing over 160,000 slaves,[24] most of whom were landed at Freetown, the colony founded in 1787 which subsequently became the capital of Sierra Leone. The naval presence also had a deterrent effect, and a study of the blockade estimates that about 825,000 additional slaves would have been transported from Africa to the Americas between 1811 and 1870 had the anti-slavery squadron not been on patrol.[25]

In America, the anti-slavery movement kindled suggestions that slaves freed in America should be returned to Africa. John Clarkson (younger brother of Thomas Clarkson) organized a fleet of fifteen ships which carried 1,190 freed slaves from Nova Scotia to Freetown in 1792. The British Treasury paid for their transportation and the emigrants were assured of free land and willing assistance in re-establishing themselves in Africa, their cradle-land. The reality proved to be otherwise.

At least sixty-seven of the emigrants died on the voyage, but the survivors scrambled ashore in happy expectation of a new life. One man,

> when he landed, found himself on the same spot from hence he had been carried off, and pointed to a particular part of the beach, where, as he relates, a woman laid hold of him, he being then a boy, and sold him to an American slave ship in the river.[26]

Clarkson gathered the pious new citizens under a giant cotton tree, where they sang hymns of gratitude for their safe arrival. The cotton tree is still there, but many of the immigrants died before they had seen a round of seasons. Thirty-eight died in the first few weeks, and a further ninety-eight with the onset of the rains.[27]

Notwithstanding numerous difficulties and disputes (largely concerning land, which was not freely available, and taxes, which the administration demanded), by the end of the year Clarkson saw the surviving immigrants housed, and starting to gain a livelihood from the soil.

THE AMERICAN DECLARATION OF INDEPENDENCE, drafted by Thomas Jefferson, opens with the words: "We hold these truths to be self-evident, that all men are created equal . . . " Privately, however, his views on humanity were less all-inclusive. Of the blacks in America, Jefferson wrote:

> They secrete less by the kidnies, and more by the glands of the skin, which gives them a very strong and disagreeable odour . . . They seem to require less sleep . . . They are more ardent after their female: but love seems with them to be more of an eager desire than a tender delicate mixture of sentiment and sensation. Their griefs are transient . . . I advance it therefore as a suspicion only, that the blacks, whether originally a distinct race, or made distinct by time and circumstances, are inferior to the whites in the endowments both of body and mind.[28]

These words echoed white prejudices of the day. Jefferson himself owned 150 slaves; and presidents James Monroe and James Madison were also slave-owners. But all felt uneasy about the institution of slavery. Indeed, Madison is said to have treated his slaves "with a consideration bordering on indulgence" and did not sell any until compelled to do so by a shortage of money in his old age,[29] and Jefferson's early draft of the Declaration of Independence included a clause "reprobating the enslaving of the inhabitants of Africa [which] was struck out in complaisance to South Carolina and Georgia, who had never attempted to restrain an importation of slaves, and who on the contrary still wished to continue it."[30]

In the northern states many slaves had already been freed by the early 1800s and although white sentiment was inclining towards the view that the abolition of slavery was a just and proper thing, white prejudice nonetheless regarded the presence of so many free blacks in their communities as a problem. At a meeting of concerned citizens held in a Washington tavern in December 1816 Henry Clay proposed a solution: send them back to Africa.

> That class of the mixed population of our country . . . neither enjoyed the immunities of freemen, nor were they subject to the incapacities of slaves, but partook in some degree of the qualities of both [he said]. From their condition, and the unconquerable prejudice resulting from their colour, they could never amalgamate with the free whites of this country. It was desirable, therefore, both as it respected them, and the residue of the population of the country, to drain them off . . .

Clay cited the example of the Sierra Leone colony, concluding:

> We have their experience before us; and can there be a nobler cause than that which, while it proposed to rid our own country of a useless and pernicious, if not dangerous portion of its population, contemplates the spreading of the arts of civilized life, and the possible redemption from ignorance and barbarism of a benighted quarter of the globe . . . [31]

The American Colonization Society was formed and with tacit government support a colony for freed slaves was eventually established on the coast of Africa. The colony was called Liberia, for freedom, and its capital named Monrovia, after the American president, James Monroe. Its beginnings were far from auspicious.

First attempts to establish a colony in Africa were directed towards Sherbro island south of Freetown in 1820; and were duly thwarted by African chiefs, who extracted gifts from the visitors with repeated assurances that land would be available, then sent them away disappointed when no more gifts were forthcoming. The following year, a second contingent of prospective settlers adopted a more determined approach to the problem of acquiring land for the colony. When initial talks and gifts failed to produce the desired agreement with chiefs on Cape Mesurado, 350 km south-east of Sierra Leone, the settlers resorted to arms, held a gun to the head of the senior chief and delivered a lecture on the advantages that a settlement would bring to the region. The Cape was sold to the settlers the next day, in exchange for trade goods worth less than $300.[32]

Though settlers of slave origin eventually succeeded in establishing viable, self-sustaining communities in both Sierra Leone and Liberia, they never became fully integrated with the indigenous populations of those regions. Experience soon taught them that survival on these particularly inhospitable stretches of coastline depended very heavily upon the adoption of African methods of agriculture and housing, for instance, but their evangelical Christianity, abstinence, and cultural conceits set them apart. Africans habitually referred to the settlers as "white men,"[33] regardless of their colour—marking a clash of cultures that was destined to reverberate through the political history of the territories.

The slaves returning to Africa from the oppressions of life in America, or rescued from ships attempting to break the blockade, had good reason to be thankful for abolition.

> They took off all the fetters from our feet, and threw them into the water [a freed slave recalled], and they gave us clothes that we might cover our nakedness, they opened the watercasks, that we might drink water to the full, and we also ate food, till we had enough.[34]

On the other hand, the indigenous West Africans who were obliged to make room for the freed slaves had reason to be doubly displeased: first, the newcomers were an additional strain on land and resources; second, abolition of the slave trade had not only disqualified a lucrative source of income, it had also left them with stock on their hands.

In 1526, when King Afonso of Kongo had complained about the number of slaves that Portuguese traders were taking from his territories, the king of Portugal had replied that Kongo had nothing else to sell (see pages 374–75). By the nineteenth century, when Europe abolished the trade, 300 years of harvesting slaves had created an efficient production and delivery system that could not be easily diverted or stopped. Without a market, the merchandise clogged the system, constituting not only a loss of revenue but also a drain on resources—slaves had to be fed.

The immediate response to these developments was of course the most obvious: slaves were set to work producing food in greater amounts than ever before. Others were applied to the task of collecting or producing the commodities which Europe was still keen to purchase. The oil-palm found growing wild in the humid forests of the Slave Coast supplied lubricants for Europe's machinery and the raw material for a product that kept its workers clean: Palmolive soap. Africa's tropical timbers were another valuable resource of the forest. From the savannas, gum arabic, found exuding from the thorn tree *Acacia senegalensis,* was exported for use as a size in the textile and printing industries. Ivory was always in demand for the foreign trade, while kola nuts found an expanding African market.

All these activities were labour-intensive; slaves provided the labour. In this way the slave trade, having spread the tentacles of commerce throughout the continent, now became an essential component of the indigenous economy's continuing viability. Slave labour was cheap. Indeed, after abolition, slaves were available in such numbers that their employment in the domestic economy was not only logical, but also a necessity.[35] Subsequently, a system of slavery emerged that was basic to the political economy of many parts of the continent. The use of slaves in Africa became more common than ever before, and enslavement actually increased.[36]

Along the coast of Sierra Leone, for instance, the availability of slave labour motivated the development of a salt industry by the Ya Kumba clan, forebears of Madame Honoria Bailor-Caulker, paramount chief of Shenge (see pages 377–79), who had dominated slave supplies to the Plantain Islands and the shores of Yawri Bay. In a self-perpetuating cycle, salt produced by slaves was transported inland by slaves and exchanged for more slaves, who were then employed on the salt pans and in plantations producing food crops (particularly cassava) to feed slaves and palm-oil for export.[37]

For Asante and its dependencies on the Gold Coast the crisis of transformation to a non-slave trading economy was especially profound. Between 1790 and 1810 slave exports fell sharply, while the efficiency of Asante slave-harvesting through tribute and war ensured that the flow of slaves into the country did not diminish. The concentration of slaves became particularly intense around Kumasi, where extensive areas of forest were cleared and slave villages established to grow crops for slaves, slave-owners, and the army.

During the first decades of the nineteenth century the slave population of central Asante became so large that it aroused fears of revolt (a development no doubt related to the Asante practice of using surplus slaves as sacrificial victims). By 1820, when diplomatic missions from Britain made it abundantly clear that the slave trade would not be resumed, the Asante rulers adopted a deliberate policy of dispersing the slave population throughout the country, particularly to areas where gold was produced and kola harvested. Tax concessions favoured the acquisition of slaves by small-scale producers, and rules governing matrilineal inheritance ensured that the large slave holdings of wealthy officials and merchants were dispersed among cousins and uncles on their death, rather than passing to eldest sons in a single bloc that was likely to be retained close to the capital, or wherever the holding was located.[38]

Elsewhere on the west coast the availability of slave labour fuelled a similar expansion of economic activity, though not always with the same restraint on the growth of individual holdings. In Ibadan, the Yoruba city of southern Nigeria, for instance, 104 families owned a total of more than 50,000 slaves by the 1860s and '70s, an average of nearly 500 per family; some individuals owned 2,000 or more.[39] These slave-holdings were made up of private armies, craftsmen, plantation workers, herders, and porters. The maximization of agricultural output was seen to be important and one ruler instigated experiments designed to produce yams large enough to constitute a single load weighing up to 40 kg. The desired result was achieved by planting the yam seedlings on large rich compost heaps of weeds, banana and plantain stalks, and earth. Subsequently this became the method of yam cultivation preferred by all producers—it was labour-intensive, but labour was not a commodity that slave-owners lacked.

Beyond the forests of West Africa, across the Sahelian savannas extending from the Atlantic coast of Senegal and the Gambia and east to Lake Chad, the political map was transformed in the early nineteenth century by a succession of religious wars, jihads, which consolidated the rule of the region's Islamic states. All the protagonists had been involved with the slave trade, and the outcome of the jihads cannot be divorced from the effect of the trade and its abolition. Islam condoned slavery,[40] a fact which doubtless contributed to its significance in the economies of the Islamic states.

During the nineteenth century, following the abolition of the Atlantic trade, 1,650,000 slaves were sold across the Sahara and through Red Sea ports, and many millions more were enslaved in the new states that the jihads had created.[41] As in the humid forest regions of West Africa, agriculture supported the Sahelian economies, with peanuts (an introduced crop) finding a lucrative market alongside the traditional exports of ivory, skins, ostrich feathers, and gum arabic.

Population data collected by French officials indicate that, by the end of the nineteenth century, slaves constituted 30 to 50 per cent of all people living in the great swathe of Sahelian grasslands extending from the Atlantic coast of Senegal to the shores of Lake Chad. Near some commercial centres the proportion reached 80 per cent.[42] Conservative estimates put the number of slaves in the Sokoto caliphate of northern Nigeria in 1900 at one-quarter of a total population of 10 million: 2.5 million slaves in a region roughly the size of California (404,815 km²). The Sokoto caliphate was probably the second largest slave society in modern history that ever existed. Only the United States in 1860, with nearly 4 million slaves, had more people in slavery than the Sokoto caliphate in 1900.[43]

The regions east of Lake Chad, and parts of the Ethiopian highlands, also witnessed an unprecedented growth in slavery during the nineteenth century, after abolition.[44] In 1820 there were only 4,500 slaves in the Nile valley between Wadi Halfa and the Fourth Cataract, for instance, amounting to approximately 4 per cent of the population. By the end of the century slaves constituted one-third of all the people living in that region. Between 1820 and 1840 Egypt responded to the abundance of slaves in these newly conquered territories on the middle Nile by enlisting them in its armies, only to find that even more new captives became available, flooding the domestic market. Egyptian soldiers were often paid in slaves, who were then sold; and the Egyptian government also accepted slaves as payment for taxes.[45]

In Ethiopia too, slavery became more prevalent—even in the Christian highlands, and especially in the southern towns, which expanded measurably with the influx of new slaves.[46] Further south still, along the coast and offshore islands of East Africa, where the avaricious incursions of the Portuguese had only briefly upset the supremacy of Arab and Swahili traders, slavery kept the wheels of commerce turning.

Clove plantations established on Zanzibar and its smaller sister island of Pemba during the first half of the nineteenth century proved to be the East African equivalent of an Asante gold mine. The plantations were of course owned by Arab or Swahili families and worked by slaves. By the 1830s the slave population of Zanzibar alone was well over 100,000 and best estimates indicate that it remained at that high level for the rest of the century. Previously, Zanzibar had been self-sufficient in food, but with the clove plantations established there was less land available for food crops and more mouths to feed. Production moved to the mainland, and thus the success of the clove industry had a knock-on effect. Rice in particular was grown along 100 kilometres of coastline directly opposite Zanzibar and Pemba, but also produced at suitable locations extending from Somalia in the north to Mozambique in the south. Grain, coconuts, and oilseeds were grown for export, with slaves providing the labour.

The East African plantation economy reached its peak between 1875 and 1884, when there were from 43,000 to 47,000 slaves working on the Kenyan coast alone—44 per cent of the total population.[47]

The story of slavery as a founding factor of commercial enterprise in nineteenth century Africa continues down the south-eastern coast; offshore to the Seychelles, the Comoros, and Madagascar; inland along the Zambezi valley and around the southernmost tip of the continent to the Cape of Good Hope. At the Cape, by sad and ironic paradox, slavery was pursued not by African or Arab entrepreneurs, but by settlers from the European nations which had so energetically set about abolishing it.

Local people provide the labour needed to cut and haul sugarcane from the canefields, Somalia

CHAPTER 40

The Climatic Context

CLIMATE EXERCISED a major influence on the slave trade, with both good and bad conditions serving to maintain the trade. The effect continued in the aftermath, when African economies relied upon a workforce of about 6 million slaves in total, and annual recruitment was ten times the number shipped from the continent each year while the Atlantic trade was at its height.

Like a grubby tidemark around the bath, abolition of the slave trade left Africa encircled by a ring of economic activity which allegedly indicated Africa's willingness to clean up its act, and was supposed to demonstrate the continent's enthusiasm for trading options which the European powers deemed legitimate now that the slave trade had been abolished. The so-called "legitimate trade" consisted of supplying Europe with raw materials and commodities that were expensive or unobtainable elsewhere: palm-oil, gold, ivory, hardwoods, rubber, wax, and gum arabic; Africans were encouraged to grow introduced crops such as groundnuts, sugar, cocoa and tea, cloves and cinnamon for the European markets, as well as the indigenous coffee and coconuts.

In retrospect, it is clear that the clean-up merely shifted the offending trade from one area of economic activity to another, leaving the so-called legitimate trade heavily tainted by its dependence upon a continuing availability of slave labour. It is true that export goods could be produced efficiently without slaves by free households employing family labour and using traditional tools.[1] For example, 70,000 individual farmers contributed to the 27,000 tonnes of groundnuts that were exported from Senegal on average each year between 1868 and 1877.[2] But this was production that fuelled a cowrie-shell economy. Each farmer's output averaged only 385 kg per year—the produce of one-tenth of a hectare or less. Big traders bought the output of small producers with cowries, imports of which soared in the 1830s (and their utility persisted: in 1952 it was still possible to buy a snack of peanuts for cowries in village markets).[3]

Thus, small-scale farming for the export market, though relatively secure and impressive in its total production, brought small returns to individual farmers. Prices were dictated by the purchasers and not related in any way to the costs of production. Furthermore, large-scale producers with capital to invest in plantations and slaves to provide the labour kept prices low, and small, independent farmers had no choice but to accept the same prices, even though they did not enjoy the same economies of scale. The independent small-scale farmers were ostensibly free, but in effect they were slaves to a slave-based economy.

The facts were self-evident. Legitimate trade was pioneered in the major slave-trading regions and developed by existing commercial enterprise. Without armies of labourers to mine, produce, or collect up the goods, and legions of porters and canoe crews to transport them to the coast, trade with Africa would have been very sluggish indeed. Production and transportation was so labour-intensive that only an enslaved or economically ensnared workforce could supply sufficient quantities of goods at a price that was low enough to match the expectations of buyers from across the seas.

The principal beneficiaries of the legitimate trade were of course the same small minority of wealthy rulers and powerful merchants who acquired positions of authority from the proceeds of the slave trade. The bulk of the population derived little or no benefit from the wealth it laboured to produce. Indeed, its living conditions and levels of personal freedom actually deteriorated as its labour was harnessed to the production and transportation demands of the expanding legitimate trade.[4] Furthermore, European imports, such as cheap cloth in particular, created a demand for manufactured goods which weakened the trading prospects of indigenous craftsmen. Firearms, on the other hand, strengthened the authority of rulers over subjects.

The sympathetically disposed may describe the forms of slavery practised in Africa prior to the advent of the slave trade as benign strategies which offered the needy a refuge from the vagaries of unpredictable ecological circumstances (see Chapter 28). The slave trade and its aftermath, which left Africa shackled to the developing industrial economies of Europe and America, transformed those marginal features of African society into central institutions upon which the economic viability of entire communities was founded.

From a purely economic point of view, the major limitation of slavery or economic ensnarement as the basis of production was that the labour pool had to be constantly replenished. This was because every slave sought to become free and the fortunate eventually succeeded, while those who remained in slavery did not maintain their numbers naturally. A working slave's lifespan was relatively short and a predominance of males meant that births among slaves did not keep pace with deaths.

Enslaved women were frequently taken as wives or concubines by free men. They bore children, but their change in status often led to assimilation and even emancipation for themselves and their offspring. This was particularly true under Islamic law, which declared that concubines could not be sold once they gave birth, and must be freed on the death of their owners. Furthermore, children born to enslaved women were deemed free from birth. Removing women and their children from the slave population in this way meant that, while the overall population size was maintained, the number of slaves declined.[5] In short, slavery could not be sustained by biological reproduction. New captives were constantly required.

In the case of the plantations established by Arabs on the spice islands of Zanzibar and Pemba, for instance, where the slave population had reached 100,000 by the 1830s and remained at that level or higher for the rest of the nineteenth century, up to 20,000 slaves had to be imported each year, simply to keep pace with an annual death rate of between 15 and 20 per cent.[6]

Estimates based on contemporary reports put the total number of slaves in the Islamic states of West Africa at the end of the nineteenth century at nearly 5 million.[7] Figures for other parts of Africa are not available, but if they brought the total for the continent up to only 6 million, and if mortality was just 10 per cent (half the maximum rate on the Zanzibar plantations), a minimum of 600,000 Africans were enslaved within the boundaries of the continent each year during the nineteenth century—about ten times the number transported across the Atlantic each year during the seventeenth century, when the trade taking slaves out of Africa was at its height. And these were people who remained in Africa, enslaved by Africans for the benefit of Africa's "legitimate trade." The social and psychological legacy of those experiences is a burden that descendants of both the enslavers and the enslaved have carried ever since.

In the final analysis, heightened death rates among enslaved and economically ensnared labour forces probably limited overall population growth in

Africa no less effectively than the export of slaves had done, more than eliminating the potential for growth that intensified production and introduced staple crops such as maize and cassava had brought to the continent.

THE ACCOUNT OF the slave trade and its aftermath given in this and previous chapters has concentrated on its social and economic dimensions. The role of climate has been only briefly mentioned. But just as wide extremes of rainfall and inherently unpredictable environmental conditions had moulded the course of human evolution—especially in regions that were only marginally suited to exploitation by human populations—so climate played a central role in the development of the slave trade.

During the early nineteenth century the Sahelian savannas, extending from the Atlantic coast of Senegal in the west to the Red Sea in the east, "for the first time in centuries" did not experience any prolonged and severe droughts such as had repeatedly undermined the region's economic development in the past. There were local droughts, but the overall production of foodstuffs, livestock, and legitimate commodities expanded—especially in the new Islamic theocracies (see page 431). A corresponding expansion in commerce occurred too, with the result that the southern desert, the savanna, and the northern forest zone probably became more closely integrated than ever before. Needless to say, the incidence of slavery also intensified during this time; consolidating the "slave mode of production."[8]

The other climatic extreme, drought, also created circumstances which consolidated the practice of enslavement. When drought brought famine, it had long been customary for the starving to pawn themselves or their children to the less stricken members of the community who had managed to accumulate surpluses of food (see pages 293–94); some chiefs had a bounden duty to provide. During the era of the slave trade these essentially benign practices became an opportunity for enrichment rather than a social duty. Slave exports peaked during famines. One ship obtained a full cargo merely by offering food.[9]

Origin myths, and traditional histories of disruption and migration, reinforced by the experiences of successive generations, prepared African communities for the realities of the environments they inhabited. In savanna regions only marginally suited to agriculture at the best of times, shifting cultivation obliged farmers to move living sites periodically. Recurring drought forced people to abandon their homes with such frequency in west-central Africa that few bothered to construct commodious or permanent dwellings which they knew they might have to leave at any time.[10]

Farmers knew they could "reap abundant harvests on the condition that the rains did not fail. But if the season continues without raining, everything withers and the people are reduced to a great scarcity of foods."[11] The only certainty was that the rains would fail with depressing but unpredictable frequency, and a drought of catastrophic severity would afflict nearly everyone once in a lifetime. It might have been some comfort to know that few would live long enough to experience a second catastrophic drought, but during the era of the slave trade the threat of enslavement lessened the chances of surviving even the first.

Portuguese records from the sixteenth to the nineteenth centuries reveal a direct correlation between ecological stress, warfare, and the export of refugees as slaves.[12] Drought, famine, and disease were a formative component of the disruption and chaos which carried the slaving frontier from the Atlantic coast to the heart of the continent, where it collided with a wave of similar proportions that had advanced from the Indian Ocean coast.

Droughts of devastating intensity afflicted the populations of west-central Africa during the 1570s and '80s; the 1640s and '50s; the 1710s and '20s, and almost continuously from 1784 to 1795.[13] These were times from which there are reports of elephants devastating the fields of farmers who had managed to raise a crop. Palm groves belonging to wealthy and prestigious elites, and valued for their oil, wine, and fibre, were felled and their starch-rich pith consumed as the last resort of starving communities.[14] Lions and leopards attacked people, and the flesh of horses which had sickened and died "was sold at high prices."[15]

During the drought of the late sixteenth century Portuguese officials reported the appearance of "marauding hordes of warriors," whom they termed the "Jaga."[16] Subsequently, the Jaga acquired a reputation for cannibalism. "Anthropophagy, while frequently exaggerated in European reports of 'Jaga' ferocity, surely existed . . . and was likely to appear under circumstances of extreme deprivation, if not as a primary food source, then as the reaction of a population under extreme duress."[17]

Many of those who survived the ravages of drought and famine subsequently succumbed to outbreaks of disease. "[There has been] serious famine over the last few years, in which the land produced no fruits because of the lack of rains," a Portuguese governor reported in February 1717. "In this year a bit of rain came," he continued, "which caused such sickness among the natives of the interior, together with hunger, that a great proportion of them died."[18] An African saying summarized the cruel irony—"hunger does not kill, it is sickness that kills."[19] Smallpox, a disease introduced from Europe to which the Africans had no natural immunity, was reported with depressing frequency, its effects reaching epidemic proportions during periods of drought.[20]

And when the rains returned at last there were fevers and other waterborne diseases to contend with: "Rain brings food in abundance but leaves no one alive to eat it."[21] Except locusts. Plagues of locusts were reported in fourteen of the twenty-five years between 1640 and 1665.[22] In 1793–94 "Locusts consumed everything growing down to the roots, including in Luanda itself. Starving people flocked into the city from the interior. Wars spread throughout the interior, but the governor was unable to muster forces to quell them."[23]

No drought passed without leaving its mark on the region and its inhabitants, but the fearsome drought which persisted for more than a decade, from 1784 to 1795, surpassed even the most catastrophic in its effects. Everywhere, people were forced to abandon their homelands. Five thousand people had occupied the Kongo kingdom's capital in 1774, for instance, but only one hundred were there to be counted in the 1790s.[24] Of the remainder, some had left the town to search for food in the surrounding countryside, others had starved; many had been sold into slavery. It can be no coincidence that the all-time peak volume of slaves sent off into the Atlantic trade from the drier latitudes of western central Africa was reached during the 1784–95 drought.[25]

Nor was the origin of groups to whom late-nineteenth-century visitors assigned independent ethnic identities, histories, and territories entirely divorced from the combined effects of ecological stress, war, and the slave trade. As the slave trade swelled in volume during the drought-stricken decades of the seventeenth and eighteenth centuries, its advancing frontier flushed hordes of refugees from marginal lands, exposing them to enslavement by communities settled in areas well-watered enough to sustain large populations through all but the worst droughts.

The network of communities straddling the fertile headwater valleys of numerous Congo River tributaries along the present-day border of Angola and Congo, which ultimately became known as the Lunda empire, was a major supplier of slaves to the Atlantic trade, for instance, and thus a leading force behind the advance of the slaving frontier. Lunda influence extended south to the floodplains of the upper Zambezi, where groups known as the Luvale and the Lozi achieved dominance—just as the Lunda had done—through slaving and trade.

The slaving frontier was extended to the north-east of the Lunda region by the Luba, and the Bemba carried it east to the lake shores they colonized on the upper Lualaba River. In the regions of central Africa where the demand for slaves on the Atlantic coast competed with demands from the Indian Ocean coast, disruption and insecurity were doubly intense. Raiding and bloodshed were not rife at all times, but the threat of capture and exile drove many to abandon the ambition of agricultural security and seek instead the safety of barely habitable rocky outcrops or narrow canyons. In west-central Africa, for instance, people retreated into the remote high forests of Kongo, or vanished into the woodlands of the Congo–Zambezi watershed, where groups of previously distinct identity and origin coalesced to form new communities, bound together by their refugee status.

It has been suggested that many of the ethnic groups known today probably "originated in flights from the slaving wars of the late seventeeth and early eighteenth centuries," for, "In the unstable universe of community and polity of western central Africa, by the eighteenth century a significant proportion . . . of those who remained behind, [identified] themselves in terms of their efforts to escape capture and the long, deadly march west to the coast."[26]

Though the underlying political and economic upheavals determining social conditions during the late seventeenth and early eighteenth centuries have been most fully examined in respect of western-central Africa,[27] there is little reason to suppose that conditions were different elsewhere on a continent so profoundly influenced by slavery, and so widely affected by extremes of climate during that period.

THE EFFECTS OF the extended drought which ravaged much of sub-Saharan Africa during the last decades of the eighteenth century were to no small degree exacerbated by the exceptionally favourable conditions which preceded it. Zululand and Natal, for instance, enjoyed consistently good rains for most of the second half of the century,[28] until being struck by a sequence of drought years no less severe than that experienced in western-central Africa during the same period. Portuguese records show that average or better than average rains had also preceded the drought in western-central Africa and, furthermore, a continent-wide review indicates that relatively humid conditions probably had prevailed for an extended period throughout the semi-arid subtropical regions of Africa prior to the drought-stricken decades of the late eighteenth century.[29]

Relatively humid conditions, with higher than average rainfall over an extended period of time encouraged people to move into regions that were previously uninhabitable. Farmers reaped good harvests from land that had never been cultivated before, and with the extension of inhabitable land and increased food supplies, it is certain that human-population growth rates rose too—creating yet another conjunction of circumstances that worked to the advantage of those involved in the slave trade.

In southern Africa the effects of the humid period were especially pronounced. Many semi-arid regions, including the Kalahari, the Karoo, and the dry north-western Cape, were considerably more humid than in later times.

There were rushy grasses, swamps, springs, and rivers in the now-barren Karoo, for instance. Antelope, buffalo, and other animals that frequent wooded grassland roamed landscapes that are now more like deserts.[30]

Cattle herders were the first beneficiaries of the green flush that better-than-average rainfalls brought to southern Africa during the second half of the eighteenth century. Cattle, converting expanses of grass into edible protein, carried the advance of Bantu-speakers into the last redoubts of Africa's indigenous hunters and gatherers.

During the colonial period, and especially under the apartheid rule which succeeded colonial government in South Africa, the spread of Bantu-speakers was commonly depicted[31] as a mass movement of people and cattle, sweeping all before them, conquering new territory. In fact, there were no massive waves of migration into southern Africa. There was no conquest, but rather "a migratory drift," and gradual territorial expansion which absorbed the region's earlier occupants into a new economy.[32]

In the cycles of change, success, and failure that no society can avoid, some of the Khoisan hunters and gatherers acquired cattle and became pastoralists; some Bantu herders lost their cattle and resorted to hunting and gathering. Everywhere, however, a recognition of property and ownership laid the foundations of an economy that was based on trade and a social order that respected wealth.

The predominance of cattle in the economies of southern and south-eastern Africa by the mid eighteenth century can be judged from the archaeological evidence of Great Zimbabwe, for instance (see Chapter 30), and from documentary accounts. Wherever travellers encountered people, they found cattle too—and the relationship was long-established. A Portuguese sailor who was shipwrecked off the Natal coast in 1593 and travelled safely through the region to Delagoa Bay wrote:

> These people are herdsmen and cultivators ... their main crop is millet which they grind between two stones or in wooden mortars to make flour. From this they make cakes, which they bake under the embers of the fire. Of the same grain they make beer, mixing it with a lot of water, which being fermented in a clay jar, cooled off and turned sour, they drink with great gusto. Their cattle are numerous, fat, tender, tasty and large, the pastures being very fertile. Their wealth consists mainly in their huge number of dehorned cows. They also subsist on cows' milk and on the butter which they make from it.[33]

Dutch seamen who likewise survived a shipwreck on the Natal coast in the 1680s, and spent nearly three years in remote parts, reported that "the country is exceedingly fertile, and incredibly populous, and full of cattle, whence it is that lions and other ravenous animals are not apt to attack men, as they find enough tame cattle to devour."[34]

The symbiotic relationship between domestic livestock and people appears to have reached its apotheosis during this period, furthering the progenitive capacity of both groups in favoured habitats where neither could have multiplied so fast without the help of the other. Cattle, and the concomitant growth in human numbers, were responsible for the distribution and social organization of the Bantu-speaking groups.

Highly stratified political systems evolved directly from the ecological requirements of cattle-herding, with a strong correlation between political stratification and the relative size of herds and settlements. At its very simplest, grazing requirements and the mechanics of herd management implied that owners of the most cattle would have access to the most land, occupy the largest settlements and hold political authority over the greatest number of people.

The Swazi, the Sotho, the Tswana, the Shona, the Ndebele, the Venda, the Xhosa, and the Zulu—all the Bantu-speaking groups of southern Africa developed economies and political systems that were founded upon the wealth of cattle. But none could depend upon cattle alone. All required large quantities of cereals as well. In the early stages of the cattle herders' migratory drift through southern latitudes, Africa's indigenous sorghums and millets had fulfilled these needs; cereal outputs increased markedly when maize was added to their agricultural repertoire.

The Portuguese introduced maize (and cassava) to East and southern Africa, just as they had to West Africa. The date of its introduction is not precisely known, though there are accounts of Portuguese settlers growing maize for the garrison at Mombasa in the 1640s, and the grain was mentioned in reports made by the Portuguese governor of Mozambique in 1750. Whatever its date of introduction, maize had become the staple crop of Mozambique by 1798 and in the same year a Portuguese envoy, Francisco Lacerda, found it being cultivated in what is now Zambia, more than 1,000 km from the Mozambique coast.[35]

As was mentioned in a previous chapter (see pages 413–14), maize offered many advantages over indigenous crops. Not only did a hectare of maize produce twice as many calories as a hectare of millet and 50 per cent more than sorghum, it was easier to grow, so that more fields could be cultivated with the same amount of labour. Furthermore, maize was not susceptible to the diseases and pests that attacked indigenous crops, and the sheathed cob protected the grain from birds, so that less was lost before harvesting. This combination of advantages enabled farmers to produce nine times more maize per unit of labour than they could from either sorghum or millet.[36]

The attractions of the new crop were obvious, and it is certain that during the periods of above average rainfall which characterized the climate of southern Africa during the second half of the eighteenth century, maize cultivation spread rapidly. It was cultivated extensively in Zululand, for example, and there is archaeological evidence suggesting both a growing dependency on the new crop and a fall in the quantities of sorghum and millet being grown in other parts of South Africa at this time.[37]

As cattle proliferated on the grasslands, people multiplied around the maize-fields. The correlation between the adoption of maize and population increases in southern Africa is inescapable; the human capacity for rapid population growth during good times was fully exercised—but bad times, catastrophically bad times, were to follow.

Maize requires fertile soils and high rainfall; the humid decades of the eighteenth century enticed farmers to break new ground, and plant the new crop where only sorghum and millets could have yielded a harvest in years of average rainfall. When drought struck at the end of the century, rainfall was either below average or totally absent year after year. Farming communities that had adopted maize as their staple crop were oversized, overextended and totally unprepared for the calamity. They could not simply revert to the more drought-resistant indigenous crops, or migrate to regions less badly affected by the drought. The land was full; there were too many people to be fed, and even if the indigenous crops could have been planted in time, sorghum and millet harvests could not sustain populations swollen by the higher productivity of maize.

The almost unbroken series of prolonged and severe droughts which struck west-central and southern Africa at the end of the eighteenth century reached its peak in the 1820s and 1830s, and appears to have signalled a general trend towards increasing aridity that can be traced throughout the continent.[38] Nothing to match the extended period of relatively humid conditions that preceded it has occurred since. In the regions of southern Africa where cattle herds proliferated on lush grasslands, and maize fuelled an increase of human population size, the sudden transition from good to bad times was especially traumatic. Survival depended upon gaining control of diminishing resources, and a wave of conquest and devastation swept over the southern African interior.

Traditional accounts attribute the upheavals which set the wave in motion to the ambitions of a Zulu leader named Shaka, who gained control of the Natal coast hinterland in the 1810s and thereafter provoked war farther afield. The Ngoni (the larger ethnic grouping of which the Zulu are a part) refer to the wars and conquests that Shaka initiated as the *Mfecane,* which means "the crushing." The Sotho and the Tswana of the interior, who were the first to experience Zulu determination to gain control of more territory and resources, refer to it as the *Difaqane*—the "scattering." They scattered, and others scattered before them.

Hardly a part of the southern African interior was not touched by the upheavals emanating from the Zululand region. Between 1816 and 1840 the political configuration of southern and central Africa was thrown into confusion. Groups under stress from deteriorating conditions in their homelands were burdened with an influx of refugees from other regions. And this at a time when the slave trade still flourished and Europeans were casting an acquisitive eye over the hinterland that lay beyond the farms and towns they had already established in the Cape.

PART 6

SETTLERS

!Kung Bushwomen rest while foraging in the Kalahari desert, Botswana

CHAPTER 41

Settlers

WHEN THE DUTCH ESTABLISHED a permanent settlement at the Cape in the 1650s the introduction of European land-use strategies clashed with those of the indigenous population. Conflict was inevitable.

The Cape of Good Hope lies as far south of the Equator as Greece is to the north of it, and early European visitors were quick to note that its Mediterranean climate was ideally suited to the production of crops which flourished in regions of warm summer sunshine and winter rainfall. Indeed, it was the only part of sub-Saharan Africa that was entirely suited to European settlement in this way. Furthermore, the Cape was strategically positioned for provisioning ships on the route to India, and devoid of Bantu farmers, whose staple millets and sorghums were adapted to the summer rainfall of tropical Africa and therefore not suited to Cape conditions.

The pastoralists whom Bartolomeu Dias and Vasco da Gama had encountered on making Europe's first landfall on the western Cape coast at the end of the fifteenth century were not Bantu, but Khoisan. Their skin was copper-hued, rather than black, and their speech—the most telling distinction—"was just as if one had heard a number of angry turkeys . . . little else but clucking and whistling," a Dutch captain noted in 1597.[1] The Khoisan languages are indeed distinguished by the exceptional number and variety of cluck, click, and tut sounds they employ, but this is a measure of their linguistic sophistication. A modern authority states unequivocally that "to speak one of [the

Khoisan languages] fluently is to exploit human phonetic ability to the full."
From the phonetic point of view,[2] these are the world's most complex languages. Far more complex than Dutch.

The Khoisans' pastoral way of life was also more complex than early
observers might have supposed. The archaeological evidence of domestic
stock in the western Cape dates back to the first century AD for sheep, and to
the seventh century AD for cattle;[3] the animals are not indigenous to the region
and therefore must have been introduced. Though precise evidence of the
development is lacking, some Khoisan hunters and gatherers (the Bushmen)
probably acquired domestic stock and herding expertise initially from Bantu
farmers entering what is now Zimbabwe and northern Botswana. As Bantu
herding and farming communities expanded southward, reaching the southern
Natal coast by the third and fourth centuries AD, Khoisan pastoralism spread[4]
west and south, around the rump of the Bantu expansion.

Climate and ecology determined the routes along which Bantu and
Khoisan pastoralism spread their separate ways through southern Africa. The
Bantu could not expand westward from the Zimbabwe corridor because the
rainfall on the rangelands lying in that direction was not enough to produce
dependable harvests from the cereal crops which customarily supplied the
essential carbohydrate component of their diet.

The Khoisan, like their prehistoric antecedents, customarily satisfied their
carbohydrate requirements by harvesting the leaves and tubers and fruits of a
wide variety of wild indigenous plants. With these resources to depend upon,
they could take domestic stock into regions the Bantu were obliged to avoid.
While the Bantu moved south, Khoisan pastoralists moved west. Drinking
water was the only limitation on their expansion in that direction, one that
intimate knowledge of the landscape enabled Khoisan pastoralists to overcome
as they spread across southern Africa to the rangelands of the western Cape.

The combination of herding and gathering strategies enabled the Khoisan
to inhabit regions that would not support the Bantu pastoralists but, as might
be expected, there were limitations. The lower productivity of gathering could
sustain only relatively low population densities. Furthermore, the rainfall
regime and nutrient-deficient soils (particularly in the south-western Cape)
produced grasslands that could only be used seasonally, not all year round.

Optimal utilization of the available grasslands in the south-western Cape
obliged the Khoisan pastoralists to migrate between seasonal pastures.[5] There
were two migration circuits: one extended south from St. Helena Bay and the
Vredenberg Peninsula, and the other headed north-east from Cape Town and
Table Bay. The Khoisan grazed their animals across the coastal pastures during

the winter months, when seasonal rains produced a flush of grass from the relatively infertile soils. At the end of winter they moved to inland valleys, where pasture left untouched along permanent rivers flowing from the mountains provided grazing during the dry summer months.

Neither winter nor summer grazing areas were rich and productive enough to support herds and people all year round, nor could the system support more than a relatively low density of people and animals. The numbers need not have been precisely known, but the equation would have been well understood: in a pastoral economy more people require more animals, but too many animals degrade the environment—and excess population is abruptly cut back.

The Khoisan population of the south-western Cape when the first European settlers arrived is estimated to have been about 50,000.[6] Overall population density was thus extremely low, but migrant pastoralists are never spread evenly over the landscape. A seasonal migration tends to crowd its participants together, so that, although the overall population density may be low, the sight of large herds and crowds of people in one place at one time of year might convince the uninitiated that the region was exceptionally productive, while the absence of man or beast in another season could suggest that the resources of the regions were underexploited. Such were the conclusions of the early visitors to the Cape, who variously applauded the abundance of beef and mutton that was available, and wrote enthusiastically of the empty lands that awaited European exploitation.

A Dutch captain visiting the Cape in August 1595 reported:[7]

> That day we bought a fine ox for a poor cutless, as also one for an old copper adze, and when we wished to have two oxen for a new copper adze they gave us yet a third large ox. The next day ... each wanted to be the first to trade, giving two fine oxen and three sheep for a seventy-pound iron rod broken into five parts ... three oxen and five sheep for a crooked knife, a shovel, a short iron bolt, with a knife and some scraps of iron, worth altogether perhaps four guilders in Holland.

In September 1601, the captains provisioning a fleet of three English ships bought 1,000 sheep and forty-two oxen for

> pieces of old iron hoops, at two pieces (of eight inches a piece) for an ox and one ... for a sheep ... These oxen are full as big as ours [the chronicler reports],[8] and were very fat, and the sheep many of them much bigger, but of a very hairy wool, yet of exceeding good flesh, fat and sweet, and (to our thinking) much better than our sheep in England.

By 1607, it was reported, Table Bay was hardly ever without some European ships,[9] their captains keen to buy oxen and sheep for pieces of "old iron hoop, not worth twopence"[10] and occasionally complaining that "there is nothing to be had but meat,"[11] although it had been noted that "the people of the Country [eat] a certain kind of root which they have, which groweth there in great abundance."[12] These were probably the bulbs and rhizomes of wild lilies, irises, and gladioli—edible, but not to the taste of European seamen.

The beginning of the seventeenth century saw the consolidation of European mercantile interest in India and the Far East. Portuguese influence and power was waning; the Dutch and the British were in the ascendant. The founding of the Dutch and British East India companies (in 1600 and 1601 respectively) gave those two nations a mercantile incentive for the expansion of their enterprises abroad, and the Cape served both as a reprovisioning station for vessels en route to and from the East.

"But to make this commerce [of the East Indies] the safer," an agent of the British East India Company wrote to his director in 1611,

> it seems desirable to me to advise Your Worship of one thing which appears to be very important, which is to establish a settlement at the Cape of Good Hope . . . When we went ashore at Saldania [the then name for Table Bay], which is near the Cape, I went two leagues inland with four or five others, and I assure Your Worship that I have never seen a better land in my life. Although it was mid-Winter the grass came up to our knees: it is full of woods and lovely rivers of fresh water, with much deer, fish and birds, and the abundance of cows and ewes is astonishing . . . The climate is very healthy, insomuch that, arriving there with many of our people sick, they all regained their health and strength within twenty days. Also it is a place made so strong by nature that a very few men can defend themselves there against many. And we found the natives of the country to be very courteous and tractable folk, and they did not give us the least annoyance during the time that we were there. As regards its position, it is almost half way on the route from Europe to the Indies, and will be no less for our journeys than is Mozambique to the Portuguese . . .

"Only wheat is lacking," another letter added, "and it would be necessary to carry some quantity of this from England for sowing, and then it would soon be abundant."[13]

The agent proposed that the Cape settlement should be populated with convicts, shipped out at a rate of 100 per year. The directors petitioned King James in 1615; and the king agreed to the plan "being a thing which may do good and can do no hurt." Convicts were made available, and there are a few records of English captains putting small numbers ashore at the Cape during the following years. But the scheme was not a success.

On an outbound voyage, Walter Peyton put ten convicts ashore at the Cape in June 1615. "We sent these miserable men on shore," his log reports,

> with each man something for his own defence, both against the wild beasts [and] heathenish people, amongst which they were to be left, namely either a half pike or ship sword to each man, beside two knives to each of them for their convenience, also to each of them his knapsack made of old canvas to carry his victuals about him, of bread they had three pound the man, and 3 or 4 hundred of Newland [Newfoundland] Fish amongst them, beside some wine and strong water which in charity was bestowed on them by sundry well disposed people in our Fleet . . . we gave them so much old canvas as made them a small tent, also I gave them half a peck of turnip seeds with other and a spade to dig the ground whereby they might set or sow them so well for future provisions . . . [14]

The men signed a joint letter of thanks to King and Company for their freedom, and undertook "to journey up into the country, to see if they could discover any thing therein, which might be beneficial unto our country and honorable Employers."

On calling at the Cape on the homeward voyage, six months later, Peyton discovered that one or two of the convicts had been killed by "evil-minded saldanians" and the rest carried away by a Portuguese ship. [15]

The Dutch were slower off the mark, but adopted a more resolute approach to the practicalities of establishing a settlement at the Cape. By the 1650s they were Europe's dominant maritime power, with a fleet of some 6,000 ships totalling at least 600,000 tonnes, and manned by perhaps 48,000 sailors. [16]

JAN VAN RIEBEECK LANDED AT Table Bay in April 1652 with instructions to establish a permanent settlement that would serve as a reprovisioning station for the large fleets of Dutch East India Company vessels that sailed from Europe to the East every year. He was to regularize the supply of meat from the Khoisan herders, build up a dairy herd, create gardens that would provide Dutch vessels with fresh fruit and vegetables, and establish a hospital in which sick seamen might recuperate.

Van Riebeeck soon found himself confronting the problem which had bedevilled foreign settlement everywhere: a shortage of labour. Land clearance; the cutting and hauling of timber; brick-making and construction of the fort, storerooms, houses, and barns; cultivation and livestock herding, fishing, salt-making . . . These tasks, in addition to the primary requirement of attending to the needs of visiting ships and their scurvy-ridden crews, were more than could be handled on an acceptable timescale by a garrison which numbered only about 100 to 200 men for most of the first decade. The crews of visiting ships were an intermittent source of additional labour, but they were often too few and too sickly to be of much use, and alternative sources—such as convicts and the indigenous Khoisan—were also inadequate: there were not enough convicts and the Khoisan were unwilling to help foreigners establish a presence on their land.

In May 1652, not two months after landing at the Cape, van Riebeeck wrote to his immediate superiors in Batavia (the Dutch East Indies, now Indonesia) requesting slaves for the settlement's dirtiest and heaviest work. He emphasized the savings their labour would effect in terms of production, but none were forthcoming—even though Batavia and Mauritius (then a Dutch possession) both employed slaves from Madagascar. In 1654 van Riebeeck took the matter in his own hands, sending two ships on separate voyages to Madagascar with instructions to purchase thirty or forty slaves, including ten girls aged between twelve and fifteen years. The first voyage failed to find a single slave; the second managed to buy just two. In fact, the port on the north-east coast of Madagascar to which van Riebeeck sent his ships had by then ceased to be a slave market.[17]

There are no records of any imported slaves arriving at the Cape until 1658; in the meantime the settlers, assisted by whatever additional and coerced labour was available, achieved some remarkable results. Buildings were constructed, gardens were cultivated, and fields of oats, tobacco, beans, and clover were sown. The crops did well. In October 1656 Van Riebeeck reported that

> the haymakers had gathered a large quantity of hay into heaps and were still busy mowing. The clover was especially fine, being knee high and standing very thick. It will be very useful for the horses during the dry season when there is hardly any grazing for them. As in the fatherland, hay will be collected annually for that purpose.[18]

Van Riebeeck was introducing European methods of crop rotation to Africa. Clover was a key ingredient, in that its capacity to fix nitrogen restored the fertility of worked-out land as well as providing feed for livestock.

The settlement had acquired a herd of 230 cattle from the Khoisan by January 1653 (less than nine months after landing in Table Bay). The Khoisan had proved reluctant to supply young breeding stock[19]—"These rogues are not at all keen to part with their cattle and sheep, although they have an abundance of fine stock," van Riebeeck wrote in November 1654[20]—but the settlers nonetheless were breeding cattle, rather than bartering for them, by 1655.

The dairy herd was already producing up to an estimated thirty-six litres of milk each day when the governing body at the Cape decided to maximize production by leasing the herd to the settlement's chief gardener, Henrik de Boom, who had shown himself to be a "steady and industrious man," and whose wife had been a dairymaid before her marriage. The terms of the lease offered the de Booms ample incentive to increase their own income, but also obliged them to supply milk and butter to the settlement at fixed prices.[21]

The move from Company to private enterprise was extended in 1657, when the Company released nine of its employees from their contracts and gave each of them freehold rights to about eight hectares of land on the fertile and well-watered eastern slopes of Table Mountain. Five were to concentrate on growing grain; four on grain, tobacco, and garden fruits; and all parties were "to breed cattle, pigs, geese, ducks, fowls etc., in fact anything from which they may derive profit . . . "[22]

With the Cape settlement now well along the road to self-sufficiency, its progress received additional impetus in 1658, when van Riebeeck's long-standing pleas for additional labour were finally answered: two shiploads of slaves arrived. In February a Dutch vessel, the *Amersfoort,* had captured a Portuguese slaver heading from Angola to Brazil. There were 500 slaves on board; the *Amersfoort* took out 250, leaving the rest—who "were getting sick and also dying"—to their fate in the "old and unserviceable" Portuguese vessel. The *Amersfoort* dropped anchor in Table Bay six weeks later, by which time deaths on board had reduced the number of slaves to 170, many of whom were ill, most of them girls and small boys "from whom for the next four or five years very little can be got," van Riebeeck complained.[23]

Another vessel, the *Hasselt,* arrived at the Cape three months later, with 228 survivors of the 271 slaves with which the ship had sailed from Dahomey at the end of February. The Guinea slaves were "a fine, strong, and healthy lot,"[24] some of whom were shipped on to Batavia while the remainder were either retained by the Company or assigned to the freeholding farmers.[25]

WHATEVER THE KHOISAN MAY HAVE thought of the settlers' original intentions it now was abundantly clear to them that the Dutch intended to stay. And conflict was inevitable. The very idea of a permanent settlement contradicted the land-use practices which had sustained the Khoisan populations hitherto. Where the Khoisan had followed a seasonal round, the Dutch stayed put—competing for land and grazing resources when the Khoisan and their herds were at the Cape, and consuming the seasonal reserves while they were away.

"In direct contradiction to the custom of the original inhabitants . . . the colonists turn their cattle out constantly in the same fields, and too in a much greater quantity than used to graze there," an early visitor remarked. Overgrazing caused the gradual replacement of nutritious grasses and herbs by unpalatable species, he noted. But, "Notwithstanding these inconveniences, the colonists remain immovable in their stone houses; which on the contrary, the Hottentots [a contemporary term for the Khoisan] on the least panic remove their huts and cattle to another place, so that the grass is nowhere eaten off too close."[26]

Faced with a growing threat to their grazing lands the Khoisan rebelled. In May 1659 they attacked suddenly and in force. The settlers' farms were destroyed and most of their livestock stolen, but the Khoisan could not take the well-defended fortress to which the settlers retreated with their surviving possessions and livestock. After months of stalemate the Khoisan alliance collapsed and their leaders were forced to come to terms. Van Riebeeck recorded details of the crucial meeting in his journal:

> They spoke for a long time about our taking every day for our own use more of the land which had belonged to them from all ages, and on which they were accustomed to pasture their cattle. They also asked, whether, if they were to come to Holland, they would be permitted to act in a similar manner, saying "it would not matter if you stayed at the Fort, but you come into the interior, selecting the best land for yourselves, and never once asking whether we like it, or whether it will put us to any inconvenience." They therefore insisted very strenuously that they should again be allowed free access to the pasture. They objected that there was not enough grass for both their cattle and ours. "Are we not right therefore to prevent you from getting any more cattle? For, if you get many cattle, you come and occupy our pasture with them, and then say the land is not wide enough for us both! Who then, with the greatest degree of justice, should give way, the natural owner, or the foreign invader?" They insisted so much on this point that we told them they had now lost that land in war, and therefore could not expect to get it back. It was our intention to keep it.[27]

By the end of the seventeenth century, Van Riebeeck's "right of conquest" had become official policy that enabled Company governors and freeburghers to claim large landholdings up to eighty kilometres from the settlement on Table Bay. During the next century the frontier advanced another 800 kilometres as hunters, traders, raiders, and cattle farmers pushed eastward into the interior.

•   •   •

THE DUTCH EAST INDIA COMPANY STOPPED providing free transportation to settlers in 1707, by which time the European population of the Cape
included about 700 company employees and a settler community of about
2,000 men, women, and children.[28] It was then decided that the expansion and
further development of the colony should depend upon the natural growth of
the settler community and the labour of imported slaves. An average of
between 200 and 300 slaves were imported each year throughout the eighteenth century, mostly from Madagascar and East Africa, but also including
small numbers from Indonesia.[29]

Company records show that the settler population of the Cape totalled
13,830 in 1793, including 4,032 men, 2,730 women, and 7,068 children.
Between them, these settlers owned a total of 14,747 slaves: 9,046 men, 3,590
women, and 2,111 children.[30] Slaves were the backbone of the colony's agricultural labour force and "cannot be dispensed with in this settlement," the
burghers protested in 1798,[31] as news of the abolition movement filtered
through from Europe. But, as elsewhere on the continent, the Cape slaves
were never a self-reproducing population; their numbers required constant
replenishment.

The Khoisan, though ostensibly free and not eligible for enslavement, were
economically ensnared. Dispossessed of land and livelihood; devastated by
smallpox—one contemporary source estimated that scarcely one in ten survived an epidemic that swept through the Khoisan population of the south-
western Cape in 1713, and they virtually disappeared from official records
thereafter[32]—they had little choice but to join the labour force.

Some Khoisan reverted to the traditional hunting-and-gathering lifestyle,
becoming the "Bushmen" that eighteenth- and nineteenth-century travellers
encountered, while the last herding groups became what a visitor described as
"the bloodhounds" of the colonial advance,

> who smell out the most fertile lands. When their kraals are discovered in
> such places several Europeans . . . soon appear and, by gifts, flattery and
> other forms of cajolery, wheedle the Hottentots into granting permission for
> them to settle alongside. But as soon as the pasture land becomes too scanty
> for the cattle of these newcomers and the Hottentots, the latter are induced
> by trifling gifts to withdraw and travel further inland.[33]

As the distance between the frontier and the authority at Cape Town increased,
the methods employed in the advance became rougher.

Of the nearly 14,000 burghers living in the Cape Colony in 1793, only just over 4,000 lived in Cape Town and its immediate surroundings. The remaining 10,000 farmed the more distant grasslands and mountain valleys through which the Khoisan had once migrated freely with their stock. The Company had established centres of local administration at Stellenbosch, fifty kilometres from Cape Town, at Swellendam, about 200 kilometres away, and at Graaf-Reinet, nearly 800 kilometres away. These centres were staffed by a company employee, the *landdrost,* with the help of a clerk and perhaps a soldier or two, but law and order was effectively in the hands of the farmers, with the wealthiest and longest-established of them having the greatest say.

The best agricultural land was, of course, the first to be occupied. Latecomers were obliged to settle in the dry interior, where pastoralism and hunting were the only viable way of life. These were the *Trekboers*—from the Dutch *boer,* meaning farmer, and *trek* meaning to pull (a wagon). In return for a small annual fee, the Company granted them the right to occupy a 6,000-acre (2,400 hectares) holding of frontier land. From among their large families, each son claimed the birthright to stake out a farm of his own on attaining adulthood. And so the frontier advanced. In theory the Trekboers were lessees; in practice they held the land as outright property that could be bought, sold, and inherited.

Like the Khoisan pastoralists they had displaced, the Trekboers were often on the move, living in their ox-drawn wagons. Where they settled, conditions were primitive; a governor of the colony described houses he saw on a tour of the frontier in 1776–77:

> they are only tumble-down barns, 40 feet by 14 or 15 feet, with clay walls and a thatched roof. These are mostly undivided; the doors were reed mats; a square hole serves as a window. The fireplace is a hole in the floor, which is usually made of clay or cowdung. There is no chimney; merely a hole in the roof to let the smoke out. I have found up to three households—children included—living together in such a dwelling. The majority, by far, of the farmers from the Overberg [beyond the mountain escarpment] come to Cape Town only once a year because of the great distance . . . and because of the difficulty of getting through the kloofs [ravines] between the mountains. To cross them they need at least 24 oxen, two teams to be changed at every halt and at least 4 spares to replace animals that are crippled or fall prey to lions. Two Hottentots are necessary as well as the farmer himself. The load usually consists of 2 vats of butter (1,000 lb in all) and 400 to 500 lbs of soap.[34]

The Trekboers kept the south-western Cape supplied with sheep, cattle and butter, acquiring in return the tea, coffee, sugar, tobacco, and essential items they required for the household, and the guns and gunpowder they needed for hunting and security. Ivory was a valuable product of the hunt while elephants still populated the frontier, game meat and skins too, but the most odious hunting undertaken at the frontier included the extermination of Khoisan who objected to the Trekboers' appropriation of their lands.

With the excuse of provocation by dispossessed Khoisan bands who stole livestock and raided farms, the frontier Boers had organized "commando" forces in the earliest stages of their advance. The "Bushman Wars" ensued, in which commandos attacked all the Khoisan communities they could find, seizing their livestock and weapons, killing or wounding the people. In one instance, a commander ordered his men to massacre thirty or forty Khoisan while still ostensibly parleying with them. He did so, he later explained, because he thought they would attack him later on.[35]

Khoisan resistance hardened as the frontier advanced during the eighteenth century. Government edicts empowered the commandos not simply to recover livestock and punish identifiable offenders, but also to wage war against all the region's Khoisan, who were now to be regarded as vermin. Slaughter was widespread. Official records show that commandos killed 503 Khoisan in 1774 alone, and 2,480 between 1786 and 1795.[36] The number of killings that passed unrecorded can only be guessed at.

The officially sanctioned campaign effectively allowed the commandos to remove the Khoisan from any land that Trekboers wished to occupy. Many Khoisan chose prudence as the better part of valour and voluntarily surrendered, but government rulings in any case allowed the Trekboers to capture and add to their labour force any Khoisan they did not kill. Commandos adopted a practice of exterminating rebellious adults but capturing children, whom they distributed among themselves along with the livestock they seized.[37] The captives were called "apprentices" and forced to work without payment until well into adult life—by which time they had nowhere else to go.

Khoisan apprentices, freed slaves, and people of mixed Khoi, slave, and European descent ultimately became the large Dutch-speaking servile population that colonists during the nineteenth century began referring to as the "Cape Coloureds."

The Khoisan who had surrendered, or were captured by the commandos, of course possessed precisely the herding and livestock management skills that would hasten the Trekboers' appropriation of resources which had sustained the Khoisan for generations; in due course the ignominy of their position was intensified by Cape government measures requiring them to render military service in support of the colonists. Many "good and faithful" Khoisan participated in the campaigns which eliminated the last vestiges of Khoisan pastoralism in the Cape.[38]

．　　．　　．

WETTER THAN AVERAGE CLIMATIC CONDITIONS during the eighteenth
century (see pages 441–42) favoured the advance of the Cape Colony frontier,
permitting Trekboers to establish their presence in the Karoo and marginal
regions that would otherwise have been uninhabitable. But the wetter climate
also favoured the consolidation of Bantu populations that had advanced south
from the Zimbabwe highlands while Khoisan pastoralism had spread across
the drier regions of northern Botswana, and south to the winter-rainfall
regime of the western Cape.

The Xhosa, a branch of the Ngoni-speakers closely related to the Zulu,
constituted the southern edge of the Bantu consolidation that was steadily
expanding westward as the Trekboers advanced east. The outlying settlements
of the two groups met in about 1770, in a fifty-kilometre-wide coastal region
known as the Zuurveld (sour field), which extends about 100 kilometres east,
and 150 kilometres west of present-day Grahamstown.

The soils of the Zuurveld are highly acidic; the vegetation it supports is
fast-growing, but much of it is harmful—even fatal—to cattle in autumn and
winter, and so the Zuurveld pasture is suitable for grazing only from about
August to January. The river valleys, however, support scrub thickets and sweet
grass which provide good grazing and browse all year round, so early settlers—both Boer and Xhosa—established homesteads in the valleys and used
the plains mainly as summer pasture.[39]

As the Zuurveld became more densely settled, however, the problems of
maintaining essential access to both winter and summer grazing intensified.
Sympathy and antagonism polarized along racial lines, and the first of what
was to be a long series of so-called "Frontier Wars" between the Trekboers and
the Xhosa broke out in 1779. It is said to have begun with a Boer cattle raid in
which a Xhosa herdsman was killed, but soon embroiled the entire Zuurveld in
fighting which inflicted heavy losses on both sides before grinding to an
inconclusive halt in 1781.[40]

During ensuing periods of uneasy peace and local conflict, the enmity
smouldering between the two groups was often smothered by mutual interest.
Many Xhosa were keen to acquire European copper, iron, and other commodities in exchange for livestock; some, particularly those who had been impoverished by misfortune, were willing to work for the settlers in return for food
and a promise of livestock with which to rebuild their herds.[41] But peaceful
coexistence between Xhosa and Boer was difficult to achieve in a region where
resources were finite and human demands constantly expanding. In June 1780
the colonist leader Adriaan van Jaarsveld put the facts plainly in a report stat-

ing that the Zuurveld could not provide pasture for the cattle of both the colonists and the Xhosa,[42] and the late-eighteenth-century droughts which afflicted the region no less severely than elsewhere on the continent emphasized his point.

Mutual suspicion and mistrust, bitterness and hate, are the words historians use to describe relations between Boer and Xhosa on the frontier in the 1790s.[43] A severe drought struck the region in 1793. Resources were more limited than ever before. Pasture was tinder dry, and conflict over access to grazing sparked off outbreaks of violence that engulfed the region in two decades of strife and warfare.

IN 1795 BRITISH FORCES TOOK the Cape Colony from the Dutch. In 1803 the Dutch regained it under the terms of the Treaty of Amiens, but were ousted again by the British in 1806, and sovereignty ultimately was confirmed in Britain's favour by a peace agreement negotiated in 1814.

Like the Dutch before them, the British were primarily interested in the Cape as "a stepping stone" on the route to their expanding interests in India and the East. But while the Cape Colony was an excellent source of meat, dairy produce, fresh vegetables, wine, and other commodities required for provisioning British vessels (not least those carrying convicts to Australia), the fact that the Cape economy ran on slave labour was embarrassing for the nation which had spearheaded the anti-slavery movement and enacted legislation abolishing the slave trade in 1807. The British adopted a pragmatic approach to the problem. While careful not to condone the slave-based economy of the Cape in so many words, their policies appeared to be distinctly pro-settler when they acceded to demands for the eastern frontier to be secured.

An official commissioner appointed to examine the frontier situation made a three-month tour of the region in 1809 and concluded that lasting peace between settlers and Xhosa could be achieved only by keeping the two groups absolutely separate. "All intercourse between the settlers and the Caffres [a contemporary term for the Bantu, sometimes spelt Kafirs or Kaffirs] should be scrupulously prevented," he advised, "until the former shall have increased considerably in numbers, and are also much more advanced in arts and industry." Meanwhile, a military force should clear the Xhosa from the Zuurveld west of the Fish River and push them back to the Keiskamma River, another fifty kilometres beyond. Finally, up to 6,000 Europeans should be imported and given small agricultural farms along the west bank of the Fish River. The eastern regions of the colony would be "fully protected by this formidable barrier" of river and settlement, he said.[44]

The military campaign began in October 1811 and ended in March 1812, with settler commandos and Khoisan units assisting British regular troops in the ruthless expulsion of the Xhosa from the Zuurveld west of the Fish River. Crops and villages were destroyed, thousands of cattle and other livestock taken. Reporting these achievements to London, the newly appointed governor of the Cape Colony, Sir John Cradock, concluded:

> I am happy to add that in the course of this service there has not been shed more Kaffir blood than would seem to be necessary to impress on the minds of these savages a proper degree of terror and respect.[45]

The Xhosa were certainly impressed enough to avoid direct confrontation with superior forces, and resorted to guerrilla tactics in their attempts to regain lost territory. During the years that followed, intermittent house-burning and cattle theft impressed such terror upon the minds of the settlers that only thirty-eight of the 145 Zuurveld farms given out after the victory of 1812 were still occupied by white farmers in 1820,[46] even though British forces and their colonial allies had by then pushed the bulk of the Xhosa population back to the Keiskamma River.

The 6,000 European settlers whose farms along the west bank of the Fish River were to be a "formidable barrier" between the Xhosa and the British Cape Colony began arriving in 1820.

CHAPTER 42

Black and White Frontiers

THE BRITISH TOOK CONTROL of the Cape from the Dutch in 1806, and in 1820 shipped 4,000 settlers to the eastern frontier as a buffer against advancing Xhosa populations. The Xhosa wanted land, the settlers desperately needed labour—a conflict of interest that was exacerbated by treachery.

The plan to settle British emigrants along the eastern border of the Cape Colony has been described as "nothing but a political manoeuvre by a Tory Government, desperate to demonstrate public concern for the unemployed in order to stave off pressures for more radical reform."[1]

Certainly there was widespread social unrest in Britain at the time, and the government was under pressure to act. Mass unemployment and political riots had followed the turmoil of the Napoleonic Wars, and theories of "overpopulation" derived from Thomas Malthus's gloomy *Essay on the Principles of Population,* published in 1798, provided a convenient explanation for these troubles. Malthus had pointed out that in all creatures—including humans—the potential to produce offspring exceeds the growth of the resources needed to feed them. If overpopulation was the problem, a growing body of influential opinion surmised, emigration was the solution.

Shiploads of convicts taken from Britain's overcrowded prisons were dispatched to Australia; attempts to populate the empty spaces of Canada with surplus free citizens were made, but abruptly halted when it became apparent that many emigrants were using their assisted passages to Canada as cheap

Herding cattle to a waterpoint on the 600-km trek across the Kalahari desert from Ghanzi to Lobatsi, Botswana

tickets to the United States.[2] The proposal to send several thousand settlers to the Cape was an attractive alternative, and in June 1819 parliament was persuaded to provide a grant of £50,000 for the emigration of roughly 4,000 settlers to the Zuurveld.

Though the emigration scheme gained a significant measure of its support in parliament from those primarily concerned about overpopulation in Britain, the government did not intend "to turn the Cape Colony into a dumping ground for paupers."[3] The emigration regulations were designed to attract farmers with capital heading a party of indentured labourers. Each party leader was required to make a deposit of £10 per adult male and would be allocated land at a rate of 100 acres per man. Applications by single individuals were declared unacceptable.

The scheme attracted an estimated 90,000 letters of application,[4] many doubtless beguiled by exaggerated reports of fertile soils and a benign climate that, it was said, would enable settlers of even "moderate income in England . . . [to] have here all that is necessary—and even some luxuries in profusion—with health and every comfort and all the soft scenery of a pleasure-ground or park around them."[5] Government and settlers alike imagined that they would find in the eastern Cape the gentle undulating landscape of eighteenth-century rural England, on which manor houses could be constructed and profitable farms established by a transposed "landed gentry" and the indentured labourers who accompanied them to the colony. One settler spelled out his ambition to become

> Lord of the Manor: To fish in all the rivers of his Settlement; to hunt all the grounds; to cut timber out of all the forest, and that the whole party should enclose his own lands and gardens and assist him in his cultivation for the first two years at least.

The government view was no less idealistic. It was envisaged that the gentry would guide their subordinate labourers in the creation of "such a System of mutual support among them as should ensure their perfect security," the then colonial Governor, Lord Charles Somerset, declared. Settlers possessing sufficient means were encouraged to engage at least ten able-bodied individuals in agricultural pursuits rather than in the maintenance of large herds of cattle, thus forming a cordon of close settlement against the inroads of savage life. On 100-acre allotments for each adult male emigrant "in the most healthy and temperate climate in the universe," distressed labourer and aspiring lord would come together in the re-creation of their vision of English landed society. Free from the "contamination of slavery," independent of native labour, and based on a "mixed body of agriculturalists and mechanics," gentry and labourer would "reciprocally create and remove wants, and thus stimulate each other" to increased productivity, social order, and social cohesion.[6]

The Utopian ideal of the enterprise was undermined not only by unrealistic expectations, however, but also by the settlers' lack of agricultural expertise. Despite government stipulations concerning essential skills and financial resources, only twelve of the sixty parties shipped to the Cape, the so-called "proprietary parties," fulfilled the stated requirements. Five parties consisted of paupers financed by their parish councils, and the remainder were made up of individuals who pooled their resources and chose leaders to negotiate on their collective behalf. Overall, just 36 per cent of the 4,000 emigrants who set sail for the Cape in 1820 were adult able-bodied men, while 20 per cent were women and no less than 44 per cent were children—an age and sex distribution which would place considerable demands on the food-producing members of the community.

Furthermore, the people selected for emigration were a far more diverse group than had been stipulated. A random survey of applications from over 500 individuals has shown that the landed gentry Lord Charles Somerset was expecting were very much a minority. Indeed, over 50 per cent of the successful applicants surveyed were unequivocally listed as skilled artisans and townspeople, while only 36 per cent described themselves as farmers or unskilled labourers—and even this figure may exaggerate the agricultural element, since many applicants probably claimed farming experience they did not possess in order to enhance their chances of selection.[7]

Four thousand settlers landed in Algoa Bay between April and June 1820 and were transported by ox-wagon to their appointed locations along the frontier. Though the circumstances they encountered did not amount to the Dystopia that hindsight predicts, it was not Utopia. Poor soils, erratic rainfall, and rivers too deeply incised to facilitate irrigation soon swept away all hope of establishing the social order of England's landed gentry in this colonial outpost. By May 1823 only 438 of the original 1,004 male grantees remained on the rural locations.[8]

The rest had moved to town. But the failure of the settlement to develop as its promoters had hoped was not due only to the infertility of the soil, or to Xhosa raids, or to three successive seasons of plant rust, drought, and flood. The 1820 settlers were as much unwilling as unable to make a living off the land, and when the task proved more arduous than anticipated "they turned with enthusiasm to the more profitable avenues of trade and manufacture."[9]

Predictably, the influx of 4,000 settlers increased the potential for trade in the frontier region, and ships calling at Algoa Bay provided a dependable outlet for export goods. The settlers were perfectly equipped to take advantage of the expanding opportunities. They were accustomed to the use of money in commercial transactions, while the Afrikaners (as the Trekboers became known) and Xhosa herders still conducted most of their business by barter and the direct exchange of services. Hard-nosed British traders soon were exchanging cheap but attractive imported iron and cotton goods with their Afrikaner and Xhosa contacts for valuable commodities such as hides and ivory, which fetched high cash prices on the English market.

THE COLONIAL GOVERNMENT HAD INTENDED that the 1820 settlers should be a buffer between the Xhosa and the colony, and that "all intercourse between the settlers and the Caffres should be scrupulously prevented,"[10] but the rapid development of trading contacts between the two groups very soon rendered all hope of such separation impossible. An early attempt to control the trade through official channels failed, but regular weekly fairs, open to all settlers and Xhosa, were an immediate success. Fifty thousand pounds of ivory and 15,000 cattle hides were traded in the seven months following the first fair in July 1824. Ivory soon peaked, but the export of hides soared to seemingly infinite heights, rising from a maximum of 6,000 per year up to 1822, to over 78,000 in 1827.[11]

Trade "cracked the official policy of non-intercourse wide open." From September 1826, licensed traders were permitted to start fairs in the interior, and in December 1830 all regulations prohibiting trading operations beyond the borders of the Cape were repealed. Within a few years, between 150 and 200 itinerant white traders were operating deep within Xhosa territory, subject to very little control from either the Cape government or that of the Xhosa chiefs.

The story of expanding contact through trade is difficult to reconcile with the persistent image of the Xhosa as a threat to the security of the colony throughout this period. Accounts of cattle-rustling and attacks on homesteads are not infrequent in the settler literature, but clearly they did not compromise the development of trading contacts, nor could they have contributed significantly to the abandonment of individual landholdings on the frontier.

The truth of the matter lies in the adjustments the settlers made to their ambitions when confronting the reality—as opposed to the idealized expectations—of life on the frontier. They soon realized that manor houses and dreams of intensive mixed farming on 100 acres of enclosed arable and pasture were impracticable, and that livestock offered the best opportunity of obtaining a good return from the land. In the first round of adaptation, therefore, holdings were sold and amalgamated into units large enough to be viable. But cattle attracted the undesirable attention of Xhosa raiders, so the second adaptation involved the adoption of sheep rather than cattle as the range animals of preference on the frontier.

A report noted in 1825 that: "Flocks of sheep are in no danger from the plundering incursions of the Caffres, for they do not value them . . . "[12] And indeed, this was true. Sheep were largely alien to Xhosa husbandry; goats were more common, but both were kept only for slaughter and neither represented a form of wealth, as was the case with cattle. Furthermore, sheep could not be driven over any great distance at speed or without rest; it would have been virtually impossible to move worthwhile numbers of sheep without being detected and highly unlikely that Xhosa warriors would risk their lives for sheep, unless driven by the exigencies of drought and hunger.[13]

So while not abandoning cattle herding entirely, the settlers increased their holdings of sheep. But not the short-haired and fat-tailed African sheep that early visitors to the Cape had found so tasty. Instead, the settlers introduced the merino, which was prized for its wool. Merino lambs were "dancing about the hills" as early as 1821, and substantial flocks were grazing the frontier pastures by the early 1830s.[14] In the event, sheep brought the settlers a twofold benefit: an animal that the Xhosa did not value enough to steal; and a product which ultimately became the mainstay of the Cape economy—wool.

Cape wool production grew in parallel with the development of England's textile industry. In 1820 Britain imported 31 per cent of its raw-wool requirement. By 1850 the proportion had risen to 49 per cent, and by 1900 to 80 per cent. Although Cape wool production never approached Australian levels, it rapidly became the colony's principal export commodity.[15] Lower shipping costs gave the Cape an advantage over its competitors, and wool soon had "become a large and valuable export from that thriving Colony." In 1842 exports amounted to about 1 million pounds weight. By 1857 the colony exported over 14 million pounds weight annually, and by 1866 over 36 million pounds, almost all of which was produced in the eastern Cape.

Wool established the value of the Cape Colony to the British economy, and convinced the British that the Xhosa must be persuaded to abandon for ever their claims to the frontier territory that the settlers had occupied.

THE XHOSA WHOSE CATTLE and kraals intermingled with the livestock and homesteads of the Trekboers on the Zuurveld at the end of the eighteenth century were the vanguard of an assertive nation that was rapidly expanding westward. But their advance was driven less by the need for grazing than by the ambition of every chief's son to stake out his own autonomous chiefdom.[16] Their numbers were not excessive. Henrich Lichtenstein, a German traveller who visited the frontier region on his travels throughout the Cape between 1803 and 1805, estimated that the two chiefs, Ndlambe and Chungwa, who occupied the 150 kilometres of territory which lay between the Sundays and the Fish rivers did not have more than 2,500 followers between them.[17]

With sporadic cattle raids and harassment of the settlers, the Xhosa on the Zuurveld demonstrated that they did not regard the frontier of the colony as a serious impediment to their expansionist tendencies—until 1811–12 that is, when the brutal campaigns of the combined British and commando forces, specifically intended to inspire "a proper degree of terror," forced the Xhosa chiefs to reassess their strategies. Formerly they had resisted suggestions that a border between the two groups should be established; after experiencing con-flict with a ruthless European military force they were inclined to believe that an agreed border might be their only hope of survival as an independent nation.[18]

The Governor of the Cape Colony, Lord Charles Somerset, exploited the Xhosa's weakened position in classic divide-and-rule fashion. He made an ally of a disaffected chief, Ngqika, and thus incited conflict between rival Xhosa factions. Ngqika's overreaching ambitions were frustrated by Ndlambe and other chiefs, who attacked him with the support of Hintsa, the Xhosa king. The victorious allies now appealed to Somerset for peace and asked him to keep out of Xhosa domestic politics in future. Somerset rejected these over-tures, provoking the fifth Frontier War in 1819.

Hintsa, Ndlambe, and other rebellious chiefs were duly defeated by the colonial forces, at which juncture Somerset turned to his ally, Ngqika, and demanded as recompense for military assistance the land lying between the Fish and Keiskamma rivers, where Ngqika himself resided. Ngqika was ap-palled: "When I look at the large extent of the fine country taken from me, I am compelled to say that, though protected, I am rather oppressed by my benefactors."[19]

Somerset's treachery prevailed. The disputed territory was ceded to the Cape Colony by treaty, but although colonial forces could always defeat the Xhosa in open conflict, they could not police the extensive frontier region to which the dispossessed and very displeased Xhosa had easy access. Xhosa guerrilla tactics kept the settlers on the alert, but also hastened the move from cattle to sheep farming, and certainly did not hinder the consolidation of trad-ing relations between the two ostensibly incompatible factions.

The sixth Frontier War erupted from this muddled background of animos-ity and mutual dependence in 1834–35. The Xhosa attacked the colony and were defeated again. Territory was the fundamental issue, but associated pressures had by then added an element of desperation to the cause. In 1834–35 severe drought and outbreaks of disease threatened the continuing viability of Xhosa communities immediately to the east of the Keiskamma,[20] and the reverberations of the *Mfecane,* the "scattering," set in motion by Shaka, the Zulu leader (see pages 444–45), were squeezing the Xhosa hard up against the colonial boundary.

Since 1825, waves of Sotho-speaking refugees from the *Mfecane* had been streaming into the frontier region from the north-east. Known collectively as Mantatees, these refugees were quickly put to work by the labour-hungry settlers. In 1828 large forces of the Ngwane people from Natal, also fleeing from the effects of the *Mfecane,* invaded Xhosa territory from the east; they were defeated, but not repelled. Most stayed to seek food and refuge among their conquerors. Some entered the colony, where they became known as the Mfengu ("seekers for service") and, like the Mantatees, were soon working for the settler community.[21]

IN A DEFINITIVE BOOK ENTITLED *The Zulu Aftermath,* the historian John Omer-Cooper describes the *Mfecane* as "one of the great formative events of African history."[22] Its origins lay in the conflicts over resources that developed among the Ngoni-speaking populations of south-east Africa in the early nineteenth century, he says, from which the Zulus emerged victorious under the autocratic, not to say despotic, leadership of Shaka.

Shaka had created a militaristic society[23] which, by its very nature, could not be confined to its small centre of origin. From a minor chiefdom less than fifty kilometres across, Zulu territory rapidly expanded into a kingdom extending more than 200 kilometres from the Tugela River to the Pongola and from the coast to the elevated inland plateau.[24]

As the Zulu triumphed over all opposition, defeated tribes were driven out of the area in every direction, declares Omer-Cooper.[25] Warfare on a scale hitherto unknown "sent defeated tribes fleeing from the storm centre, their cattle and grain stores abandoned to the victors, to fall as ravenous hordes of pillagers upon others, starting a chain reaction which spread its effects over thousands of miles."

One of the original groups was pushed to the north-east, where its chief, Sobhuza, consolidated his authority over numerous alien groups and laid the foundations of the modern Swazi state. Two other groups ousted by the Zulus, the Ngoni and the Shangana, took the northward direction, ultimately extending their influence into Malawi and all the way to Lake Victoria.

In what is now the Transvaal, a breakaway section of the Zulus themselves founded a kingdom "on the wreckage of numerous earlier tribes" and subsequently moved north again to establish the Ndebele population of Matabeleland in present-day Zimbabwe. The Ngwane and the Hlubi fled westward on to the interior plateau, while a number of displaced groups gathered in the south-west under the leadership of Moshesh to form the Basuto nation, in the mountainous region that is modern Lesotho. Another powerful group, the Kololo, was driven to abandon the high veld and undertook a long northward migration across Botswana to the upper Zambezi, eventually establishing an empire in Barotseland, homeland of the Lozi people.

And to the south of Zululand, the once densely populated Natal was devastated by refugees fleeing from the Zulu and then by Zulu armies themselves. Natal was almost swept clear of people, as its population was driven remorselessly into the frontier regions where the Xhosa were themselves desperately endeavouring to hold the line against the colonial advance. Those allowed to settle were known as the Mfengu.

The pattern of population distribution in South Africa (and to a lesser extent in Central Africa) was radically changed by widespread migration during the first decades of the nineteenth century. Where previously there had been a fairly even scatter of people, with population densities varying according to the advantages of water and soil, agglomerations of peoples emerged, often centred on relatively inhospitable terrain and separated from one another by considerable tracts of virtually empty land. A belief that the rise of the Zulus was responsible for these developments is the received wisdom of South African history.

"The Zulus are coming" is a cry that has excited millions of European readers and cinema-goers,[26] and in post-apartheid South Africa it has raised deathly fears among the Xhosa too. In both fiction and reality the Zulus are seen as the archetypal African warriors, who respect only those who can defeat them. The Zulu leader, Shaka, is seen as a social innovator to whom the idea of age-set regiments is credited; a military strategist who conceived the notion of the enflanking "cow's horns" battle formation, and a martial tactician who invented the short stabbing spear (the assegai) as a more effective killing weapon than the long throwing spear. Furthermore, the Zulu nation itself is frequently cited in anthropological texts as a classic example of a centralized state that formed of its own accord among previously stateless societies— without external influence of any sort.[27]

But how much of the Zulu legend is true? Were the conflicts, upheavals, and migrations that engulfed southern Africa in the early decades of the nineteenth century, extending even to Lake Victoria, solely a consequence of developments in a tiny distant corner of the continent—Zululand? Was Shaka the "motor" that drove the *Mfecane*?

ZULULAND RISES STEEPLY from the Indian Ocean in a series of terraces, first a coastal plain covered with dense bush, then rolling hills girdled with forest, and finally high and open grasslands. Rivers have cut deep valleys through the landscape, so that high-lying ground is at times 1,000 metres above the adjacent valley floor, and the sides of the valleys are deeply incised by feeder streams. High relief produces great variations in temperature and rainfall over short distances. The coastal terrace is hot and subtropical, while the highland climate is more temperate, with warm, wet summers, and cold dry winters. Rain-bearing winds from the Indian Ocean deposit over 1,000 mm annually on the coast; rainfall decreases inland but remains in excess of 700 mm everywhere except in river valleys that lie in the rain shadow of adjacent highlands.[28]

Variations in rainfall and elevation endowed the region with a markedly varied pattern of soils and vegetation that was ideally suited to the cattle-herding and cultivation strategies of the early Bantu immigrants. An absence of tsetse fly on the high ground, and a patchwork of seasonal grazing, made Zululand an excellent region for stock, while its wide range of soils and climate enabled cultivators to choose the environments best suited to their crops.

The earliest archaeological evidence so far unearthed in the region indicates that farmers with domestic stock were present by AD 600, when groups of up to several hundred individuals occupied villages that extended over more than eight hectares.[29] By the eighteenth century there were massive settlements of herders and cultivators on the high grasslands.[30] The deep alluvial soils of the river bends were intensively exploited; corn cobs and numerous large grindstones indicate that maize was widely grown.

As elsewhere in Africa, the onset of dry conditions in Zululand during the late eighteenth and early nineteenth centuries after decades of above-average rainfall (see page 441) was a potentially ominous development. Populations which had expanded rapidly on the combined benefits of high rainfall and the high productivity of maize could have been forced to compete for scarce resources when the climate deteriorated. This could be the catastrophic population-pressure scenario that Omer-Cooper postulates, from which the Zulus emerged supreme and Shaka set the *Mfecane* in motion.

But the archaeological evidence refutes this interpretation. Extensive surveys of Zululand have found no sign of the severe environmental deterioration that such a catastrophe presumes. In fact, there is little evidence for environmental deterioration within the area that was to come under the control of the Zulu kings. Livestock densities were close to, or even greater than, the maximum that could be supported in some areas by the end of the eighteenth century, all of which suggests "that there was no general ecological crisis" during the crucial years that saw the rise of the Zulu kingdom.[31]

The reason that the inhabitants of Zululand escaped the worst depredations of drought lies in the fact that the effects of climatic change were most severe in semi-arid regions, where communities that higher rainfall had enticed into habitats that otherwise would be uninhabitable faced a high risk of famine with the onset of drier conditions. In Zululand, with its range of habitats and generally high average rainfall, the effects of fluctuations above and below the climatic norm were less pronounced, and therefore less likely to influence population trends.

But if it was not population pressure resulting from diminishing resources that caused the conflicts from which the Zulus emerged supreme, what did? As in so many other parts of Africa, it was the influence of foreign trade. Contrary to popular legend, the Zulu state did not erupt spontaneously from among previously stateless societies, but developed as a consequence of the economic and political upheavals that foreign trade brought to adjacent regions.

The Ngoni groups who occupied territories lying to the north of Zululand had been trading with Europeans at Delagoa Bay (site of present-day Maputo) since the sixteenth century. Ivory and cattle were the principal exports, iron and copper the valued imports. But the influx of trade goods weakened the established order of livestock exchanges and marriage alliances which had previously maintained the political and economic stability of the region, offering ambitious individuals the opportunity to circumvent the power of the lineage elders, attract a following, exact tribute and build a power base of their own.[32]

No less than a dozen chiefdoms were growing in size and power, and clashing with one another and their smaller neighbours as they vied for a share of the trade that the international demand for ivory brought to Delagoa Bay during the last quarter of the eighteenth century.[33] Relations between the groups deteriorated abruptly after 1796, when destruction of the Portuguese fort by a French fleet brought the ivory trade to a halt, and animosities were intensified by the drought and famine which repeatedly afflicted groups in vulnerable habitats during the first decades of the eighteenth century.

It was during this period of economic and political stress that the advantageous environmental conditions of their homeland gave the Zulus an opportunity to turn their hitherto subordinate status into one of dominance. Under Shaka's leadership, the Zulus employed a combination of political manoeuvring and military force to gain control over neighbouring groups in the early

1820s. The moves were primarily intended to acquire the cattle and manpower which were urgently needed to strengthen the relatively weak Zulu against the threat of raids from the north, but they completely transformed the political scene.[34]

BRITISH TRADERS AND HUNTERS began venturing inland from Port Natal, present-day Durban, from about 1824. They were welcomed by Shaka as a source of manufactured goods which circumvented the Delagoa Bay trade and its intermediaries, and as potential allies in his political intrigues. The traders filled both roles eagerly, and by 1827 had become an important factor in the politics of the Zulu state; by 1829 they were pressing for Britain to extend its colonial authority from the Cape to Port Natal and its hinterland.[35]

Zululand thus entered the realm of colonial history; and the Zulu legend subsequently was spun from the accounts of a few traders (dubbed "border ruffians" by one historian), most of which were written down long after the actual events were observed or heard of by the authors.[36]

The Zulus and Shaka were certainly involved in violent warfare—with both black and British forces; a breakaway Zulu faction did found the Ndebele nation in Zimbabwe; groups of Ngoni-speakers did migrate northward and establish populations in modern Mozambique, Malawi, Zambia, and Tanzania; there were mass movements of people across southern Africa, among which the modern states of Lesotho and Swaziland were founded. But the Zulu were just one of several groups that were consolidating themselves at this time. They did not constitute the barbaric war-machine stereotyped in the literature; nor was their rise the product of dynamic, heroic nation-building. Shaka did lead an intensely militaristic nation from 1816 until his assassination in 1828; he was a brutal despot, but he was not the "motor" driving the developments which convulsed southern and south-eastern Africa in the first half of the nineteenth century. What was?

The issue remains contentious, but revisionist analysis of the historical evidence points to the conclusion that illicit slave-trading from Delagoa Bay was a very significant factor, its operations augmented by insecurity and episodes of drought and famine, and its effects rippling even to the northern and eastern Cape, where so-called native battles have been provocatively described as nothing more or less than slave-raids on refugees—the Mantatees and the Mfengu (see page 470)—engineered by settlers as a means of acquiring labour for frontier farms.

CHAPTER 43

Zulu Myths and Reality

MASSIVE POPULATION MOVEMENTS which convulsed southern
Africa in the early 1800s have been attributed to the formation and
expansion of the Zulu state in Natal. The predations of slave-traders
shipping captives from Delagoa Bay to Portuguese plantations in Brazil
are a more likely cause.

The rise of the Zulus and the *Mfecane* were so firmly established as an explanation of the conflicts and migrations that made up the history of south-east
Africa in the first half of the nineteenth century that the influence of trade was
barely considered—and the slave trade not at all—until the 1980s, when historians began to question the received wisdom. In fact, the standard story of
the Zulus and the *Mfecane* reveals more about twentieth-century historiography than it does about nineteenth-century African history: a despotic Shaka,
bloodthirsty Zulus, unrelenting black-on-black violence, migrations, and the
depopulation of interior regions were all images that suited the separatist ideologies of South Africa's white minority very well.

The role of the slave trade in the events which convulsed southern Africa
in the first half of the nineteenth century is contentious, but the belief that
slaving was the major force operating in the Delagoa Bay hinterland in
the early 1800s is fortified by a growing stack of confirmatory evidence.
The thesis is not yet proven, but it is the evidence that is sporadic, not the
slaving.[1]

Generations of Zulu youth in South Africa have been encouraged to take pride in their combative prowess

.   .   .

SUGAR WAS THE SINGLE MOST valuable item imported by England and France during the eighteenth century. Supplies came, of course, from the Caribbean islands; from the sweat of African slaves. Saint-Domingue (modern Haiti) was by far the largest producer in the Caribbean, and when its thousands of slaves rebelled in 1791 they dealt the sugar trade a blow that reverberated throughout the Caribbean and beyond. Rebellion was a constant fear on the sugar plantations, and uprisings not infrequent, but the Saint-Domingue rebellion was the only instance in which slaves actually succeeded in overthrowing their oppressors. The rebellion freed the slaves on Saint-Domingue; ironically, it also strengthened the institution of slavery elsewhere.

Sugar production on Saint-Domingue was severely disrupted by the 1790s rebellion, and it was disrupted even more widely during the early 1800s by the Napoleonic wars. The ensuing gap in the market encouraged settlers in Brazil to expand their production, and output soon rose to ten times its previous value.[2] Brazil's renowned coffee plantations were also established during the late 1790s,[3] and the overall expansion of the plantation economy inevitably increased the demand for slaves.

The majority of slaves for the Brazilian plantations were shipped from the Atlantic coast of west-central Africa; but slaves from the south-east African coast became an increasingly important contribution to the growth of Brazil's sugar and coffee production, as the search for slaving outlets moved south from Angola, around the Cape and along the coast of south and south-eastern Africa.

The earliest-known account of slaves being exported from south-eastern Africa is that of a British trader who called at Port Natal (present-day Durban) in 1719:

> Here we traded for slaves, with large brass rings, or rather collars, and several other commodities. In a fortnight we purchased 74 boys and girls. These are better slaves for working than those of Madagascar, being not only blacker but stronger.[4]

The Dutch are known to have supplied their Cape and East Indies possessions with slaves from Madagascar and Delagoa Bay (the location of present-day Maputo) until the 1750s, after which trade at the Bay was dominated by the British until the 1780s, when the Portuguese took over.

Ivory appears to have been the commodity most in demand by British and Portuguese vessels calling at Delagoa Bay and other Mozambique ports during the 1770s and 1780s. Ivory exports from Delagoa Bay alone are estimated to have reached 100,000 lb per year in the late 1780s; at least 1,500 porters would have been required to carry this ivory to the coast—doubtless they were slaves. A Portuguese friar who lived in Mozambique for seventeen years and at Delagoa Bay in 1782 and 1783 noted that local chiefs sold enemies captured in war as slaves; and official documents indicate that the annual export trade from the "two great commercial highways of the region," the Inkomati and Maputo rivers (which enter Delagoa Bay from the north and south respectively), included six to seven boatloads of ivory, hippo teeth, amber, gold, copper, agricultural products, and slaves from wars.[5]

French slavers began playing a prominent role in the south-east African trade during the first decade of the nineteenth century, supplying slaves to the sugar, coffee, and indigo plantations that had been established on the Indian Ocean islands of Mauritius and Reunion.[6] In 1812 a British captain estimated that slaves were being shipped from Portuguese settlements on the Mozambique coast to Brazil and the Indian Ocean islands at a rate of 12,000 per year. American vessels also were trading there, he said, and smuggling slaves to Brazil and the Spanish Americas.[7]

By 1822–24 the slave trade passing through Delagoa Bay had become highly organized and voluminous. Some of the African groups around the Bay were actively involved with the trade, while French and Portuguese mercenaries provoked war to obtain slaves. A commission of inquiry hearing evidence in 1828 on the Mauritius slave trade was told:

> ... in Delagoa Bay ... a connection is stated to have been formed between the Portuguese and the French slave traders, and a marauding system commenced, the object of which was the capture of the peaceable tribes inhabiting the interior of that part of Africa, to which cause is attributed the appearance since 1823, of great numbers of starving people upon the frontier of the Cape colony. The slave traders at Delagoa Bay are said to have gone out in armed parties to drive off their cattle, and destroy their grain, in the expectation that a large proportion of these wretched people would repair to the coast, in quest of subsistence, where they might be seized and embarked in the slaving vessels.[8]

In 1829 Portuguese soldiers complained to Governor Ribeiro of Lourenço Marques (now Maputo) about him "sending them on slave hunting expeditions, and mistreating them if they failed to return with a sufficient number."[9]

The immediate impact of the slave trade supplying Delagoa Bay was felt across a broad arc of territory reaching up to 300 kilometres inland from the Bay and along more than 500 kilometres of coastline. The population of this

Delagoa Bay hinterland is estimated to have ranged from about 100,000 to 180,000 in the 1820s. Portuguese records indicate that at least 1,000 and possibly up to 6,000 African males were taken from this population each year between c.1818 and the early 1830s. These are estimates based on official figures, and exclude those killed or maimed while resisting capture, or exported clandestinely. The total taken from the Delagoa Bay hinterland population during that period was "at least 20,000, and probably a very much higher number."[10]

The conflict and disruptions caused by these massive offtakes from the hinterland population set waves of unprecedented upheaval in motion. Whole peoples fled up the Limpopo, Olifants, and Levubu river systems into the eastern Transvaal.[11] The Ndebele moved first northwards then westwards into the south-eastern Transvaal, their exodus harried along by " 'brown-skinned men armed with guns,' slave-raiders from Portuguese ports."[12] Refugees fleeing south-westwards gathered in the mountains of what is now Lesotho, abandoning their independent identity to the protective leadership of Moshoeshoe and the foundation of the Sotho state. Sobhuza's proto-Swazi likewise retreated to the mountains and founded a nation; and still other groups moved on to the escarpment which forms the western edge of the Delagoa Bay hinterland.

These population movements had two factors in common: they were retreats into defensive mountain strongholds, and they were distinguished by the amalgamation of previously independent groups. Self-evidently, therefore, the moves were not related to drought and competition for scant resources, as has been suggested (one authority has cited a volcanic eruption in Indonesia in 1815, which produced a dust cloud that brought drought to the southern hemisphere and thus promoted the rise of Shaka in 1816).[13] Drought certainly had local effect from time to time, but drought did not create the demand for slaves.

The slaving hypothesis contends that the Zulu state was itself a product of the disturbances in the Delagoa Bay hinterland. The missionary Stephen Kay noted in his journal for August 1828:

> He [Shaka] was originally established near Delagoa Bay, from whence he was driven about twelve years ago, by some great convulsion there. The impetus he received appears to have gradually forced him westwards [sic] as far as Natal, where he at length seated himself with a very powerful body of adherents.

Oral histories confirm that the Zulu state was indeed moving south during the 1810s and early 1820s. Once securely ensconced among the high hills and steep valleys of present-day Zululand, its leaders established a defensive line of *amakhanda* settlements along the Mfolozi River, on the northern boundary of Zulu territory.

The *amakhanda* were essentially military outposts, occupied by conscripted soldiers and staffed by specifically assigned women who took care of the settlement's agricultural and domestic requirements. Hadrian's Wall, erected to secure the northern boundary of Roman Britain, is an analogous example from European history. But the *amakhanda* were decidedly less permanent than Hadrian's Wall. Indeed, the settlements were intended to be relocatable at short notice in response to developing contingencies.

The *amakhanda,* with their flexibility, and a sturdy combination of military and food-production capacity, symbolized the central emergency of the time and the "Zulu" success in surviving it.[14] Behind the *amakhanda* line, the Zulu state expanded with the influx of other groups escaping from the predations of slavers in the Delagoa Bay hinterland. The formation and growth of the state was thus an amalgamative process. On crossing the Mfolozi the refugees *became* Zulu.

THE WAVES OF DISRUPTION, migration, and amalgamation that the Delagoa Bay slave-traders sent rippling through the disparate communities of southern Africa doubtless would have spread to the shores of the Atlantic, were it not for the presence of white settlers who were simultaneously advancing in the opposite direction. The British settlers, who were intended to constitute an inflexible buffer between the Xhosa and the colonists, arrived at the frontier in the early 1820s, precisely when the Delagoa Bay trade began its phase of greatest expansion. The waves of disruption spreading south from Delagoa Bay hit the eastern Cape frontier and rebounded. Thus: "The arrival of the 1820 settlers in the eastern Cape had regional ramifications, and was considerably more decisive than the accession of Shaka."[15]

The Zulu state did not emerge at exactly the halfway point between Delagoa Bay and the Cape frontier, but it was, in effect, squeezed into being by forces emanating from those two extremes.

The mere presence of settlers along the colonial frontier was enough to intensify the disruptive effects spreading south from the Delagoa Bay trade, but in the event their demands exacerbated the situation. The settlers were desperately short of labour, and attempts to meet their requirements included activities that only euphemistic terminology has disguised as anything other than slave-raiding.

Many of the clashes which generations of historians have described as examples of black-on-black violence typifying an African propensity for war-fare (and need for white peacemakers) were, in fact, slave-raids—conducted with the connivance of whites and producing a supply of so-called refugees from the fighting who were subsequently sold or given out as "apprentices" to farmers in need of labour.

One such incident which took place at Dithakong, on the northern Cape frontier, in June 1823 has been the subject of intense scrutiny, not least because a government agent, John Melvill, was involved, as were an entrepreneur by the name of George Thompson and the missionary Robert Moffat, whose daughter subsequently married David Livingstone. Accounts of the Dithakong incident given by Melvill and Moffat paint a wholly humanitarian picture of events: the men claim to have restrained the brutality of local Griqua people fighting to repel invading hordes of Mantatees (see page 470); to have pro-tected women and children from its worse excesses; and to have delivered des-titute and grateful survivors to farmers willing to give them food and shelter in return for work.

In fact, the Mantatees were not an invading horde that had to be repelled; they were a displaced group that had recently settled at Dithakong. Moffat apparently changed pre-existing plans in order to make himself available for the raid; Melvill brought in three Griqua warlords and organized the necessary arms and ammunition for their forces; Moffat and Thompson reconnoitred the Mantatee positions; Moffat and Melvill guided the Griqua attack on 25 and 26 June.

The so-called battle against an invading horde was in fact a seven-hour massacre during which up to 300 Mantatees were shot dead and their villages burnt to the ground. The Griqua rounded up over 1,000 cattle, thirty-three of which were given to Melvill, "according to the custom of the country." Melvill, Moffat, and another missionary named Hamilton then enlisted armed Griqua to round up survivors. Over ninety women and children were taken back to the mission on 26–27 June. During the next few days Melvill continued to scour the country around Dithakong and rounded up at least fifty more women and children who, by his own account, did not welcome his attentions: "The women having no desire to go with us . . . and many being extremely fatigued by the exertions of the day, it was with no small difficulty that we could force them on . . . They tried every means of escaping." Another group was similarly reluctant to be saved by Melvill: "With some trouble we compelled them to go to the waggon. In this manner I soon collected about a dozen women and children."

In their published reports of the Dithakong incident, Moffat and Melvill portray themselves as men who rescued innocent victims from the violent excesses of evil chiefs, and who provided succour to survivors facing starvation. This is understandable. No other interpretation would have been acceptable to the London Missionary Society, who had assigned Moffat to the Cape, or to the British government, whom Melvill represented. But archival sources tell another story.

Melvill's comments noted above clearly indicate that the women and children he transported from Dithakong were collected by force, not rescued, and their captive status is confirmed by mission-journal entries. On 8 July Moffat wrote: "Mr. Melville [*sic*] and myself went forward with one other waggon, leaving Br. H.[amilton] to bring on the prisoners, who are, I believe, to be dispersed among the industrious Griqua." On 22 July a missionary at Griqua Town noted: "Mr. Melville sent off this morning to Graaf Reinet 15 female prisoners." This batch of prisoners was guarded and transported by Griqua, who having been "entrusted to bring them into the Colony received 100 Rix dollars" for their trouble. Melvill received payment in ammunition.[16]

As to the further distribution of the captives, the Graaf Reinet administrator was informed:

> With respect to the thirteen women of the Mantatee Tribe whom Mr. Melville has saved from destruction and sent to Graaf Reinet for protection, His Excellency [Governor of the Colony, Charles Somerset] desires that they may be placed as Apprentices for Seven Years . . . with such respectable persons . . . as in your prudence you may deem it for their advantage to entrust them to and on whose humanity you can depend.[17]

Moffat subsequently noted that these "Mantatee women, I have understood, were distributed amongst the Boers." He personally

> brought six [others] into the Colony, three were left with Mr. Baird at Beaufort from my knowledge of the care he would take of them, and two are in the care of Dr. Philip. One I brought down, at the request of Mr. Melville, for his sister, but as she had died, I made this woman over to Mr. Melville's father-in-law . . .

Somerset's instructions and Moffat's remarks draw a sanitizing veil over the distribution of the twenty or so individuals involved. It is conceivable that they were consigned to people who cared only for their welfare, but their potential as labourers must have been a significant inducement in every case, given the chronic shortage of labour in the Cape at the time. And what of the other 120 (at least) women and children that Moffat and Melvill "rescued" from death at Dithakong? Thirty or so remained with the Griqua, which effectively condemned them to slavery, as Moffat and Melvill must have known. An author reporting on "humane policy or justice to the aborigines of new settlements" noted that in the early and mid-1820s: "Amongst the Griqua . . . slaves obtained by barter, or by capture . . . are a common article of saleable property . . . They sell some of them into the Colony at a low price."[18]

The available evidence therefore shows that at least thirty of the Mantatees captured at Dithakong were probably enslaved or sold into slavery by the Griqua; another thirteen were effectively enslaved in transactions that were officially described as acts of charity. The fate of the remaining ninety (at least) captives is unrecorded, but there can be little doubt that they too helped to alleviate the Cape's chronic labour shortage.

Judicious modern estimates put the number of Mantatees involved in the so-called battle of Dithakong at about 2,000. In his initial account of events Melvill reported that 30,000 Mantatees had launched the attack, a figure he arrived at by estimating the area covered by the "enemy" and allowing one person per square yard. Within a few days the figure had been inflated to 50,000, and it was also claimed that the forces which attacked Dithakong constituted only half the total Mantatee army.

Thus the Dithakong raid generated the idea of a huge 100,000-strong Mantatee army threatening the security of the Cape. In this scenario, genuine refugees from the effects of slaving in the east became marauding bands who ravaged the countryside like locusts and threatened the entire colony. The Mantatees also were alleged to be cannibals who destroyed their victims' villages and crops. Since they were attacked wherever encountered, the resulting burnt villages and victims "rescued" from the carnage only served to fuel the fantasy.

But the lie was in the numbers. If the invading horde had been 100,000 strong, more than a few skirmishes would have been required to stop them. If refugees had been as numerous as was alleged, those "rescued" and brought into the Cape would have made a more significant contribution to the labour supply than is apparent. In fact, the shortage of labour was never less than acute anywhere in the colony, and most particularly so along the eastern frontier.

In March 1825 the Cape Governor, Lord Charles Somerset, reported to the Colonial Secretary in London that the shortage of workers had put "a stop to every undertaking, whether agricultural or of any other nature."[19] Settlers lamented that it was "utterly impossible to procure men or boys or even Hottentots to herd."[20] The Xhosa from across the Fish River had been officially barred from entering the Colony since 1812, and a declared purpose of installing the 1820 settlers along the frontier had been to curtail, if not entirely prevent, illegal immigration. Now it was abundantly clear that the viability and further development of the eastern Cape could not be secured without a substantial influx of labour.

Schemes to work the farms with indentured white labour had failed.[21] The Khoisan were not numerous enough, and the trickle of Mantatees brought in by clandestine slaving was also woefully inadequate. The frontier had already been breached by white and Xhosa traders (see page 467); now the settlers pressed for a relaxation of the embargo on black immigration, recognizing that the future of the colony depended upon the muscle and sweat of the people they had attempted to exclude from it.

The Cape administration finally responded to settler demands with Ordinance 49 of 1828, declaring that, "to procure such number of useful labourers from the Frontier Tribes as the Colonists may be desirous of engaging and it may be safe and prudent to admit," prospective black immigrants would be granted passes to enter the colony for the sole purpose of seeking work.[22] But would they come voluntarily, and in sufficient number? Mantatee labourers already in the colony were paid eighteen shillings a year, and though ostensibly "free," they lived and worked like slaves.

Ordinance 49 effectively invited the Xhosa to enslave themselves, but all who were conversant with the situation knew that the only way to obtain "voluntary" labour was to send in an army and fetch it. Within four days of the signing of Ordinance 49, the military commandant of Albany, Major Dundas, led a colonial commando across the frontier, where he joined forces with African allies and attacked an unidentified group somewhere in the south-central Transkei. Dundas and his men returned to the eastern Cape in early August with 25,000 cattle and an unrecorded number of prisoners.[23]

In late August a second attack was made across the frontier. African allies joined more than 500 well-armed white troops under the command of Lieutenant-Colonel Henry Somerset, the eldest son of Lord Charles. This huge army (allegedly totalling some 16,000 men) descended upon Ngwane communities recently settled at Mbolompo in the hour before dawn. A massacre ensued. Several hundred Ngwane were killed; forested ridges above the villages were set ablaze as British gunners raked the Ngwane escape routes with howitzer fire; droves of cattle were taken, and over 100 captives.

"I directed the whole of my force, particularly the mounted part, to collect all the women and children they could find," Somerset noted in a preliminary report. In accounts published subsequently he embroidered the bald facts in much the same way as Moffat and Melvill had done after Dithakong:

I was desirous to have restored all these persons to their people and altho[ugh] my force was very much exhausted I would have done so but I found these women positively refused to return unless I compelled them to do so, they stated that their tribe was too numerous and that they could not return, now they saw we took care of them . . . The Burghers having most kindly offered to take charge of these children to the Colony, I was glad to accede to this proposal, seeing no other way either of conveying them or securing their being taken care of.[24]

Later, another commentator observed: "The prisoners captured on that occasion became the first Kafir labourers who entered service in the Old Colony."[25] But no more raids of the Mbolompo type took place. The strategy was too crude and inefficient. The next such expedition was the sixth Frontier War of 1834–35 (see pages 469–70), motivated by pretexts deemed morally defensible, and organized on a scale that brought in not the hundred or so prisoners that Somerset had captured, but 17,000—85 per cent of whom were women and children. These were the people that became known as the Mfengu (or Fingos), alternative Mantatees who provided a more adequate and lasting solution to labour shortages in the eastern Cape.

The Mbolompo raid and the sixth Frontier War took place at a time when abolitionists were demanding that Britain should enforce in its colonies the anti-slavery legislation it had imposed at home. Britain had taken the lead in abolishing the trade and maintained a squadron of warships off West Africa with orders to impound vessels attempting to supply the Atlantic trade. Her apparent readiness to condone slavery in the Cape Colony was anomalous, to say the least.

From his office in Cape Town, Governor Bourke was keen to resolve the anomaly, but his views were not shared at the frontier, where even the military and the missionaries sympathized with the settlers' plight. Bourke's Ordinance 49 was of course intended to encourage the recruitment of free labour, in the light of which the raids that Dundas and Somerset had led across the frontier needed some explaining. Accounts of the Mbolompo massacre provoked outrage when they reached Cape Town. An English officer described Somerset's action as "one of the most disgraceful and cold-blooded acts to which the English soldier had ever been rendered accessory."

Pressed to justify the Mbolompo attack Somerset claimed that it was a defensive action, mounted to repel the "Zulu," "Chaca's people," who were reported to be invading the frontier region from the north. Herein lies the origin of the myth of Shaka, the mighty Zulus, and the *Mfecane*,[26] while the truth of the matter was that the Ngwane were moving away from the direct or indirect attention of the Delagoa Bay slavers.

Moving west across the interior, the Ngwane had run into the Griqua, who attacked them for cattle and prisoners (thereafter to be known as Mantatees). Turning southward from these attacks, they moved into the corridor of territory lying between the Zulus and the frontier, and were at once set upon by British forces raiding for "free" labour in the aftermath of Ordinance 49. Thus they were trapped in "the transcontinental *cross-fire* of interrelated European plunder systems."[27] It was the unrelenting advance of settlers from the west, and the predacious demands of slavers in the east—exacerbated by intermittent drought—that set southern Africa in turmoil during the early eighteenth century. Not Shaka, not the Zulus, not the *Mfecane*.

CHAPTER 44

The Afrikaners

THE WHITE GROUP WHICH could have become most closely integrated with Africa chose a destiny that made it the epitome of racism
on the continent.

On a small hill to the south of Pretoria the Afrikaans-speaking people of South
Africa erected a monument in honour of their past. A guidebook published in
1986 declares: "The Monument was built as a tribute to the Voortrekkers who
brought civilization to the interior. Order, geometric precision and symmetry
are therefore basic to its design."

The monument was designed in the 1930s, and shares the affectations of
grandeur which National Socialism was imposing on Germany at that time. It
is a massive square granite structure, as big as a twelve-storey building, whose
uncompromising bulk speaks of an authoritarianism that demands obedience
more than it desires respect. Notices request visitors to be silent and keep children under control; wardens watch out for violators. Women in shorts are
turned away.

In a word: the monument is uninviting. Sepulchral rather than cathedral-
like—more a tomb in which the desiccated remains of a people are stored,
than a hallowed place that keeps its dreams alive. There is no sense of human
spontaneity about it; no sign of the unrehearsed creative impulse that transforms mere craft into artistry; nothing that elicits a smile of either sympathy or
fun. It is all very serious, laden with portentous symbolism, and for those who

Descendants of Voortrekkers who settled deep in the Swartberg mountains in 1830 still lived in pioneering frontier fashion when photographed in 1962

miss the intended meaning of the graven images that confront visitors at every turn, the guidebook provides written explanation.

The outer gate is built of assegais, for instance, which "represent the power of Dingane [Shaka's successor], who sought to block the path of civilisation . . . Black wildebeest symbolise Dingane's warriors, but also the barbarism that yielded to civilisation . . . " The statue of a mother and child "symbolises the civilisation and Christianity that were maintained and developed by the women during the Great Trek." A zigzag pattern running around the top of the monument "symbolises fertility. The civilisation brought by the Voortrekkers must grow."

The Hall of Heroes is encircled by "the largest existing marble frieze in the world." Ninety-two metres long and 2.3 metres high, it consists of twenty-seven bas-relief panels depicting scenes from the Great Trek which, in their mechanically derivative imagery and execution, evoke pangs of intense admiration for the inspired excellence of the Elgin marbles. The floor of the hall is a pattern of inlaid marble rings which widen from the centre, like ripples from a stone cast into water, the guidebook declares, symbolizing "the diffusion of the spirit of sacrifice that was generated by the Voortrekkers, and that eventually spread through the entire country."

A cenotaph, placed centrally in the depths of the monument, "symbolises the resting place of Piet Retief and all the Voortrekkers who perished during the Great Trek," and a hole in the roof is positioned so that a ray of sunlight will strike the cenotaph precisely at noon on the 16th of December each year, illuminating the words: "Ons vir jou Suid-Afrika (We for thee, South Africa)."

December the 16th is the anniversary of the Battle of Blood River, at which a force of 460 Voortrekkers killed so many Zulus that the "bodies were heaped like pumpkins on a rich soil"[1] and a river otherwise known as the Ncome ran with blood and acquired a new name. The ray of sunlight striking the cenotaph "symbolises God's blessing on the work and aspirations of the Voortrekkers."

THE MEDITERRANEAN CLIMATE OF the Western Cape gave European settlers a firm toehold on the continent of Africa. The Trekboers who pushed the frontier inland doubtless saw themselves as the forerunners of an advanced civilization that was destined to rule an uncivilized continent. Ironically, however, their survival at the frontier was a measure of the extent to which they abandoned European norms and lived like the indigenous inhabitants of Africa. They hunted and lived off the land like the Khoisan; they herded cattle and small stock like the Bantu, and grew the same food crops. Indeed, they often depended upon the willingness of Africans to help them, for the regions into which they advanced were not wholly uninhabited, as Voortrekker myths imply. A display in the monument museum candidly admits: "Food became scarce as time went by and the trekkers obtained mostly sorghum, maize and sweet potatoes from the local inhabitants. By 1839, vegetable gardens and grain fields in Natal already produced crops."

Of all the European groups who have attempted to settle in Africa, the Trekboers came closest to becoming Africans. Some forthright miscegenation would have completed the process, but social inhibitions ruled against anything more than the furtive production of half-castes by white men from black women (even so, demographic analysis has shown that even the whitest of the Trekboers' descendants is at least 7 per cent black).[2]

They called themselves Afrikaners and claimed that their brief history had given them a unique affinity with the soil and soul of Africa. The indigenous Africans, who possessed not merely an affinity with the continent but an unbroken association dating back to the dawn of humanity, they regarded as benighted, inferior beings, to be dispossessed and enslaved at will. In 1898 an Afrikaner author wrote:

> According to the Boer idea, the Kaffer, the Hottentot, the Bushman belong to a lower race than the Whites. They carry, as people once rightly called it, the mark of Cain; God, the Lord, destined them to be "drawers of water and hewers of wood," as *presses* [servants] subject to the white race . . . People can only control a Kaffer or a Hottentot through fear; he must always be kept in his place; he was not to be trusted; give him only a finger and he will take the whole hand. The Boer does not believe in educating him; yes, I do not believe that I go too far when I express my feeling that the Boers as a whole doubt the existence of a Kaffer- or a Hottentot-soul.[3]

Hendrick Verwoerd, a principal architect of apartheid who became prime minister and was assassinated in 1966, presented the Bantu Education Act to parliament in 1954 (Verwoerd was then Minister for Bantu Affairs), declaring: "the natives must not be given the impression that they will graze in the greener pastures of their masters."

The apartheid policies of racial segregation and so-called "separate development" turned world opinion firmly against South Africa during the latter half of the twentieth century, and the Afrikaners defiantly took strength from their ideological isolation. Belief in a God-given destiny intensified. History became dogma, stripped of inconvenient fact and embellished with glorious myth.[4] Questioning the validity of Afrikaner ideology was taboo—especially among Afrikaners themselves. In March 1979, for instance, a band of vigilantes broke into an academic meeting and literally tarred and feathered a leading Afrikaner historian who had dared to suggest that some aspects of Voortrekker tradition might be less than totally true.[5]

Such vehement protestation disguised an unwillingness to look beyond the myth. Historians delving into the archives could not avoid uncovering evidence showing that the Voortrekkers were not paragons of virtue carrying the torch of civilization into benighted lands, as the Hall of Heroes would have its visitors believe. On the contrary, they were fugitives from official determination to eradicate an aspect of their uncivilized behaviour: slavery.

IN 1828 THERE WERE 6,598 SLAVES in the eastern districts of the Cape Colony, almost all of them owned by Afrikaner farmers. Ordinance 49, issued in July of that year, appeared to legitimize the holding of "apprentices" and other blacks who were economically enslaved to settlers; indeed, it prompted military commanders to indulge in campaigns that were tantamount to slave-raiding (see page 484), but it was also a move towards ending slavery in the Colony. One hundred and forty-seven Afrikaner farmers applied for land in the territory newly taken from the Xhosa; all were slave-owners, all were denied the land to which they claimed entitlement.[6]

With its rejection of the slave-owners' land applications the government was presenting the Afrikaners with an impossible choice: land or slaves. If they were to be allocated land for their sons and expanding families (see page 458) it would have to be worked without the assistance of slave labour. Ordinance 50, issued within days of its immediate forerunner, reinforced the message.

Ordinance 50 expressly outlawed involuntary servitude. Workers could no longer be treated as slaves. No longer would they be "subject to any compulsory service to which other of His Majesty's subjects . . . [were] not liable." Their children could not be apprenticed without parental consent. Contracts of hire for periods of more than one month had to be in writing, and no contract should be for more than one year's duration.[7] As a significant proportion of former slaves abandoned their masters, a sympathetic observer noted that "the Boers were completely deprived of labourers, and together with their children had to do all the work and tend the livestock." Another reported distressful scenes of "young and tender females" driving sheep and cattle in the absence of their fathers' slaves and servants. The Boers and their supporters on the frontier protested. Liberating servants "whom the Boers at the risk of their lives had ventured to capture among rugged rocks and civilise" was blatantly unfair, they said.

The sixth Frontier War of 1834–35 supplied a solution to the labour problems of the eastern Cape (see page 485)—but not to the satisfaction of the former slave-owning Afrikaners. Britain had passed legislation in 1833 declaring that all slaves in all colonies were to be granted full emancipation from August 1834. Slave-owners would receive financial compensation, and in the Cape former slaves would be required to stay with their masters as paid employees for a further four years. But slaves, and indeed all the inhabitants of the Colony— black and white—would be equal in law. Labourers could work for whomsoever offered the most attractive terms and conditions; farmers could no longer mete out justice as they felt fit—alleged miscreants must be brought before the court, where the case for and against would be heard and impartially judged.

The issue of compensation was mishandled and gave slave-owners legitimate cause for complaint. The sum made available by the British government was far short of the value of the slaves, and payment had to be collected in England, obliging colonial slave-owners to engage agents who charged for their services. In effect, slave-owners received only a fraction of the legitimate value of their former property.[8] But it was not simply inadequate compensation that angered slave-owning Afrikaners, nor even the idea that labourers should be free to choose their employers—no, it was the concept of social equality that rankled most.

"Equal rights, to all classes, without distinction" was the declared policy which Britain's emancipation Act brought to the Cape Colony.[9] Many (but not all) Afrikaner farmers on the frontier professed a determination to retain the "proper relations between master and servant"[10] which they had practised hitherto. Since this was no longer possible in the colony, the most determined among them decided to seek their fortune elsewhere. About 6,000 Afrikaner men, women, and children left the colony during the 1830s (about one-tenth of all whites in the Cape Colony), driving their ox-wagons across the northeast frontier with their slaves (now more properly known as servants), their cattle, their sheep, and all their movable property, especially their bibles and their guns.

"[W]e abandoned our lands and homesteads, our country and kindred," a trekker wrote subsequently, because of

> [t]he shameful and unjust proceedings with reference to the freedom of our slaves: and yet it is not so much their freedom that drove us to such lengths, as their being placed on an equal footing with Christians, contrary to the laws of God and the natural distinction of race and religion, so that it was intolerable for any decent Christian to bow down beneath such a yoke; wherefore we rather withdrew in order thus to preserve our doctrines in purity.[11]

In pursuit of purity, the Afrikaners moved into regions where their survival would depend first upon the current inhabitants' willingness to tolerate their presence, and second upon their ability to secure sufficient labour. The contradiction was not missed by contemporary observers. A newspaper of the day noted: "Farmers have been induced to withdraw from under a settled Christian Government, to seek a 'quiet life' among the gentle kings of central Africa!"[12]

Oppressive legislation was allegedly the factor which pushed the Voortrekkers from the Cape Colony, but revisionist readings[13] of the evidence suggest that the pull of land-speculation opportunities was no less powerful. A reconnaissance party sent across the north-east border in 1831 returned with encouraging reports of abundant land with "a plentiful supply of water, grass of excellent quality, and an abundance of timber." The reports inspired frontier farmers to discuss plans for leaving the colony; the first trek party crossed the colonial border in February 1834.[14]

PIET RETIEF IS THE MOST CELEBRATED of the Voortrekker leaders, but he is also notorious for having led from the rear. He joined the trek only in 1837 and, like several other Voortrekker leaders, could not be described as a self-sufficient farmer in the Trekboer tradition. Far from it. He was more a businessman than a farmer—and a businessman of dubious integrity at that— whose exploits invite the conclusion that expedience and material ambitions prompted his decision to join the trek.

Retief was born in 1780, the son of a wealthy western Cape farmer. By 1812, the property and capital his father had settled upon him had been lost in ill-advised speculation and Retief had run from his creditors to the eastern frontier. Within ten years he had accumulated considerable wealth from some dubiously conducted government contracts and speculative land deals, but by 1824 he was deep in debt again. The sale of his assets and a foray into the bootleg liquor business kept the creditors at bay for a time, but he ended up in the debtors' prison eventually and was officially declared bankrupt in June 1836. Eight months later he joined a band of trekkers leaving the colony.

The route from the colony taken by the trekkers outflanked the dense Xhosa settlement along the eastern frontier, heading north across the Orange River, then swinging east around the mountains of Lesotho. From there the route divided, some groups choosing to continue the trek northward on to the high veld currently occupied by the Ndebele, while those with Retief preferred to head for Natal.

None of the regions in which the trekkers chose to settle were totally unoccupied; indeed, by definition any place offering water and land suitable for settlement would have been occupied by Africans at one time or another in the past. But the activities of slavers supplying the Delagoa Bay trade had provoked widespread migration (see pages 478–79); drought had also disrupted residence patterns; presumably the interior during the 1830s was less densely inhabited than before. Certainly several thousand Afrikaners managed to stake out landholdings in what are now the Orange Free State and the Transvaal, and African spears raised in objection were no match for the Afrikaner guns. The Ndebele objected and were driven across the Limpopo into modern Zimbabwe, where they established a new Matabeleland at the expense of the Shona inhabitants.[15]

Being more of a speculator than a gunslinging frontiersman, Piet Retief adopted a more diplomatic approach to the matter of establishing an Afrikaner homeland in Natal. In October 1837 he led an advance party of fifteen men through Zululand to Port Natal (modern Durban), where the small community of white settlers and traders already operating in Natal readily agreed to Retief's proposal in the interests of mutual security. Retief now visited the Zulu leader, Dingane, and obtained approval for extensive Afrikaner settlement in Natal, on condition that Retief would first recover 300 head of cattle stolen from Dingane by a Sotho chief.

Regarding recovery of the cattle as little more than a formality, Retief sent advance word of Dingane's agreement back to the trekkers waiting on the Zululand border. Soon hundreds of wagons were rumbling down through the passes, and by the time Retief joined them, over 1,000 wagons were camped in groups of two and three families along the upper Tugela River and its tributaries. These premature movements were reported to Dingane, who interpreted them as preparation for an invasion.[16]

Retief recovered the stolen cattle in late January 1838 and returned them to Dingane in the company of sixty-nine Boers and some thirty Khoisan; on 4 February Dingane put his mark on a treaty Retief had drafted:

> Know all men by this—That whereas Pieter Retief, Gouvernor of the Dutch emigrant South Afrikans, has retaken my Cattle . . . which Cattle he, the said Retief, now deliver unto me: I, DINGAAN, King of the Zoolas, do hereby certify and declare that I thought fit to resign unto him, Retief, and his countrymen (on reward of the case hereabove mentioned) the Place called "Port Natal," together with all land annexed, that is to say, from Dogela [the Tugela River] to the Omsoboebo [the Umzimvubu] westward; and from the sea to the north, as far as the land may be usefull and in my possession. Which I did by this, and give unto them for their everlasting property.[17]

Dingane ostensibly gave Retief control of more than 30,000 square kilo-metres of territory: fertile river valleys, well-watered grasslands, forests, over 200 kilometres of coastline and a seaport already providing access to European goods and markets. More than enough, one would imagine, to satisfy the ambitions of a failed speculator and undischarged bankrupt.

But Dingane's generosity in itself should have been a warning. The Zulu leader had no intention of giving Zululand to the Boers. On the morning of February the sixth Dingane invited Retief and his party to a farewell celebra-tion and having enticed them, unarmed, into his kraal, promptly ordered them to be seized and taken to a neighbouring hill where each in turn was impaled on a stake and his skull smashed; Retief was the last to die.[18]

The treaty ceding Zululand to the Boers was allegedly found in a leather pouch lying with Retief's body when the remains of the murdered men were recovered by their compatriots after the Battle of Blood River. The likelihood of the pouch and treaty having been left intact by the Zulus to survive ten months of exposure to the elements has been questioned by scholars.[19] The document enshrined in Afrikaner history (and displayed on a red velvet cush-ion in the Voortrekker Museum in Pietermaritzburg) is probably a forgery con-cocted by the leader of the Boer forces at Blood River—Andries Pretorius.[20]

The massacre was observed by an English missionary, Francis Owen, who had been residing at the royal kraal for some months, attempting to impart the virtues of Christian morality to the Zulus. When the Boers were seized, Din-gane sent a messenger to Owen, advising him not to be alarmed, he was simply going to kill the Boers. Owen was thus a horrified witness to the entire episode. When it was over he hurried to Durban with the news.

Meanwhile, Dingane dispatched three regiments to attack the Boers on the upper Tugela and its tributaries. The encampments were undefended, since many of the men who might have held off the Zulu attack were away hunting or looking for farm sites (and sixty-nine had accompanied Retief). They returned to find scenes of horrific carnage. Forty-one men, fifty-six women, 185 children, and some 250 Khoisan servants had been slaughtered. Ten thou-sand cattle were driven off. When a settlement was eventually established at the site they called it *Weenen*—Weeping.

THE BATTLE OF BLOOD RIVER IN December 1838 (and sundry other skirmishes) was the Boers' revenge for the killings of the Retief party and the settlers at the Weenen encampment. Dingane capitulated and headed north, to Swaziland, where he attempted to found a new Zulu kingdom, but was defeated and died a lone fugitive c.1840. Meanwhile, his half-brother Mpande and a considerable number of dissident Zulus defected to the Afrikaners, who founded their Natal Republic in 1839 and immediately began staking out their land claims—with every sign that their concerns were not merely for land to satisfy their immediate needs, but also for property on which profit might be secured in the future.

Far from being satisfied with one 6,000-acre farm per family, "men went on staking claims right down the Umzimvubu and far beyond the Tugela . . . Soon 1,800 farms had been staked out, two or three for each family and the rest by unattached men."[21] By 1842, a community of just 6,000 men, women, and children had laid claim to almost all the fertile land[22] contained in the 30,000 square kilometres of territory that Dingane had ostensibly ceded to Piet Retief in February 1838.

The settlers acquired the labour they needed for their farms in the manner that had been customary on the Cape frontier: they seized African children. With Mpande's collaboration, Boer commandos raided the remnants of Dingane's retreating followers. Reports tell of one such raid which captured about 1,000 children, it is said, along with more than 35,000 head of cattle.[23] But soon thousands of Africans were flooding into Natal of their own accord—more than the Afrikaners could control. By 1843 the African population of the republic had risen from 10,000 to 50,000. Greatly outnumbered, with no effective system of law and order established, the Boers were in a worse plight than ever they had suffered under British rule in the Cape. Not for the last time, a white South African minority faced the problem of reconciling its need for security with its dependence on the labour of conquered people.[24]

Afrikaner commandos attempted to stem the inflow by making intimidatory attacks on neighbouring African populations, and in 1841 their leaders decreed that not more than five African families should live on one farm and that "surplus" Africans should be removed. The Afrikaners lacked the means of enforcing these decrees, but their apparent determination to persist with slavery in Natal aroused British concern. Gunships were dispatched to Port Natal and the republic was annexed by Britain in 1843. The document of submission which brought the Afrikaner Natal Republic into the British Empire included the stipulation "that there shall not be in the eye of the law any distinction of colour, origin, race, or creed; but that the protection of the law, in letter and in substance, shall be extended impartially to all alike."[25]

After the British annexation of Natal, nearly all the Afrikaners trekked back to the high veld and distributed themselves throughout the interior—

down to the Orange River and across the Vaal—creating an extensive but thinly populated frontier zone where they could sustain themselves but neither they, nor the indigenous communities, nor, for that matter, the British colonial authorities, could establish undisputed political control. Conventions agreed with the British in 1852 and 1854 formally recognized the independent authority of what would eventually become the Boers' Transvaal and Orange Free State republics, and with that the trekkers might have expected to be left alone with their problems, which were not inconsiderable.

LEFT ENTIRELY TO THEIR OWN DEVICES, with no access to European markets and therefore no means of acquiring guns and gunpowder, the Boers who trekked to the South African interior almost certainly would have ceased to exist as a distinct ethnic entity by the end of the nineteenth century. Without the props of European technology to sustain their conceit of a superior civilization, mere survival would have obliged them to consort more fully with the indigenous African population. African food crops and cultivation practices had evolved in response to local conditions; African social systems likewise were conditioned to the human and environmental imperatives of the region. Ultimately the Boers would have accepted the fact that a white skin did not automatically give its owner the ability to manage Africa to greater advantage than its indigenous inhabitants. Moreover, sheer numbers would have compelled them to accept the superiority of their black hosts: either that or they would have died out; but most probably they would have been absorbed into the African population, miscegenation neutralizing the differences and perhaps even making the best of both worlds.

Even with the contacts which the Boers managed to maintain with foreign suppliers, they drifted no small distance from the ideals of the civilized world which they professed to be introducing to the interior of southern Africa. As their capital dwindled, they acquired their guns, lead and powder, tea, sugar, and coffee from itinerant traders by barter and became increasingly impoverished. They clung to the value of Christianity and literacy as the symbols of their civilized status but could produce neither ministers nor teachers from among their own numbers.[26] In the early 1870s an observer noted that

> the children of Dutch-speaking, European parentage [are] growing up with less care bestowed upon them than upon the beasts of the field—without the ability to read or write even their mother tongue, without any instruction in the knowledge of a God that made them, having at their command no language but a limited vocabulary of semi-Dutch, semi-Hottentot words, and

those only concerning the wants or doings of themselves and the animals they tend.[27]

How far was this from the Voortrekker myth?

But the future of the Afrikaners was secured (and the fate of Africa sealed) by events that none but the most outrageously hopeful could have predicted. Diamonds were found in 1867 near the confluence of the Vaal and the Harts rivers, on the fringe of the Afrikaners' own Orange Free State; and in 1886 extensive gold deposits were discovered south of Pretoria, in the Transvaal Republic. The discoveries attracted stupendous amounts of capital investment to the dusty interior (the Cape government alone borrowed over £20 million sterling between 1872 and 1885),[28] and hastened the demarcation of landhold-ings and national boundaries in the immediate proximity of the deposits and beyond.

Thousands of prospectors rushed to the diamond fields. Some made their fortunes; but more than half—and possibly as many as 90 per cent—barely covered their costs.[29] Diamond dealers, speculators, and other entrepreneurs flexing their wallets rather than their muscles achieved the highest rates of return, especially the handful of men who eventually gained control of the entire mining industry.

And the Africans in whose homelands these riches had been discovered? Well, many joined the initial rush and succeeded in staking claims on the dia-mond fields, but the last was bought out in 1883. Meanwhile, the mines required huge amounts of labour, which offered Africans an opportunity to *earn* a living, now that their right to *make* a living from the land had been usurped by European settlers on all but a fraction of the available land area. It was paid employment, but little better than the slave labour that settlers had exacted in a previous era.

CHAPTER 45

Diamonds and Gold

THE MODERN ERA OF African history was inaugurated by the discovery of diamonds at Kimberley and gold on the Witwatersrand. Unimagined wealth awakened imperial dreams, while the mines intensified labour demands and polarized racist attitudes. Labour compounds and pass laws were just two aspects of official racial segregation instituted under British rule during the 1880s which established precedents for the apartheid laws formalized by South Africa's white government in the 1960s.

Diamonds are crystals of carbon, naturally formed only at depths of about 150 kilometres below the Earth's surface, where the immense weight of rock above exerts a pressure of 50,000 atmospheres and temperatures stand around 1,100 degrees centigrade. The purest diamonds are the whitest and brightest, but traces of other elements are sometimes incorporated in the crystal as it forms, giving a tinge of colour: most often yellow, though red, blue, green, and even black stones also occur. The radioactive decay rate of these trace elements is known and can be measured, giving the age of the diamond in which they are included. Diamonds on which this work has been done were found to be more than 3 billion years old[1]—Diamonds sparkle with fire from the core of the Archaean Earth.

Cratons—the massive inert slabs of rock which formed the core of the continents (see page 10)—are the only portions of the Earth's crust under which the pressure and temperature necessary for the creation of diamonds occurred.

Prime stones from one day's production of 5,000 carats at the Consolidated
Diamond Mines workings in Namibia

Material from the active layers beneath the cratons occasionally burst to the surface, like steam rising through porridge, leaving the vent plugged with a blue, friable rock, studded with diamonds.

Every diamond ever found was formed under a craton, and each one was carried to the surface by volcanic action. Most are found in alluvial deposits far from their source, but the antiquity and stability of Africa has left the cratonic core of the continent and its diamond-bearing volcanic intrusions uniquely intact, especially in the case of the Kaapvaal craton,[2] which constitutes the largest single portion of the South African land mass. The Kaapvaal craton is one of only two places in the world (Russia is the other) where prospectors have located the volcanic pipes through which diamonds have been transported to the surface.

Until the fifteenth century, pearls were the most precious gems; diamonds were known, but the colour and shapely proportions of emeralds, rubies, opals, and sapphires were more highly valued. Diamonds were distinguished primarily by their hardness; no element is harder—a characteristic which concealed their full potential as gems until 1456, when Louis de Berquem perfected a method of scientific faceting and thus showed how a diamond could be transformed into an unequalled reflector of light, "unleashing the interior beauty of the stone."[3]

By the nineteenth century diamonds were well established as the most precious of all gemstones. India was the primary source until the 1720s, when deposits were discovered in Brazil. In both India and Brazil diamonds were found in alluvial deposits, in sand and rock conglomerates created by erosion and carried far from their original source by massive tectonic movement and the local action of rivers during 3 billion years of Earth history. As a result of all the movement and erosion they had been exposed to, most alluvial stones were small—one carat or less. Large stones were extremely rare. Indeed, slaves in the Brazilian mines who found a stone of seventeen carats or more (about the size of a large pea) were rewarded with their freedom.[4]

The hardness of diamonds gives them a utilitarian value in some industrial processes, but gem-quality stones are useful only as rare eye-catching articles of adornment on which surplus wealth might be expended—they are strictly for the wealthy. In terms of their practical value to the inhabitants of the lands on which they were discovered, diamonds were no more useful than the cowrie shells which the slave trade had introduced to the continent. Of course, each diamond could have bought many thousand cowries, and they enslaved Africans just as surely.

A child's plaything, one among a number of pretty stones that a farmer's children had collected from the veld along the banks of the Vaal River, was the first evidence of the immense material wealth that lay in the gravels and sands of a landscape otherwise distinguished only by thorn trees and infrequent rainfall, nearly 1,000 km north-east of Cape Town. A local magistrate, W.B. Chalmers, wrote an account of the discovery in 1867 that was later summarized in a number of publications, including the London *Times*:

> ... The first diamond was discovered by pure accident. It was used for a long time by the children of a Dutch farmer, called Jacobs, as a plaything. These people are very ignorant—in fact not much better than natives ... This diamond might have been lost or thrown away ... but fortunately another Dutch farmer, a Mr. Schalk van Niekerk, a very observant man, and one more intelligent than the rest of his countrymen in this district, happened to visit Jacobs' place. Seeing the children playing with some nice stones he had a look at them, and at once took notice of the gem. He had no idea it was a diamond, but thought it was a rare-looking stone, very different from the others. He took it up, feeling it heavier than the weight of an ordinary pebble of such a size, his enquiring mind thought he would try and find out what sort of a stone it was. He offered to purchase it from Mrs. Jacobs, but she laughed at the idea of selling a stone, and told him that if he took a fancy to the stone he could have it for nothing. Niekerk then took it to O'Reilly, and asked him to find out what sort of stone it was. O'Reilly brought it to Hope Town, and showed it to everyone, and said he thought it was a diamond. But we only laughed at him ... He then took it to Colesberg; some there half believed it to be a diamond, but most ridiculed the idea ... Some gentlemen in Colesberg persuaded him to send it to Dr. Atherstone, in Graham's Town; the doctor pronounced it to be a veritable diamond ... [5]

The stone, about the size of a hazelnut, weighed $21\frac{1}{4}$ carats. After further verification in Cape Town it was bought by the Governor of the Colony, Sir Philip Wodehouse, for the sum of £500 sterling. Chalmers urged government authorities to instigate a proper search and systematic mining.

> The Colony complains about hard times [he wrote], but it deserves to be hard up when it quietly hears of the discovery of the richest of all gems in one of its Districts, and takes no steps whatever to open up the vast wealth which these gems would produce. I do not think any other colony would have treated the matter with such carelessness and cool indifference. [6]

While the government dithered, a London merchant dispatched a geologist to investigate the claim; he returned to report that the area was not diamondiferous. The stones found there had either been planted by speculators hoping to inflate land values, he said, or else had been excreted by ostriches migrating from diamond-bearing regions as yet unidentified.[7] This report tempered the ardour of international prospectors and dealers; a small number of isolated stones were found in the ensuing months, but diamond fever remained a mild local infection until March 1869, when a Griqua herdsman known as Swartboy (Black boy) to the local white farmers found a large diamond not far from the hut he was occupying while herding goats. Swartboy took the stone to Schalk van Niekerk and was doubtless overjoyed to receive for it 500 sheep, ten head of cattle, and one horse. Van Niekerk in his turn took the diamond to agents in Hope Town and received £11,000 sterling. The diamond Swartboy had found weighed eighty-three carats and became known as the Star of Africa.

A mild local infection of diamond fever now became an epidemic of major proportions. African chiefs organized systematic searches, and desperately attempted to keep out white prospectors, who arrived with plans to dig for diamonds along the banks of the Vaal. But it was by no means certain which of several chiefs had jurisdiction over the region; their resistance was uncoordinated and by July 1870, 800 prospectors were digging along the river; by October the number had soared to 5,000.[8]

Meanwhile, latecomers prospecting further afield found diamonds on farms about a day's ride from the river. On the Bulfontein farm, diamonds were picked from the mud walls of the homestead and prospectors rushed to peg claims at the site where the mud had been excavated. Diamond-bearing areas were located and pegged out on an adjacent farm, Vooruitzigt, while rumours of ninety-two diamonds recovered from a single exploratory furrow attracted other hopefuls to Du Toit's Pan, where the owner attempted to restrict access to Dutch miners only but was defeated by sheer force of numbers and ultimately agreed to permit mining by anyone who was able to pay 7s 6d per claim per month.[9] Though unaware of it at the time, the dryland prospectors had located a rare and hitherto unknown geological phenomenon: a diamond pipe, the vent of a long-extinct volcano that had transported diamonds to the Earth's surface from their point of creation 150 kilometres below.

Drawn to the diamond region by the prospect of wealth, confronting all shades of greed and ruthless ambition on a distant frontier which lacked even a vestige of legally constituted authority, the miners very commendably formulated among themselves a few simple rules that would give everyone at least a chance of making their fortune. No person should hold more than two claims, and any claim left unworked for more than eight days would be forfeited.

Each claim was thirty-one feet square (9.4 metres square); within weeks, 4,000 or so were staked out over a total area of approximately fifty to sixty acres (twenty to twenty-four hectares) in which diamonds were found.[10] Huge amounts of energy were expended.

Our first peep at the famous Du Toits pan . . . was certainly unsatisfactory [an early visitor noted], little was to be seen but dense masses of fine dust ascending heavenward. Slowly onward rolled our waggon . . . We were now all agog with interest and excitement as the scene before us gradually unfolded, and one's heart began to beat faster as the Diamond City of the Plains became more and more distinct. The strange, vague landscape of tents widened and grew whiter and clearer. It now became apparent that the dusty pall observed from afar was occasioned by the continual sifting and sorting of the precious soil by thousands of busy diggers and their vast army of native helpers. The novelty of the panorama became intensified as our waggon at last entered the great human bee-hive, and wended its way in and out among the canvas shelters dotted promiscuously here, there and everywhere, creaking and groaning through deep sand and ruts, or staggering over mighty mounds of debris. The few wooden tenements, scattered about at rare intervals, had been fashioned out of packing-cases, and the owners thereof considered themselves the aristocrats of Diggerdom.

Still moving forward, one found the mass of tents becoming denser and more bewildering in its chaotic array. Water was very scarce, and the many unwashed faces that peeped curiously as we passed seemed to match the colour of the dusty canvas abodes. Hordes of dogs and semi-nude Kafirs were everywhere, and handy Scotch carts drawn by teams of oxen, mules or horses, were noisily bumping their way along the labyrinthine roadways.[11]

In late July 1871, an African herding cattle on the Vooruitzigt property picked up a diamond on a small kopje less than two kilometres from the first diggings. The find immediately sparked off what became known as the New Rush—a term which eventually was attached to both the event and its venue. Within two days nearly 1,000 claims had been pegged out on and around the kopje. Three months later, 5,000 miners were working on the 600 to 700 claims which had proved profitable (the remainder had been abandoned), many of which had been divided into halves, quarters, and eighths. By December, about 7,000 whites and blacks were digging and sifting up to twenty metres deep—and the diamonds continued to be found. "No field has yielded diamonds in greater quantities," it was noted. "Already thousands of gems have been unearthed; and . . . the richness of some claims is almost beyond belief."[12]

"What a busy scene of life presented itself to you!" a contemporary observer wrote of the New Rush diggings.

There were hundreds of diggers, in every kind of garb . . . There were faces of every conceivable cast and colour of the human race . . . the Kaffir, the Englishman, the Hottentot, and the Dutchman, the Fingo and the German, the Yankee and the Swede, the Frenchman and the Turk, the Norwegian and the natives, the Russian and the Greek—in fact a smattering of people from every nation on the face of the earth—digging, sifting, and sorting from morning till night, day after day, month after month, until they have obtained what they consider sufficient.[13]

The site of the New Rush diggings was subsequently named Kimberley (after the British secretary of state for the colonies at the time), the richest and most famous of South Africa's diamond mines. In 1869 the Cape Colony exported 16,542 carats of diamonds; 102,500 carats were exported in 1870 and 269,000 in 1871. With the Kimberley and other mines contributing a full year's production to the 1872 figures, diamond exports almost quadrupled that year, rising to a momentous 1,080,000 carats, worth over £1.6 million sterling.[14]

Meanwhile, the diamond rush had exposed pertinent differences between Boer and British law concerning property and mineral rights. Boers claimed their farms under Orange Free State titles which permitted each adult male to farm 3,000 morgen (approximately 6,000 acres) and retain all mineral rights. But the Orange Free State had never actually exercised authority in the region where the diamonds were found, and could claim only that sovereignty passed to it automatically whenever Boers acquired land from Africans.

Under British and Cape law, on the other hand, mineral rights were retained by the state and thus remained open to public exploitation, subject to the appropriate laws.[15] In the absence of a constituted legal authority in the region, the miners and local African groups (who also claimed rights to the diamonds) unsurprisingly declared a preference for Cape law. Recognizing at last that this distant and hitherto disregarded frontier region might indeed contribute significant sums to the Colony coffers, as magistrate Chalmers had predicted, the Cape government moved swiftly to rectify its earlier dalliance. Issues of constitutional authority had to be clarified.

The diamond fields could not have been more contentiously located. They lay beyond the Orange River, which marked the northern boundary of the British Cape Colony, in a region over which the Griqua, the Tswana, the Kora, and the Tlhaping ethnic groups claimed traditional (and conflicting) rights, but which had also been staked out by white farmers who pledged allegiance to either the Orange Free State or the Transvaal Boer republics.

A British court of inquiry set up to review the issue found that the Griqua had the most valid claim, a decision which so angered the Boers that Griqua leaders subsequently appealed to the British for a promise of protection, should the menace of their thwarted neighbours ever explode into aggressive territorial invasion. The British magnanimously responded by annexing the territory. Thus by the end of 1871 what was then the world's richest diamond-producing region had become the British colony of Griqualand West.

THE KIMBERLEY MINE YIELDED more diamonds than any other comparable operation in the world, but even there the concentration was little more than one part in 3 million: nearly three tonnes of diamond-bearing rubble produced on average just under one gram of diamonds (4.8 carats to be precise, equalling 960 milligrams). The proverbial search for a needle in a haystack comes to mind, but a closer analogy would be the search for a single glass bead about the size of a pea in a three-tonne truckload of assorted rock rubble, gravel, and sand, having first dug the material from the mine, lifted it to the surface, broken it down to size with sledgehammers, sieved, and then painstakingly picked over it in the hope of finding the one glittering prize that would make the effort worth while. Large stones were found frequently enough to reignite enthusiasm for the tedious exercise but, although Kimberley was the most productive mine, most of its diamonds were small.[16]

The mines at Kimberley were quite unlike any other mining operation. Having no idea that they were excavating the vent of a diamond pipe up to 150 kilometres deep, the first diggers at Kimberley naturally enough expected that their picks and shovels would take them down to bedrock, beyond which further excavation would be futile. But the claims did not "bottom out" as expected. The yellow ground in which the first diamonds had been found ran out at about twenty metres, after which a blue ground was encountered, the true diamond-bearing material (subsequently called Kimberlite) in which even greater quantities awaited discovery.

Some claims on the Kimberley mine were abandoned before they struck the blue ground; not all sections of the pit were equally rich in diamonds, and not all miners were equally industrious. Material was removed most easily from claims around the perimeter of the pit, so they were excavated to greatest depths first, leaving blocks of ground standing in the centre like square-cut castle keeps, and giving the pit the overall appearance of an inverted doughnut. By the late 1870s the central floor of the pit was more or less level, measuring nearly 300 metres across and over ninety metres deep.

Claims were reached initially by ladders, and a complex of cart-tracks and boardwalks running between and high above intervening claims. The challenges facing miners working on one-quarter or one-eighth claims (four by two metres, little larger than a living-room carpet) are hardly to be contemplated. They had barely room to swing a pick, let alone manage the efficient removal of the blue from the pit—manually, around other working claims, over boardwalks and up ladders to the rim. Access became increasingly difficult—and perilous—as distances between the claims and the rim lengthened. Falling debris was a constant hazard; accidents were a regular occurrence.

Eventually a safer and more effective means of removing excavated material from the pit was devised. Timber stagings were constructed around the perimeter, and wire cables run down to the claims below, along each of which great tubs of excavated ground were hauled up from the claims. A veritable web of cables spanned the pit, like the spokes of a wheel. By 1874 there were 1,000 cables running to as many separate units of production, with at least 10,000 men working in the pit. Horses turned the winding gear, hauling from forty to sixty loads per day from each working claim. Steam engines introduced in the late 1870s raised daily output to 100 loads.[17]

Ox-wagons and horse carts transported the blue ground from the rim to depositing floors, where it was laid out to weather, transforming the Kimberley surroundings into an artificial landscape of ploughed fields. The blue ground took up to a year to break down (attempts to hasten the process with horse-drawn ploughs and platoons of sledgehammer-wielding labourers proved unsuccessful), after which it was sorted for diamonds—dry, and by hand in the early days; subsequently with the aid of water and mechanical riddling.

The speed with which these developments took place speaks eloquently for the human capacity to get things done. Less than one year after the first claims were pegged on the Kimberley diggings, 50,000 people were living in tents and make-do shelters in the diamond fields. By the end of 1871, there were more people at Kimberley than in Cape Town (until then the largest centre of population in southern Africa);[18] more than in either of the Boer republics, or in Natal.

The massive demand for meat, fresh vegetables, grain, and firewood stimulated the rural economy. Cattle, sheep, goats, wagons, and horses poured into Kimberley "at a deuce of a pace," a contemporary report noted,[19] as local and more distant farmers and traders seized every opportunity to grasp a share of the profits. Cash quickly replaced barter as the medium of trade. A steady stream of wagons brought goods and commodities from coastal ports to Kimberley, distances of from 600 to over 1,000 kilometres. Iron ware, picks, and shovels; timber, cables, clothing; guns, tobacco, and alcohol flooded in, but amid all the frenzied economic activity, with diamonds fuelling an economy in which thousands of pounds changed hands daily, there was one commodity of which the diggers could never get enough—labour.

.   .   .

THE MILL AND THE MINE WERE respectively the sources of the growth of industrial wealth in Britain and South Africa, but if the "dark satanic mill" is the abiding image of economic and social developments in Victorian Britain, it is the mine compound that symbolizes the early development of capitalism in South Africa. The compound system, as a particular form of working-class housing, simultaneously organized and subordinated the mine labour force to capital. On the one hand, it contributed fundamentally to the organization of the labour process through the entrenchment of a racial division of labour. On the other, it facilitated the exploitation of labour and ensured a constant supply.[20]

In effect, the Kimberley mines "had to prise a work force out of a pre-capitalist rural hinterland,"[21] but such was the extent of their influence on the economy of southern Africa that, within one year of the opening of the mines, every black society south of the Zambezi, with the exception only of the Venda and the Zulu, was represented in the diamond fields, whether by independent businessmen, artisans, or labourers.[22]

Of the 50,000 people living at Kimberley in the early 1870s, about 30,000 were Africans, of whom between 3,000 and 10,000 were permanent residents, supported by 1,000 or so heads of family who were engaged in the service economy on their own account: masons, bricklayers, carpenters, eating-house proprietors, cab owners and drivers. Approximately 10 per cent of these men actually owned diamond claims, though mostly in the poorer Bulfontein and Du Toit's Pan mines, which were steadily abandoned by whites. The remainder of the black population were migrant labourers, working on the mines for anything from a few weeks to more than a year. Government sources estimated that a total of 50,000 men worked in the Kimberley mines for varying periods each year during the early 1870s.[23]

Paradoxically, the largest number of migrants arriving to work on the Kimberley mines in any one year were those who had travelled the greatest distance. Mine returns for 1876, for example, show that 64 per cent had come from over 800 kilometres away; thousands had travelled up to 1,600 kilometres—all the way on foot. By contrast, those whose point of origin lay within eighty kilometres of Kimberley constituted less than 1 per cent of the migrant workforce.[24]

But the paradox is easily explained: those closest to the mines could make more from the economic activity that diamonds had generated by supplying local produce than by selling their labour; furthermore, they were more immediately aware of how unattractive an occupation mine labouring could be.

Indeed, there was a direct correlation between the distance travelled to the mine and length of stay: only those who had travelled from afar would tolerate the unrelenting demands of mine labour for any length of time.

Fifteen labourers worked on the average production unit in the Kimberley mine before the introduction of steam machinery.[25] Ten men worked on the claim and hauled the blue ground to the rim of the pit; five more were kept busy transporting the earth to the depositing floors and sifting for diamonds. Labourers worked from sunrise to sunset; fourteen hours in summer, ten hours in winter. They were paid from ten to thirty shillings per week, plus food consisting of maize-meal each day and one pound of meat per week, which added the value of about ten shillings to the wage.

In total, the African labour force at Kimberley was paid over £500,000 sterling per year; half of this was spent in Kimberley, each African spending an average of £5 during his sojourn in the diamond fields. Guns were a popular purchase. Indeed, it has been argued that some African leaders sent cohorts of young men to the mines expressly to acquire weapons for use in territorial disputes.[26] On the other hand, government officials of the day believed that most guns were bought for "purposes connected with legitimate and beneficial trade," particularly in ostrich feathers and ivory.[27]

In any event, the rapid turnover of migrant labour on the mines generated an equally rapid turnover in the firearms trade. Gun sales were one of the most striking sights in early Kimberley, a pioneer digger noted:

> At knock-off time our Kaffirs used to pass down streets of tented shops owned by white traders and presided over by yelling black salesmen whirling guns above their heads. These they discharged in the air crying: "Reka, reka, mona mtskeka" [Buy, buy, a gun]. A deafening din. A sight never to be forgotten.[28]

In the fifteen months between April 1873 and June 1874, 75,000 guns were sold in Kimberley.[29] But the boom was short-lived. The African gun trade was banned in 1877 (when the British adopted the Boers' long-standing practice of prohibiting the sale of guns to blacks), although Africans had already begun to demonstrate a greater interest in other commodities by then. Purchases of woollen goods alone—especially blankets—exceeded the value of gun sales by 1876, and African earnings were increasingly directed towards investment in the rural economies. Livestock was purchased to rebuild depleted herds; ploughs were bought to extend and intensify crop production. One trader alone sold 600 ploughs to African farmers in the Kimberley hinterland during the three years to 1874.[30]

Among the Sotho, in particular, the adoption of the plough led to a concurrent expansion of both local agriculture and migrant labour. "The use of the plough instead of the Kafir pick [a hoe] has enabled the Basutos either to hire ploughmen whilst they went to work, or to proceed to the [diamond fields] after a few days ploughing themselves," an official reported.[31] Approximately 3,000 Sotho made the 250-kilometre journey to the diamond fields in 1872; by 1875 three out of every four able-bodied Sotho men sought work outside Basutoland each year. Meanwhile, their households produced from thirty to forty bags of grain. When harvests were this good, the Sotho became a major supplier of grain, as well as of labour, to Kimberley. In the four years to 1874, the Sotho acquired livestock and other property to the value of over £1 million sterling from their dealing with the diamond fields.[32]

AFRICAN LABOUR HAS BEEN aptly described as the barometer of diamond wealth: "Native labour is the life of the Diamond Fields, and just as ... the supply and demand of this commodity varies so ... is the prosperity of the community gauged."[33]

In the first years of the diamond rush it was labourers who held the upper hand. Though there were at least 20,000 blacks in the diamond fields in 1872, diggers constantly complained about the shortage of labour. In fact, this was a complaint about labour costs, not shortage. Labourers were quick to appreciate the strength of their position; they refused to accept long-term contracts with any one employer and with 5,000 diggers competing for their services rapidly forced wages upward. During 1872 alone they doubled the ruling rate by continually moving to employers offering higher wages,[34] thereby creating a constant shortage of labour and straining every digger's financial resources.

One early commentator estimated that black wages accounted for approximately 86 per cent of the average digger's working costs. Black labour, a Kimberley newspaper proclaimed, was "the most expensive in the world." Furthermore, the paper continued, it was also "the most unmanageable."[35] Quite apart from the problems of short contracts and constant labour shortages, diggers had also to contend with labourers who refused to work where they considered conditions had become dangerous; many went absent without leave when pressed by the need to plant or harvest their crops; still more left the diamond fields abruptly each year when the first winter chills sent temperatures plunging below zero. And throughout, labourers knew there was more profit to be made from a stolen diamond than from a weekly wage (on one mine, diamond theft was alleged to account for three-fifths of production).[36]

In short, employers in the diamond fields could exercise little or no control over the supply, availability, cost, productivity, and honesty of their labour force. Some hankered for seasoned European labourers in preference to "raw" Africans unaccustomed to heavy manual labour. It was said that a single Irish navvy could take down a claim faster than a gang of four Africans.[37]

With 5,000 diggers competing for labour, attempts to formulate wage and employment policies that would be beneficial to all were doomed to failure, but the diggers did eventually persuade the government to pass legislation designed to bring the African labour force more in line with their requirements. Government Notice 68 of July 1872 established a depot in Kimberley at which all black labourers would be required to register on arrival, when they would be issued with a pass entitling them to seek employment. Labourers were obliged to accept contracts of employment for not less than three months and, on leaving the fields, would have to obtain another pass, certifying that they had carried out their contractual obligations to their employer's satisfaction. For their part, employers attempting to engage workers other than through the register office would be liable to a fine of £10 and three months' imprisonment.[38]

One month after the first pass laws were introduced, their conditions were further elaborated: upon registering for employment all prospective servants would be given a certificate stating the duration of their contracts and the wage they would receive. This certificate should be carried at all times; any person found without one and unable to give a satisfactory account of himself was liable to arrest and a fine of up to £5; or imprisonment for up to three months, with or without hard labour; or "corporal punishment in any number of lashes not exceeding twenty-five." In addition, any employer could search the person, residence, or property of his servants without a warrant at any time while they were employed, and within two hours of their having left his employ. All diamonds found in the possession of a servant were deemed to be the property of the employer. Any servant found guilty of diamond theft could be flogged up to a maximum of fifty lashes, and sentenced to twelve months' hard labour.

These regulations, introduced by the British government of the Cape Colony in 1872, enshrined in law a precedent of racial discrimination that was to characterize labour relations in southern Africa. Although the legislation was quite clearly intended to control black labour, government notices carefully avoided using discriminatory language. Black workers were always referred to as "servants," never as "natives." In language the law appeared colour-blind,[39] though in practice it applied exclusively to blacks. The origins of apartheid as a legally defined policy lay here.

In Kimberley, in 1872, the pass laws were vigorously enforced by the police and the courts. In December alone between 1,100 and 1,500 departing labourers were checked for exit passes. Of the 275 unable to present the required document, 250 were fined and eighteen received six lashes each in addition to a fine. Of nearly 5,000 cases that came before magistrates during 1872, most dealt with "desertion of employment" by black workers. Those found guilty received up to twelve lashes with a cat-o'-nine-tails and were then sent back to their employers.[40]

But still the diggers were not satisfied. Fifty-one thousand men were contracted for employment through the register office in 1873, but the number dropped to 43,000 in 1874 and by the end of that year most whites had concluded that registration was not the answer to their problems. Diggers declined to register their employees, complaining that the men deserted anyway, and most succeeded in eluding the police. In fact, the diggers were particularly annoyed at having paid registration fees only to see their employees desert with a contract document that guaranteed them relatively free movement on the diamond fields.[41]

The labourers found loopholes in the regulations that enabled them to evade official attempts to control their movements and choice of employer. The penalties meted out to convicted offenders were draconian, but the competitive demand for labour, and the sheer volume of workers on the diamond fields, minimized the risk of detection. Official resources were too scanty for anything more than a token level of pass-law enforcement. Exasperated employers could only redouble their complaints and demand yet tougher legislation. A Kimberley newspaper called for "class legislation, restrictive laws, and the holding in check of the coloured races till by education they are fit to be our equals . . . "[42]

First moves towards a resolution of the diggers' labour problems came not from the introduction of new laws, however, but from the repeal of a law already on the statute book. The claim-limitation law (see page 503) was repealed in 1876 and, with it, the era of the small independent diamond-producing operation ended and the era of extravagantly capitalized industrial production began.

Sixteen hundred claim-holders shared ownership of the Kimberley mine in 1872; less than five years later the number of owners had fallen to 300, of whom fewer than twenty owned more than half the mine between them. By 1879, twelve private companies or partnerships controlled three-quarters of the Kimberley mine.[43] Claims were similarly amalgamated on the other three mines. The process was inexorable. Diamonds attracted the interest of financiers with access to major sources of capital, and encouraged the finaglings of speculators who would become renowned for their ruthless business practices and the size of their personal fortunes.

In a flurry of claim purchases, company flotations, share-price manipulations, takeovers, buyouts and consolidations that ranged from the nefarious to the devious and outrageous, the entire operation of the Kimberley diamond fields was progressively brought under the control of a single company during the 1880s.[44] De Beers Consolidated Mines Limited was incorporated as the major holding company in March 1888; by 1891 it had acquired an absolute monopoly of diamond production in Kimberley and, by virtue of that fact, a controlling influence on every other commercial activity in the region.

The man principally responsible for bringing so many diverse and often opposing interests under the control of a single company was the man who created it: Cecil Rhodes, a British emigrant whose ambitions did not stop at Kimberley and De Beers. Rhodes looked beyond, to far broader horizons. The Trust Deed he drew up for De Beers Consolidated permitted the company to engage in any business enterprise, to annex land in any part of Africa, to govern foreign territories and maintain standing armies in those territories, if necessary.

Rhodes's ambitions for the company were expansive, even imperialistic, and his intentions concerning the control of De Beers were decidedly oligarchic, not to say dictatorial. Rhodes declared that four or five wealthy men, to be known as "life governors," should control the destiny of the company for the duration of their natural lifespans. These men should have substantial investments in the company and thus an overriding incentive to secure profits for the company and themselves, he said. Their wealth and lifelong appointment would shield them from the temptations of short-term gains, and their social status would give them the political access needed by a company whose success would depend as much on government policies as on the organization of production and marketing.

Rhodes proposed that the life governors' reward for such devoted attention to the company's interests should be a quarter of net profits shared between them after the distribution of dividends (to which of course they were also entitled). Objections were raised, but the proposal was accepted. Cecil Rhodes and his associates in the amalgamation of the Kimberley diamond fields, Alfred Beit, Barney Barnato and Frederic Stow, became life governors of De Beers Consolidated in May 1888.[45] De Beers made an operating profit of £1,209,780 in the twelve months to March 1890, when revenue exceeded costs by almost 52 per cent and De Beers thus made a profit of more than £50 on every £100 of diamonds sold.[46]

.   .   .

AS THE KIMBERLEY DIAMOND FIELDS WERE transformed from the pioneering enterprises of independent operators in the mid-1870s into the monolithic industrial undertaking of the late 1880s, with ownership passing to a decreasing number of individuals at each stage, employers progressively tightened their control of the labour force. Foreign capital had facilitated the amalgamation process, and its influence touched labour issues too. Goaded by financiers demanding handsome returns on their investments, and aware that labour shortages were a serious constraint on profitability, Cape administrators introduced regulations that were expressly intended to force more Africans on to the labour market.

In November 1876 the terms under which Griqualand West had been annexed to the Cape Colony were amended to give white farmers landholding rights. Locations were to be established in which the African population would reside—small enough to ensure that they could not be self-sufficient, but large enough to constitute a labour pool for farms and mines alike, and dispersed about the countryside to the convenience of white farmers and the mines. The survey delineating the locations allocated approximately 10 per cent of West Griqualand to its indigenous inhabitants and the remainder to white farmers.

African objections to these arrangements were quelled both by force of arms and by legal battles in the courts, during which the appellants found themselves obliged to sell land (at discounted prices because of the disputed title) in order to pay their legal costs. The cases were dismissed. Uprisings were crushed. Livestock was confiscated, property destroyed, and hundreds of men, women, and children were taken to Kimberley as prisoners of war and forced to work as mine labourers and domestic servants. Meanwhile, the majority of Griqualand West's black inhabitants went to live in the locations, where limited opportunities for agriculture, and the administration's imposition of a hut tax, engendered levels of impoverishment that inevitably forced hundreds to seek work on the farms and in the mines. An inspector of locations reported in 1880: "The greater part of the natives (young men) proceed to work in Kimberley for three to six months at a time . . . leaving their wives and children to take care of their stock etc."[47]

The population of Griqualand West was not large enough to satisfy more than a fraction of Kimberley's voracious labour demands, but the redistribution of land and the establishment of locations was a precedent which encouraged some employers and administrators in their belief that the colonial boundaries should be extended, bringing much greater numbers of Africans under British rule and thus exposing them to a coordinated policy of labour recruitment. Hitherto, only a relatively high level of wages could attract workers to Kimberley; furthermore, men heading for the mines had to pass through African chiefdoms and the Boer republics, where they were liable to be taxed, refused passage, molested, or robbed. It was all too arbitrary. If southern Africa was under British control, constraints could be eliminated and regular supplies of labour assured.

DURING THE MID- TO LATE 1870s Britain's Colonial Secretary, Lord Carnarvon, devised ambitious plans for a confederation which would unite the Cape Colony and Natal with the Boer republics in a single South African dominion, under the British flag. With the Transvaal Republic essentially bankrupt at the time, the Orange Free State moribund, and British interests in the Cape and Natal separated by autonomous African polities, the federation scheme seemed propitious. Not least, it would permit the establishment of a "uniform native policy" in southern Africa, one that would secure an adequate and regular flow of migrant labour for the developing economy.[48]

Carnarvon had hoped that federation could be achieved by diplomatic means, but was ultimately obliged to approve more coercive measures. The Transvaal, teetering on collapse, was annexed in 1877. British and colonial troops waged war against the Xhosa in 1877–78; against the Pedi (in the eastern Transvaal) in 1877–79; against the Zulu in 1879; and against the Sotho from 1880. Only the Sotho, in the mountain fastnesses of what is now independent Lesotho, successfully resisted the British attacks. Elsewhere the blacks were defeated. In particular, the economic and political independence of southern Africa's two most powerful black states was broken: the Pedi were dispossessed of cattle and land; the Zulu were divided into thirteen units.[49]

But dreams of federation and improved supplies of migrant labour came to nothing. The Transvaal Boers won back their independence after defeating British forces at the Battle of Majuba Hill in 1881, and British attacks on the African polities hindered, rather than enhanced the availability of labour. The influx dropped, and men were constantly leaving Kimberley to fight; the proportion of Pedi and Sotho among the workforce rose and fell with the rhythm of hostilities. To attract replacements and persuade workers to stay, employers had constantly to raise rates of pay. By the early 1880s wages were the highest they had ever been—up to £2 or more per week.[50]

Meanwhile, the Cape Colony administration had set up a Labour Commission to investigate ways and means of securing a regular supply of labour and subordinating labourers to "rigorous industrial discipline."[51] A scheme proposed by João Albasini, "an old Portuguese slave dealer," to recruit labourers from the extreme north-eastern border of the Transvaal, where he held "a sort of chieftainship" over a portion of the African population was rejected,[52] but private white recruiters became increasingly important labour suppliers, extending their operations as far as Inhambane on the Moçambique coast, well over 1,600 kilometres from Kimberley. Labour touts (black and white), who collected together the bands of Africans they found en route through the Transvaal were another source of supply. Touts promised the Africans protection, food and a safe position in Kimberley. On arrival, they were assembled in Market Square and their services offered to prospective employers at £2 a head.[53]

If these methods of recruiting labourers for the Kimberley mines appeared perilously close to enslavement, proposals for ensuring their subordination to "rigorous industrial discipline" were even more explicit. In 1879 Thomas C. Kitto, an English mining inspector with worldwide experience, completed an officially-commissioned report on the Kimberley operations:

> ... I must say the quality of labour here is the worst I have seen in any part of the world, and I cannot help contrasting it with the black labour of Brazil. I am very certain that one of the Brazilian blacks will do as much work on an average as three Kimberley blacks. The Brazilian blacks are classed from one to four, and are hired out to English companies ... The companies have to feed them ... The blacks are lodged in barracks, which are built in the form of a square, the outer wall being much higher than the inner wall; the roof slopes inside. The entrance to the place is by a large gate, over which at night stands a powerful lamp which lights up the whole place. Men and women answer to the call of their names while passing out at the gate in the morning and in the evening when entering. They retire to rest early, and an overseer locks up the premises each night and unlocks them in the morning. There is a very good feeling between the Brazilian slaves and the owners ...
>
> I believe the natives of South Africa, under European supervision, are capable of being made almost—if not quite—as good as the blacks of Brazil, provided they are dealt with in the same manner ... [54]

The Labour Commission had already recommended that the stability of the Kimberley labour force would be improved if employers were obliged to house and feed their labourers on their premises. In August 1879 this recommendation became law, and the enforced segregation of the races in South Africa began. "Localization" was the euphemism used to deflect accusations of racial discrimination. "Localization" ostensibly was intended to remove deserters, the lazy, and Africans "living at large" from the streets of Kimberley and oblige them to take up accommodation in locations in the mine fields. But of course residence in the mine locations obliged a man to take a job in the mines.

By late 1880, 22,000 African labourers were housed among seven specifically laid-out locations in the mine fields and the registrar was calling for another 10,000, the addition of which, he said, would permit employers to reduce wages to their "proper level" of ten shillings per week.[55]

The "open compounds," as they became known, provided barracks-type accommodation within high corrugated-iron fences. Gates and guards regulated access, but left the labourers free to spend such leisure time as their work permitted wherever and however they might choose. The arrangements went some way towards stabilizing the availability of labour in the mines, but appear to have concentrated the attention of both miners and mine-owners on the theft and illegal disposal of diamonds. Kimberley's elected members of parliament (Cecil Rhodes prominent among them) pressed the government to appoint a Select Committee to investigate the issue of illicit diamond buying (IDB) and propose legislative remedies.

The Select Committee accepted most of the evidence presented to it, and the Diamond Trade Act of 1882 brought in legislation designed to meet the mine-owners' demands.[56] It was an iniquitous piece of legislation. The Act set aside a fundamental tenet of British law, namely the presumption of innocence until guilt is proved. Under the Act, anyone found in possession of a diamond was presumed to be guilty unless they could show otherwise. Furthermore, persons accused of IDB offences were denied the option of trial by jury (mine-owners had protested that juries brought in too few convictions); cases would be tried by a judge sitting with two magistrates and those found guilty could expect up to fifteen years' imprisonment and fines of up to £1,000; blacks were liable to be flogged as well.

The passing of the Diamond Trade Act was accompanied by a doubling of Kimberley's white police force and the establishment of an IDB detection department with authority to "trap" anyone thought likely of succumbing to the temptation of illicit profits. The department generated a good deal of resentment among both the black and the white communities, but nonetheless contributed to a significant rise in the number of arrests and convictions achieved by the Kimberley force. In 1882 individual police officers in Kimberley made between 114 and 160 arrests each, while their counterparts in Cape Town (with a larger population) made an average of forty-five arrests each. Furthermore, not all Kimberley arrests were for illicit diamond buying; most were concerned with pass offences, desertion, and other offences relating to black labour. From 1882 onward, nearly 80 per cent of all arrests resulted in summary conviction.[57]

A consequence of zealous policing and summary justice was that Kimberley's gaol, though the largest in the Cape Colony, was always full. Indeed, its daily average of inmates was seven times the number incarcerated in Cape Town. The strain that such a large prison population placed on government services was however alleviated in 1884, when the De Beers Mining Company negotiated an arrangement to establish a privately controlled convict station and use the inmates as mine labourers. In return for the cost of erecting the convict barrack (£5,200) and the expenses of daily maintenance and discipline, the company was granted a two-year contract to exploit free convict labour. The contract was subsequently renewed. In fact, De Beers persisted with the practice of using convict labour until 1932.[58]

In evidence given to a government Select Committee in 1891, the General Manager of De Beers, G.F. Williams, described the advantages of convict labour:

> In the first place we have labour we can depend on and it is always to hand. The convicts cannot get away like ordinary labourers. We can also prevent theft better than with free boys. If the latter attempt to escape you cannot shoot them, whereas the sworn officials of the Government can shoot a convict if he attempts to escape.[59]

Convicts working in the De Beers mine were better fed than the inmates of the city gaol, and were issued with thick jerseys, moleskin trousers, felt hats, boots "when necessary," blankets, and a rudimentary mattress, but they worked two hours longer each day than prison department hard-labour regulations stipulated and were searched on entering and leaving the convict station. De Beers convicts were obliged to undress completely in the search houses and went naked to their cells, where blankets were the only available covering. At the end of his sentence, each man was confined to the cells for five days, naked and with unwieldy leather gloves locked on his hands. This practice was designed to flush out any diamonds he might have swallowed in the hope of selling once he was free.[60]

The advantages of the arrangements which the employment of convict labour had entailed were so patently obvious that it was not long before so-called free labour was housed in similar conditions and treated in a similar fashion. Beginning in 1885, the previously open compounds were converted into self-contained institutions. Once an African entered a closed compound he was denied all access to the surrounding town for the duration of his contract.[61] Labourers were paid a wage, but obliged to buy their food and any other requirements from the compound stores; they moved between the compound and the mines through enclosed subways, and the compounds were covered with a fine wire mesh to prevent stolen diamonds being thrown over the fences.

By 1889 all Kimberley's African mineworkers were accommodated in closed compounds; an arrangement which was not only profitable in its own right (De Beers made an annual profit of £10,000 from the sale of food and other goods to the compound inmates), but also exposed Africans to coercive practices which ensured that many labourers stayed beyond the duration of the customary two- or three-month contract. Long-term workers with experience were of course preferred to a constant turnover of novices.

The mines supposedly recruited their labour exclusively through the Registrar of Natives, whose duty it was to issue and renew contracts. "Those whose time has expired and don't wish to re-contract are discharged," a compound manager reported, but many were persuaded to stay on without a contract, trapped in a "legal no man's land" where they were subject to the fluctuations of the mines' labour requirements but unable to appeal to the Registrar because without a contract they could be arrested.[62]

At least one-third to one-half of the workforce housed in De Beers's largest compound between 1886 and 1895 was uncontracted, and many of these men were probably unemployed as well, for the compounds generally held more labourers than were required for a full workforce. A four-day week was also commonplace. "To work 900 men," a compound manager explained, "we want 1,400 or 1,500 men." Thus, closed compounds provided not only a constant supply of labour, but also a reserve that could be called upon as required.

GOLD DEPOSITS WERE DISCOVERED on the Witwatersrand in 1885. Within a few months, the Kimberley mining magnates had bought up the bare ranchland farms in the vicinity of the discovery for prices ranging from £7,000 to £70,000. By the end of 1887 sixty-eight gold-mining companies had been incorporated with a nominal capital of more than £3 million. Ten years later the Witwatersrand was producing one-quarter of the world's gold output. Production fell dramatically during the Anglo-Boer war (1899–1902), amounting to only 2 per cent of world output in 1901, but resumed rapidly thereafter. In 1906 the Transvaal mines produced 29.8 per cent of the world's gold; in 1907 ninety-five mines were exploiting a gold field that extended in an almost unbroken line for more than sixty kilometres.[63]

The gold-bearing ground dipped sharply from the points at which it was exposed at the surface. Vertical shafts were sunk to intercept the reef, opening up deep-level mining areas of hitherto unimagined extent. Vast amounts of capital were invested in the new industry, much of it flowing as though by predetermined intent from fortunes made in the Kimberley diamond fields. The demand for labour in the gold fields was even greater than that which the diamond mines had imposed on the African population. In 1890, 15,000 Africans were employed in the gold mines, by 1897 the daily total had risen to 69,000 and in 1912 it stood at just under 190,000.

Kimberley's closed compounds provided a model for the cheap and secure accommodation of labour in the gold mines,[64] and the history of labour supply in the diamond fields was a lesson on how the gold mines' vast labour force could best be recruited. The centralized control of recruitment was to be the primary objective. Mine-owners formed the Native Labour Supply Association in 1896, which was reorganized as the Witwatersrand Native Labour Association in 1900. Not every mine always recruited all its labour through the organization, but Wenela (as it became known) gained enough of a monopoly to offer considerable advantages to those using its services.

Wenela established recruiting stations in urban and rural areas throughout southern Africa; employers paid a fee ranging from £1 per head for men on contracts of three months or less, and up to £5 for men on a twelve-month contract, but these initial outlays were more than offset by the low wages which the centralized control of recruiting was able to impose on the workforce. In fact, wages fell as Wenela's influence on the labour market became more pervasive. In 1896 labourers earned an average of just over fifteen shillings per week; seventeen years later they were earning an average of thirteen shillings per week—and that despite the fact that labour efficiency and individual productivity had increased in the interim.[65]

The Kimberley diamond fields and the Witwatersrand gold mines established a precedent for the management of labour in Africa: it was never *employment* in the sense of a relationship which was mutually beneficial to the employer and the employee, but always the *exploitation* of an indispensable resource. The fact that the labourers came from a population that was rural, uneducated, and black encouraged employers to regard them as a race apart, with aptitudes and aspirations quite different from those of Europeans and unlikely ever to change. Recruiting authorities believed that there was no point in raising wages in line with productivity, because it would lead to only a small rise in "the native standard of living," while "the main result would be that the native would work for a shorter period . . . ," thus reducing the amount of labour available to industry.[66]

The influence of the mines' employment regime on African society in southern Africa has been pernicious—and profound. Of the 1,700,000 male Africans aged between fifteen and fifty recorded in South Africa's 1936 census, for example, 393,000 (23 per cent) were working in the country's mines and allied industries. The majority were migrants, living away from home for months at a time, in all-male compounds, segregated from surrounding communities. Farms, factories, government agencies and even employers of domestic labour perpetuated the system, in South Africa and throughout the continent. Every urban centre which developed to service the application of capital to the exploitation of African resources was surrounded by locations, compounds, and hostels in which the essential labour was housed, to the convenience of its employers but at a distance that white sensitivities deemed appropriate. On an economic level, the same sort of segregation was to be found in the industrialized nations of Europe—no loom-operator could afford to live next door to the mill-owner—but education and equality in law could change that. In Africa, colour applied an indelible stain to economic segregation, condemning blacks to subservient status on the basis of first appearances alone.

PART 7

THE SCRAMBLE

Mbuti pygmy children at Nduye, in the Ituri forest, Congo

CHAPTER 46

An Imperial Ambition

LEOPOLD II OF BELGIUM STARTED the European nations' "scramble" for territory in Africa at the end of the nineteenth century. While France, Britain, Portugal, and Germany established colonies, Leopold proclaimed himself King-Sovereign of the Congo Free State. Rubber brought great wealth to Leopold and Belgium; harvesting the crop inflicted terrible hardships upon the Congolese.

If any single individual could be said to have initiated Europe's scramble to establish proprietorial rights over the territory and resources of Africa in the late nineteenth century, it was Leopold the Second, King of the Belgians. Though Belgium was small enough to fit twice over within the surface area of Lake Victoria (and still leave room to float the Canary Islands around the edges),[1] the country was second only to Great Britain in industrial development, and its royal family had accumulated wealth enough to fund initiatives which would determine the fate of a continent. Acting entirely in his private interest, Leopold goaded the goliaths—France, Germany and Britain—and the lesser players—Portugal, the Netherlands, Spain and Italy—into formal declarations of their imperial intentions which, by mischievous design, also allocated a large section of central Africa to Leopold himself.

In November 1877 Leopold wrote, "We must obtain a slice of this *magnifique gâteau africain*";[2] by May 1885 he had obtained international approval for his Congo Free State: 2½ million square kilometres of the Congo basin, with 2,700 kilometres of navigable waterways and a wealth of resources: ivory, palm-oil, rubber, timber, copper, and, not least, a population of about 10 million people, whose labour would be called upon to facilitate the economic and social development of the region.

Leopold was absolute ruler of the Congo Free State. The Belgian parliament formally approved his wish to become king of this foreign state only on the clear understanding that Belgium would not become entangled in its affairs. It was a strictly personal undertaking. Leopold's personal fortune financed the state, Leopold determined the nature of its administration, and Leopold was the principal recipient of such profits as accrued from the undertaking.

Leopold's creation of the Congo Free State—with no support from his country and in competition with far more powerful rivals—has been described as "an extraordinary feat, explicable only by the king's qualities of will-power, perseverance, imagination, intelligence and skill in negotiation."[3] Others have been less complimentary. Leopold has been called "The King Incorporated,"[4] a ruler with few equals in the black arts of international diplomacy and finance whose actions were dominated by an imperialist vision exceeding that of any of his contemporaries. His imagination "confounds rational analysis . . . if he had died in 1875 he would be remembered as a visionary out of touch with reality, an impractical monarch who plunged into wild real estate schemes, all of which came to nothing."[5]

But Leopold lived to 1909 and, more than any man, is responsible for the image of Africa which Joseph Conrad set firmly in the public consciousness with his novel *Heart of Darkness* (1902). In an essay on exploration, Conrad bluntly described the activities of Leopold's Congo Free State as "the vilest scramble for loot that ever disfigured the history of human conscience . . ."[6]

LEOPOLD II, BORN IN 1835, had been infected with the germ of colonist ambitions by his father during the early impressionable years of his life. Leopold I reigned over a nation which industrialized rapidly and by 1845 was the most densely populated state in Europe. One in three of the population of Flanders was living off charity, for instance, giving rise to fears of social unrest. Leopold I proposed large-scale emigration as a solution to the nation's problems. Some Belgians had already emigrated to the United States, but Leopold had in mind a colony with a common language and firm economic and political links with the homeland that would accommodate substantial numbers of his subjects.[7]

The Belgian government did not share the king's enthusiasm for colonies, so Leopold was obliged to pursue his ambitions independently. The Sultan of

Turkey was approached with offers to purchase Crete; when negotiations broke down Leopold I inquired about the possibility of purchasing Cuba, but was warned off by the British government. Texas offered to cede two large tracts of land to Belgium in return for a $7 million loan, but the United States government protested that the arrangement would constitute an impermissible interference in American affairs, and Leopold was advised that the United States would soon annex Texas in any case.[8]

In 1858, Leopold heard that Denmark might be willing to sell the Faeroe Islands, but this proved to be untrue. Further afield, Caribbean islands, parts of Central and South America and even Africa were considered with keen interest. In all, fifty-one attempts to found a colony were made during the reign of Leopold I; none was successful.

Leopold II assumed the mantle of his father's colonist ambition while still heir apparent, the Duke of Brabant. In 1861 he proposed buying a portion of Borneo, then occupied by Holland, which the Dutch were willing to sell because they deemed it "not financially viable"; Sarawak attracted his interest too, and the Pacific islands which, he suggested, "would be a superb place for a penitentiary." Fiji and the Solomons came under consideration, then a province of Argentina and a small island at the confluence of the Uruguay and Paraná rivers. "Who owns this island? Could one buy it," he inquired, "and set up there a free port under the moral protection of the King of the Belgians?"[9]

Leopold II became King of the Belgians on the death of his father in December 1865 and thereafter pursued the idea of a Belgian colony with calculating, not to say demonic, vigour. The Far East, and trade with China, was the principal object of his interest at the time. When proposals for railways, mining enterprises, and commercial concessions were rejected by the Chinese, Leopold decided that the Philippines would provide an excellent base for his interests and in 1870 offered to buy the archipelago from the Spanish. Spain was ready to sell, but Leopold could not provide all the guarantees his bankers demanded; the scheme came close to success—then collapsed. New Guinea was briefly considered, then Leopold's attention turned to Tongking (now Vietnam). In 1875 he wrote: "Tongking would suit us well. The population is dense . . . and the people very friendly. A Frenchman . . . took control over I don't know how many towns with only a few men . . . " Secret negotiations with the French government ensued; in 1878 it seemed likely that a portion of Vietnam would be ceded to the King of the Belgians, but in 1881 political upheavals in France swept the scheme aside.[10]

Meanwhile, first indications of an African dimension to Leopold's colonist ambitions were developing. In early 1875, international arbitration had assigned control of Delagoa Bay on the Mozambique coast to Portugal. This left the Boers' South African Republic (the Transvaal) without access to a coastal port. President Burghers travelled to Europe, seeking capital and partners willing to build a railway linking the Transvaal and Delagoa Bay. He visited Brussels where, with the discreet backing of Leopold, detailed discussions began. Agents were sent to the Transvaal and a Belgian consulate established in Pretoria.

Leopold planned to use the railway as a foothold for acquiring the Transvaal as a colony.[11] Diamonds, recently discovered at Kimberley, doubtless sparkled prominently among his plans, and the gold strikes to come in the 1880s certainly would have brought undreamt-of wealth to his putative colony. But, as with all Leopold's colonist ambitions to date, the plan came to naught. In 1876 the bankrupt Boer republic was annexed by the British.

But Leopold had now set his sights firmly on Africa and, with the maturity of his middle years, applied his undoubted intellect and energies unswervingly to the task of establishing a colony on the continent. "I intend to find out discreetly whether there is anything doing in Africa,"[12] Leopold announced in August 1875 and aides promptly began assembling a dossier of information on the subject. The travels and travails of explorers in Africa were of particular interest to the King of the Belgians.

DAVID LIVINGSTONE WAS the pre-eminent missionary-cum-explorer of the Victorian era. Irascible and single-minded, Livingstone criss-crossed Africa between 1841 and 1873; he explored the Zambezi, "discovered" the Victoria Falls and saw enough of the slave trade for his lectures and writings to rouse the ire of Europe. By 1871, Livingstone was a household name of whom little had been heard for some time. His public was becoming anxious, so the *New York Herald* dispatched the journalist Henry Morton Stanley (who had emigrated from Britain to the United States at the age of seventeen) to Africa with the simplest of directives but the most challenging of assignments: "Find Livingstone."[13]

Stanley found the doctor at Ujiji, on the shores of Lake Tanganyika, in November 1871, and secured himself an entry in every dictionary of quotations with the greeting: "Doctor Livingstone, I presume." Their meeting reinforced popular interest in Africa, while Stanley's report that Livingstone, already unwell, intended to continue his explorations of the Great Lakes prompted the Royal Geographical Society to dispatch a relief column, under the leadership of Verney Lovett Cameron, a naval officer who had sailed with Britain's anti-slavery squadron.

The Livingstone East Coast Expedition started out from Bagamoyo, on the mainland opposite Zanzibar in March 1873. After more than the usual quota of difficulties and delays, Cameron arrived at Ujiji in February 1874, by which time Livingstone had been dead for almost a year and his embalmed body was already en route to Britain and a state burial in Westminster Abbey. Being already halfway across the continent, Cameron decided to push ahead, westward into unknown territory, rather than return to Zanzibar by the arduous route he had trodden on the inward journey. He arrived on the Atlantic coast near Benguela in present-day Angola in November 1875, almost dead from exhaustion, scurvy, and starvation.

Cameron was the first man who is known to have crossed the continent from east to west—a journey spanning twenty-six degrees of longitude which, in its wanderings and diversions, had probably blazed a trail 4,000 kilometres long. He had explored the hitherto unknown southern limits of Lake Tanganyika, identified the watershed dividing the drainage systems of the Congo and the Nile, and traversed the open floodplains from which the feeder streams of both the Congo and the Zambezi flow. Along the way he had made numerous treaties with amenable chiefs and on the strength of these had even declared a British protectorate over the Congo basin by a proclamation of 28 December 1874. The treaties and the proclamation were duly submitted to the Foreign Office for its approval.[14]

The journey across Africa had taken two years and eight months, but Cameron's announcement of his achievement was carried to London by steamship within the space of weeks (Cameron himself was still too ill to travel and did not return to Britain until April 1876). The president of the Royal Geographical Society, Sir Henry Rawlinson, presented his letters and notes to a crowded meeting of the society on the evening of 10 January 1876. Cameron had completed "one of the most arduous and successful journeys which have ever been performed into the interior of the African continent," Rawlinson announced. A report of the meeting appeared in *The Times* next day, quoting at length from Cameron's letters:

> . . . The interior is mostly a magnificent and healthy country of unspeakable richness. I have a small specimen of good coal; other minerals, such as gold, copper, iron, and silver, are abundant; and I am confident that with a wise and liberal (not lavish) expenditure of capital, one of the greatest systems of inland navigation in the world might be utilized, and in from thirty to thirty-six months, begin to repay any enterprising capitalists that might like to take it in hand . . . Nutmegs, coffee, semsem [sesame seed], groundnuts, oil palms, rice, wheat, cotton; all the productions of Southern Europe, India-rubber, copal, and sugar-cane are the vegetable productions which may be made profitable.

A canal of from twenty to thirty miles across a flat level country would connect the two great systems of the Congo and the Zambesi, water in the rains even now forming a connecting link between them. With a capital of from one million to two million pounds to begin with, a great company would have Africa open as I say in about three years, if properly worked.[15]

A subscription copy of *The Times* reached Leopold II each morning, courtesy of the night mail train to Dover, the steam ferry to Ostend and the guard on the Brussels express, who stood by to fling the paper (securely packed in a stout canister) from the train as it sped past the palace grounds at Laeken. There it was retrieved by a waiting footman and carried with all haste to the palace, where another functionary smoothed out the pages with a steam iron before the paper was delivered to the king's breakfast table.

Leopold could hardly have failed to notice Cameron's claims concerning Africa. The *Times* report of the Royal Geographical Society meeting was carried across three columns, under the heading "African Exploration," and if Leopold did not immediately begin making plans to be first of the "enterprising capitalists" whom Cameron had urged to exploit the "unspeakable riches" of the Congo basin, something of the sort was certainly prominent on the agenda he took to London in May 1876. Cameron was the first person with whom Leopold held meetings in London.[16]

Britain had repudiated Cameron's proclamation of a Congo protectorate, preferring to offer support for Portugal's prior claims[17] in return for agreements on free trade and the right of Britain's anti-slaving vessels to continue patrolling the waters off the disputed territories.[18] Diplomatic considerations thus militated against a direct declaration of interest in establishing a Belgian colony in the Congo basin, but the continuing depredations of the slave trade reported by Cameron offered the king an indirect route to the same end— philanthropy.

The publication of Livingstone's last journals in 1874, the year after his death, had created an enduring image of the horrendous trade; Cameron's journey had confirmed its prevalence; Leopold declared that he would found and finance a crusade for the suppression of the slave-trade and the enlightenment of Africa. While in London, he conferred with Cameron at Claridge's, with Sir Henry Rawlinson at the Royal Geographical Society, and took the train to Balmoral, where he told his cousin, Queen Victoria: "I have sought to meet those most interested in bringing civilization to Africa. There is an important task to be undertaken there, to which I would feel honoured to contribute."[19] King Leopold II had in mind a conference which would embellish his plans for an African colony with a veneer of esteem and respectability.

The Geographical Conference of Brussels was held at the Royal Palace in September 1876. For three days thirteen Belgians and twenty-four assorted explorers, geographers, politicians, philanthropists, missionaries, and business-men from Britain, France, Germany, Austria-Hungary, Italy, and Russia enjoyed the privileges of royalty. A special steamer collected the British delegation from Dover; aides waived customs formalities at all frontier points of entry; state carriages whisked the delegates to Brussels. At the palace, delegates were accommodated in the royal apartments; Sir Henry Rawlinson occupied a suite done out in crimson damask and gold. "Everything is red, even the Ink and the Ammunition [the toilet paper]," Rawlinson noted in a letter to his wife. "Never in any country at any time had hospitality so magnificently royal ever been dispensed . . . " remarked Baron von Richthofen, leader of the German delegation.[20]

On the evening of their arrival, the delegates were presented to their host in the throne room, lit by 7,000 candles; each was awarded the Cross of Leopold. A lavish pre-conference banquet followed, at which James Grant, who had accompanied John Speke down the Nile, found "every delicacy," cooked superbly, and the wine flowing so abundantly that he had to juggle eight glasses at the same time. A critic has remarked, however, that Leopold's hospitality was nothing more than an effective way of buying friends.[21]

Leopold addressed the opening session of the conference:

Gentlemen . . .

The subject which brings us together today is one of those which deserve to take a leading place in engaging the attention of the friends of humanity. To open up to civilisation the only part of our globe which it has not yet penetrated, to pierce the darkness in which entire populations are enveloped, is, I venture to say, a crusade worthy of this age of progress, and I am happy to perceive how much the public feeling is in favour of its accom-plishment; the tide is with us.

. . . Need I say that, in bringing you to Brussels, I have not been influ-enced by selfish views. No, gentlemen, if Belgium is small, she is happy and contented with her lot. I have no other ambition than to serve her well . . . [But] I should be happy that Brussels became, in some sort, the head-quarters of this civilising movement.

. . . I have allowed myself then to entertain the thought that it might fall within your convenience to come and discuss, and, with the authority which belongs to you, unitedly to decide the roads to follow and the means to employ for definitively planting the standard of civilisation on the soil of Central Africa . . .

Great progress has already been made, and the unknown country has been assailed on many sides . . .

My desire is, to help on, in the manner that you may point out to me, the great cause for which you have already done so much. With this object, I place myself at your disposal, and bid you a hearty welcome.[22]

Although Leopold's opening address disclaimed selfish ambition, it nonetheless concluded with a personal suggestion as to how the standard of civilization might be planted in the soil of central Africa. A line of stations might be established, extending across the continent from coast to coast, Leopold suggested, "for purposes of relief, of science, and of pacification . . . as a means of abolishing slavery, of establishing harmony among the chiefs, and of providing for them just and disinterested arbitrators, etc."[23]

The delegates offered no counter- or additional proposals—as recipients of such lavish hospitality to do so might have seemed impolite—and devoted their energies to the expansion of Leopold's suggestion into a scheme which has been aptly described as "gloriously impractical and absurd."[24]

The line of stations would span the continent from Bagamoyo to Luanda; spaced some distance apart, but maintaining regular communications with the coast. Roads would eventually be built. Meanwhile, the stations would stand as bases from which explorers could venture into the heart of the continent. There would be stores to replenish their provisions, medical facilities, observatories, and laboratories. Each station would be staffed by a team of ten or twelve men, whose number would include an astronomer, a medical naturalist, skilled artisans, and a leader who was both "a man of action and a man of science." Information on soils and climate, natural resources, and local human populations would be collected, "primarily in the service of science, and secondarily, for the advancement of commerce, industry, and civilisation."[25]

Problems of security and safety were not anticipated, a military presence was deemed unnecessary, since the stations would have "recourse to gentleness, persuasion, and that natural ascendency which emanates from the superiority of civilised man." Thus the stations were expected to become centres from which the influence of European exploration and scientific research would radiate across the surrounding countryside, "diffusing the light of civilisation among the natives."[26]

Having expanded Leopold's initial suggestion into a scheme of Utopian proportions, the conference delegates moved on to establish the International African Association, a specifically constituted body which was to be entrusted with the task of financing, constructing, staffing, and managing the stations. Two lines were drawn across the map of Africa, one roughly following the Sahel and the other extending from the Atlantic coast just south of Luanda, to

Mozambique on the Indian Ocean. The region in between was nowhere less than 2,000 km broad; it encompassed the entire Congo basin, Lake Nyasa (now Lake Malawi), Lake Tanganyika, Lake Victoria, and the upper Nile. This, the conference declared, was the region in which the International African Association would operate.[27]

Leopold was elected president of the association. Given the circumstances of its formation he could hardly have expected less—or wished for more.

THE BRUSSELS GEOGRAPHICAL CONFERENCE WAS an outstanding success for Leopold II, bringing him international recognition as the humane leader of a crusade to bring civilization to Africa. National committees were established in Belgium, Switzerland, Holland, France, Spain, Germany, Austria, and the United States to raise funds for his International Association. The British government, however, blocked the Royal Geographical Society's plans for a national committee in Britain. Repression of the slave trade was the mandate of governments, not private associations, legal experts advised; furthermore, the establishment of stations and commerce in hitherto undesignated territories would raise questions of trading rights; conflicts of interest might thus arise between the association's members that could damage international relations. Leopold appealed to Queen Victoria, but to no avail. Britain opted out of the IAA. Doubtless Leopold suffered some disappointment; on the other hand, he was spared the intimate attention of a watchdog that might have detected the wolf within the sheep's clothing. In effect, the British withdrawal strengthened his own position as a separate force in the movement to open up Africa.[28]

WHILE LEOPOLD AND HIS GUESTS WERE formulating their plans for the civilization of Africa in September 1876, Henry Morton Stanley, the man who found Livingstone and whose proven abilities were certainly deserving of the king's attention and royal hospitality, was in the depths of the continent itself, west of Lake Tanganyika, marching determinedly towards the headwaters of the Congo River. Stanley travelled under the blood-red flag of the Sultan of Zanzibar, a symbol of authority which had also given coastal slave-traders the right to pursue their interests to the heart of the continent.

Stanley's expedition was the most ambitious in Africa yet undertaken: a traverse of the continent through hitherto unexplored equatorial regions, from Zanzibar to the mouth of the Congo. Funding, courtesy of the *New York Herald* and the London *Daily Telegraph,* was as extravagant as the itinerary. The journey from coast to coast took 999 days, in the course of which the expedition covered over 11,000 km by land and water, circumnavigated both Lake Victoria and Lake Tanganyika, and followed the Congo River for 2,500 km from one of its principal sources to the sea. It was a stupendous achievement, but at tremendous cost. All three of Stanley's European companions succumbed to the rigours of the expedition, as did 173 Africans.[29]

The news of Stanley's arrival at the mouth of the Congo reached Europe in September 1877, followed in November by a full report. The IAA was at the time busy with the dispatch of its first expedition to East Africa and pressing ahead with plans for a further two (all substantially funded by Leopold himself); meanwhile, Leopold was developing some private and personal plans of his own. Stanley had confirmed that the Congo was navigable from the coast to the heart of the continent; this was as Leopold had suspected. On 17 November 1877 he wrote to the Belgian Ambassador in London:

> 1. I would like to see Stanley as soon as he has been fêted in London.
>
> 2. If Stanley appeals to me, I shall provide him with the money necessary for him to explore fully the Congo and its tributaries, and to establish stations there.
>
> 3. According to circumstances, I will endeavour to transform these stations into Belgian settlements, either afloat or on land, which would belong to us.
>
> I believe that if I commission Stanley to take possession in my name of any given place in Africa, the English would stop me. If I ask their advice they would stop me just the same. I am therefore thinking in terms of entrusting Stanley with a purely exploratory mission which will offend no-one and will provide us with stations, staffed and equipped, which we will put to good use once [the objectors] have got used to our being on the Congo.[30]

Stanley, however, was not in the least interested in the king's proposals—initially. He wanted Britain to be the beneficiary of the immense potential he had identified and hoped that the government would move quickly to annex the Congo. Stanley arrived back in Britain in late January 1878 to a hero's welcome. He was fêted, wined, and dined by royalty, and by learned societies and dignitaries in London and throughout the country. But despite intensive lobbying, and pressing the case for Britain's annexation of the Congo at every opportunity, no such move was forthcoming.

By the end of May Stanley had rattled off his two-volume account of the trans-Africa expedition *Through the Dark Continent,* and was thoroughly disillusioned with Britain's lack of enthusiasm for his proposals, tending, in characteristic fashion, to interpret them in personal terms:

> I do not understand Englishmen at all. Either they suspect me of some self-interest, or they do not believe me. My reward has been to be called a mere penny-a-liner. For the relief of Livingstone I was called an imposter . . . for trying to kindle them to action I am called . . . a hare-brained fellow totally unused to business.[31]

Stanley now turned at last to Leopold and was received at the Royal Palace in June 1878, when the broad terms of Leopold's scheme were discussed without commitment. During the autumn Stanley made a last attempt to rouse public opinion in favour of his plans to secure the Congo basin for England (he gave thirty lectures at venues across the country)—but to no avail. In December 1878 he signed a five-year contract with the King of the Belgians; eight months later he was back at the mouth of the Congo

> with the novel mission of sowing along its banks civilized settlements, to peacefully conquer and subdue it, to remould it in harmony with modern ideas into National States within whose limits . . . justice and law and order shall prevail, and murder and lawlessness and the cruel barter for slaves shall for ever cease.

Leopold had urged Stanley to keep the details of their agreement secret for as long as possible. The project should be described as a very simple and modest part of Leopold's crusade to open up Africa under the auspices of the International African Association, he said. Yet Stanley had no illusions. "The King is a clever statesman. He is supremely clever . . . " he confided in his diary.[32]

> He has not been so frank as to tell me outright what we are to strive for. Nevertheless it has been pretty evident that under the guise of an International Association he hopes to make a Belgian dependency of the Congo basin.

Just a week after landing at Banana Point, on the mouth of the Congo, Stanley's expedition was heading up-river. He describes the first easy stage of the journey in his two-volume work *The Congo and the Founding of Its Free State* (1885): the flotilla gliding along the three-mile-wide estuary to the beating of tom-toms, the mangrove swamps on the banks, the creeks from which native canoes suddenly appeared, the hot, humid, enervating air—Stanley's style is heavy and luxuriant, but so is the atmosphere of the Congo.[33] The expedition went past Boma, the principal entrepôt on the Lower Congo into which Stanley had staggered at the conclusion of his trans-Africa expedition almost exactly two years before, and past the trading posts established by French, Dutch, and Portuguese interests on the north bank of the river, in all nearly 200 kilometres of calm waters from the sea to Vivi, at the foot of Yellalla Falls, the first cataract, and the first major obstacle to the enterprise that Stanley was contracted to fulfil.

At Vivi, 240 Africans and fourteen European supervisors immediately began work on the establishment of a trading station while Stanley set about the herculean task of building a road and hauling boats and heavy equipment to the site of the next station at Isangila, eighty kilometres upstream. The Vivi station was completed by the end of January 1880—a neat collection of houses, painted inside and out, with stables for the mules, a garden, and roads to the landing stage.[34] The Isangila station was completed one year later; by then Stanley had lost six Europeans and twenty-two Africans to disease and exhaustion; he and his men had trekked 2,300 miles back and forth along thirty-eight miles of road, built three bridges, "filled a score of ravines and gullies, [and] cut through two thick forests of hard wood."[35] Ahead lay ninety miles of navigable river to Manyanga, the site Stanley had chosen for the next station. And Manyanga was less than 100 miles from Malebo Pool (subsequently named Stanley Pool), where the cataracts ended and the fully navigable Congo river system began. A station at Malebo Pool would be the key to the economic exploitation of the Upper Congo.

Meanwhile, however, members of the French National Committee of Leopold's International African Association had begun to suspect that the commendably philanthropic IAA was being replaced by a mysterious new enterprise. Reports of a commercial organization designed to exploit the wealth of the Congo leaked through the veil of secrecy which Leopold had endeavoured to draw over his initiatives. Prominent businessmen from Holland, France, and Britain were said to have invested money which, curiously, was later repaid by Belgian interests who were believed to be acting on behalf of Leopold. If these reports were true, then Stanley was not leading a philanthropic crusade on behalf of the IAA, he was carving out a colony for the Belgian king. And if Leopold could use the IAA as a front for his private enterprise, why should not the French committee of the IAA be a front for French initiatives of a similar nature?[36]

With the discreet financial support of their government, the French National Committee dispatched an expedition to Gabon in the spring of 1880 under the leadership of Pierre Savorgnan de Brazza, an Italian-born French naval officer. Brazza and his party were to follow the River Ogowe from

Gabon, already a French possession, to its headwaters and from there make such geographical explorations as circumstances permitted.

The French expedition was ostensibly a civilizing mission generously initiated by the French Committee of the IAA, but its scheduled route also offered a short cut to the Upper Congo, with obvious implications to anyone with commercial or colonial ambitions in the region. In a letter outlining the prospects of the expedition Brazza had promised that he could "plant the French flag at Stanley [Malebo] Pool before the Belgians do the same." The letter was leaked to Leopold,[37] and in due course Stanley received a message urging: "Rivals whom we cannot disregard threaten, in fact, to forestall us on the Upper Congo . . . We have no time to lose." Stanley replied:

> I am not a party in a race for the Stanley [Malebo] Pool, as I have already been in that locality just two and a half years ago and I do not intend to visit again until I can arrive with my 50 tons of goods, boats and other property.[38]

Brazza started out from the Gabon coast four months behind Stanley but he travelled light and arrived at the Pool in late August 1880, while Stanley was still struggling through the cataracts above Vivi, more than 300 kilometres from his goal. In a heady, four-week round of negotiations with local chiefs Brazza acquired a strip of territory about fifteen kilometres long on the north shore of the Pool (where the city of Brazzaville now stands), exclusive trading rights, and a treaty which placed the region under the protection of France.

Leaving a small contingent of Senegalese sailors to keep the tricolour flying over the thatched mud-hut that constituted the new French station, Brazza set off downstream for Boma and the coast in early October 1880. He called at Stanley's camp on the way, taking the time to inform Stanley of the station he had established at the Pool (but saying nothing of the treaty he had concluded) and cheekily advising the veteran explorer of monstrous difficulties ahead. It would take six months just to pass Mount Ngoma, which loomed above the camp, he said.

Using dynamite, Stanley blasted a road over the mountain in four weeks. Upstream, the Manyanga station was completed by June 1881, and Stanley set off for Malebo Pool.

Better than anyone, Stanley knew that the Pool was the gateway to the Upper Congo and its 8,000 kilometres of navigable waterways. He had journeyed down the river on his trans-Africa expedition, he knew of the resources to which the waterways would give access, and the profits that could be made from its populations (Stanley calculated at a later date that simply clothing the inhabitants of the Congo basin would require nearly 4 billion yards of cotton worth £16 million).[39] Whoever controlled the Pool controlled the wealth of the Congo basin.

The tumbledown hut, flagpole, and ill-clad guardians which constituted the French "station" on the north bank of the Pool did not impress Stanley, but the treaty Brazza had negotiated was sturdy enough. Stanley could not persuade the local chiefs to abandon its terms. They refused to supply the provisions he required; the markets were closed to him. Leave here or starve here, he was told. Prudently, Stanley withdrew to the south bank where, acceding to the extortionate demands of a chief whose status rivalled that of the men with whom Brazza had negotiated, he acquired rights and territory to match the French concession. The station his men constructed on the site was named Leopoldville (now Kinshasa), and trading began there on 5 March 1882:

> The goods are now on exhibition in the magazine. The barred windows are crowded by curious natives. Native imagination, fired by the brilliant display of cloths of all colours, silks, satins, ribbons, fancy jewellery, cutlery, pottery, crockery, glassware, guns, swords, machetes . . . etc. etc. will report that my wealth exceeds calculation! Who would have expected such a result as this three months ago? Over £500 of goods were sold by us before night.[40]

Proceeding with Leopold's earlier instructions to secure as much land as could be obtained and place it under the sovereignty of the king's enterprise "as soon as possible and without losing one minute,"[41] Stanley subsequently obtained treaties which would frustrate the development of French trading interests at the Pool, and established three stations on the Upper Congo. The most distant, nearly 2,000 kilometres above the Pool, was named Stanleyville, now Kisangani.

Stanley returned to Europe in the summer of 1884. His five years on the Congo had provided Leopold with access to the resources of the Congo basin and the territories of central Africa that lay beyond. Stations and steamboats were positioned to reap the rewards. But the cost had been enormous: in the region of £120,000, according to one estimate, and recurrent costs plus further capital expenditure were expected to be no less than £60,000 per year.[42] By 1885 Leopold had spent a total of about 11.5 million francs (£460,000) on his Congo enterprise.[43] All the money came from the king's personal fortune, which was large but not inexhaustible and the drain on resources had obliged Leopold to take out some very large loans. He displayed no inclination to economize on the Congo operation, however, though it was clear that he wanted its achievements to be measurable in economic terms. Philanthropy was to have a commercial dimension. But then even David Livingstone, the scourge of slavers and profiteers, had believed that foreign trade would be good for Africa. Commerce and Christianity were "the pioneers of civilization," he said.[44]

But exploiting the resources of the Congo as a private individual was no simple matter for a man whose regal status surely denied him the right to plead impoverishment as a motive. Leopold required international recognition, not simply for the philanthropic ideals of the International African Association he had founded, but more pressingly for the economic realities of an enterprise he had established at his own personal expense.

In October 1882 the French government formally ratified the treaty by which Brazza had annexed land on the north bank of the Malebo Pool. This move threatened the viability of the stations Stanley had built and the treaties he had negotiated. The issue was a matter of international law.[45] Sovereignty was deemed to be the prerogative of states; no private individual, company, or association could claim sovereign rights to unadjudicated territory—not even a king—which meant that Leopold's Congo acquisitions were vulnerable to takeover by any sovereign state. Such as France.

Leopold applied his consummate diplomatic skills to the problem, beginning with a subtle move of the goalposts. In late 1882 the International African Association, over which Leopold himself presided, was dissolved and the International Association of the Congo formed in its place, quite unattached to the various national associations which had been affiliated to the IAA. Though ostensibly a minor reorganization, the change in effect created Leopold Incorporated, for the new body was neither international nor an association, but a euphemism for a one-man enterprise.[46] Leopold was in total control. For the flag which would fly over the sovereign territories and possessions of the IAC, Leopold commandeered the motif of the old kingdom of Congo in Angola—a blue standard with a single gold star.

Having created a base for unilateral action, unhindered by any obligation to consult committees, Leopold now called in the favours due from an old friend and confidant, the former U.S. Ambassador to Belgium, "General" Henry S. Sanford, who had attended Leopold's 1876 Geographical Conference and had been a supporter of Leopold's Congo enterprise throughout. Sanford was not a soldier, his military title was a reward for financial contributions to the Union during the Civil War,[47] but he ranked highly in the American establishment, well-placed to present Leopold's case for recognition of the IAC to the United States.

Sanford was shaking hands with President Arthur at the White House within days of his arrival in the USA in November 1883, carrying a personal letter from Leopold. The blue flag with the golden star "now floats over seventeen stations, many territories, seven steamers engaged in the civilizing work of the Association, and over a population of many millions." Would the United States recognize the flag? United States goods exported to the Congo would not be subject to any taxes or customs duty, he assured the president.[48]

Recognition, however, required the passing of a resolution by both Houses of Congress. President Arthur made mention of Leopold's call for recognition in an address to Congress. Sanford drew up memoranda, paid calls, and gave a round of excellent dinners in the run-up to the Senate debate in early April 1884. The debate itself has been described as "rather incoherent."[49] Senators missed the crucial distinction between the IAA and the IAC; even the Secretary of State for Foreign Affairs believed the United States was being asked to support the wholly philanthropic aims of the former, rather than the more personal ambitions of the latter. Sanford did nothing to correct the misunderstanding and the Senate passed a resolution recognizing the flag of the association as the "flag of a friendly government" on 11 April 1884.

Meanwhile, back in Europe, Leopold had decided upon a direct approach as a means of dealing with the French threat to IAC possessions on the Congo. In a bold move, he offered France first option on the IAC's territories if at any time in the future the king decided to divest himself of his Congo acquisitions. It was an astonishing offer and the French government took the bait "like a hungry pike,"[50] convinced that Leopold possessed neither the financial nor the military means to maintain the IAC territories. Leopold's offer was accepted immediately. France agreed to respect the rights Leopold had claimed for his IAC in the Congo in return for pre-emptive rights—a first option on the claims. A treaty was drawn up and signed within days.

In effect, Leopold had gained his main rival's recognition of the IAC's sovereignty in the Congo. This was an important step forward, but Leopold still lacked international agreement on the frontiers of what he now increasingly referred to as the Congo Free State,[51] and could not proceed without first gaining recognition of sovereignty from Europe's other two major powers, Britain and Germany.

Britain regarded Leopold's diplomatic coup concerning French claims as a "shabby and mischievous trick"[52] that threatened to put the Congo basin in the hands of "one of the most exclusive and protectionist governments in the world."[53] Britain's newly concluded Anglo-Portuguese Treaty,[54] recognizing Portugal's claims to the Congo in return for agreements on free trade, was rendered obsolete, given that France now held the upper hand. Meanwhile, Bismarck, irritated by Britain's lack of response to inquiries concerning her claims to Angra Pequena, where German traders had established a settlement on the south-west African coast, abruptly announced (on 24 April 1884) his decision to annex the territory. A few days later, Germany formally protested against the Anglo-Portuguese Treaty (which was never ratified).

With Britain in dispute with Germany and outmanoeuvred by France, Leopold moved to take advantage of her isolation. Stanley, now back in Europe and the king's guest in Brussels, was presented with a large map of Africa and asked to outline what he considered might be the frontiers of a sovereign Congo state. The explorer marked out a territory that stretched from the coast to Lake Tanganyika, from four degrees north of the Equator to six degrees south. This included not only the entire Congo basin, but virtually all of Central Africa; the core of the continent.

The proposed frontiers of the IAC were presented to Bismarck who, while already astounded by Leopold's grandiose pretensions, saw his plans as a means of consolidating German relations with France. The French raised no objections, since they fully expected their first-option rights to become applicable before too long, and therefore could only benefit from whatever Leopold secured. Bismarck concluded that granting Leopold's wish presented no disadvantages and Germany formally recognized the sovereignty of the International Association of the Congo on 8 November 1884. Now only the objections of Britain and Portugal remained to be overcome.

IN MAY 1884, Portugal had proposed an international conference to resolve the Congo question. Bismarck responded immediately and, after sounding out the French, suggested that the conference should be held in Berlin, thus ensuring that neither Portugal nor Britain could control its agenda and deliberations.

The Berlin West Africa conference opened on 15 November 1884, just seven days after Germany had recognized the International Association of the Congo. Thirteen nations attended: Austria-Hungary, Belgium, Denmark, Great Britain, Holland, Italy, Norway, Portugal, Russia, Spain, Sweden, Turkey, and the United States. The IAC was not represented because its international status was in dispute, but it dominated the conference nonetheless: nothing could be finalized without IAC agreement. The Belgian delegation, in constant communication with Leopold, effectively represented the IAC at the conference. General Sanford attended as an observer on Leopold's behalf.

In effect, the IAC was trapped, "like a nut between the jaws of a nutcracker, by the rival pretensions of France, on the one hand, and Portugal on the other."[55] France was claiming sovereignty over both banks of Stanley [Malebo]

Pool, on the basis of the Brazza treaty, and other disputed territory; while Portugal was claiming the Congo estuary and adjacent coasts, which would deny the IAC free access to the sea. Neither Britain nor Germany wanted to see the IAC crushed out of existence, however. Bismarck saw the IAC as the best guarantor of free trade in the region, and Britain's support of the Portuguese cause was becoming an issue of diminished significance. Indeed, Britain needed German support against French claims on the lower Niger and in Egypt, so when Bismarck warned that refusal to recognize the sovereignty of the IAC would provoke an "unfriendly attitude of Germany on matters of greatest importance"[56] Britain capitulated. A formal treaty between Britain and the IAC was signed on 16 December. Similar treaties were signed by Italy, Austria-Hungary, and Holland before the end of the year.

Leopold now had the international recognition he required, leaving only the prickly issue of territory to be resolved. By virtue of the stations Stanley had established on the Congo, Leopold held the trump cards and, from his throne behind the scenes, played them in typically masterful fashion. French claims to territory extending from Stanley [Malebo] Pool and the north bank of the Congo River to the Gabon coast were recognized, and the Portuguese (after some arm-twisting by Bismarck) abandoned their claim to the estuary in return for the Cabinda enclave, north of the river. The IAC retained control of the estuary itself and, as compensation for territory conceded in the west, was granted an enormous extension of its inland territories. The Congo–Zambezi watershed was added, including Katanga (and its as-yet-undiscovered copper reserves).

Territorial conventions were signed with Germany, France, Portugal, and Belgium in short order, but Britain maintained that the frontiers claimed by Leopold were merely "some bold lines drawn through almost unexplored regions" and declined to recognize them. During the summer of 1885, however, when the responsible Foreign Office official was on holiday, documents detailing Leopold's territorial claims were delivered to London and an assistant clerk mistakenly acknowledged receipt of them without comment, a "stupid blunder" that in terms of diplomatic protocol amounted to tacit but irreversible agreement. The blunder subsequently prevented Britain from exploiting the full extent of the copper reserves discovered a few years later in what is now Zambia. Cecil Rhodes was furious.[57]

Leopold had been forced to make concessions at the conference, but these were minor compared with his gains. The Berlin Act according international recognition of the vast sovereign state that Leopold had carved out for himself in Central Africa was signed on 25 February 1885. A Belgian delegate signed on behalf of the IAC. Though never present, Leopold had dominated the

Berlin conference to such an extent that when the King of the Belgians was mentioned at the conclusion of the signing session, the audience rose and applauded loudly.[58]

The resolution permitting Leopold II to be sovereign of two independent states simultaneously (a novel role, to say the least) was passed by the Belgian parliament in April 1885. Pondering the choice of title, Leopold at first considered calling himself Emperor of the Congo, but eventually settled for the more restrained King-Sovereign of the Congo Free State. A royal decree announcing the existence of the new sovereign state was issued in May. The inhabitants of the Congo were given the news a month later.

LEOPOLD CONTINUED TO STRESS the philanthropic aspect of his Congo enterprise, but it was abundantly clear to all observers that its viability would depend upon the attention that was given to commerce. Leopold accepted financial responsibility for the administration of his Congo Free State, but fully expected private enterprise to pay for its infrastructure and economic development. A railroad, for instance, would get things moving. At Leopold's invitation, a British syndicate drew up plans for 250 kilometres of narrow-gauge railway between Matadi and Léopoldville; their investment would amount to £1,000,000, but Leopold found the demands for state assistance, land, and mineral rights excessive, and rejected the scheme. Bankers did not share Leopold's faith in the future of the Congo, and the Austrian railway company could not be persuaded to invest. Eventually the money was raised internationally; construction of the railway began in 1889, and was completed in 1898.[59]

Africans working on the construction of the railway died at a rate of 150 a month (out of a workforce of 2,000) and survivors were compelled to work "by dint of sheer force." But it was vitally necessary to complete the line, a Belgian engineer reports, "to suppress forever the far more awful tax of human porterage along . . . this sinister trail, marked with corpses."[60]

Human cost notwithstanding, the railway proved to be a tremendous economic asset to the Congo, though the boom with which its completion coincided was not due to developments that Leopold had predicted, or could even have foreseen. The first decade of the Congo Free State's existence were lean years indeed. Revenue, derived principally from ivory and palm-oil, amounted to just one-tenth of expenditure in 1887–88. The balance came from the privy purse; Leopold was spending over £100,000 a year and borrowing heavily by 1889. A lottery, launched in Belgium solely for the benefit of the Congo Free State and its allegedly philanthropic endeavours, eased the burden, but bankruptcy was averted only by a government loan of £1 million agreed in 1890.[61]

Three years later, revenues had been pushed up to one-third of expenditure but, despite supplementary government loans, it is certain that Leopold's Congo Free State would have gone under but for a "timely miracle—in the form of wild rubber." In 1890 the Congo exported just 100 tonnes of rubber; exports rose to 1,300 tonnes by 1896, to 2,000 tonnes by 1898 (when the railway was completed), and trebled to 6,000 tonnes in 1901.[62] The financial standing of the Congo Free State was transformed. In 1890 the state earned about £60,000; ten years later money was pouring into the state coffers at a rate of more than £720,000 per year. The financial difficulties of the Congo were ended, its credit rating was high, loans could be raised with ease. Soon Leopold's Free State began to accumulate budgetary surpluses.

Leopold displayed exceptional generosity in the disbursement of his new-found wealth. The Congo profits were used to fund a grandiose policy of public works and urban improvement—in Belgium. The magnificent Arcade du Cinquantenaire in Brussels, the famous Tervuren Museum, extensions to the Royal Palace, public works at Ostend, various urban building schemes—all were funded by the Congo Free State.

In 1901, the flow of funds from the Congo was even institutionalized. The "celebrated" Fondation de la Couronne was established and granted a land concession in the Congo that covered 250,000 km^2—a tenth of the entire state, eight times the size of Belgium. The products of the concession—mainly wild rubber—brought in a very high annual income, which the Foundation applied exclusively to public works in Belgium itself. A programme of long-term and "truly magnificent" projects was embarked upon.[63] The face of Brussels was to be transformed, and large tracts of urban land were acquired for the purpose. On completion, the buildings immediately became the property of the Belgian State, along with all the land which the Foundation had purchased. In all, the Belgian nation received property worth more than £2,400,000 from the Foundation.

The factor responsible for the sudden transformation of Leopold's fortunes was the invention of the pneumatic tyre, first as fitted to the mass-produced bicycle, and subsequently as an essential component of the motor car. Édouard Michelin filed a patent for the pneumatic tyre in 1891; Robert Thompson had also patented a design in 1845, as had John Dunlop in 1888, but Michelin's tyres and tubes were the first that could be removed for repair.[64]

Prior to the invention of pneumatic tyres, rubber was used principally in the production of waterproof clothing, as elastic thread, and to some extent in industry—Charles Mackintosh and Charles Goodyear were pioneers in these developments. The necessary raw materials came mainly from sources in South

America (where the waterproofing and elastic qualities of the natural latex were exploited by the Indians and had been noted by Spanish travellers in the early sixteenth century), with only minor contributions from Africa and Asia. But once Édouard Michelin had demonstrated how much more comfortable and speedy a bicycle became when fitted with pneumatic tyres, the demand for rubber soared. Car tyres (first produced in 1895), and a corresponding increase in the industrial use of rubber for hose, tubings, springs, washers, and valves, et cetera, accelerated demand still further, and created a virtually insatiable market.

The latex from which the rubber was manufactured came either from trees of the *Funtumia elastica* species, or from a vine of the genus *Landolphia*, both of which grew widely in the equatorial forests. While demand was relatively low, collection everywhere depended upon members of the indigenous population, who would take time off from their other activities to tap rubber trees and vines, rolling the latex into balls as it coagulated and delivering their production to traders.

When demand accelerated suddenly in the 1890s, entrepreneurs promptly began looking for opportunities to cultivate the crop. Seventy thousand seeds of the South American rubber tree, *Hevea brasiliensis*, smuggled out of Brazil and germinated at Kew, subsequently became the foundation of South-East Asia's rubber industry, for instance.[65] In Africa, rubber exporters were less farsighted. Their response to the increased demand was to intensify their demand on producers, the consequences of which are documented in the rise and production practices of one particularly notorious Congo concession company— Abir, the Anglo-Belgian India-Rubber Company.[66]

Founded in Antwerp in 1892, Abir was granted a concession abutting that of the Fondation de la Couronne (though only half the size, but still four times larger than Belgium), with exclusive rights to exploit all forest products for a period of thirty years. It was agreed that the local population should collect wild rubber for the company in lieu of paying taxes to the state. To enforce collection, the company was given policing rights and powers of detention, while the state would establish administrative posts for the company, supply guns and ammunition, and help keep order. In return, the State was given a 50 per cent shareholding in the company.

By 1900 Abir posts had been established throughout the concession. Once a post was in functioning order the rubber agent made a list of all the men in the villages under his control, giving each man a quota of four kilos of dry rubber per fortnight.[67] To oversee collection, armed sentries were billeted in each village, where they lived in relative luxury at the expense of the villagers and made sure that quotas were fulfilled. Villagers who fell behind were flogged, imprisoned, and even shot. Sentries whose villages failed to meet their quotas were in turn punished or fired.

Agents were also under pressure to maximize production. Hired on two-year contracts for a small basic salary plus 2 per cent commission on all the rubber collected, each agent had a quota to fill; if production fell below the quota, the value of the shortfall was deducted from his commission. With no shortage of applicants, Abir exploited a dubious privilege of being able to hire on condition that agents increased production at their assigned posts by one-half to two tonnes per month. Production could be increased either by bringing more villages under the control of the posts, or by raising quotas, thus forcing women and children to join the workforce. Both methods were used.

Abir exported nearly 1,000 tonnes of rubber in 1903, its peak year, and by 1906 had 47,000 rubber-gatherers listed on its register. By then Abir was recording annual profits of a magnitude that prompted its directors to remark that "such a result is perhaps without precedent in the annals of our industrial companies."[68]

The result of these excesses was nothing if not predictable. All the rubber within a ten-kilometre radius of the company's principal post was exhausted less than eighteen months after operations began, and a similar state of affairs advanced inexorably across the concession. There were few rubber trees in the Abir concession so the company's rubber came mainly from *Landolphia* vines which were themselves only present at a rate of two or three per hectare. The vines should be tapped sparingly and carefully to maintain a constant supply, but as workers were forced to find more rubber they adopted faster methods, such as peeling the bark, or cutting the vine into sections and placing the ends together in a collection pot. They killed the vines, and as the demand for rubber increased and the supply diminished, the more vines they destroyed. By 1904 rubber was unobtainable within an eighty-kilometre radius of all but a few Abir posts; by 1906 the entire concession was devoid of rubber.

Orders were issued against cutting vines, but ignored under the constant pressure to increase production. Attempts to establish plantations were similarly doomed to fail, since agents on two-year contracts had no incentive to look after plantations that could only benefit their successors.

This senseless overexploitation of the rubber resource was repeated on concessions throughout the Congo. Belgium (and Leopold in particular) reaped the profit. The Congo paid the price—and not simply in terms of environmental depredation; there was a human cost too. A huge cost, in social disruption, abuse, mutilation, atrocity, and murder. Appalling crimes were committed by sentries determined that villagers should fulfil their quotas, crimes that were condoned by agents who turned the blind eye of self-interest.

Reports of human-rights abuses in the Congo Free State began circulating around Europe in the early 1890s, while public opinion still regarded Leopold II as a generous and crusading philanthropist. But from 1890 onward, evidence of "an enormous and continual butchery" was steadily leaking through the veneer of the king's civilizing crusade to reveal a carnival of massacre, the Belgian parliament was told.[69] The evidence was assiduously collected and publicized, especially by Edmund Morel, whose Congo Reform Association was at the forefront of agitation for international condemnation and sanctions to be imposed on Leopold's Congo Free State.

PRIOR TO THE ARRIVAL of the concessionaires, the Congo population was estimated to be at least 20 million. An official census taken in 1911 revealed that only 8.5 million people were left. Entire regions had been depopulated.

Roger Casement, British Consul to the Free State for eleven years, travelled up-river in 1903 to make a personal investigation of the evils allegedly prevalent beyond the reach of official censure—and was appalled. A region once populated by 40,000 people now held 1,000; in another, some 6,000 people had been killed or mutilated in a period of six months.[70] Casement collected the evidence of people forced to work without pay. They told him they were given ten days to collect their rubber quota; when they failed they starved; when they pleaded that rubber was hard to find they were forced out again:

> We tried, always going further into the forest, and when we failed and our rubber was short, the soldiers came to our towns and killed us. Many were shot, some had their ears cut off; others were tied up with ropes around their necks and bodies and taken away. The white men at the posts sometimes did not know of the bad things the soldiers did to us, but it was the white men who sent the soldiers to punish us for not bringing in enough rubber.[71]

Morel uncovered evidence showing that the concessions between them employed a force of nearly 20,000 armed soldiers, plus many more thousands of "irregulars."[72] One concession alone imported close on 40,000 cartridges in a single year.[73] A Baptist missionary described how the soldiers cut off the hands of people they had shot and took them to the *commissaire*. "These hands—the hands of men, women, and children—were placed in rows before the Commissary, who counted them to see that the soldiers had not wasted cartridges," he wrote in a letter to *The Times*.[74]

> It is blood-curdling to see them (the soldiers) returning with the hands of the slain, and to find the hands of young children amongst the bigger ones evidencing their bravery . . . The rubber from this district has cost hundreds of lives, and the scenes I have witnessed, while unable to help the oppressed, have been almost enough to make me wish I were dead . . . This rubber traffic is steeped in blood . . . [75]

And it was not only the dead who lost their hands—the living were similarly mutilated. Men, women and children left to spend their lives without a hand.

So long as the evidence was verbal, Leopold and his associates were maliciously adept at countering it. Cruelty and severe punishment were attributed to "native practice"; hands had been bitten off by wild animals, they said, or removed because of cancer. But the camera changed all that. Just as the mass production of pneumatic tyres had inflated Leopold's Congo fortunes, so George Eastman's invention of the Kodak roll-film camera finally punctured it. Determined reformers took their cameras to the Congo and returned with photographs which were truly worth more than a thousand words. One horrifying picture among many shows a man named Nsala sitting on the missionary's porch, looking sorrowfully at the small hand and foot that lie before him. This was all that remained of his five-year-old daughter. She, together with his wife and son, had been killed, dismembered, cooked, and eaten by armed sentries. [76]

Leopold, self-appointed King-Sovereign of the Congo Free State, finally yielded to widespread pressure and condemnation in November 1908, when Belgium formally annexed the territory. The King of the Belgians died one year later, but was in no way cast down or even impoverished by the shame of the Congo. Indeed, the Belgian government gave him £2 million in compensation for his "sacrifices"; furthermore, although he claimed never to have profited personally from the Congo, a secret trust set up in Germany was subsequently discovered—with £1.8 million of Congo profits on deposit. [77]

JOSEPH CONRAD CAPTAINED a trading steamer on the Congo in 1890 and 1891, before the rubber boom, when ivory was still the principal item of trade. "Going up that river was like travelling back to the earliest beginnings of the world, when vegetation rioted on the earth and the big trees were kings," Conrad's narrator says in *Heart of Darkness*.

> An empty stream, a great silence, an impenetrable forest. The air was warm, thick, heavy, sluggish. There was no joy in the brilliance of sunshine. The long stretches of the waterway ran on, deserted, into the gloom of overshad-

owed distances . . . And this stillness of life did not in the least resemble a peace. It was the stillness of an implacable force brooding over an inscrutable intention.[78]

Conrad wrote *Heart of Darkness* in two months, finishing in January 1899. He had met Casement while in the Congo, and was to correspond with Morel; he made little direct contribution to the reform campaign, but humanity's eternal condemnation of Leopold and his imperial ambitions is encapsulated in the damning words which Kurtz, dishonoured custodian of the story's Inner Station, utters as he dies: "The horror, the horror."

On ceremonial occasions the Litunga (King) of the Lozi people of western
Zambia dons the cockade hat and dress uniform of a Victorian ambassador

CHAPTER 47

An African King

AFRICAN LEADERS WERE NOT invited to attend the Berlin Conference in 1884–85 at which Africa was carved out among the colonial powers, nor were they consulted. The colonial history of the Lozi people of western Zambia exemplifies the manner in which African polities were taken up, manipulated, and discarded to suit European interests.

No Africans were invited to attend the Berlin Conference of 1884, either as participants or as observers. The proceedings, though larded with expressions of good intent concerning Africa, were a strictly European affair, a round of diplomatic haggling enlivened by the frisson of high-powered scheming and competition. There was much to be won but, although the cultured gentility of the gathering and the complexity of its competing interests might suggest the proceedings were analogous to a masterly game of chess, they were more akin to a backstreet game of poker—with marked cards. "No one," remarked Bismarck,[1] "not even the most malevolent democrat, has any idea how much nullity and charlatanism there is in this diplomacy."

African leaders, no doubt, shared the European talent for diplomatic nullity or charlatanism where appropriate, but few managed to negotiate agreements with the Europeans that gained Africa more than a modicum of benefit; the Europeans got (or took) everything they wanted. It was as though the two sides were playing by different sets of rules; certainly they were speaking different languages. The treaties were drawn up, through translators, in one or another of the European languages, which gave the visitors the advantage of semantic subtlety. Many of the terms employed were untranslatable; those concerning land ownership and rights in perpetuity for instance often had no direct counterpart in African understanding and were therefore open to misrepresentation.

African leaders, however, appear to have been extraordinarily trusting of these white men with their guns and their haughty attitude of superiority. Leaders throughout the continent were persuaded or cajoled into putting their marks on the pieces of paper that were set before them. They probably believed that even if the promised benefits were not forthcoming, they could always rally their forces and throw out the interlopers. How wrong they were.

Most Africans had foreign domination thrust upon them, like it or not. Some, however, took the initiative and actively requested the foreign powers to establish a presence in their territory. Lewanika, ruler of the Lozi during the years of European penetration, was one of these. Perhaps, living on the upper Zambezi, where each year's flood rejuvenated the farmlands on the plain, he believed that the man with the piece of paper was like the trickling stream that heralded the start of the flood. Unstoppable; inevitable; a development that could be turned to advantage.

In any event, Lewanika ceded 200,000 square miles of territorial and mineral rights in Barotseland[2] in exchange for a piece of paper promising education, civilization, and the establishment of industrial enterprises.[3] Nothing was forthcoming, not even the annual payment of £2,000, with which Lewanika and his indunas (councillors) planned to arm themselves against the threats of their warring neighbours, the Ndebele. British officials did however make a practice of addressing Lewanika as "King of the Lozi," and he was invited to the coronation of Edward VII, along with heads of state from Europe and around the world.

Lewanika was born in 1842, at a time when the Lozi were under the subjugation of invaders from the south, the Kololo, who were themselves moving away from the upheavals and huge population movements convulsing southern Africa at the time (see page 471). The Lozi ultimately regained control, and by the time Lewanika became Litunga (ruler) in 1878 they were firmly established on the Zambezi floodplain.[4]

On the inherently impoverished soils of the Central African Plateau agriculture was generally extensive rather than intensive, people were obliged to be more or less constantly on the move, clearing new land as their fields became infertile. But on the Zambezi floodplain, where the annual inundation revitalized favourably situated expanses of land, the same fields could be cultivated year after year. The Lozi established compact villages on mounds that dotted the plain, from which they farmed the surrounding wetlands as the retreat of the flood permitted.[5] In average years, the waters begin to rise in December; by March the plain is inundated, the mounds are uninhabitable and the Lozi take to their canoes and paddle across to villages lining the escarpment on the eastern edge of the plain. This move, known as the *Kuomboka,* is an annual pageant of splendid high ceremony.[6]

The ecological circumstances exploited by the Lozi on the Zambezi floodplain are almost identical to those found on the inland Niger delta (see Chapter 23), with the difference that whereas people on the Niger developed an almost symbiotic system of mutual dependence, the Lozi had a form of centralized government. The process probably began with barter. The floodplain facilitated permanent settlement but it did not provide all the necessities of life, so the Lozi turned to their forest-dwelling neighbours on the escarpment for canoes and other forest products, for instance, and supplied fish, livestock, and grain in return. Subsequently, this kind of economic interdependence became Lozi domination, not always benign, with the subject groups obliged to supply an annual tribute of their products in return for being absorbed into the Lozi system. They also supplied labour, though slavery may be a more accurate description, since in many cases people were captured for the sole purpose of furthering the development of the Lozi state.[7]

Irrigation ditches and deep-water canals were dug across the plain by captive labour. Artificial mounds were raised on the plain as living sites became scarce, and captives—or slaves—laboured in the fields, kept house, and were even available for execution by proxy should their owners be found guilty of a capital offence.

Twenty-five groups succumbed to Lozi domination.[8] Rebellion does not appear to have been an option for them and, as succeeding generations followed their subservient roles in life, they became integral elements of the Lozi population. But they could never become *true* Lozi. That status was reserved for those whose name and family history could be traced directly to an ancestral mound on the floodplain.[9]

The title, Litunga, though generally interpreted as ruler or king, actually means "of the earth" in the Lozi language. Traditionally, the Lozi say "the Litunga is the earth, and the earth is the Litunga";[10] he holds the land in trust for the people. Neither Litunga nor induna nor individual Lozi could *own* land, but all had sublimated a stark recognition of their dependence upon the floodplain into something approaching reverence for their homeland. This sense of belonging gave the region an element of ethnographic as well as topographic durability.

· · ·

IN DECEMBER, the Barotse plain extends westward from the escarpment to the horizon, where the Zambezi flows from north to south, unseen, beneath a shimmering heat-haze. Villages and trees stand on numerous prominences; cattle graze distant rangelands; fields are cultivated, near and far. Shoals of dugout canoes lie in the shallows of the harbour at the foot of the escarpment. Flocks of waterbirds follow the canal, which offers a short cut to the main stream. People walk along the banks in the shade of black umbrellas (more often used to shelter from the sun than from the rain). Even at a distance their voices are audible. The clatter of an outboard interrupts for a moment, quickly fades, then is replaced by the sound of water dribbling from a canoe-paddle.

The Zambezi drains a wedge of Africa not much smaller than France. The rains fall mainly between October and December. By January, hundreds of tributaries have carried the portion of the deluge which the land could not hold down to the main stream of the Zambezi. The river rises and steadily transforms the broad shallow valley of its upper reaches into a lake 150 kilometres long and fifty kilometres across at its widest point. This vast body of water (two metres deep on average) moves southward at a brisk walking pace, hastening the decomposition of dead vegetation and depositing substantial quantities of enriching sediments.

Seen from the escarpment, the initial advance of the flood is magical. Patches of water appear among the distant rangelands, shining like quicksilver; as the flood swells, village mounds become islands. In a matter of days the plain becomes a vast lagoon, reflecting a deep blue tropical sky, beautiful as any south-sea idyll. A few more days and the blue lagoon is transformed to vivid green as grass and water plants, prompted by the sudden inundation, grow rapidly with the rising water. These are uniquely adapted species; as the water level peaks, they surface across the entire extent of the flood. Open water persists only on lagoons and along permanent channels, but canoes still move freely, making tracks through the green that gently close behind them.

The flood approaches its peak in March, when only the highest mounds stand clear of the water. Fields are inundated, villages are awash, and people find themselves sharing a fast-diminishing living space with a disagreeable number of rodents and reptiles. It is time for the *Kuomboka*.

The indunas have conferred. The drums thunder across the flooded plain, signalling that the move to high ground will be made two days hence; summoning appointed subjects to prepare for the traditional ritual of transporting the Litunga and his household from the royal residence at Lealui to the palace at Limulunga, twenty kilometres away, on the edge of the escarpment.

The Litunga travels in the *nalikwanda,* a flat-bottomed barge thirty-one metres long and three and a half metres across the beam. The barge is built of broad planks, nailed and sewn together with fibre made from tree roots; its sides, over a metre high, are painted in stripes of black and white. A white canopy is set amidships to accommodate the Litunga, his immediate attendants and guests. Ninety-six volunteers have been granted the honour of paddling the *nalikwanda* to Limulunga. The route is haphazard and the voyage takes most of the day. There are stories of exhausted paddlers being tossed over the side in disgrace, to be rescued by accompanying canoes, or else left to take their chances among the crocodiles. That was in times past; physical incapacity has been treated more tolerantly in modern times.

A fleet of ten lesser barges accompanies the *nalikwanda,* each with its appointed passengers and purpose, and as the royal fleet advances across the flooded plain it is joined by numerous smaller canoes; some bearing families who have timed their move to coincide with that of the Litunga, others who perhaps have already made their move, or who live elsewhere, and have returned for the ceremony. Many Lozi say that tradition compels them to take part in the *Kuomboka,* whether or not they still live on the plain.

A canal leads from the floodplain to the harbour at Limulunga, and cheering crowds surge forward to line the banks as the *nalikwanda* hoves into view. The paddlers accelerate; spray flashes in the sunlight. Suddenly, within metres of the shore, each man turns about and in a frenzy of paddling, the barge is raced back down the canal in reverse. High-pitched yodelling cries rise above the roar of the crowd. The paddlers stop, turn again, and once more the barge surges towards the shore. Then again the paddlers turn and drive the barge towards the plain. Three times they approach the shore, three times they reverse, each time raising the cheers and cries of the crowd to greater volume and pitch. Finally, they drive the *nalikwanda* ashore. The crowd falls silent. The paddlers stand to attention and, after a well-judged interval, the Litunga emerges from the canopy and steps ashore.

When the Litunga boards the *nalikwanda* at Lealui he customarily wears a light European-style suit, a pearl-grey frock coat and a trilby hat; when he leaves the barge at Limulunga he is dressed in a splendid uniform of dark-blue serge ornately embroidered with gold braid, with matching cockade hat complete with a plume of white egret feathers. This sartorial transformation is an integral part of the *Kuomboka* tradition which delights unsuspecting visitors who, should they ask, are likely to be told that the uniform was given to

Lewanika by Queen Victoria. At least one report claims that Lewanika actually had asked the Queen for a submarine with which to hunt the ferocious Zambezi crocodiles, but was given an admiral's dress uniform instead[11]—no doubt because the submarine had yet to be invented.

WHEN DAVID LIVINGSTONE AND his companions reached the Barotse plain in June 1851 (when the Kololo were in control), they might have supposed themselves to be the first Europeans ever to visit the region. But, to their surprise, they found the chief and his followers dressed in "green baize, red drugget, calico and cheap, gaudy cloth, some in garments of European manufacture." In fact, though nearly 2,500 kilometres from the ocean, Livingstone had reached the southern limit of the Atlantic slave trade.[12] He was told that local chiefs had long since been in the habit of sending slaves up the Zambezi to be exchanged for articles of European manufacture. A gun or a bolt of cloth, for instance, could be acquired for the price of a boy apiece.[13] Slaves from the upper Zambezi were marched to the Angola coast, and shipped from there to Brazil—a voyage of twenty-five days, Livingstone reported.[14]

Livingstone returned in 1853, when he found a Portuguese slave-trader actually in residence on the escarpment. Silva Porto was well ensconced, with the Portuguese flag flying above his stockade, cabbages in the garden and supplies sufficient to entertain Livingstone and present him with Dutch cheeses and preserved pears.[15] But Livingstone was reluctant to be associated with the man. "The prospects . . . are very dark in this bloody land," he reported.

Twenty-five years later, by which time Europe's emergent colonial ambitions had alerted Portugal to the strategic value of establishing a trans-Africa link between its east- and west-coast territories,[16] another Portuguese traveller reached Lealui via the west coast slave route. Serpa Pinto arrived just days after Lubosi (as Lewanika was then known) had been installed as Litunga. Summoned to the ruler's presence he encountered a young man of lofty stature and proportionately stout, seated on a high-backed chair, with councillors to either side and about 1,000 people squatting round about. Serpa Pinto was struck by the Litunga's liking for European attire, presumably acquired by the sale of slaves.

> He wore a cashmere mantle over a coloured shirt, and, in lieu of a cravat, had a numerous collection of amulets hanging on his chest.
> His drawers were of coloured cashmere, displaying Scotch thread stockings, perfectly white, and he had on a pair of low well polished shoes.
> A large counterpane of smart colours, lieu of a capote, and a soft grey hat, adorned with two large and beautiful ostrich-feathers, completed the costume of the great potentate.[17]

Serpa Pinto told Lubosi that he had come as the envoy of the king of Portugal with the aim of facilitating commerce between the two countries. He wanted to open a road along which Lubosi and his subjects could outfit themselves with European goods. Lubosi liked the idea, but his Lozi Council took a dislike to Serpa Pinto and before long had contrived to make life so uncomfortable for him that his plan to open up a route to Mozambique was abandoned and he travelled south to Durban instead.[18]

Meanwhile, as the Portuguese fell from favour, alternative trading options were advancing from the south, following the trails blazed by David Livingstone and fellow missionaries. An English hunter and trader, George Westbeech, brought wagon-loads of goods all the way from Port Elizabeth and Grahamstown, more than 2,500 kilometres away, across the Boer republics, skirting the Kalahari. Westbeech upturned his wagons so that they could be floated across the Zambezi as rafts while the oxen swam alongside. On his first foray across the river he acquired enough ivory to make a profit of £12,000 on the expedition. Subsequently he was granted exclusive rights to hunt elephants in Barotseland, and up to fifteen tonnes of ivory were sent out each year.[19] The Lozi recognized in Westbeech a quality not much evident in the traders they had encountered hitherto—integrity. They found they could trust him and his agents to fulfil a promise. This, and the superior goods he provided, brought Westbeech a monopoly of trade in the region, thus hastening the end of the slave trade, weakening the position of the Portuguese, and giving the British a sound introduction to a large portion of central Africa.

Missionaries were the first to take advantage of Westbeech's achievement. David Livingstone had died in 1873, but his impassioned reports on the slave trade in central Africa had turned many a charitable soul towards the missionary cause. Most gave money; some devoted their lives to it.

Frederick Stanley Arnot, of the austere Plymouth Brethren persuasion, arrived on George Westbeech's doorstep, so to speak, in August 1882. He was twenty-four old and had travelled to the banks of the Zambezi with three donkeys carrying all his worldly goods: "One suit of clothes, one knife, fork and spoon, one plate, cup, some soap, beads, calico, wheat-meal, tea, sugar, coffee, a little powder and lead."[20]

With an introduction from Westbeech, Arnot arrived at Lealui in late November 1882. He stayed nearly eighteen months, learned the language, suffered considerable privation and, perhaps by virtue of being so alone and so single-minded, earned the respect of the Lozi. Like Westbeech, he was trusted. Lubosi allowed him to open a school, and even sent two of his own children for tuition, though with the caveat that the word of God should not feature in the lessons. "Yes, yes, that is good, to read, write and to know numbers," Lubosi told Arnot. "But don't, don't teach them the Word of God; it is not nice . . . We know quite enough about God and dying."[21]

In February 1883, as the Zambezi flooded the plain, Arnot was invited to accompany Lubosi on the voyage from Lealui to the high ground. Earlier travellers had noted that the Lozi moved from the flooded plain each year, and had remarked upon the size of the Litunga's barge, but Arnot's account of the 1883 event is the first record of the *Kuomboka* ceremony—though he does not name it as such.

Two thousand canoes accompanied the Litunga's barge, which was over twelve metres long, Arnot reports. The chair of state and drums stood amidships; pots of food were cooked over fires set on thick layers of clay; councillors sat while headmen and chiefs punted and paddled with long poles. A gang of slaves was bailing constantly, and three or four ship's carpenters were busy with bundles of bark-string oakum, stopping innumerable leaks and earnestly longing for dry land.

This first account of the *Kuomboka* is quoted in a book on Arnot and on his experiences among the Lozi.[22] It is not all a pretty story. Though generally charitable to his hosts, Arnot also described a society of terrible barbarity. Strangulation was a common form of punishment for minor crimes, usually intended to inflict only a temporary loss of consciousness, but often causing permanent loss of life.[23] Human sacrifice was commonplace, and people believed to be witches were burned to death with horrible frequency. A newly built house, a canoe, or a drum had to be sanctified with human blood before it could be used, Arnot reports.[24] The sacrificial victim was usually a child. Fingers and toes were cut off, and when enough blood had flowed the child was killed, dismembered, and flung into the river.

Like many African societies, the Lozi believed that misfortune was always the result of malevolent human intent—in short, witchcraft. People brought to trial accused of witchcraft were obliged to wash their hands in a deep cauldron of boiling water; blistering was held to be proof of guilt and the victim was marched off to be burned before a howling mob . . . "Not a day passes but someone is tried and burnt," Arnot reported,

> the details of scenes I have been forced to witness in this line are too horrible to put on paper; many a guiltless victim is marched off to the horrid pile. Two hundred yards or so from my hut there lies a perfect Golgotha of skulls and human bones.

He protested to Lubosi:

If they consider it a fair trial of whiteness or blackness of heart, as they call it, then let both the accuser and the accused put their hands in the boiling water. [Lubosi] is strongly in favour, and would try any means to stop this fearful system of murder which is thinning out many of his best men, but the nation is so strongly in favour of the practice that he can do nothing.[25]

Lubosi himself fell foul of Lozi suspicions shortly after Arnot's departure in April 1884, but escaped the rebellion and on re-establishing his rule by force in November 1885, embarked upon a merciless rout of the vanquished.

Visiting Lealui a few weeks later, George Westbeech wrote in his diary:[26]

The flat from Lia-liue to Mongu, a distance of twelve miles without a bush, is even now covered with skeletons and grinning skulls . . . [Lubosi] now, I am sorry to say, began to show his capacity in the killing line, for all who were caught or came to surrender themselves, trusting to his former clemency, were immediately killed; even the women, wives of rebels, were ripped open by the assegai and thus left to die. Others were taken to the plain . . . their arms and legs broken and left for the [hyenas] to finish . . . Boys and girls of any tender age were carried off to the nearest lagoons and thrown to the crocodiles, which swarm in them, and by all I can gather, as many, if not more, were killed by these means, than fell in the fight.

To commemorate his reinstatement, Lubosi adopted the name Lewanika, meaning conqueror. Sixteen years later, in 1902, the King of England would shake his hand. Lewanika would be in Westminster Abbey, resplendent in frock coat and kid gloves, with top hat on his knees, seated among the distinguished guests (including Leopold II, King of the Belgians) at the coronation of Edward VII. He would have an audience with the king at Buckingham Palace, discussions at the Foreign Office, and would be the guest of honour at functions around the country. Crowds welcomed him; dignitaries applauded his speeches warmly.

The transformation from murderous despot to distinguished potentate can be said to have begun with the arrival in Barotseland of François Coillard, a French Protestant missionary. It was not so much that he effected the change, but that he was the catalyst in a course of events which changed Lewanika.

Coillard arrived at Lealui in March 1886, while the shadow of Lewanika's punitive massacres still lay over Barotseland. He was introduced to the Litunga by George Westbeech and immediately upset the polite formality of the occasion by complaining about the filthy and dilapidated accommodation he had been offered.[27] But such forthright and uncompromising behaviour seems to have been an important factor in the relationship which Coillard established with Lewanika. At the time Lewanika was in dire need of someone he could trust. Coillard was fifty-two years old, with white hair and full-flowing beard. An elderly, impressive man to whom Lewanika later declared: "When I once saw you that was enough, I gave myself to you."[28]

Coillard became a confidant; close enough to sit with Lewanika in a sacred grove beneath a mysterious large-fronded tree brought to Barotseland by a witch doctor from the coast and demonstrate that the fruit hanging in great bunches from the "tree" were edible (whereupon bananas became a first right of the Litunga);[29] trusted enough for Lewanika to seek his advice on the external influences then threatening to affect the future of Barotseland.

THE PROFITS ACCRUING from the discovery of diamonds and gold in South Africa had encouraged speculators to cast an avaricious eye northward. There were legends of gold in Matabeleland (now Zimbabwe) and by late 1887 ten groups were haggling with Lobengula, leader of the Matabele, for the mineral rights to that country. The men seeking the concessions had plenty of beads, cloth, and fine talk, but not too many scruples in their baggage, and Lobengula was finally persuaded to put his elephant seal on a treaty of perpetual amity with a group offering £1,200 a year, 1,000 rifles, 100,000 rounds of ammunition, and a gunboat on the Zambezi with which Lobengula intended to attack his traditional enemies, among whom were the Lozi.[30]

Rhodes was the man behind the Matabeleland agreement of 1888; Lobengula received the rifles, the ammunition and £1,200 a year, but never did get the gunboat. Even so, word that the agreement had been signed was enough to rouse considerable alarm in Barotseland. Lewanika turned to Coillard, begging him to write to Queen Victoria asking that Barotseland be given protectorate status, such as Britain had bestowed on Basutoland and, more pertinently, on Bechuanaland in 1885. Coillard wrote to the Administrator of Bechuanaland in January 1889:

> I am urgently requested by Lewanika, the King of the Barotse, to write to your excellency, and through you to her Majesty the Queen's Government. The King Lewanika is most anxious to solicit that the Protectorate of the British Government should soon be extended to him and his people . . . [31]

Coillard's letter took some months to reach London and the reply was similarly delayed. The truth of the matter was that Britain had little interest in taking on responsibility for Barotseland. The Bechuanaland Protectorate had been declared in response to Germany's annexation of South-West Africa in 1884, when Britain had feared the Germans might extend their territory in South-West Africa to link up with the Boers in the Transvaal. The Bechuanaland Protectorate blocked that possibility.

Meanwhile, an enterprising fellow by the name of Harry Ware had arrived at Lealui, laden with gifts of clothes, blankets, rifles, and ammunition. It was an auspicious moment. George Westbeech had died a few months before, leaving the Lozi without a reliable trading connection. But Ware wanted more than trade, he was after a mineral concession. And ultimately he was granted one. With Coillard acting as interpreter and adviser, wooed by gifts and the promise of £200 each year, plus a royalty of 4 per cent on total output, Ware was granted a twenty-year concession to mine minerals and precious stones on the plateau to the east of the floodplain. The agreement was signed on 28 June 1889: "I, Lewanika, King of the Barotsi nation . . . "[32]

The land area covered by the Ware grant was considerable and very loosely defined (the northern boundary was a cattle path, and no eastern limit was specified), but since the Lozi heartland was excluded, Lewanika and the chiefs had every reason to be pleased with the deal. It would provide a revenue from land which was principally inhabited by a subservient group—the Toka—and which, having been conceded to European interests, might now serve as a buffer to invasions by the Matabele. Furthermore, Coillard advised that the Ware concession marked the first step towards achieving British protection for Barotseland.[33] For Lewanika it was a personal triumph, strengthening his influence among the chiefs and thus his position as Litunga.

With the agreement in his baggage, Ware did not linger to look for gold or diamonds on the plateau, but hurried south and, on reaching Kimberley in October, sold his concession to two speculators for £500. In December, after some hard bargaining, the speculators in turn sold it on. To Cecil Rhodes. For £9,000 and 10,000 shares in his British South Africa Company.[34]

In writing of the deal Rhodes remarked that he did think the price excessive; which gives some clue to the scale of his ambitions in Africa in 1889. Rhodes was already immensely rich; he had gained overall control of the Kimberley diamond mines, and had major interests in the development of the gold-mining industry in the Transvaal. Wealth and ruthless business acumen had brought political influence and fuelled grandiose plans for a British Empire in Africa, stretching from the Cape to Cairo, as magnificent as the Indian Raj, ruled by Rhodes and his men. But first he had to have exclusive rights to the land. And at a time when the European powers were scrambling for spheres of influence around the world, that meant keeping others out.

The granting of Protectorate status had kept the Germans out of Bechuanaland; an agreement with Lobengula forestalled Boer and Portuguese ambitions in Matabeleland; but what of Barotseland? Rhodes had to have that too. And here there is a suggestion of connivance between the Company and the British Government which was to have a detrimental and irreversible effect upon the future of Barotseland.

While Rhodes was in London petitioning for a royal charter, Lewanika's request for royal protection was still under consideration at the Colonial Office. Clearly, the Company's interest in central Africa could also serve to offset the British government's lack of interest in Barotseland. In any event, whether by coincidence, convenience or connivance, the Company was granted a royal charter without limits for the whole of the African interior, including, of course, Barotseland. The Colonial Office answered Lewanika's request, advising that, under the terms of its Royal Charter, the Company would provide Lewanika and his people with the fullest protection. Furthermore, Rhodes pledged the Company to pay for the arrangements.

With a royal charter and vast financial reserves giving him a virtual free hand throughout central Africa, Rhodes bought the Ware concession (I have "got Barotse," he wrote to a colleague)[35] and dispatched an envoy to Lewanika with instructions to secure an agreement giving the Company control over all of Barotseland. The envoy, Frank Elliot Lochner, arrived at Lealui in April 1890. Lewanika and the chiefs were highly suspicious of the agreement he sought, but Lochner ultimately overcame their objections with a quite shameless misrepresentation of the Company as an arm of the British government and himself as an ambassador of Queen Victoria.[36] He had been sent to offer the queen's protection to Barotseland, he told Lewanika. He was seeking an alliance as well as a concession, he said, and a refusal would be interpreted as an unfriendly act which might drive the queen to impose her friendship on Barotseland by force.

Leavening his threats with enticements, Lochner distributed gifts extravagantly, improved the terms (at Coillard's insistence), and celebrated the queen's birthday with a party and firework display which won him many supporters.[37] Meanwhile, an envoy from Bechuanaland arrived to offer praise for the Protectorate status enjoyed by that country.

Lewanika signed the Lochner Concession on 26 June 1890. The document stated that the king and his successors in perpetuity would receive an annual payment of £2,000. The Company would aid and assist in the education and civilization of the native subjects of the king by the establishment, maintenance, and endowment of schools and industrial establishments, and by the extension and equipment of telegraphs, and of regular services of postal and transport communication. Finally, as a sign of the amicable relations between the king and the Company, the Company would appoint and maintain a British Resident, with appropriate staff and furnishings, to reside permanently with the king.[38]

On the key issue of Protectorate status the agreement was equivocal, to say the least: "this agreement shall be considered in the light of a treaty between my said Barotse nation and the government of Her Britannic Majesty Queen Victoria." Lochner himself assumed the role of protector: "I, Frank Elliot Lochner, on behalf of the said Company, hereby undertake and agree to protect the said King and nation from all outside interference and attack."

In return for its promises the Company acquired sole, absolute, exclusive and perpetual right and power, without royalty or deduction, to all commercial trading, import and export, mining and construction enterprise over the whole of the territory of the said nation, or any future extension thereof, including all subject and dependent territory. The Lochner agreement enlarged the Rhodes empire by more than 200,000 square miles. "See how things grow," Rhodes is reported to have remarked, gleefully, on receiving word of Lochner's achievement.[39]

On the face of it, the Lochner agreement promised Lewanika everything he could have wished, for himself and for Barotseland. And, if gold had been discovered in the headwaters of the Zambezi; if some lucky prospector had stubbed his toe on a nugget of copper—perhaps even if the soils of the plateau had been rich enough to sustain European-style agriculture—Rhodes's British South Africa Company might have fulfilled its obligations. Lewanika might have had schools and railways, telephone lines, industry and trade, bringing to Barotseland the prosperity he had been promised.

But the gold was in Matabeleland; the fabulously rich copper belt lay 600 kilometres to the east (and extended beyond Rhodes's reach to Katanga, in Leopold's Congo Free State), and settlers were not attracted to Barotseland. And as investment offered greater profit elsewhere, the British South Africa Company defaulted on every commitment it had made to Lewanika. There was no social or industrial development whatsoever. The Company invested nothing and kept its administrative costs to an absolute minimum. Education was left to the missionaries; not one penny of the £2,000 annuity was paid for seven years, and then it was reduced to £850 per year with no back-payment of the £14,000 owing under the agreement; the promised resident finally arrived in 1897, seven years late; he was a young man with a small unimpressive entourage who very soon distanced himself from Lozi concerns.

Barotseland was destined to become a backwater, but Lewanika and the Lozi chiefs would not allow it to be ignored. Doubts about the validity of the Lochner agreement were raised and Lewanika ultimately realized that he had signed an agreement with a commercial company which had no authority to offer the protection of Queen Victoria. Barotseland's so-called "Protectorate" status was meaningless. Lewanika was outraged. He protested to the British government that he had been cheated by Lochner, and that the concessions he had granted were therefore invalid. A memorandum from the desk of the Colonial Secretary in London noted that, yes, "Mr. Lochner may have made too free a use of her Majesty's name in communicating with Lewanika."[40] Even so, the government concluded that the agreement must stand. The situation could be ameliorated, but not reversed.

In the event, amelioration amounted to little more than a series of patronizing letters and gestures in response to the Lozi's unremitting protest. Britain finally relented in 1924, when the administration of Northern Rhodesia passed from the British South Africa Company to the Colonial Office. By then the territorial backwater had become a stagnant labour pool, from which were drawn the thousands of men required to dig profits from the Company's more rewarding enterprises elsewhere in central and southern Africa. In some districts around half the able-bodied male population would be away at any one time, while the other half would be resting between contracts. There was no work for them at home, apart from the occasional hunting safari. Barotseland was one of the most neglected territories in Africa; and would remain so. In 1959 an observer described the country as "probably the most backward part of central Africa, or the most unspoilt, depending on your point of view."[41]

Backward? Or unspoilt? Many visitors will have inclined to the latter point of view, admiring Barotseland as a rare picture of Africa in its pristine state, complete with wonderful traditions of indigenous ceremony. But Rhodes and his men had meddled too deeply in the affairs of Barotseland for their involvement to have left anything untouched. The picture which visitors admired was as much a product of the Company's involvement as was the backwardness which the Lozi themselves deplored. The Company had fostered the growth of a ruling elite whose interests were favoured by the prevailing circumstances. The rulers could afford pretentious ceremonies; they were thoroughly compromised and their extravaganzas only blunted the thrust of Lozi complaints against the Company.

The annuity paid from 1897 (albeit reduced), plus traditional tribute and the benefits of slave labour, enabled the king and his court to live well. From 1902 their well-being was supplemented by a share of receipts from the newly introduced hut tax. This tax was perhaps the aspect of company rule most despised by the Lozi at large. Its purpose was twofold; one explicit, the other implicit. The first was to produce a revenue which might help to make the administration of Barotseland self-financing, thus reducing Company contributions. The second was to oblige people with no immediate source of income to seek employment, preferably in Company mines, thus helping the Company to meet its labour requirements.

In fact, Barotseland enjoyed some years of relative prosperity around the turn of the century, despite the inadequacies of Company rule. Lewanika ruled like a monarch in medieval Europe. Up to one-third of his subjects were serfs and slaves working for the king, state, and the elite. Canals and irrigation networks were dug, food was plentiful, and the Lozi were never more united behind their ruler than when the Company arranged for Lewanika, King of the Barotse, to attend the coronation of King Edward VII in 1902.[42]

THE CORONATION OF EDWARD VII is fundamental to the tradition of extravagant royal events which are generally thought to be a very ancient part of England's heritage.[43] In fact, such royal events are a tradition invented in and for the twentieth century. The coronations of William IV (1830) and Victoria (1837) were disorganized affairs which attracted little attention. Victoria's Diamond Jubilee celebration in 1897 gave some indication of the effect which could be achieved, however, and the coronation of Edward VII was fully intended to display the imperial might and magnificence of Great Britain, the Empire builder. Rulers from around the world were invited, including Lewanika, King of the Barotse.

The coronation was planned to the last detail—and that last detail may very well have been the question of what Lewanika should wear. When the problem arose, the Secretary of State for Colonial Affairs suggested that Lewanika should be made an Honorary Colonel of the Barotse Native Police and wear their uniform for the coronation. This idea was vetoed by the High Commissioner, and the problem then ascended rapidly through the echelons of authority to the pinnacle of ceremonial power, the monarch himself.

By happy coincidence, the king took a particular interest in uniforms; he was an expert on the subject and is even said to have made a hobby of designing uniforms. Doubtless the king had approved the design of the new uniforms with which Britain's ambassadors had recently been issued. Certainly he was aware that the introduction of these new outfits had created a redundant stock of the old style, which were richly adorned with gold braid. Lewanika should be attired in one of those, the king ordained.[44] And thus the Litunga acquired the uniform which has become part of the *Kuomboka* tradition. Not an admiral's uniform, as is often reported, but a surplus dress uniform of a Victorian ambassador; not a gift from Queen Victoria, but the suggestion of her son, Edward; not given in lieu of a submarine, but as something to wear at the coronation.

"Shall you not feel embarrassed at your first interview [with Edward VII]?" Coillard asked as Lewanika was preparing to leave. "Oh no," Lewanika replied, "when we kings get together we always find plenty to talk about."[45]

In fact, Lewanika was with the king for no more than ten minutes. He was received cordially, heartily welcomed, and wished a safe journey home, the London *Times* reported.[46] Most of Lewanika's time in England was spent away from London. He visited agricultural shows, attended functions in county towns, and was treated with a patronizing and amused gentility. A local newspaper reported that Lewanika "shows no sign of his past barbaric habits," and one of his hosts subsequently wrote of the "childlike simplicity of the Barotse nature," going on to describe Lewanika and his entourage "crawling upstairs to their beds, like exaggerated black beetles, laughing and chattering like boys newly home from school."

It is clear that the British at all levels of society regarded their guest as a novelty—the tamed savage. Lewanika's attitude towards his hosts is less transparent. He conducted himself with immense dignity, though he must have known from the start that the visit would not achieve its principal aim. Lewanika had requested an opportunity for full discussions with the government on the question of Barotseland's relationship with the British South Africa Company; he might even have expected to discuss the matter with the king. The Lozi knew they had been cheated by Rhodes's men. They wanted to divest themselves of Company rule absolutely, but no opportunities for discussion were provided. Lewanika was fobbed off with social niceties, while his dignified behaviour probably enhanced the image of the Company as a benign benefactor of savage Africa.

Whatever the failings of his visit to England, Lewanika returned to Barotseland with a keen sense of ceremony. A missionary newsletter reported his arrival:[47]

> Lewanika and his entourage were conveyed across the last miles of the plain in carriages drawn by four horses, with coachmen in full livery, even to gloves. His subjects lined the route. Servants unrolled a red carpet on the ground and the King descended from his carriage, and seated himself gravely on his throne—a great gilded armchair covered with blue silk and gold embroidery in the empire style. He was wearing the rich uniform of an Indian prince, trimmed with gold lace; his sword was at his side, and his costume was completed with a peaked cap and chamois gloves of dazzling whiteness . . .

The *Kuomboka* following Lewanika's return was a gala event. A life-size model of an elephant, designed and partially constructed by the Litunga himself, surmounted the pavilion of the *nalikwanda*. The drums thundered, the people sang and the king was in his glory. He showed Coillard some harness bells strung along the roof of the pavilion. "What I want," he explained, "is a number of big bells—camel bells—hung from one end to the other, so that at each stroke of the paddles there may be a mighty ringing."[48]

But while Lewanika toyed with the trappings of kingship, his kingdom slipped from him. He complained that so much had been taken away and so little done: no public works, nothing to promote the development of the country. "We sometimes are caused to feel as if we are a conquered nation, while we have made an agreement between our nation and the Imperial Government," one appeal noted.[49]

By way of response the Lozi were instructed to be more respectful to their foreign rulers. All Africans should treat all whites with scrupulous courtesy and respect, a directive ordered. Hats should be raised to all white men. The Lozi royal salute should be given to high-ranking officials and a suitable salute of lower degree should be given to lower-ranking officials. And the final blow to Lozi kingship was delivered in October 1907 when the Administrator ordered that "the title of 'King' as applied to Lewanika and that of 'Prince' to Letia [Lewanika's son], are to be discontinued and discountenanced."[50] It was felt that the title drew an inappropriate analogy with the imperial British monarch and elevated Lewanika above other chiefs. Henceforth he would be a Paramount Chief, just like the other chiefs in what became Northern Rhodesia in 1911, when Barotseland was reduced to the status of a province (one of seven) within that colonial entity.[51]

Throughout the decline of Lozi autonomy and royal authority there were factions that blamed Lewanika as much as they blamed the Company for the trend of events. They would have overthrown him—had they been able—but the Company took care to surround Lewanika and his supporters with a buffer of comfortable living; the old man was thoroughly compromised. He died in January 1916, aged seventy-four, having lived just long enough to see natural calamity add cruelly to the neglect from which his country had already suffered. The Zambezi did not flood the plain in 1915; there was no *Kuomboka* that year, crops failed, and an epidemic of pleuropneumonia killed thousands of cattle. The death of Lewanika left the Lozi impoverished by more than the loss of a king.

Baobab tree on a land boundary at Mtito Andei, Kenya

CHAPTER 48

Drawing the Line

AFRICA'S COLONIAL BOUNDARIES WERE decided upon in Europe by negotiators with little consideration for local conditions. The boundaries cut through at least 177 ethnic "culture areas," dividing pre-existing economic and social units and distorting the development of entire regions.

On the cross-border road between Tanga in Tanzania and Mombasa in Kenya, Zingibari is distinguished from other villages along the route by a small horde of gesticulating gentlemen with bicycles who rush forward to greet travellers alighting from the bus. The bicycles are all of the sturdy, sit-up-and-beg variety, imported from India or China. The protective wrappings of polythene and brown paper in which they were bought still adorn the frames and mudguards of the newest of them; pedals have disintegrated on the oldest, leaving only the spindles for propulsion; brakes are inoperative; spokes are missing (the remainder strategically arranged in groups of four around the rim); tyres are often worn to the canvas . . . but saddles are universally large and padded; the luggage rack is well-upholstered too.

Whatever their defects, these bicycles offer at least a modicum of passenger comfort. They are, in fact, the Zingibari "taxi service" and anyone contemplating a visit to Jassini on the Kenya/Tanzania border would be silly not to take a ride astride the luggage rack of a bicycle adapted to carry two. Jassini was once a border-crossing point, but since the tarred road (and bus route) via Lunga-Lunga was opened in the 1960s the village has become a backwater, accessible only via fourteen kilometres of sandy trails winding through abandoned coconut and cashew plantations, and across expanses of scrub grassland dotted with homesteads and adjacent plots of maize and cassava. The ride cost 800 Tanzanian shillings—less than two U.S. dollars.

No one in the Tanga region local-government office could offer any information concerning Jassini. Indeed, local government seemed unaware of the village's existence. There were no regional maps to indicate its location, no knowledge of which local-government ward and division was responsible for its administration, no list of its elected council members, no idea of its health, education, and water services. A flurry of interest was aroused by a secretary who announced that she knew someone who came from the area, but closer inquiry proved her to have been mistaken, or misled. "They don't want to know about the rural areas," the Regional Local Government Officer said (himself not overly interested in the hitherto uncelebrated Jassini village), "they come to the towns and they want to forget the villages. They forget completely."

At Jassini, the villagers were not surprised to hear of the government's ignorance concerning their existence and whereabouts. No one could recall when last a motor vehicle had come to the village. With the closing of the border crossing, the existing sand road had rapidly reverted to scrub, and the tracks that remained were suitable only for foot traffic and the occasional bicycle. Thirty households occupied the village in the mid-1990s, amounting to a population of less than 300.

Hassan Tenga was born in Jassini in 1922 and his father had been born at Kwendwa on a nearby island around 1890; he could not say when the family had moved to Jassini, but he clearly remembered his grandfather's stories of animosity and fighting between their people—the WaDigo—and the Maasai. "Sometimes we beat them; sometimes they beat us. But that was all before the 1890s," he was told. "The fighting stopped when the Germans came and made this place part of their colony."

The Germans established sisal estates, coconut and cashew plantations; people worked for them. The Germans were not bad, Hassan's father had said, they were sometimes cruel—they lashed people who did not work hard enough—but not bad. Hassan himself grew up in what he recalls as a period of steadily mounting prosperity under colonial rule. The Germans and the British colonial government which took over the territory after the First World War introduced machinery, made roads, built schools and hospitals. "All good things, no bad things," he says, "things got better day after day."

Hassan remembers the 1930s in particular as a golden age among the palms, a time when the benefits and costs of the colonial experience balanced out in favour of the indigenous population and offered a promising future. "I saw with my own eyes more than 200 households in Jassini, farming and fishing for themselves. Some worked on the sisal estates as well. And there was justice," he adds with a flourish, "more justice than when the chiefs made the laws; more justice than today."

Jassini in the 1990s is a classic example of the "unspoilt or undeveloped" paradox so often encountered in Africa. It is a beautiful, softly shaded, and tranquil village, with the proper mix of adults and children, bustle and inactivity, ordered and natural aspects that are typical of communities living undemandingly within the ecological constraints of their environment.

No technological aid or national development scheme has touched Jassini. No electricity; no water supply. Not a corrugated iron roof, a commercially made brick or concrete block in sight. Not even a shop. A few households keep small stocks of soap, tea, matches, and other commodities for sale but otherwise the village is self-supporting; importing very little, exporting virtually nothing. Villagers harvest cashews and coconuts from the neglected plantations but not in quantities that merit the effort required to get them to market. The alluvial soils are very fertile—indeed, under irrigation from the Umbwa river, the region once exported significant quantities of rice to Mombasa, and to the clove plantations on Pemba and Zanzibar (see page 432). Nowadays household gardens produce sufficient maize and cassava with a minimum of effort, as well as bananas and sugar cane, while the ocean is a convenient source of fish. Goats and small numbers of cattle graze on the surrounding grasslands.

The layout of the village is determined by the baobabs looming from its midst: great bulging trees that seem poised to push the houses aside. But a house never stands in one place for too long. Made of mud-brick and wattle, thatched with palm fronds, each remains inhabitable for only four years or so—but time is the only expense of building another, and people have time enough.

The reason for Jassini's apparent abandonment by the Tanzanian authorities is its proximity to Kenya. Indeed, the international boundary bisects the village. Alawe Shale has built his house in Tanzania, but grows his cassava in Kenya. Furahini is stripping fronds from palms in Kenya, but will use them to rethatch her house in Tanzania. The villagers fetch water from wells in Kenya; they use Kenyan currency. "Tanzanian shillings are useless here," Ezekiel explains, "Tanzanian shops are far away and don't have things we want, so we buy from Kenyan traders and they won't give you anything for Tanzanian shillings."

The international boundary between Tanzania and Kenya was defined in an Anglo-German agreement, and the history of the surveys which established its alignment through the mangrove swamps and shifting water-courses of the tidal estuary on which Jassini is situated is an edifying introduction to the problems which the European concept of nations and boundaries brought to Africa. A relevant portion of the official Anglo-German Treaty, signed in 1900, reads:

> I. The boundary follows the left bank of the Ngobwe to about the point No. 13 on [the surveyor's] Map. But inasmuch as since the drawing of the map the Ngobwe had altered its course, the exact point No. 13 has not been taken as a boundary, but a point situated on a branch of the river flowing out of the rice-fields . . . This point has been marked by a tall mangrove-post painted with tar.
>
> II. From this point the boundary follows N.70 E. (astronomical) in a straight line to point No. 5 (large baobab tree on the high part of the bank). On this line several mangrove-poles have been planted in the rice-fields and in the mangrove forest. The line is cut through the forest.
>
> III. On the high bank the boundary goes from the baobab at No. 5 past a second baobab to a third baobab. Two blocks of cement have been placed in the intervening space, and marks have been cut upon the baobabs.
>
> IV. From the third baobab the boundary turns to the line drawn by Sir Arthur Hardinge and Mr. Meyer. On this connecting-line two blocks of cement have been placed (one in the middle and one at the end) . . . One cement block has been placed at the point where a path coming from the house of the D.O.A.G. (German East Africa Company's) Settlement crosses the frontier. The frontier passes a few metres west of point No. 12, strikes point No. 2, and turns to point No. 11 (white ant-hill known as Dr. Stuhlmann's hill) . . . [1]

Though baobabs, mangrove poles, and anthills may seem inadequate for the purpose of defining a permanent and legally binding international boundary, baobabs at least are prominent features of the landscape and relatively long-lived. Local African groups customarily identified particular baobabs as territorial markers.[2] But not even baobabs live for ever, especially not those growing on the high banks of shifting estuarine waterways.

In 1993, nearly 100 years after the initial survey, none of the baobabs specified as markers in the Anglo-German boundary agreement could be located. The boundary was in fact re-surveyed in 1956, and a series of metre-high concrete markers erected which are relatively easy to find amid a scattering of baobabs, young and old, none of which stands directly on the line of the boundary.

The markers erected in 1956 doubtless will prove more durable than those they replace, but no formal amendment to the written description of the boundary has ever been made. In terms of international law, the 1900 agreement remains the most recent (and therefore legally binding) description of the boundary: "... from the baobab at No. 5 past a second baobab to a third baobab ... "

Does the discrepancy matter? Probably not. Certainly the residents of Jassini are unaffected by the specific location of the boundary, and the governments of Kenya and Tanzania are hardly likely to make the location of missing baobabs an issue of international dispute, but in terms of general significance the siting of the Kenya/Tanzania boundary through the Jassini hinterland matters a great deal.

The 1892 survey team identified the region as one of considerable agricultural potential, with rich alluvial soils and an ample supply of water making it "capable of receiving a population twenty times as numerous as at present."[3] At the end of the nineteenth century it was natural calamity (especially rinderpest, see page 589) and the threat of Maasai raids that left the region underpopulated and its resources largely unexploited. At the end of the twentieth century it is the boundary itself which restricts development. The Tanzanian government has withheld services and actively discouraged people from exploiting the border region. In 1975 the residents of Jassini were instructed to move to a village some kilometres distant, where services would be provided. They refused, and have since been left to their own devices: a dwindling population in a region of considerable potential.

AFRICA IS THE MOST STABLE of the Earth's continental land masses—the most ancient rocks, a fount of life itself, the cradle of humanity—and yet it is also the most divided continent on Earth. It was Africa's misfortune, not only to have been plundered by Europe, but also to have been colonized at a time when the concept of the "nation state" was firmly entrenched as a primary determinant of the historical process. Beginning with the French Revolution of 1789, or perhaps with Britain's Glorious Revolution of a century earlier, Europe experienced convulsions of nation-building during the nineteenth century.

From a mere handful in the 1850s, Europe had spawned a score of independent nations by the end of the century. The process was carried abroad, to wherever the founding nations had commercial or strategic interests. Africa was especially vulnerable, with the consequence that today the continent is divided into forty-six states (plus five offshore island states), more than three times the number in Asia (whose land-surface area is almost 50 per cent larger); nearly four times the number in South America.[4]

The boundaries dividing Africa's forty-six nations add up to more than 46,000 kilometres (compared with under 42,000 kilometres in all Asia). Not surprisingly, most African states have more than one neighbour; twenty have four or more; Tanzania and Zambia each have eight; Congo and the Sudan each have nine. Fifteen African states are entirely landlocked, more than in the rest of the world put together,[5] and no country in Africa is free from problems of access, security, and economic instability that are directly attributable to the boundaries they inherited from the colonial era.

The boundary between Senegal and the Gambia is a classic example. The Gambia, 500 kilometres long but in places only twenty kilometres wide, lies astride the navigable section of the Gambia River—"a worm-like intrusion into the State of Senegal," as one commentator has observed.[6] Apart from some small sections, the boundary is entirely geometrical, consisting of arcs and straight lines that in some cases run directly through villages, severing trade routes and dividing populations between French- and English-speaking administrations.

And yet the Gambia River is one of the easiest and most extensively navigable rivers in Africa. But for the boundary it would undoubtedly have become the principal artery of trade for both Senegal and landlocked Mali as well as the Gambia. In the event, the French colonial authorities were obliged to use the inferior Senegal River as a means of access to the inland territories they had colonized. A railway from Saint-Louis to Dakar (the first in West Africa) eased problems on the river, and the need to use the river at all was finally overcome in 1923, with the completion of a line from Dakar to Bamako on the Niger. This became the artery along which produce was transported from the interior to the coast, while the Gambia River—which could have served the entire hinterland at a fraction of the cost—carried only produce from the Gambia itself.

Throughout the continent, railways were seen as a solution to Africa's transportation problems from which tremendous economic advantages would accrue. In many regions, porters, each carrying a load of fifteen kg (or more) on their heads, were the time-honoured way of transporting goods and head-loading remained the only option until the arrival of the railway. And the railway brought huge economic benefits. When the East African railway reached Uganda in 1901, for instance, the cost of transporting cotton to the coast was reduced from £200 to £2.40 per tonne.[7]

But railways also accelerated the fragmentation of Africa. Constructed to facilitate the transportation of goods from inland areas to the coast, they inevitably hastened the drainage of resources, produce, and manpower away from the periphery towards central concentrations of urban centres, ports and the associated economic activity.

Boundaries, by definition, determine which regions are central and which are peripheral to the interests of the state; railways exacerbate the situation. Few railways in Africa cross international frontiers; most do not even approach them. Over 90 per cent of frontiers in West Africa, for instance, are more than eighty kilometres from the national railway. Furthermore, many regions that are within eighty kilometres of a railway cannot use it because they are on the wrong side of an international boundary. A large section of eastern Ghana—separated from the rest of the country by the Volta River and dam—could make good use of the Togolese railway, for instance, were it not for the dividing line that the British and German colonial authorities somewhat arbitrarily imposed upon the region.[8]

As with railways, so too with roads. They also serve principally the core of the nation, with disproportionately few in the border regions and even fewer that actually cross international boundaries. Nigeria, for example, shares an 800-kilometre boundary with its neighbour Benin, but only one surfaced road joins the two nations. The boundary areas of both countries have been poorly served by their national governments in terms of communications and services; indeed, 53 per cent of the Benin–Nigeria boundary remains unsurveyed and unmarked,[9] leaving the residents of these areas uncertain as to which country they reside in.

The anomaly arose following the Anglo-French Agreement of 1889. Colonial administrators agreed that the boundary should extend from the coast to the Niger River, but only the strategically sensitive and economically important sections were accurately surveyed. Elsewhere compromise prevailed; stone cairns and temporary signposts were erected to demonstrate "the existence of a real frontier between the territories of the two European nations,"[10] creating territorial uncertainties that have persisted to the present day, including the disputed ownership of a number of border villages.

Villagers, however, have not been greatly troubled by the uncertainties of their national identity. Even where the boundary was completely demarcated, the authorities found that people did not pretend to understand the distinction. "We regard the boundary as separating the English and the French, not the Yoruba," a local chief declared.[11]

A survey shows that no fewer than 177 ethnic "culture areas" in Africa are divided by national boundaries. Every land boundary cuts through at least one. The Nigeria–Cameroon boundary divides fourteen, while the boundaries of Burkina Faso cut through twenty-one.[12] But these divisions are hardly noticed:

kinship, ethnic, and economic links are far stronger than the obligations of national identity. Indeed, the nations created by the colonial powers were certain to become "very leaky vessels,"[13] with wealth and trade leaking from one to another in a quite uncontrolled manner.

Smuggling—or "unofficial trade" as it is euphemistically known—is a continent-wide activity of major proportions. In a pioneering inquiry, the United States Department of Commerce estimated that "unofficial trade" accounts for nine-tenths of all trade in the Republic of Benin.[14] Likewise, it is certain that only a relatively small proportion of the diamonds mined in Sierra Leone, Zaire, and Angola are sold through official channels; thousands of litres of Nigeria's cheap petrol leak across its borders; commodities such as cocoa, coffee, cotton, and groundnuts persistently find their way to the markets that offer the best price.

Kano state in northern Nigeria harvested 285,000 tonnes of wheat in 1988, but only 15,000 tonnes—just over 5 per cent—found its way to the country's official flour mills. "What happened to the rest is anybody's guess," *West Africa*'s correspondent remarked.[15]

NO SINGLE MOTIVE CAN ACCOUNT FOR Europe's headlong rush to partition Africa in the last decade of the nineteenth century. Strategic considerations, commercial pressures, diplomatic intrigue, philanthropic intentions, evangelization, and grandiose ambition all featured in one or more of the bilateral negotiations by which the European powers divided up the continent among themselves. But whatever the motives, once the lines on the map had been drawn the colonizers found themselves confronting a common problem: economic viability.

The fact is that while South Africa had proved to be—quite literally—a gold mine, and Leopold's dubious methods had wrested a fortune from the Congo, the figures showed that the continent was neither a good investment nor particularly relevant to European economies. During the 1870s, for instance, Africa accounted for little more than 5 per cent of Britain's trade—and most of that came from Egypt and South Africa. Even Rhodes's British South Africa Company did not pay a single dividend during the thirty-three years it administered Rhodesia.[16]

British financiers and treasury officials were largely unmoved by the glowing reports sent home by explorers, missionaries, and commercial agents. Ivory was a diminishing resource, they said, agriculture and mining were plagued by labour problems, and the climate was not conducive to European settlement. In 1890, when moved to respond to yet another call for more investment in

Africa, a former British Governor of the Gold Coast, Sir John Pope-Hennessy, entitled the article he contributed to an influential journal of the day "Is Central Africa Worth Having?" and had no difficulty at all convincing himself that the answer was an emphatic "No."[17]

In the event, three of the four major powers that embarked upon the process of colonizing Africa really had no choice in the matter once Leopold II had introduced the novel idea of seeking international recognition of the Congo as a sovereign state. Portugal had claims of first right to protect; Britain and France had rival interests which one would surely take over should the other not establish effective occupation, as the Berlin Treaty demanded. "I agree with you that there is something absurd in the sudden Scramble for colonies," Lord Derby, Britain's Colonial Secretary, wrote to Lord Granville at the Foreign Office while the Berlin Conference was in progress, " . . . but there is a difference between wanting new acquisitions and keeping what we have . . . "[18]

Germany, the fourth major colonizing power, was under no such pressure of prior commitment. Pressure from within the country was another matter, however. Many Germans wanted the government to acquire territory abroad, especially in Africa where they envisaged a sort of German "India" on the "Dark Continent." Emigration would provide an outlet for Germany's rapidly expanding population, they argued, and colonies would be a market for the country's burgeoning industrial output. National fervour played a role too, generating a sense that this was Germany's last chance "to make up for the omissions of centuries" and establish a position of power on the world-historical stage.[19]

Bismarck steadfastly resisted the call for colonies. "So long as I am Chancellor," he told a senior councillor at the Foreign Ministry, "we shan't pursue a colonial policy."[20] He repeated the vow to other officials and in the Reichstag stressed the cost and impracticalities of maintaining colonies abroad; colonies would be an absurd liability, he said. Then in May 1884, Bismarck suddenly changed his mind. He ordered the German flag to be raised over Togo and Cameroon in July of that year, over Angra Pequena (South-West Africa, now Namibia) in August, and over East Africa in February 1885, exciting the whole German nation "to cry out joyfully, at last, at last!," a contemporary commentator noted.[21]

The abrupt volte-face was motivated primarily by domestic political considerations,[22] and the foundation of a "second Reich" did indeed add a flush of charismatic prestige to Bismarck's political standing, but his enthusiasm for colonies was soon overwhelmed by the problems of their administration. Bismarck had expected the companies to assume responsibility for the "flag" and the cost of colonial rule,[23] while the Reich would merely offer "protection." The companies did not fulfil his expectations. Within a few years the national dream of a colonial empire had turned into a nightmare. In October 1899 Bismarck curtly advised the German Consul-General in Zanzibar that he had "had enough of colonies";[24] a few months later he was forced to sign a humiliating letter of resignation as Chancellor. Bismarck, the man who had created the German Reich, retired from the international arena.

Germany's colonial empire, whose rapidly mounting administrative and economic problems had contributed significantly to Bismarck's downfall, survived intact until the First World War (and became the responsibility of the allied powers thereafter). It was the most short-lived of the colonial regimes in Africa. German rule lasted for little more than thirty years. Yet it generated more official reports, statistical collations, and technical publications than any other part of colonial Africa, some so thorough that it is possible to trace the precise value of even the horns and hoofs sent year by year from each colony to the Fatherland.[25]

Stereotypes notwithstanding, it is abundantly clear that Germany approached the problems of colonial administration with characteristic thoroughness, and introduced the beginnings of a coordinated development programme to the territories they controlled. Each of the German colonies achieved a miniature *Wirtschaftswunder* (economic miracle) during the last decade of German rule.[26] Pioneering health, education, and agricultural services began to offer the African populations a measure of recompense for the trauma and abuses they had suffered during the first two decades of German rule.

In 1914, just months before the outbreak of war, the Reichstag passed resolutions committing Germany to policies of public welfare in its colonies that were far more comprehensive than any other operating in Africa at the time.[27] The German legislation insisted that the African family structure must be preserved; minimum wages and maximum working hours must be negotiated and respected.

In theory, a policy of social paternalism, originally developed to answer the needs of the growing working class in Germany, was to be extended to the African colonies. In practice, the First World War ruled against its implementation.

CHAPTER 49

Resistance

"THE THIN WHITE LINE" of colonial authority in Africa was tested at several points but never broken. The newly invented machine-gun was a formidable instrument of colonial power, but the devastating onslaughts of drought, disease, and rinderpest (cattle plague) in the 1890s were no less influential.

Here we are, three white men in the heart of Africa, with 20 Nigger soldiers and 50 Nigger police, 68 miles from doctors or reinforcements, administering and policing a district inhabited by half a million well armed savages who have only quite recently come into touch with the white man . . . the position is most humourous to my mind.[1]

A sense of humour was probably an essential qualification for administrative officers in the early 1900s, for "the thin white line" of colonial authority was stretched to the point of absurdity throughout Africa. Colonial administrations were woefully lacking in men and resources. The colonial government of Nyasaland (Malawi), for instance, was established in 1891 with a budget of £10,000 per year, enough to employ ten European civilians and two military officers, seventy Sikhs from a Punjab regiment, and eighty-five armed porters from the Zanzibar coast—and this for a territory of some 94,000 km^2 with a population of between 1 and 2 millions.[2]

The Uganda government, with a territory and population more than twice as large as Nyasaland, started out (in 1894) with an allocation of £50,000 per

Soldiers buried in the graveyard at Fort Pearson on the Tugela River in Natal, South Africa, died during the Zulu War of 1879

year, and was thus able to recruit 200 Sudanese troops to enforce its administrative policies. Northern Nigeria received £100,000 from 1900, which paid for six civilian administrators and a force of 2,000 soldiers (mostly ex-slaves) led by 120 British officers to control a population of 10 million who also owed allegiance to a series of powerful Muslim leaders, any one of which could have fielded a force many times larger than the entire colonial garrison.

Initially, European governments had expected European capital to shoulder the cost of transforming Africa. Selected chartered companies would pay for the administration and security of the territories, it was agreed, in return for exclusive rights to exploit the resources they had discovered and would develop. But European capital did not respond to the extent required. As the amount of investment required rose, enthusiasm fell. The British Imperial East Africa Company laid out about ten shillings of capital for every square mile of the territory it was supposed to develop and administer, and German East Africa was no better off.[3]

Only the British South Africa Company, drawing on the fortune Rhodes had garnered from the rapidly expanding South African economy, could mobilize anything approaching the capital needed to establish an adequate administration—and even its resources were stretched: "it is simply imperative that we must economise all along the line . . . ," Company headquarters told a district administrator in 1891, "the Bank will not advance another shilling. Rhodes has got an awful sickener of the Police. They are horribly expensive and do nothing but grumble. They must be reduced to a minimum."[4]

As the failings of the chartered companies mounted, the colonial powers were obliged to raise their grants-in-aid. Some five to ten years after the start of colonial rule, most territories were receiving grants at ten times the initial rate. Thereafter, as the colonies advanced towards economic self-sufficiency, grants declined. By about 1914 they had been almost entirely replaced by local revenues.[5]

The thirty-year transition from dependency to economic self-sufficiency marks a continent-wide submission to colonial rule. It was a process which demanded the active collaboration of the African population—and at often considerable cost to themselves. Individuals and groups found themselves obliged to give up land, accede to government demands for labour, accept the imperatives of a cash economy, pay taxes, and submit to the rule of foreign law. The change was vast and all-embracing (truly a "fantastic invasion")[6]—why did the Africans allow it to happen, when "the thin white line" was so vulnerable?

.   .   .

THE RURAL FAMILIES that constituted the vast majority of the African population had little choice in the matter. Their lives were already subject to the vagaries of climate and obligations to their leaders and their kin. Where circumstances were oppressive (such as where slavery persisted), they may even have welcomed the change, seeing perhaps the prospect of a brighter future.

But Africa's leaders had a choice; behind the gifts, the treaties, and the promises they saw the events of the late nineteenth century as the augury of a fundamental change in the nature of the relationship that had existed between Africa and Europe for over 300 years. Where previously the Europeans had been content to trade for African commodities, they now intended to take control of production and distribution as well. Clearly, some accommodation would be advantageous to both parties but an overwhelming majority of African leaders were vehemently opposed to Europe's colonial ambitions and determined, above all, to retain their sovereignty and independence.[7]

Lewanika, King of the Lozi (see Chapter 47), endeavoured to retain his sovereignty through compromise and negotiation. Likewise, Makombe Hanga, ruler of Barue in central Mozambique, told a white visitor in 1895:

> I see how you white men advance more and more in Africa, on all sides of my country companies are at work . . . My country will also have to take up these reforms and I am quite prepared to open it up . . . I should also like to have good roads and railways . . . But I will remain the Makombe my fathers have been.[8]

Other leaders, perhaps more realistic in their assessment of European intentions, rejected colonial advances outright. In 1891, for instance, Prempeh I of the Asante in modern Ghana answered a British offer of Protectorate status with these words:

> The suggestion that Asante in its present state should come and enjoy the protection of Her Majesty the Queen and Empress of India I may say is a matter of very serious consideration, and which I am happy to say we have arrived at this conclusion, that my kingdom of Asante will never commit itself to any such policy. Asante must remain as of old at the same time to remain friendly with all white men.[9]

In 1890 Machemba, leader of the Yao people in what is now Tanzania, told the German commander, Hermann von Wissman:

> I have listened to your words but can find no reason why I should obey you—I would rather die first . . . I do not fall at your feet, for you are God's

creature just as I am . . . I am Sultan here in my land. You are Sultan there in yours. Yet listen, I do not say to you that you should obey me: for I know that you are a free man . . . As for me, I will not come to you, and if you are strong enough, then come and fetch me.[10]

Hendrik Witbooi, leader of the Nama in South-West Africa, told the German administrator, Theodor von Leutwein, in 1894 that "the Lord God has established various kingdoms in the world. Therefore I know and believe that it is no sin or crime that I should wish to remain the independent chief of my land and people."[11]

In 1895, Wobogo, the King of the Mossi (in modern Burkina Faso), told an officer commanding French colonial forces:

I know that the whites wish to kill me in order to take my country, and yet you claim that they will help me to organize my country. But I find my country good just as it is. I have no need of them. I know what is necessary for me and what I want: I have my own merchants: also, consider yourself fortunate that I do not order your head to be cut off. Go away now, and above all, never come back.

These cries of defiance were made by articulate men who, in some cases, also possessed the wherewithal to back their words with action. When Menelik II (1844–1913) of Ethiopia learned that the European powers had declared their intention of dividing up Africa among themselves, he let it be known that his country was not available for such treatment. Indeed, in a pronouncement addressed to the heads of state of Britain, France, Germany, Italy, and Russia in 1891, Menelik appealed for help with his own territorial claims:

I have no intention at all of being an indifferent spectator, if the distant Powers hold the idea of dividing up Africa, Ethiopia having been for the past fourteen centuries, an island of Christians in a sea of Pagans.

Since the All-Powerful has protected Ethiopia up until now, I am hopeful that He will keep and enlarge it also in the future, and I do not think for a moment that He will divide Ethiopia among the other Powers.

Formerly the boundary of Ethiopia was the sea. Failing the use of force and failing the aid of the Christians, our boundary on the sea fell into the hands of the Muslims. Today we do not pretend to be able to recover our sea coast by force; but we hope that the Christian Powers, advised by our Saviour, Jesus Christ, will restore our seacoast boundary to us, or that they will give us at least a few points along the coast.[12]

Far from helping Menelik recover lost territory, Britain and France actually connived to assist Italy in launching a campaign to annex Ethiopia. The Italians had already seized the Red Sea port of Massawa (in 1885, making Ethiopia a landlocked state) and negotiated a treaty which ceded Eritrea to Italy in return for recognition of the Emperor's sovereignty over the rest of Ethiopia, a very large loan, and the right to import goods (including arms and ammunition) through Italian territory.

Now they wanted more. Seizing on misinterpretations arising from differences in the Amharic and Italian texts of the treaty, Italy picked a quarrel and self-righteously invaded northern Ethiopia in 1890. Menelik protested but left the Italians alone while surreptitiously importing large quantities of firearms—from France and Russia in particular—and consolidating Ethiopia's other boundaries. In September 1895 he moved a force of 100,000 men, most of them armed with modern weapons, to the north. After a number of skirmishes, the final confrontation was fought out at Adowa, on 1 March 1896.[13]

The Ethiopians inflicted a terrible defeat on the Italians. During the battle, 3,179 Italian officers and men were killed, plus about 2,000 locally recruited troops. Many more were wounded, or missing. In all, the Italians lost over 40 per cent of their fighting force, and all their *matériel,* including artillery and 11,000 rifles.[14]

But the price of victory had been high. The Ethiopians had lost about 7,000 dead and 10,000 wounded. Menelik pondered the possibility of seizing the initiative and pressing forward to reclaim Eritrea. But supply lines were already overextended, food was scarce, and water supplies uncertain. Furthermore, the men were tired of fighting. Menelik led his army back to Addis Ababa, where a peace treaty signed in October 1896 recognized the absolute independence of Ethiopia and the sovereignty of its emperor.[15]

Eritrea remained an Italian colony despite Menelik's defeat of the Italian forces but Ethiopia was the only African state that successfully resisted European colonization. Ethiopia's mountainous and deeply rifted terrain, and the unifying influence of a powerful Christian hierarchy, doubtless were potent weapons in Menelik's armoury; but this did not diminish his achievement.

Elsewhere on the continent resistance was crushed, either by conquest or by attrition. Leaders were killed or captured and deported. Lat Dior of Cayor (in modern Senegal) was killed in action; Samori Ture, who waged an eight-year campaign (1891–98) of "remarkable tenacity and military skill" against the French in West Africa, was captured and deported to Gabon, where he died two years later. Abushiri, the hero of East African resistance, was captured and hanged by the Germans; Lobengula of the Ndebele died in flight, Prempeh I of the Asante was exiled to the Seychelles, along with Mwanga of the Buganda and Kabarega of the Bunyoro. Behazin of Dahomey and Cetswayo of the Zulu were also banished and spent the remainder of their lives in exile.[16]

But even though "the thin white line" was weak and African resistance strong, advances in European technology rendered the outcome inevitable. First, the introduction of quinine as a prophylactic (in the 1850s) reduced European deaths from malaria by about four-fifths, making military operations possible in even the most badly infested regions; second, European troops were armed with superior weapons—which the signatories to the Brussels Convention of 1890 had agreed not to sell to Africans.[17]

While African troops were armed mostly with early-nineteenth-century muskets which took at least one minute to load, had a range of only eighty metres, and misfired at least three times in ten, European troops had breech-loading rifles from 1866 and repeating rifles from 1885. But it was the Maxim machine-gun, patented in 1884, which delivered the most deadly blow. Capable of firing eleven bullets a second into the ranks and defences of opposing forces, the Maxim gun devastated the palisaded strongholds of East Africa and the baked-mud defences of the savanna.[18] With the Maxim gun on their side, French forces suffered not a single casualty when driving the Tukulor from Segou in modern Mali, and the British killed at least 10,800 Sudanese at Omdurman with a loss of just 49 dead.

In a poem entitled "The Modern Traveller," Hilaire Belloc summed up the military situation in Africa with a blunt couplet:

> Whatever happens, we have got
> The Maxim Gun, and they have not.[19]

Neither spears nor stockpiles of antiquated muzzle-loading muskets could challenge Europe's new death-dealing technology. "War now be no war," a bewildered Fulani warrior complained,

> I [see] Maxim-gun kill Fulani five hundred yards away, eight hundred yards far away. It no be blackman . . . fight, it be white man one-side war. It no good . . . slave-raiding not so bad as big battle where white man kill black man long way away. Black man not get near kill white man. If he come near he die.[20]

THE EARLY COLONIAL period has been described as a time that fostered widespread war and revolutionary change in Africa. Some accounts of African history during this period amount to a paean glorifying African resistance to colonial conquest,[21] which at least corrects the widely shared assumptions of passive submission found in other accounts:

> Backed by their wealth and increasing mastery of science, the European kings and soldiers carried all before them. In doing so they found it easy—and convenient—to treat Africans either as savages or as helpless children.[22]

Africans were neither helpless nor savages, but nor were they universally committed to resisting the colonial invasion. Episodes of resistance and conquest occurred in parts of nearly every African colony, it is true, but they were mostly small actions, spread over twenty or even thirty years. Conquest, where it occurred, was but one aspect of a slow process of infiltration, much of which was completely bloodless.[23]

In fact, given the fragility of the thin white line and the feeble resources at the disposal of the new rulers, any attempt to characterize the early colonial period in terms of conquest and resistance-to-conquest is seriously misleading.[24] More relevance must be attached to the indigenous and wholly inescapable dynamic which determined not only the fates of Africans and colonists alike, but also the entire course of human evolution—human ecology.

Demographers have estimated that by 1900 the human population of Africa was about 129 million. It had been a long slow haul from the 47 million who had populated the continent in 1500.[25] During that same 400 years the world population (excluding Africa) had risen from just under 500 million to almost 2,000 million. Africa's growth rate was restrained by the slave trade to some extent, but more consistently by the interrelated constraints of food production, labour availability, fertility, and disease. African populations could not escape from the cycles of boom and bust described in a previous chapter, even though the introduction of more productive crops and labour-saving technology had loosened the shackles a little.

Of the 129 million people estimated to have been living in Africa at the turn of the century, fewer than half of 1 per cent (645,000) could have been actively engaged in resisting the colonial invasion—even if all recorded instances had occurred simultaneously. Lengthy periods of time and vast expanses of territory were totally unaffected by resistance movements, to the extent that resistance clearly has more relevance as a feature of Africa's modern political history than as a determinant of the colonization process.

While resistance leaders became the heroes of national independence movements, the majority of the African population continued as before, more concerned with the day-to-day imperatives of life than with the grievances of their leaders. And the period in question—the thirty years from 1885 to

1914—saw Africa afflicted by a series of debilitating natural calamities. Calamities of biblical proportions. It was as though nature had contrived to weaken Africa just when Europe decided to take over the continent.

CLIMATE HAS ALWAYS BEEN an extenuating factor in African history. As has been described in previous chapters, a series of better-than-average rains induced population growth, human dispersal, and the establishment of villages on previously uninhabitable land. A return to average rainfall conditions inevitably caused distress. Worse-than-average rains brought disaster.

During the twenty-five years from 1870 to 1895, forty-six of the seventy-two locations from which evidence of past rainfall has been recovered (from soils, lakes, and river beds) experienced better-than-average conditions; six had average rainfall, twenty worse-than-average. The Angola coast and parts of modern Nigeria were dry; conditions in southern Africa were variable; but the Rift Valley, the Sahara, most of West and North Africa were exceptionally wet. Wells dotted the western Sahara (indicating the presence of ample grazing), and stands of forest grew to maturity in now barren regions of Mauritania and Mali.[26]

This was a period when Lake Chad overflowed, the Senegal and Niger rivers regularly rose to flood deep depressions along their banks, and the farming potential of these rejuvenated lands was unconstrained. Wheat production on the Niger Bend region during the 1870s and 1880s thrived to the extent that grain was exported to surrounding areas. Harvests were also continually good in southern Algeria, Namibia, and the otherwise dry regions of South Africa and Botswana. The wetter conditions are confirmed by numerous quantitative measurements of rainfall and river flow. Rainfall at Freetown in Sierra Leone, for instance, averaged 35 per cent above the mean from 1880 to 1895; the Nile discharge was also 35 per cent greater.

Thus the generation that would bear the brunt of the colonial incursions was born and reared during a period of exceptionally good conditions across the greater part of the continent. Consequently, the human population was in a boom phase. Numbers were increasing—perhaps even to the extent that the labour demands of the new economic regime might have been satisfied without causing labour shortages at home.

The good times peaked in the early 1890s, however, and thereafter conditions deteriorated dramatically. A map of Africa illustrating the rainfall data for the period from 1870 to 1895 bears a healthy flush of plus signs, indicating better-than-average rainfall, but the map for the following twenty-five years is covered with minuses. Only the Canary Islands and Morocco enjoyed better-than-average rainfall between 1895 and 1920; conditions were average in

Tunisia and variable in Mozambique, but at sixty-two locations across the continent, worse-than-average conditions prevailed.[27]

With the sudden decline in rainfall, lake levels fell, and river flow decreased dramatically. Drought was severe and widespread. The Sahel, well-watered for the previous twenty-five years, suffered year after year of extreme drought. After years of plenty, harvests failed in farming regions extending from Algeria and West Africa southward to the Kalahari. In southern Africa, unrelieved desiccation prompted the establishment of a commission to investigate the problem,[28] and there was even a serious proposal to flood the Kalahari (by canal from the Okavango River) in an attempt to replicate the beneficial effects of the "good" rains.

The instances seem repetitive, but the correlations between climatically induced upheavals in the human condition and major shifts in the course of African history are clearly more than mere coincidence. At the turn of the century, an African population weaned on the surpluses of previous decades was severely weakened by the austerities of drought. No wonder resistance to European colonization was not more widespread and sustained. For many Africans "the thin white line" might have seemed more like a lifeline than the advancing boundary of an aggressive foreign power, especially where it was represented by missions, churches, and schools speaking of a future in which the crushing cycles of the past would be relieved by European technology.

But worse-than-average rainfall was not the only calamity visited upon African communities during the early years of the colonial period. There were even greater catastrophes ahead. Indeed, drought and famine were merely the cruel preliminaries which increased susceptibility to the plagues that would follow.

Outbreaks of cholera, typhus, and smallpox were frequent among malnourished communities during the 1890s; jiggers (sand-fleas), introduced from Brazil via Angola in 1872, had spread along caravan routes across the continent to Zanzibar by 1898, causing terrible suffering to people who were unaware of the danger. "Those who keep the feet clean and look after them daily to extract the jiggers have little to fear from this plague," Oscar Baumann, a German traveller noted in 1894.

> But left to themselves, the sand-flea larvae will grow to the size of a pea and finally break out into sores. When these appear in large numbers, they can cause blood poisoning and death. Particularly in areas where the sand-flea occurs for the first time, and where its treatment is unknown, its impact can be devastating. We saw people in Uzinza [in modern Tanzania] whose limbs had disintegrated. Whole villages had died out on account of this vexation.[29]

From the Great Lakes region, where it was reported that smallpox had already reduced communities to one-tenth of their former size, jigger infestations had left the survivors incapable of working in their fields—harvests were left standing.[30] Elsewhere, locusts destroyed crops before they ripened.[31] But the worst plagues were yet to come.

Rinderpest (cattle plague) killed between 90 and 95 per cent of all cattle in Africa between 1889 and the early 1900s. The disease first appeared in Somaliland in 1889, and spread rapidly to Ethiopia, the Sudan, and East Africa. Via the pastoralists of the Sahel corridor, the plague spread to West Africa; along the Rift Valley its devastation extended to the Zambezi, where its advance was halted—but only temporarily. The plague finally crossed the river early in 1896, and by March it was advancing through Bechuanaland [Botswana] at a rate of forty kilometres a day. Attempts to halt its progress through South Africa failed; by November 1897 the entire continent had been infected and even the animals on Cecil Rhodes's estate at Groote Schuur, near Cape Town, were dying of rinderpest.[32]

The rinderpest epidemic has been described as the greatest natural calamity ever to befall the African continent, a calamity which has no parallel elsewhere.[33]

RINDERPEST IS A VIRUS DISEASE, very highly contagious, which manifests itself in fever, restlessness, loss of appetite, blood-stained diarrhoea, and often also nasal discharges. Some animals become maniacal; the great majority weaken rapidly and die.

The disease has a long history.[34] It was known in classical times and appears to have maintained a reservoir of infection on the Russian steppes, from where epidemics periodically erupted to ravage the Middle East and Europe. The disease was brought to sub-Saharan Africa by Italian forces in 1889, with infected cattle they had imported from India, Aden, and South Russia to feed the troops then occupying Massawa. Indigenous herds, previously unexposed to the disease, lacked immunity and rapidly succumbed.

The epidemic seemed to gain in virulence as it spread—and cattle were not the only animals affected. Sheep and goats died too, and the disease virtually eliminated the populations of buffalo, giraffe, and eland that it touched, as well as most small antelopes, warthogs, bush pigs and forest hogs.

In South Africa, drastic attempts were made to halt the advance of the disease. A barbed-wire fence, 1,600 km long, was erected from Bechuanaland to the Cape–Natal coast. Police patrolled the fence; disinfection points were established; infected herds were shot—in all, over £1 million was spent on trying to keep the disease out of South Africa,[35] but to no avail. Two and a half million cattle died south of the fence; 5.5 million south of the Zambezi, and up to 95 per cent of the cattle in Africa's pastoral regions generally.[36]

The consequences of the catastrophe were immense, not only in terms of the hunger and death that followed the plague, but also in terms of its social and psychological impact. Cattle had long been accepted as a form of wealth that endowed their owners with power and authority. Almost instantaneously, rinderpest swept away the wealth of tropical Africa. The pastoralist aristocrats were ruined. Where herds had numbered tens of thousands, only a few dozen animals survived.[37] "The Fulani [in northern Nigeria], having lost all, or nearly all their cattle, became demented: many are said to have done away with themselves. Some roamed the bush calling imaginary cattle."[38]

Oscar Baumann, who travelled through German East Africa in 1891, estimated that fully two-thirds of the Maasai population died as a consequence of the rinderpest. And nothing of the old way of life was left to sustain the survivors:

> There were women like skeletons with the madness of starvation in their eyes . . . "warriors" scarcely able to crawl on all fours, and apathetic, languishing elders. These people would eat anything, dead donkeys were a feast for them, but they did not distain bones, hides, or even the horns of slaughtered cattle . . . They were refugees from Serengeti, where the famine had depopulated entire districts, and came as beggars to their kinfolk at Mutyek who had barely enough to feed themselves.[39]

Captain Frederick Lugard, assigned to establish the British colonial presence in East Africa, observed similar tragedies on his journeys through Kenya and Uganda in the early 1890s: "Constantly we pass dead buffaloes, carcases a month or so old," he noted in his diary, "mostly uneaten by vultures or hyenas . . . Everywhere in the paths are heaps of bones and horns of dead oxen. It must have been a fearful plague which has swept away every living ox, and the wild buffalo also . . . "

With their cattle dead, Lugard saw surviving pastoralists eating "the fruits of the earth" which previously they had never touched.

> They are forced to cultivate but apparently don't know how and produce nothing. Otherwise by this time their fields would be full of crops. It is close on six months since I passed and there is now no more food than there was then. They are half-starved-looking, most of them, and covered with Itch— a most filthy looking disease which is most contagious, and the body is covered with open sores like smallpox.[40]

Lugard concluded: "The enormous extent of the devastation [rinderpest] has caused in Africa can hardly be exaggerated."[41] Africans everywhere were starving, diseased, demoralized, and anxious to be friends. But Lugard, the arch-colonialist, saw an advantage in their plight. The rinderpest, he wrote "in some respects . . . has favoured our enterprise. Powerful and warlike as the pastoral tribes are, their pride has been humbled and our progress facilitated by this awful visitation. The advent of the white man had not else been so peaceful."[42]

Furthermore, the removal of domestic cattle from Africa's tropical savannas and wooded grasslands weakened not only the African capacity to resist the colonial invasion; it also weakened their ability to reoccupy the ranges they had formerly exploited—with demographic consequences which compounded the already devastating effects of the rinderpest.

No animals clip the sward as thoroughly and as repeatedly as a herd of cattle under human control. From the first flush of green until the dry season inhibits growth, cattle keep the pastures very short indeed. It has been shown that heavy grazing actually stimulates some grasses to produce more fodder (see page 102), but it also ensures that no tree or shrub seedling can grow to more than a few centimetres in height. Their rootstocks develop formidably however, and in the absence of grazing animals the plants rapidly make up for all the growth they lost in previous years. In the space of a season or two, pasture is transformed into wooded grassland and shady thornbush thickets, creating ideal conditions for the spread of the tsetse fly.

The empire of the tsetse, initially diminished by the drastic reduction of the wild-animal populations which constituted the primary food source of the blood-feeding fly, recovered ground quickly as wild-animal numbers rose again, and extended its domain across the wooded grassland that had grown up in the absence of cattle. The wild animals carry trypanosomes in their bloodstream, the parasite which causes sleeping sickness (trypanosomiasis) in people and domestic stock (see page 242). The wild hosts are immune, but when parasites are ingested by a feeding tsetse and released into the bloodstream of a vulnerable person or animal from which the fly takes a subsequent meal—then the consequences often are fatal.

It has been shown that since the constituent elements of the trypanosome cycle—the parasites, the wild-animal hosts, the insect vector, and the potential victims—have coexisted in Africa for a long time, they must have achieved a degree of ecological balance that ensured the survival of all parties.[43] The disease was endemic, but people and their cattle kept it under control. Pioneers were exposed to the acute dangers of the disease, but as people and their herds established control, contact with the vector was reduced. Individuals and cattle undoubtedly continued to contract sleeping sickness from time to time, but the frequency was relatively low.

Rinderpest disrupted that ecological balance, and in susceptible regions the tsetse fly not only extended its range but the hitherto merely endemic sleeping sickness rapidly assumed epidemic proportions. The disruption was especially marked in the former cattle-herding regions of East Africa. Cases of trypanosomiasis were reported from southern Uganda in 1902,[44] and the disease had killed 200,000 people by 1906[45]—two of every three who had survived the famine, pestilence, and war that had afflicted the area during the previous decade.

THE OVERALL EFFECT of the rinderpest plague, compounded by initial depopulation and the subsequent migration of people away from the bite of the tsetse fly, was to shift the ecological balance of the trypanosome cycle heavily in favour of wild-animal populations. In East Africa in particular, areas which had once supported large and relatively prosperous populations of herders and farmers were transformed into tsetse-infested bush and woodland inhabited only by wild animals.[46] Influential conservationists during the colonial period assumed that these regions were precious examples of African environments which had existed since time began. Believing that the plains and woodlands packed with animals were a manifestation of "natural" perfection, untouched by humanity, they declared that they should be preserved from human depredation for evermore. Most are now tsetse-infested game parks: Serengeti, the Masai Mara, Tsavo, Selous, Ruaha, Luangwa, Kafue, Wankie, Okavango, Kruger . . .

CHAPTER 50

Rebellion

OPPRESSIVE POLICIES INSPIRED rebellions against German colonial rule in South-West Africa and German East Africa (present-day Tanzania). Both were crushed, giving Africans a sobering foretaste of the ruthless methods they would see employed in the Boer War (1899–1902) and the First World War (1914–18).

At the outbreak of the First World War in August 1914, Major H.G. von Doering, the Governor of German Togo, suggested to his counterparts in the British Gold Coast (now Ghana) and French Dahomey (now Benin) that Togo should be declared neutral, so that their African subjects would be spared the spectacle of Europeans fighting one another.[1] A nice sentiment, especially as expressed by a representative of the nation which had killed tens of thousands of Africans in the suppression of rebellion in its own colonies during the past decade.

There is a difference between resistance and rebellion, and while African resistance to the colonial invasions had sputtered ineffectively, its drive and potential dissipated by a lack of shared conviction and coordinated effort, oppressive colonial regimes tended to unite people. This was especially so in the German colonies, where even those who had suffered the recent calamities of drought, rinderpest, famine, and disease were roused to rebellion by the European determination to wrench some reward from their investment in Africa. Oppressed to the point beyond which there was nothing more to lose, the people rebelled.

Herero cattle herdsman and his grandson on the fringes of the Kalahari
desert, Namibia

In South-West Africa, the plagues which marked the turn of the century had reduced Nama and Herero pastoralists to a state of abject subjugation. Over 250,000 cattle had died. A proud and independent people were humbled and starving. In desperation, the pastoralists sold land to white settlers to pay for vaccinations, to buy new cattle, or simply to buy food and save their families from starvation.

As white ranchers took over the African grazing lands, white traders simultaneously stripped the surviving pastoralists of their remaining rights, cattle, and possessions. The traders extended loans of food and essentials to the few remaining African stockholders, then subsequently demanded their livestock as repayment. Totally impoverished, the Herero were forced to accept employment as labourers on private farms or public works, encouraging Governor Theodor von Leutwein to report to Berlin that the Herero were adapting to the colonial situation with admirable good sense.

Like Lugard in East Africa (see page 591), Leutwein believed the plagues and the famine had enabled him to tame the colony without a war. With the completion of a railway from the coast at Swakopmund to Windhoek, and a telegraph line beside it, the colony began attracting more immigrants, and more capital. The number of white settlers rose sharply in the aftermath of the rinderpest, from 2,000 in 1896 to 4,700 in 1903.

Leutwein is reputed to have treated the Herero leaders with "studied politeness," but the same cannot be said of the administrators and settlers who employed Herero workers on the farms and public works. Brutal floggings and rape were commonplace, even murders went unpunished. Leutwein deplored what he privately called the "barbarous" conduct of the settlers, but did nothing to stop it. On 12 January 1904 the Herero took action themselves. In a series of attacks on isolated farms and settlements they killed every German male who was capable of bearing arms. Within a matter of days over 100 had been killed, including the most hated traders. Some of the victims were stabbed and hacked to death, others were tortured and mutilated, but all women and children, missionaries, and Europeans of other nationalities were spared.[2]

It was a violent and short-lived rebellion, brought to a halt by machine-guns defending the garrison towns to which the Germans retreated, but it provoked a devastating response. While Leutwein attempted to negotiate, settlers exacted reprisals and, in June 1904, General Lothar von Trotha arrived at Swakopmund with German reinforcements and the Kaiser's order to crush the revolt by "fair means or foul." This was an order that turned a small war into a great catastrophe.[3]

Spurning Leutwein's suggestions of compromise, Trotha drove the Herero into the fringes of the Kalahari desert and erected a line of guard posts behind them, sealing off 250 kilometres of the desert border. With some 8,000 men and 16,000 women and children, along with the remnants of their stock, trapped between the desert and the withering fire of the German guns, Trotha issued a formal proclamation:

> I, the Great General of the German soldiers, address this letter to the Herero people. The Herero are no longer considered German subjects. They have murdered, stolen, cut off ears and other parts from wounded soldiers, and now refuse to fight on, out of cowardice. I have this to say to them . . . the Herero people will have to leave the country. Otherwise I shall force them to do so by means of guns. Within the German boundaries, every Herero, whether armed or unarmed, with or without cattle, will be shot. I shall not accept any more women or children. I shall drive them back to their people. Otherwise I shall order shots to be fired at them.
> Signed: the Great General of the Mighty Kaiser, von Trotha.

Expulsion or extermination. The great general's notorious *Vernichtungsbefehl* (extermination order) was withdrawn two months after its proclamation (on orders from Berlin), but not before Hendrik Witbooi, leader of the Nama people in the south of the colony, had concluded that he and his people might be the next victims of German belligerence.

Though already eighty years old, Witbooi raised and led a Nama rebellion against the German authorities. For more than a year Nama guerrillas—who never numbered more than 1,500, less than half of whom were armed with modern rifles—held up to 15,000 German troops at bay. The end came in October 1905, when Witbooi was mortally wounded during an attack on German supply lines. Thereafter, Nama unity crumbled, the survivors capitulated and in return for their lives agreed to be settled in a reserve near their capital, Gibeon.

General von Trotha sailed for Germany in November 1905. The campaign against the Herero and Nama had required a force of 17,000 German troops and cost £20 million. Trotha was awarded the Order of Merit for his devotion to the Fatherland. Africa remembers his inhumanity.

Of the 24,000 Herero men, women and children who were trapped on the edge of the Kalahari, 5,000 somehow found their way to safety in Bechuana-land or the Cape. The majority died in the *sandveld*, or crept back to the west where they were hunted down like game by Trotha's army. Many Herero sur-rendered and were sent to work in forced-labour camps—a total of 9,000 by the summer of 1905. But many more must have died of starvation or were killed in the raids on Herero villages that continued until November 1905. After Trotha was recalled, a further 6,000 emaciated Herero and 2,000 Nama were taken prisoner.[4]

Sending sick people to labour camps was a death sentence. The work was arduous in the extreme, the food meagre, and medical supplies non-existent. By 1907 the Germans reported that over half the 15,000 Herero and 2,000 Nama prisoners had died in the camps. When a census was taken in 1911, only half the Nama estimated a decade before (9,800 out of 20,000) and less than a quarter of the original number of Herero (15,000 out of 80,000) were found to have survived the war.

Seventy-five per cent of the entire Nama and Herero population had died. Trotha's extermination order was almost fulfilled. South-West Africa was a defeated and vacant land—ripe for German settlers and the entrenchment of German influence which persists even since the country became the independent nation of Namibia in 1990.

ON A MORNING LATE IN July 1905, men from the village of Nandete in the Matumbi Hills, about 200 kilometres south of Dar es Salaam in the then German East Africa, climbed the stony path towards the cotton-fields. The cotton was ripening well after the rains, but the men were dissatisfied. Two elders, Ngulumbalyo Mandai and Lindimyo Machela, stepped forward and with symbolic deliberation wrenched three plants from the ground. This was a declaration of war against the German Empire.[5]

One of the aims of German colonization in East Africa had been to provide Germany with a reliable source of raw cotton. Cotton did eventually become Tanganyika's second most important export crop (after sisal),[6] with production based around the shores of Lake Victoria. Early attempts to grow the crop were concentrated in the coastal regions, however, where villagers were ordered to establish communal plots on which each adult male would work for a set number of days each year under the authority of an appointed headman. By the beginning of the 1904–5 season, some 4,000 hectares of communal plots (ranging from about one to fourteen hectares in size) had been laid out and an estimated 160,000 men were under obligation to work on the cotton plots.[7]

The idea had been that the headman, the workers, and the *Kommunalverband* (the European-controlled district development committee) would receive one-third of the market price for their crop. But the payments received by the workers were derisory or non-existent while the demand for their labour mounted. Large numbers of workers refused to accept the miserly thirty-five cents each was offered for their first year's work. For many there was no payment at all the following year while the demand for labour in the cotton-fields increased everywhere and even doubled in some instances. Villagers became convinced "that the government had devised a new means of obliging [them] to carry out a hated task for nothing."[8] Defections were widespread, not simply because the demands of the cotton-fields were financially unrewarding, but also because the concept of communal cultivation itself was an anathema to the people of the Matumbi Hills. Interviewed in the Dar es Salaam gaol (where he had been confined for his failings on the cotton scheme), headman Pazi Kitoweo explained that his people "would pay hut tax and also clear roads, but they would not work on communal plots."[9]

The people of the Matumbi Hills (and the southern region in general) were what anthropologists call an acephalous group—literally meaning "headless"—without a recognized leader or chief. Each household was independent and responsible for its own affairs, and linked to the group as a whole only by language, kinship, and trading or barter ties, and their beliefs. Among the last, a belief in the power of the spirit world was common to villagers throughout the region, and for months a prophet named Kinjikitile Ngwale had been spreading abroad his vision of a spiritual force that would enable the people to drive the Germans from their country. Kinjikitile lived at Ngarambe, on the western slopes of the Matumbi Hills, and was said to be possessed by the snake spirit, Hongo, who in turn served Bokero, a highly venerated deity.

It was said that "Hongo was to Bokero as Jesus is to God," which lent considerable strength to Kinjikitile's contentions. As disaffection with the German regime mounted, people flocked to the huge spirit-hut he had constructed, where his preachings welded local beliefs in divinity, possession, and medicines into a new dynamic that promised the people unity, leadership, and protection. He distributed a medicine—*maji* (water)—which, he said, would turn German bullets to water. By combining territorial authority and divine possession in this way, Kinjikitile created a cult with exactly the qualities needed to inspire widespread popular rebellion. Unite and drive out the Germans was this prophet's message.[10]

Kinjikitile took the title Bokero and employed assistants called *hongo*. He sent agents to command each area and by mid-1905 his secret mass movement had united supporters throughout the Matumbi Hills and a considerable distance beyond. The elders of Nandete were awaiting his word that day late in July, when the headman ordered them to carry his tax chest to Kilwa. Patience snapped. Without waiting to consult Kinjikitile they uprooted the cotton plants and sounded the war drums. The *Maji-Maji* rebellion had begun.

The Germans were taken completely by surprise. Their patrols were attacked, civilians murdered, and for a month it seemed that Kinjikitile's prophecy had come true. The Germans were driven from the Matumbi Hills and neighbouring Kichi, their bullets seemingly as ineffective as water. Kinjikitile was quickly captured and hanged, but his defiant cry from the scaffold, claiming that the *hongo* had already taken *maji* to Kilosa in the heart of the country, and to Mahenge, the main German garrison in the southern Highlands, was no empty boast.

Rebellion erupted throughout the region. People joined the movement firmly believing "that the maji from Ngarambe could liquify a German bullet." "This is not war. We shall not die. We shall only kill," a leader told his men. The *maji* united even formerly antagonistic groups. "Truly we were firmly united," a participant later recalled. "There was no tribalism in obeying the leaders."[11]

The terrible truth of the *maji* was revealed at Mahenge on 30 August 1905, when two large columns—composed of several different groups—advanced on the garrison, each led by a *hongo* armed only with a millet stalk.[12] "All those who took the *maji* united as if they were of one clan," it was remembered. Provided they did not turn their backs, they were assured, German bullets could not harm them. A mission worker described the attack and its outcome:

> Two machine guns, Europeans, and soldiers rained death and destruction among the ranks of the advancing enemy. Although we saw the ranks thin, the survivors maintained order for about a quarter of an hour, marching closer amidst a hail of bullets. But then the ranks broke apart and took cover behind numerous small rocks ... Then suddenly the cry rang out: "New enemy on the Gambira [eastern] side!" Everyone looked in that direction, and there ... a second column of at least 1,200 men was advancing towards us. Fire was opened on them immediately. The enemy sought to reach Mahenge village at the double. There they were hidden by the houses and stormed up the road towards the boma. As soon as they reappeared within range they were met by deafening fire. The first attackers were only three paces from the firing line when they sank to the ground, struck down by deadly bullets ... When no more enemy could be seen, the Station Commander climbed down from the top of the boma tower ... and distributed champagne.[13]

Despite the failure of the *maji* at Mahenge, the rebellion continued. At its height, over twenty different ethnic groups were involved[14] throughout the central and southern region, launching guerrilla-style attacks on German outposts and supply lines. The Germans shipped in reinforcements. Even so, they could not crush the movement by direct military means and ultimately resorted to more underhand tactics. Governor von Götzen concluded that a famine would flush out the more intransigent rebels. His military commander agreed:

"Only hunger and want can bring about a final submission. Military actions alone will remain more or less a drop in the ocean."[15]

Accordingly, three columns advanced through the region, pursuing a scorched-earth policy—creating famine. People were forced from their homes, villages were burned to the ground; food crops that could not be taken away or given to loyal groups were destroyed. Leaders of the rebellion and suspected collaborators were captured, shot, or hanged—the last of them on 18 July 1908, almost three years to the day since the men of Nandete had uprooted the cotton.

Official German reports state that 75,000 people died in the crushing of the rebellion, but testimonies and other evidence collected in the 1960s suggest that in fact between 250,000 and 300,000 people died (perhaps one-third of the area's total population), most of them from starvation. In return the rebels killed fifteen Europeans and 389 Africans attached to the German forces.[16]

Paraphrasing Tacitus' verdict on the Roman warfare in Germany, a commentator wrote that "the Germans in East Africa made a solitude and called it peace."[17] The *Maji-Maji* districts were at peace again, but it was the peace of the wilderness. Survivors attempting to re-establish themselves in the region found it transformed, with forest encroaching on the village sites and game reoccupying previously cultivated land. More ominously, the tsetse fly was there too. In fact, what rinderpest had done for pastoralists in other parts of Africa, war and famine did for agriculturists in the southern regions of German East Africa. Vast areas of their homeland were uninhabitable; from its midst the British colonial administration carved out the world's largest game park—the Selous. "The people of southern Tanganyika had lost not only a hope of regaining freedom. They had lost a battle in their long war with nature."[18]

GERMANY'S COLONIAL WHITE-ON-BLACK AGGRESSION notwithstanding, the Anglo-Boer War of 1899–1902 had exposed Africans to the spectacle of Europeans fighting one another more than a decade before Major H.G. von Doering, the Governor of German Togo, made his pious plea that Togo should be declared neutral in the First World War. Of course, the Anglo-Boer War was confined to South Africa, but its consequences in terms of modern warfare were profound enough to reverberate throughout the continent and, indeed, the world.

The Anglo-Boer War was a rehearsal for the First World War and beyond, imposing the primacy of the military-industrial complex upon national economies, demonstrating how a nation's industry and manpower could be mobilized on a huge scale to fight abroad, and refining the tactical horrors of twentieth-century warfare: the machine-gun, barbed wire, trenches, concentration camps . . .

The war was provoked by British attempts to break the Boer stranglehold on development of the gold-mining industry in the Transvaal. By the late 1890s, a dependable flow of South African gold had become fundamental to London's new-found status as the financial capital of the world. In Pretoria, however, gold-mining was viewed from a different perspective. President Kruger and his government saw the presence of gold beneath the veld as an endowment which should serve primarily the interests of the Afrikaner farming community, not international financiers. The industry was therefore controlled by the state on that basis—as a source of tax and customs revenue, with little or no incentive offered for further development.

With the connivance of the British government, Cecil Rhodes had attempted to provoke an insurrection in 1895 (the notorious Jameson Raid)[19] that would overthrow the Transvaal government from within. Its failure hardened the Boer position in subsequent diplomatic attempts to resolve the impasse, leaving the Pretoria government (with the support of the Orange Free State republic) no alternative but to go to war for the right to control the Transvaal's gold-mining industry.

Hostilities opened in October 1899. Both sides believed the war would be over by Christmas. In the event it dragged on until the last day of May 1902. Britain mobilized a total of 448,000 men during that time, of whom 22,000 died (13,250 from disease);[20] in monetary terms, victory cost the British taxpayer £222 million. The Boers mobilized 88,000 men (including overseas volunteers and colonial rebels) and lost over 7,000 dead. The conflict laid waste to large areas of the conquered Boer states, left the Boers in penury, but forged an Afrikaner nation strong enough to win the peace.[21]

The war had opened conventionally enough, with the Boers engaging British forces on several fronts and laying siege to towns in the Cape and Natal. After rushing in reinforcements, the British responded with counterattacks which rapidly advanced to capture Bloemfontein (the Orange Free State capital) in March, Johannesburg in May and Pretoria in early June 1900. In September Britain formally annexed the Transvaal.

The war seemed all but won. President Kruger left the country via Mozambique for Switzerland (where he died four years later), but the surviving Boer commanders were not ready to give up. They resorted to guerrilla tactics, deploying their forces in small mounted units which could evade capture while continuing to harass the British army by attacking supply lines, disorganizing communications, and sometimes inflicting quite startling casualties on the army of occupation.

Stung by the prospect of an interminable guerrilla war, the British erected nearly 6,000 kilometres of barbed-wire barricades and installed armed Africans in a total of 8,000 blockhouses guarding the lines. This was intended to limit the mobility of the Boer units. To reduce their operational efficiency still further, the British commander, Lord Kitchener, ordered that the farmhouses of combatant Boers should be burned, their crops destroyed, their livestock removed, and their families herded into concentration camps.

By October 1901 the population of the concentration camps stood at 111,619.[22] Conditions were appalling, lacking even the minimal requirements of clean water, food, and shelter that are essential to survival. Typhoid, dysentery, and measles were rampant, nursing care totally inadequate. Between June 1901 and May 1902, 27,927 Boer refugees perished in the British concentration camps, a death toll that amounted to twice the number of men killed in action on both sides, and represented perhaps 10 per cent of the Boer population of the two republics. More than 22,000 of the victims were children under the age of sixteen; more than 4,000 were adult women.[23]

The hardships suffered by Boer civilians in the concentration camps aroused a storm of criticism, around which opposition to the war crystallized. In Britain, Lloyd George, leader of the parliamentary opposition, likened Kitchener's tactics to those of Herod, who had also "attempted to crush a little race by killing its young sons and daughters."[24]

The deaths, hardship, and humiliation suffered by women and children in British concentration camps during the Anglo-Boer War are etched deep in the collective memory of the Afrikaner people. Like the Battle of Blood River (see page 489), the loss and grief became a crucial element of the Afrikaners' belief in a God-given right to exist which they exercised with such wilful power during the later part of the twentieth century.

The story of Afrikaner suffering during the Anglo-Boer War is relatively well known. That indigenous blacks suffered no less severely is hardly known at all. At the outbreak of war, both parties had tacitly agreed to refrain "from involving the African peoples in their fighting, except as unarmed servants and scouts and, on the British side, as guards." It was to be a white man's war. But in a country where blacks outnumbered whites by a ratio of four to one, it was hardly possible that the black population could be mere spectators, unaffected by three years of devastation and waste.

In fact, the effects of the war rippled through the entire subcontinent. Thousands of men were thrown out of work by the suspension of production in many mines, and by the dislocation of the migrant labour system that followed. Rural communities, whose self-sufficiency already had been subverted by the labour demands of the mining industry, were now obliged to support large numbers of returning miners, on whose wages they had come to depend. Blacks became embroiled, often involuntarily, in some of the most celebrated episodes of the war, such as the sieges of Mafeking, Kimberley, and Ladysmith. More than 100,000 were directly involved as scouts, spies, guards, servants, and messengers for the white armies and, despite protestations to the contrary, at least 10,000 and possibly as many as 30,000 blacks were fighting with the British as armed combatants by the end of the war.[25]

Nor did blacks escape the effects of Kitchener's "scorched earth" policy. Indeed, more blacks were rounded up and incarcerated in concentration camps than whites; and more of them died. Though the records are often incomplete, it is clear that at least 115,700 Africans had been sent to the camps by the end of May 1902, of whom 14,154 died.[26]

Throughout it all, however, the war generated a mood of optimistic expectation among many blacks. The early military successes of the British, and their rapid annexations of the Orange Free State and the Transvaal, encouraged a belief that a new future was dawning, one in which black interests would be safeguarded and their status and influence in South African society progressively advanced.[27]

In the Boer republics especially, a black elite was convinced that British victory would be followed by an extension of political, educational, and commercial opportunities for blacks. Expectations had been raised by British hints that the limited political rights enjoyed by blacks in the Cape (where men of any origin could vote provided they owned property) would be extended to the former republics. Some even believed that the object of the war was to expel the Boers from their farms and return the land to its original African occupants. In anticipation of this happy outcome, enterprising individuals actually moved on to some of the farms which Kitchener's men had forced Afrikaners to vacate. They rebuilt the homes, planted crops, established gardens, and generally prospered from the rise in market prices which the war brought in its wake.

Not surprisingly, difficulties arose when Boers returned to their farms after the cessation of hostilities. In some districts the new occupants refused to leave. Returning to his farm in the Vryheid district, even Louis Botha, former Commandant-General of Boer forces in the Transvaal and the man who signed the peace agreement, was run off his own land by former tenants shouting that he "had no business there, and . . . had better leave."[28]

The truth of the matter was contained in the formal Peace of Vereeniging that was signed in Pretoria on 31 May 1902. Amid undertakings concerning the repatriation of prisoners, amnesties, the protection of the Dutch language in the courts, economic safeguards, relief for the victims of war, and the promise of eventual self-government, Clause Eight resolved that no decision would be taken on the question of extending political rights to blacks until self-government had been restored to the former republics.

Clause Eight of the Peace of Vereeniging effectively postponed the introduction of a non-racial franchise indefinitely, casting aside British hints of reform. Left to their own devices neither British settlers nor Afrikaner farmers would voluntarily grant political rights to blacks in the Transvaal and the Orange Free State.

Far from improving the lot of South Africa's black population, the end of the war brought only the disillusion of unfulfilled expectation. For every £4 sterling officially assessed as war compensation to Africans in the Transvaal, for instance, only £1 was ever paid out. Boer farmers, on the other hand, not only received more generous compensation, but were also given legal title to their lands and access to agricultural credits that enabled them to introduce advanced farming technology.

Furthermore, the discriminatory legislation which Africans had hoped to see abolished was largely retained by the British and in some instances even reinforced and extended after the war. State control over workers was intensified and wages in the mining industry reduced. Indeed, Britain's overriding objective was to return the gold-mining industry to full production and to create the conditions necessary to improve the industry's productivity.[29] Britain set out to create a modernized state compatible with the needs of mining capital, and this was to be the most enduring legacy of the period.

Writing in December 1900, as British military successes were raising African hopes, a prescient contributor to an African newspaper warned:

> At the end of the war the whites will all unite to formulate some scheme by which they may make the native industrious . . . and though we are rejoicing over the defeat of the Boers, the truth is that it will be fortunate for us if for three years we obtain the same wages from the English as we got in the past at Johannesburg.[30]

SHORTLY AFTER BRITAIN had declared war against Germany in August 1914, a Foreign Office memorandum noted that "we want as many German colonies as we can get to use as pawns when negotiating peace terms."[31] With such views circulating in Europe, von Doering, the Governor of German Togo, had little chance of receiving an agreeable response to his appeal that Togo should remain neutral. In fact, British forces in the Gold Coast were mobilized four days *before* the British declaration of war. Indeed, the first shots of the First World War were fired in the Anglo-French invasion of Togo which began shortly thereafter,[32] and the surrender of German forces on 26 August 1914 was the first allied victory.

By the time of the armistice in November 1918, more than 2 million Africans had contributed directly to the European war effort, either as soldiers or as porters and labourers; more than 200,000 gave their lives.[33] From a continent-wide population of about 130 million the figures seem low when compared with allied and German losses that amounted to millions of deaths, but for the population of a continent only marginally involved with the politics of the conflict the impact was widespread, deep, and enduring.

There was some strategic justification for the allies to carry Europe's war to Africa—in military terms it was important that Germany's offensive capacity should be disabled—but territorial aggrandisement provided an additional incentive.

Apart from the negotiating pawns mentioned above, Britain also made a secret deal with Italy, agreeing that her entry into the war on the allied side would be rewarded with British support for an extension of Italian territories in Africa.[34] Belgium, although at first keen to invoke the perpetual neutrality of the Congo under Article Ten of the Berlin Act, eagerly seized upon German transgressions as an excuse to join in the invasion of German territory, hoping to secure a good bargaining position in the peace settlement. The French invasion of Cameroon likewise was inspired in no small part by a determination to retrieve territory reluctantly ceded to Germany in 1911, and South Africa joined the allied cause (defying rabid Afrikaner support for Germany) in the hopes of securing South-West Africa as a fifth province.

German ports at Lomé in Togo, Douala in Cameroon, Swakopmund and Lüderitz in South-West Africa were occupied soon after the outbreak of war. In East Africa, Dar es Salaam and Tanga were bombarded by British cruisers and thus rendered unavailable to German ships (though neither port was actually taken until later in the war).

The strategic phase of the war in Africa was thus completed in a matter of weeks, and the first stages of the territorial phase also proceeded rapidly, with Togo taken in August 1914, and South-West Africa capitulating after a three-month campaign launched by South African forces in 1915. The campaign in Cameroon took until early 1916 to achieve success, but it was in East Africa that operations were most protracted. Indeed, General Paul von Lettow-Vorbeck and the German East African forces kept the allies engaged throughout the war, and did not abandon the cause until three days after the armistice had been signed in Europe, when they surrendered in north-eastern Rhodesia.[35]

Like the allies, Germany had expected to use the war in Europe as an excuse to secure territorial gains in Africa. Early defeats eliminated all hope of that but, in East Africa at least, German forces remained active for the duration of the war, obliging the allies to keep troops and resources in Africa that might otherwise have been deployed on the European front. Lettow-Vorbeck fought an astute guerrilla campaign. It was "an ice-cream war,"[36] with German forces melting away whenever threatened by opposing forces. In this way, Lettow-Vorbeck managed to keep some 160,000 allied troops engaged with a force which never exceeded 15,000 men.

The men deployed in Africa by both the allies and German forces were overwhelmingly African. Only in South-West Africa were they excluded from the campaigns, and this was only because the South African generals were reluctant to arm their African population, and the Germans dared not, after having so brutally repressed the Herero and Nama rebellions. Elsewhere, Ghanaians and Dahomeans fought the Togolese; Nigerians fought the Cameroonians; West Africans were shipped around the continent to join Kenyans fighting in German East Africa.

Over 1 million African troops were recruited during the war; in addition, carriers were required on a massive scale—up to three for every soldier in the field.[37] In the early stages of the war recruitment was largely voluntary, or organized by chiefs who were instructed to deliver the numbers required of them by the local District Officer. In the British colonies, military bands were used to attract potential recruits, who were often enticed to join by "big promises, free food, fine uniforms" and all the trappings which African young men might never again have the chance to grasp.[38]

"Many people went off to fight" believing theirs would be an easy task, an East African veteran recalled. "Many people were dying, but they used to speak . . . as if nobody was dying in the war."[39] When the truth filtered back to the villages, voluntary recruitment became a thing of the past, and the authorities resorted to a harsher means of maintaining the supply of manpower.

In French West Africa, where all African males between the ages of twenty and twenty-eight were already obliged to do four years compulsory military service, there was a standing army of 14,785 men at the outbreak of war. During 1915–16 the authorities ordered the recruitment of an additional 50,000 men, and thus began what has been described as a *véritable chasse à l'homme,* and "a new slave trade." Chiefs given quotas to fill rounded up strangers and former slaves, to avoid enlisting their immediate dependants or kinsmen, and since few could prove their date of birth, many men above and below military age were forcibly recruited.[40]

Similarly, when incentives failed to attract volunteers to the war effort in Mozambique, "all able-bodied men in some regions were simply seized, bound, and hauled off either to labour or to fight."[41] In the Congo, up to 260,000 porters were impressed by the Belgians during the East African campaign. In Northern Rhodesia, forced recruitment of porters meant that for a large part of the war over one-third of all adult males in the territory were engaged on carrier service. In British East Africa, an ordinance of 1915 made all males between the ages of eighteen and forty-five liable for military service.[42]

More than 50,000 African troops and over 1 million carriers were deployed during the East Africa campaign alone, of whom more than 100,000 died.[43] During the latter part of the war, as allied losses in Europe mounted to horrific dimensions, the British War Office secretly requested 6,000 East and West African troops to be used as supply companies on the Western Front. The request was rejected. African troops might be deployed in the Middle East, the Colonial Office conceded, "but *not* against German troops in Europe."[44]

The French government entertained no such compunction. By the end of the war, the French colonies in Africa had sent 450,000 soldiers (50,000 from Algeria) to fight in Europe, and the minister responsible boasted that the numbers could have been "easily trebled or quadrupled" if African recruitment had begun sooner.[45] When the fighting was over, France even contributed African troops to the army of occupation in the Rhineland. Many Germans were outraged. Years later, Hitler wrote in *Mein Kampf* of France's attempt at "contamination by Negro blood on the Rhine," arousing fears that the Rhineland might become "the hunting ground of African Negro hordes."[46]

THE HISTORY BOOKS MAY AROUSE admiration for some strategic decision, or horror at some tactical blunder; the novels can conjure up a tingle of excitement, but it is the numbers that constitute the most telling and durable evocations of the war. They are impossible to forget.

A survey of the First World War and its consequences in Africa concluded that more than 2.5 million Africans, or nearly 2 per cent of the population of the continent, were involved in war work of some kind. "The slave trade at its height never reached a tenth of the numbers involved in any one year."[47] It was a war that Africa had done nothing to provoke and from which Africa had nothing to gain. For every African that was directly involved with the war, another dozen of his kin—men, women, and children—were affected by it. And this so soon after the traumas of drought and rinderpest, tsetse fly and disease that had accompanied the upheavals of colonization. Surely, now, at last, Africa deserved some time at peace.

On Sunday mornings, Witwatersrand gold-mine labourers perform a
programme of "native" dances for visitors to the mines

CHAPTER 51

The Invention of Africa

BETWEEN THE FIRST AND THE SECOND WORLD WARS, colonial governments accepted more responsibility for the welfare of the African colonies than ever before. Establishing effective administrations tacitly amounted to redefining the continent, however. The constantly changing institutions of non-literate societies were set in the written word of law; origin myths were transformed into tribal histories; socioeconomic distinctions made one tribe better than another.

Peace. After the centuries of cruel travail which culminated with the ravages of the First World War, the 1920s did indeed bring a semblance of peace to Africa, permeating the history books and contemporary accounts of the period with a sense of a continent resting; its human population exhausted but recuperating, and preparing to pick up the pieces and build a history of its own. Of course, this impression may be only a reaction to the apparently unending litany of distress that went before. Certainly, oppressive regimes of forced labour, famine, and untimely death continued during the 1920s and '30s, but not even the most avid anti-colonialist could deny that many parts of Africa enjoyed a period of continuous peace and security once the First World War was over and the various colonial administrative systems began functioning more effectively.[1]

Peace was secured by the new map of Africa. The colonial partition had simplified political relationships on the continent. Where formerly there had been hundreds of independent clans and lineages, putative city states, kingdoms and empires with shifting and indeterminate frontiers, there were now just fifty or so states with fixed boundaries and capital cities. The colonial boundaries divided many communities (see page 575), sacrificing their liberties and rights to the "dead hand of colonialism and international law,"[2] it is true, but whatever the iniquities of the colonial boundaries, they also contributed to peace on the continent. Virtually all the wars that have flared up in Africa since the colonial period have been fought within national boundaries, not across them.

Peace and security greatly facilitated economic activity and social and physical mobility within each colony, stimulating a diffusion of new ideas, new techniques, new tastes and new fashions which accelerated the pace of modernization throughout the continent. Each colonial government introduced a judicial system based on European law (complete with wig and gown in the British colonies), and established a civil administration. Furthermore, the establishment of an economic base in the colonies, plus famine relief and campaigns against epidemic diseases, stimulated a 37.5 per cent increase in the population of Africa (from 120 million to 165 million) between 1880 and 1935, despite a net loss during the early colonial period.[3]

Prior to 1914, it was primarily the fortune-seeking speculator who was attracted to the idea of investing large amounts of capital in Africa. After 1918, by which time many ambitious dreams had turned into expensive nightmares and speculators had woken up to the realities of African economics, the colonial governments were obliged to accept responsibility for the welfare and development of their African colonies, though enthusiasm for the undertaking was not widespread at a time when Europe itself was struggling to repair the devastations of war.

The overriding priority of governments was to make the African colonies economically self-supporting, which meant developing export trade, and the prospects were not encouraging. In 1913, for example, Africa as a whole had accounted for about 7 per cent and 10 per cent respectively of the external trade (excluding gold) of Britain and France. But most trade had been with South Africa, Egypt, and Algeria. Tropical Africa had accounted for less than 2 per cent of Britain's trade, and less than 1 per cent of that of France. The Belgian Congo in 1912 had contributed only 1 per cent of Belgian trade, and in 1910 Germany's African colonies had accounted for less than 1 per cent of Germany's external trade.[4] Clearly, achieving economic self-sufficiency in the colonies would be a long haul, twenty to thirty years in most cases, with deficits in the meantime supported by imperial grants-in-aid, grudgingly given.[5]

But the obligation was inescapable. The mandates under which the League of Nations had assigned the German territories in Africa to the colonial powers after the First World War stipulated that they should be governed as "a sacred trust of civilization" until they were able "to stand on their own feet in the arduous conditions of the modern world."[6] In other words, the colonial powers must not merely govern, but must also develop the colonies into functioning members of the world community—economically and politically—according to the prevailing capitalist model of the nation state.

Viewed with hindsight, the paternalistic conceit of the colonial authorities is breathtaking. Africa was looked upon as the neglected child of the modern world, who must be nurtured and "civilized" as a child is reared to adulthood. And the men (always men) performing this task were the product of an educational system that considered itself supremely suited for the job. The headmaster of Harrow (second only to Eton in the British educational hierarchy) declared that:

> An English headmaster, as he looks to the future of his pupils, will not forget that they are destined to be citizens of the greatest empire under heaven; he will teach them patriotism . . . He will inspire them with faith in the divinely ordained mission of their country and their race.[7]

Edward Lumley, who spent twenty-two years delivering Britain's "divinely ordained mission" to the people of Tanganyika between 1923 and 1945, has noted: "The District Commissioner had to be a man of many parts." To qualify for the post he had to have an honours degree from a good university (most came from Oxford or Cambridge, or Trinity College Dublin, in Lumley's day) and was also expected to have some kind of athletic record. "Bookworms were not considered good material for a job that called for great physical endurance."

During the course of up to ten years in junior positions the aspirant District Commissioner was required to become fluent in the native language of the territory and to pass an examination in the criminal code. On appointment, he became the de facto ruler of his domain. He tried all court cases that were within his capacity as magistrate and occasionally was given extended jurisdiction by the High Court. He advised the tribal chiefs on political matters, supervised their administrative functions, and checked the finances of the native treasuries.

"The D.C. was also responsible for the economic well-being of his Africans," Lumley wrote in his memoir published in 1976.[8]

> He had to see that they planted enough food crops for their needs. He also had to assist them with advice as to the best means of earning the money to pay their taxes. This might take the form of encouraging them to plant cot-

ton or coffee, or even [as Lumley once did] instruct them on preparing beeswax and extracting it from the hives of the wild bees.

The colonial assumption of superior knowledge in all things was based first on the convictions of late-nineteenth-century Europe, and second on the belief that Africa had had no history or culture worthy of the name until the European colonizers accepted the "sacred trust of civilization."

It was not without consequence that "the European movement into Africa coincided with the nineteenth- and twentieth-century peak of racism and cultural chauvinism in Europe itself."[9] The combined achievements of commerce, Christianity, and military force had given Europe a very high opinion of itself, which even some scientific thinking was persuaded to support. Social Darwinism put Europeans at the top of the evolutionary ladder; Africans were close to the bottom, a rung or two above the inhabitants of Tierra del Fuego and Tasmania. Authoritative history books disseminated the view that

> the main body of the Africans, the Negro peoples who remained in their tropical homeland between the Sahara and the Limpopo, had . . . no history. They had stayed, for untold centuries, sunk in barbarism. Such, it might almost seem, had been nature's decree . . . So they remained stagnant, neither going forward nor going back. Nowhere in the world, save perhaps in some miasmic swamps of South America or in some derelict Pacific Islands, was human life so stagnant. The heart of Africa was scarcely beating.[10]

Given that Africa was assumed to have had no history before the arrival of the Europeans, it is hardly an exaggeration to say that Europe *created* the image of Africa that the colonial period bequeathed to the world. Having drawn the boundaries of nation states and undertaken to establish a civilizing government in each, with hierarchical administration and military support, Africa and the lives of its inhabitants were restructured to fit the European idea of how it should be.

In their efforts to establish nationwide government, colonial administrators effectively "set about inventing African traditions for Africans" that would make the process more acceptable to the indigenous population.[11] Kingship was a classic example. Africa possessed dozens of rudimentary kings (or so the colonizers believed), and the "theology" of an omniscient, omnipotent, and omnipresent "Imperial Monarchy" readily took root in the British colonies.[12] The Kaiser acquired similar status in the German colonies. Faced with the more difficult task of incorporating Africans into a republican tradition, the French abolished kingship in their territories and invited Africans to declare their allegiance to the motherland, La France.

The nation state itself was still a relatively recent phenomenon when the colonizing process got under way. Likewise, the traditions of king and country, of church, school, and regiment, were also artefacts of European social restructuring of the late nineteenth century. But the First World War had given all these things a patina of use that was readily interpreted as a sign of enduring antiquity. Respect for the traditional was probably at its height in the aftermath of the war, and the colonizers were predisposed to look favourably upon whatever they took to be traditional in Africa. They began to codify and promulgate the traditions they identified.

Between 1905 and 1914 about eighty books on African ethnography had been published in Europe;[13] most were devoted to particular groups and written by serving administrators. During that same period, Germany had sponsored ten ethnographic expeditions which visited most parts of tropical Africa. The Belgians had sponsored a study of the Zande (in the south-western Sudan), and Belgian sociologists had devised a questionnaire to elicit a series of ethnographies from missionaries and others. The British had also been active. The Sudan government had commissioned ethnographic surveys from C.G. Seligman (who subsequently became professor of ethnology in London) in 1909–12, and the Colonial Office had appointed Northcote Thomas to make a series of ethnographic studies in southern Nigeria and Sierra Leone. An expedition to the Congo by the Hungarian Emil Torday in 1907–9 had been made at the behest of the British Museum (whose ethnographic collections had been compared unfavourably with those of the Berlin Museum). In French West Africa a number of officials had made a speciality of ethnographic studies, and in 1917 a committee for historical and scientific studies in the French territories was established in Dakar.[14]

In the post–First World War years, African studies moved on from the mere recording of "primitive" peoples and their physical characteristics to the study of their institutions, customs, beliefs and modes of livelihood. In British West Africa three "government anthropologists," R.S. Rattray, C.K. Meek and P.A. Talbot, were appointed to make studies in the Gold Coast, Nigeria and Central Africa respectively. On a more purely academic level, Bronislaw Malinowski, whose work among Pacific islanders had pioneered a new concept of field work, was a formative influence on the study E.E. Evans-Pritchard was to make of the Nuer people in the Sudan; linguists investigated the grammatical structure and phonetics of African languages; agricultural experts assessed African food-production capabilities.

Collectively, administrators and academics identified the "traditions" of social practice which supposedly distinguished one group from another and drew lines on maps which assigned each group to a particular territory. They wrote down names and addresses and dates of birth, and set in print the laws by which people must conduct their lives.

In this way literacy transformed the flexibility of customary practice into hard, immutable, prescriptive law. Customary law had always taken contemporary assessments into account when making its judgements, but once a particular set of interpretations was codified in colonial law it became rigid and unable to reflect change in the future. In land-tenure disputes, for instance, "colonial officers expected the courts to enforce long-established custom rather than current opinion."[15] Common official stereotypes about African customary land law thus came to be used by colonial officials in assessing the legality of current decisions, and so came to be incorporated in "customary" systems of tenure.

The most far-reaching inventions of tradition in colonial Africa probably occurred precisely when European administrators believed they were respecting age-old African custom, whereas "What were called customary law, customary land-rights, customary political structure and so on, were in fact *all* invented by colonial codification."[16]

The colonizers claimed that they were merely confirming the significance of existing traditions, but traditions in Africa (and everywhere else for that matter) are merely accepted modes of behaviour that currently function to the benefit of society as a whole. They persist so long as their benefit is evident, and fade away when it is not. No tradition lasts for ever. Change and adaptability is the very essence of human existence—nowhere more so than in Africa. The paradox is painfully evident: by creating an image of Africa steeped in unchanging tradition, the colonizers condemned the continent to live in a reconstructed moment of its past, complete with natives in traditional dress, wild animals, and pristine landscapes. The paradox could not stand unresolved for ever, but it hindered development for decades.

TRIBALISM IS THE MOST PERNICIOUS of the traditions which the colonial period bequeathed to Africa. The word "tribe" has been in use since Roman times, when it referred to any one of the three families that originally lived in Rome, but the Oxford English Dictionary asserts that the word "tribalism" was coined only in 1886, in a reference claiming that "no national life, much less civilisation, was possible under the system of Celtic tribalism." Be that as it may, any reference to tribalism in the twentieth century immediately brings Africa to mind.

There are ethnic groups living in close proximity in other parts of the world who are highly antagonistic towards one another—the Serbs and the

Croats, the Israelis and the Palestinians—but their aggressions are attributed more readily to religion than to tribal differences. Tribalism, by contrast, has a distinctly dark and nasty African connotation: the Maasai and the Kikuyu in Kenya; the Zulu and the Xhosa in South Africa; the Yoruba, Hausa, and Igbo in Nigeria; the Hutu and the Tutsi in Rwanda and Burundi. These and other groups have at times seemed determined to eliminate each other simply because they claimed differences of birthright.

But the different groups often have more in common than separates them. The Xhosa and Zulu languages, for instance, are 70 per cent concordant. "If they were writing sophisticated poetry maybe they would be unintelligible to one another," a linguist has remarked,[17] "but in general speech they can understand each other perfectly." Furthermore, the norms and values which govern the social interaction, marriage and family, and belief systems of the two groups are essentially the same.[18]

Research on Zulu ethnicity has shown the concept of the Zulu as a discrete ethnic group did not emerge until the 1870s.[19] This was the period when British forces were fighting Africans they identified as "Zooloos" in Natal, and it is not inconceivable that Xhosa identity may have been forged in similar fashion during the wars fought between settlers and Africans on the frontier of the Eastern Cape in the early decades of the nineteenth century.

In Kenya, the conviction that the Kikuyu and Maasai were sworn enemies, which had motivated a good deal of colonial policy, was a fiction, invented by the colonial administration for their own convenience.[20] There was sporadic fighting, but the Kikuyu fought among themselves as much as they fought with the Maasai. The Kikuyu traded with the Maasai, they intermarried and shared important aspects of social and ritual practice; the Kikuyu language is heavily indebted to Maasai, all the words relating to cattle, for instance, are taken from the Maasai. And even the word for God is shared: Ngai in Kikuyu; Nkai, or E'Ngai in Maasai.

In Nigeria, although broad cultural identities—pan-Igbo, pan-Hausa, and pan-Yoruba—had emerged before the missionaries and the British administration arrived to make their mark on the social landscape, they did not correspond to the colonial notion of static tribal identities. They were a reality, but they waxed and waned under changing conditions; they were units of inclusivity as often as of exclusivity, which embodied the notion of linguistic and cultural affinity rather than a rigid idea of shared descent.[21]

In Zambia, the chief of a little-known group once ventured to remark: "My people were not Soli until 1937 when the Bwana D.C. told us we were."[22] Indeed, *ethnic thinking*—that is, the perception of unity as the inevitable outcome of common origin—was rare in Africa (though not completely unknown) before it was applied by the colonial authorities.[23] Thus, ethnicity (meaning tribalism) was not a cultural characteristic that was deeply rooted in the African past; it was a consciously crafted ideological tradition that was introduced during the colonial present.[24]

Colonial policies in Tanganyika exemplified the belief that every African belonged to a tribe, just as every European belonged to a nation. Tribes were defined as cultural units, with a common language, a single social system, and established customary law. Tribal membership was hereditary, and different tribes were related genealogically, so that Africa's history could be looked upon as a huge family tree of tribes.[25] Since the incoming British administration was convinced that the Germans had completely destroyed all pre-existing African social systems, their British successors devoted considerable effort to identifying tribes and finding the chief. "Each tribe must be considered as a distinct unit . . . Each tribe must be under a chief," one provincial commissioner told his staff in 1926.[26]

These concepts bore little relation to Tanganyika's kaleidoscopic history, but they were the shifting sands on which the colonial administrators imposed a new political geography. And once the process was in motion, it was enthusiastically reinforced by the Africans themselves. They inhabited a world of social and economic uncertainty in which the invented histories offered at least a hope of order and continuity. Africans wanted effective units of action no less than the colonial administrators wanted effective units of government. And so, because "Europeans believed Africans belonged to tribes; Africans built tribes to belong to."[27]

And with the tribes came the chiefs. There were always individuals with personal motives for collaborating with the identification of tribal units that they could lead. Throughout Africa, tribal identities were catalysts which enabled ambitious individuals and groups to achieve positions of status, dominance, and wealth that might otherwise have been unattainable. Tribes became the franchise from which politicians launched the drive for national independence. Tribes were also an ideological refuge in times of stress—during famine, elections, or even in the matter of getting a job—when ethnic sentiment polarized into a sense of "them and us" that often erupted in bloodshed.

IT IS NO ACCIDENT that Rwanda and Burundi are the most densely populated countries in Africa. They are also the most fertile. Tucked away at the very heart of the continent, at elevations that average about 2,000 metres above sea level and enjoy copious rainfall on soils of volcanic origin, this is exceptionally good farming country. In 1993, Rwanda and Burundi supported

312 and 233 persons per square kilometre respectively.[28] Burundi in particular had a greater proportion of its land surface under permanent cultivation and pasture than any other country in Africa: 87 per cent. Rwanda had less, 59 per cent, but even that was equal to the proportion of arable and pasture land in the Netherlands, Europe's most densely populated nation (with 448 persons per square kilometre).[29]

Rwanda and Burundi were part of German East Africa until the end of the First World War. Neither territory had escaped the famine, rinderpest, and epidemics which ravaged tropical Africa at the end of the nineteenth century. Nor had they recovered fully when the Germans arrived to "pacify" the region and impose colonial rule, but both countries contained individuals and groups who were prepared to cooperate with the process in return for greater authority in local political and economic affairs.

German ethnographic researches in the early 1900s[30] reported that Ruanda–Urundi (as the territories were then known) was inhabited by three ethnic groups: the Twa, the Hutu, and the Tutsi. The Twa were pygmy hunters and gatherers who were thought to have been in the region since time immemorial; the Hutu were Bantu-speaking agriculturists who came later, and the Tutsi were pastoralists of Hamitic origin, they declared, who were assumed to have invaded Ruanda–Urundi sometime later still. The penetration of the Tutsi was said to have been a slow and peaceful process, during the course of which the Tutsi adopted the Bantu language of the Hutu (as had the Twa), so that all three groups spoke the same language, with only minor local modifications.

In appearance, however, the three groups were said to be strikingly different.[31] The Tutsi were reported to be tall, handsome, slender, and well-proportioned. The Twa were grotesque little creatures whom the Germans referred to as dwarfs. Between the two stood the stocky aboriginal Bantu, the Hutu. Though anthropologists have since shown that these physical characteristics are neither so general nor so sharply defined as described by the German ethnographers, they are persistently cited as fact.

The Tutsi comprised only about 12 to 15 per cent of the Ruanda–Urundi population, with the Hutu accounting for about 85 per cent (and the Twa making up the balance), but it was from among the Tutsi that the Germans sought collaborators to assist the colonization process.

The cattle culture, with its haughty conceit and dedication to the accumulation of wealth, gave the Tutsi an aristocratic demeanour with which the German colonizers readily identified. Their ethnographers were told that the Tutsi wielded almost total political and economic power over the Hutu (and of course the Twa), owning not only all the cattle but, theoretically at least, all the land as well. The countries were ruled by princes, *ganwa,* they learned, who were in turn answerable to the *mwami,* the absolute and semi-divine sovereign whose symbol of authority was a drum hung with the genitals of slaughtered enemies.[32]

The chiefs whom the Germans selected to hold positions of authority in the colonial administration were exclusively Tutsi.

The Germans were very impressed with the natural fertility of their jewel in the highlands of central Africa and its capacity to sustain large numbers of people, but their attempts to establish commercial crops such as cotton, tobacco, and rice were not a success. In 1913 Dr. Richard Kandt, the energetic senior administrator in Ruanda, decided that coffee would be the thing. Coffee, he said, grew well even on ground the Hutu considered uncultivable. Furthermore, coffee could be planted in the banana groves, where the soil was rich and moist and the bananas would provide protection from sun and wind. The cost of establishing the plantation would be high, he admitted in a lengthy memorandum.[33] But

> should we be frightened because of the high costs? Brazil was also not originally a coffee country, Ceylon not a tea country, and the Malay states not a rubber country. This last example shows how with favourable conditions a completely new productive character can be stamped rapidly on a country.

Kandt proposed that with a determined concentration of energy and effort, 1 million coffee trees could be planted in 1914, and increased by 1 million a year; by 1920 there would be 6 million coffee trees in Ruanda–Urundi, producing about 1 kg of coffee per tree. Ruanda–Urundi would become the coffee farm of Germany, he said. Ruanda and Urundi alone could meet German demands, with enough left over for the world market. The economy of German East Africa would be diversified, and the enormous labour potential of Ruanda–Urundi put to good use at last. Coffee was the German vision of Ruanda–Urundi's economic future. Like many other visions, it was shattered by the First World War.

BELGIAN FORCES INVADED RUANDA–Urundi from the Congo in April 1916, and occupied the territories for the remainder of the war. In the preliminary round of negotiations to determine the fate of the former German territories, Belgium let it be known that "she intend[ed] to derive from her considerable military effort in Africa as great a benefit as possible." Ruanda–Urundi was "fertile, rich in cattle, and favourable for white colonization" and the Belgians were not shy in acknowledging that they would use the territories they had occupied as a pawn to gain profit elsewhere—in either Europe or Africa.

What the Belgians wanted most was a slice of Angola bordering the south bank of the Congo River. The deals concluded at the Berlin conference of 1884–85 had denied Portugal sovereignty over the entire mouth of the river, and the Congo state had thus been guaranteed access to the Atlantic, along with a slender extension of territory bordered by Angola on one side and the Cabinda enclave on the other (see pages 541–42). "This compromise at the time seemed a victory," a Belgian diplomat subsequently noted, "not until later did we see its inconveniences."[34]

The inconveniences were exactly those of a property-owner whose gate and driveway are too narrow for all the traffic that requires access. Security was a problem too: the neighbours were simply too close for comfort; from their territory the vital river access could be severed with ease.

Acquiring the southern bank of the Congo would solve all these problems but, since a victory against Germany in Central Africa in no way constituted grounds for claiming reparations from Portugal, some bold—not to say devi-ous—negotiations were called for. In May 1919 Belgium proposed a three-way deal: Britain should take over Ruanda–Urundi from Belgium; Belgium should acquire the Congo south bank from Portugal; and Portugal should be given the south-east corner of German East Africa that Britain had conquered.

The British were embarrassed by the unashamedly acquisitive nature of the Belgian plans, but not averse to the suggestion that Ruanda–Urundi should become part of British East Africa. The first stage of the three-way deal was successfully accomplished when Ruanda–Urundi was formally ceded to Bel-gium by the Mandates Commission but, with the negotiating pawn firmly in hand, both British and Belgian expectations were scuppered by Portuguese intractability. The Portuguese could not be persuaded to exchange a slice of Angola for a chunk of the former German East Africa. Belgium was doubly afflicted by the outcome: she failed to ease the difficulties of access to the Atlantic, and she was burdened with the duty of governing Ruanda–Urundi as "a sacred trust of civilization" until the countries were able "to stand on their own feet in the arduous conditions of the modern world," as the League of Nations mandate stipulated.

Belgium's acquisition of Ruanda–Urundi was one of the greatest ironies in the history of Africa—and perhaps the greatest tragedy too. Belgian statesmen did not want the tiny landlocked territory—indeed, it could only add to their problems in the Congo—and they themselves admitted that the inhabitants would be better off if Ruanda–Urundi remained part of the former German

East Africa.[35] But this was Belgium's reward for victory. The green fertile hills, the tall slender Tutsi, the stocky Hutu and the dwarf-like Twa became Belgium's responsibility.

THE BELGIAN RESPONSE TO "civilization's sacred trust" concerning Ruanda–Urundi was to treat the territories as an extension of the Belgian Congo. The two tiny countries became economically subservient to the greedy monster on their western flank. There was no mineral wealth to be exploited in either Ruanda or Urundi, but high population densities made them a valuable labour pool for the copper mines in Katanga. In 1930, for example, more than 2 per cent of the entire able-bodied male population of Ruanda–Urundi was working in the Congo, most of them in Katanga.[36]

Those who remained behind had a yearly quota of compulsory unpaid labour to fulfil; "only" twenty-nine days, it is true, and supposedly (but not always) to be set against taxes. Much of the compulsory labour was applied to the cultivation of crops, but in a highland landscape where communications were rudimentary, much more was engaged in simply carrying the produce from rural areas to the distribution centres. Ruanda–Urundi's natural fertility and success with introduced crops such as beans, sweet potatoes, cassava, and potatoes made it the "breadbasket" of the Belgian Congo.

Coffee, the dream of Ruanda's last German administrator, was introduced to Ruanda–Urundi by the Belgians in 1925, beginning with an experimental "coffee programme" which obliged each chief and sub-chief to cultivate a half-hectare of the crop. Encouraging results led to the systematic extension of coffee-growing throughout the territory. Ruanda exported fifty tonnes of coffee in 1929, and had increased its annual output to 2,000 tonnes by 1937.

By the 1930s the cash economy was a fact of life throughout colonial Africa. Only the most destitute or isolated individuals could escape the necessity to earn money. Wherever privilege could grant favours, tribal affinities became important: people holding positions of power and authority were morally obliged to assist their kin. In Ruanda–Urundi, favour was disproportionately in the hands of the Tutsi, and colonial rule had eroded the reciprocal balance of their relationship with the Hutu (and the Twa) into what was essentially no more than a master–servant attitude.

Writing in 1931, after seventeen years of intimate contact with the Hutu and the Tutsi, a Belgian missionary concluded that the two groups shared a common culture.[37] Nonetheless, the minority group was more beneficially placed in the colonial hierarchy. And how could you tell them apart? Those at either end of the physical continuum—the stereotypically tall slender Tutsi and the short stocky Hutu—were easily identified, but between these extremes there were thousands, if not the majority of the population, whose physical appearance was no clue at all. Generations of intermarriage, migration, and changes in occupation and economic standing had blurred the tribal distinction. But no matter. In 1926 the Belgian authorities introduced an identity card to clarify the issue. By law, the card had to specify which tribe the holder belonged to. Where appearance was indecisive and proof of ancestry was lacking, a simple formula was applied: those with ten cows or more were classified as Tutsi, those with less were Hutu.[38]

PART 8

THE FIRST DANCE
OF FREEDOM

Schoolchildren in Lagos, Nigeria

CHAPTER 52

The Emergent Elite

EDUCATION STIMULATES PEOPLE "to want what they do not have."
In Africa, those whose aptitude qualified them for education to university level studied abroad, where contact with political activists taught
them to want independence for their countries. Their numbers were
small, but the gulf that education opened up between the elite and the
majority of Africans was very large indeed.

Taye Babaleye, a senior Administrative Officer at the International Institute of
Tropical Agriculture in Ibadan, Nigeria, remembers village life "as a kind of
paradise—a place where you felt that life was never going to end, but would
go on for ever" amid the forest trees, the gardens, the warmth, the rain, the
smell of damp earth, the comfort of family, and a sense of life without need.

But Taye's father had decided that his children would not remain tied to
the life of a village farmer as he had been. Education would be the means of
their escape. He vowed to send at least the first-born of each of his six wives to
secondary school. The cocoa and coffee trees he had planted would provide
the necessary cash, along with the proceeds of kola nuts and palm-oil collected
from the forest. And he succeeded—the first-born of his last wife was in the
third year when he died in 1976.

Education is widely respected in Africa. So much so among the Fang people of Gabon that parents who in the past would have dipped a spear in the
water which was used to wash a new-born son, began using a pencil instead.[1]

But while the pencil may indeed be mightier than the spear in the long term, the short-term effect of education in rural African communities was not wholly favourable: schools emptied the villages and filled the cities. At the end of each school year thousands of young able-bodied people left the sparsely populated regions where labour was short and moved to urban centres where jobs are scarce.

In the early 1970s, when the International Institute of Tropical Agriculture began operations at Ibadan with a brief to improve the utilization of available resources in tropical Africa, a survey found that educated people were a major export of the agricultural sector. Ninety-four per cent of children with no schooling stayed in their villages, but 84 per cent of primary-school leavers and 100 per cent of secondary-school graduates left for the urban centres. Of the secondary-school graduates, just 10 per cent moved on to higher education, 31 per cent became apprentices, skilled labourers or were self-employed, while the remainder—59 per cent—were either unskilled labourers or unemployed. "This out-migration of the educated from farm families represents a major export of the agricultural sector," the survey concluded.[2]

There can be little doubt that the 59 per cent who were either unemployed or working as labourers in the urban centres could have made a very useful contribution to the improvement of resource utilization in the villages they had left behind. But education had given them a glimpse of broader horizons and policy-makers had in effect declared that national development could not begin in the village. A literate middle class was required to run the country and build a market economy. "Let it be remembered," John K. Galbraith wrote in a commentary on the challenges facing undeveloped countries, "there is no literate population on this planet that is poor, no illiterate population that is otherwise than poor."[3]

And to paraphrase another commentator on development in Africa: children should be equipped with basic literacy, and "stimulated to want what they do not have."[4]

IN 1920, SIR GORDON GUGGISBERG, then Governor of the Gold Coast (present-day Ghana), declared:

> One of the greatest mistakes of the education in the past has been this, that it has taught the African to become a European instead of remaining African. This is entirely wrong and the Government recognizes it. In future, our education will aim at making an African remain an African and taking interest in his own country.[5]

The British colonial administration established Achimota College, the first secondary school in the Gold Coast, in 1927 at Guggisberg's instigation, but evidence of an emphasis on Africa in the syllabus is not forthcoming—there or anywhere else in colonial Africa. On the contrary, the persistent use of European textbooks led to contradictions between the content of colonial education and the reality of Africa which verged on the ludicrous. On a hot afternoon in the tropics, a class would be given a lesson on the seasons of the year: spring, summer, autumn, and winter. They would learn about the Alps and the Rhine, but nothing about the Atlas Mountains or the Zambezi. Students in British colonies would write essays on "how we defeated the Spanish Armada in 1588"; those in the French colonies would learn from their textbooks that "the Gauls, our ancestors, had blue eyes." Bemba children, who could name fifty or sixty indigenous plant species by the age of six, were taught about European flowers—and roses at that.[6]

Dr. Kofi Busia, who was prime minister of Ghana from 1969 to 1972, wrote of the estrangement which he had experienced as a consequence of the colonial education system:

> At the end of my first year at secondary school ... I went home to Wenchi for the Christmas vacation. I had not been home for four years, and on that visit, I became painfully aware of my isolation. I understood our community far less than the boys of my own age who had never been to school. Over the years, as I went through college and university, I felt increasingly that the education I received taught me more and more about Europe and less and less about my own society.[7]

But only a tiny number of African children received levels of education which were likely to induce such a degree of estrangement. Kofi Busia belonged to a very privileged elite indeed. Very few schools for Africans provided classes beyond primary/secondary level, or eighth or ninth grade.

In 1938 there were probably no more than 11,000 Africans receiving secondary education in all of sub-Saharan Africa (with a total population of more than 165 million). Only in South Africa, the Gold Coast, and Sierra Leone did the figures approach even one-tenth of 1 per cent of the population.[8]

Secondary schools, where they existed, covered very large catchment areas. Together with Achimota, Fourah Bay College in Sierra Leone (founded in 1827 and the first school in sub-Saharan Africa to offer secondary education to Africans) attracted students from all parts of British West Africa. Makerere College in Uganda likewise catered for students from all over East Africa. In southern Africa, the Free Church of Scotland had founded schools offering secondary education to Africans at Lovedale in the eastern Cape, and in Nyasaland (present-day Malawi).

In French West Africa, able and determined students from families wealthy enough to afford the expense found their way to the government's William Ponty School in Dakar, Senegal. The school had been established primarily for expatriate children; only 1,500 African students completed courses there in the twenty-one years between 1918 and 1939—though children of school age probably averaged at least 8 million in number throughout the period.

By the 1930s, just four institutions—Lovedale, Makerere, Achimota, and Ponty—were offering education up to university-entrance standard to the eligible among sub-Saharan Africa's 165 million inhabitants. Lovedale had in fact established the Fort Hare University College, where Africans could take degrees from the University of South Africa (which catered for the white population), but the number of graduates it produced was pitifully small: an average of fewer than four students per year acquired degrees between 1923 and 1936. At Achimota, thirty-seven students were working for degrees from London University in 1938. At Fourah Bay College in Sierra Leone two or three students each year obtained degrees awarded by the University of Durham.

As the privileged few reached the heights of education available in Africa, further advancement of their talents inevitably meant travelling overseas. For them, education had succeeded in stimulating wants that could only be satisfied beyond the boundaries of the continent, boundaries drawn in the social as well as the geographical context.

Though the details of courses taken by West Africans studying overseas in the early colonial period are still insufficiently known, law appears to have been the most popular subject.[9] This was, of course, European law—with its emphasis on individual and property rights—which the colonial administrations had determined should be the foundation of social justice in Africa. By the late 1920s there were already about sixty London-qualified lawyers practising in both Sierra Leone and Nigeria. Medicine attracted a smaller share of talent but in 1913 there were seven African doctors in Nigeria who had qualified in Britain. Between 1930 and 1940 an annual average of sixty-two West Africans (other than law students) were studying at British universities, plus about a dozen from East Africa in 1939 (though most of these were white).

In France, most African students came from North Africa, though the government of French West Africa did send twenty-three Ponty graduates to France on teacher-training courses in the early 1920s. Just nine students from French West Africa went to French universities in subsequent years (mostly for veterinary studies, but including one who took a degree in arts—Léopold

Sédar Senghor) and a total of perhaps no more than twelve black students from French West Africa obtained university degrees between 1905 and 1940. In the late 1920s there were just two African lawyers in the region.

North America also attracted its share of African students, particularly from South Africa, where American missionary connections were especially strong. More than 150 black South Africans went to study in the United States during the first decades of the colonial period. The first Kenyan (a Maasai) went to the United States in 1908. Twenty Nigerians followed between 1920 and 1937, most of them sent by missionary societies to pursue religious studies. Twelve more arrived in 1938; most went to Lincoln University in Pennsylvania, a black university whose graduates have included Nnamdi Azikiwe (1931) and Kwame Nkrumah (1939), who would later become the first presidents of independent Nigeria and Ghana respectively.

The Africans who were educated abroad during the 1920s and '30s were born and raised during the colonial period, their memories untrammelled by personal experience of the pre-colonial past, their minds filled with the precepts of an education whose emphasis on the individual and competitive achievement had stimulated some vigorous strains of ambition. The elite had suggestions and comments to make. Simply to apply their talents to the smooth—or even improved—running of the existing system was not enough. A new agenda was emerging—the call for self-government and national independence.

In an address given at Howard University in 1954, Nnamdi Azikiwe spoke of his student days in the United States: "Here ... I learned the rudiments of the humanities, the anatomy of the social sciences, and the grammar of politics."[10]

THE EMERGENCE AND CONSOLIDATION OF movements calling for African independence coincided with the growth of the Soviet Union as a world power. It was inevitable that the two developments should interact; indeed, in theory at least they were mutually supportive: Africa offered the Soviets fertile ground for the spread of communism abroad, while the Soviet Union presented Africans with a stirring example of an oppressive regime successfully overthrown.

Shortly after the Bolshevik revolution in 1917, Lenin pledged the support of the Soviet Union to all colonized peoples. When Marx and Engels were defining the principles of communism in the mid nineteenth century, colonialism was not yet an issue in global economics and Africa was not well known. Lenin, however, frequently referred to Africa in his utterances on imperialism, nationalism, and the colonial question. Indeed, Africa—with minimal industrialization and a predominantly rural population—might have seemed ideally poised to move directly from quasi-feudalism to communism without passing through the capitalist phase which the communists were committed to eradicating from the rest of the world.

The Comintern (an organization founded in Moscow in 1919 by delegates from twelve nations for the avowed purpose of promoting communism abroad) sought to exert its influence on Africa through a network of Communist parties and affiliated organizations in Europe and the United States.

The French Communist Party was directed to

> draw up a tactical plan of action and to examine the practical tasks that it will need to pursue to induce the native masses to support the communist effort and at the same time to take up arms against capitalism and imperialism

in the French African colonies.[11] Through the Pan-African movement (founded in America at the turn of the century principally to promote the interests of Afro-Americans), the communist ideal reached African students in the United States and subsequently spread to their counterparts in Britain.

Kwame Nkrumah, Nnamdi Azikiwe, Hastings Banda, Jomo Kenyatta, Léopold Senghor, and others who would later play a prominent role in the political development of independent Africa were exposed to the communist ideal in the 1920s and 1930s. Kenyatta actually studied in Moscow at an institute founded in 1930 to train the cadres of the communist movement, and he wrote articles attacking British rule, white settlers, and missionaries in Africa for communist journals.[12]

There was, of course, a fundamental contradiction in the strategy adopted by the Comintern to promote its cause in Africa: the Africans it was courting in Europe and America were the bourgeois elite of the continent—the privileged, not the oppressed. And indeed, although socialist ideals were prominent among the themes used by African activists to rally support for the anti-colonialist cause, the introduction of communism to Africa was not their principal aim.

Communist parties were established in some African countries; Soviet aid was solicited and welcomed; socialism was often the professed faith; but the overriding aim was to replace colonial administrations with independent governments of a different colour. They would be black governments not white, but still dependent upon revenues flowing from a capitalist economic system and blessed with the unstinting support of a population that was over 80 per cent rural, predominantly illiterate, and universally habituated to the autocratic rule of those in power.

SUCH CIVILIZATION OR SOCIAL UPGRADING as had resulted from the colonial interlude was essentially an urban phenomenon. The rural population was largely unaffected and might even have been persuaded that colonial government promised more advantages than disadvantages for the future.

Colonial agricultural services had introduced improved crops and technical services. Lorries and the expansion of road networks brought food aid more readily in times of hardship. Education took young people away from the villages, it was true, but then child mortality had fallen as a result of improvements in health care. In fact, education itself contributed to the improvements: even the simple hygiene lessons given to girls at primary schools have been found to halve infant mortality rates.[13]

Africa's population increased at an unprecedented rate during the mid-decades of the colonial period, rising from 142 million in 1920 to 200 million by the late 1940s, a trend that was set to continue, taking Africa's population to nearly 300 million as nations across the continent achieved their independence in the 1960s.[14]

But even then, more than 80 per cent of Africa's population was still living in the villages as before, eating staple crops the people grew themselves, working to produce a cash crop surplus that would pay for essentials and their children's schooling. Fewer than 20 per cent of the continent's population lived in urban centres in the early 1960s, compared with more than 60 per cent in Europe and North America, whence came the educational systems and political ideals that had inspired Africa's new leaders.

An urban population amounting to 20 per cent of the total is an average for the entire continent (the precise United Nations figure is 18.4 per cent). The figure of course varies from country to country, across a very wide range. The urban population of South Africa constituted 46.7 per cent of its total in 1960. Among the countries of North Africa the figure averaged just over 30 per cent. In tropical Africa, only the Congo Republic (the former French Congo) had an urban population that constituted more than 30 per cent of the whole in 1960; Ghana had 23.3 per cent, Congo 22.3 per cent, Nigeria 13.1 per cent, Kenya 7.4 per cent. Urban populations were smallest as a proportion of the total in tropical Africa's most densely populated countries: 2.4 per cent in Rwanda, 2.2 per cent in Burundi.[15]

. . .

EDUCATION AND FOREIGN TRAVEL HAD TAUGHT the privileged elite how to conduct high-level discussions of diplomatic, economic and political issues in the corridors of power, but among the illiterate villagers who had been persuaded to elect them to parliament, their intellectual achievements and national ambitions were rendered meaningless by the "Robin Hood" syndrome. From the villagers' point of view, the attractions of the democracy that independence had brought were centred exclusively on the prospect of having a local representative at the centre of power—a wealthy, influential man who could capture a share of whatever was available and bring it back to the village.

These men were the sons of the rural community; the village was their constituency; their obligations to the nation as a whole were secondary. Thus issues which demanded attention on a national level—the provision of roads and social services, for instance—became subject to the arguments of local interest, with conclusions tending to favour the most powerful groups.

Conversely, African leaders discovered that their political initiatives—though addressing issues of national importance—were inevitably interpreted as moves designed to benefit their own natal communities and—with more sinister implications—ethnic group. When Jaramogi Oginga Odinga attempted to form a radical socialist party in Kenya, for instance, he found that support came not from the disadvantaged across the length and breadth of the country, whom his proposed reforms were intended to benefit, but almost exclusively from all sections—rich and poor—of the Luo, his own ethnic group. Similarly, despite Chief Obafemi Awolowo's all-embracing socialist rhetoric in the early years of Nigerian independence, he became the hero not of the working class of Nigeria as a whole but of nearly all classes in Yorubaland.

"On balance, it can be legitimately argued that whenever there has been near confrontation and competition between the forces of ethnicity on one side and the forces of class-consciousness on the other, ethnicity has almost invariably triumphed in Africa," an article on nation-building and changing political values in Africa concluded.[16]

Thus the tribal distinctions that were established to facilitate administration during the colonial period in Africa became substitutes for the social and economic distinctions which have inspired political reform throughout history and around the world. The pain of injustice has fuelled the pressure for fair and stable government everywhere. In Africa, the injustices of colonial rule inspired nationalist movements that united the most diverse of ethnic groups in the drive for independence. Once independence had been achieved, however, the nationalist movements all too often fractured into political groupings of purely ethnic dimensions, whose struggles for power and wealth not only left national issues inadequately addressed and injustices largely unremedied, but also polarized economic and social discontent along ethnic lines—with some dreadful consequences.

The British practice of ruling their African colonies indirectly, through a network of district officers and chiefs, went some way towards ensuring that all districts and therefore all ethnic groups were represented among the educated and literate elite that became politically active during the colonial period. The French system produced educated Africans who were known as the *assimilés*—those who could be assimilated into the superior culture and administration which France had brought to Africa—and they too came from all corners of the colonies. Educated Africans in the Portuguese colonies were similarly known as the *assimilados* (with the further distinction that those fluent in Portuguese were known as the *civilisados*), and in the Belgian territories educated Africans were called the *évolués*—those who had "evolved" from savagery to civilization, thanks to the Belgians.

The availability of education during the colonial period was of course the key to the ethnic composition of the cohorts of activists clamouring for independence. Where opportunities for education and advanced study had been broadly based, hopes of establishing democratic governments in which tribal divisions might be diverted to the practical purpose of parliamentary opposition were justified. With hindsight, however, it is painfully obvious that no such hopes existed for Rwanda and Burundi, where colonial administrators had decided at an early stage that only the Tutsi were worthy of being educated.

Hans Meyer, who travelled through Rwanda and Burundi while the territories were part of German East Africa, wrote:

> The longer one has travelled in negro countries, and the better one has got acquainted with the negro character, the more one is impressed with the proud reserve of the Tutsi . . . The tall fellows stand still and relaxed, leaning on their spears while watching the Europeans pass or approach, as if this unusual sight did not impress them in the least . . .
>
> The Tutsi consider themselves as the top of the creation from the standpoint of intelligent and political genius [Meyer noted], [and] to be rich and powerful and to enjoy life by doing nothing is the symbol of all wisdom for the Tutsi, the ideal for which he strives with utmost shrewdness and unscrupulousness.[17]

Both the German and the Belgian administrations established some government schools in Rwanda and Burundi during the early colonial period, but the Church and mission stations were always the principal sources of education in the region. The missionaries, however, regarded education primarily as a means of evangelization, convinced that Africans could spread the Christian faith more widely and more effectively than white missionaries. For their part, the Tutsis regarded education as a means of consolidating their power, shrewdly aware that close affiliation with the Church and the colonial administration could only enhance their position as a minority group holding a position of superior status over a deprived majority.

In the early 1930s, the resident Catholic Bishop, Léon Classe, negotiated a "Contrat Scolaire" with the Belgian administration by which the government schools were phased out and the Catholic Church assumed responsibility for the entire educational system. The contract carried a significant financial incentive. Each pupil was worth forty-seven francs in government subsidies to the Church, each qualified teacher worth 600 francs per class of twenty-five pupils.[18]

In return for the subsidies, the Church accepted an obligation to broaden the curriculum and produce not just African evangelists, priests and teachers, but also Africans who were educated to fill secular roles. And here Church and State were in perfect agreement as to what was required: "You must choose the Tutsi," Classe told the missionaries, "because the government will probably refuse Hutu teachers . . . In the government the positions in every branch of the administration, even the unimportant ones, will be reserved henceforth for young Tutsi."[19]

By the early 1930s and until well after the Second World War, the consensus of opinion among Belgian administrators was that the Tutsi should remain the sole recipients of secular and missionary education.[20] The administration wanted a Tutsi bureaucracy, and the Church's education programme supplied it, thus consolidating the ethnic definitions of an artificial and iniquitous class structure. Bishop Classe envisaged a Christian ruling class, a "racial aristocracy," he said. It did not matter that some schools were hopelessly overcrowded, and others not very good. A streaming system guaranteed that the Tutsi were given the best of what was available. However sub-standard the general level of education, the nobility was assured of special attention,[21] and the Belgians thus imposed an ethnic definition of eligibility on the emerging political class.

But education was not completely withheld from the Hutu. "We must not . . . neglect the classes of Hutu young people and children," Bishop Classe told the teaching Fathers. "They also need to be schooled and educated, and they will take up places in mine workings and industry."[22]

The opportunities for Hutu advancement beyond the levels that Bishop Classe had decreed were extremely limited. A few Hutu displayed enough aptitude and religious conviction to qualify as candidates for the priesthood, on the assumption that as priests they would spread the faith among their people, and the Catholic seminaries were virtually the only route to higher education open to the Hutu until 1956. Some did indeed become priests; others left the seminaries to pursue secular careers. In fact, the first Rwandese to achieve anything approaching a university education was a Hutu former seminarist, Anastase Makuza, who graduated from the Centre Universitaire of Kisantu (Congo) in 1955 with a degree in political and administrative sciences.

Despite his outstanding achievements, Makuza could not find a job worthy of his qualifications. His application for a post in the government administration was turned down; a position as research assistant at the Institut pour la Recherche Scientifique en Afrique Centrale was not open to him because, Makuza has said, "the IRSAC was 150 per cent Tutsi." He even looked for a job in Burundi before ending up as a typist in a government office in Kibuye, Rwanda. In 1957 Makuza was promoted to the rank of administrative assistant and subsequently transferred to Kigali, the Rwandan capital. By then, however, Makuza was already a potential revolutionary.[23]

From about 1956 onwards, the number of educated Hutu in Rwanda looking for employment to match their talents grew year by year, but few posts other than as lowly clerks were open to them. Among this relatively small but highly articulate Hutu elite, frustration generated by the Tutsi monopoly of all sectors of the administration and economy rapidly hardened into a determination to break Tutsi domination. Social injustices were attributed to racial discrimination, with the implication that redressing the racial balance of power would restore the rights of the deprived.

In March 1957, the Hutu elite published the *Hutu Manifesto*, a radical document which challenged every aspect of Rwanda's prevailing economic and administrative system. The *Manifesto* identified the central issue as "the political monopoly of one race, the Tutsi race, which, given the present structural framework, becomes a social and economic monopoly." Instances of political, social and cultural injustice were cited, and measures specifically designed to achieve "the integral and collective promotion of the Hutu" were proposed, including the abandonment of class prejudice, the recognition of individual landed property, the promotion of Hutus to public office, and the extension of educational opportunities at all levels to Hutu children. "Never before had such a devastating critique of the *ancien régime* been publicly set forth by its opponents."[24]

The *Hutu Manifesto* urged the Belgian administration to take "more positive and unambiguous measures to achieve the political and economic emancipation of the Hutu," but it aroused only minor and belated official response. In

December 1958, the Vice-Governor-General, Jean-Paul Harroy, finally conceded that "the Hutu–Tutsi question posed an undeniable problem" and proposed that official usage of the terms Hutu and Tutsi should be abolished.[25] The Hutu rejected the proposal, claiming that it was mere "Tutsi obfuscation."[26] The Tutsi, meanwhile, were left free to interpret Belgian silence and inaction as tacit approval of their claims to supremacy.

CHAPTER 53

Spoils of War

THE SECOND WORLD WAR FORESHADOWED the end of colonialism in Africa, though experts believed that decades of preparation
would be required before self-government was merited. In the event,
nationalist pressure and unrest (such as the Mau Mau rebellion in
Kenya), brought independence much sooner—long before the proposed standards of preparedness had been attained.

The Second World War was of decisive importance to Africa. Though the war
itself temporarily restrained demands for self-rule, Africa's involvement in the
conflict strengthened her case. Just as the initial rise of fascism in Europe during the 1930s had strengthened support for the countervailing socialist movement, so the conflict that defeated the global ambitions of the fascists also
accelerated the spread of anti-colonial sentiment.

But it was not only a matter of political sentiment. The war also demonstrated that Africa was an invaluable member of the world community. The
Congo, for instance, effectively became the locus of Belgium's independent
existence for the duration of the war after German forces overran Europe in
1940, providing the London-based government-in-exile with 85 per cent of its
funding.[1] And the African colonies contributed significant numbers of men to
the war effort. Over 160,000 African troops were recruited from the French
colonies in North and West Africa, for instance;[2] and by the end of the war
more than 374,000 Africans from the British colonies were serving in fighting
and ancillary units, along with 210,000 whites from southern Africa.[3]

Queen Elizabeth II with President Kenyatta, who led Kenya to independence from Britain, in the rose garden at State House, Nairobi

African manpower made a valuable contribution to the war effort but Africa's mineral resources were nothing less than indispensable to the allied victory. With enemy action disrupting access to established sources of essential iron, tin, copper, and zinc, the allies turned to Africa. The development of the atom bomb, for instance, which brought the war with Japan to an abrupt end, was utterly dependent upon supplies of uranium from the Belgian Congo.[4]

The wartime demand for strategic raw materials benefited even the least-developed colonies, such as Angola and Moçambique. In British West Africa, the increased production of iron in Sierra Leone and tin in Nigeria—together with the development of processing facilities—contributed to a doubling of the region's export trade from $176 million to $344 million between 1938 and 1946.[5] In southern Africa, manufacturing industry expanded at a dramatic rate. Southern Rhodesia, for instance, effectively created an iron and steel industry from scratch and the colony's gross industrial output more than trebled between 1938 and 1946, rising from just over $20 million to more than $68 million. Industrial enterprises developed at an equally astonishing rate in South Africa during the war, building the country into the industrial giant of the continent, with gross industrial production totalling more than $1 billion in 1945.[6]

In 1941, at the darkest moment of the war, with German forces in control of Europe and poised to invade Britain, Prime Minister Winston Churchill crossed the Atlantic to plead for American aid. He and President Franklin D. Roosevelt met secretly aboard warships anchored in Placentia Bay, Newfoundland. There, over a period of four days, the two leaders of the free world drew up the Atlantic Charter, and thrashed out the Lend-Lease arrangement that enabled the United States to supply essential military equipment and supplies without enraging Americans determined to keep their country out of the war.

Roosevelt insisted that the post-war objectives enshrined in the Atlantic Charter should include a commitment to self-determination for all colonies. Clause Three of the charter stated:

> They [the British and United States governments] respect the right of all peoples to choose the form of government under which they will live; and they wish to see sovereign rights and self-government restored to those who have been forcibly deprived of them.[7]

Roosevelt's demands are alleged to have brought Churchill close to apoplexy, but it is more likely that the two wily politicians had been careful to choose a form of words which allowed both of them to claim satisfaction.[8] With Britain virtually bankrupt and threatened with invasion a fudge was the best that Churchill could hope for. Back in England, he told the House of Commons that the Atlantic Charter was intended to apply to the "states and nations of Europe . . . under the Nazi yoke" and not to the British colonies, an interpretation which outraged African activists.[9] All over the continent letters and articles appeared in local newspapers insisting that the Atlantic Charter should indeed apply to Africa. Inadvertently, Churchill had given Africa's emergent political organizations a unifying theme: independence.

From Roosevelt's point of view, as the leader of a nation bred in the tradition of anti-imperialism, demands for a commitment to self-determination might have been obligatory. A supplementary document from the State Department underlined the American position, to the extent of declaring that a timetable to independence should be drawn up: "It is accordingly, the duty and purpose of each nation having political ties with colonial peoples . . . to fix at the earliest practicable moment, dates upon which the colonial peoples shall be accorded the status of full independence . . . " American public opinion echoed the sentiment, with the press to the fore. In an open letter to the English people the editors of *Life* magazine declared in 1942: "One thing we are sure we are *not* fighting for is to hold the British empire together . . . "[10]

Whatever Churchill may have told the House of Commons, his government was fully aware that American enthusiasm for independence probably entailed the end of the British Empire.[11] But for all its fine sentiment, a clause in the Atlantic Charter calling for "access on equal terms to the trade and to the raw material of the world" indicates that Roosevelt's noble demands were not wholly without self-interest.

The war gave a tremendous boost to the growth of American technological, industrial, and financial power. It was clear that, once the conflict was over, America's economic well-being could be sustained only by a vast expansion of export markets. Africa, where America's pre-war trade had been negligible (except in South Africa and Morocco), was an obvious target.

The point was not missed by British colonial officers. Noting the enthusiasm with which Pan-American Airways and the Socony-Vacuum oil company (later renamed Mobil) were establishing bases in Africa, the Colonial Office advised Churchill that the Americans seemed to be aiming for "a permanent position of economic predominance." American troops (including blacks) and a sudden influx of Camel cigarettes, chewing-gum, jeeps, and modern radios stimulated new tastes and aspirations among African consumers; widespread rumours to the effect that the Americans would take over the West African colonies once the war was over were reported.[12]

By then, however, the colonial powers could have been in no doubt that the days of their imperial authority in Africa were numbered. Their major allies—the United States in the west, and the Soviet Union in the east—were both committed to seeing the end of colonialism in Africa, albeit with political philosophies diametrically opposed.

France's capacity to make a prior commitment to self-determination for her African colonies as the Atlantic Charter required was complicated by the fact that during the war there were, in effect, two French governments: the Vichy government under Marshal Pétain; and the Free French government-in-exile led by General de Gaulle. The Vichy government controlled metropolitan France and the North African colonies (Algeria, Morocco and Tunisia) in collaboration with the occupying German forces; the Free French controlled the West African colonies in collaboration with the allies.

In 1942, when the Atlantic Charter was drawn up and the allies were planning the invasions that would expel the Axis forces from Algeria, Morocco, and Tunisia, the Vichy government began making plans for the post-war development of the French colonies. A ten-year plan (1942–52) produced by a group of "technocrats" anticipated that the economic future of France would be based on industrial development financed by private enterprise, with state funds available if private enterprise could not cope. A sum of 736 billion francs was budgeted for state intervention, of which only a modest 84 billion francs was allocated specifically to the colonies.

The ten-year plan did not envisage the setting up of productive capacity in the colonies that might compete with industry at home; on the contrary, the intention was that "the colonies and the mother country [should] form a *community*" which protected French industry by guaranteeing its markets abroad. The Vichy plan was never formally ratified; nevertheless, it stood as the framework of France's post-war economic policy for the colonies.[13]

Meanwhile, as Vichy France filed away its plan for the *economic* arrangements that would link France and its colonies after the war, the Free French convened a conference at which the *political* links were defined.

The French Africa Conference was held in Brazzaville, French Equatorial Africa, in early 1944. General de Gaulle attended, along with the Governor-Generals of the French territories and colonial service staff; representatives of the African elite also attended, but were not allowed to participate in the discussions.

There can be no doubt that the Brazzaville conference was convened partly in response to the demands of the Atlantic Charter, and its conclusions were equally clear—"any idea of autonomy, or any possibility of evolution outside the French Empire, or of self-government in the colonies, even in the distant future" was unambiguously rejected. Instead, representatives of the colonies would be elected to the French Legislative Assembly, thus conceding a measure of self-determination which tied the colonies even more closely to metropolitan France than before. Among the African elite who felt themselves eligible for election to the assembly, reaction is said to have been "joyous." Jean Aubame, who subsequently became a deputy from Gabon, wrote: "The Brazzaville Conference may be regarded as a veritable Declaration of the Rights of African Man: a declaration as yet timid, incomplete, and reticent, perhaps, but rich in possibilities."[14]

The Americans were less enthusiastic about the decisions made at Brazzaville, but the French were no less suspicious of America's post-war ambitions. Furthermore, they were overridingly anxious to regain the political power France had exercised in world affairs before the war. De Gaulle asked Roosevelt:[15]

> How can she do this if she is excluded from the organization of the great world powers and their decisions, if she loses her African and Asian territories—in short, if the settlement of the War definitely imposes upon her the psychology of the vanquished?

The British government during this period was more concerned with the realities of the present than with plans for the future. A Colonial Development and Welfare Act passed in 1940 provided a modest £50 million for the following ten years (increased to £120 million in 1945) and Churchill's Colonial Secretary informed parliament in July 1943 that Britain's goal regarding the colonies could be defined as "self-government within the framework of the British Empire." No absolute commitment was given, much less a timetable.

The conventional view within the Colonial Office after the war was that the principal African territories would need another sixty or eighty years of British rule before self-government was merited.[16] And the Americans, with convictions about self-determination modified by their own desire to have control of strategic bases in the Pacific and elsewhere, were leaning towards an even more pessimistic view. Asked in 1943 how long it might take dependent territories such as the Belgian Congo to achieve self-government, a senior American official is said to have replied,[17] "more than one hundred years." For parts of the Portuguese Empire, he thought a thousand years would be required.

African activists, stirred by the events of the war and encouraged by anti-colonial sentiments abroad, wanted much more and much sooner. In October 1945 the sixth Pan-African Congress was convened in Manchester, England. The movement had changed greatly during the war. Very few American blacks travelled to Manchester; for the first time this was predominantly a congress of Africa's young leaders. Kwame Nkrumah and Jomo Kenyatta were there, along with trade unionists, lawyers, teachers, and writers from East, West and South

Africa. The resolutions passed by the congress included a forthright challenge to the colonial powers:

> The delegates believe in peace. How could it be otherwise, when for centuries the African peoples have been the victims of violence and slavery? Yet if the Western world is still determined to rule mankind by force, then Africans, as a last resort, may have to appeal to force in the effort to achieve freedom, even if force destroys them and the world.
>
> We are determined to be free. We want education. We want the right to earn a decent living; the right to express our thoughts and emotions, to adopt and create forms of beauty. We demand for Black Africa autonomy and independence, so far and no further than it is possible in this One World for groups and peoples to rule themselves subject to inevitable world unity and federation.
>
> We are not ashamed to have been an age-long patient people. We continue willingly to sacrifice and strive. But we are unwilling to starve any longer while doing the world's drudgery, in order to support by our poverty and ignorance a false aristocracy and a discarded imperialism . . .
>
> Therefore, we shall complain, appeal and arraign. We will make the world listen to the facts of our condition. We will fight in every way we can for freedom, democracy and social betterment.[18]

SOUTH AFRICA WAS THE FIRST NATION on the continent to achieve independence, but although Britain renounced its sovereign authority in 1910—more than thirty years before Roosevelt and Churchill drew up the Atlantic Charter—the move did not mean independence and self-determination for the country's majority black population. On the contrary, the arrangements merely transferred sovereignty from whites in Europe to whites in South Africa, enshrining in law a racial philosophy ensuring that blacks in South Africa would be the last on the continent to achieve full emancipation.

The idea of a federation unifying the Cape Colony, Natal, and the Transvaal and Orange Free State Boer republics was not new. British ministers pressed for it in the 1870s (see page 515); Rhodes dreamt of creating a state that extended from the Cape to the Zambezi and beyond. But it was not so much external ambitions as the internal complexities of government, trade, railway, and customs agreements which brought delegates from the four regions to a convention that would prepare a constitution for a united South Africa.

The convention assembled in Durban in October 1908. There were thirty delegates with voting rights: twelve from the Cape Colony, eight from the Transvaal, and five each from the Orange Free State and Natal. All were white and male. Fourteen were Afrikaners, sixteen were of British origin.

The constitution which emerged from the convention created a unitary state with parliamentary sovereignty. The four colonies became the four provinces of the Union of South Africa, with a central government legally supreme over all local institutions. The constitution followed the British model, but with key differences that were to have momentous consequences,[19] especially on the crucial question of franchise laws, which differed significantly in the four colonies.

In the Transvaal and the Orange Free State only white men (and not white women), were entitled to vote or to become members of parliament. In Natal, all white men could vote, and so too could any Africans, Indians, and Coloureds who satisfied certain economic criteria (though in practice few qualified). In the Cape Colony, however, any man of any race could vote or become a member of parliament provided he was literate and earned £50 a year or owned a house and land worth £75 pounds.

In fact, no black man ever sat in the Cape colonial parliament;[20] in 1909 whites comprised 85 per cent of registered voters; 10 per cent were Coloured and just 5 per cent were African. Nonetheless, delegates from the Cape proposed a uniform franchise based on the Cape model for the entire country. The other three delegations were adamantly opposed, but all parties finally settled on a compromise that would restrict membership of parliament to white men, while allowing the franchise laws of each colony to remain in force in each province. The Cape's lingering liberalism was further protected by a clause stipulating that any bill proposing to alter the franchise laws would require the support of two-thirds of both houses of parliament in a joint sitting.

The constitution was ratified by the British parliament in London despite protests concerning the de facto colour bar that it enshrined in law. On 31 May 1910, eight years to the day since he had laid down his arms as a leader of the Afrikaner republics, Louis Botha became prime minister of the Union of South Africa, with a population of 4 million Africans, 500,000 Coloureds, 150,000 Indians, and 1,275,000 whites.

The outcome was not what the Africans who had supported the British cause in the Boer War had hoped for—and worse was to come. The Nationalist party under D.F. Malan won power in 1948. Within months they exploited constitutional loopholes resulting from the compromises of 1908, and packed the Senate with co-opted members to gain the two-thirds majority needed to revoke the entrenched clause under which blacks, Coloureds, and Indians had been able to vote in the Cape. The last vestige of liberalism was expunged from the constitution, and the official policy of apartheid (an Afrikaans word meaning separateness, pronounced "apart-hate") grew like a cancer in its place. Henceforward, only whites could vote in South African elections.

Meanwhile, the *assimilés*—the educated black elite of the French African colonies—had acquired the right to vote in French elections. Faithful to the promises of the Brazzaville Conference, France abolished colonial practices like forced labour and the much-hated *indigénat* (which allowed the administration to impose penal sanctions on French "subjects" that did not apply to French citizens), and granted French citizenship to all inhabitants of the African colonies. Local assemblies were established for each territory, and federal assemblies for the two main regions of French West Africa and French Equatorial Africa. Twenty-four deputies were elected to represent African interests at the French Constituent Assembly in Paris.

For the first time, political activity was unrestricted in the French African colonies; freedom of the press and association was established, trade unions were encouraged. In Paris, however, the activities of the African deputies were restricted, not least by the limitation of numbers. The tiny band was almost lost among the six hundred others who made up the Constituent Assembly in 1945. Indeed, in all but colour they were indistinguishable. They were looked upon and saw themselves as Frenchmen, sharing French traditions of loyalty, willingly subservient to French government and culture, and proud to be citizens of a world power. Their professed aim was to secure for Africans the same rights and privileges enjoyed by metropolitan Frenchmen. There was no mention of self-determination or independence. "Our programme," said the two deputies from Senegal, Léopold Senghor and Amadou Lamine-Guèye, "can be summarised in a very simple formula: a single category of Frenchmen, having exactly the same rights since all are subject to the same duties, including dying for the same country."[21]

But however loyal and deserving its sentiment, advancement of the African cause was fraught with difficulty. Most of the African deputies had never been to France before; their numbers were insignificant and they had no experience of parliamentary procedure. Furthermore, under French law they were supposed to be representatives of the entire French nation, and as concerned with the post-war reconstruction of France as with affairs in distant colonies.

"Let us be frank," a moderate African councillor said in 1951, "the coloured representatives obtained absolutely nothing . . . They did not even succeed in capturing for a few moments the attention of an Assembly indifferent to the point of insolence."[22]

THE FRENCH HAD HOPED TO retain control over the colonies in the post-war era by appearing to give Africans a voice in the affairs of *la plus grande France*. The British, on the other hand, had taken the view that although there was as yet little demand for self-government among the African population at large, the rise of nationalism was inevitable, and in 1946 began planning to give the Africans control over their own affairs.

A government committee was assigned the task of planning "a new approach" to Africa, by way not only of economic and social advance, but also of political progress. The report submitted by the committee in May 1947 implied a virtual revolution in African policy, proposing a programme of preparation for self-government, so that the transfer of power could be carried out "with the minimum of friction, the maximum of goodwill for this country and the greatest possible degree of efficiency."[23] Power would be transferred in stages, according to the circumstances in each colony, beginning with the democratization of African local government and ending with African ministries responsible to democratically elected assemblies.[24] This signalled the end of indirect rule. The chiefs, previously the go-betweens of British colonial administration, were to make way for the educated elite.

The report stressed that

> ... internal self-government cannot be achieved until territorial unity has become a reality, sufficient numbers of Africans have emerged qualified by their training and character to manage their own affairs on a territorial scale and the political leaders have become representative of and responsible to the people.[25]

Such caveats notwithstanding, the report predicted that, "Perhaps within a generation many of the principal territories of the Colonial Empire will have attained or be within sight of the goal of full responsibility for local affairs."[26]

All but the black population of South Africa were independent within a generation—some in less than half that time—but the transfer of power did not proceed with the efficiency, goodwill, and lack of friction that had been deemed desirable. The British government had concluded that it was better to concede too much power too soon than too little too late, but events moved faster than anticipated.

Rioting in Accra in 1948 persuaded the Colonial Office to hasten the introduction of direct elections and a quasi-ministerial system in Gold Coast. In fact, the timetable to independence was shortened by fifteen years, thus sweeping aside all hope of nurturing moderate politicians to lead the independent nation. The 1951 elections were won by the more extreme Convention People's Party and its leader, the "Marxian Socialist" Kwame Nkrumah,[27] had to be let out of gaol in order to form a government.

The precipitate transfer of power in Gold Coast inevitably raised expectations throughout Africa. The ballot box and directly elected assemblies, which the colonial governments had planned to use as bargaining counters, introducing them stage by stage as the colonies advanced towards political maturity, had been conceded prematurely, thus contributing to the development of nationalism as a popular movement. "Wittingly and unwittingly, the British had sown the wind of colonial concessions and reaped the whirlwind of African nationalism."[28]

In East and Central Africa, British plans for African self-determination were complicated by the presence of white settlers who, though not excessively numerous, viewed the prospect of black government with a degree of alarm that had to be accommodated. Land was the major issue, particularly in the so-called white highlands of Kenya, where settlers had displaced an African population of largely Kikuyu ethnic origin. The Kikuyu were the largest group in Kenya, numbering more than 1 million—one-fifth of the country's African population.

Jomo Kenyatta, who had returned to Africa in 1946 as a leader of national aspirations, was a Kikuyu who had studied anthropology in London and completed a thesis on the Kikuyu—*Facing Mount Kenya*—that was published in 1938. Though Kenyatta appeared willing to act as the government's accredited African conscience within a developing constitutional framework, militant factions within the Kikuyu movements had a more radical agenda. Strikes were provoked in Mombasa and Nairobi. In the highlands, impoverished and dispossessed Kikuyu were urged to take violent action—not against the whites and their colonial government directly, but against Kikuyu who were suspected of supporting the government plans. Outbreaks of arson, cattle-maiming, and personal violence became rife and in October 1952 a state of emergency was declared. Four years of intensive military operations ensued, beginning with small-scale operations and evolving rapidly into all-out guerrilla warfare, as the British government struggled to defeat an elusive enemy—Mau Mau.[29]

Nearly 2,000 loyalist Kikuyu were murdered in the Mau Mau uprisings. The death toll among the rebels and their supporters was listed as 11,500. Thirty-two whites were killed in the four years of the emergency—fewer than died in traffic accidents in Nairobi during the same period.[30]

Kenyatta's role in the Mau Mau uprising was equivocal. He denounced the movement at a public meeting held in August 1952, even using a traditional Kikuyu curse condemning Mau Mau to oblivion. "Mau Mau has spoiled the country," he told the 25,000-strong Kikuyu audience. "Let Mau Mau perish for ever. All people should search for Mau Mau and kill it."[31] Some whites believed that Kenyatta had meant just what he said; some Kikuyu knew the words had been chosen to satisfy the government and would be taken seriously by only the weaker members of the Mau Mau movement. In any event, Kenyatta was arrested along with other leading Kikuyu politicians when the state of emergency was declared, and charged with masterminding the Mau Mau movement.

The trial lasted five months, and found Kenyatta guilty of persuading the Kikuyu to murder, to burn, and to commit evil atrocities. "You have let loose upon this land a flood of misery and unhappiness affecting the lives of all races in it, including your own people,"[32] the judge told him when delivering the verdict. Kenyatta was sentenced to seven years' hard labour, to be followed by an indefinite period of restriction. He was released in 1961, elected to the newly constituted parliament in 1962 and installed as President of independent Kenya in 1963.

AT THE HEIGHT OF the Mau Mau emergency, Britain deployed eleven infantry battalions and a squadron of heavy bombers to supplement local forces of 21,000 policemen and a Kikuyu Home Guard some 25,000 strong. With British forces so heavily engaged, the conflict was a major item of news in Britain itself, the stories of debasing secret oaths, guerrilla war, and atrocity tending to confirm popular prejudice concerning Africa.

Among those who were teenagers at the time some, whose interest in the Africa of the stamp-album and the illustrated magazines inclined their attention towards reports emanating from Kenya, were struck by a comparison commentators made as they attempted to find a cause for the uprising in the broader context of colonial affairs.

Look at the Belgian Congo, they said. No rebellions or demands for independence were heard from that corner of the continent, though it was the richest colony in Africa. The Congo was at peace. Kenya was at war. What were the Belgians doing that the British had failed to do? The answer, short and brutal, is—nothing.

While the rise of nationalism drove Britain and France to the conclusion that African independence was inevitable, Belgium reacted with blithe indifference. Independence for the Belgian colonies was not on the agenda; nor did Africans participate in the administration of the Belgian colonies to an extent that would prepare them for government. Such total unpreparedness was to have catastrophic consequences. The peace that seemed so enviable in the early 1950s was merely the lull before the storm.

CHAPTER 54

First Dance of Freedom[1]

THE BELGIAN CONGO WAS among the least prepared of the nations that became independent in the 1960s. Chaos and rebellion erupted within days of the independence ceremonies. But the Congo was strategically important, and America's meddling in the Congo's affairs typifies the manner in which African countries thus became pawns in the Cold War. CIA agents planned to assassinate the Congo's first prime minister, the Soviet-leaning Patrice Lumumba, and U.S. support for Joseph Mobutu was designed to frustrate Soviet ambitions in the region.

During the Second World War, with Belgium overrun by German forces, the Belgian Congo was already independent in the sense that it was not controlled from Europe. Furthermore, because its resources were vital to the Allied war effort (see pages 637–39), the wartime administration of the Congo not only governed its own affairs, but was also able to develop a highly profitable economy.

The demands of the war made the Congo wealthy, the logistics of wartime production made its administration efficient, and the Belgians saw no reason to change the arrangements once the war was over. Indeed, a ten-year development plan drawn up in the late 1940s essentially promised more of the same, offering only a first step in the progressive transformation of the Congo from a country almost entirely dependent on the export of raw materials to one with a balanced economy.[2] Production and profits rose accordingly. Mining output—

King Baudouin of Belgium and President Mobutu at the commencement of a
state visit commemorating the Congo's ten years of independence

the backbone of the country's development—increased by more than 60 per cent in the ten years to 1955; the volume of industrial production tripled; hydroelectric-power generation quadrupled. External trade rose in similar measure, with the value of exports increasing nearly fourfold and imports rising more than five times in value.[3]

By 1959, the Congo was producing 9 per cent of the world's copper, 49 per cent of its cobalt, 69 per cent of its industrial diamonds, and 6.5 per cent of its tin. Palm-oil, cotton, and coffee alone contributed £53 million to the country's exports.[4] No other colony in Africa could boast of such riches, so profitably exploited. No wonder commentators looked upon the Congo as a paragon of colonial virtue. The country was highly profitable, efficient, and peaceful.

The achievements of the Belgians in the Congo rested on an alliance of government, the Catholic Church and the mining corporations, which the demands of self-sufficiency had consolidated during the war. In essence, the government provided the administration, the Church attended to matters of education and moral welfare, and the mining industry produced the revenue required to support the whole enterprise. By convention, colonial matters rarely featured in Belgian politics, and the Belgian public were content to own the richest colony in Africa without concern for what happened there. Consequently, Congo affairs were left to a cabal of Belgian officials, churchmen, and businessmen whose activities were virtually exempt from outside scrutiny.

The Belgian Congo's contribution to the war effort imposed huge demands upon the indigenous population, including at least sixty days of obligatory labour per year for every male African living in "customary society."[5] The demands were not appreciably lessened in the post-war years but the health, primary education, and industrial training programmes available in the Congo in the early 1950s were more advanced than in any other African colony.

The missionary effort was strikingly successful. By 1950 more than one-third of the population were professed Christians;[6] in 1955, 10 per cent of the Congo population were attending school, compared with 7 per cent in the Gold Coast, 6 per cent in India, and just 3 per cent in French Equatorial Africa.[7] The government had made basic health care widely available at local clinics; officials toured the rural districts regularly, dispensing law and order, ensuring that villagers produced crops efficiently, maintained the roads, and were available for work on the mines and plantations. Mining corporations in the east of the country provided housing, welfare schemes, and technical training for their labour force.

The Belgians appear to have believed that with the alliance of government,

Church, and industry providing paternalistic leadership, Christian education, and a measure of material reward, the African population would be content with Belgian rule for ever. A contrary note was sounded in the early 1950s by Antoine A.J. Van Bilsen, a professor of international studies, whose newspaper and journal articles attempted to alert his fellow countrymen to the need for a change of colonial policy. In 1956 Van Bilsen published a *Plan de Trente Ans pour l'Émancipation de l'Afrique Belge,* urging that the Congo could not escape the "liberation forces on the move in Africa" and should therefore "prepare the stages of an ineluctable evolution."[8]

Van Bilsen proposed that the emancipation of the Congo should proceed in stages over a period of thirty years towards the goal of a Belgo-Congolese federal union (he carefully avoided the word *indépendence*). His proposals met with scorn and abuse from many quarters and with indifference from the government. The Minister for the Congo is reported to have spoken contemptuously of "irresponsible strategists who fix dates . . . Such an attitude shows that they either know nothing or that they understand nothing of Africa."[9]

Whether it was Van Bilsen or the Minister for the Congo who understood Africa more fully, the Congolese themselves were aware of the "liberation forces on the move in Africa" and a vocal minority wanted to ensure that the Congo too would be among the countries they touched. Activists were few, and the influence of charismatic individuals therefore disproportionately large. Patrice Lumumba was among the most charismatic.

Lumumba was born in 1925, so it was during the 1950s that he entered his thirties, the stage of life when talent and ambition are likely to be most aggressively combined. A tall, thin, intense man, he had attended school only at the primary level, but his intelligence and remarkable energy had thereafter led him to a variety of jobs in different parts of the country. He spent several years working as a postal clerk in Stanleyville (now Kisangani), where he edited the journal of the postal workers' union and contributed articles to the newspapers on political subjects. In 1956 he was charged with embezzlement and spent a year in gaol, where he used the time to write a book, *Le Congo, Terre d'Avenir— Est-Il Menacé?* (The Congo, land of the future—is it threatened?).[10] "The essential wish of the Congolese elite," he wrote, "is to be 'Belgians' and to have the right to the same freedom and the same rights."

Opportunities for the Congolese elite to enjoy the same freedom and rights as Belgians were extremely limited at the time. Racial segregation was rampant in both the social and the economic spheres. In 1955, for instance, more than 1 million Congolese were in paid employment, but their total remuneration barely exceeded the total paid to the 20,000 Belgians then working in the country—an average black-to-white wage ratio of 1 to 40.[11]

The administration could boast that 10 per cent of the population was at school in 1955, as noted above, but educational facilities above the primary level were so limited that only 136 children completed full secondary education in 1959. Thus it is hardly surprising that only three Congolese held posts in the top three grades of the civil service in that year; the remaining 4,872 posts were all held by Belgians. There were no Congolese doctors, lawyers, army officers, or secondary-school teachers. As many as 35,244 Congolese were employed as primary-school teachers, it is true, but of these only 10,000 had completed a full teacher-training course; 12,000 had done an emergency training course; 13,000 had no training at all.[12]

Education in the Congo was of course the responsibility of the Church, and although it had failed to make an impact on the secular administration its success in the ecclesiastical field was significant: the first Congolese priest was ordained in 1917, the first Congolese bishop was consecrated in 1956. By 1959 there were already more than 600 Congolese priests ministering to communities throughout the country.[13]

In 1948 the Belgians had introduced a scheme whereby Africans who were literate, of good behaviour and free of such uncivilized practices as polygamy and sorcery, could apply for a *Carte du Mérite Civique,* but its promises of social integration were so imprecise that hardly any Congolese bothered to apply—fewer than 500 cards were issued in five years. The *évolués,* as they were known (see page 633), wanted more. The whites were dedicatedly opposed to anything that might appear to promise equal status. By way of compromise, the government introduced a new status in 1952, *immatriculation.*

To qualify for this promise of elevated status, an applicant had to satisfy Belgian officials that he was sufficiently educated and "penetrated with European civilisation and conforms to it," a hurdle which many whites would undoubtedly have failed to pass. In the course of their inquiries, the officials made the most intimate examination of a candidate's lifestyle, interrogating him about his relationship with his wife and friends and even subjecting his house to inspection. "Every room in the house, from the living room, bedroom and kitchen to the bathroom, are explored from top to bottom, in order to uncover anything which is incompatible with the requirements of civilised life," Lumumba reported in *Le Congo, Terre d'Avenir.*[14]

As a gesture of Belgian goodwill, the *immatriculation* decree was an unmitigated failure. Only about 200 Congolese qualified over a period of five years, and they soon found that the *immatriculation* brought them no closer to the emancipated European lifestyle they so avidly desired. They gained the right to be tried in the same courts as whites, but social and economic integration remained as distant as ever. "Frankly speaking, the *immatriculés* are deeply disappointed," Patrice Lumumba (who was one of them) wrote in his book, "despite his juridical status, his standard of living, his social position, and his . . . needs inherent in the life of any civilized man—the Congolese *immatriculé* is, with rare exceptions, economically and socially [no different from] any other Congolese."[15] In other words, despite fulfilling the conditions which had promised integration, the *évolués* were still denied access to the social and economic world of the Europeans. In the eyes of the Belgians they were still Africans—black, and inferior.

In their attempts to gain a share of European privilege, the *évolués* had been obliged to set themselves apart from the mass of the Congo population. Indeed, the mere fact of applying for the *immatriculation* required them to demonstrate the distance separating them from the non-*évolués,* and expressions of contempt for the "ignorant and backward" masses were commonplace. But the inadequacies of the *immatriculation* inspired a change of heart. With the colonial door shut fast on their ambitions to share European privilege, the disappointed *évolués* redirected their energies: instead of struggling ineffectively to join the European-dominated regime from below, they would impose themselves upon it from above—with the help of the "ignorant and backward" masses.

Slogans of African nationalism began emanating from *évolué* circles: independence, liberation from the chains of colonialism. On 28 December 1958, Patrice Lumumba addressed a meeting of the Mouvement National Congolais (MNC) which he had founded shortly before:

> The Mouvement National Congolais has as its basic aim the liberation of the Congolese people from the colonial regime, and its accession to independence . . . we wish to bid farewell to the old regime, this regime of subjection which deprives our nationals of enjoyment of the acknowledged rights of any human individual and any free citizen . . . Africa is irresistibly engaged in a merciless struggle for its liberation against the colonizer. Our compatriots must join us in order to serve the national cause more effectively and to carry out the will of a people determined to free itself from the chains of paternalism and colonialism.

By this time, the rising tide of nationalism had persuaded even the Belgians that some modification of their plans for the future of the Congo was required. A study group was set up in July 1958 consisting entirely of Belgians. Local-government elections were proposed, to be followed some time later by the creation of provincial and national assemblies. These modest recommendations, presented in Brussels in December that year, were thought to be a major advance. The date upon which the proposals would be announced was set as

13 January 1959. Nine days before, on 4 January 1959, the *pax belgica* was shattered. Violent riots broke out in Léopoldville.

African crowds ran wild through the streets, looting, burning, and attacking Europeans. The Force Publique was called out and the riot was put down with considerable savagery. Official figures put African casualties at forty-nine dead and 241 wounded; unofficial reports say that more than 200 died. The immediate cause of the riots was the refusal of permission for a scheduled Sunday afternoon political rally; Lumumba's inflammatory speech the previous week may also have been a contributory factor, but a subsequent Belgian investigation spoke of widespread discontent and frustration.

The government stuck to its plans, however. On 13 January the new proposals were announced (and in many quarters were interpreted as a hastily prepared response to the riots): elections to the communal and territorial councils would be held in December 1959, more Africans would be appointed to the various advisory councils, and the new statute would take effect immediately. Furthermore, King Baudouin stated publicly and for the first time that Belgium intended to grant the Congo full independence.[16] Van Bilsen had proposed thirty years; in the event, Belgium would hand over everything in less than eighteen months.

With elections to be held within a year, in a vast and disparate nation with no previous experience of the democratic process, the frenetic political activity which followed the Belgian announcement took on a predictable and ominous hue—tribalism. By November 1959, as many as fifty-three political parties were officially registered; a few months later the number had increased to 120. Among them, only Lumumba's Mouvement National Congolais championed Congolese nationalism. Virtually every other party had been formed to promote tribal interests.

Joseph Kasavubu, for instance, dreamt of reuniting the Bakongo people (who had been divided by the colonial boundaries of the French Congo, the Belgian Congo, and Angola), and rebuilding the fabled Kongo empire that had grown rich on the slave trade in the sixteenth and seventeenth centuries (see pages 374–75). Under Kasavubu's leadership, Abako—the Alliance des Ba-Kongo—became a militant political organization advocating Bakongo secession more than it championed the cause of national independence.

In Katanga province, 1,600 kilometres to the south-east, Moïse Tshombe was forging another major tribal party with secessionist ambitions. The Confédération des Associations Tribales du Katanga, known as Conakat, drew most support from southern Katanga, source of the copper which constituted the Congo's most valuable export. Under Tshombe's leadership and with the support of the local Belgian mining interests, Conakat advocated autonomy for Katanga and the retention of close ties with Belgium. Tshombe's electoral support was tribal, but his motivations undoubtedly were influenced by commercial considerations.

By the end of 1959, political fervour had ignited growing disorder throughout the Congo. There were disturbances in Stanleyville; the Bakongo region was a tinderbox of political tension, and in Kasai province tribal war had already broken out between the Lulua and Baluba. Furthermore, the December elections held in accordance with the announcement made in January had been boycotted in many parts of the country. The prospects for a peaceful transfer of power were slim. Belgian public opinion was appalled by talk of Belgian forces being deployed in the Congo.

With the vain hope of halting the rush to violence, the Belgian government convened a round-table conference in January 1960. Ninety-six Congolese delegates from thirteen political groups were invited to Brussels, including Kasavubu, Tshombe, and Lumumba. It was the first time ever that the Belgian authorities had consulted the Congolese concerning the future of their country. The Belgian negotiators had been hoping for an agreement to a phased transfer of power over a period of about four years. The Congolese, excited by the prospect of power and aware that Belgium had neither the stomach nor the ability to enforce Belgian preferences, wanted independence on 1 June 1960. The ensuing discussions persuaded them to concede an extra thirty days of colonial rule, but no more. Thus, on 27 January 1960, with virtually no time for adequate preparation, Belgium agreed that the Congo should become an independent nation six months later, on 30 June 1960. Elections for the 137 seats in the National Assembly were scheduled for May.

Lumumba's MNC won thirty-three seats, the largest single total, but could form a government only with a cumbersome coalition of twelve different parties—including some bitter rivals. Lumumba—thirty-five years old, volatile to the point of irrationality, ill-prepared, and deeply resentful of Belgian attempts to keep him from power—became the Congo's first prime minister. Kasavubu became head of state. Tshombe, appointed president of the Katanga provincial government, was highly dissatisfied with Katanga's share of ministerial influence in the independent government.

The independence-day celebrations opened with pomp and ceremony in the new Palais de la Nation, a building erected the previous year as the Belgian Governor-General's residence but hastily converted into a national assembly. King Baudouin gave the opening address. The text had been drafted by his advisers in Belgium without reference to the Congolese or even the responsible minister, and was paternalistic in the extreme. The king began by praising the early Belgian colonizers, especially Léopold II, and then listed the sacrifices which Belgium had made for the Congo. He warned the Congolese not to make hasty reforms and to beware of foreign countries which might try to interfere. It was now the job of the Congolese, he concluded, to show Belgium that she had been right to trust them.

The Congolese were not impressed. As President, Kasavubu replied in moderate terms, but omitted from his prepared text the final passage which had paid tribute to the king. Meanwhile, Lumumba could be seen scribbling furiously on the draft of his own speech. When called upon, Lumumba launched into a rousing nationalistic speech, better suited to a local election rally than to a ceremonial occasion of international significance. Deliberately rude and vindictive, he contrasted the king's representation of colonial history with the humiliations which the Congolese had suffered under Belgian rule. Finally, he spoke of what Africans could achieve. "We shall show the whole world," he said, "what the black man can do when he is allowed to work in freedom and we shall make of the Congo a shining example for the whole of Africa."[17]

The Congolese applauded warmly, but the Belgians were deeply shaken and regarded the speech as a bitter insult. They felt Lumumba had deliberately humiliated them before the whole world. The official lunch was delayed for two hours while the king and Belgian ministers debated whether to boycott it and return at once to Belgium. They stayed, but the lunch was hardly the celebratory affair that had been anticipated.

The Congo became an independent nation on the 30th of June 1960, a Thursday. On the following Monday the new government was confronted by its first crisis. In the lower ranks of the Force Publique, the Congo's 25,000-man army, resentment over low pay and lack of promotion had been simmering for weeks. Now they felt that the promises of independence had passed them by. The government was Congolese, but the army was still controlled by 1,100 Belgian officers (not unreasonably, since the first contingent of Congolese officer cadets sent to Belgium for training was not due to return until 1963). A protest meeting held at a garrison near Léopoldville demanded immediate Africanization of the officer corps and ended in a riot, threatening mutiny.

Lumumba offered the troops minor concessions and appealed for discipline. Their response was anything but encouraging so, on the 6th of July he capitulated, announcing the immediate dismissal of the senior Belgian officers and subsequently agreeing that the entire officer corps should be replaced by Congolese. Victor Lundula, whose military experience was limited to service as a sergeant in the Second World War, was appointed army commander. The man appointed to be his chief of staff, Joseph Mobutu, had served in the Force

Publique for seven years, but only as a clerk, and had left in 1956 to become a journalist. At the time of his appointment as army chief of staff, Mobutu was Lumumba's private secretary.

The sudden removal of authority unleashed mutiny at army barracks across the country. Violence and disorder was widespread. In scores of incidents, whites were humiliated, beaten, and raped; priests and nuns were singled out for special insult. Within days, 25,000 Belgians had fled, most of them across the Congo River to the French Congo (which became independent the following month—August 1960) or by road to neighbouring states. In response the Belgians mobilized their forces, flying in reinforcements that eventually took the number of Belgian troops in the Congo to nearly 10,000. Lumumba became convinced that Belgium was trying to reimpose its rule.

Meanwhile, on 11 July Moïse Tshombe took advantage of the unrest to declare independence for Katanga. Under the guise of protecting Belgian interests, Belgian troops in Katanga disarmed and expelled Congolese army units from the province—a move open to interpretation as tacit recognition of Katangan independence which predictably intensified Lumumba's paranoia concerning Belgian intentions.

The plight of the Congo was now desperate. Government authority had collapsed. The army, regarded only a week before as the most reliable organization in the country, had degenerated into a wild and dangerous rabble. The white population, on whom the administration and the economy depended, was fleeing in thousands. The major cities were in turmoil. The Katanga secession threatened to break the country apart.

Blaming the Belgians for the chaos, Lumumba severed diplomatic relations with the former colonial power and appealed to the United Nations for military assistance in resisting what he called the Belgian "aggression." The UN asked Belgium to withdraw (but set no date), instigated a technical-assistance programme for the Congo and organized a major airlift of troops from other African countries; within three days, 3,500 UN troops arrived in the Congo, the advance contingent of forces which eventually mounted to 19,000 men from twenty-six countries. But Lumumba was not satisfied. On 16 July he threatened to call on the Soviet Union for help if Belgian troops were not evacuated within twenty-four hours, and repeated the threat a few days later.

By the end of July, UN troops had been deployed in five of the Congo's six provinces, allowing Belgian troops to be withdrawn. The sixth province was secessionist Katanga, where Tshombe insisted the Belgians should remain to keep order and warned that UN forces would be attacked if they attempted to enter the province. When UN Secretary-General Dag Hammarskjöld flew in and commenced a round of intense shuttle diplomacy, attempting to negotiate a settlement, Lumumba accused him of being a Belgian "puppet" and complained that the UN was not doing enough to end the Katanga secession. In the UN Security Council the Soviet Union also accused Hammarskjöld of acting as a western stooge.

Soviet planes began flying food supplies to the Congo in early August, and a shipment of 100 trucks was dispatched. Lumumba requested Soviet military aid on the 15th of August and by the end of the month he had fifteen Ilyushin aircraft, a supply of arms, and more than 300 Soviet-bloc technicians at his disposal, including military advisers. As the Congo slid further into chaos, Lumumba could think only of crushing Tshombe and the Katanga secession. Negotiation was not on his agenda. Hammarskjöld now feared that Lumumba's increasingly irrational behaviour would wreck the United Nations as well as the Congo. By accepting Soviet military aid, Lumumba had raised the Congo struggle for power to the level of a Cold War confrontation. The United States viewed developments in the Congo with increasing alarm. On 19 July 1960, less than three weeks after Congolese independence, the U.S. ambassador in Brussels advised Washington by cable that Lumumba had

> maneuvered himself into a position of opposition to West, resistance to United Nations and increasing dependence on Soviet Union and on Congolese supporters who are pursuing Soviet ends . . . only prudent, therefore, to plan on basis that Lumumba government threatens our vital interests in Congo and Africa generally. A principal objective of political and diplomatic action must therefore be to destroy Lumumba government as now constituted, but at the same time we must find or develop another horse to back which would be acceptable in rest of Africa and defensible against Soviet political attack.[18]

The Congo situation was discussed at a meeting of the U.S. National Security Council held on 18 August 1960. Under-Secretary of State Douglas Dillon advised the meeting that Lumumba was "working to serve the purpose of the Soviets." CIA director Allen Dulles added that Lumumba was in "Soviet pay."

President Eisenhower's reaction to warnings that Lumumba might succeed in forcing the UN to leave the Congo was one of outrage. He protested that it was not the Congolese who objected to UN support—"we [are] talking of one man forcing us out of the Congo; of Lumumba supported by the Soviets."[19] The president's remarks at this and other meetings were interpreted by CIA director Allen Dulles as "implicit authorization" to assassinate Lumumba.

An agent was dispatched to Léopoldville. An initial assassination plan required someone to apply a dose of poison to Lumumba's toothbrush; alternatively, a high-powered rifle with telescopic scope and silencer was proposed.

But before either toothbrush or rifle could be deployed, the Congolese had themselves removed Lumumba from power. In a radio broadcast on 5 September, President Kasavubu, urged on by American diplomats, Belgian political advisers, and Congolese supporters, announced that he had dismissed Lumumba as prime minister. When the news reached Lumumba, he in turn rushed to the radio station and announced that he had dismissed Kasavubu as president. Confusion ensued. Some parts of the Congo declared their support for Lumumba, others for Kasavubu and Ileo (another candidate), and parliament voted to annul both decisions.

With arrests and counter-arrests by the contending parties threatening yet another round of violent disturbance, the impasse was resolved on the evening of 14 September when the twenty-nine-year-old army chief of staff, Colonel Joseph Mobutu, announced that he was taking power in the name of the army. He declared that he was "neutralizing" Kasavubu, Lumumba, Ileo, and all other politicians for the time being, and recalling the cream of Congolese students studying abroad to help him run the country in cooperation with the United Nations until the end of the year. Then, in a move that warmed the hearts of the CIA agents who had been indoctrinating him for weeks, Mobutu ordered the Soviet and Czechoslovak embassies to get out of the Congo within forty-eight hours.

Mobutu's coup caused uproar at the United Nations, exposing the depth of the rift that separated Soviet and western ideologies. In a speech to the General Assembly on 22 September the Soviet leader, Nikita Khrushchev, launched a vitriolic attack on the United Nations handling of the Congo affair, directing his venom at the Secretary-General in particular. The executive machinery of the United Nations was "one-sided," he said. Hammarskjöld had been chosen by the western powers; therefore he reflected western views. The pro-western "bias" was "particularly glaring" in the case of the Congo, where the Secretary-General had "virtually adopted the position of the colonialists." This was a "very dangerous matter," Khrushchev concluded. To rectify matters he proposed "abolishing the post of Secretary-General" and replacing it with a troika, a three-man executive representing the world's three major blocs: western, socialist, and neutralist. This, he said, would safeguard the interests of all states and ensure there was no repetition of the Congo experience.[20]

Khrushchev's attack served to confirm Western suspicions concerning Soviet ambitions in Africa. The *New York Times* described the Soviet leader's speech as a "declaration of war" on the United Nations. Hammarskjöld himself was not surprised. He shared the American view that the Soviets were trying to establish a power base in Africa, and had expected that his attempts to apply the Security Council mandate in an impartial manner would conflict with the

Soviet ambition. In a cable to a colleague he described Khrushchev's speech as the "greatest compliment so far paid" to the United Nations. It meant, he said, that the Soviet leader had recognized that the organization was the "main obstacle to an expansion of empire in Africa." The "very venom" of Khrushchev's attack, he said, was a "recognition of defeat."[21]

The troika proposal was voted down, but throughout the wrangle, Hammarskjöld's staunchest supporters—the Americans—were also his greatest liability. Every time they spoke in defence of the Secretary-General they lent weight to Khrushchev's claim that he had been following United States orders in his handling of the Congo crisis. The Secretary-General attempted to keep some distance between himself and his American admirers, but the concordance of their views was undeniable. It was not so much that Hammarskjöld was following the orders of the United States, more perhaps that the United States was seizing an opportunity to follow the United Nations into Africa— establishing a firm power base on the continent in the guise of countering a Soviet threat to do the same.

TRUE TO HIS PROMISE, Mobutu restored constitutional government to the Congo at the end of 1960, reinstating Kasavubu as president. Over the next few years, Mobutu used the fragile security provided by the United Nations presence to build up the army and his own position as a military strongman. The UN forces withdrew after Katanga finally abandoned its secessionist ambitions in 1963; President Kasavubu invited Tshombe to form a national government as prime minister, precipitating a political power struggle which Mobutu resolved by staging a second coup in October 1965.

Mobutu was by then firmly in command of a well-organized and disciplined 25,000-man army. On taking power once again, he announced that his military high command had named him president and that he would rule for five years. He then proceeded to reduce the power of parliament, suspend all provincial assemblies, assume command of the police and have a number of suspected rivals executed. The following year he took over the office of prime minister, a post he subsequently relinquished—though he remained president, with his absolute control of political affairs enshrined in a new constitution promulgated in 1967. Three years later, Mobutu introduced an "African authenticity" campaign, which began by renaming the Congo "Zaire" and gave African names to cities and villages and geographical features throughout the country. The policy was later extended to personal names—all citizens were required to take an African name. The president changed his name from Joseph-Désiré Mobutu to Mobutu Sese Seko Kuku Ngbendu Wa Za Banga, meaning "the all-powerful warrior who, because of his endurance and inflexible will to win, sweeps from conquest to conquest leaving fire in his wake."[22]

And Patrice Lumumba? Though deposed by Mobutu on 14 September 1960, after just seventy-six days in office, Lumumba continued to live at the prime minister's residence in Léopoldville, guarded by an inner ring of UN troops in the garden to prevent his arrest and surrounded by an outer ring of Mobutu's troops on the perimeter to prevent his escape. Hence the difficulty of obtaining access to his toothbrush that the CIA agents had experienced. Meanwhile, Lumumba's supporters regrouped in Stanleyville. At the end of November Lumumba decided to join them—a fatal move. He was arrested en route and handed over to Mobutu's army.

Lumumba was consigned to a military prison, but his supporters continued to have an unsettling effect on the country at large. Kasavubu invited Lumumba to join the government, where his influence might have been beneficial. Lumumba refused, at which Kasavubu and his advisers decided that he should be sent to Elisabethville, the Katangan capital, where the errant Tshombe was in charge.

On 17 January 1961, Lumumba and two colleagues were flown to Katanga, where a Swedish warrant officer with the United Nations forces witnessed their arrival:

> The first to leave the aeroplane was a smartly dressed African. He was followed by three other Africans, blind-folded and with their hands tied behind their backs. The first of the prisoners to alight had a small beard [Lumumba]. As they came down the stairs, some of the *gendarmes* ran to them, pushed them, kicked them and brutally struck them with rifle butts; one of the prisoners fell to the ground. After about one minute the three prisoners were placed in a jeep which drove off . . . [23]

Neither Lumumba nor his two companions were ever seen again. It is believed they were taken to a farmhouse on the outskirts of Elisabethville, where they died at the hands of Katangese officials and Belgian mercenaries.[24] Lumumba's death established him as one of the most famous political martyrs of modern times. Even Mobutu praised him, raising the public image of Lumumba as a pan-African socialist to the status of a unifying cult—while he himself cultivated the strictly non-socialist western connections that had underwritten his accession and would support his reign.

CHAPTER 55

Dreams and Nightmares

THE DREAMS OF AFRICA BECOMING a continent of peaceful democratic states quickly evaporated. More than seventy coups occurred in the first thirty years of independence. By the 1990s few states preserved even the vestiges of democracy. One-party states, presidents-for-life, and military rule became the norm; resources were squandered as the elite accumulated wealth and the majority of Africans suffered. Nigeria and Rwanda exemplify the nightmare; South Africa preserves a flickering hope of transforming dreams into reality.

At the United Nations in October 1960, the General Assembly passed a resolution declaring that "unpreparedness should not be a pretext for delaying independence."[1] Nor was it. Sixteen former colonies in a state of varying but generally inadequate preparedness became independent in 1960; by 1965 the total of newly independent states in Africa had risen to thirty-eight, and another seven were added in the ten years to 1975.[2] Zimbabwe shook off settler rule in 1980, and a black government was elected to power in South Africa in 1994.

With the terrible exception of the Congo, the transfer of power was accomplished more efficiently than might have been expected, and with an encouraging degree of goodwill and optimism. The Sierra Leone leader, Milton Margai, burst into tears when the British Colonial Secretary asked him to specify the date on which his country should become independent; "I never expected to live long enough to be asked that question," he said. On attaining

Kenya farmer at the maize harvest, the future in his hands

power in Kenya, Jomo Kenyatta took pains to allay the fears of the white settlers. Referring to his imprisonment (see pages 647–48) he told an audience of suspicious whites:

> Jomo Kenyatta has no intention of retaliating or looking backwards. We are going to forget the past and look to the future. I have suffered imprisonment and detention; but that is gone, and I am not going to remember it. Let us join hands and work for the benefit of Kenya . . .

The audience rose and gave him a standing ovation.[3]

The economic and social circumstances in Africa's newly independent states also augured well for the future. The former colonies were poor, it is true, but by no means the world's poorest countries. Ghana's annual national income per head in 1960 was £70, for instance, and Nigeria's was £29; in India, the comparable figure was £25.[4] Furthermore, the post-war boom in commodity prices had enabled the colonial governments to implement social and economic development plans which had brought noticeable improvements to the lives of most people. All the former colonies had experienced more than ten years of constant economic growth, and plans for the future were based on the assumption that the trend would continue.

Dreams of rapid economic transformation were certainly naive, but hopes for sound continuing growth were not unreasonable. And real growth did occur. Figures from the World Bank Development Report 1992 show that between 1965 and 1980 sub-Saharan Africa's gross domestic product per head (at constant prices) grew at an average of 1.5 per cent per year, compared with India's 1.3 per cent.[5]

The nationalists of course believed that colonialism had retarded development, and the more idealistic of them expected their countries to race ahead after independence. Some, like Nkrumah, saw independence as an opportunity to catch up with advanced countries and win respect so long denied. Not for them a minimalist style of government geared to the interests and potential of the agricultural societies that constituted more than 80 per cent of the population. No, they dreamt of creating modern nation states, complete with the complex development plans and bureaucratic controls of the industrial world in which the elite aspired to live.

Among their dreams, Africa's new leaders shared a passionate belief in the power of their "Africanness"—an expression which is customarily defined in terms of the perceived differences between Africans and Europeans, between blacks and whites. Léopold Senghor, leader of independent Senegal and member of the Académie Française, wrote poems (in French) in praise of *négritude*.

Julius Nyerere, leader of independent Tanzania, contrasted the Africans' sense of shared identity with the individualism of Europeans: "Africans all over the continent, without a word being spoken . . . looked at the European, looked at one another, and knew that in relation to the European they were one."[6]

As the era of independence dawned, Nyerere was among the most passionate of those who dreamt of a new and unified Africa. "For the sake of all African states, large or small," Nyerere declared in 1963, "our goal must be a United States of Africa. Only this can really give Africa the future her people deserve after centuries of economic uncertainty and social oppression." Nyerere identified the national boundaries inherited from the colonial era as a serious threat to African unity. "The boundaries which divide African states are so nonsensical," he said, "that without our sense of unity they would be a cause of friction." But they must stay. Independent Africa had no choice but to keep them, Nyerere argued, even though every country embraced areas which would belong to another if principles of ethnic or political geography were considered.

> . . . for us to start making "claims" on each other's territory would be to play into the hands of those who wish to keep Africa weak so as to improve their own relative strength in the future [he said], and it might well lead us to the tragic absurdity of spending money on armaments while our people die for want of medical attention or starve from want of knowledge.[7]

In May 1963, representatives of thirty African nations met in Addis Ababa, the Ethiopian capital, to establish the Organization of African Unity (OAU). A professed intention of the OAU was to provide Africa with a powerful independent voice in world affairs—African unity was high on the agenda. The thirty heads of state attending the inaugural sessions agreed to retain the boundaries of the former colonies, and signed a Charter of African Unity pledging themselves to respect "the territorial integrity of every state and its inalienable right to an independent existence."

The heads of state took due heed of Nyerere's warning that conflict between African nations posed a serious threat to the future peace and prosperity of the continent. But an empty chair at the conference table warned of yet more ominous dangers. Sylvanus Olympio, the President of Togo, should have occupied the thirty-first chair, but he had been assassinated four months earlier; shot dead at the gates of the American Embassy in Lomé by a group of dissatisfied ex-servicemen under the leadership of a twenty-five-year-old sergeant, Étienne Eyadema.

The assassination of Sylvanus Olympio was black Africa's first *coup d'état.*

The regime which replaced him was not admitted to the OAU Conference of Heads of State in Addis Ababa, but the exclusion in itself acknowledged a sober truth. The African leaders dreamt of unity and pledged to respect the territorial integrity of nations, but it was not conflict *between* nations that threatened Africa's future. No, the potential for strife *within* nations posed a far greater threat.

MORE THAN SEVENTY COUPS OCCURRED in thirty-two of Africa's independent nations between the assassination of Sylvanus Olympio in 1963 and the overthrow of Zaire's President Mobutu in 1997. Of the states represented at the inaugural session of the OAU, only five (Cameroon, Ivory Coast, Senegal, Tanzania, and Tunisia) had not suffered a violent change of government by 1997 (other nations which have not experienced coups were not represented at the conference).[8] Benin (formerly Dahomey), for instance, suffered the trauma of six coups, five different constitutions and twelve heads of state during its first ten years of independence. The leading light of African nationalism, Kwame Nkrumah, was deposed in 1966; in that same year Nigeria—the country which had seemed better prepared for independence than any other African nation—was struck by the first of five coups in twenty years.[9]

The surge of optimism which had accompanied the transfer of power in Africa had been especially evident in the case of Nigeria. With the continent's largest population, experienced politicians, an efficient civil service and the benefit of a strong, diversified economy, Nigeria was expected to be at the forefront of economic and political progress in Africa—leading the continent's transition from an undeveloped to a developed region.

As a consequence of straddling the linguistic cradle-land of the Bantu people (see page 184), Nigeria is home to the largest number of ethnic and language groups in Africa. From among these, three main alliances had emerged in the run-up to independence, each with a geographic as well as a linguistic and ethnic dimension. The north was predominantly inhabited by people speaking Hausa; the east by the Igbo and associated groups; the west by the Yoruba.

Geographic, environmental, economic, religious, and cultural factors, plus the lingering effects of the slave trade and forced labour, all served to distinguish the three groups one from another. The promise of independence politicized those differences as each group struggled for a position of strength in constitutional negotiations with the British. Regional ambitions occasionally seemed irreconcilable, but were eventually assuaged by mutual agreement that independent Nigeria should have a federal constitution. Regional governments would handle local affairs, and a federal government would control national interests. The arrangement seemed a sensible compromise. Outwardly at least, Nigeria entered the era of independence as a promising example of a carefully balanced and stable parliamentary democracy.[10]

Behind the scenes, however, the picture was not so reassuring. Politicians on all sides were engaged in a reckless scramble for power and profit. At every level, from federal ministry to village dispensary, politicians and people in authority used their positions to the benefit of their own group and the detriment of others. Public funds were regularly commandeered for political and personal gain. Nigeria's leaders constructed sturdy empires of wealth and patronage. In return for keeping them in power, their supporters were given jobs, contracts, loans, scholarships—whatever was available. There was no question of having to account for illicit disbursements, for everyone in government was culpable.

Nigerian politics rapidly degenerated into a corrupt and bitter struggle for the spoils of office. As the regions competed for the largest share of federal revenue, for the location of industries, and for appointments to public office, political debate was routinely conducted in acrimonious and abusive language—tribal affiliations were constantly exploited.

The scramble went on for six years, frittering away the wealth and potential of the country, leaving the vast majority of the population impoverished and demeaned by the avaricious behaviour of their elected leaders. The electorate was disgusted, but there was no chance of voting the politicians out of office: democracy itself had been corrupted.

On 15 January 1966, a group of young army majors launched an attempt to overthrow the regime by force. In Lagos, they seized the federal prime minister, Sir Abubakar Tafawa Balewa, executed him at the roadside and dumped his body in a ditch; in Ibadan the premier of the Western Region, Chief Akintola, was killed by rebel troops in a brief gun battle; in Kaduna, the Sardauna of Sokoto, premier of the Northern Region, was shot dead at his residence. The systematic killings also accounted for a number of senior army officers on the rebels' death list.

From army headquarters in Lagos, the army commander, Major-General Aguiyi-Ironsi, rallied loyal troops at garrisons around the country and swiftly gained control of the situation. The rebels surrendered and the military regime assumed power, with General Ironsi as its leader.

In the South, as discredited ministers and politicians were swept from office, the military takeover was widely applauded. In the North, however, there were suspicions about the motive of the majors' rebellion. All but one of the seven principal conspirators were from the East's major tribe, the Igbo.

They had murdered the North's two most important leaders, Tafawa Balewa and the Sardauna of Sokoto, and virtually all the senior Northern army officers. Yet no Igbo politician or regional premier had been killed, and only one senior Igbo officer (and that appeared to have been by mistake). Furthermore, the result of the coup had been to wrest power from the North and install a military government led by another Igbo: General Ironsi. Northerners became increasingly convinced that the majors' coup had been part of an Igbo conspiracy to gain control of the country.

Ironsi's subsequent actions did nothing to dampen Northern suspicions. He dallied over the fate of the conspirators, whom Southerners said should be released as heroes, while Northerners demanded they should be tried for mutiny and murder. He declared there was no place for regionalism and tribal consciousness in the new regime, yet the gaps which the majors' rebellion had created in the army were filled predominantly by Igbos. He appointed an Igbo to head an advisory commission and in late May confirmed Northern suspicions with the sudden announcement of a new constitution. Nigeria was no longer a federation, he declared in a broadcast. The regions were abolished. The regional civil services would be unified in a single national body. All political and tribal organizations were proscribed and political activity was banned.

Reaction was swift. Anti-government demonstrations in the North flared into riots during which several hundred Igbos were killed. Shaken, Ironsi gave assurances that no major constitutional changes would be made without consultation, but Northern unrest was now uncontainable.

Northern officers mounted their counter-coup at the end of July. Ironsi was seized, flogged, and executed; scores of Eastern officers and other ranks were rounded up and killed. Political manoeuvrings in the aftermath of the coup established a moderate Northerner, Lt-Col. Yakubu Gowon, as leader and the Northern and Western Regions united in favour of retaining a federal form of government. But the East was alienated. Lt-Col. Emeka Ojukwu, military governor of the Eastern Region, refused to accept Gowon as leader and declared that the coup had divided Nigeria into two parts—Igbo versus the rest. Ojukwu's defiant words provoked another round of violence in the North.

This time the killing was on a far more terrible scale than before, and the purpose was not simply vengeance but to drive Easterners out of the North altogether. "All the envy, resentment and mistrust that Northerners felt for the minority Eastern communities living in their midst burst out with explosive force into a pogrom that the authorities made no attempt to stop."[11] Disgruntled politicians, civil servants, and students urged the mobs on to the streets and the Northern army joined in. Thousands of Easterners were killed or maimed; thousands more fled—from the North and from other parts of Nigeria as the climate of fear touched Igbos everywhere. Traders, artisans, clerks, labourers, civil servants, and academics abandoned everything to join the exodus. By the end of the year, more than 1 million refugees, many wounded, exhausted or in shock, had sought safety in the East.

On 30 May 1967, a year after the first riots against the Igbo in the North, Ojukwu announced that the Eastern Region was seceding from the Nigerian Federation and amid scenes of jubilation proclaimed the independence of the new state of Biafra. Nigeria's civil war began little more than a month later.

"To Keep Nigeria One is a Task that Must be Done," posters published by the Federal Government announced during the war (above a crude drawing of a boot crushing the Biafran leader). Biafra surrendered in January 1970, after thirty months of courageous resistance. In defeat the Biafrans met not reprisals and crushing humiliation, as had been expected, but only the hand of reconciliation from the victors. An amnesty was extended to all who had fought against the federal government; Biafran rebels were reabsorbed in the federal army; Igbo civil servants returned to their posts in the government, and Igbo property in the North and other regions was restored to its owners. No reparations were demanded; no medals for service in the war were awarded. "In the history of warfare, there can rarely have been such a bloodless end and such a merciful aftermath."[12]

A condition of the peace terms[13] was that Nigeria should no longer be administered as three regions, but should be divided into many more states. Under continuing military rule, Nigeria's political and social landscape was transformed during this period by the interaction of two factors: the multiplication of states, and the wealth that oil revenues poured into the government's coffers. Instead of three strong regions with divisive tribal affiliations fighting to control the centre, thirty small states competed for influence and their share of the nation's wealth, making Nigeria a "unitary state with a strong decentralising component."[14] The change averted the threat of tribal conflict on a national scale, but left Nigerian politics as corrupt and self-serving as before.

Nigeria's problems during the 1970s and 1980s were exacerbated by an embarrassment of riches. The country was by no means rich at independence, but valuable cash crops at least brought a measure of economic security to most regions and to all levels of society. Oil production began in 1958, and oil revenues increased steadily until 1973, when oil-price rises provided unimagined wealth. Between 1968 and 1977 government revenue multiplied by a factor of thirty-four. But oil was a product linked only by money to the rest of the economy. Its earnings overvalued Nigeria's currency, so that the value of cash-crop exports collapsed while cheap imports undercut local industry.[15] Consequently, by cruel irony, while Nigeria earned fabulous amounts of wealth, the growth of per capita GDP slowed to 1.7 per cent a year during the 1970s, and declined to 1.1 per cent a year during the 1980s.[16]

Nigeria was under civilian rule from 1979 to 1983 before the army again seized power "to save this nation from imminent collapse." Elections for a restoration of civilian rule were held ten years later, but declared invalid when the electorate voted overwhelmingly for a presidential candidate, Moshood Abiola (a southerner of considerable wealth and influence), of whom the military did not approve. Military rule was resumed, and has continued. Meanwhile, the population more than doubled, from 42 million at independence to 92 million thirty years later and was projected to reach 95 million by the year 2000; wealth became more than ever concentrated in the hands of the few, while the average annual per capita income remained only U.S.$310 in 1993,[17] leaving Nigerians to wonder if democracy and an equitable distribution of the nation's wealth were possible in their country.

Or in Africa as a whole. By 1989, just seven of the forty-five states in sub-Saharan Africa preserved even the vestiges of democracy. Only Botswana held regular competitive elections. In the remainder, democracy had either been stifled by military rule, as in Nigeria, or abandoned in favour of one-party systems, as in Kenya and the Ivory Coast, for example, where heads of state transformed themselves into presidents-for-life and politicians voicing opposition were locked up (or worse).

The example of Botswana as an exception is instructive. Diamonds endowed Botswana with the world's fastest-growing economy[18] during the years following its independence in 1966, and the country's relatively small population (1.5 million in 1996) belonged almost exclusively to a single ethnic group—the Tswana (the Khoisan population of Botswana numbered fewer than 40,000, of whom only a small proportion live exclusively as hunters and gatherers). Prosperity and shared identity favour stability; lack of them polarizes dissent.

RWANDA WAS NEITHER PROSPEROUS nor blessed with a shared national identity at independence in July 1961. In making its hasty preparations for the handover of power, the Belgian colonial administration had attempted to satisfy the political demands of the Hutu and counter the recalcitrance of the Tutsi with proposals for a stage-by-stage process to independence for Ruanda–Urundi. Far from easing growing tensions in Rwanda (or Burundi), however, the Belgian proposals merely intensified passions.

With the Tutsi comprising only a small minority of the population, a Hutu victory in the forthcoming elections was guaranteed. Anxious, no doubt, to curry favour with the prospective leaders of independent Rwanda, the Belgians chose this moment of high tension to reverse their allegiances in the country. Throughout the colonial period, they had supported the Tutsi elite and connived with their subjugation of the Hutu. Now they changed sides and began backing the Hutu, even to the extent of declining to intervene as Hutu activists incited murderous attacks on the Tutsi. "Because of the force of circumstances, we have to take sides. We cannot remain neutral and passive," an officer commanding Belgian forces in Rwanda reported to his superiors.[19]

In early 1960, the colonial authorities began dismissing Tutsi chiefs and appointing Hutus to the freshly vacated posts. The new chiefs immediately organized the persecution of the Tutsi in the regions they now controlled, precipitating a mass exodus which eventually drove some 130,000 Rwandese Tutsi to take refuge in the Congo, Burundi, Tanzania, and Uganda. Communal elections held in July 1960 gave the Parti du Mouvement de l'Émancipation Hutu (Parmehutu) control of 210 of 229 *communes*; Tutsi candidates retained control of the remaining nineteen. Where the Tutsi had controlled the entire country just months before, the Hutu had suddenly taken their place; and in the *communes* the new *bourgmestres* readily adopted the "feudal"-style rule that the Tutsi had pursued, often in a manner no less oppressive than that of their predecessors.

The United Nations, obliged to grapple with the deteriorating Rwanda situation in parallel with its operations in the Congo, viewed developments with concern. While not in the least inclined to support Tutsi yearnings for the supremacy they had enjoyed in the colonial era, the Hutu seemed even less worthy of support. The UN called upon Belgium to organize some form of national reconciliation, an aim described by a senior Belgian adviser as "perfectly useless." A National Reconciliation Conference was convened nonetheless, in Ostend, with predictably inconclusive results. Meanwhile, the Belgian authorities colluded with the Hutu leaders to arrange what was subsequently described as a "legal coup."

On 28 January 1961, Rwanda's elected councillors and *bourgmestres* were called to an emergency meeting at Gitarama, the birthplace of the Hutu leader, Grégoire Kayibanda, where "the sovereign democratic Republic of Rwanda" was declared by acclamation before a crowd of 25,000 people. The UN had little choice but to accept the de facto independence of the territory; Belgium was relieved of responsibility for an increasingly chaotic situation.[20]

Legislative elections held under UN supervision in September 1961 confirmed Hutu supremacy; Rwanda became formally independent on 1 July 1962, under a republican government, with Grégoire Kayibanda as its president.

.   .   .

AT THE TIME OF INDEPENDENCE, official statistics showed that the Tutsi constituted only 9 per cent of the Rwanda population. In the interests of peace and harmony, a newly independent nation might have been expected to advocate assimilation, to do away with the identity cards which defined ethnic origin (see pages 620–21), and proclaim that the people were no longer either Hutu or Tutsi, they were Rwandans. There was already enough intermarriage and interdependence for such a policy to have succeeded.

But no. Uniquely in Africa, Rwandan nationalism had not been aroused by aims to drive out a colonial regime, it had been inspired by ambitions to take over an oppressive indigenous hegemony which the colonial authorities had installed and supported. Once in power, with an unassailable majority, the Hutu elite sought not reconciliation and national unity, but absolute supremacy.

Soon after independence, an official policy of ethnic quotas was introduced. Since the Tutsi represented only 9 per cent of the Rwanda population, no more than 9 per cent of students and children in school should be Tutsi; likewise, in the civil service and any other area of employment, the Tutsi should comprise no more than 9 per cent of the workforce.[21]

Meanwhile, sporadic violence continued: "150 Tutsi were killed around [Butare] in September–October 1961, 3,000 houses were burnt down and 22,000 people were displaced. New waves of refugees went on foot to the refugee camps in Uganda." The intention was clear: by fair means or foul, the Tutsi should be encouraged to leave. A United Nations report commented:

> The developments of these last eighteen months have brought about the racial dictatorship of one party . . . An oppressive system has been replaced by another one . . . It is quite possible that some day we will witness violent reactions on the part of the Tutsi.[22]

In fact they had already started. Since late 1960, small commandos of Tutsi exiles, called *Inyenzi* (cockroaches) by the Hutu, had been launching attacks from the Congo, Burundi, Tanzania, and Uganda, hoping to return by force. Though they had no chance of success—the Rwandese army was largely controlled by Belgians and could call upon Belgian paratroopers in a crisis— *Inyenzi* attacks on Hutu officials led to ferocious and indiscriminate reprisals. A United States investigating committee reported:

The biggest killings followed a large *Inyenzi* attack from Burundi on December 23, 1963. Hutu gangs killed an estimated ten thousand Tutsi, while the government executed about twenty prominent Tutsi, some of whose names had been on a list of prospective future ministers in a Tutsi-led government that had been found on the body of one of the attackers.[23]

Grégoire Kayibanda established a regime of such stifling authoritarianism that even its prime beneficiaries, the Hutu elite, found cause for complaint. As Kayibanda recognized a growing need to rally support for his rule, he turned again on the old enemies, the Tutsi, encouraging vigilantes to scrutinize the schools, the university, the civil service and even private businesses to ensure that the ethnic-quota policy was being respected. Not surprisingly, the "purification" campaign was carried out most vigorously by those of the educated elite who could expect to take over the posts occupied by allegedly surplus Tutsi.

The economic and psychological effects of the hatred generated by the "purification" campaign throughout the country set off another massive wave of Tutsi emigration. Furthermore, far from strengthening support for Kayibanda, the vigilante campaigns became a focus of opposition against him. On 5 July 1973, the senior army commander, Major-General Juvénal Habyarimana, took power. Kayibanda was imprisoned (where he is said to have been starved to death by his gaolers), and more than fifty of his supporters were killed over the next few years.[24]

As with the regime of Kayibanda before him, Habyarimana's "Second Republic" rapidly became a self-serving institution which fomented dissent among those excluded from the circles of privilege. Especially as rising oil prices and falling commodity revenues brought the economy of the country close to collapse by the late 1980s, and available sources of privilege shrank accordingly.

Meanwhile, refugee numbers in the surrounding states had mounted to at least 400,000, according to the United Nations High Commission for Refugees (UNHCR), and probably as many as 700,000 according to informal sources.[25] From among them, Tutsi leaders and a number of prominent Hutu opponents of the Habyarimana regime collaborated to recruit and arm what they called the Rwandese Patriotic Front (RPF). The RPF was preparing to invade, though insisting that its aim was not to reimpose Tutsi hegemony in Rwanda, only to overthrow a corrupt regime and establish democratic government. In mid-1990 agents in the Rwanda army and government advised that the Habyarimana regime was on the verge of collapse. One push and it would topple, they said.

The RPF attacked from Uganda in early October 1990 and were defeated within days, an outcome which owed as much to the support of French and Belgian troops (brought in to "protect their nationals") and Zairean troops as to the efficacy of the Rwanda army. In practical terms the invasion prompted Habyarimana to enlarge the Rwanda army very significantly. In October 1990 it had comprised about 5,000 men; one year later the number had risen to 24,000 and soared to over 35,000 during 1993. To arm this greatly enlarged force, France "enabled" the Rwanda government to buy assorted arms to the value of $6 million from Egypt during 1992. South Africa supplied arms worth $5.9 million; the United States had been a long-term supplier, though its military sales to Rwanda in 1993 alone are estimated to have been worth $600,000. All this weaponry for the most densely populated country in Africa: a small impoverished land on the brink of economic collapse.

But expansion of the country's military might at the expense of more sympathetic social initiatives was not the only consequence of the invasion. Predictably, reprisals ensued, not only against the Rwandese Tutsis who were accused of having collaborated with the RPF, but also against Hutus from the south, branded as "the enemy within," who were opposed to the government and thought likely to have close links with the Tutsi.

An International Commission on Human Rights subsequently established that the Rwandese government had killed about 2,000 Rwandese between October 1990 and January 1993, most of them Tutsi or Hutu belonging to opposition parties, and that "authorities at the highest level, including the President of the Republic, consented to the abuses." Furthermore, the commission found that the president and the government had encouraged armed militia to take "the lead in violence against Tutsi and members of the political opposition, thus 'privatising' violence formerly carried out by the state itself."[26]

Events now took a different turn. With the tacit support of the Uganda military, a reorganized RPF—whose numbers had expanded to nearly 12,000 by the end of 1992 and exceeded 25,000 in April 1994—launched a number of successful guerrilla attacks, striking targets across the length and breadth of the country. Realizing that the RPF was a force to be reckoned with, and under international pressure to do something about the government killings and the refugees, Habyarimana negotiated an agreement with the RPF leadership in August 1993. The Arusha Accords (the negotiations took place in Arusha, northern Tanzania) committed Rwanda to a number of radical reforms. There was to be a transitional government with the RPF guaranteed a share of power; a commission to oversee the safe return of the refugees; and a new army with the RPF contributing 40 per cent of the troops and 50 per cent of the high command.

All this was too much for the extremists in Habyarimana's government and the opposition. To them the Arusha Accords were tantamount to handing power back to the despised Tutsi elite. At the extremists' instigation, Radio Rwanda and an independent radio station began broadcasting a torrent of anti-government propaganda: denouncing the Arusha Accords, declaring that the RPF intended to reinstate the Tutsi hegemony of old, branding all Tutsi as RPF supporters, and exhorting listeners to kill Tutsi civilians and Hutu sympathizers.

The president did nothing to stop the broadcasts, probably because to have done so would have enraged the extremists still more, but he had already gone too far.

On 6 April 1994, an aircraft bringing President Habyarimana back from talks in Arusha was shot down as it came in to land at Kigali airport. Everyone on board was killed. The government immediately blamed Belgian UN troops but, although the crash has never been fully explained, circumstantial evidence strongly suggests that extremists intent on sabotaging the Arusha Accords were responsible.[27]

Killings on the scale of genocide began within hours of the president's death, and continued for three months. No one knows exactly how many people were killed. The only actual body counts were made in Kigali, where aid agencies coordinated the collection and mass burial of 60,000 bodies, and in Western Uganda, where the authorities estimated that about 40,000 bodies had floated across Lake Victoria from Rwanda and had been buried locally.

The definitive United Nations report concluded that 500,000 people had been killed,[28] but this could be conservative. An estimate arrived at by deducting the known number of Tutsi survivors (in the refugee centres) from 1991 census figures (adjusted to take account of a 3.2 per cent population growth rate), concludes that between 800,000 and 850,000 Tutsi died in the genocide, plus between 10,000 and 30,000 Hutu. The Tutsi population had been reduced from about 930,000 to no more than 130,000 in the space of 100 days.[29] For every Tutsi remaining alive, seven had died.

Killing on this scale did not result from random conflict and outrage. It had been organized and planned. The organizers of the Rwanda genocide are known, and have been named.[30] Members of the president's entourage and top-ranking officers in the Ministry of Defence were responsible for the organization and coordination—and even some bankers and businessmen were involved in the planning of the "final solution." At the local level, the slaughter was directed by the *gendarmerie,* the *préfets,* the *bourgmestres,* sundry civil servants and sympathizers.

The killings began in Kigali during the night of the president's death. In less than thirty-six hours the 1,500-man presidential guard had disposed of most of the "priority targets": politicians, journalists, and civil-rights activists. Away from the capital, groups of specially recruited militia, numbering about 50,000 country-wide, received their orders to murder through a chain of command that extended from the government to the *préfets, bourgmestres,* and local councillors.

The militia carried out their gruesome task with a variety of weapons— AK-47 assault rifles, grenades, and pangas (the all-purpose, heavy-bladed machetes). Some killed their victims with a club, studded with nails. A 1,200-page report on the Rwanda genocide contains the testimonies of survivors and helpless onlookers who witnessed some of the killings. The scale and brutality are horrifying: rape, torture, mutilation, unspeakably cruel murder; mothers forced to watch their children die before being killed themselves; children forced to kill their families. Mutilations were common, and macabre ritual was evident: "Brutality here does not end with murder. At massacre sites, corpses, many of them those of children, have been methodically dismembered and the body parts stacked neatly in separate piles."[31] Page after page, the reports are numbing to the point of disbelief. Inhuman. How could people do these terrible things?

They say that the militia was compelled to do it; that there is a strong authoritarian tradition in Rwandese culture, and an equally strong acceptance of group identity. When the authorities gave orders to kill and most of the group complied, it took a brave man indeed to abandon the crowd and refuse to join in. For one thing, such heroism was not without personal danger. And the same applied to the men who passed on the orders. "The vast majority of civil servants carried out their murderous duties with attitudes varying from careerist eagerness to sullen obediency."[32]

But however readily the orders were passed on, and however willingly the militia performed their assigned duties, the killings could not have been so thorough without the active participation of ordinary villagers. And the terrible truth revealed by the survivors' testimonies is that the main agents of the genocide were people who turned on their neighbours and slaughtered them.

Not so long before, the villagers all had been Rwandans, living together— working, trading, marrying—for the most part distinguished only by the invidious ethnic identity card which the Belgians had introduced and which the Hutu had refused to abolish. Now they were distinguished by life and death. There was compulsion, of course, but also evidence that years of indoctrination had convinced many people that the *Inyenzi* should die. Even where people were forced to take part in the killings they were helped along by the mental and emotional lubricant of ideology. "I regret what I did . . . I am ashamed, but what would you have done if you had been in my place?" a confessed killer pleaded. "Either you took part in the massacre or you were massacred yourself. So I took weapons and I defended the members of my tribe against the Tutsi."[33]

The terrible irony of the Rwanda genocide was that having reduced the country to anarchy and chaos, it allowed the RPF to take control. Hundreds of thousands of people, fearing Tutsi retribution, fled in panic from town to town as the RPF advanced across the breadth of the country. In Gisenyi province, on Rwanda's western border, more than one million crossed into Zaire in less than a week before the RPF took Gisenyi on 18 July 1994. On the same day, the RPF high command in Kigali formed a new government. Of its twenty-two ministers, sixteen were Hutu—including the president and the prime minister.

In the space of 100 days, civil war and genocide had killed more than 10 per cent of the population and forced another 30 per cent into exile. Those remaining in the country were traumatized and in complete disarray. Many had lost their houses and all they possessed; many more were displaced and living far from their homes; the psychological effects of their experiences were profound and not likely to be easily erased. The country's infrastructure had been left in ruins—no water or electricity in the towns, houses everywhere looted, with doors and window frames removed and even light-switches prised from the walls. From his exile in Zaire, the Rwandese chief of staff promised that "The RPF will rule over a desert."

"RWANDA IS OUR NIGHTMARE, South Africa is our dream," wrote the Nigerian Nobel Prize–winning novelist, Wole Soyinka, in May 1994, in an article entitled "The Bloodsoaked Quilt of Africa." In April that year, as Rwanda had descended into chaos, South Africa had raised the hopes of humanity to Utopian heights. Free elections had taken place on 26 April 1994. For the first time ever, the black majority of the country's 22.7 million electorate had voted. As had been expected, the African National Congress (ANC) secured a convincing majority in a multiracial parliament with a power-sharing government. Nelson Mandela, the man gaoled for treason in 1964 and released only in 1990, became president.

The events which occurred simultaneously in Rwanda and South Africa in April 1994 were at opposite extremes of human social behaviour; they demonstrate the depths and the heights to which humanity may fall or rise as it contends with the fundamentals of human existence. At root it is a matter of numbers and available resources; at the operational level it is a matter of leadership calibre and accountability.

Rwanda is the most densely populated country in Africa. By the late 1980s, with over 90 per cent of Rwandans living directly off the land, and a population growth rate of 3.2 per cent per year (one of the highest in the world), land shortage was acute and Rwanda was finding it increasingly difficult to feed itself. When the economy collapsed and the elite were left struggling to maintain their privileged status, they pleaded that Rwanda was overpopulated, and emphatically unable to accommodate the refugees whose return the RPF was threatening to facilitate. "The glass is full," President Habyarimana was fond of saying, "and I have nowhere to put the rest of the water."[34]

The proposition that growing population density inevitably leads to a country's economic and social decline has yet to be proved,[35] and has been convincingly dismissed in the case of Rwanda,[36] but it was a powerful weapon in the hands of the Rwanda elite. After a century of tribal indoctrination, the regime readily found supporters for the contention that the Tutsi were to blame for the country's problems and must be expelled. The irony is, of course, that only the removal of significant numbers of Hutu could have eased the problem of land shortages—the Tutsi were minority landowners.

In any event, war and genocide are an ineffective means of adjusting population size. The Khmer Rouge killed 12 per cent of the Cambodian population between 1975 and 1979, for instance, but within four years the country's population size had recovered and grown to more than its pre-1975 figure. The human capacity for population increase is such that the Rwandese population will overtake its 1994 levels in under three years, demographers from the United Nations Population Fund have estimated.[37] In other words, the terrible slaughter in Rwanda made only a blip on the demographic record, one that will be swiftly expunged, leaving only the memory of a nightmare to complicate the already formidable difficulties of reconciling numbers and resources in Rwanda.

In South Africa, also riven by racial divides and ruled by a minority, the white government and its black opponents viewed the country's mounting difficulties from a shared perspective as they negotiated the route to majority rule. Both parties accepted the inescapable facts of demography and concluded that the amount of resources must be increased and distributed more equitably.

The demographic facts were daunting. South Africa's population had trebled under apartheid, from 12,671,000 in 1951 to an estimated 38,900,000 in 1991. Furthermore, the black-to-white ratio of the population had also changed significantly during that period. In 1951, whites represented just over 21 per cent of the population, Coloureds and Asians accounted for nearly 11 per cent, and the remaining 68 per cent were blacks. A census conducted in 1985 revealed that the proportion of whites in the South African population had dropped by one-third, to an estimated 14 per cent; Coloureds and Asians had dropped slightly too, to 10 per cent—blacks now accounted for 76 per cent of the population.

Despite a steady inflow of white immigrants and official attempts to encourage large families among whites and contraception among blacks (in 1991 South Africa had twice as many family-planning clinics as health clinics),[38] the numerical strength of the whites was diminishing, and the trend was set to continue. Projections indicated that whites would make up only 9 per cent of the population by the year 2010, when blacks would comprise a full 83 per cent, numbering more than 53 million.[39]

Demographic changes on this scale not only altered the balance of racial power, but also threatened to bring the South African economy grinding to a halt if blacks did not participate in it more, as both producers and consumers. No less significantly, the growth of the black population undermined apartheid, which had been planned on the assumption that the black population at the end of the century would be only half what it actually became.

Quite apart from its brutal indignities, the apartheid state was a preposterous extravagance. Three parliamentary chambers, ten departments of education, health, and welfare (one for each "race" and one for each non-independent Homeland), large military and state security establishments, and the financially dependent Homelands all combined to place an enormous burden on the country's finances. Sanctions and a spate of disinvestment increased the load. In 1987, World Bank figures showed that South Africa's growth rate was among the lowest in the world. The gross domestic product per capita actually decreased by 1.1 per cent between 1980 and 1987.[40]

The pressure was insupportable, the facts inescapable. Apartheid would have to go, and with it white rule.

Ideological pressures certainly played a role in bringing down the apartheid regime in South Africa. The significance of the ANC's unyielding campaign of resistance is undeniable; anti-apartheid movements around the world seriously affected South Africa's international relations; and the ban on South African participation in international sporting events was something that many whites were anxious to see lifted. But there was nothing ideological about the relinquishing of power. It was not inspired by a sudden awakening to the injustices of apartheid, the move was strictly pragmatic: apartheid was no longer affordable.

Black victory at the polls in 1994 returned South Africa to the mainstream of African history, banishing the last of white rule from the continent. The change appeared to have been brought about by an urgent need to avoid disastrous conflict, but the threat of conflict—important though it had been—was only the surface tension of a deeper reality. In the end, the elites of two groups—black and white—both recognized the inescapable facts of numbers and resources.

Only a negotiated settlement could hope to contain, and then plan to relieve, the mounting pressures of population growth, urbanization, poverty, health, and education that the country was facing—anything else threatened chaos of Rwandese dimensions. It was no use simply blaming the whites or calling for them to be evicted from the land—there were not enough of them to make any difference. The demographers had predicted that by the year 2000 there would be 24 million Africans living in the urban areas, where they would outnumber urban whites by a factor of five to one and would expect to be gainfully employed.

And employment was now the key issue, in South Africa, in the continent, and in the world beyond. Throughout the greater part of humanity's existence, a shortage of labour had restrained the species development. For thousands of generations, people had struggled with the fact that there were barely enough of them to produce the food they needed to survive. Resources were ample, but numbers insufficient. Now the problem was reversed. Medical advances in the twentieth century had lengthened lifespans and increased fertility; in Africa, population growth rates had soared to unprecedented levels. Between 1950 and 1990, the total population of Africa multiplied threefold, from 200 million to 600 million; and in 1994 the UN Population Fund predicted that the number would double again in the next twenty-five years—despite the effects of war, Aids, and malnutrition.[41]

Meanwhile, as numbers rose food production had suffered a serious collapse. The evidence suggests that sub-Saharan Africa's per capita food output was on average adequate in the 1960s, but declined by around 1 per cent per year over the next twenty years.[42] The demand for cash crops and agricultural exports contributed significantly to the decline (farms that grew vegetables and flowers for export to Europe, for example, no longer produced food for Africa); so did the move to the cities.

In 1990, Africa as a whole was neither overpopulated nor underpopulated, but its numbers and resources were unevenly distributed. Rwanda was densely packed and running short of land, Zaire had abundant land and a shortage of labour. South Africa had both land and labour, but agriculture had been industrialized and labour that in a previous era would have been employed on the land, was gravitating towards the urban areas, looking for jobs.

By 1994, nearly 400,000 people entered the South African labour market each year—the majority of them black—but in the previous ten years fewer than ten out of every hundred had been able to find a job in the mainstream business sector. In 1994, at least 20 per cent of South Africa's labour force was unemployed, and the finance ministry calculated that simply to prevent unemployment rising would require an annual economic growth rate of 3.5 per cent; to reduce the absolute numbers of unemployed a sustainable growth rate of 7.5 per cent was needed.[43]

Such a level of growth will be difficult to achieve, threatening South Africa with the nightmare of internal strife and dissension if the dreams of independence are not fulfilled.

The scenes at polling stations throughout South Africa in April 1994, when millions of people assembled to vote, waiting patiently in queues that wove erratically through rural homesteads, townships, and suburban streets, must stand as one of the most heartening events in modern history. It was the first time that most of the electors had voted, and the first time that any national election had received such a degree of worldwide approval and support. Never before had the international media reported so extensively on an item of good news from Africa. After so much war, drought, and catastrophe, the world stopped and looked at the true face of Africa and Africans.

The South African election brought Nelson Mandela to power—a man whose strengths had been preserved intact by twenty-seven years of incarceration. By imprisoning him indefinitely, the apartheid regime had sought to remove Mandela's influence from the mainstream of political development, but in fact they had intensified it. Nelson Mandela emerged from prison perfectly equipped for his role in the new South Africa—unbowed by the oppression and indignities of the white regime, untainted by the failures and corruption of independent black Africa, steeled by years of study and reflection.

Nelson Mandela and the shift in political power that he represents affirm the value of integrity and ideals in an era when economic pragmatism is the dominant theme of world affairs. He and South Africa offer hope for all humanity—yes, hope from a continent that for too long has seemed to generate nothing but despair.

SPEAKING IN MAY 1995, a Catholic theologian in Rwanda, Laurien Ntezimana, confessed to having been shocked by the genocide in his country, but not astonished. People live behind a mask, he said, which the winds of history occasionally blow aside. The genocide was shocking, but only those who were naive about human nature could be astonished. He told an inquiring reporter: "I have the impression that you have not yet discovered man, either in his grandeur or in his misery; he can always surprise us."[44]

Appendix A: Some Metric Equivalents

1 centimetre (cm) = 0.394 inch

1 metre = 1.094 yards
1 kilometre = 0.6214 mile

1 kilogram = 2.205 lb

1 metric ton (1 tonne) = 0.984 long (UK)
ton; 1.1025 short (U.S.) tons

10 tonnes per hectare = 3.9 long (UK) tons
per acre

1 cubic centimetre (cc) = 0.061 cubic inch
1 millilitre (ml) = (UK) 0.035 fluid oz; (U.S.)
0.034 fluid oz
1 litre (= 1,000 ml) = (UK) 35.19 fluid oz *or*
1.76 pints *or* 0.22 gallon (U.S.) 33.82
fluid oz *or* 2.11 pints *or* 0.26 gallon
1 square metre = 1.196 square yards
1 square kilometre = 0.386 square mile
1 hectare = 2.471 acres

1° centigrade = 1.8° Fahrenheit

1 inch = 25.4 millimetres (mm)
1 foot = 0.348 metre (m)
1 yard = 0.9144 metre (m)
1 mile = 1.609 kilometres (km)

1 ounce (oz) = 28.35 grams (g)
1 pound (lb) = 0.4536 kilogram (kg)
1 hundredweight (cwt) = 50.8 kg
1 long (UK) ton (20 cwt) = 1.016 metric
tons
1 short (U.S.) ton (2,000 lb) = 0.907 metric
ton
1 long (UK) ton per acre = 2.5 tonnes per
hectare

1 cubic inch = 16.33 cubic centimetres (cc)

1 pint = (UK) 568 millilitres (ml); (U.S.) 473
millilitres (ml)
1 gallon = (UK) 4.55 litres (l); (U.S.) 3.78
litres (l)

1 square yard = 0.836 square metre
1 acre = 0.405 hectare (ha)
1 square mile = 259 hectares = 2.59 square
kilometres

1° Fahrenheit = 0.55° centigrade

In this book 1 billion = 1,000,000,000.
The league was equivalent to approximately 5 km or 3 miles.

APPENDIX B: MAPS AND CHART

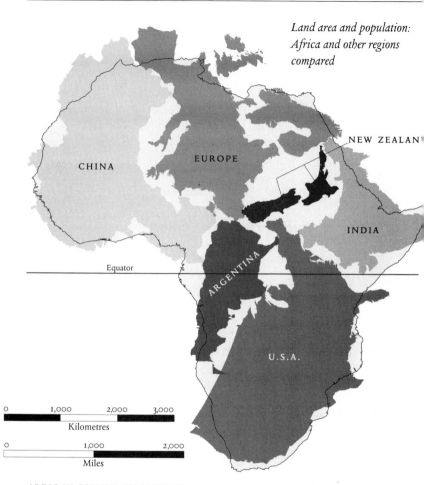

Land area and population: Africa and other regions compared

AREAS IN SQUARE KILOMETRES

China	9,604,733
U.S.A.	9,370,705
India	3,290,251
Europe	4,940,999
Argentina	2,769,139
New Zealand	268,894
TOTAL	30,244,721
AFRICA	30,343,551

POPULATIONS

China	1,234,300,000
U.S.A.	265,800,000
India	955,000,000
Europe	727,700,000
Argentina	35,000,000
New Zealand	3,600,000
TOTAL	3,221,400,400
AFRICA	748,100,000

MAP 1. Africa is large enough to encompass large portions of the rest of the world's land mass, though those areas support more than four times as many people. (Sources: Guthrie, 1986, p. 83; United Nations, *World Population 1996*)

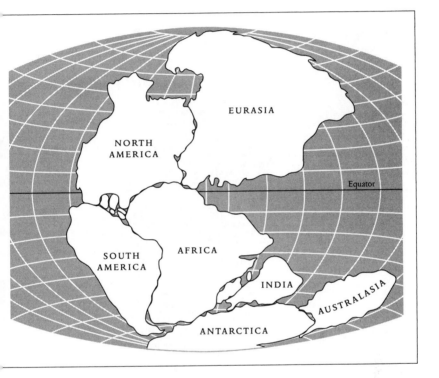

MAP 2. Pangaea, 200 million years ago (after Curtis and Barnes, 1989, p. 1013)

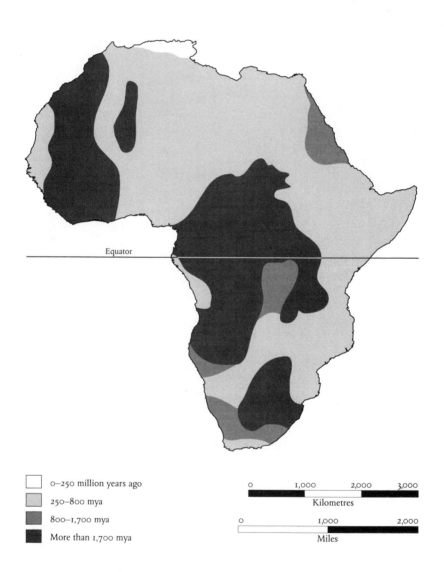

Equator

0–250 million years ago

250–800 mya

800–1,700 mya

More than 1,700 mya

MAP 3. The age of the African continental crust (after Nisbet, 1991, p. 28)

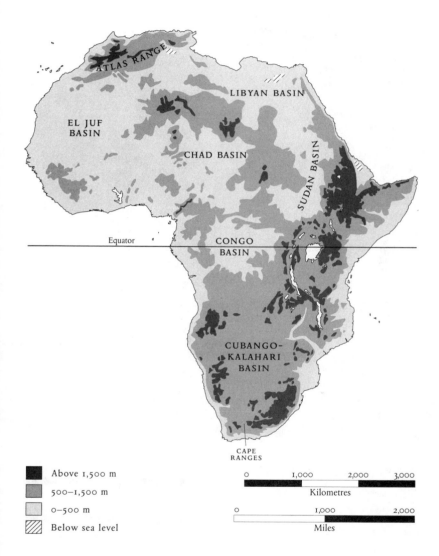

MAP 4. Relief and morphology of Africa (after Cooke, 1978, p. 18, Fig. 2.1)

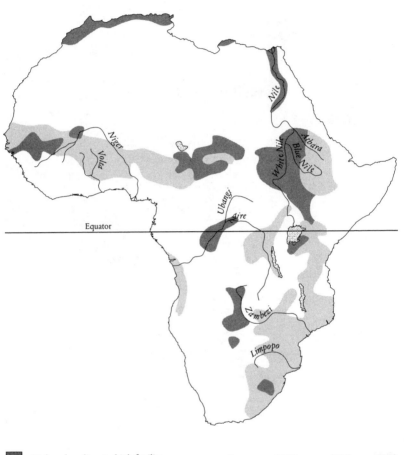

High and medium-to-high fertility

Medium fertility

Low fertility

Areas of water

0   1,000   2,000   3,000

Kilometres

0   1,000   2,000

Miles

MAP 5. Inherent fertility of African soils (after FAO, 1991, pp. 2, 41)

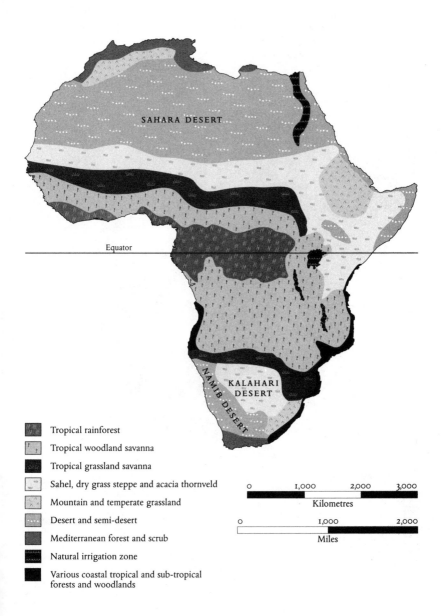

SAHARA DESERT

Equator

NAMIB DESERT

KALAHARI
DESERT

Tropical rainforest
Tropical woodland savanna
Tropical grassland savanna
Sahel, dry grass steppe and acacia thornveld
Mountain and temperate grassland
Desert and semi-desert
Mediterranean forest and scrub
Natural irrigation zone
Various coastal tropical and sub-tropical
forests and woodlands

| 0 | 1,000 | 2,000 | 3,000 |
Kilometres

| 0 | 1,000 | 2,000 |
Miles

MAP 6. The vegetation of modern Africa (after Shillington, 1989, 1.1)

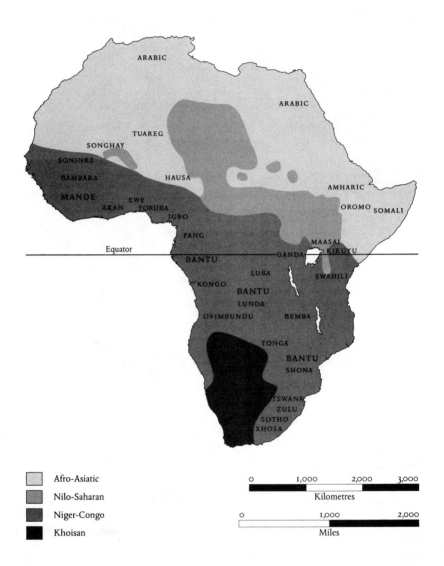

MAP 7. The languages of Africa (after Shillington, 1989, p. 50, 4.1)

MAP 8. The countries of Africa

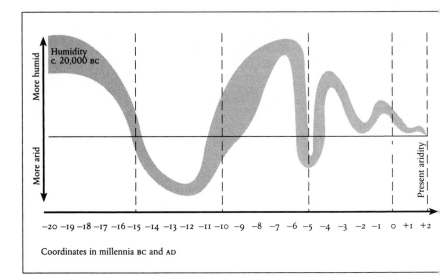

CLIMATIC CHANGE in Africa. The chart shows the extent to which climatic conditions in the Sahara have been more humid and more arid than at present over the last 22,000 years. It is to be expected that conditions elsewhere in Africa have been similarly variable. The width of the curve reflects divergences between regions, contradictory evidence, and variations in dating. (After Muzzolini, 1993, p. 228)

NOTES

PROLOGUE

1. Charles Guthrie, in Hansen and McMillan, 1986, p. 83
2. Lonsdale, 1981, p. 139
3. McNeill, 1977, p. 104
4. McEvedy, p. 37
5. J.C. Caldwell, 1985, in Unesco, 1981–93, vol. 7, p. 483

CHAPTER I
Building a Continent

1. T.N. Clifford, in Clifford and Gass, 1970, p. 14
2. Anhaeusser, in Tarling, 1978, p. 97
3. Cloud, p. 176
4. Cloud, p. 174; Cahen, p. 423; Cocks, p. 26
5. Hunter and Hamilton, in Tarling, 1978, p. 112
6. Nisbet, p. 61
7. Cocks, pp. 44–45
8. The Geological Society of South Africa, p. 14
9. Hunter and Hamilton, p. 109

10. (a) BIC minerals contributed 8,500 million rands to the South African economy in 1995, when 1.6 rands equalled 1.0 U.S. dollar. GNP: South Africa, $118 billion; Tanzania, $2.5 billion; Malawi, $2.03 billion (1993 figures). Population: South Africa, 35.28 million; Tanzania, 28.2 million; Malawi, 9.7 million (1993 estimates). Minerals Bureau of South

Africa, 1996, mineral production statistics for 1995, Department of Mineral and Energy Affairs, Johannesburg. (b) SBS World Guide, pp. 397, 399, 576, 584, 619, 621

11. The Geological Society of South Africa, p. 2

12. Von Gruenewaldt, quoted in Hunter and Hamilton

13. Minerals Bureau of South Africa, 1996

14. World Bank Report 1994, quoted in the *Guardian* leader, 18 May 1994

15. Hammerbeck and Allcock. Calculations assume unfolded Barberton Mountain Land to be two-thirds the present area of Lesotho (30,345 km^2), thus approximating to Wales (20,760 km^2) and Massachusetts (20,265 km^2)

16. Viljoen and Viljoen, in Clifford and Gass, p. 42

CHAPTER 2
Transitions

1. S.L. Miller, 1953, 1974

2. In particular C.K. Brain, who began research on the evolution of the earliest known animals after retiring from a career which had included pioneering studies into the origins and behaviour of early man. See especially: Brain, 1981, 1993 (ed.)

3. Dick, quoted in Goodacre, p. 261

4. Hallam

5. Jerome E. Dobson, p. 188

6. Du Toit, 1929

7. Young, p. 20, quoted in Jerome E. Dobson, p. 188

8. Nance, Worsley, and Moody; Murphy and Nance. The authors present their supercontinent cycle as a model which builds on an earlier description of episodic plate motions known as the Wilson cycle. See J.T. Wilson

9. Clifford and Gass, p. 18

10. Nance, Worsley, and Moody, p. 48; Partridge

11. McCauley *et al.*

12. Said, cited in McCauley *et al.*

13. Charig, p. 110

14. Gow

CHAPTER 3
Missing Links

1. Desmond Morris

2. Linnaeus

3. Simons, 1992, p. 199

4. Van Valen and Sloan, 1965a, 1965b

5. Napier and Napier, p. 23

6. Simons, 1992, p. 205

7. Simons, cited in Napier and Napier, p. 23

8. Napier and Napier, p. 23

9. Simons, 1967, p. 29

10. Flenley, p. 2

11. Myers

12. Nisbet, p. 164

13. Tewolde, p. 2

CHAPTER 4
Origins and Climate

1. Berger

2. Imbrie, p. 411

3. Urey

4. Urey, pp. 491, 497

5. Hays, Imbrie, and Shackleton; Shackleton and Opdyke

6. Neil Roberts, p. 176

7. Shackleton *et al.*

8. Kingdon, p. 13

9. Cooke, p. 19

10. Noted in *Science,* 1994, vol. 264, p. 955

11. Foley, 1994

12. Andrew Hill, 1987, p. 59

13. Foley, 1994, p. 287

CHAPTER 5
The Real World

1. Andrew Hill, 1994

2. Hill and Ward, p. 52; C. Guthrie, p. 83

3. R.E.F. Leakey

4. A. Hill *et al.*, 1991; A. Hill, 1995

5. A. Hill, 1994, p. 138; A. Hill, 1995, p. 183

6. A. Hill *et al.*, 1985, p. 760

7. Andrew Hill, 1985

8. A. Hill *et al.*, 1992

9. Curtis and Barnes, pp. 222–28

10. Quade, Cerling, and Bowman, cited in Andrew Hill, 1994a, p. 15

11. Kingston, Marino, and Hill

12. Vrba, 1980, 1985a, 1985b, 1992

13. Coppens

14. Coppens, p. 66

CHAPTER 6
Footsteps

1. Johanson, White, and Coppens

2. Andrew Hill, pers. comm., 1976; Reader, 1981, p. 236, (2nd edn) 1988a, p. 226

3. Darwin, 1871

4. Reader, 1988a, chap. 4; see also *Nature,* 23 May 1996, for further evidence concerning the identity of the person responsible.

5. Raymond Dart

6. R. Dart

7. ibid., p. 209

8. ibid., pp. 207–8

9. R. McNeill Alexander, p. 84

10. Steudel

11. C.O. Lovejoy

12. ibid.

13. Sinclair, Leakey, and Norton-Griffiths

14. Schaller and Lowther

CHAPTER 7
The Cutting Edge

1. Johanson

2. Johanson, White, and Coppens

3. Susman, Stern, and Jungers

4. Speth, 1989, p. 330

5. Stefansson, p. 234, cited in Speth, 1989, pp. 329–43

6. Høygaard, cited in Speth, 1989, p. 334

7. Blumenschine

8. Speth, 1989

9. Hatley and Kappelman

10. Wood, quoting Walker and Leakey

11. Andrew Hill, 1985; Ward and Hill

12. White, Suwa, and Asfaw

13. Walker, Leakey, Harris, and Brown; A. Walker

14. A. Walker

15. Bishop, Pickword, and Hill

16. Blumenschine

17. McBrearty and Moniz

CHAPTER 8
In the Mind's Eye

1. Isaac, p. 495, in Isaac and McCown

2. Feibel

3. Harris and Capaldo

4. Blumenschine, cited in Harris and Capaldo

5. Leakey, Tobias, and Napier

6. P.V. Tobias, p. 708

7. Leakey and Walker; Walker and Leakey (eds.)

8. Swisher *et al.*

9. Aiello and Wheeler

10. Gowlett, 1992b, p. 342

11. M.D. Leakey, p. 86

12. J. Desmond Clark, 1989, p. 570

CHAPTER 9
Cool Systems

1. Eighty thousand kilometres: Curtis and Barnes, p. 753

2. ibid., p. 768

3. Harrison, Tanner, Pilbeam, and Baker, p. 488

4. Wheeler, 1991, p. 118

5. Curtis and Barnes, p. 777

6. Harrison *et al.*, p. 452

7. ibid.

8. Wheeler, 1991, p. 119

9. Harrison *et al.*, p. 453

10. Wheeler, 1984, p. 91

11. ibid., p. 93

12. Wheeler, 1988, p. 64

13. Wheeler, 1992, p. 359

14. P.E. Wheeler, pers. comm., 8 March 1995

15. Aiello and Wheeler

16. ibid., table I

17. Wheeler, 1984, p. 97

CHAPTER 10
Out of Africa

1. Bräuer, 1984, 1989

2. See Stringer and McKie for the evidence for these dates and a discussion of alternative interpretations of global colonization.

3. A.C. Wilson *et al.*, 1985

4. Cann, Stoneking, and Wilson

5. Stoneking, Bhatia, and Wilson

6. Cann, Stoneking, and Wilson; Reader, 1988a, pp. 29–32

7. A.C. Wilson *et al.*, 1987

8. *Newsweek*

9. For a review of the issues see Mirazon and Foley

10. Cavalli-Sforza

11. Rouhani and Jones

CHAPTER 11
On Home Ground

1. J. Desmond Clark, 1967, cited in Richard H.V. Bell, p. 198

2. Richard H.V. Bell, in Huntley and Walker, p. 197

3. Coe

4. French, cited in Richard H.V. Bell, p. 200; Jewiss, cited in Richard H.V. Bell, p. 200

5. McNaughton, p. 698

6. ibid.

7. ibid., p. 697

8. McKey *et al.*, cited in Richard H.V. Bell, p. 213

9. Richard H.V. Bell, p. 205

CHAPTER 12
Word of Mouth

1. Wrangham

2. ibid., p. iii, quoted in Haraway, 1992, p. 178

3. R. Wrangham, August 1984, pers. comm., Harvard

4. Lieberman, 1992, p. 135

5. Lieberman, 1985, cited in Bradshaw, p. 629

6. Lieberman, 1992, p. 134

7. Pinker, quoted in *New Scientist,* 26 February 1994, p. 46

8. Ruhlen, in Ross, p. 71, and in Robert Wright, p. 67

9. Traill, in Tobias (ed.), 1978

10. R.I.M. Dunbar, 1992a, 1992b, 1993

11. Reader, 1988b, p. 217

12. R.I.M. Dunbar, 1992a, p. 29

13. ibid., p. 30

14. Robin Dunbar

CHAPTER 13
Ancestral Economies

1. Hubbell, cited in Winterhalder, p. 321
2. Hobbes
3. Herskovits, pp. 15–16, 69, 88, cited in Winterhalder, p. 321
4. Sahlins, in Lee and DeVore, p. 86
5. Haraway, p. 199
6. Coon, 1939, in Coon, 1948
7. Haraway, chap. 8
8. Reader, 1988a, p. 125
9. H.J. Deacon, 1993, in Aitken, Mellars, and Stringer
10. Lawrence H. Robbins *et al.*
11. M. Sahlins, quoted in Richard B. Lee, 1979, p. 2
12. Richard B. Lee, 1979, pp. xvii–xviii
13. Marshall
14. Laurens van der Post, p. 3, quoted in Edwin N. Wilmsen, 1989, p. 9
15. Richard B. Lee, 1979
16. R.B. Lee, 1968, p. 39
17. ibid., 1969, pp. 14–22, 60–63
18. ibid., 1968, p. 40
19. Lee and DeVore
20. ibid., p. ix
21. Laughlin, in Lee and DeVore, p. 304
22. Washburn and Lancaster, in Lee and DeVore, pp. 293, 303
23. Calculated from Richard B. Lee, 1979, p. 48
24. World Resources Institute, p. 238
25. Richard B. Lee, 1979, p. 48
26. World Resources Institute, p. 237
27. Nancy Howell, in Ward and Weiss, p. 30
28. Richard B. Lee, 1979, p. 310
29. ibid., p. 317
30. ibid., pp. 326–29
31. Speth, 1990, p. 165
32. Richard B. Lee, 1979, p. 1
33. Edwin N. Wilmsen, p. 3
34. R.B. Lee, 1965, cited in Edwin N. Wilmsen, p. 304
35. Edwin Wilmsen, 1978, 1982, cited in Speth, 1990, p. 164
36. Cited in Edwin N. Wilmsen

37. Bentley

38. R.B. Lee, 1979, p. 205

39. Speth, 1990, p. 158

40. ibid., p. 152

41. Richard B. Lee, 1982, in Leacock and Lee, p. 40; cited in Speth, 1990, p. 159

42. Stefansson, p. 234, quoted in Marvin Harris, p. 42

43. Speth, 1990, p. 155

44. Trussell, cited in Bentley, p. 96

45. Speth, 1990, p. 150

46. Spielmann, cited in Speth, 1990, p. 150

CHAPTER 14
The Human Potential

1. Speth, 1990, p. 152

2. Campbell, p. 123

3. Houston, in Sinclair and Norton-Griffiths, pp. 266–67, 276–77. Cited by R. Potts in R. Foley, p. 137

4. Louis Leakey

5. MacArthur and Wilson

6. Stini, in Garine and Harrison, pp. 32–3

7. Stini, p. 33

8. Hassan, 1981, p. 196

9. ibid., p. 58

10. Wheeler, 1992, p. 359

11. Hassan, 1981, p. 33

12. Hall and Rosillo-Calle, in Ominde and Juma, p. 50

13. World Resources Institute, p. 238

14. Coale

15. Hassan, 1981, p. 140. Population doubling in 130 years gives fifteen doublings in 2,000 years; 150 doubled fifteen times gives 4.9 million.

16. Cohen, p. 102, citing J.D. Clark, 1970, pp. 81, 108

17. Deacon and Thackeray, in J.C. Vogel, p. 379

18. J.D. Clark, 1970, p. 108

19. Louis Leakey

20. Brain and Sillen

21. Terra Amata in France: H. de Lumley, in Butzer and Isaac. Torralba and Ambrona in Spain: F.C. Howell; Freeman, in Butzer and Isaac. Vertesszollos in Hungary: Kretzoi and Vertes

22. John Gowlett, p. 115

23. John Parkington, 1991, pers. comm., Cape Town

24. Neil Roberts, p. 175

CHAPTER 15
Climate and Culture

1. J.D. Clark, 1976, in Harlan, de Wet, and Stemler (eds.), p. 67

2. ibid.

3. Tim White

4. Hilary Deacon, 1992, pers. comm., Royal Society meeting, 26 February 1992. See also H.J. Deacon, 1993

5. Paul S. Martin. See also L.S.B. Leakey, and P.S. Martin

6. Hays, Imbrie, and Shackleton, p. 1129

7. Deacon and Thackeray, in J.C. Vogel, p. 379

8. Halstead, pp. 168–69

9. H.J. Deacon, 1989, p. 560

10. Yellen

11. Gibbons

12. Yellen, p. 553

13. ibid., p. 554

14. Alison S. Brooks *et al.*, p. 552

15. John Gowlett, p. 103

16. CLIMAP Project Members, 1976

17. Neil Roberts, p. 175

18. Van Zinderen Bakker, p. 82

19. Grove, 1993, in Shaw, Sinclair, Andah, and Okpoko, pp. 34–35

20. Brooks and Robertshaw, in Gamble and Soffer, p. 133

21. J. Deacon, in Gamble and Soffer, p. 175

22. Van Zinderen Bakker, p. 79

23. Mitchell, in Gamble and Soffer, p. 195

24. Brooks and Robertshaw, in Gamble and Soffer, p. 137

25. Alan Hamilton, p. 88

26. Calculated from Alan Hamilton, p. 88, and World Resources Institute, p. 64

27. Brooks and Robertshaw, in Gamble and Soffer, pp. 137–38

28. ibid., p. 160

29. K.W. Butzer, cited in Van Zinderen Bakker, p. 91

30. Nick Walker, in Gamble and Soffer, p. 211

31. Brooks and Robertshaw, in Gamble and Soffer, pp. 145, 147

32. Slocum, in Reiter, p. 46. Cited in Haraway, p. 334

33. J. Deacon, in Gamble and Soffer, p. 179

34. Sarnthein, p. 46

35. Nick Walker, in Gamble and Soffer, p. 211

36. J.A.J. Gowlett, 1992a, p. 357

37. Oakley, p. 70

38. Phillipson, 1985, p. 89

39. Brooks and Robertshaw, in Gamble and Soffer, pp. 156–57

40. Wendorf, in Wendorf (ed.)

41. Close and Wendorf, 1990, in Gamble and Soffer, pp. 51–53

CHAPTER 16
The Beginnings of Agriculture

1. H.J. Deacon, 1989, pp. 557–58

2. Cowling; Van Rensburg; Myers

3. H.J. Deacon, 1989, pp. 557–58

4. Wendorf and Schild, 1980, pp. 264–65

5. Wendorf and Schild, 1989, in Wendorf, Schild, and Close, pp. 820–21. Cited in Shaw et al., p. 180

6. Hillman and Hather, in Wendorf, Schild, and Close, p. 180. Cited in Shaw *et al.*, p. 175

7. Wetterstrom, in Shaw *et al.*, pp. 178–79

8. Hassan, 1980, in Williams and Faure

9. ibid., p. 438

10. Rzoska, p. 148

11. Daniel A. Livingstone, in Williams and Faure, p. 341

12. A.T. Grove, in Shaw *et al.*, p. 35

13. Karl W. Butzer, 1980, in Williams and Faure, p. 272

14. Close and Wendorf, 1992, in Gebauer and Price, p. 63

15. Muzzolini, in Shaw *et al.*, p. 229

CHAPTER 17
Renewable Resources

1. Classon; Grigson, in Milles, Williams, and Gardner, pp. 77–109. Cited in Wendorf and Schild, 1995

2. Clutton-Brock, 1992, p. 382

3. Andrew B. Smith, 1992, p. 128

4. R.G. Klein, p. 126

5. Close and Wendorf, 1992, in Gebauer and Price, pp. 63–72

6. Wendorf (ed.), 1968, cited in Wendorf and Schild, 1984, p. 127

7. Christopher Ehret, in Shaw *et al.*, pp. 104–25

8. Phillipson, 1995, pers. comm., Cambridge

9. Other opinions cited in Wendorf and Schild, 1995, p. 124

10. Clutton-Brock, 1993, in Shaw *et al.*, pp. 68–69

11. Andrew B. Smith, 1992, p. 54

12. Loftus *et al.*

13. Close and Wendorf, 1992, in Gebauer and Price, pp. 63–72

14. Wendorf and Schild (eds.), 1990; Wendorf and Schild, 1984, in Clark and Brandt, p. 95

15. Playa, from the Spanish, meaning "shore," describes a flat area, free of vegetation and usually salty, lying at the bottom of a desert basin and dry except after rain (OED).

16. Wendorf and Schild (eds.), 1980, p. 269

17. ibid., pp. 335–36

18. Wendorf and Schild, 1995, p. 120

19. Wasylikowa, in Shaw *et al.*, pp. 154–64

20. El Hadidi, in Wendorf and Schild (eds.), 1980, p. 348

21. Stemler, in Clark and Brandt, pp. 127–31

22. Harlan, De Wet, and Stemler, in Harlan, De Wet, and Stemler (eds.), pp. 3–19

23. Roland Oliver, 1993, pers. comm., 26 April 1993

24. Clutton-Brock, 1993, p. 70

25. Stemler, p. 130

26. Roset, in A.E. Close, pp. 189–210. Cited in R. Haaland, 1992, p. 47

27. Banks, in Wendorf and Schild (eds.), 1980, pp. 301–2

28. R. Haaland, 1992, p. 48

29. Phillipson, 1985, p. 123

30. Hassan, 1986, p. 69

31. Hassan, 1980, in Williams and Faure, p. 447

CHAPTER 18
The Pastoral Scene

1. Clutton-Brock, 1992, p. 384

2. Zeuner, p. 199

3. Ingold, p. 138

4. Clutton-Brock, 1987, pp. 67, 137

5. Frederick J. Simoons, 1971, p. 434

6. Clutton-Brock, 1987, p. 67

7. Armelagos, in Clark and Brandt, p. 146

8. Marvin Harris, p. 140

9. Norman Kretchmer, p. 71

10. McCracken, p. 497

11. Cuatrecasas, Lockwood, and Caldwell, cited in McCracken

12. Cook and Kajubi

13. Johnson, Cole, and Ahern, p. 5

14. Norman Kretchmer, p. 76

15. N. Kretchmer *et al.*, cited in F.J. Simoons, p. 88

16. Muzzolini, in Shaw *et al.*, p. 228

17. Frederick J. Simoons, 1971, 1973

18. ibid., 1971, p. 437

19. McDonald

20. Andrew B. Smith, 1984, in Clark and Brandt, p. 86; Andrew B. Smith, 1992, p. 58

21. F.J. Simoons, 1971, p. 437; Lhote

22. Andrew B. Smith, 1992, p. 59

23. Roderick J. McIntosh, 1992, p. 12

24. Andrew B. Smith, 1992, p. 70

25. Among present-day pastoralists, such as the Maasai in East Africa, each family of eight persons requires a herd of at least forty cattle (including cows, calves, and bulls) to remain viable. With this ratio of stock to people, up to 525,000 families could have exploited the pastoralist potential of the Sahara during those good times—perhaps as many as 4,200,000 men, women, and children. See Pratt and Gwynne, pp. 35–37.

26. Nash, p. 214, cited in Andrew B. Smith, 1992, p. 128

27. Andrew B. Smith, 1992, p. 131

28. Barthelme, in Clark and Brandt, pp. 200–205

29. Ambrose, in Clark and Brandt, pp. 212–39

30. Ambrose, pp. 232–33

31. Monod, p. 134, cited in Peter Robertshaw, 1989, p. 208

32. Ambrose and DeNiro, cited in Peter Robertshaw, 1993, in Shaw *et al.*, p. 368

33. Ehret: 1971, p. 32; and 1974, p. 52, cited in Ambrose, in Clark and Brandt, p. 234

34. Peter Robertshaw, 1993, in Shaw *et al.*, p. 365

CHAPTER 19
The Impact of Iron

1. The form and content of these introductory paragraphs follow that of Phillipson, 1977a

2. Greenberg. Greenberg used the term "Niger–Kordofanian" for the group that includes the Bantu languages. Subsequently this has been replaced by the term "Niger–Congo."

3. Sanders

4. Greenberg, p. 51, cited in Oliver, p. 42

5. Dalby, 1981, in Unesco, vol. 1, p. 309

6. Nurse, in J.E.G. Sutton (ed.), 1996, p. 65

7. Malcolm Guthrie

8. Vansina, 1990, p. 55

9. See Phillipson, 1977b

10. E. Wilmsen, 1992, pers. comm., Johannesburg, 30 January 1992

11. Colin Renfrew, 1993, talk on BBC World Service, 13 October 1993

12. Wertime and Muhly, cited in Phillipson, 1985, p. 189

13. Shillington, 1989, p. 39

14. E.W. Herbert, 1984, p. 4

15. Grébénart, cited in S.K. McIntosh, 1994

16. Killick *et al.*, p. 390

17. E.W. Herbert, 1984, p. 10

18. Doran

19. Phillipson, 1985, p. 151

20. R.C.C. Law, in Oliver and Fage (eds.), vol. 2, pp. 87–147

21. Shillington, 1989, p. 46

22. Mauny, in Oliver and Fage (eds.), vol. 2, pp. 272–341

23. Phillipson, 1985, p. 151

24. Tylecote, cited in S.K. McIntosh, 1994

25. Oliver, p. 65

26. Oslisly, in J.E.G. Sutton (ed.), pp. 324–31

27. Taylor and Marchant, in J.E.G. Sutton, pp. 283–95

28. Shillington, 1989, p. 59

29. Randi Haaland, 1985, in Haaland and Shinnie, p. 67

30. Maclean, in J.E.G. Sutton (ed.), pp. 296–302

31. Randi Haaland, 1980

CHAPTER 20
The Nile

1. Karl Butzer, 1976, p. 83, cited in O'Connor, in Shaw *et al.*, p. 572

2. ibid., p. 572

3. Kitchen, in Shaw *et al.*, p. 601

4. John Gowlett, p. 181

5. Adams, 1977, quoted in Connah, 1987, p. 25

6. Connah, 1987, p. 66

7. Kitchen, in Shaw *et al.*, p. 587

8. Breasted, vol. 2, 486–87, cited in Davidson, 1991, p. 57

9. Breasted, vol. 1, paras. 333–36, 353, cited in Davidson, 1991, p. 55

10. Shinnie, pp. 162–63

11. Budge, reproduced in Shinnie, pp. 90–91

12. Arkell, p. 174, cited in Shinnie, p. 165

13. Shinnie, p. 166

14. Paraphrasing Adams, 1977, cited in note 5 above

15. John Alexander, p. 61

CHAPTER 21
The Periplus of the Erythraean Sea

1. Rickman cited in Reader, 1988b, pp. 225–26

2. ibid.

3. Casson, 1986, pp. 183–90, 201–8, 239–43, cited in Casson, 1989, p. 285

4. Casson, 1989, p. 12

5. ibid., p. 94

6. ibid., p. 10

7. ibid., p. 17

8. "*Periplus*" in Casson, 1989, p. 61

9. Davidson, 1991, p. 25

CHAPTER 22
Aksum

1. Salt, pp. 451–53, cited in Casson, 1989, p. 103

2. Anfray, in Unesco, vol. 2, p. 366

3. Casson, 1989, p. 103

4. "Aksum" is the spelling customarily used to denote the ancient city. "Axum" generally refers to the modern city, though some authors use it for both the ancient and the modern city.

5. Kobish[ch]anov, in Unesco, vol. 2, p. 384

6. Fattovich, p. 22

7. Goody, p. 25

8. Ehret, 1979, p. 161

9. Fattovich, pp. 17–18

10. Van Beek

11. Yalden, 1983

12. ibid.

13. Vavilov, 1926, 1951

14. Jack R. Harlan

15. Hawkes; D.R. Harris; J.T. Williams

16. Sauer, cited in Brandt, in Clark and Brandt, p. 174

17. F.J. Simoons, p. 9

18. Glyn Jones, p. 40

19. Ethiopian Central Statistical Office, 1984. Cited in Glyn Jones, p. 39

20. Glyn Jones, p. 37

21. Contenson, in Unesco, vol. 2, pp. 341–61

22. Fattovich, p. 17

23. Karl W. Butzer, 1981, p. 489

24. ibid., p. 473

25. ibid., p. 477

26. Munro-Hay, 1993, in Shaw *et al.*, p. 615

27. Casson, 1989, p. 53

28. Kobishchanov, pp. 104–5, 265, cited in Karl W. Butzer, 1981, p. 472

29. Karl W. Butzer, 1981, p. 473

30. Mohr, p. 236, cited in Karl W. Butzer, 1981, p. 473

31. Munro-Hay, 1991, p. 17

32. Karl W. Butzer, 1981, p. 488

33. Kobish[ch]anov, in Unesco, vol. 2, p. 394

34. Kobishchanov, p. 175, cited in Connah, 1987, p. 93

35. Phillipson, 1994, p. 2

36. Buxton, pp. 89–90, cited in Connah, 1987, p. 78

37. Karl W. Butzer, 1981, p. 492

38. ibid., pp. 489–90

39. For an account and interpretation of the legend see Hancock

CHAPTER 23
Cities without Citadels

1. Susan Keech McIntosh and Roderick J. McIntosh, in Shaw *et al.*, p. 622

2. ibid., pp. 622–23

3. Bovill; Levtzion. Both cited in R.J. and S.K. McIntosh, 1988, vol. 20, p. 147

4. Susan Keech McIntosh and Roderick J. McIntosh, in Shaw *et al.*, p. 622

5. S.K. and R.J. McIntosh, 1980

6. R.J. McIntosh, 1991

7. S.K. and R.J. McIntosh, 1980, p. 308

8. ibid., p. 333

9. ibid., p. 337

10. ibid., p. 335

11. Lowe-McConnell, in A.T. Grove (ed.), 1984, pp. 101–40

12. S.K. and R.J. McIntosh, 1980, p. 337

13. A.T. Grove, 1984, in A.T. Grove (ed.), 1984, p. 10

14. ibid., p. 15

15. R.J. McIntosh, 1993, p. 198

16. R.J. and S.K. McIntosh, 1984, in Clark and Brandt, pp. 171–72

17. R.J. McIntosh: 1992, p. 32; 1983

18. Barth, p. 1088, cited in R.J. McIntosh, 1992, p. 33

19. R.J. McIntosh, 1992, p. 33

20. Susan Keech McIntosh and Roderick J. McIntosh, in Shaw *et al.*, pp. 631–33

21. ibid., p. 632

22. ibid., p. 633

23. R.J. McIrtosh, 1991, p. 206

24. ibid., p. 204

25. R.J. McIntosh, 1994, pers. comm., Jenne, 30 January 1994

CHAPTER 24
Disease and Affliction

1. McNeill, 1977, p. 104

2. McEvedy, p. 37

3. J.C. Caldwell, in Unesco, vol. 7, 1985, p. 483

4. The parasites and disease organisms in question were transmitted from the environment to the human host, rather than from person to person. In virgin territory, without reinfection, they would have disappeared from the human population

5. Ransford, pp. 125–26

6. Giblin, pp. 61–62

7. Collins, in Harrison, 1982, p. 81

8. Ruffer, p. 18, cited in McNeill, 1977, p. 44

9. Ransford, p. 152

10. Harrison *et al.*, p. 517

11. Ransford, pp. 44–45

12. Mattingly

13. Harrison *et al.*, p. 233

14. McNeill, 1977, p. 47

15. Harrison *et al.*, p. 231

16. Frank B. Livingstone

17. Andrew Dobson, p. 414

18. McNeill, 1977, p. 51

19. Hull, pp. 879–906, cited in McNeill, 1977, p. 312

20. Phillips

21. Iliffe, 1995, p. 68

22. Lonsdale, 1981, p. 139

CHAPTER 25
Successful Harvests

1. Felix Nweke, 1992, pers. comm., Ibadan, International Institute of Tropical Agriculture, 12 October 1992

2. FAO, p. 43

3. J.R. Harlan, 1976, p. 200

4. Harlan, De Wet, and Stemler, in Harlan, De Wet, and Stemler (eds.), pp. 3–19

5. Marnham, p. 18

6. Braudel, cited in Unesco, 1981, vol. 1, p. 5

7. Unesco, 1981, vol. 1, p. 5

8. H.J.W. Mutsaers, 1992, pers. comm., Ibadan, International Institute of Tropical Agriculture, 14 October 1992

9. Iliffe, 1995, p. 112

10. Nweke, p. 14

11. Akobundu, p. 682

12. Fox, cited in Edholm, in Van Loon *et al.*, p. 20

13. Allan Hill

14. Pimental, cited in Ward, Sutherland, and Sutherland, p. 571

15. Ward, Sutherland, and Sutherland, pp. 571–72

16. Adams, 1989; Grove and Sutton

17. Vansina, 1990, pp. 85, 88, 172, 215; J.E.G. Sutton, 1989

18. Pitcairn

19. Ludwig, in Ruthenberg, p. 94

20. ibid.

21. Ukara Divisional Secretary's Office reports, 1988

22. Ludwig, in Ruthenberg, p. 91

23. Paulssen, cited in Ludwig, in Ruthenberg, p. 89

24. Malcolm

25. Colson, 1971b, in *Cambridge History of Africa,* vol. 3, p. 199

26. Marion Johnson, 1984, in Gregory, Cordell, and Gervais, p. 77

27. Marion Johnson, 1984

28. Moss, p. 266

29. Calef

30. National Parks Board of South Africa statistics, supplied by the Environment and Development Group, Oxford, 1996

31. C. Darwin, p. 117

32. Reader, 1972

33. Mayr, cited in Parker and Graham, vol. 34, p. 296

34. Parker and Graham, pts I and II

35. ibid., pt II, p. 25

CHAPTER 26
The Implications of Trade

1. Kopytoff, in Karp, pp. 3–84

2. Susan K. McIntosh, 1992, p. 5

3. ibid.

4. Leonard Thompson, 1990, p. 27

5. Lugard, 31 Oct. 1890, in Perham

6. Thomas N. Huffman, 1992, pers. comm., Harts Rivier, South Africa, 1 February 1992

7. Martin Hall, 1987a, pp. 39–40

8. Thomas N. Huffman, 1993a, p. 223

9. From the barter of essential goods and services between individuals and groups to the development of a trading economy is not a long step, but the transition takes time. It also requires a medium of exchange that will establish the agreed value of a variety of goods—in other words, a form of money, so that people could for example sell a chicken and buy a kilo of rice without having to find someone who both wanted a chicken and had rice to dispose of, as the barter system required

10. Edwin Wilmsen, 1992, pers. comm., Johannesburg, 30 January 1992

11. Hopkins, p. 53

12. Waldecker, no. 75, p. 9, cited in J. Alexander, in Shaw *et al.*, p. 652

13. Multhauf, p. 4

14. John Alexander, 1994, pers. comm., Cambridge, 5 July 1994

15. Paul E. Lovejoy, 1986, p. 12

16. Multhauf, p. 3. Estimates of the amount of salt required by cattle vary. Two sources cited give 36.5 kg and 10.3 kg annually per cow

17. W. Bosman, 1705, cited in Multhauf, p. 21

18. Paul E. Lovejoy, 1986, p. 86

19. Sutton, 1990, p. 17

20. Paul E. Lovejoy, 1986, p. 50

21. Connah, 1991, p. 483

22. Cameron, vol. 1, p. 232

23. Paul E. Lovejoy, 1986, p. 40

24. Mauny, in *Cambridge History of Africa,* vol. 2, p. 281

25. Blench, in Shaw *et al.*, pp. 88, 93

26. Bulliet, cited in Oliver, p. 131

27. Caton-Thompson, cited in Clutton-Brock, 1993, in Shaw *et al.*, p. 67

28. Rowley-Conwy, cited in Clutton-Brock, 1993, p. 66

29. Philip D. Curtin, 1984, p. 21

30. Lawrence

31. Vines, p. 22

32. Quoted in Vines, p. 25

33. Banks-Smith

34. Philip D. Curtin, 1984, p. 21

35. Nachtigal, vol. 2, p. 97

36. Hopkins, p. 48

37. Levene

38. Breunig

39. Robert Smith, p. 518

40. Hopkins, p. 72

41. S.K. and R.J. McIntosh, p. 446

42. Hopkins, p. 47

43. Iliffe, 1995, p. 82

44. Oliver, 1991, p. 137

45. Iliffe, 1995, p. 82

CHAPTER 27
Outposts and Inroads

1. Also known as the Ibo, though this is the anglicized version of the term; Igbo is the mother-tongue rendering.

2. Uchendu, in Miers and Kopytoff, p. 123

3. Shaw, 1970, 1977

4. Sutton, 1991, p. 146

5. Cradock, p. 9

6. Lawal; Posnansky; Shaw, 1975

7. Cradock, p. 9

8. Wansbrough, in Dalby (ed.), p. 89, cited in Levtzion and Hopkins, p. 1

9. National Geographic Society, p. 153

10. Levtzion and Hopkins, p. 81

11. Oliver, 1991, p. 99

12. Conrad and Fisher, p. 21

13. David Conrad, 1994, pers. comm., Bamako, Mali, 21 February 1994

14. George E. Brooks, 1994

15. Garrard

16. ibid., p. 449

17. Hopkins, p. 82

18. Levtzion and Hopkins, pp. 27–28

19. ibid., pp. 80–81, 110

20. The actual phrase in Levtzion and Hopkins, p. 81, is: "over a country inhabited by tribes of the Sudan whose dwellings are continuous."

21. Levtzion, pp. 23–25

22. J.E.G. Sutton, 1982

23. Eugenia W. Herbert

24. T. Monod, "Le Ma'den Ijâfen," pp. 286–320, cited (without source) in Eugenia W. Herbert, p. 114

25. Eugenia W. Herbert, pp. 114–15

26. Hopkins, p. 46

CHAPTER 28
Merrie Africa

1. Hopkins, p. 26

2. Fage, in Hair (ed.), p. 23

3. Meillassoux, "Introduction," in Meillassoux (ed.)

4. Miers and Kopytoff, p. 72

5. Quoted in Reader, 1988b, p. 223

6. Quoted without reference to source in Meillassoux, p. 95

7. Barbara and Allen Isaacman, in Miers and Kopytoff, pp. 107–8

8. Miers and Kopytoff, p. 66

9. ibid., p. 7

10. ibid., p. 11

11. ibid., p. 10

12. Uchendu, in Miers and Kopytoff, p. 125

13. Miers and Kopytoff, p. 32

14. Hopkins, p. 24

15. Baier and Lovejoy, in Miers and Kopytoff, p. 400

16. Connah, 1987, p. 134

17. Vansina, 1990, p. 156

18. Hopkins, p. 10

19. Gauthier, p. 171, quoted in Hopkins, p. 27

20. Cited in Iliffe, 1987, p. 9

21. Rodney, 1970, p. 36, cited in Hopkins, p. 27

CHAPTER 29
Bananas and Cattle

1. Marees, p. 162

2. International Food Policy Research Institute, p. 31

3. These introductory paragraphs are drawn from Christopher C. Wrigley

4. De Langhe, Swennen, and Vuysteke, in J.E.G. Sutton (ed.), p. 149

5. ibid., p. 150

6. Simmonds, 1966, quoted in De Langhe, Swennen, and Vuysteke, p. 150; Simmonds, 1962

7. Somatic mutation is that which occurs when plants are propagated from cuttings. It occurs much more rarely than the mutations which arise in the seeds of sexual reproduction. Bananas never produce seeds, so cuttings are the only viable means of propagation and somatic mutation the only means by which new cultivars could arise.

8. Felix E. Chami, 1994, pers. comm., Cambridge, British Institute in East Africa conference, 4–7 July 1994

9. De Langhe, Swennen, and Vuysteke, in J.E. G. Sutton (ed.), p. 148

10. Berchem, cited in De Langhe, Swennen, and Vuysteke, p. 147

11. Vansina, 1992, p. 64

12. De Langhe, Swennen, and Vuysteke, p. 154

13. Schoenbrun, 1990

14. ibid., 1993a, 1993b

15. ibid., 1993b, p. 23

16. ibid., 1993a, p. 52

17. ibid., p. 53

18. ibid., p. 48

19. J.E.G. Sutton, 1993, p. 59

20. ibid., 1990, p. 5

21. ibid., 1990, p. 10; 1993, p. 52

22. ibid., 1990, p. 10

23. ibid., p. 15

24. ibid.

25. ibid., p. 16

26. Speke, p. 201

27. ibid., p. 202

28. Sanders

29. Chris Wrigley; Schoenbrun, 1990

30. J.E.G. Sutton, 1993, p. 40

CHAPTER 30
Cattle and Gold

1. Peter S. Garlake, 1992, pers. comm., Borrowdale Homestead, Zimbabwe, 16 June 1992

2. Schmidt-Neilsen, pp. 79–80, cited in Andrew B. Smith, 1992, p. 104

3. John E.G. Sutton, 1993, p. 59

4. Tainton, cited in Andrew B. Smith, 1992, p. 135

5. Martin Hall, 1987a, pp. 77–78

6. Tyson and Lindesay

7. Thomas N. Huffman, 1993b

8. ibid., 1982, p. 145

9. Peter Garlake, 1973, p. 157

10. Pratt and Gwynne, cited in Andrew B. Smith, 1986, in Hall and Smith, p. 36

11. Dyson-Hudson, in Cernea, p. 173, cited in Andrew B. Smith, 1992, p. 109

12. Shillington, 1989, pp. 127–28

13. Quoted in J.E.G. Sutton, 1990, p. 66

14. Trimingham, in Chittick and Rotberg, pp. 115–46

15. Nisbet, p. 55

16. Peter S. Garlake, 1978

17. Brain, 1974, cited in Peter S. Garlake, 1978, p. 487

18. Graeme Barker, cited in Peter S. Garlake, 1978, p. 483

19. T.N. Huffman, 1996

20. Huffman and Vogel, p. 61

21. ibid., p. 68

22. Tuffnell

23. Peter S. Garlake, 1973, p. 120

24. T.N. Huffman, 1987, p. 18

25. Peter S. Garlake, 1973, pp. 131–33

26. T.N. Huffman, 1972, p. 362

27. Connah, 1987, p. 211

28. ibid., p. 212

29. T.N. Huffman, 1987, p. 1

30. ibid., 1981, cited in Connah, 1987, p. 197

31. D.N. Beach, in Birmingham and Martin, p. 256

32. David N. Beach, 1980, p. 46

33. D.N. Beach, 1983, p. 256

34. Summers

35. Phimister, cited in Connah, 1987, p. 213

36. McCrea and Pinchuk, p. 86

CHAPTER 31
"I Speak of Africa and Golden Joys"

1. William Shakespeare, *Henry IV,* part 2, v.iii.104. First published 1600

2. Eldred D. Jones

3. Snow, p. 5

4. Chang, p. 36

5. Snow, p. 21; Chang, p. 36

6. Chang, p. 42

7. Snow, Plate 1 (opposite p. 138)

8. Pacheco Pereira, p. 61

9. Unger, in Teixeira da Mota, pp. 229–49, cited in George E. Brooks, 1993, p. 123

10. McNeill, 1979, p. 302

11. Mercer, pp. 17–18, 59, 64, 112, 115–19, cited in Crosby, p. 80

12. George E. Brooks, 1993, p. 146

13. ibid., p. 122

14. Mercer, pp. 148–59, cited in Crosby, p. 87

15. Mercer, pp. 222–38

16. Azurara (trans. and ed. Beazley and Prestage, 1896, 1899), Hakluyt Society, Ser. 2, vol. 100, pp. 244–45. Gomes Eannes de Azurara was royal librarian, chronicler, and keeper of the archives of Portugal. His account of the Portuguese voyages from 1433 to 1448 was completed in February 1453 and is distinguished by the care he took to obtain the accounts of eyewitnesses or of participants in what he describes.

17. Crone, p. 9

18. ibid.

19. Crosby, p. 77

20. Azurara, in Beazley and Prestage, 1896, vol. 95, p. 30

21. ibid., p. 33

22. ibid., p. 35

23. ibid., 1899, vol. 100, p. 320, n. 74

24. ibid., 1896, vol. 95, p. 36

25. ibid., p. 37

26. ibid., pp. 44–50

27. ibid., pp. 54–57

28. Donnan, vol. 1, p. 24

29. Azurara, in Beazley and Prestage, 1896, vol. 95, pp. 81–82

30. ibid., 1896, vol. 95, p. 91, and 1899, vol. 100, pp. xii–xiii, 145, 255

CHAPTER 32
Portuguese Initiatives

1. Blake, 1977, p. 21

2. Azurara, in Beazley and Prestage, 1968, vol. 95, p. 83

3. Sintra, in Crone, p. 84

4. George E. Brooks, 1993, p. 124

5. Azurara, in Beazley and Prestage, 1896, vol. 95, p. 37

6. Cadamosto, in Crone, p. 20

7. Blake, 1977, pp. 16–17

8. Cadamosto, in Crone, p. 17; George E. Brooks, 1993, p. 127

9. Azurara, in Beazley and Prestage, 1896, vol. 95, p. 83

10. Da Silva Rego, p. 17; Boxer, 1968, p. 7

11. Cadamosto, in Crone, p. 17

12. George E. Brooks, 1993, pp. 127–28

13. Cadamosto, in Crone, p. 17

14. George E. Brooks, 1993, p. 143

15. ibid., 1987, pp. 146–47

16. Blake: 1942, vol. 1, pp. 67–69; 1977, pp. 26–28

17. George E. Brooks, 1993, p. 54

18. Pacheco Pereira, in Kimble, p. 118

19. Wilks, p. 336

20. Iliffe, 1995, p. 129

21. *Times Atlas,* map 89

22. Iliffe, 1995, p. 130

23. Blake, 1942, p. 13

24. ibid., 1977, pp. 98–99

25. ibid., 1942, pp. 70–77; 1977, p. 99; Pacheco Pereira, in Kimble, pp. 119–20

26. Blake, 1942, p. 77

27. ibid., p. 142

28. Pacheco Pereira, in Kimble, pp. 142–43

29. ibid., p. 148

30. Axelson, p. 14, n. 5

31. ibid., pp. 12–22

32. Hart

33. Axelson, p. 15

34. ibid., p. 18

35. ibid.

36. ibid., App. III

37. ibid., p. 22

CHAPTER 33
In Search of Prester John

1. Brian J. Barker, p. 5

2. Crawford, 1958, pp. 5, 212

3. Skelton, in Crawford, 1958, pp. 212–15

4. Tamrat, p. 256

5. ibid., p. 257

6. Crawford, 1958, p. 5

7. Tamrat, p. 266

8. ibid., p. 254

9. Crawford, 1958, pp. 13–20

10. ibid., pp. 17–18

11. Álvares (trans. Beckingham and Huntingford, 1961), pp. 369–76

12. Tamrat, p. 287

13. Álvares, pp. 369–76

14. Pacheco Pereira, in Kimble, p. 153. Cited in Axelson, p. 33

15. Ravenstein

16. ibid., p. 6

17. ibid., p. 8

18. ibid., pp. 9–13

19. Axelson, pp. 19, 37

20. ibid., p. 37

21. ibid., p. 38

22. Ravenstein, pp. 17–18

23. ibid., p. 21

24. ibid., p. 24

25. Axelson, p. 44

26. Ravenstein, p. 39

27. ibid., p. 46

28. Boxer, 1968, pp. 13–14

29. Axelson, p. 47

30. Ravenstein, p. 89

31. Axelson, p. 47

32. Ravenstein, pp. 93–94

CHAPTER 34
Harnessed to Europe

1. Axelson, p. 58

2. ibid, pp. 108–9

3. ibid., pp. 110–11

4. Thomas N. Huffman, 1995, pers. comm., 11 November 1995

5. R.J. McIntosh, 1995, pers. comm., 17 November 1995

6. Álvares (trans. Beckingham and Huntingford, 1961)

7. ibid., p. 512

8. ibid., p. 191

9. ibid., p. 198

10. ibid., p. 141

11. ibid., p. 189

12. ibid., p. 132

13. ibid., pp. 136–37

14. ibid., p. 514

15. ibid., p. 166

16. Aksum/Axum: see Chapter 22, n. 4, above

17. Álvares (trans. Beckingham and Huntingford, 1961), p. 515

18. ibid., pp. 502–6

19. ibid., p. 516

20. ibid., p. 509

CHAPTER 35
Nothing Else to Sell

1. Adam Jones, 1986, 1987a, 1987b

2. Davidson, 1991, 1992; Oliver and Fage; *Cambridge History of Africa*; Unesco; Shillington; Oliver

3. Caldwell, in Unesco, vol. 7, p. 483

4. Oliver, p. 246

5. ibid., p. 147

6. ibid., p. 145

7. Boxer, 1969, pp. 98–99

8. ibid., p. 99

9. Thornton, p. 151

10. ibid., pp. 155–56

11. George E. Brooks, 1993, p. 141

12. Boxer, 1969, p. 100

13. Adapted from translation by Davidson, 1991, pp. 223–25

14. Iliffe, 1995, p. 130

CHAPTER 36
The Atlantic Slave Trade

1. Achebe, p. 121 (1972 edn)

2. But though related here as Honoria Bailor-Caulker told the story in Freetown, 5 October 1991, subsequent checking has shown it to be only partially true. Cardinal Newman wrote the hymn "Amazing Grace" in 1833, not John Newton, who lived from 1725 to 1807.

3. Francis Childe, 1992, pers. comm., ex United Nations office, Dakar, Senegal

4. P.D. Curtin, 1969, p. 268. Cited in Iliffe, 1995, p. 131

5. Paul E. Lovejoy, 1989, p. 368

6. Inikori, 1984, in Unesco, vol. 5, pp. 80–82

7. Iliffe, 1995, p. 131

8. Saunders, p. 59

9. Vogt: 1973; 1979, pp. 57–58, 72, cited in Paul E. Lovejoy, 1983, p. 37

10. Paul E. Lovejoy, 1983, p. 19

11. Kaplan, p. 319

12. Blake, 1977 (2nd edn), p. 77

13. ibid., p. 75

14. ibid., pp. 107–9

15. Boxer, 1968, p. 20

16. P.D. Curtin, 1969, pp. 268, 287. Cited in Iliffe, 1995, p. 131

17. Donnan, vol. 1, pp. 14–15

18. ibid., p. 42

19. ibid., p. 16

20. George E. Brooks, 1993, pp. 148–49

21. Donnan, vol. 1, p. 17

22. ibid., p. 10

23. Markham, p. 5. This transcription uses modern English orthography.

24. ibid., pp. 6–7

25. Donnan, vol. 1, p. 46

26. ibid., p. 47

27. Markham, pp. 16–17

28. ibid., p. 52

29. Donnan, vol. 1, p. 51

30. Markham, p. 64

31. Donnan, vol. 1, p. 59

32. M.W.S. Hawkins, p. 67

33. Donnan, vol. 1, p. 98

34. ibid., p. 101

35. K.G. Davies, p. 59

36. Newton, in Martin and Spurrell, pp. ix–x

37. ibid., pp. 95–96

38. ibid., pp. xii–xiii

39. ibid., p. 32

40. ibid., p. 42

41. ibid., p. 95

42. Isert, p. 175

43. J.C. Miller, 1988, p. 5

44. Walvin, p. 46

45. ibid., p. 47

46. J.C. Miller, 1988, p. 338

47. Galenson, p. 43

48. Klein and Engerman, in Anstey and Hair, p. 117

49. Newton, in Martin and Spurrell, p. 103

50. ibid., p. 29

51. J.C. Miller, 1988, p. 411

52. Falconbridge, quoted in Walvin, p. 50

CHAPTER 37
African Slave Traders

1. Hopkins, p. 105

2. Metcalf, 1987b, p. 385; Hopkins, p. 110

3. Herbert, p. 126

4. ibid.

5. ibid., p. 132

6. ibid., p. 201

7. ibid., p. 132

8. Ryder, 1969, p. 61, cited in Hogendorn and Johnson, p. 30

9. Ryder, 1959, cited in Hogendorn and Johnson, p. 109

10. Paul E. Lovejoy, 1988

11. C.H. Robinson, p. 46, cited in Hogendorn and Johnson, p. 129

12. Hogendorn and Johnson, p. 6

13. ibid., p. 5

14. Gray and Bell, cited in Hogendorn and Johnson, p. 34

15. Hogendorn and Johnson, p. 83

16. ibid., p. 30

17. ibid., p. 101

18. Paul E. Lovejoy, 1983, p. 19

19. Hogendorn and Johnson, p. 58

20. ibid., p. 111

21. ibid., p. 110

22. Johnston, pp. 131–32, quoted in Herbert, p. 124, who notes that, although Johnston was referring to the Congo in the mid nineteenth century, "his comment might have applied to any region or any moment during this period."

23. Johnson, 1966

24. Metcalf, 1987a, p. 35

25. ibid., p. 34

26. ibid., 1987b, p. 379

27. Miles's barter lists are analysed in papers by George Metcalf, 1987a, 1987b, from which the figures quoted in these paragraphs are taken.

28. Metcalf, 1987a, p. 37

29. ibid., pp. 29–33

30. References cited in Metcalf, 1987a, p. 32, n. 15

31. Robin Law, 1991, p. 208

32. Donnan, vol. 2

33. Forde

34. Hair, 1990, p. 359

35. ibid., pp. 361, 363

36. Forde, pp. 8, 36

37. ibid., p. 19

38. ibid., p. 50

39. ibid., p. 57

CHAPTER 38
Africa Transformed

1. Robbins *et al.*, 1993

2. Hogendorn and Johnson, p. 108

3. J.C. Miller, 1988, pp. 71, 73

4. Paul E. Lovejoy: 1983, p. 22; 1989

5. Manning, 1990, p. 24

6. David Eltis, 1990, p. 491

7. ibid., 1987

8. Eltis and Jennings, p. 958, quoted in Paul E. Lovejoy, 1989, p. 367

9. Paul E. Lovejoy, 1989, p. 367

10. Vansina, 1985

11. J.C. Miller, 1988, p. 149

12. ibid., pp. 153–54

13. ibid., pp. 154–55

14. James L.A. Webb, p. 222

15. Park, pp. 231–33, quoted in Donnan, vol. 2, p. 635

16. Edwards

17. ibid., pp. 15–16

18. Johnson, 1976, in Anstey and Hair, p. 31

19. Moore, quoted in Donnan, vol. 2, p. 396

20. William James, 1789. Testimony quoted in Donnan, vol. 2, p. 598
21. Curtin and Vansina
22. Hair, 1965, p. 203
23. ibid., p. 200
24. J.C. Miller, 1988, p. 71
25. Thomas and Bean
26. Manning, 1988, in Daget, cited in Paul E. Lovejoy, 1989, p. 385
27. Manning, 1990, p. 60
28. ibid., p. 84
29. ibid., 1988, quoted in Paul E. Lovejoy, 1989, p. 387
30. J.C. Miller, 1988, p. 141
31. ibid., p. 140
32. Miracle
33. Thomas N. Huffman, 1993b
34. Duarte Lopez, 1591, quoted in Miracle
35. Barbot, vol. 5, p. 197, quoted in Miracle, p. 43
36. Miracle, p. 43
37. Johnson, 1976, p. 18
38. Iliffe, 1995, p. 129
39. Gemery and Hogendorn, in Dewey and Hopkins, p. 247
40. Kea, p. 197, quoted in Gemery and Hogendorn, p. 248
41. P.D. Curtin, 1975, p. 324, cited in Richards, p. 44
42. J.C. Miller, 1988, p. 88
43. Gemery and Hogendorn, p. 248
44. Inikori, 1977, p. 349
45. Johnson, 1976, p. 19
46. Richards, pp. 46–47
47. Inikori, 1977, p. 367
48. Metcalf, 1987b, p. 384
49. ibid., p. 385
50. Inikori, 1977, p. 350
51. Paul E. Lovejoy, 1983, p. 106

CHAPTER 39
The Aftermath

1. Hopkins, p. 103
2. Iliffe, 1995, p. 135
3. ibid., p. 145

4. J.C. Miller, 1988, pp. 113–14

5. Iliffe, 1995, p. 142

6. ibid., p. 139

7. Forde, pp. 140–48

8. Burton: 1864, chap. 13: "Of the So-Called Amazons and the Dahoman Army"; 1865

9. Iliffe, 1995, p. 144

10. Robin Law, 1990, p. 213

11. Dalzell, quoted in Donnan, vol. 2, p. 596

12. Gomer Williams, p. 551

13. ibid., p. 576

14. Burton, 1864, pp. 232–33

15. ibid., p. 235, n. 54

16. ibid., pp. 235–36

17. Asante—often spelt Ashanti, which was a transliteration from the language of the Ga people, a neighbouring group whose pronunciation of the name differs from that of the Asante themselves

18. Iliffe, 1995, p. 144

19. Manning, 1990, p. 151

20. Villiers, pp. 78–81, cited in Manning, 1990, p. 151

21. Donnan, vol. 2, p. 592

22. Paul E. Lovejoy, 1983, pp. 283–87

23. ibid., p. 19

24. Iliffe, 1995, p. 148

25. LeVeen, cited in Hopkins, p. 113

26. Clarkson, quoted in West, p. 44

27. West, pp. 44–45

28. Jefferson, quoted in West, p. 95

29. Burns, quoted in West, p. 89

30. Jefferson, p. 253, quoted in West, p. 89

31. Quoted in West, p. 99

32. ibid., p. 114

33. Ashmun, p. 25, quoted in West, p. 121

34. Ali Eisami Gazirmabe, in P.D. Curtin (ed.), 1967, p. 214, quoted in Iliffe, 1995, p. 148

35. Paul E. Lovejoy, 1983, p. 163

36. ibid., 1989, p. 365

37. ibid., 1983, p. 162

38. ibid., p. 167

39. ibid., p. 174

40. As did the Bible, namely Leviticus 25:44–46: "Both thy bondmen, and thy bond-maids, which thou shalt have, shall be of the heathen that are about you; of them shall ye buy bondmen and bondmaids . . . of the children of strangers . . . shall ye buy . . . and they shall be your possession."

41. Paul E. Lovejoy, 1983, p. 184

42. ibid., pp. 184–85

43. ibid., 1989, p. 392

44. ibid., 1983, p. 185

45. ibid., p. 203

46. ibid., p. 185

47. ibid., pp. 224–25

CHAPTER 40
The Climatic Context

1. Hopkins, p. 125

2. Iliffe, 1995, p. 149

3. Hogendorn and Johnson, pp. 112, 153

4. Shillington, 1989, p. 238

5. Paul E. Lovejoy, 1983, p. 7

6. ibid., p. 224

7. ibid., 1989, p. 392

8. ibid., 1983, pp. 9–11

9. Iliffe, 1995, p. 133

10. J.C. Miller, 1988, p. 157

11. ibid., 1982, p. 22

12. ibid., p. 32

13. ibid., p. 21

14. ibid., p. 26

15. ibid., p. 40

16. ibid., p. 25

17. ibid., p. 26

18. ibid., p. 46

19. ibid., p. 23

20. ibid., p. 21

21. ibid., p. 23

22. ibid., p. 21

23. ibid., p. 53

24. Hilton, p. 219, quoted in J.C. Miller, 1988, p. 155

25. J.C. Miller, 1988, p. 159

26. ibid., pp. 38–39

27. J. C. Miller, 1988

28. Thomas N. Huffman, 1986, p. 293, citing Martin Hall, 1976

29. Nicholson, in Hansen and McMillan, p. 117

30. Nicholson, p. 115

31. The single most influential body of work contributing to this view was Theal, 1882–1919

32. Leonard Thompson, 1990, p. 15

33. Boxer (ed.), 1959, pp. 121–22, quoted in Shillington, 1989, p. 155

34. Bird, p. 46, quoted in Leonard Thompson, 1990, p. 21

35. Miracle, pp. 48–49

36. Thomas N. Huffman, 1993b

37. ibid., 1986, pp. 292–93

38. Nicholson, p. 115

CHAPTER 41
Settlers

1. Raven-Hart, p. 19

2. Traill, in Philip V.T. Tobias, p. 139

3. Andrew B. Smith, 1992, p. 203

4. The means by which Khoisan pastoralism was carried forward is a subject of speculation. It could have been achieved by a founding group of Khoisan herders colonizing new territory as their numbers increased, or by the practice of pastoralism spreading from group to group across regions already inhabited by the Khoisan.

5. Andrew B. Smith, 1992, pp. 193–200

6. Elphick and Giliomee, p. 3

7. Raven-Hart, p. 17

8. ibid., p. 23

9. ibid., p. 35

10. ibid., p. 32

11. ibid., p. 40

12. ibid., p. 33

13. ibid., p. 61

14. ibid., pp. 72–73

15. ibid., p. 75

16. Leonard Thompson, 1990, p. 33

17. Elphick and Giliomee, p. 111

18. ibid., p. 70

19. ibid., p. 10

20. Thom, vol. 1, p. 270, quoted in Andrew B. Smith, 1983, p. 260

21. Abbott, pp. 10–11

22. Davenport and Hunt, p. 2

23. Leibbrandt, p. 113

24. ibid., p. 118

25. Elphick and Giliomee, p. 112

26. Sparrman, p. 251, quoted in Andrew B. Smith, 1983, p. 261

27. Moodie, vol. 1, p. 205, quoted in Shillington, 1989, pp. 215–16

28. Leonard Thompson, 1990, p. 35

29. Elphick and Giliomee, pp. 112–16

30. Leonard Thompson, 1990, pp. 35–36

31. Elphick and Giliomee, p. 138

32. ibid., p. 21

33. Mentzel, pt. 1, p. 36, quoted in Davenport and Hunt, p. 11

34. Hendrik Swellengrebel, p. 348, quoted in Leonard Thompson, 1990, p. 48

35. Elphick and Giliomee, p. 26

36. ibid., p. 27

37. Leonard Thompson, 1990, p. 49

38. Elphick and Giliomee, pp. 27–28

39. ibid., p. 422

40. Shillington, 1989, p. 219

41. Elphick and Giliomee, p. 432

42. ibid., p. 434

43. ibid., p. 439

44. Moodie, pt 5, pp. 17–19, quoted in Leonard Thompson, 1990, p. 54

45. Maclennan, quoted in Leonard Thompson, 1990, p. 55

46. Elphick and Giliomee, pp. 481–82

CHAPTER 42
Black and White Frontiers

1. Peires, in Elphick and Giliomee, p. 474

2. ibid., p. 474

3. ibid.; H.J.M. Johnston

4. Bryer and Hunt, p. 17

5. Crais, p. 129

6. Quoted in Crais, p. 130

7. Bryer and Hunt, pp. 41–42

8. Peires, p. 475

9. ibid.

10. Quoted in Leonard Thompson, 1990, p. 54

11. Peires, p. 485

12. Quoted in A.C.M. Webb, p. 45

13. ibid., p. 44

14. Bryer and Hunt, p. 66

15. Crais, p. 133

16. Peires, p. 480

17. Lichtenstein, vol. 1, p. 347, cited in Peires, p. 480

18. Peires, p. 481

19. Brownlee, in G. Thompson, vol. 2, p. 200, quoted in Peires, pp. 482–83

20. J.S. Galbraith, pp. 100ff, quoted in A.C.M. Webb, p. 45

21. Peires, p. 486

22. Omer-Cooper, p. 4

23. Gluckman, 1960

24. Shillington, 1989, p. 260

25. Omer-Cooper, pp. 3–4

26. Donald R. Morris, 1965/1968. Feature films: *Zulu* (1964); *Zulu Dawn* (1979)

27. Lowie, 1927, 1950; Service, cited in Raum, p. 125

28. Guy, pp. 4–7

29. Maggs

30. Tim Maggs, 1992, pers. comm., Pietermaritzburg, 23 January 1992

31. Martin Hall, 1987b, p. 126

32. Bonner; Borland, cited in Martin Hall, 1987a, p. 128

33. John B. Wright, pp. 4–5

34. ibid., p. 9

35. ibid., p. 22

36. Raum, p. 127

CHAPTER 43
Zulu Myths and Reality

1. Cobbing, 1991, pp. 7, 11

2. Rice, p. 269, cited in Vail and White, p. 17

3. Allen F. Isaacman, p. 86, cited in Alpers, p. 188

4. Bannister, p. xxxii, quoted in Eldredge, in Carolyn Hamilton

5. Eldredge, in Carolyn Hamilton, pp. 129–30

6. Paul E. Lovejoy, 1983, p. 60

7. Eldredge, p. 132

8. British Parliamentary Papers . . . , p. 38, quoted in Cobbing, 1991, p. 9

9. A.K. Smith, quoted in Cobbing, 1991, p. 35

10. Cobbing, 1988, pp. 504–5

11. ibid., p. 506

12. ibid., 1991, p. 15

13. Ballard, p. 360, cited in Cobbing, 1991, p. 19

14. Cobbing, 1991, p. 17

15. ibid., 1988, p. 517

16. George Thompson, vol. 1, chaps. 15, 16; Isaac Schapera, 1951, pp. 94–99, quoted in Cobbing: 1988, p. 493; 1991, p. 24

17. Theal, 1897–1905, vol. 16, p. 223, quoted in Cobbing, 1991, p. 25

18. Bannister, p. 228, quoted in Cobbing, 1988, p. 492

19. Theal, 1897–1905, vol. 20, pp. 400–401, quoted in Cobbing, 1988, p. 501

20. Philipps

21. Newton-King, in Marks and Atmore, pp. 182–91, cited in Cobbing, 1988, p. 494

22. Peires, in Elphick and Giliomee, p. 486

23. Cobbing: 1988, p. 502; 1991, p. 34

24. Van Warmelo, p. 255, quoted in Cobbing, 1988, p. 503

25. Bird, vol. 1, p. 123, quoted in Cobbing, 1988, p. 503

26. Cobbing, 1991, p. 34

27. ibid., 1988, p. 509

CHAPTER 44
The Afrikaners

1. Quoted without attribution in Donald R. Morris, 1968, p. 149

2. Heese, p. 21, cited in Elphick and Giliomee, p. 202

3. Oordt, p. 13, quoted in Leonard Thompson, 1985, p. 85

4. Leonard Thompson, 1985

5. ibid., p. 145

6. Elphick and Giliomee, p. 500

7. ibid., pp. 47–48

8. Leonard Thompson, 1985, p. 147

9. Chase, vol. 1, pp. 66–67, quoted in Du Toit and Giliomee, p. 112

10. Retief, published in the *Grahamstown Journal,* 2 February 1837, quoted in Du Toit and Giliomee, p. 214

11. Steenkamp, in Bird, vol. 1, p. 459, quoted in Leonard Thompson, 1985, p. 149

12. Norman Etherington, p. 17

13. ibid., pp. 3–21

14. Elphick and Giliomee, p. 505

15. Leonard Thompson, 1990, p. 90

16. Donald R. Morris, 1966, p. 140

17. Davenport and Hunt, pp. 19–20

18. Eric A. Walker, pp. 147–65; Cory

19. Leonard Thompson, 1990, p. 91, n. 45

20. Richner, p. 24

21. Eric A. Walker, p. 249, quoted in Norman Etherington, p. 19

22. Leonard Thompson, 1990, p. 91

23. Richner, p. 24

24. Leonard Thompson, 1990, p. 92

25. Bird, vol. 2, p. 146, quoted in Leonard Thompson, 1990, p. 93

26. Du Toit and Giliomee, p. 21

27. *Cape Monthly Magazine,* p. 130, quoted in Giliomee, in Vail, pp. 32–33

28. Iliffe, 1995, p. 179

29. Worger, p. 22

CHAPTER 45
Diamonds and Gold

1. Boyd and Gurney, p. 473

2. Diamonds are found in association with all the continent's cratons; some deposits in West Africa are very rich indeed, but all are alluvial.

3. Robert Vicat Turrell, p. 4

4. ibid.

5. Quoted in Robertson, p. 70

6. ibid., p. 117

7. Worger, p. 9

8. Robert Vicat Turrell, p. 1

9. Robertson, pp. 221–22

10. Worger, pp. 16–17

11. Beet, pp. 19–21, quoted in Rotberg, 1988, pp. 55–56

12. John Robinson, p. 211, quoted in Rotberg, 1988, p. 56

13. Chapman, pp. 122–23, 145–46, quoted in Rotberg, 1987, p. 56

14. Robert Vicat Turrell, p. 10

15. Worger, p. 14

16. Robert Vicat Turrell, pp. 5–6, and p. 240, n. 11

17. ibid., p. 18

18. Worger, p. 15

19. Shillington, 1982, in Marks and Rathbone, p. 105

20. Rob Turrell, 1982, in Marks and Rathbone, p. 45

21. Rob Turrell, 1984, p. 74

22. Worger, p. 72

23. ibid., p. 71

24. ibid., p. 75

25. Rob Turrell, 1982, p. 50

26. Shillington, 1989, p. 320

27. Worger, p. 76

28. Quoted in Robert Vicat Turrell, p. 61

29. ibid., p. 61

30. Shillington, 1982, p. 105

31. Quoted in Worger, p. 83

32. ibid., pp. 82–83

33. Quoted in Robert Vicat Turrell, p. 57

34. Worger, p. 20

35. ibid., p. 112

36. ibid., p. 128

37. Robert Vicat Turrell, p. 21

38. Worger, pp. 115–16

39. ibid., p. 117

40. ibid.

41. ibid., p. 118

42. Quoted in Worger, p. 118

43. ibid., pp. 38, 42

44. Robert Vicat Turrell, pp. 206–27, for a concise and objective account of the process

45. Worger, pp. 226–27

46. ibid., p. 255

47. ibid., pp. 94–96

48. ibid., pp. 97–98; Norman A. Etherington, p. 235

49. Worger, p. 98

50. ibid., p. 101

51. Rob Turrell, 1982, p. 54

52. Robert Vicat Turrell, p. 91

53. Rob Turrell, 1982, p. 55

54. Quoted in Rob Turrell, 1982, p. 56

55. Rob Turrell, 1982, p. 57

56. ibid., p. 61

57. Worger, pp. 135–36

58. Rob Turrell, 1982, p. 65

59. Quoted in Rob Turrell, 1982, p. 65

60. Rob Turrell, 1984, p. 70

61. ibid., p. 61

62. ibid., p. 71

63. Van Der Horst, p. 126; Mendelsohn and Potgieter, pp. 6–9; Richardson and Van-Helten, in Marks and Rathbone, p. 78

64. Rob Turrell, 1984, p. 59

65. Van Der Horst, pp. 134, 192, 205

66. ibid., p. 197

CHAPTER 46
An Imperial Ambition

1. Lake Victoria, 68,800 km^2; Belgium, 30,520 km^2; Canary Islands, 7,275 km^2

2. Jean Stengers, 1988, in Förster, Mommsen, and Robinson, pp. 229–46

3. Emerson, p. 121

4. Ascherson

5. John S. Galbraith, p. 373

6. Conrad, 1926, p. 25

7. Emerson, p. 25

8. ibid.

9. ibid., pp. 28, 29

10. ibid., pp. 58–62

11. ibid., p. 61

12. Quoted in Emerson, p. 72

13. Henry Morton Stanley, 1872

14. Anstey, p. 54

15. *The Times,* 11 January 1876, p. 11 (news report)

16. Emerson, p. 74

17. Based on the grounds of prior discovery, Diogo Cão having reached the Congo estuary in 1483 and subsequently established relations with local rulers (see page 344)

18. Anstey, pp. 54–55

19. Quoted in Emerson, p. 76

20. Pakenham, p. 22

21. Bauer, p. 67, quoted in Bederman, pp. 66–67

22. Banning, pp. 152–54

23. ibid., p. 154

24. Severin, p. 249, quoted in Bederman, p. 71

25. Banning, pp. 107–9, 113

26. ibid., pp. 109, 113

27. Bederman, p. 73

28. Emerson, pp. 80–81

29. ibid., p. 82; Pakenham, p. 37, says 114 Africans died

30. Emerson, p. 85; Pakenham, p. 38

31. Lady Dorothy Stanley, p. 289, quoted in Pakenham, p. 59

32. Hird, p. 177, quoted in Emerson, p. 91

33. Emerson, p. 92

34. ibid.

35. Quoted (without attribution) in Bierman, p. 228

36. Pakenham, p. 146

37. ibid., pp. 146, 149

38. Maurice, p. 34, quoted in Bierman, p. 227

39. Pakenham, p. 247

40. Henry Morton Stanley, 1885, vol. 1, pp. 379–80, quoted in Emerson, p. 95

41. Hird, pp. 183–84, quoted in Emerson, p. 96

42. Pakenham, pp. 155, 161

43. Jean Stengers, 1988, p. 235

44. Monk, p. 21, quoted in Rotberg, 1970, p. 44

45. Jean Stengers, 1988, p. 239

46. John S. Galbraith, p. 383

47. Pakenham, p. 243

48. ibid., p. 244

49. Emerson, p. 104

50. Pakenham, p. 246

51. Jean Stengers, 1988, p. 239

52. ibid., 1967, p. 162, in Gifford and Louis, 1967, quoted in Pakenham, p. 247

53. Quoted in Emerson, p. 106

54. Anstey, p. 241

55. Crowe, p. 156

56. Cited in Louis, 1967, in Gifford and Louis, 1967, p. 203, quoted in Pakenham, p. 249

57. Emerson, pp. 120–21

58. ibid., p. 118

59. ibid., pp. 143–48

60. Sherry, p. 32

61. J. Stengers, 1969, in Gann and Duigan, p. 272

62. ibid.

63. ibid., p. 273

64. *New Scientist,* 28 September 1991, p. 28

65. Woodruff, p. 41

66. Harms

67. ibid., pp. 78–79

68. ibid., p. 81

69. Morel, 1904, p. 103

70. Roger Casement, quoted in Morel, 1904, p. 236

71. Casement, pp. 60–62, quoted in Pakenham, p. 599

72. Morel, 1920, p. 118

73. ibid., 1904, p. 147

74. Quoted in Morel, 1904, pp. 110–11

75. Quoted in Morel, 1920, pp. 121–22

76. Morel, 1904, p. 445, and photograph facing p. 144

77. Pakenham, p. 663

78. Conrad, 1902, p. 48

CHAPTER 47
An African King

1. Otto von Bismarck (undated), quoted in Crowe, p. viii

2. The Lozi called their homeland *Bulozi,* which was mistakenly recorded as Barotse; thus Barotseland.

3. The Lochner Concession, 1890. Appendix B in Clay, pp. 160–61

4. Gluckman, 1951, in Colson and Gluckman; Prins

5. Trapnell and Clothier

6. Kalaluka

7. Reefe, vol. 1, p. 197

8. Gluckman, 1951, pp. 7–8

9. ibid., p. 19. See also Mainga

10. Litunga Ilute Yeta, pers. comm., Limulunga, 6 March 1990

11. See Robins

12. Oswell, vol. 1, p. 245

13. Schapera, 1960, pp. 41, 43 (n. 4)

14. ibid., p. 234

15. ibid., pp. 205–7

16. Nowell

17. Pinto, vol. 2, p. 4

18. ibid., pp. 44–49

19. Tabler, pp. 6–7

20. F.S. Arnot, 1914, p. 5, cited in Clay, p. 29

21. Baker, pp. 67–70

22. ibid.

23. Mackintosh, pp. 359–60, cited in Clay, p. 53

24. Fred S. Arnot, 1899, p. 75

25. ibid., p. 76

26. Tabler, p. 47

27. Mackintosh, p. 327, cited in Clay, p. 48

28. ibid., p. 330, cited in Clay, p. 48

29. Coillard, p. 278, n. 1

30. The Rudd Concession, 1888. Text in Rouillard, pp. 219–20, cited in Rotberg, 1988, p. 262

31. Baxter, 1951, pp. 39–40, cited in Clay, pp. 61–62

32. The Ware Concession, 1889. In Clay, App. A, pp. 158–59

33. Coillard, p. 357

34. Baxter, 1963, p. 7, cited in Clay, p. 62

35. Rotberg, 1988, p. 324

36. Caplan, p. 51

37. Coillard, 1897, pp. 384–87

38. The Lochner Concession, 1890. In Clay, App. B, pp. 160–61

39. Quoted in Caplan, p. 70, n. 74

40. Colonial Office to Foreign Office, 1891. Quoted in Caplan, p. 51

41. Fraenkal, p. 92, quoted in Caplan, p. 184

42. Clay, p. 124

43. Cannadine, in Hobsbawm and Ranger, pp. 101–64, esp. 133–38

44. Clay, p. 124

45. Mackintosh, p. 430, quoted in Clay, p. 124

46. *The Times,* 30 May 1902, p. 10

47. *News from Barotsiland,* 1903, vol. 19, p. 5

48. Coillard, 1904, in *News from Barotsiland,* vol. 23, p. 11

49. Quoted in Caplan, p. 96

50. ibid., p. 100

51. ibid., p. 102

CHAPTER 48
Drawing the Line

1. Quoted in McEwan, 1971, p. 141

2. David Sperling, 1993, pers. comm., University of Nairobi, 20 July

3. C.S. Smith, p. 426

4. J.R.V. Prescott: 1979, p. 3; 1987, p. 242 (N.B.: Statistics published before the break-up of the Soviet Union)

5. Griffiths, p. 204

6. Quoted in Darkoh, p. 62

7. Pingali, Bigot, and Binswanger, p. 47

8. Griffiths, p. 213

9. McEwan, 1991, p. 62

10. Hertslet, p. 799, quoted in McEwan, 1991, p. 69

11. V. Prescott, p. 103, quoted in McEwan, 1991, p. 69

12. Asiwaju, pp. 252–59

13. Davidson, 1992, p. 203

14. Allen, p. 134, cited in Davidson, 1992, p. 213

15. Quoted in Davidson, 1992, pp. 213–14

16. Iliffe, 1995, p. 192

17. Hennessy

18. Quoted in Pakenham, p. 217

19. Bade, in Förster, Mommsen, and Robinson, pp. 120–47

20. Holstein, Rich, and Fischer, pp. 138, 161, quoted in Pakenham, p. 203

21. Quoted in Bade, p. 139

22. ibid.

23. ibid., p. 146

24. Quoted in ibid., p. 147

25. Gann, in Duigan and Gann, 1975, p. 213

26. Gann, p. 250

27. ibid., pp. 238–39

CHAPTER 49
Resistance

1. Meinertzhagen, quoted by Ranger, 1969, in Gann and Duigan, p. 295

2. Oliver, p. 187

3. Ranger, 1969, p. 295

4. Quoted in ibid., p. 294

5. Oliver and Fage, p. 174

6. Conrad, 1902; Marnham

7. Boahen, 1985b, in Unesco, vol. 7, p. 3

8. Quoted in A. Isaacman, pp. 128–29

9. Quoted in Fynn, in Crowder, 1971, pp. 43–44

10. Quoted in Davidson, 1964, pp. 357–58

11. Quoted in Iliffe, 1968, in Kiboydya, cited by Ranger, 1985, in Unesco, 1985, p. 49

12. Quoted in Boahen, 1985b, p. 4

13. Akpan, in Unesco, vol. 7, p. 270

14. ibid., p. 272

15. Pakenham, p. 485

16. Boahen, 1985b, p. 7; Mwanzi, in Unesco, vol. 7, p. 161; Hargreaves, 1969, in Gann and Duigan, p. 207

17. Boahen, 1985b, p. 39

18. Iliffe, 1995, pp. 192–93

19. Hilaire Belloc, *Cautionary Tales,* London, 1907

20. Crozier, p. 149, quoted in Ellis, p. 96

21. See Unesco, vol. 7

22. Davidson, 1963, p. 68

23. Lonsdale, 1985, p. 722, cited in Oliver, p. 188

24. Oliver, p. 188

25. Caldwell, in Unesco, vol. 7, p. 483

26. Nicholson, in Hansen and McMillan, p. 115

27. Nicholson, p. 116

28. ibid., p. 117

29. Kjekshus, p. 135

30. J.N.P. Davies, p. 16

31. Iliffe, 1979, p. 125

32. Van Onselen, p. 473

33. J.N.P. Davies, p. 12

34. ibid., pp. 12–20

35. Van Onselen, p. 474

36. J.N.P. Davies, p. 14

37. Kjekshus, p. 128

38. Quoted in J.N.P. Davies, p. 14

39. Quoted in Kjekshus, p. 130

40. Quoted in J.N.P. Davies, p. 17

41. Quoted in Kjekshus, p. 130

42. Quoted in J.N.P. Davies, p. 17

43. Ford, p. 494, cited in Kjekshus, p. 166

44. Lambrecht, p. 18

45. H.H. Bell, cited in Kjekshus, p. 165

46. Richard D. Waller

CHAPTER 50
Rebellion

1. Cornevin, p. 208, cited in Crowder, 1985, in Unesco, vol. 7, p. 284

2. Pakenham, pp. 608–9

3. Pakenham, pp. 609–10

4. Figures cited in Pakenham, p. 615

5. Iliffe, 1979, p. 168

6. Coulson, p. 38

7. Estimates calculated from figures in Iliffe, 1967, pp. 498–99

8. ibid., p. 498

9. ibid.

10. ibid., 1979, p. 170

11. Quoted in ibid., p. 174

12. Pakenham, p. 620

13. Quoted in Iliffe, 1979, p. 179

14. Gwassa, p. 202, in Ranger and Kimambo, pp. 202–17, quoted in Mwanzi, in Unesco, vol. 7, p. 167

15. Quoted in Pakenham, p. 622

16. Iliffe, 1979, p. 200

17. Quoted in Kjekshus, p. 151

18. Iliffe, 1979, p. 202

19. See Rotberg, 1988, chap. 19

20. Warwick, pp. 3, 17

21. Oliver, p. 184

22. Pakenham, p. 578

23. Warwick, p. 145

24. Quoted in ibid., p. 145

25. ibid., pp. 4–5

26. ibid., p. 145

27. ibid., p. 163

28. Quoted in ibid., p. 165

29. ibid., pp. 182–83

30. Quoted in ibid., p. 163

31. Quoted (without attribution) in Strandman, p. 339

32. Eric J. Grove, cited in Killingray, p. 39

33. Page, p. 14

34. Hess

35. Page, p. 12

36. Boyd

37. Crowder, 1985, in Unesco, 1985, pp. 292–93

38. Page, p. 6

39. ibid.

40. Crowder, 1985, p. 295

41. Isaacman and Isaacman, pp. 157–58, quoted in Page, p. 6

42. Crowder, 1985, p. 295

43. Hodges, p. 115

44. Killingray, p. 49

45. Andrew and Kanya-Forstner, p. 16

46. Page, p. 15

47. Crowder, 1985, p. 295

CHAPTER 51
The Invention of Africa

1. Boahen, 1985a, in Unesco, vol. 7, p. 785

2. Afigbo, in Unesco, vol. 7, p. 493

3. Boahen, 1985a, p. 795

4. Andrew D. Roberts, 1990b, in Andrew Roberts, 1990a, p. 25

5. Oliver and Fage, p. 180

6. Quoted in Oliver and Fage, p. 184

7. Quoted in Ranger, 1983, in Hobsbawm and Ranger, p. 216

8. Lumley, pp. 10–11

9. Curtin *et al.*, 1978, p. 484

10. Coupland, p. 3

11. Ranger, 1983, pp. 211–62

12. ibid., p. 212

13. Andrew D. Roberts, 1990b, pp. 24–76

14. ibid., pp. 38, 53

15. Colson, 1971a, in Duigan and Gann, 1971, p. 196

16. Ranger, 1983, p. 250 (emphasis in the original)

17. C. Ehret, 1991, pers. comm., University of California, Los Angeles, 30 April

18. de Haas, p. 25

19. Nicholas Cope, 1992, pers. comm., London, 17 March; Cope

20. Muriuki, pp. 98–100; Godfrey Muriuki, 1987, pers. comm., Nairobi, 14 January

21. Ajayi, cited in Sharp and McAllister, p. 19

22. Argyle, p. 9, quoted in de Haas, p. 23

23. Comaroff and Comaroff: 1991, 1992, cited in *Anthrop. Today,* vol. 9, pt 5, 1993, p. 19

24. Vail, p. 7

25. Iliffe, 1979, pp. 323–24

26. ibid., pp. 322–23

27. ibid., p. 324

28. SBS *World Guide*

29. ibid., *World Resources 1986,* pp. 256–57

30. Summarized in chap. 11 of W.R. Louis, 1963

31. W.R. Louis, 1963, p. 112

32. ibid., p. 110

33. Quoted in ibid., pp. 174–75

34. Quoted in ibid., p. 233

35. ibid., p. 259

36. Coquery-Vidrovitch, 1985, in Unesco, vol. 7, p. 365

37. Lemarchand, 1994, p. 14

38. de Waal, pp. 1–2

CHAPTER 52
The Emergent Elite

1. Iliffe, 1995, p. 222

2. International Institute of Tropical Agriculture, p. 35

3. John K. Galbraith, p. 12

4. Douglas Rimmer, in D. Rimmer, p. 9

5. Quoted in Boahen, 1985a, in Unesco, vol. 7, pp. 800–801

6. W. Rodney, 1988, pp. 246–47

7. Quoted in ibid., p. 246

8. Andrew D. Roberts, 1990a, pp. 227–30

9. ibid.

10. Azikiwe, p. 13

11. Quoted in Thiam and Mulira, in Unesco, vol. 8, p. 800

12. Meredith, p. 5

13. Iliffe, 1995, p. 241

14. Caldwell, in Unesco, vol. 7, pp. 483, 486

15. World Resources Institute, 1986, p. 248

16. Unesco, 1993, p. 488

17. Quoted in Lemarchand, 1970, p. 42

18. Linden, p. 163

19. Quoted in ibid., p. 163. Classe actually used the terms Batusi and Bahutu, Tusi being a contemporary version of the name, and the Ba- prefix indicating "a person of . . ." In this book the modern usages, Tutsi and Hutu, are applied throughout.

20. Lemarchand, 1970, p. 74

21. Linden, p. 164

22. Quoted in ibid., p. 164

23. Lemarchand, 1970, p. 139

24. ibid., p. 149

25. ibid., p. 152

26. Linden, p. 250

CHAPTER 53
Spoils of War

1. Cited in Crowder, 1993, in Unesco, vol. 8, p. 92

2. Coquery-Vidrovitch, 1993, in Unesco, vol. 8, p. 292

3. Duigan and Gann, 1970, p. 19

4. Dummett, p. 392

5. Coquery-Vidrovitch, 1993, p. 292 (pounds converted to dollars at the wartime rate of U.S.$4 to £1)

6. Duigan and Gann, 1970, p. 19

7. Quoted in Shillington, 1989, p. 372

8. W.R. Louis, 1977

9. Lynch, in Gifford and Louis, 1982, p. 74

10. *Life* magazine, 12 October 1942, quoted in Gifford and Louis, 1982, p. 33

11. Louis and Robinson, in Gifford and Louis, 1982, pp. 34–35

12. John D. Hargreaves, p. 55

13. Coquery-Vidrovitch, 1993, p. 294

14. Gifford and Louis, 1982, p. 192

15. Quoted in ibid., p. 92

16. Meredith, p. 38

17. ibid., p. 36

18. Quoted in Legum, p. 137

19. Leonard Thompson, 1990, pp. 150–53

20. ibid., p. 150

21. Quoted in Meredith, p. 21

22. ibid., p. 26

23. ibid., p. 39

24. Louis and Robinson, in Gifford and Louis, 1982, p. 42

25. John D. Hargreaves, p. 99

26. Quoted in Meredith, p. 39

27. ibid., p. 51

28. Louis and Robinson, p. 43

29. John D. Hargreaves, p. 130

30. Meredith, p. 68

31. Quoted in Meredith, p. 65

32. Quoted in ibid., p. 70

CHAPTER 54
First Dance of Freedom

1. Meredith. The title, "First Dance of Freedom," is taken from Byron, 1821–22, *Detached Thoughts*: "I sometimes wish I was the owner of Africa; to do at once what Wilberforce will do in time, viz—sweep Slavery from her desarts, and look upon the first dance of their Freedom."

2. Hoskyns, p. 19

3. Jean Stengers, 1982, in Gifford and Louis, 1982, pp. 305–6

4. Hoskyns, p. 14

5. Crowder, 1993, in Unesco, vol. 8, p. 94

6. Hastings, pp. 43–44, cited in John D. Hargreaves, p. 176

7. Jean Stengers, 1982, p. 308

8. Quoted in ibid., p. 323

9. Quoted in Meredith, p. 83

10. Lumumba

11. Jean Stengers, p. 306

12. Hoskyns, pp. 12–13

13. Jean Stengers, 1982, pp. 308–9

14. Quoted in Meredith, pp. 29–30

15. Quoted in Jean Stengers, 1982, p. 318

16. Hoskyns, p. 10

17. ibid., pp. 85–86

18. Quoted in Kalb, p. 27

19. ibid., pp. 53–55

20. Quoted in ibid., p. 111

21. Quoted in ibid., p. 111

22. Lipschutz and Rasmussen, pp. 274–75; the *Guardian,* 1996, "Pass notes [on Mobutu]," *Guardian* pt 2, p. 3, 4 November

23. Hoskyns, p. 308

24. Meredith, p. 150

CHAPTER 55
Dreams and Nightmares

1. Mazrui, p. 43

2. Unesco, vol. 8, table 15.1

3. Quoted in Meredith, p. 122

4. World Bank, 1992, pp. 220–21, 268–69, cited in Iliffe, 1995, p. 252

5. ibid.

6. Quoted in Unesco, vol. 8, p. 11

7. Nyerere, pp. 1–2

8. Unesco, vol. 8, pp. 456–61. Among nations which were not represented at the Addis Ababa OAU conference in 1963, Angola, Botswana, Kenya, Malawi, Mozambique, Zambia, and Zimbabwe have also been free of coups—though not without internal strife.

9. Unesco, vol. 8, p. 456

10. The essence of this and following paragraphs is drawn from chap. 21 of Meredith

11. Meredith, p. 210

12. St. Jorre, quoted in Meredith, p. 218

13. Obasanjo, p. 126, quoted in Iliffe, 1995, p. 258

14. Iliffe, 1995, p. 258

15. ibid., p. 255

16. World Bank, 1993, pp. 240, 288, quoted in Iliffe, 1995, p. 255

17. SBS *World Guide* (4th edn), p. 472

18. World Bank, 1994, quoted in a *Guardian* leader, 18 May 1994

19. Quoted in Prunier, p. 49

20. Unesco, vol. 8, pp. 213–14; Prunier, p. 53

21. Cited in Prunier, p. 60

22. Quoted in ibid., p. 53

23. Africa Rights, p. 12

24. Prunier, p. 82

25. ibid., p. 63

26. Vassall-Adams, p. 25

27. See esp. Prunier, pp. 213–29

28. ibid., pp. 262–63

29. ibid., pp. 264–65

30. Africa Rights, pp. 16, 100–176

31. *The Economist,* quoted in Prunier, p. 256

32. Prunier, p. 246

33. ibid., p. 247

34. Quoted in Africa Rights, p. 16

35. Uvin, p. 195, cited in Africa Rights, p. 16

36. David Waller, p. 19, cited in Africa Rights, p. 17

37. United Nations Population Fund, 1994, cited in the *Guardian,* 13 August 1994

38. J.C. and P. Caldwell, p. 227

39. Leonard Thompson, p. 243

40. ibid., p. 241

41. United Nations Population Fund, 1994, cited in the *Guardian,* 13 August 1994

42. Platteau, in Drèze and Sen, vol. 2, p. 281, cited in Iliffe, 1995, p. 266

43. Walsh

44. Hilsum

BIBLIOGRAPHY

ABBOTT, C.W., 1949, *The History of Buttermaking in South Africa*, Pretoria, Department of Agriculture (Agricultural Research Series 17, Bulletin 300)

ACHEBE, CHINUA, 1958, *Things Fall Apart*, London, Heinemann (African Writers series)

ADAMS, W.Y., 1977, *Nubia: Corridor to Africa*, London, Allen Lane

ADAMS, W.Y., 1989, "Definition and development in African indigenous irrigation," *Azania*, vol. 24, pp. 12–20

AFIGBO, A.E., 1985, "The social repercussions of colonial rule: the new social structures," in Unesco, 1985, vol. 7, pp. 487–507

AFRICA RIGHTS, 1995, *Rwanda—Death, Despair and Defiance*, London, Africa Rights

AIELLO, LESLIE C., and WHEELER, PETER, 1995, "The expensive-tissue hypothesis—the brain and the digestive system in human and primate evolution," *Curr. Anthrop.*, 36(2), pp. 199–221

AITKEN, M.J., MELLARS, P.A., and STRINGER, C.B. (eds.), 1993, "The origin of modern humans and the impact of science-based dating," *Phil. Trans. Biol. Sci.* (Royal Society, London), 1280

AJAYI, JACOB ADE, 1993, "Historical perspectives on ethnicity and nationalism in Nigeria," cited in *Anthrop. Today*, vol. 9, pt 5.

AKOBUNDU, I.O., 1991, "Weeds in human affairs in sub-Saharan Africa—implications for sustainable food production," *Weed Technol.*, vol. 5, pp. 680–90

AKPAN, M.B., 1985, "Liberia and Ethiopia, 1880–1914: the survival of two African states," in Unesco, 1985, vol. 7, pp. 249–82

ALEXANDER, J., 1993, "The salt industries of west Africa: a preliminary study," in Shaw *et al.* (eds.) 1993, pp. 652–57

ALEXANDER, JOHN, 1993, "Beyond the Nile. The influence of Egypt and Nubia in the sub-Saharan Africa," *Expedition*, vol. 35 (pt 2), pp. 51–61

ALEXANDER, R. MCNEILL, 1992, "Human locomotion," in *Cambridge Encyclopedia of Human Evolution*, pp. 80–85

ALLEN, C., *et al.*, 1989, *Benin, the Congo, Burkina Faso*, London/New York, Pinter

ALPERS, EDWARD A., 1975, *Ivory and Slaves in East Central Africa—Changing Patterns of International Trade to the Later Nineteenth Century*, London, Heinemann

ÁLVARES, *see* Beckingham and Huntingford

AMBROSE, STANLEY H., 1984, "The introduction of pastoral adaptations to the highlands of East Africa," in Clark and Brandt, pp. 212–39

AMBROSE, S.H., and DENIRO, M.J., 1986, "Reconstruction of African human diet using bone collagen carbon and nitrogen isotope ratios," *Nature*, 319, pp. 321–24

ANDREW, C.M., and KANYA-FORSTNER, A.S., 1978, "France, Africa and the First World War," *J. Afr. Hist.*, vol. 19, pp. 11–23

ANFRAY, F., 1981, "The civilization of Aksum from the first to the seventh century," in Unesco, 1981, vol. 2, pp. 362–80

ANHAEUSSER, C.R., "The geological evolution of the primitive Earth—evidence from the Barberton Mountain Land," in Tarling, p. 97

ANSTEY, ROGER, 1962, *Britain and the Congo in the nineteenth century*, Oxford, Clarendon Press

ANSTEY, R., and HAIR, P.E.H. (eds.), 1976, *Liverpool, the African Slave Trade, and Abolition: Essays to Illustrate Current Knowledge and Research*, Widnes, Historical Society of Lancashire and Cheshire (Occasional series, vol. 2)

ARGYLE, W.J., 1971, "A critique of one rural–urban dichotomy," unpublished MS

ARKELL, A.J., 1961, *A History of the Sudan: from Earliest Times to 1821*, London, Athlone Press

ARMELAGOS, G.J., *et al.*, 1984, "Effects of nutritional change on the skeletal biology of Northeast African (Sudanese Nubian) populations," in Clark and Brandt, pp. 132–46

ARNOT, FRED S., 1899, *Garenganze; or Seven Years' Pioneer Mission Work in Central Africa*, London, Hawkins

ARNOT, F.S., 1914, *Missionary Travels in Central Africa*, Bath, Echoes of Service

ASCHERSON, NEAL, 1963, *The King Incorporated: Leopold the Second in the Age of Trusts*, London

ASHMUN, JEHUDI, 1826, *History of the American Colony in Liberia*, Washington, D.C.

ASIWAJU, A.I., 1983, *Partitioned Africans: Ethnic Relations across Africa's International Boundaries 1884–1984*, London, Hurst

AXELSON, ERIC, 1940/1969, *South-east Africa 1488–1530*, London, Longman (1940), New York, Kraus (1969)

AZIKIWE, B.N., 1961, *Zik: a Selection from the Speeches of Nnamdi Azikiwe*, Cambridge, Cambridge University Press

AZURARA, *see* Beazley and Prestage

BADE, KLAUS J., 1988, "Imperial Germany and west Africa: colonial movement, business interests, and Bismarck's 'colonial policies,'" in Förster, Mommsen, and Robinson, pp. 120–47

BAIER, STEPHEN, and LOVEJOY, PAUL E., 1977, "The Tuareg of the central Sudan," in Miers and Kopytoff, pp. 391–411

BAKER, E., 1923, *The Life and Exploration of F.S. Arnot,* London, Seeley, Service

BALLARD, CHARLES, 1986, "Drought and economic stress: South Africa in the 1800s," *J. Interdisc. Hist.,* vol. 17, pt 2

BANKS, K.M., 1980, "Ceramics of the Western Desert," in Wendorf and Schild (eds.), 1980, pp. 299–315

BANKS-SMITH, NANCY, 1990, the *Guardian,* 1 October (television review)

BANNING, EMILE, 1877, *Africa and the Brussels Geographical Conference,* London, Sampson Low

BANNISTER, S., 1830 (repr. 1968), *Humane Policy, or Justice to the Aborigines of New Settlements,* London

BARBOT, JOHN, 1678, "A description of the coasts of north and south Guinea," in Churchill and John

BARKER, BRIAN J., 1989, *Dias and Da Gama: the Portuguese Discovery of the Cape Sea-route,* Cape Town, Struik

BARKER, GRAEME, 1978, "Economic models for the Manekweni zimbabwe, Mozambique," *Azania,* vol. 13, pp. 71–100

BARTH, F., 1956, "Ecological relationships of ethnic groups in Swat, North Pakistan," *Am. Anthrop.,* vol. 58, pp. 1079–89

BARTHELME, JOHN W., 1984, "Early evidence for animal domestication in Eastern Africa," in Clark and Brandt, pp. 200–205

BAUER, LUDWIG, 1934, *Leopold the Unloved: King of the Belgians and of Money,* London, Cassell

BAXTER, T.W., 1951, "The Barotse concessions," 2 pts, *N. Rhod. J.,* vol. 1, nos. 3, 4

BAXTER, T.W., 1963, *The Concessions of Northern Rhodesia,* National Archives of Rhodesia and Nyasaland (Occasional Papers 1)

BEACH, DAVID N., 1980, *The Shona and Zimbabwe, 900–1850,* London, Heinemann

BEACH, D.N., 1983, "The Zimbabwe plateau and its peoples," in Birmingham and Martin, vol. 1, pp. 245–77

BEAZLEY, C.R., and PRESTAGE, E. (trans. & eds.), 1896, 1899: Azurara, G.E. de, c.1450, *The Chronicle of the Discovery and Conquest of Guinea* [1441–48], 2 vols., Cambridge, Hakluyt Society, Ser. 2, vols. 95, 100

BECKINGHAM, C.F., and HUNTINGFORD, G.W.B. (trans.), 1961: Álvares, Francisco, 1540, *The Prester John of the Indies,* Cambridge, Hakluyt Society, Ser. 2, vols. 114, 115, pp. 369–76

BEDERMAN, SANFORD H., 1989, "The 1876 Brussels geographical conference and the charade of European cooperation in African exploration," *Terrae Incogn.,* vol. 21, pp. 63–73

BEET, GEORGE, 1931, *The Grand Old Days of the Diamond Fields: Memories of Past Times with the Diggers of Diamondia,* Cape Town

BELL, H.H., 1910, "Sleeping sickness in Uganda," *Scott. Geogr. Mag.,* vol. 26, pp. 478–85

BELL, RICHARD H.V., 1982, "The effects of soil nutrient availability on community structure in African ecosystems," in Huntley and Walker

BENTLEY, GILLIAN R., 1985, "Hunter-gatherer energetics and fertility: a reassessment of the !Kung San," *Hum. Ecol.,* 13(1), pp. 79–108

BERCHEM, J., 1989–90, "Sprachbeziehungen im Bereich des Kulturwortsschatzes zwischen den Bantusprachen und dem Malagasy," *Sprache Gesch. Afr.,* vol. 10/11, pp. 9–169

BERGER, A., 1988, "Milankovitch and climate," *Rev. Geophys.,* vol. 26 (pt 4), pp. 624–57

BERTHELET, A., and CHAVAILLON, J. (eds.), 1993, *The Use of Tools by Human and Non-human Primates,* Oxford, Clarendon Press

BIERMAN, JOHN, 1991, *Dark Safari, the Life behind the Legend of Henry Morton Stanley,* London, Hodder & Stoughton

BIRD, JOHN, 1888, *The Annals of Natal, 1495 to 1845,* 2 vols., Pietermaritzburg

BIRMINGHAM, D., and MARTIN, P. (eds.), 1983, *History of Central Africa,* 2 vols., London, Longman

BISHOP, W.W., PICKFORD, M., and HILL, A., 1975, "New evidence regarding the Quaternary geology, archaeology and hominids of Chesowanja, Kenya," *Nature,* 258, pp. 204–8

BLAKE, JOHN W., 1942, *Europeans in West Africa,* 2 vols., Cambridge, Hakluyt Society

BLAKE, JOHN W., 1977, *West Africa. Quest for God and Gold 1454–1578* (2nd edn), London, Curzon Press

BLENCH, R., 1993, "Ethnographic and linguistic evidence for the prehistory of African ruminant livestock, horses and ponies," in Shaw *et al.* (eds.), 1993, pp. 71–103

BLUMENSCHINE, ROBERT J., 1986, *Early Hominid Scavenging Opportunities: Implications of Carcass Availability in the Serengeti and Ngorongoro Ecosystems,* Oxford, British Archaeological Reports (International series 283)

BOAHEN, A. ADU, 1985a, "Colonialism in Africa: its impact and significance," in Unesco, 1985, vol. 7, pp. 782–809

BOAHEN, A. ADU, 1985b, "Africa and the colonial challenge," in Unesco, vol. 7, pp. 1–18

BONNER, P., 1982, *Kings, Commoners and Concessionaires,* Cambridge, Cambridge University Press

BORLAND, C.H., 1982, "How basic is 'basic' vocabulary?," *Curr. Anthrop.,* vol. 23, pp. 315–16

BOVILL, E.W., 1968, *The Golden Trade of the Moors,* Oxford, Oxford University Press

BOXER, C.R., 1968, *Four Centuries of Portuguese Expansion, 1415–1825: A Succinct Survey,* Johannesburg, Witwatersrand University Press

BOXER, C.R., 1969, *The Portuguese Seaborne Empire, 1415–1825,* London, Hutchinson

BOXER, C.R. (ed.), 1959, *The Tragic History of the Sea, 1589–1622,* Cambridge, Cambridge University Press

BOYD, F.R., and GURNEY, J.J., 1986, "Diamonds and the African lithosphere," *Science,* vol. 232, pp. 472–77

BOYD, WILLIAM, 1983, *An Ice-cream War,* London, Hamish Hamilton

BRADSHAW, JOHN L., 1988, "The evolution of human lateral asymmetries: new evidence and second thoughts," *J. Hum. Evol.,* 17, pp. 615–37

BRAIN, C.K., 1974, "Human food remains from the Iron Age at Zimbabwe," *S. Afr. J. Sci.,* vol. 70, pp. 303–9

BRAIN, C.K., 1981, *The Hunters or the Hunted? An Introduction to African Cave Taphonomy,* Chicago, Chicago University Press

BRAIN, C.K. (ed.), 1993, *Swartkrans. A Cave's Chronicle of Early Man,* Pretoria, Transvaal Museum (Monograph 8)

BRAIN, C.K., and SILLEN, A., 1988, "Evidence from the Swartkrans cave for the earliest use of fire," *Nature,* 336, pp. 464–66

BRANDT, STEVEN A., 1984, "New perspectives on the origins of food production in Ethiopia," in Clark and Brandt, pp. 174–90

BRAUDEL, F., 1969, *Écrits sur l'Histoire,* Paris, Flammarion

BRÄUER, GÜNTER, 1984, "A craniological approach to the origin of anatomically modern *Homo sapiens* in Africa and implications for the appearance of modern Europeans," in Smith and Spencer, pp. 327–410

BRÄUER, GÜNTER, 1989, "The evolution of modern humans: a comparison of the African and non-African evidence," in Mellars and Stringer, pp. 123–54

BREASTED, J.H., 1906–7, *Ancient Records of Egypt,* 5 vols., Chicago, University of Chicago Press

BREUNIG, PETER, 1994, "Gajiganna: early settlement and environment in the Chad Basin," paper presented at Society of Africanist Archaeologists Conference, Bloomington, 28 April to 1 May 1994

BRITISH PARLIAMENTARY PAPERS 292 (1829), *Report of the Commissioners of Inquiry upon the Slave Trade at Mauritius, 12 March 1828,* p. 38, Shannon, Irish University Press, 1969 (British Parliamentary Papers ser.: Slave Trade 76), quoted in Cobbing, 1991

BROOKS, A.S., and ROBERTSHAW, P., 1990, "The glacial maximum in tropical Africa," in Gamble and Soffer, p. 133ff

BROOKS, ALISON S., *et al.,* 1995, "Dating and context of three Middle Stone Age sites with bone points in the Upper Semliki Valley, Zaire," *Science,* 268, p. 552

BROOKS, GEORGE E., 1993, *Landlords and Strangers. Ecology, Society and Trade in Western Africa, 1000–1630,* Oxford, Westview Press

BROOKS, GEORGE E., 1994, "Climate, ecology and trade in western Africa during the past two millennia," paper presented at African–American–Japanese Scholars Conference for Cooperation in the Educational, Cultural and Environmental Spheres in Africa, Tokyo, December 1994

BROWNLEE, J., 1827, "Account of the Amakosae or southern Caffers," in G. Thompson, p. 200

BRYER, LYNNE, and HUNT, KEITH S., 1987, *The 1820 Settlers,* Cape Town, Don Nelson

BUDGE, E.A.W., 1907, *The Egyptian Sudan: Its History and Monuments,* vol. 2, London

BULLIET, RICHARD W., 1975, *The Camel and the Wheel,* Cambridge, Mass., Harvard University Press

BURNS, EDWARD MCNALL, 1938, *James Madison,* New Brunswick, NJ, Rutgers University Press

BURTON, RICHARD, 1864, *A Mission to Gelele, King of Dahomey* (ed. with an introduction and notes by Newbury, C.W., 1966), London, Routledge & Kegan Paul

BURTON, RICHARD, 1865 [On the Amazons of Dahomey], in *Trans. Ethnol. Soc., Lond.,* vol. 3, p. 405.

BUTZER, K.W., 1973, "Pleistocene 'periglacial' phenomena in southern Africa," *Boreas,* 2(1), pp. 1–11

BUTZER, KARL, 1976, *Early Hydraulic Civilization in Egypt: A Study in Cultural Ecology,* Chicago, University of Chicago Press

BUTZER, KARL W., 1980, "Pleistocene history of the Nile Valley in Egypt and Lower Nubia," in Williams and Faure, pp. 248–76

BUTZER, KARL W., 1981, "Rise and fall of Axum, Ethiopia: a geo-archaeological interpretation," *Am. Antiq.,* vol. 46 (pt 3), pp. 471–95

BUTZER, K.W., and ISAAC, G.LL. (eds.), 1975, *After the Australopithecines,* The Hague, Mouton

BUXTON, B.R., 1970, *The Abyssinians,* London, Thames & Hudson

CAHEN, LUCIEN, *et al.,* 1984, *The Geochronology and Evolution of Africa,* Oxford, Clarendon Press

CALDWELL, J.C., 1985, "The social repercussions of colonial rule: demographic aspects," in Unesco, 1985, vol. 7, pp. 458–86

CALDWELL, J.C., and P., 1993, "The South African fertility decline," *Pop. Dev. Rev.,* vol. 19, pp. 220–27

CALEF, GEORGE, 1988, "Maximum rate of increase in African elephants," *Afr. J. Ecol.,* 26, pp. 323–27

CAMBRIDGE ENCYCLOPEDIA OF HUMAN EVOLUTION, 1992, Cambridge, Cambridge University Press

CAMBRIDGE HISTORY OF AFRICA, see Oliver and Fage (eds.), 1975–86

CAMERON, V.L., 1877, *Across Africa,* 2 vols., London

CAMPBELL, BERNARD, 1983, *Human Ecology,* London, Heinemann

CANN, R.L., STONEKING, M., and WILSON, A.C., 1987, "Mitochondrial DNA and human evolution," *Nature,* 325, pp. 31–36

CANNADINE, DAVID, 1983, "The context, performance and meaning of ritual: the British monarchy and the 'invention of tradition,' c. 1820–1977," in Hobsbawm and Ranger, pp. 101–64

CAPE MONTHLY MAGAZINE, 1873, "Our agricultural population," *Cape Monthly Magazine,* vol. 6, no. 33 (March)

CAPLAN, GERALD L., *The Elites of Barotseland, 1878–1969. A Political History of Zambia's Western Province,* London, Hurst

CASEMENT, R., 1933, *Report,* London, Parliamentary Papers

CASSON, LIONEL, 1986, *Ships and Seamanship in the Ancient World,* Lawrenceville, NJ, Princeton University Press

CASSON, LIONEL, 1989, *The Periplus Maris Erythraei,* Lawrenceville, NJ, Princeton University Press

CATON-THOMPSON, G., 1934, "The camel in dynastic Egypt," *Man,* vol. 34, p. 21

CAVALLI-SFORZA, LUIGI LUCA, 1991, "Genes, people and languages," *Sci. Am.,* 1991 (11), pp. 71–78

CERNEA, M.M. (ed.), 1985, *Putting People First,* Oxford, Oxford University Press

CHANG, KUEI-SHENG, 1971, "Ming maritime enterprise and China's knowledge of Africa," *Terrae Incogn.,* vol. 3, pp. 33–44

CHAPMAN, CHARLES, 1872, *A Voyage from Southampton to Cape Town . . . and Illustrations of the Diamond Fields,* London

CHARIG, ALAN, 1979, *A New Look at the Dinosaurs,* London, British Museum (Natural History)

CHASE, J.C. (ed.), 1843, *The Natal Papers,* 2 vols., Grahamstown

CHITTICK, H.N., and ROTBERG, R.I. (eds.), 1975, *East Africa and the Orient: Cultural Syntheses in Pre-colonial Times,* New York, Africana Press

CHURCHILL, AWNSHAM and JOHN (eds.), 1732, *A Collection of Voyages and Travels,* 6 vols., London

CLARK, J. DESMOND, 1967, *Atlas of African Prehistory,* Chicago, Ill., University of Chicago Press

CLARK, J.D., 1970, *The Prehistory of Africa,* New York, Praeger

CLARK, J.D., 1976, "Prehistoric populations and pressures favoring plant domestication in Africa," in Harlan, de Wet, and Stemler (eds.), 1976, pp. 67–105

CLARK, J. DESMOND, 1989, "The origin and spread of modern humans: a broad perspective on the African evidence," in Mellars and Stringer, pp. 565–88

CLARK, J.D., and BRANDT, S.A. (eds.), 1984, *From Hunters to Farmers. The Causes and Consequences of Food Production in Africa,* Berkeley, University of California Press

CLARKSON, JOHN, 1792, extracts from diary, in *Sierra Leone Studies,* Freetown, March 1927

CLASSON, A.T., 1980, "The animal remains from Tell es Sinn compared with those from Bouqras," *Anatolica,* 7, pp. 35–52

CLAY, GERVAS, 1968, *Your Friend, Lewanika. The Life and Times of Lubosi Lewanika, Litunga of Barotseland,* London, Chatto & Windus

CLIFFORD, T.N., and GASS, I.G. (eds.), 1970, *African Magmatism & Tectonics,* Edinburgh, Oliver & Boyd

CLIMAP PROJECT MEMBERS, 1976, "The surface of the ice age earth," *Science,* 191, pp. 1131–7

CLOSE, A.E. (ed.), 1987, *Prehistory of Arid North Africa,* Dallas, Tex., Southern Methodist University Press

CLOSE, ANGELA E., and WENDORF, FRED, 1990, "North Africa at 18000 BP," in Gamble and Soffer, pp. 41–57

CLOSE, A.E., and WENDORF, F., 1992, "The beginnings of food production in the Eastern Sahara," in Gebauer and Price, pp. 63–72

CLOUD, PRESTON, 1988, *Oasis in Space: Earth History from the Beginning,* New York, W.W. Norton

CLUTTON-BROCK, JULIET, 1987, *A Natural History of Domesticated Animals,* Cambridge, Cambridge University Press

CLUTTON-BROCK, JULIET, 1992, "Domestication of animals," in *Cambridge Encyclopedia of Human Evolution,* pp. 380–85

CLUTTON-BROCK, JULIET, 1993, "The spread of domestic animals in Africa," in Shaw *et al.* (eds.), 1993, pp. 61–70

CLUTTON-BROCK, JULIET (ed.), 1989, *The Walking Larder: Patterns of Domestication, Pastoralism, and Predation,* London, Unwin Hyman

COALE, A.J., 1974, *Sci. Am.,* vol. 231, September

COBBING, JULIAN, 1988, "The Mfecane as alibi: thoughts on Dithakong and Mbolompo," *J. Afr. Hist.,* vol. 29, pp. 487–519

COBBING, JULIAN, 1991, "Ousting the Mfecane: reply to Elizabeth Eldredge," paper presented to the Colloquium on the "Mfecane" Aftermath, University of the Witwatersrand, 6–9 September 1991 (MS)

COCKS, L.M.R. (ed.), 1981, *The Evolving Earth,* Cambridge, Cambridge University Press for the British Museum (Natural History), London

COE, M., 1981, "Body size and the extinction of the Pleistocene megafauna," *Palaeoecol. Afr.,* 13, p. 141

COHEN, MARK N., 1977, *The Food Crisis in Prehistory, Overpopulation and the Origins of Agriculture,* New Haven, Conn., Yale University Press

COILLARD, FRANÇOIS, 1897, *On the Threshold of Central Africa. A Record of Twenty Years' Pioneering among the Barotsi of the Upper Zambesi,* London, Hodder & Stoughton

COLLINS, K.J., 1982, "Energy expenditure, productivity and endemic disease," in Harrison, G.A. (ed.), 1982, pp. 65–84

COLSON, ELIZABETH, 1971a, "The impact of the colonial period on the definition of land rights," in Duigan and Gann (eds.), 1971, pp. 193–215

COLSON, ELIZABETH, 1971b, "The impact of the colonial period on the definition of land rights," in *Cambridge History of Africa,* vol. 3

COLSON, E., and GLUCKMAN, M. (eds.), 1951, *Seven Tribes of British Central Africa,* London, Oxford University Press

COMAROFF, JOHN, and JEAN, 1991, *Of Revelation and Revolution: Christianity, Colonialism and Consciousness in South Africa,* Chicago, University of Chicago Press

COMAROFF, JOHN, and JEAN, 1992, *Ethnography and the Historical Imagination,* Boulder, Colo., Westview Press

CONNAH, GRAHAM, 1987, *African Civilizations: Precolonial Cities and States in Tropical Africa: An Archaeological Perspective,* Cambridge, Cambridge University Press

CONNAH, GRAHAM, 1991, "The salt of Bunyoro: seeking the origins of an African kingdom," *Antiquity,* vol. 65, pp. 479–94

CONRAD, D.C., and FISHER, H.J., 1982, "The conquest that never was," *Hist. Afr.,* vol. 9, pp. 21–59, and vol. 10, pp. 53–78

CONRAD, JOSEPH, 1902, *The Heart of Darkness;* Penguin edn, London, 1976

CONRAD, JOSEPH, 1926, *Last Essays,* London, Dent

CONTENSON, H. DE, 1981, "Pre-Aksumite culture," in Unesco, 1981, vol. 2, pp. 341–61

COOK, G.C., and KAJUBI, S.K., 1966, "Tribal incidence of lactase deficiency in Uganda," *The Lancet,* 2 April, pp. 725–30

COOKE, H.B.S., 1982, in *Cambridge History of Africa,* vol. 1, p. 19

COON, CARLETON S., 1939, *The Races of Europe,* New York, Macmillan

COON, CARLETON S. (ed.), 1948, *A Reader in Anthropology,* New York, Holt

COPE, NICHOLAS, 1993, *To Bind the Nation: Soloman kaDinuzulu and Zulu Nationalism, 1913–1933,* Pietermaritzburg, University of Natal Press

COPPENS, YVES, 1994, "The east side story: the origin of humankind," *Sci. Am.,* vol. 270 (pt 5), pp. 62–69

COQUERY-VIDROVITCH, C., 1985, "The colonial economy of the former French, Belgian and Portuguese zones, 1914–35," in Unesco, 1985, vol. 7, pp. 351–81

COQUERY-VIDROVITCH, CATHERINE, 1993, "Economic changes in Africa in the world context," in Unesco, 1993, vol. 8, pp. 285–316

CORNEVIN, R., 1962, *Histoire du Togo,* Paris, Berger-Levrault

CORRUCCINI, R., and CIOCHON, R. (eds.), 1994, *Integrative Paths to the Past: Paleoanthropological Advances in Honor of F. Clark Howell,* Englewood Cliffs, NJ, Prentice-Hall

CORY, G. (ed.), 1926, *The Diary of Rev. Francis Owen,* Cape Town

COULSON, ANDREW, 1982, *Tanzania: a Political Economy,* Oxford, Clarendon Press

COUPLAND, R., 1928, *Kirk on the Zambezi,* Oxford, Clarendon Press

COWLING, RICHARD, 1992, *The Ecology of the Fynbos,* Oxford, Oxford University Press

CRADOCK, P.T., 1991, "Man and metal in ancient Nigeria," *Brit. Mus. Mag.* (London), vol. 6, pt 1

CRAIS, CLIFTON C., 1986, "Gentry and labour in three Eastern Cape districts," *S. Afr. Hist. J.,* vol. 18, pp. 125–46

CRAWFORD, O.G.S., 1958, *Ethiopian Itineraries, c.1400–1524,* Cambridge, Hakluyt Society (Ser. 2, vol. 109)

CRONE, G.R., 1937, *The Voyages of Cadamosto and Other Documents on Western Africa in the Second Half of the Fifteenth Century,* Cambridge, Hakluyt Society (Ser. 2, vol. 80)

CROSBY, ALFRED W., 1986, *Ecological Imperialism—the Biological Expansion of Europe, 900–1900,* Cambridge, Cambridge University Press

CROWDER, M., 1985, "The First World War and its consequences," in Unesco, 1985, vol. 7, pp. 283–311

CROWDER, M., 1993, "Africa under British and Belgian domination 1935–45," in Unesco, 1993, vol. 8, pp. 76–101

CROWDER, M. (ed.), 1971, *West African Resistance,* London, Hutchinson

CROWE, S.E., 1942, *The Berlin West African Conference 1884–1885,* London, Longman

CROZIER, F.P., 1937, *The Men I Killed,* London, Cape

CUATRECASAS, P., LOCKWOOD, D.H., and CALDWELL, J.R., 1965, "Lactase deficiency in the adult," *The Lancet,* 2 January, pp. 14–18

CURTIN, P.D., 1969, *The Atlantic Slave Trade: a Census,* Madison, University of Wisconsin Press

CURTIN, P.D. (ed.), 1967, *Africa Remembered: Narratives by West Africans from the Era of the Slave Trade,* Madison, University of Wisconsin Press

CURTIN, P.D., 1975, *Economic Change in Precolonial Africa,* Madison, University of Wisconsin Press

CURTIN, PHILIP D., 1984, *Cross-cultural Trade in World History,* Cambridge, Cambridge University Press

CURTIN, PHILIP D., and VANSINA, JAN, 1964, "Sources of the nineteenth century Atlantic slave trade," *J. Afr. Hist.,* vol. 5, pp. 185–208

CURTIN, P., FEIERMAN, S., THOMPSON, L., VANSINA, J., 1978, *African History,* London, Longman

CURTIS, H., and BARNES, N.S., 1989, *Biology,* 5th edn, New York, Worth

DA SILVA REGO, A., 1967, *Portuguese Colonization in the Sixteenth Century: a Study of the Royal Ordinances (Regimentos),* Johannesburg, Witwatersrand University Press

DAGET, S. (ed.), 1988, *Actes du Colloque sur la Traite des Noirs,* Paris/Nantes

DALBY, D., 1981, "The language map of Africa," in Unesco, 1981, vol. 1, pp. 309–15

DALBY, D. (ed.), 1970, *Language and History in Africa,* London, Cass

DALZELL, ARCHIBALD, 1793, *The History of Dahomey, an Inland Kingdom of Africa, Compiled from Authentic Sources,* London; 1967, fac. edn, London, Frank Cass

DARKOH, M.B.K., 1983, *Contemporary Political Map and African Unity,* London

DART, RAYMOND, 1925, "*Australopithecus africanus*: the man-ape of South Africa," *Nature,* vol. 115, pp. 195–99

DART, R., 1953, "The predatory transition from ape to man," *Int. Anthrop. Ling. Rev.,* vol. 1, pp. 201–18

DARWIN, C., 1859, *The Origin of Species by Means of Natural Selection,* Penguin edn, London, 1968

DARWIN, CHARLES, 1871, *The Descent of Man,* London

DAVENPORT, T.R.H., and HUNT, K.S. (eds.), 1974, *The Right to the Land,* Cape Town, David Philip

DAVIDSON, BASIL, 1963, *Guide to African History,* London

DAVIDSON, BASIL, 1964, *The African Past,* London, Longman

DAVIDSON, BASIL, 1991, *African Civilization Revisited: from Antiquity to Modern Times,* Trenton, NJ, Africa World Press

DAVIDSON, BASIL, 1992, *Black Man's Burden,* London, James Currey

DAVIES, J.N.P., 1979, *Pestilence and Disease in the history of Africa,* Johannesburg, Witwatersrand University Press (Raymond Dart Lecture 14)

DAVIES, K.G., 1957, *The Royal African Company,* London

DE HAAS, MARY, 1987, *Natal/KwaZulu: Present Realities, Future Hopes,* Durban, Centre for Adult Education, University of Natal

DE LANGHE, E., SWENNEN, R., and VUYSTEKE, D., 1996, "Plantain in the early Bantu world," in Sutton, J.E.G. (ed.), 1996, pp. 147–60

DE LUMLEY, H., 1975, "Cultural evolution in France in its paleoecological setting during the middle Pleistocene," in Butzer and Isaac, pp. 745–808

DE WAAL, ALEX, 1994, "Genocide in Rwanda," *Anthrop. Today,* vol. 10, pt 3

DEACON, H.J., 1976, *Where Hunters Gathered: A Study of Holocene Stone Age People in the Eastern Cape,* Claremont, South African Archaeological Society (Monograph 1)

DEACON, H.J., 1989, "Late Pleistocene palaeoecology and archaeology in the Southern Cape, South Africa," in Mellars and Stringer, pp. 547–64

DEACON, H.J., 1993, "Southern Africa and modern human origins," in Aitken, Mellars, and Stringer

DEACON, H.J., and THACKERAY, J.F., 1984, "Late Pleistocene environmental changes in distribution and density of humans through time . . . ," in Vogel, J.C. (ed.), 1984, pp. 375–90

DEACON, J., 1990, "Changes in the archaeological record in South Africa at 18000 BP," in Gamble and Soffer, pp. 170–88

DELSON, E. (ed.), 1985, *Ancestors: the Hard Evidence*, New York, Alan R. Liss

DEWEY, CLIVE, and HOPKINS, A.G. (eds.), 1978, *The Imperial Impact: Studies in the Economic History of Africa and India*, London, Athlone Press

DICK, THOMAS, 1838, quoted in Goodacre

DOBSON, ANDREW, 1993, "People and disease," in *Cambridge Encyclopedia of Human Evolution*, pp. 411–20

DOBSON, JEROME E., 1992, "Spatial logic in paleogeography and the explanation of continental drift," *Ann. Ass. Am. Geogr.*, vol. 82 (pt 2), pp. 187–206

DONNAN, E. (ed.), 1930–35, *Documents Illustrative of the History of the Slave Trade to America*, 4 vols., Washington, D.C.

DORAN, MICHAEL F., 1977, "The maritime provenance of iron technology in West Africa," *Terrae Incogn.*, 9, pp. 89–98

DRÈZE, J., and SEN, A. (eds.), 1990–91, *The Political Economy of Hunger*, 3 vols., Oxford

DU TOIT, ALEX L., 1929, "On a geological comparison of South Africa with South America," *Proc. Geol. Soc. S. Afr.*, vol. 31, pp. 19–40

DU TOIT, ANDRÉ, and GILIOMEE, HERMANN (eds.), 1983, *Afrikaner Political Thought. Analysis and Documents*, vol. 1: *1780–1850*, Cape Town, David Philip

DUIGAN, PETER J., and GANN, L.H. (eds.), 1970, 1971, *Colonialism in Africa 1870–1960*, vol. 2 (1970), vol. 3 (1971): *Profiles of Change: African Society and Colonial Rule*, Cambridge, Cambridge University Press

DUIGAN, PETER, and GANN, LEWIS H. (eds.), 1975, *Colonialism in Africa*, vol. 4: *The Economics of Colonialism*, Cambridge, Cambridge University Press

DUMMETT, RAYMOND, 1985, "Africa's strategic minerals during the Second World War," *J. Afr. Hist.*, vol. 26

DUNBAR, R.I.M., 1992a, "Why gossip is good for you," *New Sci.*, 21 November, pp. 21–31

DUNBAR, R.I.M., 1992b, "Neocortex size as a constant on group size in primates," *J. Hum. Evol.*, vol. 22, pp. 219–33

DUNBAR, R.I.M., 1993, "Co-evolution of neocortex size, group size, and language in humans," *Behav. Brain Sci.*, vol. 16, pp. 681–735

DUNBAR, ROBIN, 1996, *Grooming, Gossip and the Evolution of Language*, London, Faber

DYSON-HUDSON, N., 1985, "Pastoral production systems and livestock development projects: an East African perspective," in Cernea, pp. 157–86

THE ECONOMIST, 1994, "Rwanda: no end in sight," 23 April

EDHOLM, O.G., 1979, "Nutrition and physical working capacity," in Van Loon, Staudt, and Zander, pp. 18–23

EDWARDS, PAUL (ed.), 1989, *The Life of Olaudah Equiano, or Gustavus Vassa the African,* London, Longman

EHRET, C., 1971, *Southern Nilotic History,* Evanston, Ill., Northwestern University Press

EHRET, C., 1974, *Ethiopians and East Africans: the Problems of Contacts,* Nairobi, East African Publishing House

EHRET, C., 1979, "On the antiquity of agriculture in Ethiopia," *J. Afr. Hist.,* vol. 20, pp. 161–77

EHRET, CHRISTOPHER, 1993, "Nilo-Saharans and the Saharo-Sudanese Neolithic," in Shaw *et al.* (eds.), 1993, pp. 104–25

EL HADIDI, M. NABIL, 1980, "Vegetation of the Nubian Desert (Nabta Region)," in Wendorf and Schild (eds.), 1980, pp. 345–51

ELDREDGE, ELIZABETH A., 1995, "Sources of conflict in Southern Africa c.1800–1830," in Hamilton, Carolyn (ed.), pp. 129–30

ELLIS, JOHN, 1993, *The Social History of the Machine-gun,* London, Pimlico

ELPHICK, RICHARD, and GILIOMEE, H. (eds.), 1989, *The Shaping of South African Society, 1652–1840,* Cape Town, Maskew Miller Longman

ELTIS, DAVID, 1987, *Economic Growth and the Ending of the Transatlantic Slave Trade,* New York, Oxford University Press

ELTIS, DAVID, 1990, "The volume, age/sex ratios, and African impact of the slave trade: some refinements of Paul Lovejoy's review of the literature," *J. Afr. Hist.,* vol. 31, pp. 485–92

ELTIS, D., and JENNINGS, LAWRENCE C., 1988, "Trade between Western Africa and the Atlantic world in the pre-Colonial era," *Am. Hist. Rev.,* vol. 43, pt 4, pp. 936–59

EMERSON, BARBARA C., 1979, *Leopold II of the Belgians—King of Colonialism,* London, Weidenfeld & Nicolson

ETHERINGTON, NORMAN A., 1979, "Labour supply and the genesis of South African confederation in the 1870s," *J. Afr. Hist.,* vol. 20, pp. 235–53

ETHERINGTON, NORMAN, 1991, "The Great Trek in relation to the Mfecane: a reassessment," *S. Afr. Hist. J.,* vol. 25, pp. 3–21

FAGE, JOHN D., 1990, "States and social cohesion in black Africa," in Hair (ed.), 1990, pp. 18–37

FALCONBRIDGE, ALEXANDER, 1788, *An Account of the Slave Trade on the Coast of Africa,* London

FAO, 1991, *World Soil Resources Report 66,* Rome, Food and Agriculture Organization of the United Nations

FATTOVICH, RUDOLFO, 1990, "Remarks on the Pre-Axumite period in northern Ethiopia," *J. Ethiop. Stud.,* vol. 23, pp. 1–34

FEIBEL, CRAIG S., 1994, "Landscape evolution in the Plio-Pleistocene Turkana basin, Kenya and Ethiopia," paper given at Society of Africanist Archaeologists Conference, Bloomington, 28 April to 1 May 1994

FLENLEY, JOHN R., 1979, *The Equatorial Rain Forest: a Geological History,* London, Butterworth

FOLEY, R. (ed.), 1984, *Hominid Evolution and Community Ecology: Prehistoric Human Adaptation in Biological Perspective,* London, Academic Press

FOLEY, ROBERT A., 1994, "Speciation, extinction and climatic change in hominid evolution," *J. Hum. Evol.,* vol. 26, pp. 275–89

FORD, J., 1971, *The Role of the Trypanosomiases in African Ecology: a Study of the Tsetse Fly Problem,* Oxford, Clarendon Press

FORDE, DARYLL (ed.), 1956, *Efik Traders of Old Calabar,* Oxford, Oxford University Press

FÖRSTER, S., MOMMSEN, W.J., and ROBINSON, R. (eds.), 1988, *Bismarck, Europe, and Africa. The Berlin Africa Conference 1884–1885 and the Onset of Partition,* London, German Historical Institute

FOX, R.H., 1953, "A study of energy expenditure of Africans engaged in various rural activities," Ph.D. thesis, University of London

FRAENKAL, PETER, 1959, *Wayaleshi,* London

FREEMAN, L., 1975, "Acheulian sites and stratigraphy in Iberia and the Maghreb," in Butzer and Isaac

FRENCH, M.H., 1957, "Nutritional value of tropical grasses and fodders," *Herb. Abstr.,* 27, pp. 1–9

FYNN, J.K., 1971, "Ghana-Asante (Ashanti)," in Crowder (ed.), 1971, pp. 19–52

GALBRAITH, JOHN K., 1992, "The challenge to the South: seven basic principles," *South Letter* (The South Centre, Geneva and Dar es Salaam), no. 14, pp. 12–13

GALBRAITH, J.S., 1963, *Reluctant Empire,* Berkeley, University of California Press

GALBRAITH, JOHN S., 1971, "Gordon, MacKinnon, and Leopold: the scramble for Africa 1876–84," *Vict. Stud.,* vol. 14, pp. 369–88

GALENSON, DAVID W., 1986, *Traders, Planters, and Slaves. Market Behaviour in Early English America,* Cambridge, Cambridge University Press

GAMBLE, C.S., and SOFFER, O., 1990, *The World at 18000 BP,* vol. 2: *Low Latitudes,* London, Unwin Hyman

GANN, L.H., 1975, "Economic development in Germany's African Empire, 1884–1914," in Duigan and Gann (eds.), 1975, pp. 213–55

GANN, L.H., and DUIGAN, P. (eds.), 1969, *Colonialism in Africa 1870–1960,* vol. 1, *The History and Politics of Colonialism 1870–1914,* Cambridge, Cambridge University Press

GARINE, I. DE, and HARRISON, G.A. (eds.), 1988, *Coping with Uncertainty in Food Supply,* Oxford, Oxford University Press

GARLAKE, PETER, 1973, *Great Zimbabwe,* London, Thames & Hudson

GARLAKE, PETER S., 1978, "Pastoralism and zimbabwes," *J. Afr. Hist.,* vol. 14, pp. 479–93

GARRARD, TIMOTHY F., 1982, "Myth and metrology: the early trans-Saharan gold trade," *J. Afr. Hist.,* vol. 23, pp. 443–61

GAUTHIER, E.F., 1943, *L'Afrique Noire Occidentale,* Paris

GEBAUER, A.B., and PRICE, T.D. (eds.), 1992

GEMERY, H.A., and HOGENDORN, H.S., 1978, "Technological change, slavery and the slave trade," in Dewey and Hopkins, pp. 243–58

GEOLOGICAL SOCIETY OF SOUTH AFRICA, 1992, *Some Superlatives of Geology in Southern Africa,* Johannésburg

GIBBONS, ANN, 1995, "Old dates for modern behavior," *Science,* 268, pp. 495–96

GIBLIN, JAMES, 1990, "Trypanosomiasis control in African history: an evaded issue," *J. Afr. Hist.,* vol. 31, pp. 59–80

GIFFORD, P., and LOUIS, W.R. (eds.), 1967, *France and Britain in Africa. Imperial Rivalry and Colonial Rule,* New Haven, Conn., Yale University Press

GIFFORD, PROSSER, and LOUIS, W.R. (eds.), 1982, *The Transfer of Power in Africa: Decolonization 1940–1960,* New Haven, Conn., Yale University Press

GILIOMEE, H., 1989, "The beginnings of Afrikaner ethnic consciousness, 1850–1915," in Vail (ed.), 1989, pp. 21–54

GLUCKMAN, MAX, 1951, "The Lozi of Barotseland in North-western Rhodesia," in Colson and Gluckman

GLUCKMAN, MAX, 1960, "The rise of a Zulu empire," *Sci. Am.,* vol. 202, pt 4 (April), pp. 157–68

GOODACRE, ALAN, 1991, "Continental drift," *Nature,* vol. 354

GOODY, JACK, 1971, *Technology, Tradition and the State in Africa,* Cambridge, Cambridge University Press

GOW, C.E., 1985, "A new skull of Megazostrodon (mammalia, Triconodonta) from the Elliot Formation (Lower Jurassic) of Southern Africa," *Palaeont. Afr.,* 26 (pt 2), pp. 13–23

GOWLETT, JOHN, 1984, *Ascent to Civilization,* London, Collins

GOWLETT, J.A.J., 1992a, "Tools—the palaeolithic record," in *Cambridge Encyclopedia of Human Evolution,* pp. 350–60

GOWLETT, J.A.J., 1992b, "Early human mental abilities," in *Cambridge Encyclopedia of Human Evolution,* p. 342

GRAY, ALBERT, and BELL, H.C.P. (eds.), 1887, 1890, *The Voyage of François Pyrard of Laval to the East Indies, the Maldives, the Moluccas, and Brazil,* London

GRÉBÉNART, D., 1988, *Les Premiers Métallurgistes en Afrique Occidentale,* Paris/Abidjan, Éditions Errance/Les Nouvelles Éditions Africaines

GREENBERG, JOSEPH H., 1966, *The Languages of Africa,* The Hague, Mouton

GREGORY, J.W., CORDELL, D.D., and GERVAIS, R. (eds.), 1984, *African Historical Demography,* Edinburgh, African Studies Centre, University of Edinburgh

GRIFFITHS, IEUAN, 1986, "The scramble for Africa: inherited political boundaries," *Geogr. J.,* vol. 152, pp. 204–16

GRIGSON, C., 1989, "Size and sex: evidence for domestication of cattle in the Near East," in Milles, Williams, and Gardner, pp. 77–109

GROVE, A.T., 1984, "The environmental setting," in Grove, A.T. (ed.), 1984

GROVE, A.T., 1993, "Africa's climate in the Holocene," in Shaw *et al.,* pp. 34–35

GROVE, A.T. (ed.), 1984, *The Niger and Its Neighbours: Environmental History and Hydrobiology, Human Use and Health Hazards of the Major West African Rivers,* Rotterdam, Balkema

GROVE, A.T., and SUTTON, J.E.G., 1989, "Agricultural terracing south of the Sahara," *Azania,* vol. 24, pp. 114–22

GROVE, ERIC J., 1976, "The first shots of the Great War: the Anglo-French conquest of Togo, 1914," *Army Q.*, July

GUARDIAN, 1996, "Pass notes" [on Mobutu], *Guardian* pt 2, p. 3, 4 November

GUTHRIE, CHARLES, 1986, "The African environment," in Hansen and McMillan

GUTHRIE, MALCOLM, 1967–70, *Comparative Bantu: An Introduction to the Comparative Linguistics and Prehistory of the Bantu Languages*, 4 vols., Farnborough, Gregg

GUY, JEFFERSON J., 1979, *The Destruction of the Zulu Kingdom: the Civil War in Zululand 1879–1884*, London, Longman

GWASSA, G.C.K., 1972, "Kinjitile and the ideology of Maji Maji," in Ranger and Kimambo, pp. 202–17

HAALAND, RANDI, 1980, "Man's role in the changing habitat of Mema during the old kingdom of Ghana," *Norweg. Archaeol. Rev.*, 13, pp. 31–46

HAALAND, RANDI, 1985, "Iron production, its socio-cultural context and ecological implications," in Haaland and Shinnie, pp. 50–72

HAALAND, R., 1992, "Fish, pots and grain: Early and Mid-Holocene adaptations in the Central Sudan," *Afr. Archaeol. Rev.*, 10, pp. 43–64

HAALAND, R., and SHINNIE, P.L. (eds.), 1985, *African Iron Working: Ancient and Traditional*, Oslo, Norwegian University Press

HAIR, P.E.H., 1965, "The enslavement of Koelle's informants," *J. Afr. Hist.*, vol. 6, pp. 193–203

HAIR, P.E.H., 1990, "Antera Duke of Old Calabar—a little more about an African entrepreneur," *History in Africa*, vol. 17, pp. 359–65

HAIR, P.E.H. (ed.), 1990, *Black Africa in Time-Perspective*, Liverpool, Centre for African Studies, University of Liverpool

HALL, DAVID O., and ROSILLO-CALLE, FRANCISCO, 1991, "African forests and grasslands: sources or sinks of greenhouse gases?," in Ominde and Juma

HALL, MARTIN, 1976, "Dendroclimatology, rainfall and human adaptation in the Late Iron Age of Natal and Zululand," *Ann. Natal Mus.*, vol. 22, pp. 693–703

HALL, MARTIN, 1987a, *The Changing Past: Farmers, Kings and Traders in Southern Africa 200 to 1860*, Cape Town, David Philip

HALL, MARTIN, 1987b, "Archaeology and modes of production in pre-colonial southern Africa," *J.S. Afr. Stud.*, vol. 14, pp. 1–17

HALL, M., and SMITH, A.B. (eds.), 1986, "Prehistoric pastoralism in southern Africa," *S. Afr. Archaeol. Soc.* (Goodwin Ser. no. 5)

HALLAM, A., 1975, "Alfred Wegener and the hypothesis of continental drift," *Sci. Am.*, vol. 232(2), pp. 88–97

HALSTEAD, L.B., 1982, *The Search for the Past*, New York, Doubleday

HAMILTON, ALAN, 1976, "Significance of patterns of distribution shown by forest plants and animals in tropical Africa for the reconstruction of Upper Pleistocene palaeoenvironments," *Palaeoecol. Afr.*, 9, pp. 63–97

HAMILTON, CAROLYN (ed.), 1995, *The Mfecane Aftermath*, Johannesburg, Witwatersrand University Press

HAMMERBECK, E.C.I., and ALLCOCK, R.J., 1985, *Geological Map of South Africa,* Geological Society of South Africa

HANCOCK, GRAHAM, 1992, *The Sign and the Seal,* London, Heinemann

HANSEN, ART, and MCMILLAN, DELLA E. (eds.), 1986, *Food in sub-Saharan Africa,* Boulder, Colo., Lynne Reiner

HARAWAY, DONNA, 1992, *Primate Visions. Gender, Race and Nature in the World of Modern Science,* London, Verso

HARGREAVES, J.D., 1969, "West African states and the European conquest," in Gann and Duigan, pp. 199–219

HARGREAVES, JOHN D., 1988, *Decolonisation in Africa,* London, Longman

HARLAN, JACK R., 1971, "Agricultural origins: centers and noncenters," *Science,* 174, pp. 468–74

HARLAN, J.R., 1976, *Crops and Man,* Madison, University of Wisconsin Press

HARLAN, J.R., DE WET, J.M.J., and STEMLER, A.B.L. (eds.), 1976a, *Origins of African Plant Domestication,* The Hague, Mouton

HARLAN, JACK R., DE WET, J.M.J., and STEMLER, ANN, 1976b, "Plant domestication and indigenous African agriculture," in Harlan, de Wet, and Stemler (eds.), pp. 3–19

HARMS, ROBERT, 1975, "The end of red rubber: a reassessment," *J. Afr. Hist.,* vol. 16, pp. 73–88

HARRIS, D.R., 1990, "Vavilov's concept . . . ," *Biol. J. LS,* vol. 39, pp. 7–16

HARRIS, J.W.K., and CAPALDO, S.D., 1993, "The earliest stone tools: their implications for an understanding of the activities and behaviour of late Pliocene hominids," in Berthelet and Chavaillon, pp. 196–224

HARRIS, MARVIN, 1986, *Good to Eat: Riddles of Food and Culture,* London, Allen & Unwin

HARRISON, G.A. (ed.), 1982, *Energy and Effort,* London, Taylor & Francis

HARRISON, G.A., TANNER, H.J.M., PILBEAM, D.R., and BAKER, P.T., 1992, *Human Biology,* Oxford, Oxford Science Publications

HART, HENRY, 1952, *Sea Roads to the Indies: an Account of the Voyages and Exploits of the Portuguese Navigators, together with the Life and Times of Dom Vasco da Gama,* London, William Hodge

HASSAN, FEKRI A., 1980, "Prehistoric sites along the Main Nile," in Williams and Faure, pp. 421–50

HASSAN, FEKRI A., 1981, *Demographic Archaeology,* London, Academic Press

HASSAN, FEKRI A., 1986, "Desert environment and origins of agriculture in Egypt," *Norw. Archaeol. Rev.,* 19, pp. 63–77

HASTINGS, ADRIAN, 1979, *A History of African Christianity,* Cambridge

HATLEY, T., and KAPPELMAN, J., 1980, "Bears, pigs and plio-pleistocene hominids: a case for the exploitation of below-ground food resources," *Hum. Ecol.,* vol. 8 (pt 4), pp. 371–87

HAWKES, J.G., 1990, "N.I. Vavilov—the man and his work," *Biol. J. LS,* vol. 39, pp. 3–6

HAWKINS, JOHN, *The Voyages,* ed. Clements R. Markham, 1878, Cambridge, Hakluyt Society, vol. 57

HAWKINS, M.W.S., 1888, *Plymouth Armada Heroes*, London

HAYS, J.D., IMBRIE, J., and SHACKLETON, N.J., 1976, "Variations in the Earth's orbit: pacemaker of the ice ages," *Science*, vol. 194, pp. 1121–32

HEESE, J.A., 1971, *Die Herkoms van die Afrikaner 1657–1867*, Cape Town

HEINTZ, B., and JONES, A. (eds.), 1987, "European sources for sub-Saharan Africa before 1900: use and abuse," *Paid.* (Stuttgart), vol. 33

HENDRIK SWELLENGREBEL *see* Swellengrebel

HENNESSY, J. POPE, 1890, "Is Central Africa worth having?," *The Nineteenth Century*, September, pp. 478–87

HERBERT, EUGENIA W., 1984, *Red Gold of Africa: Copper in Precolonial History and Culture*, Madison, University of Wisconsin Press

HERSKOVITS, M.J., 1952 [1940], *Economic Anthropology*, New York, Alfred A. Knopf

HERTSLET, SIR E., 1909, *The Map of Africa by Treaty*, 3rd edn, London, HMSO, vol. 2

HESS, R.L., 1963, "Italy and Africa: colonial ambitions in the First World War," *J. Afr. Hist.*, vol. 4, pp. 105–26

HILL, ALLAN, 1986, *Insights into Child Mortality in the Sahel from some Small-scale Studies in Mali*, New York, Population Council (Fertility Determinants Research Notes 12)

HILL, ANDREW, 1985, "Early hominid from Baringo, Kenya," *Nature*, vol. 315, pp. 222–24

HILL, ANDREW, 1987, "Causes of perceived faunal change in the later Neogene of East Africa," *J. Hum. Evol.*, vol. 16, pp. 583–96

HILL, ANDREW, 1994, "Late Miocene and early Pliocene hominoids from Africa," in Corruccini and Ciochon, pp. 123–45

HILL, A., 1995, "Faunal and environmental change in the neogene of East Africa: evidence from the Tugen Hills Sequence, Baringo District, Kenya," in Vrba *et al.* (eds.), 1995, pp. 178–93

HILL, ANDREW, and WARD, STEVEN, 1988, "Origin of the Hominidae: the record of African large hominoid evolution between 14 My and 4 My," *Yb. Phys. Anthrop.*, vol. 31, p. 52

HILL, ANDREW *et al.*, 1985, "Neogene palaeontology and geochronology of the Baringo Basin, Kenya," *J. Hum. Evol.*, vol. 14, p. 760

HILL, A., *et al.*, 1991, "Kipsaramon: a lower Miocene hominoid site in the Tugen Hills, Baringo District, Kenya," *J. Hum. Evol.*, vol. 20, pp. 67–75

HILL, A., *et al.*, 1992, "Earliest *Homo*," *Nature*, 355, pp. 719–22

HILLMAN, G.E.M., and HATHER, J., 1989, "Wild plant foods and diet at late paleolithic Wadi Kubbaniya: the evidence from charred remains," in Wendorf, Schild, and Close, pp. 162–242

HILSUM, LINDSAY, 1996, "Rwanda—the Betrayal," *Witness*, Channel 4 TV, 16 May

HILTON, ANNE, 1985, *The Kingdom of Kongo*, Oxford, Clarendon Press

HIRD, FRANK, 1935, *H.M. Stanley: The Authorised Life*, London

HOBBES, THOMAS (1588–1679), *Leviathan*, pt I, chap. 13

HOBSBAWM, ERIC, and RANGER, TERENCE (eds.), 1983, *The Invention of Tradition*, Cambridge, Cambridge University Press

HODGES, G.W.T., 1978, "African manpower statistics for the British forces in East Africa, 1914–1918," *J. Afr. Hist.,* vol. 19, pp. 101–16

HOGENDORN, JAN, and JOHNSON, MARION, 1986, *The Shell Money of the Slave Trade,* Cambridge, Cambridge University Press

HOLSTEIN, F. VON (ed. Rich, N., and Fischer, M.), 1957, *The Holstein Papers,* vol. 2 (diaries), Cambridge, Cambridge University Press

HOPKINS, A.G., 1973, *An Economic History of West Africa,* London, Longman

HOSKYNS, CATHERINE, 1965, *The Congo since Independence: January 1960–December 1961,* Oxford, Oxford University Press

HOUSTON, D.C., 1979, "The adaptations of scavengers," in Sinclair and Norton-Griffiths

HOWELL, F.C., 1966, "Observations on the earlier phases of the European lower paleolithic," *Am. Anthrop.,* 68 (pt 2), pp. 88–201

HOWELL, NANCY, 1976, "Towards a uniformitarian theory of human paleodemography," in Ward and Weiss, pp. 26–40

HØYGAARD, A., 1940, "Studies on the nutrition and physiopathology of Eskimos . . . 1936–7," *Norske VidenskAkad. Oslo,* Skr. 1. *Mat.-Naturvidensk. Klasse 1940* (pt 9), pp. 1–176

HUBBELL, S., 1988, *A Book of Bees,* New York, Random House

HUFFMAN, T.N., 1972, "The rise and fall of Zimbabwe," *J. Afr. Hist.,* vol. 13, pp. 353–66

HUFFMAN, T.N., 1981, "Snakes and birds: expressive space at Great Zimbabwe," *Afr. Stud.,* vol. 40, pp. 131–50

HUFFMAN, THOMAS N., 1982, "Archaeology and ethnohistory of the African iron age," *Ann. Rev. Anthrop.,* vol. 11, pp. 133–50

HUFFMAN, THOMAS N., 1986, "Archaeological evidence and conventional explanations of Southern Bantu settlement patterns," *Africa,* vol. 56, pp. 280–98

HUFFMAN, T.N., 1987, *Symbols in Stone. Unravelling the Mystery of Great Zimbabwe,* Johannesburg, Witwatersrand University Press

HUFFMAN, THOMAS N., 1993a, "Broederstroom and the central cattle pattern," *S. Afr. J. Sci.,* vol. 89, pp. 220–26

HUFFMAN, THOMAS N., 1993b, "Climatic change during the Iron Age," paper presented at an International Congress in Honour of Dr. Mary Douglas Leakey's Outstanding Contribution to Palaeoanthropology, Arusha, Tanzania, 8–15 August 1993

HUFFMAN, T.N., 1996, *Sacred Leadership: Space and Gender in Ancient Zimbabwe,* Johannesburg, Witwatersrand University Press

HUFFMAN, T.N., and VOGEL, J.C., 1991, "The chronology of Great Zimbabwe," *S. Afr. Archaeol. Bull.,* vol. 46, pp. 61–70

HULL, THOMAS G., 1963, *Diseases Transmitted from Animals to Man,* 5th edn, Springfield, Ill.

HUNTER, D.R., and HAMILTON, P.J., 1978, "The Bushveld complex," in Tarling

HUNTLEY, B.J., and WALKER, B.H. (eds.), 1982, *Ecology of Tropical Ecosystems,* Berlin, Springer-Verlag

ILIFFE, J., 1967, "The organization of the Maji Maji rebellion," *J. Afr. Hist.,* vol. 9, pp. 495–512

ILIFFE, J., 1968, "The Herero and Nama risings," in Kiboydya

ILIFFE, J., 1979, *A Modern History of Tanganyika*, Cambridge, Cambridge University Press

ILIFFE, J., 1987, *The African Poor*, Cambridge, Cambridge University Press

ILIFFE, J., 1995, *Africans, the History of a Continent*, Cambridge, Cambridge University Press

IMBRIE, JOHN, 1982, "Astronomical theory of the Pleistocene Ice Ages: a brief historical review," *Icarus*, vol. 50, p. 411

INGOLD, TIM, 1980, *Hunters, Pastoralists and Ranchers*, Cambridge, Cambridge University Press

INIKORI, J.E., 1977, "The import of firearms into West Africa 1705–1807: a quantitative analysis," *J. Afr. Hist.*, vol. 28, pp. 339–68

INIKORI, J.E., 1984, [Estimates of the volume of the slave trade], in Unesco, 1984, vol. 5

INTERNATIONAL FOOD POLICY RESEARCH INSTITUTE (IFPRI), 1991, *Facts and Figures: International Agricultural Research*, New York, Rockefeller Foundation

INTERNATIONAL INSTITUTE OF TROPICAL AGRICULTURE (IITA), 1971, *Annual Report*, Ibadan

ISAAC, GLYNN, 1976, "The activities of early African hominids," in Isaac and McCown

ISAAC, GLYNN LL., and MCCOWN, ELIZABETH R. (eds.), 1976, *Human Origins—Louis Leakey and the East African evidence*, Menlo Park, Calif., W.A. Benjamin

ISAACMAN, ALLEN F., 1972, *Mozambique—the Africanization of a European Institution: the Zambezi Prazos, 1750–1902*, Madison, University of Wisconsin Press

ISAACMAN, A., 1976, *Anti-colonial Activity in the Zambesi Valley 1850–1921*, Berkeley, University of California Press

ISAACMAN, A.F., and ISAACMAN B., 1976, *The Tradition of Resistance in Mozambique: the Zambesi Valley 1850–1921*, London, Heinemann

ISAACMAN, BARBARA and ALLEN, 1977, "Slavery and social stratification among the Sena of Mozambique," in Miers and Kopytoff, pp. 105–20

ISERT, PAUL ERDMANN (1788) 1992, *Letters on West Africa and the Slave Trade*, Oxford, Oxford University Press

JEFFERSON, THOMAS, 1782, *Notes on Virginia*

JEWISS, O.R., 1966, "Morphological and physiological aspects of growth in grasses during the vegetative phase," in Milthorpe and Ivins

JOHANSON, D.C., 1978, "Ethiopia yields first 'Family' of early man," *Nat. Geogr.*, December, Washington, D.C., pp. 790–811

JOHANSON, D.C., WHITE, T.D., and COPPENS, Y., 1978, "A new species of the genus Australopithecus (Primates: Hominidae) from the Pliocene of Eastern Africa," *Kirtlandia* (Cleveland, Ohio), vol. 28, pp. 1–14

JOHNSON, MARION, 1966, "The ounce in eighteenth-century West African trade," *J. Afr. Hist.*, vol. 7, pp. 197–214

JOHNSON, MARION, 1976, in Anstey and Hair, p. 31

JOHNSON, MARION, 1984, "Elephants and towns," in Gregory, Cordell, and Gervais

JOHNSON, R.C., COLE, R.E., and AHERN, F.M., 1981, "Genetic interpretation of racial and ethnic differences in lactose absorption and tolerance: a review," *Hum. Biol.*, 53, pp. 1–13

JOHNSTON, H.H., 1884, *The River Congo from Its Mouth to Bolobo*, London

JOHNSTON, H.J.M., 1972, *British Emigration Policy 1815–1830: Shovelling Out Paupers*, Oxford, Clarendon Press

JONES, ADAM, 1986, "Semper aliquid veteris: printed sources for the history of the Ivory and Gold Coasts," *J. Afr. Hist.*, vol. 27, pp. 215–35

JONES, ADAM, 1987a, *Raw, Medium, Well Done: a Critical Review of Editorial and Quasi-editorial Work of pre-1885 European Sources for sub-Saharan Africa, 1960–1986*, Madison, University of Wisconsin Press

JONES, ADAM, 1987b, "The dark continent: a preliminary study of the geographic coverage in European sources 1400–1880," in Heintz and Jones, pp. 19–26

JONES, ELDRED D., 1971, *The Elizabethan Image of Africa*, Amherst, Mass., Folger Shakespeare Library

JONES, GLYN, 1988, "Endemic crop plants of Ethiopia: 1. T'ef (Eragrostis tef)," *Walia*, vol. 11, pp. 37–43

KALALUKA, L., 1979, *Kuomboka*, Lusaka, Zambia, Neczam

KALB, MADELEINE G., 1982, *The Congo Cables: the Cold War in Africa—from Eisenhower to Kennedy*, New York, Macmillan

KAPLAN, MARION, 1991, *The Portuguese: The Land and Its People*, London, Viking

KARP, IVAN (ed.), 1987, *The African Frontier*, Bloomington, Indiana University Press

KEA, R.A., 1971, "Firearms and warfare on the Gold and Slave Coasts from the sixteenth to the nineteenth centuries," *J. Afr. Hist.*, vol. 12, pp. 185–213

KIBOYDYA, G. (ed.), 1968, *Aspects of South African History*, Dar es Salaam, East African Publishing House

KILLICK, D.J., VAN DER MERWE, N.J., GORDON, R.B., GRÉBÉNART, D., 1988, "Reassessment of the evidence for early metallurgy in Niger, West Africa," *J. Archaeol. Sci.*, 15, pp. 267–394

KILLINGRAY, DAVID, 1978, "Repercussions of World War I in the Gold Coast," *J. Afr. Hist.*, vol. 19, pp. 39–59

KIMBLE, GEORGE H.T. (trans. and ed.), 1937, Pacheco Pereira, Duarte, 1506, *Esmeraldo de situ orbis*, Cambridge, Hakluyt Society (Ser. II, vol. 79)

KINGDON, JONATHAN, 1989, *Island Africa*, Princeton, NJ, Princeton University Press

KINGSTON, J.D., MARINO, D.D., and HILL, A., 1994, "Isotopic evidence for Neogene hominid paleoenvironments in the Kenya Rift Valley," *Science*, vol. 264, pp. 955–59

KITCHEN, K.A., 1993, "The land of Punt," in Shaw *et al.* (eds.), 1993, pp. 587–608

KJEKSHUS, H., 1977, *Ecology Control and Economic Development in East African History: Tanganyika 1850–1950*, London, Heinemann

KLEIN, HERBERT S., and ENGERMAN, STANLEY L., 1976, "Slave mortality on British ships 1791–1797," in Anstey and Hair

KLEIN, R.G., 1994, "Wild bovines of the African Quaternary," in Wendorf and Schild, 1995

KOBISHCHANOV, Y.M. (trans. L.T. Kapitanoff), 1979, *Axum* (ed. J.W. Michels), London, Pennsylvania State University Press

KOBISH(CH)ANOV, Y.M., 1981, "Aksum: political system, economics and culture, first to fourth century," in Unesco, 1981, vol. 2, pp. 381–400

KOPYTOFF, IGOR, 1987, "The internal African frontier," in Karp, pp. 3–84

KRETCHMER, N., et al., 1971, "Intestinal absorption of lactose in Nigerian ethnic groups," The Lancet, ii, pp. 392–95

KRETCHMER, NORMAN, 1972, "Lactose and lactase," Sci. Am., 227(4), pp. 70–78

KRETZOI, M., AND VERTES, L., 1965, "Upper Biharian (Intermindel) pebble industry occupation site in western Hungary," Curr. Anthrop., 6, pp. 74–87

LAMBRECHT, F.L., 1964, "Aspects of evolution and ecology of tsetse and trypanosomiasis in the prehistoric African environment," J. Afr. Hist., vol. 5, pp. 1–24

LAUGHLIN, W.S., 1968, "Hunting: an integrated biobehavior system and its evolutionary importance," in Lee and DeVore, pp. 304–20

LAW, R.C.C., 1978, "North Africa in the age of Phoenician and Greek colonisation," in Cambridge History of Africa, vol. 2, pp. 87–147

LAW, ROBIN, 1990, "Further light on Bullfinch Lambe and the 'Emperor of Pawpaw:' King Agaja of Dahomey's letter to King George I of England 1726," Hist. Afr., vol. 17, pp. 211–26

LAW, ROBIN, 1991, The Slave Coast of West Africa 1550–1750. The Impact of the Atlantic Slave Trade on an African Society, Oxford, Clarendon Press

LAWAL, B., 1973, "Dating problems at Igbo-Ukwu," J. Afr. Hist., vol. 14, pp. 1–8

LAWRENCE, T.E., 1919, Arab Bulletin (Cairo), no. 111, 24 May

LEACOCK, ELEANOR R., and LEE, RICHARD B., 1982, Politics and History in Band Society, Cambridge, Cambridge University Press

LEAKEY, L.S.B., 1966, "Africa and Pleistocene overkill?," Nature, 212, p. 1615

LEAKEY, L.S.B., TOBIAS, P.V., and NAPIER, J.R., 1964, "A new species of the genus Homo from Olduvai Gorge," Nature, 202, pp. 7–9

LEAKEY, LOUIS, n.d., tape of California lecture

LEAKEY, M.D., 1979, Olduvai Gorge: My Search for Early Man, London, Collins

LEAKEY, R.E.F., 1969, "New cercopithecidae from the Chemeron Beds of Lake Baringo, Kenya," in Fossil Vertebrates of Africa, vol. 1, London, Academic Press, pp. 53–69

LEAKEY, R.E.F., and WALKER, A.C., 1985, "Homo erectus unearthed," Nat. Geogr. Mag., 168, pp. 625–29

LEE R.B., 1965, "Subsistence ecology of !Kung Bushmen," Ph.D. dissertation (anthropology), Berkeley, University of California

LEE R.B., 1968, "What hunters do for a living, or, how to make out on scarce resources," in Lee and DeVore, pp. 30–48

LEE R.B., 1969, "Eating Christmas in the Kalahari," Nat. Hist., December

LEE, RICHARD B., 1979, The !Kung San: Men, Women and Work in a Foraging Society, Cambridge, Cambridge University Press

LEE, RICHARD B., 1982, "Politics, sexual and non-sexual, in an egalitarian society," in Leacock and Lee, pp. 37–59

LEE R.B., and DEVORE, I. (eds.), 1968, *Man the Hunter*, Chicago, Aldine

LEGUM, COLIN, 1962, *Pan-Africanism—a Short Political Guide*, London, Pall Mall

LEIBBRANDT, H.C.V. (ed.), 1897, "Riebeeck's journal," pt 2, "January 1656 to December 1658," in *Precis of the Archives*, Cape Town, Cape of Good Hope, Government Printer

LEMARCHAND, RENÉ, 1970, *Rwanda and Burundi*, London, Pall Mall

LEMARCHAND, RENÉ, 1994, *Burundi—Ethnocide as Discourse and Practice*, Cambridge, Cambridge University Press

LEVEEN, E. PHILLIP, 1971, "British slave trade suppression policies 1821–1865: impact and implications," Ph.D. thesis, University of California at Berkeley

LEVENE, FLEUR, 1991, "The salt and the wounds," *Observer* magazine (London), 20 October 1991

LEVTZION, N., 1973, *Ancient Ghana and Mali*, London, Methuen

LEVTZION, N., and HOPKINS, J.F.P., 1981, *Corpus of Early Arabic Sources for West African History*, Cambridge, Cambridge University Press

LHOTE, H., 1959, *The Search for the Tassili Frescoes*, London, Hutchinson

LICHTENSTEIN, H., 1812–15, repr. 1928/30, *Travels in Southern Africa in the Years 1803, 1804, 1805 and 1806*, Cape Town

LIEBERMAN, PHILIP, 1985, "On the evolution of human syntactic ability: its pre-adaptive bases—motor control and speech," *J. Hum. Evol.*, 14, pp. 657–68

LIEBERMAN, PHILIP, 1992, "Human speech and language," in *Cambridge Encyclopedia of Human Evolution*

LINDEN, IAN, 1977, *Church and Revolution in Rwanda*, Manchester, Manchester University Press

LINNAEUS, CAROLUS, 1735, *Systema Naturae*

LIPSCHUTZ, M.R., and RASMUSSEN, R.K. (comps.), 1989, *Dictionary of African Historical Biography*, Berkeley, University of California Press

LIVINGSTONE, DANIEL A., 1980, "Environmental changes in the Nile headwaters," in Williams and Faure, pp. 335–55

LIVINGSTONE, FRANK B., 1958, "Anthropological implications of sickle cell gene distribution in West Africa," *Am. Anthrop.*, vol. 60, pp. 533–62

LOFTUS, R.T., *et al.*, 1994, "Evidence for two independent domestications of cattle," *Proc. Nat. Acad. Sci. N.Y.*, 91, pp. 2757–61

LONSDALE, JOHN D., 1981, "State and social processes in Africa: a historiographical survey," *Afr. Stud. Rev.*, vol. 24, pp. 139–225

LONSDALE, JOHN, 1985, "The European scramble and conquest in African history," *Cambridge History of Africa*, vol. 6, pp. 680–766

LOUIS, W.R., 1963, *Ruanda-Urundi 1884–1919*, Oxford, Clarendon Press

LOUIS, W.R., 1967, *Great Britain and Germany's Lost Colonies 1914–1919*, London

LOUIS, W.R., 1977, *Imperialism at Bay*, Oxford, Clarendon Press

LOUIS, W.R., and ROBINSON, R., 1982, "The United States and the liquidation of the British Empire in Tropical Africa, 1941–1951," in Gifford, Prosser, and Louis, W.R.

LOVEJOY, C.O., 1981, "The origin of man," *Science*, vol. 211, pp. 341–50

LOVEJOY, PAUL E., 1983, *Transformations in Slavery. A History of Slavery in Africa*, Cambridge, Cambridge University Press

LOVEJOY, PAUL E., 1986, *Salt of the Desert Sun: a History of Salt Production and Trade in the Central Sudan*, Cambridge, Cambridge University Press

LOVEJOY, PAUL E., 1988, "Concubinage and the status of women slaves in early colonial north Nigeria," *J. Afr. Hist.*, vol. 29, pp. 245–66

LOVEJOY, PAUL E., 1989, "The impact of the Atlantic slave trade on Africa: a review of the literature," *J. Afr. Hist.*, vol. 30, pp. 365–94

LOWE-MCCONNELL, R.H., 1984, "The biology of the river systems with particular reference to the fishes," in Grove, A.T. (ed.), 1984, pp. 101–40

LOWIE, R.H., 1927, *The Origins of the State*, New York, Harcourt & Brace

LOWIE, R.H., 1950, *Social Organization*, London, Routledge & Kegan Paul

LUDWIG, H.-D., 1968, "Permanent farming on Ukara: impact of land shortage on husbandry practices," in Ruthenberg, pp. 88–135

LUMLEY, EDWARD K., 1976, *Forgotten Mandate: A British District Officer in Tanganyika*, London, Hurst

LUMUMBA P., 1961 (Brussels), Eng. trans. pub. 1962: *Congo, My Country*, London

LYNCH, HOLLIS R., 1982, in Gifford, Prosser, and Louis, W.R.

MACARTHUR, R.H., and WILSON, E.O., 1967, *The Theory of Island Biogeography*, Princeton, NJ, Princeton University Press

MCBREARTY, SALLY, and MONIZ, MARC, 1991, "The archaeology of gender. Prostitutes or providers? Hunting, tool use, and sex roles in earliest *Homo*," in Dale Walde and Noreen D. Willows (eds.), *Proc. 22nd Ann. Conf. Archaeol. Ass. Univ. Calgary*

MCCAULEY, JOHN F., *et al.*, 1986, "Paleodrainages of the Eastern Sahara—the Radar rivers revisited (SIR-A/B implications for a Mid-Tertiary Trans-African Drainage System)," *IEEE Trans. Geosci. Remote Sens. GE-24* (pt 4), pp. 624–47

MCCRACKEN, ROBERT D., 1971, "Lactose deficiency: an example of dietary evolution," *Curr. Anthrop.*, 12, pp. 479–519

MCCREA, BARBARA, and PINCHUK, TONY, 1990, *Zimbabwe and Botswana. The Rough Guide*, London, Harrap/Columbus

MCDONALD, MARY, 1994, "An early pastoralist site in Dakhleh Oasis, Egypt," paper presented at Society of Africanist Archaeologists 12th Biennial Conference, Bloomington, Indiana, 28 April to 1 May 1994

MCEVEDY, COLIN, 1980, *The Penguin Atlas of African History*, London

MCEWAN, ALEC C., 1971, *International Boundaries of East Africa*, Oxford, Clarendon Press

MCEWAN, ALEC C., 1991, "The establishment of the Nigeria/Benin boundary, 1889–1989," *Geogr. J.*, vol. 157, pp. 62–70

MCINTOSH, R.J., 1983, "Floodplain morphology and human occupation of the upper Inland Delta of the Niger," *Geogr. J.*, vol. 149, pp. 182–201

MCINTOSH, R.J., 1991, "Early urban clusters in China and Africa," *J. Fld Archaeol.*, vol. 18, pp. 199–212

MCINTOSH, R.J., 1992, "Historical view of the semiarid tropics," paper presented at the 1992 Carter Lecture Series, Center for African Studies, University of Florida. (MS)

MCINTOSH, R.J., 1993, "The pulse model: genesis and accommodation of specialization in the middle Niger," *J. Afr. Hist.,* vol. 34, pp. 181–220

MCINTOSH, R.J., and S.K., 1984, "Early Iron Age economy in the inland Niger Delta (Mali)," in Clark and Brandt, pp. 158–72

MCINTOSH, R.J., and S.K., 1988, "From *siècles obscurs* to revolutionary centuries in the middle Niger," *Wld Archeol.,* vol. 20, pp. 141–65

MCINTOSH, SUSAN K., 1992, "Reflections on structure and process in African intermediate societies," paper presented to American Anthropological Association, San Francisco, 2–6 December 1992. (MS)

MCINTOSH, S.K., 1994, "Changing perceptions of West Africa's past: archaeological research since 1988," *J. Archaeol. Res.*

MCINTOSH, S.K., and R.J., 1980, "Prehistorical investigations in the region of Jenne, Mali," *Brit. Archaeol. Reps,* Oxford

MCINTOSH, SUSAN KEECH and RODERICK J., 1993, "Cities without citadels: understanding urban origins along the middle Niger," in Shaw *et al.* (eds.), 1993, pp. 621–41

MCKEY, D., *et al.*, 1978, "Phenolic content of vegetation in two African rainforests: ecological implications," *Science,* 202, pp. 61–64

MACKINTOSH, C.W., 1907, *Coillard of the Zambezi,* London, T. Fisher Unwin

MACLEAN, M. RACHEL, 1994, "Late Stone Age and Early Stone Age settlement in the Interlacustrine region: a district case study," in Sutton, J.E.G. (ed.), 1996, pp. 296–302

MACLENNAN, DONALD, 1986, *A Proper Degree of Terror,* Johannesburg

MCNAUGHTON, S.J., 1979, "Grazing as an optimization process: grass-ungulate relationships in the Serengeti," *Am. Nat.,* 113(5), pp. 691–703

MCNEILL, WILLIAM H., 1977, *Plagues and Peoples,* New York, Doubleday

MCNEILL, W.H., 1979, *A World History,* Oxford, Oxford University Press

MAGGS, TIM, 1980, "Msuluzi confluence: a seventh century Early Iron Age site on the Tugela River," *Ann. Natal Mus.,* vol. 24, pp. 111–45

MAINGA, MUTUMBA, 1973, *Bulozi under the Luyana Kings, Political Evolution and State Formation in Pre-colonial Zambia,* London, Longman

MALCOLM, D.W., 1934, *Report on Ukara,* Mwanza, Provincial Offices (13 pp. MS.)

MANNING, PATRICK, 1988, "The impact of slave exports on the population of the western coast of Africa 1700–1850," in Daget

MANNING, PATRICK, 1990, *Slavery and African Life—Occidental, Oriental and African Slave Trades,* Cambridge, Cambridge University Press

MAREES, PIETER DE (1602), *Description and Historical Account of the Gold Coast of Guinea,* trans. and ed. Albert Van Dantzig and Adam Jones, 1987, British Academy, Oxford University Press

MARKHAM, CLEMENTS R. (ed.), 1878, *John Hawkins. The Voyages,* Cambridge, Hakluyt Society, vol. 57

MARKS, S., and ATMORE, A. (eds.), 1980, *Economy and Society in Pre-industrial South Africa,* London, Longman

MARKS, SHULA, and RATHBONE, RICHARD (eds.), 1982, *Industrialization and Social Change in South Africa: African Class Formation, Culture, and Consciousness, 1870–1930,* New York, Longman

MARNHAM, PATRICK, 1987, *Fantastic Invasion*, London, Penguin Books

MARSHALL, JOHN, 1957, "Ecology of the !Kung Bushmen of the Kalahari," senior honors thesis in anthropology, Harvard University (Cambridge, Mass.)

MARTIN, BERNARD, and SPURRELL, MARK (eds.), 1962, *John Newton, The Journal of a Slave Trader—1750–1754*, London, Epworth

MARTIN, PAUL S., 1966, "African and Pleistocene overkill," *Nature*, 212, pp. 339–42. *See also* Leakey, 1966, and Martin, 1967

MARTIN, P.S., 1967, "Overkill at Olduvai gorge," *Nature*, 215, pp. 212–13

MATTINGLY, P.F., 1983, "The palaeogeography of mosquito-borne disease," *Biol. J. LS*, vol. 199, pp. 185–210

MAUNY, R., 1978, "Trans-Saharan contacts and the Iron Age in west Africa," in *Cambridge History of Africa*, vol. 2, pp. 272–341

MAURICE, ALBERT (ed.), 1957, *The Unpublished Letters of H.M. Stanley*, London

MAYR, ERNST, 1965, *Animal Species and Evolution*, Cambridge, Mass., Harvard University Press

MAZRUI, ALI A., 1978, *Political Values and the Educated Class in Africa*, London, Heinemann

MEILLASSOUX, C., 1991, *The Anthropology of Slavery*, London, Athlone Press

MEILLASSOUX, C. (ed.), 1971, *The Development of Indigenous Trade and Markets in West Africa*, London

MEINERTZHAGEN, RICHARD, 1957, *Kenya Diary, 1902–1906*, Edinburgh

MELLARS, PAUL, and STRINGER, CHRIS (eds.), 1989, *The Human Revolution—Behavioural and Biological Perspectives on the Origins of Modern Humans*, Edinburgh, Edinburgh University Press

MENDELSOHN, F., and POTGIETER, C.T. (eds.), 1986, *Guidebook to Sites of Geological and Mining Interest on the Central Witwatersrand*, Geological Society of South Africa

MENTZEL, O.F., 1741, *A Complete and Authentic Geographical and Topographical Description of the . . . Cape of Good Hope*, Cape Town, 1921

MERCER, JOHN, 1980, *The Canary Islands, Their Prehistory, Conquest and Survival*, London, Rex Collings

MEREDITH, M., 1984, *The First Dance of Freedom*, London, Hamish Hamilton

METCALF, GEORGE, 1987a, "Gold, assortments and the trade ounce: Fante merchants and the problem of supply and demand in the 1770s," *J. Afr. Hist.*, vol. 28, pp. 27–41

METCALF, GEORGE, 1987b, "A microcosm of why Africans sold slaves: Akan consumption patterns in the 1770s," *J. Afr. Hist.*, vol. 28, pp. 377–94

MIERS, SUZANNE, and KOPYTOFF, IGOR (eds.), 1977, *Slavery in Africa: Historical and Anthropological Perspectives*, Madison, University of Wisconsin Press

MILLER, J.C., 1982, "The significance of drought, disease and famine in the agriculturally marginal zones of west Central Africa," *J. Afr. Hist.*, vol. 23, pp. 17–61

MILLER, J.C., 1988, *Way of Death: Merchant Capitalism and the Angolan Slave Trade 1730–1830*, Madison, University of Wisconsin Press

MILLER, S.L., 1953, "A production of amino acids under possible primitive earth conditions," *Science*, Washington, D.C., vol. 117, pp. 528–29

MILLER, S.L., 1974, "The first laboratory synthesis of organic compounds under primitive earth conditions," in Neyman, pp. 228–42

MILLES, A., WILLIAMS, D., and GARDNER, N. (eds.), 1980, *The Beginnings of Agriculture*, Oxford, British Archaeological Reports (International Ser. 496)

MILTHORPE, F.L., and IVINS, J.D. (eds.), 1966, *The Growth of Cereals and Grasses*, London, Butterworth

MIRACLE, MARVIN P., 1965, "The introduction and spread of maize in Africa," *J. Afr. Hist.*, vol. 6, pp. 39–55

MIRAZON, MARTA, and FOLEY, ROBERT, 1994, "Multiple dispersals and modern human origins," *Evol. Anthrop.*, 3(2), pp. 48–60

MITCHELL, PETER, 1990, in Gamble and Soffer

MOHR, P.A., 1971, *The Geology of Ethiopia*, Addis Ababa, Haile Selassie I University Press

MONK, WILLIAM (ed.), 1858, *Dr. Livingstone's Cambridge Lectures*, London

MONOD, T. (ed.), 1975, *Pastoralism in Tropical Africa*, London, International African Institute, pp. 1–183 (see "Introduction")

MOODIE, D. (ed.), 1960, *The Record: or a Series of Official Papers Relative to the Conditions and Treatment of the Native Tribes of South Africa, 1838, 1842*, Cape Town, Balkema (fac. repr.)

MOORE, FRANCIS, 1738, *Travels into the Inland Parts of Africa*, London

MOREL, E.D., 1904, *King Leopold's Rule in Africa*, London

MOREL, E.D., 1920, *The Black Man's Burden*, Manchester

MORRIS, DESMOND, 1967, *The Naked Ape*, London

MORRIS, DONALD R., 1965, *The Washing of the Spears. The Rise and Fall of the Zulu Nation*, New York, Simon & Schuster; 1968, London, Sphere Books

MOSS, CYNTHIA, 1988, *Elephant Memories*, London, Elm Tree Books

MULTHAUF, ROBERT P., 1978, *Neptune's Gift. A History of Common Salt*, Baltimore, Md./London, Johns Hopkins University Press

MUNRO-HAY, STUART, 1991, *An African Civilisation, the Aksumite Kingdom of Northern Ethiopia*, Edinburgh, Edinburgh University Press

MUNRO-HAY, STUART, 1993, "State development and urbanism in modern Ethiopia," in Shaw *et al.* (eds.), 1993, pp. 609–21

MURIUKI, GODFREY, 1975, *A History of the Kikuyu*, Nairobi, Oxford University Press

MURPHY, J. BRENDAN, and NANCE, R. DAMIAN, 1992, "Mountain belts and the supercontinent cycle," *Sci. Am.*, April, pp. 34–41

MUZZOLINI, A., 1993, "The emergence of a food-producing economy in the Sahara," in Shaw *et al.* (eds.), 1993, pp. 227–39

MWANZI, H.A., 1985, "African initiatives and resistance in East Africa," in Unesco, 1985, vol. 7, pp. 149–68

MYERS, NORMAN, 1994, "Seeds of hope," *Guardian*, 12 May, science section, pp. 14–15

NACHTIGAL, GUSTAV, 1980, *Sahara and Sudan*, vol. 2, *Bornu, Kanem, Ennedi*, trans. A.G.B. and H.H. Fisher, New York, Holmes & Meier

NANCE, R. DAMIAN, WORSLEY, THOMAS R., and MOODY, JUDITH B., 1988, "The supercontinent cycle," *Sci. Am.*, July, pp. 44–51

NAPIER, J.R., and P.H., 1985, *The Natural History of the Primates*, British Museum (Natural History), Cambridge, Cambridge University Press

NASH, T.A.M., 1969, *Africa's Bane*, London, Collins

NATIONAL GEOGRAPHIC SOCIETY, 1983, *People and Places of the Past*, Washington, D.C.

NEWBURY, C.W. (ed.), 1966, *Burton, Richard, 1864. A Mission to Gelele, King of Dahomey*, London, Routledge & Kegan Paul

NEWS FROM BAROTSILAND, see Société des Missions Évangéliques

NEWSWEEK, 1988, "The African Eve," New York, 11 January

NEWTON, JOHN, 1750–1754, *The Journal of a Slave Trader*, ed. with introd. by Bernard Martin and Mark Spurrell, 1962, London, Epworth Press

NEWTON-KING, S., 1980, "The labour market of the Cape Colony, 1807–1828," in Marks and Atmore, pp. 182–91

NEYMAN, J. (ed.), 1974, *The Heritage of Copernicus: Theories Pleasing to the Mind*, Cambridge, Mass., MIT Press

NICHOLSON, SHARON E., 1986, "Climate, drought and famine in Africa," in Hansen and McMillan, pp. 107–29

NISBET, EUAN, 1991, *Living Earth: A Short History of Life and Its Home*, London, Chapman & Hall

NOWELL, C., 1982, *The Rose-coloured Map. Portugal's Attempt to Build an African Empire*, Lisbon

NURSE, DEREK, 1996, "'Historical' classifications of the Bantu languages," in Sutton (ed.), 1996, pp. 65–81

NWEKE, F.I., *et al.*, 1991, *Production Costs in the Yam-based Cropping Systems of Southeastern Nigeria*, Ibadan, International Institute of Tropical Africa (RCMP Research Monograph 6)

NYERERE, JULIUS K., 1963, "A United States of Africa," *J. Mod. Afr. Stud.*, vol. 1, pt 1, pp. 1–6

OAKLEY, KENNETH P., 1972, *Man the Tool-maker*, London, British Museum (Natural History)

OBASANJO, O., 1981, *My Command*, London

O'CONNOR, DAVID, 1993, "Urbanism in bronze age Egypt and northeast Africa," in Shaw *et al.* (eds.), 1993, pp. 570–86

OLIVER, ROLAND, 1991, *The African Experience*, London, Weidenfeld & Nicolson

OLIVER, R., and FAGE, J., 1962/1988, *A Short History of Africa*, London, Penguin Books

OLIVER, R., and FAGE, J.D. (eds.), 1975–86, *Cambridge History of Africa*, 8 vols., Cambridge, Cambridge University Press

OMER-COOPER, JOHN D., 1966, *The Zulu Aftermath. A Nineteenth Century Revolution in Bantu Africa*, London, Longman

OMINDE, S.H., and JUMA, CALESTOUS (eds.), 1991, *A Change in the Weather: African Perspectives on Climatic Change*, Nairobi, ACTS Press

OORDT, J.F. VAN, 1898, *Paul Kruger en de opkomst van de Zuid-Afrikaansche Republiek*, Amsterdam/Cape Town

OSLISLY, RICHARD, 1996, "The middle Ogooué valley [Gabon]: cultural changes and palaeoclimatic implications of the last four millennia," in Sutton (ed.), 1996, pp. 324–31

OSWELL, W. EDWARD, 1900, *William Cotton Oswell: Hunter and Explorer*, 2 vols., London, Heinemann

PACHECO PEREIRA, DUARTE, 1506, *Esmeraldo de situ orbis*, trans. and ed. George H.T. Kimble, 1937, Cambridge, Hakluyt Society (Ser. II, vol. 79)

PAGE, MELVIN E. (ed.), 1987, *Africa and the First World War*, London, Macmillan

PAKENHAM, THOMAS, 1991, *The Scramble for Africa*, London, Weidenfeld & Nicolson

PARK, MUNGO, 1813, *Travels to the Interior of Africa*, London

PARKER, I.S.C., and GRAHAM, A.D., 1989, "Elephant decline: downward trends in African elephant distribution and numbers," 2 pts, *Int. J. Environ. Stud.*, vol. 34, pp. 287–305, and vol. 35, pp. 13–26

PARTRIDGE, TIM C., 1994, "Between two oceans," Johannesburg, pp. 1–2 (unpub. draft MS.)

PAULSSEN, F., 1913, "Rechtsanschauung der Eingeboren auf Ukara," *Baessler Archiv*, 4(I)

PEIRES, J.B., 1989, "The British and the Cape," in Elphick and Giliomee, pp. 472–518

PERHAM, M., 1956, *Lugard*, vol. 1: *The Years of Adventure 1886–1898*, London

PHILIPPS, THOMAS, 1960, *Philipps, 1820 Settler* (ed. A. Jones), Pietermaritzburg

PHILLIPS, PERROT, 1992, "Banking on it," *Weekend Guardian*, 3 October

PHILLIPSON, D.W., 1977a, "The spread of the Bantu language," *Sci. Am.*, 236(4), pp. 106–14

PHILLIPSON, D.W., 1977b, *The Later Prehistory of Eastern and Southern Africa*, London, Heinemann

PHILLIPSON, D.W., 1985, 2nd edn 1996, *African Archaeology*, Cambridge, Cambridge University Press

PHILLIPSON, D.W., 1994, "Aksum: the ancient capital of Christian Ethiopia" (unpub. summary MS.)

PHIMISTER, I.R., 1976, "Pre-colonial gold mining in southern Zambezia: a reassessment," *Afr. Soc. Res.*, vol. 21, pp. 1–30

PIMENTAL, D., 1974, *Energy Use in Food Production*, Ithaca, NY, Cornell University Press

PINGALI, P., BIGOT, Y., and BINSWANGER, H.P. (eds.), 1987, *Agricultural Mechanization and the Evolution of Farming Systems in Sub-Saharan Africa*, Baltimore, Md., Johns Hopkins University Press

PINKER, STEVEN, 1994, *The Language Instinct*, London, Allen Lane

PINTO, SERPA, 1881, *How I Crossed Africa*, 2 vols., London, Sampson Low

PISCES, N.G., et al. (eds.), 1994, *Proceeds of the Ocean Drilling Program. Scientific Results*, vol. 138

PITCAIRN, A., 1925, *Report on Ukara Island*, Mwanza, Provincial Offices (MS.)

PLATTEAU, J.-P., 1991, "The food crisis in Africa," in Drèze and Sen, vol. 2

POSNANSKY, M., 1973, "Aspects of early West African trade," *Wld Archaeol.*, vol. 5, pt 2, pp. 149–62

PRATT, D.J., and GWYNNE, M.D., 1977, *Rangeland Management and Ecology in East Africa*, London, Hodder & Stoughton

PRESCOTT, J.R.V., 1979, "Africa's boundary problems," *Optima,* vol. 26, pt 1, pp. 3–21

PRESCOTT, J.R.V., 1987, *Political Frontiers and Boundaries,* London, Allen & Unwin

PRESCOTT, V., 1971, *The Evolution of Nigeria's International and Regional Boundaries,* Vancouver, Tantalus

PRINS, GWYN, 1980, *The Hidden Hippopotamus. Reappraisal in African History: The Early Colonial Experience in Western Zambia,* Cambridge, Cambridge University Press

PRUNIER, GÉRARD, 1995, *The Rwanda Crisis 1959–1994. History of a Genocide,* London, Hurst

QUADE, J., CERLING, T.E., and BOWMAN, J.R., 1989, "Development of Asian monsoon revealed by marked ecological shift during the latest Miocene in northern Pakistan," *Nature,* vol. 342, pp. 163–66

RANGER, T.O., 1969, in Gann and Duigan

RANGER, T.O., 1983, "The invention of tradition in colonial Africa," in Hobsbawm and Ranger, pp. 211–62

RANGER, T.O., 1985, "African initiatives and resistance in the face of partition and conquest," in Unesco, 1985, vol. 7, pp. 45–62

RANGER, T.O., and KIMAMBO, I.N. (eds.), 1972, *The Historical Study of African Religion,* London, Heinemann

RANSFORD, O., 1983, *Bid the Sickness Cease. Disease in the History of Black Africa,* London, John Murray

RAUM, JOHANNES W., 1989, "Historical concepts and the evolutionary interpretation of the emergence of states: the case of the Zulu reconsidered," *Z. Ethnol.,* vol. 114, pp. 125–38

RAVEN-HART, R., 1967, *Before Van Riebeeck: Callers at South Africa from 1488 to 1652,* Cape Town, Struik

RAVENSTEIN, E.G. (ed.), 1898, *The First Voyage of Vasco da Gama,* Cambridge, Hakluyt Society, Ser. 1, vol. 42

READER, JOHN, 1972, "Too many elephants," *Smithsonian,* vol. 3(4), pp. 26–31

READER, JOHN, 1981, 1988a, *Missing Links,* London, Collins (1981); 2nd edn., London, Penguin Books (1988a)

READER, JOHN, 1988b, *Man on Earth,* London, Collins

REEFE, THOMAS Q., 1983, "The societies of the eastern savanna," in Birmingham and Martin, vol. 1

REITER, RAYNA R. (ed.), 1975, *Towards an Anthropology of Women,* New York, Monthly Review Press

RETIEF, PIET, 1837, "[The Voortrekker] Manifesto," in the *Grahamstown Journal,* 2 February

RICE, C.D., 1975, *The Rise and Fall of Black Slavery,* London

RICHARDS, W.A., 1980, "The import of firearms into West Africa in the eighteenth century," *J. Afr. Hist.,* vol. 21, pp. 43–59

RICHARDSON, PETER, and VAN-HELTEN, JEAN JACQUES, 1982, "Labour in the South African gold mining industry, 1886–1914," in Marks and Rathbone, pp. 77–98

RICHNER, JURG, 1991, "Eastern frontier slaving and its extension into the Transorangia and Natal, 1770–1843," paper presented to the Colloquium on the "Mfecane" Aftermath, University of the Witwatersrand, 6–9 September 1991 (MS.)

RICKMAN, G.E., 1980, *The Corn Supply of Ancient Rome,* Oxford, Oxford University Press

RIMMER, DOUGLAS, 1991, *The Africas of 1961 and 1991,* in Rimmer, D. (ed.), pp. 1–15

RIMMER, D. (ed.), 1991, *Africa 30 Years On,* London, James Currey

ROBBINS, LAWRENCE H., *et al.,* 1992, "The 'aquatic civilization of Middle Africa' surfaces in Southern Africa," paper presented at the Society of Africanist Archaeologists Symposium, University of California, Los Angeles, March 1992

ROBBINS, L.H., *et al.,* 1993, "Prehistoric mining and new discoveries of rock art at the Tsodilo Hills, Botswana," *Nyame Akuma,* no. 40, pp. 2–5

ROBERTS, ANDREW D., 1990a, "The imperial mind," in Roberts, Andrew D. (ed.)

ROBERTS, ANDREW D. (ed.), 1990b, *The Colonial Moment in Africa,* Cambridge, Cambridge University Press

ROBERTS, NEIL, 1992, "Climatic change in the past," in *Cambridge Encyclopedia of Human Evolution,* pp. 174–78

ROBERTSHAW, PETER, 1989, "The development of pastoralism in East Africa," in Clutton-Brock (ed.), 1989, pp. 207–14

ROBERTSHAW, PETER, 1993, "The beginnings of food production in southwestern Kenya," in Shaw *et al.* (eds.), 1993, pp. 358–71

ROBERTSON, MARIAN, 1974, *Diamond Fever. South African Diamond History 1866–9 from Primary Sources,* Cape Town, Oxford University Press

ROBINS, ERIC, 1966, "An ebbing reign on the flooded plain," *Life* magazine (New York), 1 April

ROBINSON, C.H., 1896, *Hausaland,* London

ROBINSON, JOHN (ed.), 1872, *Notes on Natal: An Old Colonist's Book for New Settlers,* Durban

RODNEY, WALTER, 1970, *A History of the Upper Guinea Coast, 1545–1800,* Oxford

RODNEY, W., 1988, *How Europe Underdeveloped Africa,* London, Bogle L'Ouverture Publications

ROSET, J.P., 1987, "Paleoclimatic and cultural conditions of neolithic development in the early holocene of northern Niger," in Close (ed.), 1987, pp. 189–210

ROSS, PHILIP E., 1991, "Hard words," *Sci. Am.,* 264(4), pp. 71–79

ROTBERG, ROBERT I. (ed.), 1970, *Africa and Its Explorers: Motives, Methods, and Impact,* London, Oxford University Press

ROTBERG, ROBERT I., 1988, *The Founder. Cecil Rhodes and the Pursuit of Power,* New York, Oxford University Press

ROUHANI, SHAHIN, and JONES, STEVE, 1992, "Bottlenecks in human evolution," in *Cambridge Encyclopedia of Human Evolution,* pp. 281–83

ROUILLARD, NANCY (ed.), 1936, *Matabele Thompson: an Autobiography,* London

ROWLEY-CONWY, PETER, 1988, "The camel in the Nile Valley," *J. Egypt. Archaeol.,* vol. 74, pp. 245–48

RUFFER, M.A., 1921, *Studies in Paleopathology of Egypt,* Chicago

RUHLEN, MERRITT, 1991, in Ross, p. 71, and Wright, Robert, p. 67

RUTHENBERG, HANS (ed.), 1968, *Smallholder Farming and Smallholder Development in Tanzania. Ten Case Studies,* Munich, Weltforum Verlag

RYDER, A.F.C., 1959, "An early Portuguese trading voyage to the Forcados River," *J. Hist. Soc. Nigeria,* vol. 1, no. 4

RYDER, A.F.C., 1969, *Benin and the Europeans 1485–1897,* London

RZOSKA, J., 1976, *The Nile: Biology of an Ancient River,* The Hague, Junk BV (Monogr. Biol. 29)

SAHLINS, MARSHALL, 1968, "Notes on the original affluent society," in Lee and DeVore, pp. 85–89

SAID, R., 1981, *The Geological Evolution of the River Nile,* New York, Springer-Verlag

SALT, HENRY, 1814, *A Voyage to Abyssinia,* London

SANDERS, EDITH R., 1969, "The hamitic myth: its origins and functions in time perspective," *J. Afr. Hist.,* 10, pp. 521–32

SARNTHEIN, MICHAEL, 1978, "Sand deserts during glacial maximum and climatic optimum," *Nature,* 272, pp. 43–46

SAUER, C.O., 1952, *Agricultural Origins and Dispersals,* New York Geographic Society

SAUNDERS, A.C. DE C.M., 1982, *A Social History of the Black Slaves and Freemen in Portugal 1441–1555,* Cambridge, Cambridge University Press

SBS *WORLD GUIDE* (4TH EDN), 1995, Reed Reference, Australia. Original edn pub. London, Michael O'Mara Books, 1990

SCHALLER, G.B., and LOWTHER, G.R., 1969, "The relevance of carnivore behavior to the study of early hominids," *SW. J. Anthrop.,* vol. 25 (pt 4), pp. 307–41

SCHAPERA, ISAAC (ed.), 1951, *Apprenticeship at Kuruman,* London

SCHAPERA, I. (ed.), 1960, *Livingstone's Private Journals 1851–1853,* London, Chatto & Windus

SCHMIDT-NEILSEN, K., 1964, *Desert Animals,* Oxford, Oxford University Press

SCHOENBRUN, DAVID L., 1990, "Early history in Eastern Africa's Great Lakes Region: linguistic, ecological and archaeological approaches ca. 500 B.C. to A.D. 1000," Ph.D. thesis, University of California at Los Angeles

SCHOENBRUN, DAVID L., 1993a, "Cattle herds and banana gardens," *Afr. Archaeol. Rev.,* vol. 11, pp. 39–72

SCHOENBRUN, DAVID L., 1993b, "We are what we eat; ancient agriculture between the Great Lakes," *J. Afr. Hist.,* vol. 34, pp. 1–31

SEELEY, T.D., 1989, "The honey bee colony as a superorganism," *Am. Sci.,* 77, pp. 546–53

SERVICE, E.R., 1975, *Origins of the State and Civilization,* New York, W.W. Norton

SEVERIN, TIMOTHY, 1973, *The African Adventure,* New York, Dutton

SHACKLETON, N.J., AND OPDYKE, N.D., 1973, "Oxygen isotope and paleomagnetic stratigraphy of equatorial Pacific core V28–238: oxygen isotope temperatures and ice volumes on a 10^5 and 10^6 year scale," *Quat. Res.,* vol. 3, pp. 39–55

SHACKLETON, N.J., *et al.,* 1994, "A new late Neogene time-scale: application to leg 138 sites," in Pisces

SHARP, JOHN, and MCALLISTER, PAT, 1993, "Ethnicity, identity and nationalism: international insights and the South African debate," *Anthrop. Today,* vol. 9, pt 5, pp. 18–20

SHAW, THURSTAN, 1970, *Igbo-Ukwu,* 2 vols., London, Faber & Faber

SHAW, THURSTAN, 1975, "Those Igbo-Ukwu radiocarbon dates: facts, fictions and probabilities," *J. Afr. Hist.,* vol. 16, pp. 503–17

SHAW, THURSTAN, 1977, *Unearthing Igbo-Ukwu,* Ibadan, Oxford University Press

SHAW, THURSTAN, SINCLAIR, PAUL, ANDAH, BASSEY, and OKPOKO, ALEX (eds.), 1993, *The Archaeology of Africa: Food, Metals and Towns,* pp. 32–42, London, Routledge

SHERRY, NORMAN, 1971, *Conrad's Western World,* Cambridge, Cambridge University Press

SHILLINGTON, KEVIN, 1982, "The impact of diamond discoveries on the Kimberley hinterland," in Marks and Rathbone, pp. 99–118

SHILLINGTON, KEVIN, 1989, *History of Africa,* London, Macmillan

SHINNIE, P.L., 1978, *Meroë. An Ancient Civilization of the Sudan,* London, Thames & Hudson

SIMMONDS, N.W., 1962, *The Evolution of the Edible Bananas,* London, Longman

SIMMONDS, N.W., 1966, *Bananas,* 2nd edn, London, Longman

SIMONS, ELWYN, 1967, "The earliest apes," *Sci. Am.,* December

SIMONS, ELWYN, 1972, *Primate Evolution: an Introduction to Man's Place in Nature,* New York, Macmillan

SIMONS, ELWYN, 1992, "The fossil history of primates," in *Cambridge Encyclopedia of Human Evolution,* pp. 199–208

SIMOONS, F.J., 1965, "Some questions on the economic prehistory of Ethiopia," *J. Afr. Hist.,* vol. 6, pp. 1–13

SIMOONS, FREDERICK J., 1971, "The antiquity of dairying in Asia and Africa," *Geogr. Rev.,* 61, pp. 431–39

SIMOONS, F.J., 1973, "The determinants of dairying and milk use in the Old World: ecological, physiological and cultural," *Ecol. Fd Nutr.,* 2, pp. 83–90

SINCLAIR, A.R.E., LEAKEY, M.D., and NORTON-GRIFFITHS, M., 1986, "Migration and hominid bipedalism," *Nature,* vol. 324, pp. 307–8

SINCLAIR, A.R.E., and NORTON-GRIFFITHS, M. (eds.), 1979, *Serengeti: Dynamics of an Ecosystem,* Chicago, University of Chicago Press

SKELTON, R.A., 1956, "An Ethiopian embassy to Western Europe in 1306," in Crawford, pp. 212–15

SLOCUM, SALLY, 1975, "Woman the gatherer: male bias in anthropology," in Reiter

SMITH, ANDREW B., 1983, "The disruption of Khoi society in the seventeenth century," *African Seminar Collected Papers,* vol. 3, pp. 257–71, Centre for African Studies, University of Cape Town

SMITH, ANDREW B., 1984, "Origins of the Neolithic in the Sahara," in Clark and Brandt, pp. 84–92

SMITH, ANDREW B., 1986, "Competition, conflict and clientship: Khoi and San relationships in the western Cape," in Hall and Smith, pp. 36–41

SMITH, ANDREW B., 1992, *Pastoralism in Africa: Origins and Development Ecology*, London, Hurst

SMITH, A.K., 1970, "The struggle for control of southern Mozambique, 1770–1835" (Ph.D. thesis, University of California at Los Angeles), quoted in Cobbing, 1991, p. 35

SMITH, C.S., 1894, "The Anglo-German boundary in East Equatorial Africa. Proceedings of the British Commission, 1892," *Geogr. J.*, vol. 4, pp. 424–37

SMITH, F.H., and SPENCER, F. (eds.), 1984, *The Origins of Modern Humans: A World Survey of the Fossil Evidence*, New York, Alan R. Liss

SMITH, ROBERT, 1970, "The canoe in West African history," *J. Afr. Hist.*, vol. 11, pp. 515–33

SNOW, PHILIP, 1988, *The Star Raft—China's Encounter with Africa*, London, Weidenfeld & Nicolson

SOCIÉTÉ DES MISSIONS ÉVANGÉLIQUES, *News from Barotsiland* (Paris), 1898–1916

SPARRMAN, A., 1785, *A Voyage to the Cape of Good Hope*, 2 vols., London, Robinson

SPEKE, JOHN HANNING, 1863, *Journal of the Discovery of the Source of the Nile*, Everyman edn, London, 1969

SPETH, JOHN D., 1989, "Early hominid hunting and scavenging: the role of meat as an energy source," *J. Hum. Evol.*, vol. 18, p. 330

SPETH, JOHN D., 1990, "Seasonality, resource stress, and food sharing in so-called 'Egalitarian' foraging societies," *J. Anthrop. Archaeol.*, 9, pp. 148–88

SPIELMANN, KATHERINE A., 1989, "A review: dietary restrictions on hunter-gatherer women and the implications for fertility and infant mortality," *Hum. Ecol.*, 17(3), pp. 321–45

STANLEY, HENRY MORTON, 1872, *How I Found Livingstone*, London

STANLEY, HENRY MORTON, 1885, *The Congo and the Founding of Its Free State*, 2 vols., London

STANLEY, LADY DOROTHY (ed.), 1909, *The Autobiography of Sir Henry Morton Stanley*, London

STEENKAMP, ANNA, 1843, in Bird, vol. 1, p. 459

STEFANSSON, V., 1944, *Arctic Manual*, New York, Macmillan

STEMLER, ANN, 1984, "The transition from food collecting to food production in northern Africa," in Clark and Brandt, pp. 127–31

STENGERS, J., 1967, in Gifford and Louis (eds.), 1967

STENGERS, J., 1969, "The Congo Free State and the Belgian Congo," in Gann and Duigan, pp. 261–92

STENGERS, JEAN, 1982, "Precipitous decolonization: the case of the Belgian Congo," in Gifford and Louis, 1982

STENGERS, JEAN, 1988, "Leopold II and the Association Internationale du Congo," in Förster, Mommsen, and Robinson (eds.), pp. 229–46

STEUDEL, KAREN L., 1994, "Locomotor energetics and hominid evolution," *Evol. Anthrop.*, vol. 3 (pt 2), pp. 42–47

STINI, W.A., 1988, "Food, seasonality and human evolution," in Garine and Harrison, pp. 32–51

ST. JORRE, JOHN DE, 1972, *The Nigerian Civil War*, London, Hodder & Stoughton

STONEKING, M., BHATIA, K., and WILSON, A.C., 1986, "Rate of sequence divergence estimated from restriction maps of mitochondrial DNA from Papua New Guinea," *Cold Spring Harbor Symp. Quant. Biol.*, 51, pp. 433–39

STRANDMAN, HARTMAN POGGE VON, 1969, "Review of: Louis, W.R., 1967. Great Britain and Germany's lost colonies 1914–1919" (London), *J. Afr. Hist.*, vol. 9, p. 339

STRINGER, CHRIS, and MCKIE, ROBIN, 1996, *African Exodus*, London, Cape

SUMMERS, ROGER, 1969, *Ancient Mining in Rhodesia and Adjacent Areas*, Salisbury, National Museums and Monuments of Rhodesia

SUSMAN, R.L., STERN, JR, J.T., and JUNGERS, W.L., 1985, "Locomotor adaptations in the Hadar hominids," in Delson

SUTTON, J.E.G., 1982, "Archaeology in West Africa: a review of recent work and a further list of radiocarbon dates," *J. Afr. Hist.*, vol. 23, pp. 291–313

SUTTON, J.E.G., 1989, "Towards a history of cultivating the fields," *Azania*, vol. 24, pp. 98–112

SUTTON, J.E.G., 1990, *A Thousand Years of East Africa*, Nairobi, British Institute in East Africa

SUTTON, J.E.G., 1991, "The international factor at Igbo-Ukwu," *Afr. Archaeol. Rev.*, vol. 9, pp. 145–60

SUTTON, JOHN E.G., 1993, "The antecedents of the interlacustrine kingdoms," *J. Afr. Hist.*, vol. 34, pp. 33–64

SUTTON, J.E.G. (ed.), 1996, "The growth of farming communities in Africa from the equator southwards," *Azania* (Nairobi), vols. 29–30

SWELLENGREBEL, HENDRIK, 1982, "Hendrik Swellengrebel to C. de Grijselaw, 26 June, 1783. A few considerations about the Cape," in *Briefwisseling van Hendrick Swellengrebel jr. oor Kaapse sake, 1778–1792*, Cape Town (1982), quoted in Leonard Thompson, 1990, p. 48

SWISHER, CARL, *et al.*, 1994, "Age of the earliest known hominids in Java, Indonesia," *Science*, 263, pp. 1118–21

TABLER, E.C. (ed.), 1963, *Trade and Travel in Early Barotseland: The Diaries of George Westbeech, 1885–1888, and Captain Norman MacLeod, 1875–1876*, London, Chatto & Windus

TAINTON, N.M., 1981, *Veld and Pasture Management in South Africa*, Pietermaritzburg, Shuter & Shooter

TAMRAT, TADESSE, 1972, *Church and State in Ethiopia*, Oxford, Clarendon Press

TARLING, D.H. (ed.), 1978, *Evolution of the Earth's Crust*, London, Academic Press

TAYLOR, DAVID, and MARCHANT, ROBERT, 1996, "Human impact in the Interlacustrine region: longterm pollen records from the Rukiga highlands," in Sutton (ed.), 1996, pp. 283–95

TEIXEIRA DA MOTA, VICE-ALMIRANTE A., 1987, *In Memoriam*, Lisbon

TEWOLDE, BERHAN, 1992, "Amani forest [Tanzania] study," cited in *The Environmental Problems of Northern Ethiopia*, Addis Ababa, Department of the Environment (Ethiopia)

THEAL, G.M., 1882–1919, *History of South Africa*, 11 vols., London

THEAL, G.M., 1897–1905, *Records of the Cape Colony*, 36 vols., London

THIAM, IBA DER, and MULIRA, JAMES, 1985, "Africa and the socialist countries," in Unesco, 1985, vol. 8, pp. 798–828

THOM, H.B. (ed.), 1952, *Journals of Jan van Riebeeck,* 3 vols., Cape Town

THOMAS, ROBERT P., and BEAN, RICHARD, 1974, "The fishers of men: the profits of the slave trade," *J. Econ. Hist.,* vol. 34, pp. 885–914

THOMPSON, GEORGE, 1827, *Travels and Adventures in Southern Africa* (ed. V. Forbes), London, repr. Cape Town, 1967–68

THOMPSON, LEONARD, 1985, *The Political Mythology of Apartheid,* New Haven, Conn., Yale University Press

THOMPSON, LEONARD, 1990, *A History of South Africa,* New Haven, Conn., Yale University Press

THORNTON, JOHN, 1984, "The development of an African Catholic church in the kingdom of Kongo 1491–1750," *J. Afr. Hist.,* vol. 25, pp. 147–67

THE TIMES ATLAS, 1985, London, Times Books

TOBIAS, P.V., 1991, *Olduvai Gorge,* vol. 4: *The Skulls, Endocasts and Teeth of* Homo habilis, Cambridge, Cambridge University Press

TOBIAS, PHILIP V.T. (ed.), 1978, *The Bushmen: San hunters and herders of Southern Africa,* Cape Town, Human & Rousseau

TRAILL, A., 1978, "The languages of the Bushmen," in Tobias, Philip V.T., p. 139

TRAPNELL, C.G., and Clothier, J.N., 1937 (repr. 1957), *The Soils, Vegetation and Agricultural Systems of North Western Rhodesia. Ecological Survey,* Lusaka, Zambia

TRIMINGHAM, J.S., 1975, "The Arab geographers and the East African coast," in Chittick and Rotberg, pp. 115–46

TRUSSELL, J., 1978, "Menarche and fatness: re-examination of the critical body composition hypothesis," *Science,* 200, pp. 1506–9

TUFNELL, RICHARD N., 1994, "Zimbabwe costing," Kirkcudbrightshire (unpub.)

TURRELL, ROB [R.V.], 1982, "Kimberley: labour and compounds 1871–1888," in Marks and Rathbone, pp. 45–76

TURRELL, ROB [R.V.], 1984, "Kimberley's model compounds," *J. Afr. Hist.,* vol. 25, pp. 59–75

TURRELL, ROBERT VICAT, 1987, *Capital and Labour of the Kimberley Diamond Fields 1871–1890,* Cambridge, Cambridge University Press

TYLECOTE, T.F., 1975, "Iron smelting at Taruga, Nigeria," *J. Hist. Metall. Soc.,* 9, pp. 49–56

TYSON, P.D., and LINDESAY, J.A., 1992, "The climate of the last 2,000 years in southern Africa," *Holocene,* vol. 2, pp. 271–78

UCHENDU, VICTOR, 1977, "Slaves and Slavery in Igboland, Nigeria," in Miers and Kopytoff, pp. 121–32

UKARA DIVISIONAL SECRETARY'S OFFICE, *Reports,* 1988

UNESCO, 1981–93, *General History of Africa* (ed. J. Ki-Zerbo *et al.*), 8 vols., London, Heinemann

UNGER, R.W., 1987, "Portuguese shipbuilding and the early voyages to the Guinea coast," in Teixeira da Mota, pp. 229–49

UREY, HAROLD C., 1948, "Oxygen isotopes in nature and in the laboratory," *Science,* vol. 108, pp. 489–96

UVIN, PETER, 1994, *The International Organization of Hunger,* London, Kegan Paul

VAIL, LEROY (ed.), 1989, *The Creation of Tribalism in* Southern Africa, London, James Currey

VAIL, LEROY, and WHITE, LANDEG, 1980, *Capitalism and Colonialism in Mozambique. A Study of Quelimane District,* Minneapolis, University of Minnesota Press

VAN BEEK, G.W., 1967, "Monuments of Axum in the light of south Arabian archaeology," *J. Am. Orient. Soc.,* 87, pp. 113–22

VAN DER HORST, SHEILA, 1942, *Native Labour in South Africa,* Johannesburg

VAN DER POST, LAURENS, 1958, *The Lost World of the Kalahari,* New York, William Morrow

VAN LOON, J.H., STAUDT, F.J., and ZANDER, J. (eds.), 1979, *Ergonomics in Tropical Agriculture and Forestry. Proc. 5th Jt Ergon. Symp.,* Wageningen

VAN ONSELEN, C., 1972, "Reaction to rinderpest in Southern Africa 1896–97," *J. Afr. Hist.,* vol. 13, pp. 473–88

VAN RENSBURG, T.F.J., n.d., *An Introduction to Fynbos,* Pretoria, South African Department of Environmental Affairs

VAN VALEN, L., and SLOAN, R.E., 1965a, "A middle Paleocene primate," *Nature,* vol. 207, pp. 435–36

VAN VALEN, L., and SLOAN, R.E., 1965b, "The earliest primates," *Science,* vol. 150, pp. 743–45

VAN WARMELO, M.J. (ed.), 1938, *History of the Matigwane and the AmaNgwane Tribe,* Pretoria

VAN ZINDEREN BAKKER, E.M., 1982, "African palaeoenvironments 18,000 years before present," *Palaeoecol. Afr.,* 15, pp. 79–99

VANSINA, JAN, 1985, *Oral Tradition as History,* Madison, University of Wisconsin Press

VANSINA, JAN, 1990, *Paths in the Rainforest: Towards a History of Political Tradition in Equatorial Africa,* Madison, University of Wisconsin Press; London, James Currey

VASSALL-ADAMS, GUY, 1994, *Rwanda—an Agenda for International Action,* Oxford, Oxfam

VAVILOV, N.I., 1926, *Studies on the Origin of Cultivated Plants,* Leningrad, Institute of Applied Botany and Plant Breeding

VAVILOV, N.I., 1951, "The origin, variation, immunity and breeding of cultivated plants," *Chron. Bot.,* 13, pp. 1–364

VILJOEN, M.J., and VILJOEN, R.P., 1970, "Archaean vulcanicity and continental evolution in the Barberton Region, Transvaal," in Clifford and Gass, p. 42

VILLIERS, PATRICK, 1982, *Traite des Noirs et Navires Négriers au XVIIIe Siècle,* Grenoble

VINES, GAIL, 1992, "Winning streak for sheiks," *New Sci.,* vol. 136, pp. 22–25

VOGEL, F., and SPERLING, K. (eds.), 1987, *Human Genetics: Proc. 7th Int. Congr.,* Berlin, Springer

VOGEL, J.C. (ed.), 1984, *Late Cainozoic Palaeoclimates of the Southern Hemisphere,* Rotterdam, Balkema

VOGT, JOHN L., 1973, "The early São Tomé-Príncipe slave trade with Mina, 1500–1540," *Int. J. Afr. Hist. Stud.*, vol. 6, pt 3, pp. 453–67

VOGT, JOHN L., 1979, *Portuguese Rule on the Gold Coast, 1469–1682*, Athens: University of Georgia Press

VRBA, ELISABETH S., 1980, "Evolution, species and fossils: how does life evolve?," *S. Afr. J. Sci.*, vol. 76, pp. 61–84

VRBA, ELISABETH S., 1985a, "Environment and evolution: alternative causes of the temporal distribution of evolutionary events," *S. Afr. J. Sci.*, vol. 81, pp. 229–36

VRBA, ELISABETH S., 1985b, "African Bovidae: evolutionary events since the Miocene," *S. Afr. J. Sci.*, vol. 81, pp. 263–67

VRBA, ELISABETH S., 1992, "Mammals as a key to evolutionary theory," *J. Mamm.*, vol. 73 (pt 1), pp. 1–28

VRBA, E.S., DENTON, G.H., PARTRIDGE, T.C., and BURKLE, L.H. (eds.), 1995, *Paleoclimate and Evolution, with Emphasis on Human Origins*, New Haven, Conn., Yale University Press

WALDECKER, B., 1967, "Sel et salines en Afrique," *Bull. Cent. d'Étude Probl. Soc. Indig.*, nos. 75, 76, pp. 9–54

WALKER, A., 1981, "Diet and teeth—dietary hypotheses and human evolution," *Phil. Trans. R. Soc. Lond. B*, 292, pp. 57–64

WALKER, A.C., LEAKEY, R.E.F., HARRIS, J.M., and BROWN, F.H., 1986, "2.5 Myr *Australopithecus boisei* from west of Lake Turkana, Kenya," *Nature*, 322, pp. 517–22

WALKER, ALAN, and LEAKEY, R.E.F. (eds.), 1993, *The Nariokotome* Homo erectus *skeleton*, Cambridge, Mass., Harvard University Press

WALKER, ALAN, and LEAKEY, RICHARD E.F., 1978, "The hominids of East Turkana," *Sci. Am.*, August 1978

WALKER, ERIC A., 1938, *The Great Trek*, London

WALKER, NICK, 1990, "Zimbabwe at 18000bp," in Gamble and Soffer, pp. 206–13

WALLER, DAVID, 1993, *Rwanda: Which Way Now?*, Oxford, Oxfam

WALLER, RICHARD D., 1990, "Tsetse fly in western Narok, Kenya," *J. Afr. Hist.*, vol. 31, pp. 81–101

WALSH, DAVID, 1994, "South Africa—the legacy," *Guardian* education supplement, 26 April

WALVIN, JAMES, 1992, *Black Ivory—a History of British Slavery*, London, HarperCollins

WANSBROUGH, J., 1970, "Africa and the Arab geographers," in Dalby (ed.), pp. 89–101

WARD, G.M., SUTHERLAND, T.M., and SUTHERLAND, J.M., 1980, "Animals as an energy source in Third World agriculture," *Science*, vol. 208, pp. 571–74

WARD, R.H., and WEISS, K.M. (eds.), 1976, *The Demographic Evolution of Human Populations*, London, Academic Press

WARD, STEVEN, and HILL, ANDREW, 1987, "Pliocene hominid partial mandible from Tabarin, Baringo, Kenya," *Am. J. Phys. Anthrop.*, 72, pp. 21–37

WARWICK, PETER, 1983, *Black People and the South African War 1899–1902*, Cambridge, Cambridge University Press

WASHBURN, SHERWOOD L., and LANCASTER, C.S., 1968, "The evolution of hunting," in Lee and DeVore, pp. 293–303

WASYLIKOWA *et al.*, 1993, "Examination of botanical remains from early Neolithic houses at Nabta Playa, Western Desert, Egypt, with special reference to sorghum grains," in Shaw *et al.* (eds.), 1993, pp. 154–64

WEBB, A.C.M., 1978, "The immediate consequences of the sixth frontier war on the farming community of Albany," *S. Afr. Hist. J.,* vol. 10, pp. 38–48

WEBB, JAMES L.A., 1993, "The horse and slave trade between the western Sahara and Senegambia," *J. Afr. Hist.,* vol. 34, pp. 221–46

WENDORF, FRED, 1968, "A Nubian final paleolithic graveyard near Jebel Sahaba, Sudan," in Wendorf (ed.), 1968, pp. 954–95

WENDORF, FRED (ed.), 1968, *The Prehistory of Nubia,* vols. 1 and 2, Dallas, Tex., Southern Methodist University Press

WENDORF, FRED, and SCHILD, ROMUALD (eds.), 1980, *Prehistory of the Eastern Sahara,* London, Academic Press

WENDORF, FRED, and SCHILD, ROMUALD, 1984, "The emergence of food production in the Egyptian Sahara," in Clark and Brandt, pp. 93–101

WENDORF, FRED D., and SCHILD, ROMUALD, 1989, "Summary and synthesis," in Wendorf, Schild, and Close, pp. 768–824

WENDORF, FRED, and SCHILD, ROMUALD, 1995, "Are the early Holocene cattle in the Eastern Sahara domestic or wild?" *Evol. Anthrop.* 3(4), pp. 118–28

WENDORF, F., SCHILD, R., and CLOSE, A.E. (eds.), 1989, *The Prehistory of Wadi Kubbaniya,* vol. 3: *Late Palaeolithic Archaeology,* Dallas, Tex., Southern Methodist University Press

WERTIME, T.A., and MUHLY, J.D., 1980, *The Coming of the Age of Iron,* New Haven, Conn., Yale University Press

WEST, RICHARD, 1970, *Back to Africa—a History of Sierra Leone and Liberia,* London, Jonathan Cape

WETTERSTROM, WILMA, 1993, "Foraging and farming in Egypt: the transition from hunting and gathering to horticulture in the Nile valley," in Shaw *et al.* (eds.), 1993, pp. 165–226

WHEELER, P.E., 1984, "The evolution of bipedality and loss of functional body hair in hominids," *J. Hum. Evol.,* 13, pp. 91–98

WHEELER, P.E., 1988, "Stand tall and stay cool," *New Sci.* (London), 12 May

WHEELER, P.E., 1991, "The influence of bipedalism on the energy and water budgets of early hominids," *J. Hum. Evol.,* 21, pp. 117–36

WHEELER, P.E., 1992, "The thermoregulatory advantages of large body size for hominids foraging in savannah environments," *J. Hum. Evol.,* 23, pp. 351–62

WHITE, TIM, 1987, "Cannibals at Klasies?," *Sagittarius* (magazine of the South African Museum), 2(2), pp. 6–9

WHITE, TIM D., SUWA, G., and ASFAW, B., 1994, "*Australopithecus ramidus,* a new species of early hominid from Aramis, Ethiopia," *Nature,* 371, pp. 306–12

WILKS, IVOR, 1982, "Wangara, Akan and Portuguese in the fifteenth and sixteenth centuries," *J. Afr. Hist.,* vol. 23, pp. 333–49

WILLIAMS, GOMER, 1897, *History of the Liverpool Privateers,* London, Heinemann

WILLIAMS, J.T., 1990, "Vavilov's centres . . . ," *Biol. J. LS,* vol. 39, pp. 89–93

WILLIAMS, M.A.J., and FAURE, H. (eds.), 1980, *The Sahara and the Nile,* Rotterdam, Balkema

WILMSEN, EDWIN, 1978, "Seasonal effects of dietary intake on Kalahari San," *Fed. Proc.,* 37, pp. 65–72

WILMSEN, EDWIN, 1982, "Studies in diet, nutrition, and fertility among a group of Kalahari Bushmen in Botswana," *Soc. Sci. Inf.* (Sage, London/Beverly Hills), 21(1), pp. 95–125

WILMSEN, EDWIN N., 1989, *Land Filled with Flies. A Political Economy of the Kalahari,* Chicago, University of Chicago Press

WILSON, A.C., *et al.,* 1985, "Mitochondrial DNA and two perspectives of evolutionary genetics," *Biol. J. LS,* 26, pp. 375–400

WILSON, A.C., *et al.,* 1987, "Mitochondrial clans and the age of our common mother," in Vogel and Sperling, pp. 158–64

WILSON, J.T., 1966, "Did the Atlantic close and reopen?," *Nature,* vol. 211, pp. 676–81

WINTERHALDER, BRUCE, 1993, "Work, resources and population in foraging societies," *Man* (N.S.), 28, pp. 321–40

WOOD, B., 1992, "Evolution of australopithecines," in *Cambridge Encyclopedia of Human Evolution,* p. 236, quoting Walker and Leakey, 1978, p. 61

WOODRUFF, WILLIAM, 1958, *The Rise of the British Rubber Industry,* Liverpool, Liverpool University Press

WORGER, WILLIAM H., 1987, *South Africa's City of Diamonds: Mine Workers and Monopoly Capitalism in Kimberley, 1867–1895,* New Haven, Conn., Yale University Press

WORLD BANK, 1992, *Development Report, 1992,* Washington, D.C., World Bank

WORLD BANK, 1993, *World Development Report 1993,* Washington, D.C., World Bank

WORLD BANK REPORT, 1994, Washington, D.C., World Bank

WORLD RESOURCES INSTITUTE, 1986, *World Resources, An Assessment of the Resource Base that Supports the Global Economy,* New York, Basic Books

WRANGHAM, RICHARD, 1975, "The behavioural ecology of chimpanzees in Gombe National Park, Tanzania," Ph.D. thesis, Cambridge

WRIGHT, JOHN B., 1995, "Political transformations in Natal in the late eighteenth century and early nineteenth century," paper presented to the Colloquium on the "Mfecane" Aftermath, University of the Witwatersrand, 6–9 September 1991, pp. 4–5 (MS.)

WRIGHT, ROBERT, 1991, "Quest for the mother tongue," *Atl. Mon.,* April 1991, pp. 39–68

WRIGLEY, CHRIS, 1987, "Cattle and language between the lakes," *Sprache Gesch. Afr.,* vol. 8, pp. 247–80

WRIGLEY, CHRISTOPHER C., 1989, "Bananas in Buganda," *Azania,* vol. 24, pp. 64–70

YALDEN, D.W., 1983, "The extent of the high ground in Ethiopia compared to the rest of Africa," *SINET*: Ethiop. J. Sci., 6(1), pp. 35–38

YELLEN, JOHN E., *et al.,* 1995, "A Middle Stone Age worked bone industry from Katanda, Upper Semlike Valley, Zaire," *Science,* 268, pp. 553–56

YOUNG, PATRICK, 1976, *Drifting Continents, Shifting Seas,* New York, Franklin Watts

ZEUNER, F.E., 1963, *A History of Domesticated Animals,* London, Hutchinson

INDEX

Italicized page numbers refer to photographs

A NOTE ON THE TYPE

The text of this book was set in Monotype Columbus,
a contemporary face designed specifically for
digital typesetting by Patricia Saunders. Named for
Christopher Columbus, and released on the quincentenary
of his 1492 voyage from Spain to the Americas,
Monotype Columbus has a distinctly Spanish flavor
to its letter forms. Saunders did, in fact, draw inspiration
from fonts created by Jorge Coci in sixteenth-century
Spain, as well as from italic fonts by the brilliant
typographer Robert Granjon, to create
this lively and highly readable new face.

Composed by North Market Street Graphics,
Lancaster, Pennsylvania

Designed by Cassandra J. Pappas